DISCOVERING BIBLICAL EQUALITY

COMPLEMENTARITY WITHOUT HIERARCHY

GENERAL EDITORS
Ronald W. Pierce AND
Rebecca Merrill Groothuis

CONTRIBUTING EDITOR
Gordon D. Fee

InterVarsity Press
Downers Grove, Illinois

InterVarsity Press
P.O. Box 1400, Downers Grove, IL 60515-1426
World Wide Web: www.ivpress.com
E-mail: mail@ivpress.com

InterVarsity Press® is the book-publishing division of InterVarsity Christian Fellowship/USA®, a student movement active on campus at hundreds of universities, colleges and schools of nursing in the United States of America, and a member movement of the International Fellowship of Evangelical Students. For information about local and regional activities, write Public Relations Dept., InterVarsity Christian Fellowship/USA, 6400 Schroeder Rd., P.O. Box 7895, Madison, WI 53707-7895, or visit the IVCF website at <www.intervarsity.org>.

ISBN 0-8308-2729-3

Printed in the United States of America ∞

Library of Congress Cataloging-in-Publication Data

Discovering biblical equality: complementarity without hierarchy /
Ronald W. Pierce and Rebecca Merrill Groothuis, general editors;
Gordon D. Fee, contributing editor.
    p. cm.
  Includes bibliographical references and indexes.
  ISBN 0-8308-2729-3 (pbk.: alk. paper)
  1. Sex role—Biblical teaching. 2. Equality—Biblical teaching. 3.
Evangelicalism. I. Pierce, Ronald W., 1946- II. Groothuis, Rebecca
Merrill. III. Fee, Gordon D.
  BS680.S53D57 2004
  270'.082—dc22

                   2004017264

P	22	21	20	19	18	17	16	15	14	13	12	11	10	9	8	7	6	5	4	3	2	1
Y	22	21	20	19	18	17	16	15	14	13	12	11	10	09	08	07	06	05	04				

CONTENTS

ABBREVIATIONS

ABD	*Anchor Bible Dictionary*
AOAT	Alter Orient und Altes Testament
ASV	American Standard Version
AV	Authorized Version (= KJV, King James Version)
BA	*Biblical Archaeologist*
BBE	The Bible in Basic English (Cambridge University Press, 1949)
BBR	*Bulletin for Biblical Research*
BDAG	Bauer, Danker, Arndt, Gingrich, *Greek-English Lexicon of the New Testament*
BDF	Blass, Debrunner, Funk, *A Greek Grammar of the New Testament*
BGU	Aegyptische Urkunden aus den Königlichen (Staatlichen) Museen zu Berlin
BZAW	Beihefte zur Zeitschrift für die alttestamentliche Wissenschaft
CBQ	*Catholic Biblical Quarterly*
CEV	Contemporary English Version
DBY	Darby Translation
DNTT	*Dictionary of New Testament Theology*
EvQ	*Evangelical Quarterly*
HALOT	Koehler, Baumgartner, Stamm et al., *The Hebrew and Aramaic Lexicon of the Old Testament*
HTR	*Harvard Theological Review*
ICC	International Critical Commentary (Edinburgh: T & T Clark)
JAOS	*Journal of the American Oriental Society*
JB	Jerusalem Bible
JBCerf	*La Bible de Jérusalem* (Éditions du Cerf)
JBL	*Journal of Biblical Literature*
JETS	*Journal of the Evangelical Theological Society*
JPT	*Journal of Pentecostal Theology*
JSNT	*Journal for the Study of the New Testament*
JSOT	*Journal for the Study of the Old Testament*
*JSOT*Sup	*Journal for the Study of the Old Testament* Supplement Series
KJV	King James Version (= AV, Authorized Version)
LCL	Loeb Classical Library (Harvard University)
LSJ	Liddell, Scott, Jones, *Greek-English Lexicon*
LXX	The Septuagint (Greek translation of the Hebrew Bible)
NAB	New American Bible
NABr	New American Bible (revised)
NAC	New American Commentary

NASB	New American Standard Bible
NASU	New American Standard Bible Updated
NCB	New Century Bible Commentary
NCV	Holy Bible: New Century Version
NEB	New English Bible
NIBC	New International Bible Commentary
NICNT	New International Commentary on the New Testament
NICOT	New International Commentary on the Old Testament
NIGTC	New International Greek Testament Commentary
NIV	New International Version
NJB	New Jerusalem Bible
NKJV	New King James Version
NLT	New Living Translation
NovT	*Novum Testamentum*
NRSV	New Revised Standard Version
NTS	*New Testament Studies*
OBO	Orbis Biblicus et Orientalis
PNTC	The Pillar New Testament Commentary
RBMW	*Recovering Biblical Manhood and Womanhood: A Response to Evangelical Feminism,* ed. John Piper and Wayne Grudem (Wheaton, Ill.: Crossway, 1991)
REB	Revised English Bible
RestQ	*Restoration Quarterly*
RevExp	*Review and Expositor*
RSV	Revised Standard Version
SBLDS	Society of Biblical Literature Dissertation Series
SBLMS	Society of Biblical Literature Monograph Series
SP	Sacra Pagina
TDNT	*Theological Dictionary of the New Testament*
TEV	Today's English Version [= Good News Bible]
TLG	Thesaurus Linguae Graecae
TNIV	Today's New International Version
TNTC	Tyndale New Testament Commentary
TrinJ	*Trinity Journal*
TynBul	*Tyndale Bulletin*
*VT*Sup	*Vetus Testamentum* Supplements
WBC	Word Biblical Commentary
WTJ	*Westminster Theological Journal*
WUNT	Wissenschaftliche Untersuchungen zum Neuen Testament
ZAW	*Zeitschrift für die alttestamentliche Wissenschaft*

PREFACE

Discovering Biblical Equality is the result of a collaborative effort of a diverse group of evangelical scholars united here by two convictions: that the Bible is the fully inspired and authoritative Word of God, and that it teaches gender equality in church, home and society. Each of the editors had independently contemplated such a volume for some years before God brought us together in 2000 to begin the project in earnest. After four years of watching this collection emerge, and on behalf of all those contributing to its final form, we would like to thank several groups and individuals who, by God's grace, have made it possible.

First, we could not have accomplished this task without the support of our families. Ron's wife Pat Pierce and their adult children Debi and Brett were a constant source of encouragement (in addition to Brett's reading and making helpful suggestions on many of the chapters). Doug Groothuis served in a number of unofficial yet indispensable capacities—as consultant, manuscript reviewer, research assistant, typist, prayer warrior, and occasional writer and editor. Paul and Jean Merrill also prayed faithfully and effectually throughout.

Second, we would like to thank Gordon Fee, whose invaluable contribution to this project far exceeded what is normally expected of a contributing editor. We are especially grateful for his willingness to provide two chapters as a late fill-in, in addition to the two chapters he was originally assigned to write. Maudine Fee's astute comments as unofficial manuscript reviewer are also greatly appreciated.

Others have also supported and prayed for this work from the beginning, including those from our churches, academic organizations (colleagues and students), and the staff and members of Christians for Biblical Equality.

We also want to thank Talbot School of Theology for providing Ron with a research sabbatical to work on this project, as well as Biola University who supplied two research grants for additional editorial assistance from Sarah Moore, Sheryl A. Silzer and Geoffrey S. Smith.

Finally, we very much appreciate the work of the InterVarsity Press editorial staff, especially Jim Hoover, who readily accepted the project and skillfully managed it to its completion. His patience, guidance and expertise have been indispensable.

Ronald W. Pierce
Rebecca Merrill Groothuis

INTRODUCTION

Rebecca Merrill Groothuis and Ronald W. Pierce

I f you hold to my teaching, you are really my disciples. Then you will know the truth, and the truth will set you free" (Jn 8:31-32). So promised Jesus Christ, the Lord of the church and the cosmos. The cause of Christ is advanced only as truth is recognized, affirmed and lived out with wisdom and integrity. Truth must be brought to the world as well as to the church. Doctrine that falls short of the truth not only impedes believers from walking in the full freedom of the gospel of grace and truth but also hinders unbelievers from coming to salvation through the work of Jesus Christ.

This book is born of the conviction that both the world and the church urgently need to hear and take to heart the message of biblical equality, because it is at once true, logical, biblical and beneficial. The essential message of biblical equality is simple and straightforward: Gender, in and of itself, neither privileges nor curtails one's ability to be used to advance the kingdom or to glorify God in any dimension of ministry, mission, society or family. The differences between men and women do not justify granting men unique and perpetual prerogatives of leadership and authority not shared by women. Biblical equality, therefore, denies that there is any created or otherwise God-ordained hierarchy *based solely on gender.* Egalitarianism recognizes patterns of authority in the family, church and society—it is not anarchistic—but rejects the notion that any office, ministry or opportunity should be denied anyone on the grounds of gender alone. This is because women and men are made equally in God's image and likeness (Gen 1:27), are equally fallen (Rom 3:23), equally redeemable through Christ's life, death and resurrection (Jn 3:16), equally participants in the new-covenant community (Gal 3:28), equally heirs of God in Christ (1 Pet 3:7), and equally able to be filled and empowered by the Holy Spirit for life and ministry (Acts 2:17).

Consequently, any limits placed on the gifts and abilities of women should be challenged through a rigorous investigation of the biblical texts—rightly interpreted and harmonized with the whole of God's Word. Biblical egalitarianism (as opposed to any brand of secular or pagan feminism) is biblically based and kingdom focused. It does not rest its arguments on secular political movements or a theologically liberal denial of the Scripture's full and objective truth and authority for all time. Moreover, biblical egalitarians apply the basic historical-grammatical method of interpretation and the best principles of theologizing to their task. They make no appeal to "women's consciousness" as normative; neither do they feel free to dispense with or underplay any aspect of sacred Scripture, since it is all equally God-breathed and profitable for all of life (2 Tim 3:15-17). Biblical equality, while concerned about the false limits and stereotypes that have fettered women, is not "woman centered" but God-centered and concerned with the biblical liberation of both women and men for the cause of Christ in our day and beyond. For when women are denied their gifts and callings, men suffer from the omission as well.

The Purpose of the Book

This book is part of an ongoing controversy among evangelical Christians over the meaning of gender, ministry and marriage. Though varying expressions of an exclusive male leadership have persisted in the church and home over the last two millennia, a remnant has always been present to speak on behalf of biblical equality between men and women. This voice became stronger and clearer after the Reformation, especially at the turn of the nineteenth and twentieth centuries, and during recent decades has been expressed by a host of evangelicals who hold firmly to the inspiration and authority of Scripture. This volume is built on the faithful work of those who have preceded us.

A threefold goal has guided the writing and editing of this collection of essays. First, we have sought to present a positive explanation and a fresh defense of biblical equality in a format that may be useful as a resource for teachers, students and laypersons who have a serious interest in "the gender question." To this end, the book is academic and persuasive in tone and may be read alongside similar texts that defend the male leadership position.[1]

---

[1]Such as John Piper and Wayne Grudem, eds., *Recovering Biblical Manhood and Womanhood: A Response to Evangelical Feminism* (Wheaton, Ill.: Crossway, 1991), or Robert L. Saucy and Judith K. TenElshof, eds., *Women and Men in Ministry: A Complementary Perspective* (Chicago: Moody Press, 2001).

Second, we have sought to foster a dialogue that will draw in those who share our evangelical heritage yet disagree with or have questions about the biblical equality position. In order to offer a fuller, more informative picture of gender equality, we have widened the scope of our discussion beyond the usual biblical texts to cover a range of theological, historical, hermeneutical, psychological and practical perspectives. Thus we hope that there were will be something in this book that will be helpful and relevant for everyone. We are convinced that an ongoing constructive dialogue among evangelicals can lead us all to a better understanding of God's Word and God's will for our life together as the body of Christ.

Third, and perhaps most important, we wish to encourage women as well as men to celebrate God's gift of gender complementarity in the context of mutually shared partnerships, without the trappings of male hierarchy that traditionally have accompanied such relationships, whether in marriage, in ministry or in the context of cross-gender friendships. Further, it is our desire that women called to ministry will be better able to discover and develop their gifts and exercise them in fruitful ministry.

Evangelicals and Gender: Two Views

While there is a spectrum of views on this topic, the most fundamental divide is over one basic question: Are there any aspects of leadership denied to women and reserved for men strictly on the basis of what one cannot change, one's gender? Many of those who answer yes prefer to be called "complementarians" because they believe that the differences between men and women—differences which, in their view, empower men and restrict women in certain ways—are complementary. Yet this term must be challenged because egalitarians also believe in gender complementarity—but *complementarity without hierarchy.* How, then, should we speak of the differing views?

It is vitally important to meaningful discussion—especially between Christians—to use terms that are accurate and respectful representations of each view. Speaking of and to each other in a Christlike manner is crucial. Toward this end, we must take a moment to offer a brief explanation of how we really differ on this issue. Though there is much common ground that we share, at the end of the day two distinctive positions emerge.

Male leadership. This position sets forth a male leadership that restricts women from full participation in certain ministries and decision-making responsibilities. The emphasis is on male leadership rather than shared leadership in the church and home. For the greater part of church history this position has been expressed in such terms as *patriarchy, hierarchy, headship* (interpreted to mean "leadership"), *authority* and *tradition*. However, such language has been shunned recently by many proponents of the view, due to some negative connotations and misuse. Despite its drawbacks, however, this terminology continues to identify accurately the essential distinction of the position. According to this view, men are seen as responsible under God for the leadership of both church and home, though they should serve in these roles with an attitude of humility. Women may have a limited degree of input into leadership and decision making, but in the end they must submit to the decisions of their husbands and/or male church elders (though disagreement still exists within this position as to how exactly this theory is to be worked out in practice).

The long tenure of this view as the majority opinion in the church has led to it being called "the traditional view." But since this could be perceived to have a negative implication (being *only traditional* as opposed to being *biblical*), and because the traditional view had understood women to be personally inferior to men, new terminology was sought. By the end of the 1980s the idea of "biblical manhood and womanhood" expressed in terms of gender "complementarity" became the language of preference for a number of proponents of male leadership.[2] Concurrent with this terminology is the contention that God created male and female as equal but "distinct" (to be "complements" of one another) *and* that female submission to male leadership is inherent in the gender distinction (from which it would follow that belief in gender equality must somehow deny gender complementarity).

Gender equality. For those holding to gender equality, the most common descriptives have been *evangelical feminism, egalitarianism* and *biblical equality*. As with the terms applied to the male leadership view, there have been negative implications and pejorative uses of these terms in the debate. For example, though *feminism* accurately describes the aspect of this position that seeks to be more supportive of a woman's freedom and opportunity to serve alongside men in ministry and marriage, the qualifier *evangelical* is helpful in distinguishing evangelical feminism from the unbiblical aspects of liberal religious and secular feminism. The term *egalitarian* has been used by some opponents to suggest that evangelicals who hold this position admit to no significant gender differences between men and women other than the anatomical, though such an extreme egalitarianism has never been held by evangelical proponents of gender equality. Finally, *biblical* is added to the concept of gender

---

[2]Piper and Grudem, "Preface," *RBMW,* pp. xiii-xv; Saucy and TenElshof, "A Problem in the Church," in *Women and Men,* pp. 26-30.

equality in order to distinguish evangelicals from those who seek gender equality primarily because of cultural pressure, personal agendas or equal-rights politics, rather than out of obedience to the Bible.

With regard to the idea of "complementarity," it should be noted that from the time of the first wave of the modern women's movement at the turn of the nineteenth and twentieth centuries, many have argued that women should participate equally with men precisely *because* they bring complementary gender qualities to marriage, ministry and society. Thus the most recent term for the male leadership position has often been employed by those who have held the opposite view![3] Of course, the difference lies not in the basic meaning of the term ("to complete one another") but in the different implications argued by each side. In the gender debate, this term may well be more helpful in identifying a point of agreement between the opposing views than indicating their disagreements. This is why we have chosen to use the term in our title, *Discovering Biblical Equality: Complementarity Without Hierarchy.*

Though we speak strongly in favor of unity, points of agreement and dialogue, it must be noted at the start that we see no middle ground on this question. The notion of complementarity is helpful and must be pursued, but two essential questions remain. Are all avenues of ministry and leadership open to women as well as men, or are women restricted from certain roles and subordinated to male authority on the basis of gender alone? Likewise, do wives share equally with husbands in leadership and decision making in marriage, or does the husband have a unique responsibility and privilege to make final decisions, based on his gender alone? The answers to these questions will continue to distinguish clearly between the male leadership and gender equality positions.

In view of all these considerations, it is probably most fitting to refer to those who believe in restricting leadership to men as simply advocates of male leadership, or patriarchalists (because they affirm male authority over women), or traditionalists (since they reflect what has been the dominant tradition of the church, however much they may critique some extreme aspects of this tradition), or hierarchicalists (because they affirm hierarchy at a point where egalitarians affirm equality).

The debate between those who promote male leadership and those who promote gender equality cannot be rightly settled by name calling, issuing propaganda or evading this divisive issue. It can be approached with integrity only through care-

---

[3]See, for example, Mary J. Evans, *Woman in the Bible* (Downers Grove, Ill.: InterVarsity Press, 1983), p. 132; also Mary Stewart Van Leeuwen et al., eds., *After Eden: Facing the Challenge of Gender Reconciliation* (Grand Rapids, Mich.: Eerdmans, 1993), pp. 23-24.

ful scholarly investigation of what the Bible teaches about the nature, gifts and callings of women and men. To that end this book is offered. *Discovering Biblical Equality* is the first multiauthored volume to comprehensively, systematically and consistently articulate an egalitarian position based on the tenets of biblical teaching.[4] While the authors are aware of and responsive to the traditionalist alternative, the overall spirit of the book is more affirming of God's gifting of women and men than it is critical of those who dispute biblical equality.

An Overview of Discovering Biblical Equality

All five sections of the book contribute in different and complementary ways to an understanding of biblical equality. Part one provides a needed historical backdrop to the contemporary debate. Ruth Tucker skillfully surveys the changing roles of women in ministry from the early church through the eighteenth century. Janette Hassey focuses on the pivotal but often neglected topic of evangelical women in the nineteenth and early twentieth centuries. (Some may be surprised to learn that an egalitarian perspective within evangelicalism did not wait for the secular feminism of the 1960s.) Ronald Pierce takes stock of more recent developments among evangelical egalitarians, with a bibliographic survey of the 1970s through the beginning of the twenty-first century.

Part two zeroes in on the crucial topic of biblical support for gender equality and challenges traditionalist interpretations and applications. Richard Hess investigates the foundational Genesis passages on human origins, roles and destiny and finds no created hierarchy of gender. Ronald Pierce engages the challenging topic of women under the Old Testament law by putting the Jewish theocracy into a larger perspective. Linda Belleville considers the many and varied women leaders in the Bible and explains their significance to the gender debate. Jesus' treatment of women is a crucial matter, since he was God incarnate. Aída Besançon Spencer finds that Jesus affirmed women in ways often missed by students of the Bible and draws out the implications of this important truth. Gordon Fee offers a compelling explanation of the ecclesiological significance of Paul's declaration that in Christ there is neither male nor female. Craig Keener, Gordon Fee, I. Howard Marshall, Linda Belleville and Peter Davids address key New Testament passages taken by some to imply a divinely mandated subordination of women; they argue that this conclusion does not follow from

---

[4]Earlier multiauthored volumes include Alvera Mickelsen, ed., *Women, Authority and the Bible* (Downers Grove, Ill.: InterVarsity Press, 1986), and Kathy Keay, ed., *Men, Women and God: Evangelicals on Feminism* (London: Marshall Pickering, 1987).

a close reading and analysis of the texts. They leave no stone unturned in their careful assessment of these important and often-misunderstood passages.

Part three explores critical theological dimensions of the gender debate, with respect to Spirit gifting as the criterion for ministry (Gordon Fee), the nature of authority in the New Testament (Walter Liefeld), biblical priesthood and the pastorate (Stanley Grenz), gendered language for God (Judy Brown) and the doctrine of the subordination of Christ (Kevin Giles). Rebecca Merrill Groothuis offers an analysis of a key hermeneutical principle used by patriarchalists to justify women's subordination—that women are equal to men in being but permanently unequal in role—and finds it logically wanting.

In part four Roger Nicole and Gordon Fee discuss the purpose and place of hermeneutics (the method of biblical interpretation) in the gender debate. William Webb's exposition of a "redemptive hermeneutic" draws out parallels between the texts on slavery and the texts on women's submission. In another chapter Webb argues that endorsing biblical equality does not lead to the sanctioning of homosexual practices. Sulia and Karen Mason show that evangelical egalitarianism, unlike modern secular feminism, logically leads to supporting the value of unborn human life and opposing abortion on demand.

Part five offers practical information and insights on working out the principles of biblical equality in the church, in marriage and in our personal lives. Joan Burgess Winfrey writes of the need for proper self-esteem in women, a need best answered by the egalitarian viewpoint. Judith and Jack Balswick paint a helpful and insightful picture of marriage as a partnership of equals. Cynthia Neal Kimball discusses both the natural and the cultural differences between men and women as they bear on our life together in the church. Mimi Haddad and Alvera Mickelsen present ways that the message of biblical equality can be shared creatively and practically with the church. Alice Matthews concludes this volume by wrestling with the vexed issue of how traditionalists and egalitarians can get along and even move toward reconciliation in Christ, despite their deep differences.

All of the contributors to *Discovering Biblical Equality* have applied their expertise to the cause of helping Christians discover the truth, goodness and joy of gender complementarity without hierarchy. They do so out of their love for Christ and God's Word, as well as their desire to see the kingdom of God flourish more fully. It is our hope and prayer that the reader may be like the noble Bereans who, with open minds and hopeful hearts, examined the Scriptures to test the truth of Paul's message (Acts 17:11).

PART I

SETTING THE STAGE

The Historical Backdrop

1

THE CHANGING ROLES
OF WOMEN IN MINISTRY

The Early Church Through the 18th Century

Ruth A. Tucker

Martyrs, mystics, mothers, scholars, visionaries, missionaries, reformers, rebels—any attempt to categorize and summarize women and their activities, involvement and roles in Christian faith and ministry over eighteen centuries is daunting. But there is good news. No longer are scholars lamenting the paucity of sources. Primary and secondary works abound, and women's names are finding their way into general texts and monographs as never before. No more do Patricia Hill's words (written in 1985) ring true: "As so frequently happens in the writing of history, the women have simply disappeared."[1]

Yet the story of women—whether incorporated into a broader historical narrative or confined to gender-specific accounts—is difficult to encapsulate. The temptation has been to focus on extraordinary women whose lives exemplified what would have been deemed notable if achieved by their male counterparts. Women have thus been judged by the male standard—assumed to be the only standard by which to reckon success. But by this standard women never fully made the mark. The consequence has often led to a distorted picture. On the one hand, women's contributions have been magnified beyond their actual significance; and on the other hand, the story of women has become the story of male discrimination and dominance.

If told from the "underside," the pages of women's history would reveal tender

---

[1]Patricia Hill, *The World Their Household: The American Woman's Foreign Missions Movement and Cultural Transformation, 1870-1920* (Ann Arbor: University of Michigan, 1985), p. 2.

scenes of nursing the sick, feeding the hungry, tending graves, mending clothes, planting flowers, singing psalms and leading bedtime prayers. But the impartial reporter's eye would also peer behind closed doors to expose infanticide, idleness, cursing, gossip, child abuse and thievery. That women professed faith in Christ did not make them immune from evildoing. And the celebrated "saints" were as susceptible to sin as were the nameless lowly ones whose voices have long been stilled in the grave.

In actuality, the story of women in the Christian church is no different from the story of humankind that began in the Garden—a story that promises incredible potential but is severely limited by sin, failure and fallenness. Thus as we look to our past to understand women of faith, we must first look around and see each other as we are. Human nature has not changed—nor has the temptation to gloss over the failings of those we would feature as our foremothers. But our goal is, and ought to be, to present an honest portrait and to allow any achievement to stand as a monument to God's grace. When we reflect on our colorful heritage, we see the good and the bad—a heritage flavored by sacrifice and self-denial and stories of success, but also flawed by frustration and failure. Yet never should we even imagine that what we read is the whole story.

Martyrs

Many of the accounts of women in the early church relate to martyrdom and are told in a way aimed to enhance Christian faith. Like their male counterparts, these women were often remembered for their courage and unfaltering faith in the face of persecution. A woman martyr became an instant heroine as the sum total of her life was judged by the way she conducted herself during torture and death.

Perpetua and Felicitas, her servant, are the most notable of the many women who gave their lives for the faith during the Roman persecution in the early centuries of the Christian era. In A.D. 202, under Septimus Severus, these two were confined to prison with a group of Christians. On the day of execution they were led to the arena, where they were first gored by wild heifers and then beheaded by a gladiator.

As new believers—catechists who were apparently preparing for baptism—they may have had options other than martyrdom that would not have required them to deny the faith publicly. Perpetua had a young child, and she, with Felicitas, might have been permitted to separate from the group and return home with her father, who had come for her. Today a young mother in such circumstances might in good conscience eagerly pursue such a course. But Perpetua (and perhaps equally Felicitas) wanted to make a public stand for the faith, and for that sacrifice they have been remembered through the centuries.

Perpetua's "ambivalent position regarding her son reveals some potential ambiguity regarding the roles of mother and martyr," writes Joyce Salisbury. "Did one have to renounce the maternal role in order to seek Christian spiritual perfection in the same way that Perpetua renounced her expected role?" The answer to that question is at least a qualified yes.[2]

Some decades later under Emperor Decius, Alexandria in North Africa became a center for persecution of Christians. Here the response was mixed. Some suffered unto death; others denied the faith and escaped. The account of Eusebius is as inspiring as it is chilling:

> They led a woman called Quinta, who was a believer, to the temple of an idol, and attempted to force her to worship, but when she turned away in disgust, they tied her by the feet, and dragged her through the whole city, over the rough stones of the paved streets, dashing her against the millstones, and scourging her at the same time, until they brought her to the same place, where they stoned her. (*Ecclesiastical History* 6.41)

In another instance of torture, "they seized that admirable virgin, Apollonia, then in advanced age, and beating her jaws, they broke out all her teeth, and kindling a fire before the city, threatened to burn her alive unless she would repeat their impious expressions." She initially hesitated, "but when suffered to go, she suddenly sprang into the fire and was consumed" (Eusebius *Ecclesiastical History* 6.41).

Not all professing Christians, however, responded as did Quinta and Apollonia. Many women and men denied the faith in the face of torture and persecution, as Eusebius goes on to reveal. Some denied the faith outright. Advancing to the altars, they "boldly asserted that they had never before been Christians. . . . Some, also, after enduring the torture for a time, at last renounced" (Eusebius *Ecclesiastical History* 6.41).

But those who died for their faith—the named and the unnamed—made a sacrifice that has served the church through the ages. Tertullian's famous maxim "The blood of the martyrs is the seed of the church" captures a truth that is easily forgotten in an age of cheap grace. There was a profoundly simple theology of martyrdom in the early church that burned in the hearts of those faithful martyrs—a theology that said the truth was worth dying for.

---

[2]Joyce E. Salisbury, *Perpetua's Passion: The Death and Memory of a Young Roman Woman* (New York: Routledge, 1997), p. 87.

Mothers of the Church

No study of theology is complete without addressing the foundational teachings of the church fathers—patristics, as they are known. From Irenaeus to Augustine, these men had a profound influence on how biblical teachings would be understood through the centuries that followed. There is no comparable group of church mothers. There were actual mothers—such as Monica the mother of St. Augustine, who holds a place of honor in the church largely because of her faithful prayers for her wayward son as recounted in his classic writing *The Confessions.* There were other great mothers in the course of church history—most notably Susanna Wesley— but they were known primarily for nurturing their famous sons. The theologians, from Augustine to Aquinas to Luther and Wesley and Barth, were men. Women were excluded from this elite club. "No Daughters of Eve Allowed" would have been a fitting sign on the clubhouse door. The woman, so the argument ran, was the one tempted by Satan and the first to fall into sin. She was more easily deceived than the man and thus would have been a menacing presence in the ivory towers of theological discussion and decision-making forums.

Yet despite the obstacles there were women who gravitated to the study of Scripture and the formulation of theology. They were typically women of some wealth who joined in community to study and serve those in need. It was within such experiments with ascetic living that women most often found opportunities for learning and for ministry in the church of the early centuries. In this era monastic communities were less formal than they later became, and they were frequently confined to a Roman matron's home or attached to a church or cathedral. The activities of the women were wide ranging and varied—though always with an overarching focus on personal holiness and care for those in need.

An example is the community surrounding Marcella in fourth-century Rome. These women renounced their wealth and fashion finery, donned brown dresses and went out into the streets to serve the needy. But they often developed reputations for more than humanitarian service and holy living. Marcella was also known for her keen mind and understanding of the Bible. She was a close associate of Jerome (who translated the Vulgate Bible), and when he was away from Rome, he referred those who sought his counsel to her. "If an argument arose about some evidence from Scripture," he wrote, "the question was pursued with her as the judge."[3]

---

[3]Jerome *Epistle* 127.2-7, quoted in Elizabeth A. Clark, *Women in the Early Church*, Message of the Fathers of the Church 13 (Wilmington, Del.: Glazier, 1983), pp. 205-8.

Another woman whose name is associated with early monastic life is Paula, a widow and mother of five children. She too was a friend of Jerome and worked closely with him on his translation of the Vulgate Bible. Later she followed him to Palestine, where she founded a monastery for women. Here as elsewhere she was known primarily for good works, her reputation largely built on Jerome's high praise of her.

But her name was also associated with his in a negative light. Both Paula and Jerome promoted the practice—and the ideal—of celibacy. Indeed it was considered impossible to live a truly holy life without sexual abstinence. For Paula and Jerome, however, this ideal did not preclude a close friendship—so close that it would be associated with scandal. "Before I knew the house of saintly Paula," wrote Jerome, "my praises were sung through the city." But that changed due to an "evil report." He lamented that "the only fault found in me is my sex, and that only when Paula comes to Jerusalem."[4]

Throughout medieval times there were women who challenged the established church to return to holiness and women who claimed theological insight through visions and revelations. But never did they reach the stature of the great theologians such as Gregory the Great or Hildebrand or Anselm or Thomas Aquinas or Peter Lombard. The *fathers* laid the foundation for biblical and theological dogma, and their successors carried on that tradition to modern times.

Medieval Monastics

Women's monasticism began in the fourth and fifth centuries and continued to grow during the centuries that followed. Initially most convents were small and privately owned and operated, typically with close connections to an aristocratic family. Later women's orders were founded that paralleled male monasticism and spread into more remote geographical areas.

Beginning in the eighth and ninth centuries, there was a steep decline in women's monasticism, largely as a result of the monastic reform movements—reform with a distinctly masculine flavor. The number of new convents was strictly limited, and the activity of nuns was severely regulated. There were exceptions, however, such as educated and highly respected Lioba, who served a long tenure as the missionary abbess of Bischofsheim in Germany, beginning in 748. In that capacity she had regular contact with a wide range of people—from villagers to bishops—who often

---

[4]Quoted in *The Letters of Abelard and Heloise*, trans. Betty Radice (New York: Penguin, 1974), p. 98.

came to her for counsel on church matters.[5] By the twelfth century women's monasticism was on the rise again, at least in numbers.

In many respects, however, the convent provided a less than healthy atmosphere. The strict cloistering of nuns under the authoritarian rule of an abbess sometimes led to what would today be deemed mental disorders—though at the time it was viewed as piety on the road to perfection. In his book *Holy Anorexia* Rudolph Bell writes of young women who walked barefoot in snow, slept on boards, beat themselves until the blood ran, or deprived themselves of food to the point that they nearly starved themselves to death—all in an effort to please God.[6] Cloistering also led to dissatisfaction with monastic life, and even open rebellion. In the late sixth century some forty nuns, led by the infamous Chrodield, kidnapped their abbess, held her in custody at a nearby church, and then returned and plundered the convent.[7] In a few instances convents were little more than brothels, as was alleged by the bishops of Chartres and Rouen. Indeed, according to a monastic leader, the nuns in many of the convents in France during the twelfth century were involved in prostitution.[8]

Even when there was outward success, the celibate life did not necessarily lend itself to a sense of contentment and spiritual growth, as is illustrated by the story of Heloise. She was caught up in the most notorious scandal of the twelfth century—the scandal of a pregnant teenage student who had been seduced by her teacher twice her age. Peter Abelard was not just a teacher; he was a monk and a philosopher who had a reputation for brilliance and a quick wit. But he paid a heavy price for his sin. He was attacked in his apartment and castrated. He repented of his wrongdoing and went on to become one of the great thinkers of his era—only to have his writings condemned shortly before he died.

Heloise did not repent. She longed to be the mistress—if not the wife—of the man she loved. But Abelard was committed to a life of celibacy. She entered a convent at his insistence, though her heart was not in it. "I can expect no reward for this from God," she lamented, "for it is certain that I have done nothing as yet for love of him. . . . I would have had no hesitation, God knows, in following you or

[5]Eleanor McLaughlin, "Women, Power and the Pursuit of Holiness in Medieval Christianity," in *Women of Spirit: Female Leaders in the Jewish and Christian Traditions*, ed. Rosemary Radford Ruether and Eleanor McLaughlin (New York: Simon & Schuster, 1979), p. 105.
[6]Rudolph Bell, *Holy Anorexia* (Chicago: University of Chicago Press, 1985).
[7]Lina Eckenstein, *Women Under Monasticism* (New York: Russell & Russell, 1896), pp. 67-68.
[8]Will Durant, *Age of Faith* (New York: Simon & Schuster, 1950), p. 806.

going ahead at your bidding to the flames of hell." Abelard responded by pleading with her not to focus on him but rather to "have compassion on Him who suffered willingly for your redemption."

Heloise outlived Abelard and became one of the great abbesses of medieval monasticism. Peter the Venerable, who ruled over some two thousand Cluniac houses, praised her for having "surpassed all women" and "almost every man" in her faithful ministry. Whether she ever came to terms with the pain of frustrated love and with monastic life is a secret she took with her to the grave.[9]

Despite tight restrictions and other negative aspects of monastic life for women, the number of convents significantly increased in the twelfth and thirteenth centuries—though never at a pace to accommodate the number of women seeking to enter the religious life.[10] One of the reasons for the clamor for convent life was a new sense of respect and veneration for certain nuns whose celebrated status was gained largely through visions, dreams and revelations.

Mystics

Mystical forms of spirituality had long been associated with monastic life, but it was "the German nunneries," according to historian Will Durant, that "tended to be havens of intense mysticism." By the thirteenth century female mystics outnumbered men far beyond the borders of Germany, and "their ecstasies were more frequent and more often accompanied by paramystical phenomena."[11]

One of the most revered mystics of this era was Hildegard of Bingen (1098-1179), who ruled as abbess of the Benedictine convent of Disebodenberg. She counseled emperors, popes and bishops, deriving her authority from her claim to direct communion with God. She testified of being guided by a Divine Light—a power that directed her writing and teaching. This did not involve a dream or a trance:

> Ever since I was a child I have always seen this vision in my soul, right up to the present time, when I am over seventy. . . . I do not hear these things with my outer ears, nor do I perceive them with the rational parts of my mind, nor with any combination of my five senses; but only in my soul, with my outer eyes open. . . . Whatever I see or learn in this vision, I hold in my memory for a long time; so that when

---

[9]*Letters of Abelard and Heloise,* pp. 9-55, 117, 129-31, 147.

[10]Caroline W. Bynum, *Jesus as Mother: Studies in the Spirituality of the High Middle Ages* (Berkeley: University of California Press, 1982), p. 14.

[11]Durant, *Age of Faith,* p. 806.

I recall what I have seen and heard, I simultaneously see and hear and understand and, as it were, learn in this moment what I understand. But what I do not see, I do not understand, because I am unlearned.[12]

The most dominant theme of Hildegard's words of wisdom was reform of the church. She spoke out strongly against immorality and corruption associated with the church—from the lowliest priest to the pope. "While her tone is apocalyptic and provocative," writes Fiona Maddocks, "her attitude is hard-line, reactionary rather than revolutionary. Her principal target is . . . the clergy, who in her eyes had neglected their duties and sought temporal power and wealth over spiritual humility."[13] And she did not limit her call for renewal and reform to the clergy. She called on all sinners to repent before it was too late. The alternative was endless agony, as depicted in her visions: "I saw a great fire, black, red, and white, and in it horrible fiery vipers spitting flame; and there the vipers tortured the souls of those who had been slaves of the sin of uncharitableness."[14]

But Hildegard primarily aimed her arrows at the clergy, and amazingly, her ministry was under church sanction. She did not mince words: "Woe to those who have breasts and will not nurse God's children!" Speaking of such bold challenges to the clergy and her "gender-bending metaphors," Kathleen Norris writes: "It is inconceivable today that a Roman Catholic nun might receive papal permission to go on preaching journeys through Germany, and use the opportunity to lambaste the clergy for negligence in their pastoral duties."[15]

Hildegard's authority was derived not only from her visions but also through her status as a powerful abbess. The same was true for Gertrude of Hefla (also known as Gertrude the Great). But many of the noted medieval mystics maintained a more solitary way of life. Julian of Norwich, for example, lived as a hermit in a small cell built into a church wall. From that cell she received visitors and circulated her revelations, a series of sixteen, which came to her on one day in 1373, together forming her widely heralded work *Revelations of Divine Love.* An important theme of her revelations was the necessity of pain and suffering in order to progress spiritually. She also broached a more controversial topic—the

[12]Hildegard of Bingen, *Mystical Writings,* ed. Fiona Bowie and Oliver Davies, trans. Robert Carver (New York: Crossroad, 1992), pp. 144-46.

[13]Fiona Maddocks, *Hildegard of Bingen: The Woman of Her Age* (New York: Doubleday, 2001), p. 216.

[14]Quoted in Henry Osborn Taylor, *The Medieval Mind* (Cambridge, Mass.: Harvard University Press, 1949), pp. 470-71.

[15]Kathleen Norris, *Amazing Grace: A Vocabulary of Faith* (New York: Riverhead Books, 1998), p. 234.

feminine side of God. God came to her as a mother, as did Jesus. Yet she was self-effacing regarding her own standing as a woman, referring to herself as "lewd, feeble and frail" and insisting that she was not going against Paul's prohibition on women's preaching since she was merely testifying to the grace God had given her.[16]

Still another well-known mystic of late medieval times was Catherine of Siena, who is remembered more for her good works and strict asceticism than for her mystical spirituality. It was a visionary experience, however, that launched Catherine into ministry. Her vision captured the frivolity of a street festival, the allure of worldly pleasure: "Suddenly Christ appeared with his mother and a host of saints. Placing a gold ring on her finger, he took Catherine as his bride."[17]

As the bride of Jesus, Catherine claimed the role of a sin-bearer for all those who were too obstinate to live godly lives. To God she vowed to "gather together all our sins, all our faults, all our human miseries, and I'll make a great bunch of them all and carry them all on my shoulders . . . to the foot of the throne of your infinite mercy."[18] But her ministry involved far more than a figurative collecting of sins; she spent most of her days in the streets of Siena in selfless service to the sick and needy. During the plague of 1374 "she was indefatigable by day and night," healing those who were deemed hopeless by local physicians.[19]

The activity for which she is most remembered is her effort to reform the papacy—and closely tied to that reform effort was her insistence that the pope move back to Rome from Avignon, which she dubbed "the Babylon of the West." She led a delegation on a march to Avignon and managed to get an audience with Pope Gregory XI, who did return to Rome shortly before he died. Her efforts to bring about reform, however, were hindered by the Great Schism, during which time the papacy had more than one claimant to the throne, with popes in Rome and Avignon. Yet Catherine persevered, refusing to give up despite the insurmountable obstacles. Her voluminous correspondence with popes and other church officials stands as a monument to one woman's call for sinners to repent.

---

[16]Edmund College and James Walsh, "Editing Julian of Norwich's *Revelations:* A Progress Report," *Medieval Studies* 38 (1976): 421.

[17]Donald Weinstein and Rudolph Bell, *Saints and Society: the Two Worlds of Western Christendom, 1000-1700* (Chicago: University of Chicago Press, 1982), p. 39.

[18]Quoted in Michael De la Bedoyere, *Catherine: Saint of Siena* (London: Hollis and Carter, 1947), p. 40.

[19]Phillip Schaff, *History of the Christian Church* (Grand Rapids, Mich.: Eerdmans, 1979), 6:196.

Reformers

The sixteenth century is a watershed in the history of the church—and no less so regarding women in church history. In less than a generation, the Protestant Reformers introduced radical changes not only in clerical life but also in everyday life, and there were significant changes in the very tone of the faith. Not surprisingly, there were changes in women's ministry as well.

Eleanor McLaughlin suggests that medieval Christianity was characterized by what is often perceived as a "feminine" notion of spirituality, exemplified in an "image of God, who was Mother as well as Father" and emphasizing "Love more than Intellect."[20] This "feminine" spirituality was in many ways turned on its head with the Reformation, especially with the Reformation's emphasis on the biblical text and its discrediting of mystical and visionary experiences. Likewise, most of the Reformers discredited the monastic system that allowed women opportunities for "professional" ministry.

There was, however, continuity between medieval and Reformation times as well. Like their Catholic predecessors, Reformers often made disparaging references to women. Thomas Aquinas had thought that women were weaker than men "both of mind and of body," and Luther was known for his impetuous slurs on womanhood.

Yet women's voices were hardly silenced within Protestantism. Luther and Calvin and other leading Reformers sought out women for advice and assistance. And women were Reformers in their own right—often challenging the words and actions of their male counterparts. But like their Roman Catholic sisters before them, they rarely overstepped their bounds. For instance, they often couched their strong words in terms of deprecation, frequently referring to themselves as weak, lowly, unworthy and "only a woman."

Katie Von Bora Luther is recognized as the "first lady" of the Reformation, though her ministry was not nearly so extensive as that of other Protestant women who would follow her. The story of this feisty nun's escape from the monastery is well known, as is her subsequent marriage to Martin Luther. Their marriage opened the way for the minister's wife and family to have an important role in the church. She cared for a large household and managed a farm on the side, all the while serving as a partner to the great Reformer.

Argula von Stauffer (1492-1554) was Luther's most outspoken defender in the public arena, gaining her the label of "insolent daughter of Eve" from her Catholic

---

[20]McLaughlin, "Women, Power," p. 102.

opponents. For more than forty years she risked her life and the well-being of her family for the cause of the Protestant Reformation. In a letter to Catholic authorities she asked, "What have Luther and Melanchthon taught save the Word of God?" She taunted them for condemning Luther but not refuting him. In 1523, as a young mother, she boldly defended her views in a debate before the diet of the Empire Nurnberg.[21]

Stauffer (also known by her husband's last name, von Grumbach) was persecuted not only by state officials but also by her husband, whose very livelihood was in jeopardy because of her activities. Luther recognized her sacrificial work in a letter to a friend:

> The Duke of Bavaria rages above measure, killing, crushing and persecuting the gospel with all his might. That most noble woman, Argula von Stauffer, is there making a valiant fight with great spirit, boldness of speech and knowledge of Christ. . . . Her husband, who treats her tyrannically, has been deposed from his prefecture. . . . She alone, among these monsters, carries on with firm faith, though, she admits, not without inner trembling. She is a singular instrument of Christ.[22]

Stauffer's boldness was rooted in her conviction that she was following in a long line of ordinary people uniquely designated to serve God. "The extraordinarily militant roles of Deborah, Jael, Esther, Judith become archetypal," writes Peter Matheson. "Womanly 'shamefacedness,' like all human shame, is thus overcome by the imperative of grace which makes them leaders and thinkers. . . . This perception then unlocks for Argula the reluctance of all true prophets to speak. . . . All normal categories have been turned upside down."[23]

She was twice imprisoned, the second time when she was seventy, shortly before her death. Her crimes amounted to far more than oral protest and circulating books and tracts against Catholic doctrines. She had conducted religious meetings in her home and officiated at secret funerals in cemeteries.[24]

Katherine Zell was another Reformer who boldly challenged the religious establishment, including her fellow Reformers. From her childhood she was, by her own testimony, "a student and sort of church mother," always eager to engage "learned

[21]Ibid., pp. 97-98.

[22]Martin Luther, quoted in ibid., p. 106.

[23]Peter Matheson, introduction to *Argula Von Grumbach: A Woman's Voice in the Reformation*, ed. Peter Matheson (Edinburgh: T & T Clark, 1995), pp. 38-39.

[24]Roland H. Bainton, *Women of the Reformation in Germany and Italy* (Minneapolis: Augsburg, 1971), p. 108.

men" in theological conversations. Her marriage to Matthew Zell, a priest turned Protestant preacher, set the stage for her wide-ranging, lifelong ministry. She headed a vast refugee ministry that helped families fleeing the Peasants' War; she wrote tracts, edited a hymnbook and served as a full partner in her husband's ministry. She boldly defended Anabaptists and others who were persecuted by Catholics and Protestants alike. "Why do you rail at Schwenckfeld?" she demanded of a Lutheran leader. "You talk as if you would have him burned like the poor Servetus at Geneva." She lamented that the Anabaptists—Christians "who accept Christ in all the essentials as we do"—were "pursued as by a hunter with dogs chasing wild boars."[25]

Zell was accused of seeking to become "Doctor Katrina" and "usurping the office of preacher" following her husband's death. She responded to the charges by citing Mary Magdalene, "who with no thought of being an apostle, came to tell the disciples that she had encountered the risen Lord."[26]

She was a prolific writer and today is known largely through her writings. "She stands out from other lay pamphleteers and writers in several ways," writes Elsie McKee.

> The most important is the length of time during which she published, from 1524 until 1558. . . . The amount and especially the diversity of her writings are another surprise. . . . Her literary legacy includes a wide range of genres, from devotional meditations and pastoral counsel and religious instruction to polemical theology, from autobiographical and historical apologetics to a sermon and petitions to Strasbourg's city council for civic reform, as well as personal correspondence.[27]

Religion was very politicized during the Reformation era, and where Protestants ruled, Catholics were persecuted and convents were closed. But in Catholic lands, convents flourished and renewal movements took root. One of the most celebrated of the Catholic monastic reformers was Teresa of Ávila (1515-1582), a Carmelite nun who was known for her visionary mysticism seeking to bring God inside oneself—"perfect union of the soul with God." Her best-known mystical trance was the experience of her heart being pierced by a spear of divine love. But her ministry involved far more than mystical ecstasy. She brought renewal to Car-

---

[25]Katherine Zell, quoted in ibid., pp. 65, 73.
[26]Zell, quoted in ibid., pp. 66-67.
[27]Elsie Anne McKee, *Katharina Schultz Zell: The Life and Thought of a Sixteenth-Century Reformer* (Boston: Brill, 1999), I:xii.

melite convents and established fifteen new houses in less than two decades. For this ministry she was both revered and despised. One leading cleric accused her of being a "restless gadabout, disobedient, contumacious woman who promulgates pernicious doctrines under pretense of devotion . . . and teaches theology as if she were a doctor of the Church."[28]

Rebels with a Cause

In the centuries following the Reformation, women continued to make their mark in ministry—though most often in sectarian movements that emerged outside the established churches. Indeed, throughout Christian history women have readily found opportunities to serve in the developing stages of religious movements but then have faced opposition as these groups moved into the mainstream of institutionalized Christianity.

Anne Hutchinson (1591-1643) is an example of such a woman. She attained a place of prominence among the English Puritans but found that her rebel mentality was not appreciated when the Puritans became the "established church" of the Massachusetts Bay Colony. It is true that she had been a controversial figure before she immigrated to New England. But in old England the Puritan divines were often so consumed with their own rebel cause that they had little time to deal with rebels in their midst—especially someone of her standing in the community (she was the wife of the well-respected William Hutchinson and the mother of fifteen children).

In the Bay Colony, Anne Hutchinson found a welcome acceptance among women, and she quickly established herself as a leader of them—especially through her expertise in midwifery and childcare. But her greatest influence was in the spiritual arena. A student of the Bible, she began holding weekly meetings in her home for the express purpose of elucidating—and often challenging—the Sunday sermons. John Cotton, her minister, initially praised her ministry for encouraging "many of the women (and their husbands) . . . to inquire more seriously after the Lord Jesus Christ."[29]

That Hutchinson was gaining a large following among both women and men was itself enough to make her suspect in the eyes of many of the church leaders, but her exposition of Scripture seriously challenged the theological framework of

---

[28]Quoted in Roland H. Bainton, *Women of the Reformation From Spain to Scandinavia* (Minneapolis: Augsburg, 1977), p. 56.

[29]John Cotton, "The Way of the Congregational Churches Cleared" (1648), in *The Antinomian Controversy*, ed. David D. Hall (Middletown, Conn.: Wesleyan University Press, 1968), p. 412.

Puritan preaching, and this was intolerable. According to Selma Williams, "She offered her own version of the . . . Covenant of Grace: each person's actions to be
guided by his or her own conscience and inner morality; each person to communicate directly with God, without need of outside supervision."[30] And not only were
women included in her circle, but the "Hutchinsonians," as they were called, included many men as well. The women, "as by an Eve," railed a Colonial minister,
"catch their husbands also." For such heresy she was brought to trial, convicted and
banished from the Bay Colony.[31]

In the decades following Hutchinson's banishment, there would be other
women who would test the tolerance of the officials of the Bay Colony. One was
Mary Dyer, a follower of Hutchinson who later, while visiting England, became a
Quaker (Society of Friends). Despite laws against the entry of Quakers into the
colony, Dyer returned to Boston to testify of her new faith. She was twice banished,
but each time she returned, only to be sentenced to hang. She was reprieved at the
last moment and sent away again, but she returned and was hanged in Boston in
the spring of 1660.[32] Her death caused many of the colonists to protest the
"wicked law," but it was not sufficient to prevent the "witch" executions in Salem
only three decades later.

So prominent were women among the Quakers that in the early years they were
rumored to be a cult of women. The most noted Quaker woman was Margaret Fell
Fox (1614-1702). She did not join the Society of Friends until her late thirties, as
the mother of nine children and wife of the wealthy Judge Thomas Fell. After her
husband died, she assumed a more active, aggressive leadership role and was twice
imprisoned for conducting illegal meetings, with one prison term extending for
four years amid deplorable conditions. In 1669, at the age of fifty-five, she married
George Fox, the founder and leader of the Quakers, ten years her junior. Their active ministries often kept them apart, and after he died she continued to give direction to the movement for more than a decade.[33]

Margaret Fell Fox served as a role model and an outspoken advocate of equality

---

[30]Selma Williams, *Divine Rebel: The Life of Anne Marbury Hutchinson* (New York: Holt, Rinehart and Win-
ston, 1981), p. 121.

[31]John Winthrop, *Winthrop's Journal: History of New England, 1630-1649*, 2 vols., ed. James K. Hosmer
(New York: Scribner, 1908), 1:240.

[32]Horatio Rogers, *Mary Dyer of Rhode Island* (Providence, R.I.: Preston and Rounds, 1896), quoted in
The Quaker Reader, ed. Jessamyn West (New York: Viking, 1962), p. 175.

[33]Ruth A. Tucker and Walter Liefeld, *Daughters of the Church: Women and Ministry from New Testament Times
to the Present* (Grand Rapids, Mich.: Zondervan, 1987), pp. 229-32.

for women in society and among the Quakers. She did not mince words in challenging the male establishment. In her booklet *Women's Speaking Justified, Proved and Allowed Of by the Scriptures* she wrote: "But all this opposing of women's speaking, hath arisen out of the bottomless pit."[34] She also spoke out strongly for pacifism and laid the groundwork for that Quaker principle in 1660 through her writing entitled "Declaration and an Information."[35]

Like the Quakers, the early Methodists were perceived as an extremist movement outside the religious mainstream. And as among the Quakers, Methodist women had very prominent roles in the early years—though John Wesley was sensitive about that fact and about being labeled a Quaker because of the large number of women preachers in his ranks.

Susanna Wesley, the mother of John and Charles (and seventeen other children), is perhaps rightly regarded as "the mother of Methodism"—not because she was an active Methodist herself but because of her enormous influence over her two sons. A strong and spirited woman, she challenged her husband's efforts to control her political views, and when he later abandoned her and the children, she preached sermons to his Anglican parishioners. Indeed, she preached so well that there was standing room only for those who came to hear her expound the Scripture. When her husband returned, she stepped down from the pulpit, but her influence in the home continued. She was far more a pragmatist than any sort of modern-day feminist—as were her sons. Their agenda was not equal rights for women but the preaching of the gospel, and women's voices were needed as much as were men's.[36]

John Wesley later referred to his mother as a "preacher of righteousness," a description that aptly fits many of the early Methodist women. Margaret Davidson, Sarah Crosby, Sarah Mallet and others all preached in front of large crowds—though sometimes stepping down from the pulpit or breaking their sermons into short exhortations with hymns interspersed, and being careful not to speak in a high, shrill voice.[37] Most of these women ministered among the working-class, poorer elements of society. Other women mixed easily with royalty and the upper classes of society. Lady Selina, Countess of Huntingdon, donated large sums for the training of Methodist ministers, and she became actively involved in theological

---

[34]Margaret Fell (Fox), *Women's Speaking Justified, Proved and Allowed Of by the Scriptures* (London, 1667), p. 10.

[35]Tucker and Liefeld, *Daughters of the Church*, p. 230.

[36]Ibid., pp. 236-38.

[37]Ibid., pp. 240-41.

issues and ministry placement—showing favor to those who supported George Whitefield's Calvinism as opposed to Wesley's Arminianism. For decades the "Huntingdon Connection" was a power to be reckoned with.[38]

Of all the early Methodist women, the one who stands out the most for faithful service is Mary Bosanquet Fletcher (1739-1815), who actively served in the ministry from age eighteen until her death at seventy-six. Born into wealth, she used her inheritance to found an orphanage, where she served for two decades while preaching and leading Methodist societies on the side. In 1781, at the age of forty-two, she married John Fletcher, one of the most respected Wesleyan theologians and a close associate of John Wesley. Four years later he died, and Mary continued in the ministry as a widow for thirty years. She was a powerful preacher and sometimes spoke to crowds as large as three thousand. She regularly spoke at the "tythe barn," a facility that drew large numbers of itinerant ministers who regarded her as a pastor to pastors. Even after the age of seventy, she continued to preach at as many as six meetings a week.[39]

For John Wesley and other churchmen over the centuries, coming to terms with women preachers was not an easy matter. He was convinced that the apostle Paul did not permit women to preach under ordinary circumstances. But he was also convinced that "the whole world of God termed Methodism is an extraordinary dispensation" and thus did "not fall under the ordinary rules of discipline." To Mary Fletcher, whose ministry was often criticized, Wesley wrote: "I think the strength of the cause rests there—on you having an *extraordinary* call."[40]

Mary Fletcher stood in a long line of women who had served faithfully from the time of Mary Magdalene, Phoebe and Lydia—a line that includes Perpetua, Marcella, Paula, Lioba, Hildegard, Katherine Zell, Teresa of Ávila and Margaret Fell Fox. These women were convinced of their extraordinary call to preach the gospel, and their gifts made a way for them in various and often remarkable ministries through the history of the church.

---

[38]Earl Kent Brown, *Women of Mr. Wesley's Methodism* (New York: Edwin Mellen, 1983), pp. 105, 185-98.
[39]Ruth A. Tucker, *Private Lives of Pastors' Wives* (Grand Rapids, Mich.: Zondervan, 1988), pp. 62-70.
[40]John Wesley, quoted in Brown, *Women of Mr. Wesley's Methodism*, pp. 27-28.

2

EVANGELICAL WOMEN
IN MINISTRY A CENTURY AGO

The 19th and Early 20th Centuries

Janette Hassey

In 1927 the Moody Bible Institute *Alumni News* proudly published a letter containing an astounding personal account of the ministry of Mabel C. Thomas, a 1913 MBI graduate. Thomas, called to the pastorate in a Kansas church, had preached, taught weekly Bible classes and baptized dozens of converts. She concluded her letter with praise, since she "could not have met the many and varied opportunities for service without the training of MBI."[1]

At the beginning of the twentieth century, evangelical churches in America grappled with two thorny issues—theological liberalism and feminist demands for women's equal rights. Many evangelicals responded to the first challenge by reasserting scriptural inspiration and inerrancy. Some of these same "proto-fundamentalists"[2] were convinced that a literal approach to the Bible, and especially to prophecy, demanded equality for women in church ministry.

Today, however, female graduates of MBI and other evangelical institutions rarely enter the pastorate or pulpit. Why do evangelical groups that once welcomed women as pastors and preachers now prohibit or discourage such ministry? How could evangelicals a century ago have held high their inerrant, verbally inspired Bi-

---

[1]Mabel C. Thomas, letter in *Moody Alumni News*, June 1927, p. 12.

[2]The term *fundamentalist* is used here in the classic sense, referring to the theologically conservative Protestant organizations that emerged in the early twentieth century, such as the Independent Fundamental Churches of America (IFCA). This early fundamentalism arose largely as a response by evangelicals to the growing movement of theological liberalism. See also N. J. Cohen, ed., *The Fundamentalist Phenomenon: A View from Within, a Response from Without* (Grand Rapids, Mich.: Eerdmans, 1990).

ble in one hand while blessing the ministries of women preachers, pastors, Bible teachers and evangelists with the other? This chapter will analyze these provocative historical questions.

While investigating women's roles in early fundamentalist circles, I found that fundamentalism a century ago was neither exclusively male dominated nor inherently antifeminist.[3] Specifically, when I examined the life and ministry of transitional evangelical figures such as Dwight L. Moody and A. J. Gordon, or of self-avowed fundamentalists such as W. B. Riley and J. R. Straton, I discovered key leaders who saw their support of women preachers as consistent with their biblical literalism.

These historical findings counter the popular but misleading claim that evangelical feminism, or biblical equality, is simply an accommodation to recent secular feminist and theologically liberal movements for women's rights. Rather, evangelical feminism in America first surfaced in the mid-nineteenth century and accelerated into the early twentieth century. Even before concern for women's equality had coalesced into a social/religious movement, a number of evangelical women had stepped out into public ministry as part of the revival activity of the Second Great Awakening in the early nineteenth century.

Evangelical Women and the Early Bible Institutes

Bible institutes provided a significant training ground for evangelical women who entered public ministry a century ago. Many women received formal biblical and theological training for the first time. Nationally prominent evangelical leaders— Moody in Chicago, A. B. Simpson in New York, Gordon in Boston and Riley in Minneapolis—established major Bible institutes that dominated the movement. Each man's openness to women's public ministry decisively affected women's roles in each school and also influenced the church at large.

Albert B. Simpson (1843-1919) established North America's first Bible institute in 1883—the Missionary Training College for Home and Foreign Missions in New York City. In 1887 the school relocated to Nyack, New York. In 1897 Simpson formed the Christian and Missionary Alliance (C&MA). Simpson gave women a prominent place in church ministry, encouraging women's participation

---

[3]For an in-depth account of my research (including bibliography and appendices), which this chapter summarizes, see Janette Hassey, *No Time for Silence: Evangelical Women in Public Ministry Around the Turn of the Century* (Grand Rapids, Mich.: Zondervan, 1986; reprint Minneapolis: Christians for Biblical Equality).

and leadership in virtually every phase of early C&MA life.[4] He included women on the executive board committee, employed them as Bible professors, and supported female evangelists and branch officers (the early C&MA equivalent to a local minister).[5] Simpson's school at Nyack required women to practice preaching in chapel along with men. Having women in church leadership was consistent with Simpson's lay missionary concept—that ordinary people given basic Bible training could evangelize the lost just as effectively as could seminary-trained clergy.

In 1889 Baptist pastor A. J. Gordon opened the Boston Missionary Training School, later called Gordon Bible College. He claimed that a sanctified, Holy Spirit-filled life, not gender, qualified one for church ministry. In "Women as Evangelists" his wife Maria Gordon described how Gordon's training prepared women to "answer any call of the Spirit."[6] Yearbooks clearly document the wide ministry of women graduates serving as preachers, pastors and Bible teachers.

William Bell Riley, pastor of First Baptist Church in Minneapolis, opened what was perhaps the most aggressive of the fundamentalist Bible schools in 1902. Riley's Northwestern Bible and Missionary Training School employed women preachers in its extension department, while alumnae preached, pastored and evangelized with official school recognition.

Major evangelical schools such as Nyack, Gordon and Northwestern provided women with the training to preach, enter the pastorate and teach Bible while committed to a high view of scriptural authority. Leading the pack was Moody Bible Institute of Chicago, opened by Dwight L. Moody in 1889 as the Bible Institute of the Chicago Evangelization Society.

MBI women openly served as pastors, evangelists, pulpit supply preachers, Bible teachers and even in the ordained ministry. The school's official publication, *Moody Monthly*, listed Lottie Osborn Sheidler as the first woman to graduate from the pastor's course, in August 1929. The activities of alumnae provide the most important indication of MBI's openness to women in public ministry. Equipped at Moody with the skills they needed, female graduates served as pastors and preached in a wide range of denominations.

---

[4]John H. Cable, *A History of the Missionary Training Institute, 1883-1933* (Nyack, N.Y.: Nyack College, 1933), p. 20 (available at A. B. Simpson Historical Library, C&MA headquarters building, Nyack, N.Y.).

[5]Wendell W. Price, "The Role of Women in Ministry of the Christian and Missionary Alliance," D.Min. diss., San Francisco Theological Seminary, 1977.

[6]Mrs. A. J. (Maria) Gordon, "Women as Evangelists," *Northfield Echoes* I (1894): 151.

Although MBI leaders may not have always explicitly encouraged women to preach, pastor or seek ordination, their implicit endorsement of women in those authoritative roles for over forty years cannot be denied. MBI offers the clearest documentation of a turn-of-the-century evangelical educational institution outside of the Wesleyan holiness camp that actively promoted public church ministry for women. None questioned Moody's commitment to a verbally inspired, inerrant Bible. Consequently, the early MBI stands as an appropriate educational symbol of "fundamentalist feminism."

Denominational Approaches to Women in Ministry

Of the Methodist groups, holiness churches were the most open to women's public ministry. For them, the Holy Spirit's second work of grace, not necessarily ordination or education, properly qualified a person to preach. The Free Methodists, Wesleyan Methodists and Church of the Nazarene all promoted equality for women. The Salvation Army admitted women to all ranks of leadership. Newly formed Pentecostal denominations of the early twentieth century continued this holiness practice, often employing Spirit-baptized women as pastors, evangelists and healers.

Roles for women in Baptist circles differed widely. The Free Will Baptists ordained women, and the German and Swedish Baptists encouraged women as pastors and evangelists. American Baptist churches in the North ordained dozens of women in the first quarter of the twentieth century. In contrast, Southern Baptist women who desired to preach or pastor faced enormous opposition.

Smaller groups, such as Bible-believing Quakers, Evangelical Mennonites and the Advent Christian Church, also endorsed women's public church leadership. With their historic emphasis on a seminary-trained clergy, Presbyterian, Episcopal and Lutheran churches largely excluded women from the pastorate by limiting seminary education to males. Only the revivalistic Cumberland Presbyterians, who waived the traditional educational requirements for the ministry, utilized women in leadership to a greater extent. In the wake of the modernist-fundamentalist conflict around the 1920s, groups of conservative Christians began to leave existing denominations and form new associations such as the Independent Fundamental Churches of America (IFCA). Until 1930 this organization welcomed ordained women as members.

Several factors undoubtedly influenced denominational openness toward women in public ministry. The relative freedom for women in the holiness wing of

Methodism points to the influence of theology, especially with respect to the doctrine of the Holy Spirit, in opening doors for women. The wide divergence of practice among Baptists—generally more restrictive in the South—illustrates the impact of regionalism on evangelical feminism. The preaching ministry of some Cumberland Presbyterian women represents the powerful force of revivalism in changing traditional roles for women. The surge of women into Congregational pastorates at this time exemplifies the impact of form of church government on opportunities for women.

The Evangelical Free Church denomination, formed in the 1880s, was revivalist in spirit, congregational in church government, premillennial and "Bible-only" in theology, and concentrated among pietist Scandinavian immigrants in the upper Midwest region. The Free Church utilized women as evangelists, Bible teachers and pastors. The committee that drafted the 1908 constitution for the incorporation of the Swedish Evangelical Free Church of America intended that men and women have equal status in the church. The rules for ordination in 1925 state that "a candidate for ordination shall request a reference from the church of which he or she is a member."[7] Two key leaders of the Free Church, Fredrik Franson and John Gustaf Princell, wrote in public support of women's preaching ministry.

Evangelical Egalitarian Biblical Exegesis

In looking historically at evangelical feminist biblical exegesis concerning women's public church ministry, we will consider ten representative documents written by evangelicals committed to the authority of Scripture. These publications spanned almost seventy years (1859-1926) and helped open doors for women to minister. Thanks partly to the circulation of these books, pamphlets and articles, evangelical women who preached and pastored understood their public ministry to be consistent with their commitment to biblical authority.

Methodist holiness leader Phoebe Palmer (1807-1874) wrote *Promise of the Father* in 1859 to defend the call and need of women to speak in public. She asserted that the gift of the Spirit promised by the Father arrived at Pentecost and was received by both men and women. She argued for the right of women to preach Christ when so led by the Holy Spirit. Palmer's ministry and writing influenced Catherine Booth, Frances Willard and B. T. Roberts.

After hearing Palmer preach, Salvation Army founder Catherine Booth (1829-

---

[7]Della E. Olson, *A Woman of Her Times* (Minneapolis: Free Church Press, 1977), p. 81.

1890) was appalled to read a local minister's violent "scriptural" attack on Palmer and other women preachers. Booth responded with a letter, which was expanded and published as the pamphlet *Female Ministry* in 1859. Booth quoted from Palmer and closely paralleled Palmer's exegesis. For Booth, the Bible urges women gifted and called by the Spirit to preach.

Methodist temperance leader Frances Willard (1839-1898) professed sanctification under Palmer's ministry. Willard wrote *Women in the Pulpit* in 1888 to defend women's ordination. Her book displayed familiarity with the writings of both Palmer and Booth. She found close to forty biblical texts in support of women's public ministry.

Free Church leader Fredrik Franson wrote the article "Prophesying Daughters" in 1889 in response to criticism of his advocacy of female evangelists. He concluded that Scripture overwhelmingly supports women's public ministry and the church must never silence women gifted as apostles, prophets, evangelists or shepherds. For Franson, the Bible cannot forbid what the Spirit blesses. A premillennial dispensationalist like Gordon, Franson interpreted women in the pulpit as an essential sign of the end times.

Converted under Palmer's ministry, B. T. Roberts fought for women's ordination within the Free Methodist denomination. In 1891 Roberts wrote *Ordaining Women*, a scriptural argument emphasizing parallels between slavery and the women's issue. Just as opponents of abolition who appealed to the Bible were greatly mistaken on slavery, so were the opponents of women's ordination.

Baptist A. J. Gordon attended a convention where conservatives forbade a female missionary to speak. In response Gordon wrote "The Ministry of Women" in 1894 to vindicate scripturally the preaching of female missionaries. According to Joel 2:28, female prophecy today should not be the exception but the rule.

When Methodist medical doctor and reformer Katharine Bushnell (1856-1946) sensed God's call to China as a missionary, she agreed on one condition: that God prove to her that Paul did not forbid women's preaching. A scholar of both Hebrew and Greek, Bushnell studied the Bible in depth and then assembled the results of her years of research in a Bible correspondence course for women. In 1919 these lessons were published in book form as *God's Word to Women: One Hundred Bible Studies on Woman's Place in the Divine Economy.*[8] Bushnell exegeted Old Testament pas-

---

[8]Katharine Bushnell, *God's Word to Women* (Oakland, Calif.: K. C. Bushnell, c. 1923; reprint, North Collins, N.Y.: Ray B. Munson, 1976).

sages at length, devoting twenty lessons to Genesis 1–3. She charged that a misunderstanding of Genesis 3:16 lay behind the misinterpretation of Paul's words. Bushnell saw no contradiction between belief in women's equal status in the church and a high view of Scripture as infallible. Because her technical scholarship went over the heads of many untrained laypeople, in 1919 Jessie Penn-Lewis published, with Bushnell's permission, *The Magna Charta of Women*, which presented *God's Word to Women* in simplified form.

In 1926 Lee Anna Starr published *The Bible Status of Woman*, which frequently quoted Bushnell's work. Skilled in both Hebrew and Greek, Starr was ordained by the Methodist Protestant Church and ministered as a local pastor. Dismayed that "modern" women might reject Christianity as a whole because of supposed biblical teachings on women's subordination, Starr sought to correct that misunderstanding in an intellectually viable way.

After welcoming female evangelist Uldine Utley to his pulpit, John Roach Straton came under criticism from those who held that allowing a female to preach constituted a denial of biblical authority. To refute these charges, in 1926 Straton wrote *Does the Bible Forbid Women to Preach and Pray in Public?* He grounded his support of women's preaching in the doctrine of the Holy Spirit, seen in Joel 2 and Acts 2. This pamphlet by such a militant fundamentalist proves that a commitment to both biblical inerrancy and women's public church ministry was feasible in the early twentieth century.

These ten documents reveal two general approaches in early evangelical feminist exegesis. Those authors who argued primarily for women's right to preach tended to focus on the Joel 2-Acts 2 prophecy-fulfillment passages, which state that "your daughters shall prophesy." They viewed Pentecost as the pivotal event in women's liberation. Other writers pushed for women's equality in all spheres of life, not just the pulpit. They stressed the broader theological issues of creation-redemption. They saw the incarnation of Christ and his victory on the cross over Satan as the crucial event for women, since Christ's atonement ameliorates the effects of the Fall.

Without evangelical publications such as these, the rise of women to positions of leadership in evangelical, Bible-believing circles would have been inconceivable. Evangelical women preached, pastored and taught the Bible in the late nineteenth and early twentieth centuries because they and many other evangelicals were convinced that their ministry entailed obedience to God's Word, not rebellious disobedience.

Reasons for the Rise of Evangelical Women in Public Ministry

Why did so many evangelical women find pulpits and pastorates open to them for the first time in the late nineteenth and early twentieth centuries? Evangelical theology, a charismatic style of church leadership, and social activism provide keys to understanding this phenomenon.

Evangelical theology. Evangelical women entered the pulpit because significant elements of their own theology supported such a practice. At interdenominational Bible institutes and conferences, many evangelicals rubbed shoulders with other Christians whose theology promoted an egalitarian concept of women in ministry, including the Quakers, the United Brethren and those in the Salvation Army. In addition, the interaction of holiness churches and even some Pentecostal groups with other branches of evangelicalism significantly influenced views toward women. For example, Moody Bible Institute opposed Aimee Semple McPherson's Pentecostal doctrine of healing but not her right to preach or pastor.

Along with Bible institutes, Bible conferences served as key agencies in the promotion of premillennial and fundamentalist theology among evangelical laypeople. The earliest Bible conferences welcomed women preachers and Bible teachers, thus exposing thousands of conference participants to women in positions of authoritative leadership. In 1880 Moody, for example, organized the Northfield Conference, which frequently featured women such as Maria Gordon. Winona Lake Bible Conference, founded in 1895 and closely tied to MBI, widely publicized the public ministry of women from MBI, the Salvation Army and elsewhere.

An emphasis among evangelicals on the sanctifying, empowering work of the Holy Spirit usually corresponded to increasing openness to the exercise of women's gifts. Bishop Alma White, founder of the Pillar of Fire Church, declared that "so long as the Holy Spirit operates in the world, women must necessarily preach the Gospel."[9] Moody, Gordon, Simpson and Franson also emphasized a second work of the Holy Spirit in the life of a Christian to provide power for witness and missions.

Franson clearly tied his use of female evangelists to the urgent needs he sensed in worldwide missions:

> Brothers, the harvest is great and the laborers are few. If the ladies want to help out
> in the fields during the harvest time, then I think we should let them bind as many
> sheaves as they can. It is better that women bind the sheaves, than that the sheaves

---

[9]Alma White, *Woman's Ministry* (London: Pillar of Fire, n.d.), p. 2.

get lost. When one has been sent out on the field and heard the real cries for help from dozens of places, places to which one cannot possibly reach, then one cannot help but think, "It seems strange that only such a few verses of Scripture, about which there are so many disputes, should be made such obstacles to hinder those who otherwise would have responded to these calls for help."[10]

These pietistic evangelicals sought personal holiness expressed concretely in evangelistic witness and missionary concern. Given that context, who dared silence a sanctified woman who was Spirit-led to preach and testify? "It was the theology of the movement and the essential nature of the place of public testimony in the holiness experience which gave many an otherwise timid woman the authority and power to speak out 'as the Holy Spirit led her.'"[11]

Eschatology and prophetic interest as well as emphasis on the Holy Spirit contributed to new attitudes toward women's ministry. For many premillennialists, Joel's description of "prophesying daughters" in the last days took on vital significance (Joel 2:28). Franson concluded that "we seem to see Psalm 68:12 being fulfilled in our day, 'the Lord gives the command: the women who proclaim the good tidings are a great host.'"[12] Since Christ's second coming would be preceded by a special outpouring of the Holy Spirit, many interpreted the increase in women preachers as visible evidence of such an outpouring.

Truly convinced that the end was near and that at Christ's return the unconverted faced damnation in hell, turn-of-the-century premillennialists urgently pursued fervent evangelism and intensely promoted worldwide missions. Faced with what they considered an emergency situation with eternal souls at stake, these evangelicals often enlisted male and female workers alike to preach the gospel to a dying world.

Bible institute founder Charles H. Pridgeon based his forceful appeal for women in ministry on the reality of hell and the imminent return of Christ in these "last days."

If it was "last days" on Pentecost, it certainly is now. Millions are perishing for the bread of life. If there is not only a present world that needs regeneration, but also a hereafter of heaven and hell, we who have the light can realize our awful responsibil-

---

[10]Fredrik Franson, quoted in Edvard P. Torjesen, *Fredrik Franson: A Model for Worldwide Evangelism* (Pasadena, Calif.: William Carey Library, 1983), p. 47.

[11]Melvin Easterday Dieter, *The Holiness Revival in the Nineteenth Century* (Metuchen, N.J.: Scarecrow, 1980), p. 42.

[12]Franson, quoted in Torjesen, *Franson*, p. 62.

ity. Our forces need to be mobilized and that not only of men but also women and children. The question of the ministry of women is more than just an academic question. The force of men who offer for His service is inadequate. Souls are perishing. There is no time to argue whether it be a man or woman that performs the service. The need must be met. The dying one that is saved will be saved just as well by whomsoever brings the Word of Life. We can split hairs, look wise, and hold up some possible meaning of a text or two of Scripture when the whole trend of God's Word is on the other side; millions are going to hell while we delay.[13]

It was said that God's obvious use of women preachers to convert sinners proved he was blessing their ministry. Surely God would not put such a seal of approval on women's disobedience, proponents argued. Arguing that women are morally superior and consequently have the potential to be even more effective preachers than men, T. DeWitt Talmage said women preachers "have a pathos and a power in their religious utterances that men can never reach."[14]

There were, of course, those who disputed women's biblical right to preach publicly—but not always with clear knowledge of what they were disputing. When Christian Golder accused proponents of women's ordination of denying biblical inspiration and charged that "in order to emancipate woman, one must first divorce himself from the Word of God," he had not read the evangelical feminist interpretations that were circulating.[15] When P. D. Stephenson blamed the women's movement on "free thinkers, Socialists, agnostics, evolutionists and other foes of the Bible and Evangelical Christianity," he failed to account for advocates of biblical inspiration who also fought for women's equality.[16] The editor of the *Western Recorder*, who opposed women's public ministry, finally conceded that some faithful disciples do believe Scripture yet do not silence women.[17]

At any rate, it was obvious that one's commitment to biblical authority was not the deciding factor in whether to oppose or endorse women's ministry; inerrantists sat on both sides of the fence. Most evangelicals at this time were obliged to toler-

---

[13]Charles H. Pridgeon, *The Ministry of Women* (Gibsonia, Penn.: Pittsburgh Bible Institute, n.d.), pp. 26-28. Pridgeon (1863-1932), a Presbyterian minister who worked as an evangelist with Moody, had contact with Simpson and professed sanctification in 1892. He founded Pittsburgh Bible Institute with his wife, Louise Shepard Pridgeon, in 1901.

[14]T. DeWitt Talmage, *Woman: Her Power and Privileges* (New York: J. S. Ogilvie, 1888), p. 16.

[15]Christian Golder, *History of the Deaconess Movement in the Christian Church* (Cincinnati, Ohio: Jennings and Pye, 1903), p. 528.

[16]P. D. Stephenson, *The Woman Question* (Charlotte, N.C.: Presbyterian Publishing, 1899), p. 227.

[17]"Editorial Response," *Western Recorder*, February 8, 1923, p. 8.

ate legitimate interdenominational differences of opinion on such issues as sacraments, church government, Calvinism and even women's ministry.

Charismatic church leadership. Evangelical women experienced increased freedom to preach and pastor in those circles that emphasized Spirit-given gifts of leadership (Greek *charismata*) as the essential qualification for ministry. In the early charismatic stages of the revivalist, holiness and fundamentalist movements, evangelicals often perceived women to be as spiritually gifted as men.

Revivalism, which emphasized personal conversion and testimony, tended to loosen institutional structure and foster informal, spontaneous worship; women enjoyed new opportunities to preach in such settings.[18] The emphasis on charismatic authority and lay leadership resulted in relaxed educational requirements for the clergy. Most early fundamentalists continued with this concept of a nonprofessional ministry, sending workers with only Bible institute training or less into gospel ministry and pastorates. Turn-of-the-century women, barred from most evangelical seminaries, could attend Bible institutes and prepare equally with men for ministry in revivalistic churches.

Doors to public ministry were more open to the daughters and wives of evangelical men holding egalitarian views. Presbyterian minister A. T. Pierson, for example, agreed with his close friend A. J. Gordon on the need for wider opportunities for women in ministry.[19] Pierson fully supported his own daughter, who served as a pastor and evangelist in Vermont.

The wife-husband team ministry approach of women such as Phoebe Palmer, Catherine Booth and Hannah Whitall Smith exemplified the importance of male support for women in public ministry. Similarly, women like Josephine Princell and Maria Gordon were able to teach along with their husbands at newly opened Bible institutes.

Social activism. Between the 1880s and the adoption in 1920 of the Nineteenth Amendment, which gave women the vote, the United States completed its transition from an agricultural society to a worldwide industrial power. Social factors such as accelerating immigration, rapid urbanization and industrialization trans-

---

[18]Martha Tomhave Blauvelt, "Women and Revivalism," in vol. I of *Women and Religion in America*, ed. Rosemary Radford Ruether and Rosemary Skinner Keller (San Francisco: Harper & Row, 1981), discusses the early-nineteenth-century setting. The major exceptions to the rule were the revivalistic churches in the South.

[19]Dana Lee Robert, "Arthur Tappan Pierson and Forward Movements of Late-Nineteenth-Century Evangelicalism," Ph.D. diss., Yale University, 1984, pp. 308-10.

formed American life after the Civil War and prepared the ground for various reform movements.

Most nineteenth-century feminists had championed other reform movements
such as abolition or temperance. By the turn of the century, the feminist movement
encompassed a wide spectrum of advocates and reform platforms. Religious or
evangelical feminism held up religion or Scripture as woman's basis for equality. In
contrast, secular feminism, exemplified by Elizabeth Cady Stanton, grounded
equality for women in natural law or Enlightenment philosophy, rejecting traditional religion and the Bible as degrading to women.

The social activism of this period provided a positive context for many evangelical women to enter public church ministry. Temperance and suffrage did what the
abolition movement had done in antebellum America: they provided an impetus
for women's rights.

As socially concerned women spoke out on behalf of slaves or victims of alcohol
abuse, they found the power and reason to speak out on their own behalf. Women
trained through temperance and suffrage work to organize and speak publicly
gained the confidence and experience needed for local church leadership. In 1910
Stanton Coit called every suffrage platform a pulpit and each suffragist a
preacher.[20] In many evangelical churches, the first woman to preach from the pulpit
was a temperance or suffrage worker.

Evangelical women in church leadership were often associated with the Women's
Christian Temperance Union (WCTU), an organization that grew out of the 1873-
1874 crusade of Midwestern Protestant women to close saloons.[21] The strategy of
"gospel temperance" relied on religious conversion to reform both the drunkard and
the liquor industry. Frances Willard, WCTU president from 1879 until 1898, developed the Union into the largest, most powerful and most influential organization of
women in the nineteenth century, enlisting more than two million members worldwide by 1897. The WCTU enabled many women to develop a changing role for
themselves and served as a base for other causes and reforms.[22]

---

[20]Stanton Coit, *Women in Church and State* (London: West London Ethical Society, 1910), p. 27.

[21]Barbara Leslie Epstein, *Politics of Domesticity: Women, Evangelism and Temperance in Nineteenth-Century America*
    (Middletown, Conn.: Wesleyan University Press, 1981); Susan Dye Lee, "Evangelical Domesticity:
    The Woman's Temperance Crusade of 1873-74," in *Women in New Worlds*, ed. Hilah F. Thomas and
    Rosemary Skinner Keller, 2 vols. (Nashville, Tenn: Abingdon, 1981-1982), 1:293-309.

[22]Ruth Bordin, *Woman and Temperance: The Quest for Power and Liberty, 1873-1900* (Philadelphia: Temple
    University Press, 1981); Carolyn DeSwarte Gifford, "For God and Home and Native Land: The
    W.C.T.U.'s Image of Woman in the Late Nineteenth Century," in *Women in New Worlds*, 1:310-27.

Many evangelical leaders openly promoted women's gospel temperance work. Moody utilized Willard herself in his campaigns, Maria Gordon led the Boston-area WCTU, and Josephine Princell of the Free Church organized a Swedish WCTU. MBI approvingly advertised the temperance work of several WCTU representatives, such as national evangelist Helen L. Byrnes.

Suffrage was likewise a major issue to millions of American women of this era, including evangelical women in public ministry. Willard combined temperance and suffrage advocacies. Many evangelical women followed her challenge to support suffrage as a matter of Christian duty. Pious women, they argued, could use their votes to elevate American society. In fact, the National American Woman Suffrage Association (NAWSA) depended on the support of evangelical women. Many churches also supported these women. William Bell Riley, citing Willard as a convincing argument for women's right to preach, opened his church to suffrage meetings.

Anna Howard Shaw represented the overlap in evangelical women's leadership in both church ministry and the temperance and suffrage movements. Rev. Shaw, ordained by the Methodist Protestant Church, served as superintendent of the WCTU Department of Franchise from 1888 to 1892. She resigned from her pastorate to lecture and organize woman's suffrage, serving as NAWSA president from 1904 to 1915. For Shaw, the right to vote was a key to woman's freedom.

Winona Bible Conference speaker Viola D. Romans also symbolized the relationship between the temperance and suffrage crusades and evangelical women in ministry. Romans, a suffragist and WCTU representative, lectured in 1914 on equality with men in home and church, basing her presentation on Genesis.

> I am a suffragist. . . . I understand most of you here are suffragists. . . . My grandmother was a Quaker preacher. I was brought up with the idea in the home and church that we had co-privileges along with our brothers. . . . God blessed them and set them at much the same work, that of replenishing the earth and subduing it. He said not a word about subduing each other.[23]

The story of Christabel Pankhurst ties together many of the factors that led to the rise of women in public church leadership a century ago.[24] A strategist of the militant suffrage crusade in Britain before World War I, Pankhurst developed her leadership and public speaking skills in women's struggle to gain the vote. After her conversion to premillennial fundamentalist Christianity, a reporter wrote that "she

---

[23]Viola D. Romans, "The Nation's Call," *Winona Echoes*, August 1914, pp. 349-50.
[24]David Mitchell, *The Fighting Pankhursts: A Study in Tenacity* (New York: Macmillan, 1967).

has been converted to Christianity of a somewhat rigid type, which brings her into great demand as a lecturer in churches on literal inspiration."

Like D. L. Moody, Catherine Booth and others, Pankhurst influenced evangelicalism on both sides of the ocean. She began her public ministry in 1921 and gained new fame in America as a prominent preacher for the premillennial cause, traveling nationwide to speak at Bible conferences, including Winona. A frequent visitor at Moody Bible Institute, Pankhurst preached at Straton's Calvary Baptist Church in New York City in 1924 and then at the National Bible Institute. For more than twenty years she attracted immense audiences and rallied premillennialists; she claimed that thousands were converted through her evangelistic preaching.

In a sense Pankhurst represented the end of an era. Shortly after her time, other conservative evangelical women who were called to preach began to find the pulpits of revival tents, fundamentalist churches, Bible conferences and Bible institutes off limits.

Reasons for the Decline of Women in Public Ministry

What can account for the gradual decline of public ministry opportunities for evangelical women between the world wars? First, fundamentalist separatist subcultures emerged which tended to harden on the women's issue. Second, as fundamentalism institutionalized, women were squeezed out of leadership roles. Third, the conservative Protestant backlash against changing social values resulted in restrictions on women in ministry. Finally, a more literalist view of Scripture among fundamentalists meant less flexibility in interpreting the subject of women in ministry.

Separatist fundamentalist subcultures. Between the world wars, fundamentalists lost the battle for control of mainline denominations and schools; in regrouping, they created a host of separate institutions. Whereas the nineteenth-century evangelical empire had stood near the center of American culture, the fundamentalism of the 1930s withdrew and formed distinct subcultures. Part of the movement veered in a militant, separatist, extremist direction, often allied with far right-wing politics. In that process of narrowing, opportunities for women also tightened.

Although united briefly in the initial attack on modernist theology, fundamentalism began to splinter in defeat. A growing disputatious, antiecumenical attitude among fundamentalists eliminated earlier cooperative interdenominational undertakings such as WCTU meetings. The Pentecostal practices of tongues and healing and even Methodist perfectionism increasingly antagonized fundamentalists.

The feminist heritage was lost even among the holiness churches, except where it was institutionalized, as in the Salvation Army. By World War II most evangelicals could go a lifetime never having heard a woman preacher or pastor, and girls grew up with fewer and fewer role models of women in public ministry.

Significantly, fundamentalism widened geographically during the same decades in which it narrowed denominationally. Whereas early fundamentalist strength had lain in the urban North, the welcoming into their fold of southern conservative cousins like the Southern Baptists produced a shift of strength to the southern Bible Belt. This change paralleled the establishment of Dallas Seminary, a fundamentalist graduate school in the South. Southern conservative social values, which traditionally included the subordinate place of women in society and church, typified an increasingly large segment of the fundamentalist constituency.

The early fundamentalist involvement in social action waned as the movement became more rigid. Historical distance from earlier temperance and suffrage crusades decreased one's chances of hearing evangelical women speak publicly in church. The secular feminist movement certainly lost steam and direction after the passage of the Nineteenth Amendment granted women the vote in 1920. As evangelicals turned from active social concern and reform to institution-building and theological squabbles, women lost opportunities to speak out on behalf of others as they had done in support of temperance and suffrage.

Institutionalization. Both Moody Bible Institute and the Evangelical Free Church illustrate the process of institutionalization and its effect on women's roles. Changes in educational programs in these denominations furnish one indication of this change. MBI, for instance, began in the 1880s as a practical training center for women and men in lay ministry. MBI's inauguration of a graduate school a century later suggests an enormous transformation. Similarly, early Free churches typically supported itinerant lay evangelists rather than seminary-trained pastors. The establishment of doctoral programs at Trinity University later in the twentieth century also indicates immense institutional transition.

With the rising social status of many churches came the demand for professional, seminary-trained clergy in place of charismatic lay ministry. As frontier churches previously viewed as home mission fields increased in numbers and wealth, congregations could afford to support a married man as minister. Some considered the presence of a female pastor a tacit acknowledgment of a church's poverty.

Educational attainment and credentials often replaced spiritual gifts as the essential leadership qualifications. The establishment of interdenominational Dallas Theological Seminary in 1924—the nation's first strictly fundamentalist seminary—symbolized this shift.[25] Lewis Sperry Chafer, undoubtedly influenced by Charles Scofield's view on women while teaching at Philadelphia College of the Bible, was the founder of Dallas. Emerging from the modernist-fundamentalist debates of the 1920s, it admitted only born-again male college graduates endowed with ministry gifts. Chafer clearly distinguished his school from Bible institutes, claiming that "those Bible courses which have been designed for laymen and Christian workers generally are not adequate as a foundational Bible training for the preacher or teacher."[26]

In the first quarter of the twentieth century, Bible institutes furnished a large slice of local church leadership and influenced theology accordingly. Later, Dallas and similar schools began training the men who went on to administer and teach at Bible institutes.[27] When evangelical churches were clamoring for seminary-trained pastors, Dallas sent out only men to fill those posts. Other seminaries trained women but discouraged them from preaching and pastoral roles.

By the mid-twentieth century, churches increasingly directed women gifted to minister away from pulpit and pastoral duties toward safer spheres of service. Since World War I, the rapidly rising field of religious or Christian education has drawn trained women into its fold. A female Bible institute graduate who in 1910 might have pastored a small church or traveled as an itinerant revivalist would by 1940 more likely serve as a director of religious education.

Professionalization affected women's service on the mission field as well. Foreign missions continued as an acceptable ministry option for women throughout the twentieth century. But the shift to overseas specialties in medicine, education, agriculture and construction influenced perceptions of appropriate roles for women. Before specialization, churches sent missionaries primarily as preachers, church planters and Bible teachers, with women filling those positions along with

---

[25]Rudolf A. Renfer, "A History of Dallas Theological Seminary," Ph.D. diss., University of Texas, 1959.

[26]Lewis Sperry Chafer, "Effective Ministerial Training," *Evangelical Theological College Bulletin*, May 1925, p. 9.

[27]An examination of the educational background of the men who teach Bible and theology on MBI's faculty listed in the 1985-1986 catalog illustrates the phenomenal impact of Dallas. Thirteen of the nineteen Bible and theology professors graduated from Dallas. The dean of education and chairs of five departments—Bible, Theology, Pastoral Studies, Evangelism and Christian Education—also graduated from Dallas.

men. As specialization increased, women more often than not filled supportive roles as men handled preaching and pastoring. And female missionaries unused to preaching overseas felt less comfortable in American pulpits on furlough.

In summary, women found declining opportunities for leadership in evangelical churches, schools and agencies as institutionalization squelched earlier gift-based forms of ministry.[28] In worship as well as in education, routinization set in. In a shift toward more regulated and formalized church services, praying and speaking were no longer left to chance. Structured rather than spontaneous worship tended to exclude women from public participation.

Fundamentalist reaction to social change. Opposition to women's public ministry was part of a post-World War I reaction to vocal, extreme feminism and a perceived decline in womanhood. Dress, appearance and habits constituted the most conspicuous signs of American women's growing independence. Shorter skirts, bobbed hair, cosmetics, public smoking and drinking—these externals marked the "liberated" woman. More substantially, the expansion of women into the workforce produced growing economic independence.

The onset of the Depression undoubtedly accelerated the return of fundamentalists and evangelicals to traditional values. Evangelicals feared that cultural trends toward women's freedom in dress, habits, morals and occupations might destroy the family. As churches identified women preachers and pastors with the secular women's movement, opposition rose. Hoping to save the American home, many evangelicals narrowed their view of appropriate women's roles. The attack by John R. Rice, a separatist fundamentalist, against *Bobbed Hair, Bossy Wives and Women Preachers* illustrates how these issues connected in this era.[29]

The backlash in conservative Protestant circles against changing social mores can be traced in *Moody Monthly* magazines of the 1930s. Numerous articles appeared on the "new woman," exposing the ill effects of modern morality. The disturbing shifts in the roles and behavior of women in American society frightened conservative Christians. Convinced that the survival of the traditional family and of the entire social order was at stake, many evangelicals tightened their approach to women in church ministry. Might not women's leadership there give encouragement to other destructive tendencies?

---

[28]See David Moberg, *The Church as a Social Institution* (Englewood Cliffs, N.J.: Prentice-Hall, 1962), and H. Richard Niebuhr, *The Social Sources of Denominationalism* (New York: Henry Holt, 1929), on the institutionalization process in religious groups.

[29]John R. Rice, *Bobbed Hair, Bossy Wives and Women Preachers* (Wheaton, Ill.: Sword of the Lord, 1941).

MBI and other evangelical institutions began to advocate a more limited role expectation for women in an effort to maintain traditional family and moral values. In the process, evangelicals took away ministry opportunities from women.

Fundamentalist exegesis. In reaction to perceived threats to the family and society, many fundamentalist institutions revised their earlier perspectives on biblical teaching on women. Fundamentalists no longer interpreted the passages in I Timothy 2 or I Corinthians 14 as occasional advice for specific problems; instead these passages were regarded as giving transcultural principles for all times and places.

In the early twentieth century, fundamentalists had tightened the lines around the concept of inerrancy; it became one of the Fundamentals and was understood to require a literalistic interpretation of Scripture. Opposition to women ministers may have been formalized as a byproduct. Just as the South had employed extremely authoritative and literalistic views of Scripture to justify slavery, the North adopted similar attitudes toward women after the modernist battles. As this type of literalism became entrenched, fundamentalists interpreted passages about women more rigidly.

Opportunities for women to preach and pastor declined as evangelical churches identified such service as contrary to Scripture. Support of women's public ministry came to be seen as a denial of biblical inerrancy. Straton's 1926 pamphlet was one of the last publications from the fundamentalist camp arguing for women's right to preach. Few evangelical men followed in the steps of Moody, Gordon, Simpson, Franson, Riley and Straton to publicly defend women preachers. When the publications containing feminist exegesis from the evangelical perspective went out of print, little appeared to replace them.[30] Unable or unwilling to view women's public ministry as consistent with Scripture, evangelical churches increasingly labeled their pulpits "For Men Only."

This shift in biblical exegesis produced theological reformulation. For example, the same premillennialism used by Gordon and Franson to advocate women preachers was utilized by later writers to restrict women. Certain dispensationalists began to interpret women's leadership as an *evil* sign of the end times, identifying such women with the whore of Babylon.

Turn-of-the-century evangelicals committed to the imminent, premillennial return of Christ had put their intense convictions into action. The urgent need to mobilize workers to spread the gospel worldwide left no time for one sex to remain

---

[30]Only recently have reprints of these books, pamphlets and articles been made available.

silent. Later premillennialists apparently retained intellectual assent to Christ's soon return but relaxed considerably on the urgency of evangelizing the world. They proved more concerned with opposing evolution than promoting evangelism, and thus evangelical recruitment of female preachers subsided.

Although knowledge of the past does not and should not dictate the future, it helps illumine how recent attitudes toward women developed. For several decades at the end of the nineteenth century and beginning of the twentieth, evangelical churches did not leave the public gifts of women in the church buried. We, in turn, dare not bury the accounts of those courageous, committed pioneer women.

3

CONTEMPORARY EVANGELICALS
FOR GENDER EQUALITY

Ronald W. Pierce

Over the last several decades a new chapter has been written in the history of the evangelical egalitarian movement in North America and Great Britain.[1] With its roots in the writings and ministries of Christians from previous centuries,[2] it has revived the message that "the prejudice of the past has obscured the teachings of God's Word."[3]

A review of the literature reveals a progression in the movement as evangelical egalitarians discovered their roots in the 1970s, defined the parameters of their position in the 1980s, and refined their theology, while making it more accessible for the church, from the 1990s to the present. They affirmed the essentials of their theologically conservative background, especially the inspiration and authority of Scripture, while arguing that restrictive roles for women do not reflect an accurate interpretation of the texts.

Evangelicals during this time were united in their opposition to the more radical religious and secular forms of feminism, yet they remained divided on the *"evangelical* feminist" question. Books were published, position statements written, and organizations formed, distinguishing those who emphasized male leadership from those advocating gender equality.

---

[1]This chapter focuses primarily on books and national debates in the United States, although important work was also being done abroad during this time. Certain contributions from the United Kingdom, Australia and Canada are mentioned below where appropriate.

[2]Ruth A. Tucker argues, "Well-reasoned books articulating Christian feminism have appeared since the Reformation" (*Women in the Maze: Questions and Answers on Biblical Equality* [Downers Grove, Ill.: InterVarsity Press, 1992], p. 216). See chapters one and two above.

[3]Lee Anna Starr, *The Bible Status of Woman* (1926; reprint Zarephath, N.J.: Pillar of Fire, 1955), p. 7.

Biblical Equality Movement: The 1970s

Although it followed in the wake of modern secular feminism, the biblical equality movement that emerged in the mid-1970s was, in fact, a resurgence or "second wave" of the women's movement of the previous century. Evangelical egalitarians are ideologically much more closely aligned with the evangelical activists and women preachers of the nineteenth and early twentieth centuries than with the various non-Christian and liberal forms of feminism that developed in the latter half of the past century.[4]

In 1963 Betty Friedan's *The Feminine Mystique*[5] exposed the "Victorian stereotype" imposed on women during the mid-twentieth century. By this time fundamentalists like Charles Ryrie in *The Place of Women in the Church* (1958)[6] were defending this stereotype as "the biblical view." It was against this backdrop that Letha Scanzoni and Nancy Hardesty published their popular volume *All We're Meant to Be* (1974),[7] presenting their understanding of an egalitarian Christian woman "made in a multifaceted way and drawn from life itself."[8]

The following year, as the Evangelical Women's Caucus was being organized,[9] Paul Jewett's *Man as Male and Female*[10] hit the market. Virginia Mollenkott proclaimed him "the first male evangelical" to argue from "*all* the Scriptures" that the idea of female subordination is incompatible with the creation accounts, Jesus' teaching and Paul *in Galatians*.[11] Though contributing some helpful work on these texts, Jew-

---

[4]See Rebecca Merrill Groothuis, *Women Caught in the Conflict: The Culture War Between Traditionalism and Feminism* (Grand Rapids, Mich.: Baker, 1994; reprint Eugene, Ore.: Wipf & Stock, 1997), chaps. 3-4, esp. pp. 44-47.

[5]Betty Friedan, *The Feminine Mystique* (New York: W. W. Norton, 1963). She also helped establish the National Organization for Women (NOW).

[6]Charles C. Ryrie, *The Place of Women in the Church* (New York: Macmillan, 1958).

[7]Letha Scanzoni and Nancy Hardesty, *All We're Meant to Be: A Biblical Approach to Women's Liberation* (Waco, Tex.: Word, 1974).

[8]Quoted in Ruth A. Tucker and Walter L. Liefeld, *Daughters of the Church: Women and Ministry from New Testament Times to the Present* (Grand Rapids, Mich.: Zondervan/Academie, 1987), p. 411.

[9]Originally one of six task forces within Evangelicals for Social Action, it first consisted of a few women who were concerned about gender issues in church and society. They addressed such topics as the Equal Rights Amendment, inclusive language, ordination of women and discriminatory hiring policies in Christian institutions. Their first national conference in 1975 was called "Women in Transition: A Biblical Approach to Feminism." In 1990 the organization changed its name to Evangelical & Ecumenical Women's Caucus.

[10]Paul K. Jewett, *Man as Male and Female: A Study in Sexual Relationships from a Theological Point of View* (Grand Rapids, Mich.: Eerdmans, 1975).

[11]Virginia Mollenkott, foreword to ibid., p. 9 (italics mine).

ett contended that the apostle's practice "did not always match his profound and revolutionary insight"[12] and that his restrictions on women were based on an "incorrect rabbinic understanding of the second creation account alone."[13] Though Jewett's work was otherwise important to the movement,[14] in his treatment of the bulk of Paul's letters he placed himself outside the boundaries of mainstream evangelicalism.

Thus Patricia Gundry's *Woman Be Free!* (1977)[15] should be hailed as the first unambiguous expression of contemporary evangelical egalitarianism. In it she exposed three traditionalist threats designed to hold women down: that gender equality will lead to (1) loss of femininity, (2) destruction of home, family and society, and (3) denial of the inspiration of the Bible.[16] Following the exegetical work of Lee Anna Starr, she argued, in contrast to Jewett, that the seemingly restrictive passages had been misinterpreted. Though others echoed Gundry's concerns,[17] no other publication at this time had quite the same impact on the evangelical community.

In 1978 the gender issue was given a platform at the national meeting of the Evangelical Theological Society (ETS), in a debate between E. Margaret Howe and Robert Saucy over the question of ordination. Howe's argument for ordaining women announced a new position in a society whose doctrinal statement was then focused primarily on the inerrancy of Scripture.

Throughout the 1970s "biblical feminism" was regarded as an oxymoron by most evangelicals, as well as by liberal and secular feminists. Few from the conservative camp dared to follow Gundry and Howe into these dangerous waters. During this time neo-evangelicals like Jewett provided both a bridge by which mainstream evangelicals could relate to the gender debate and a foil against which they would struggle. Many saw the need for a more scholarly defense of gender equality that remained consistent with all of Scripture.

---

[12]Publisher's back-cover summary of *Man as Male and Female*.

[13]Jewett, *Man as Male and Female*, p. 119.

[14]For example, Jewett's emphasis on Galatians 3:28 as the "Magna Carta of Humanity" and his understanding of the image of God in Genesis 1 were adopted and developed by many evangelicals. Nevertheless, his assessment of Paul as a Christian with an "uneasy conscience" and his rejection of the bulk of Paul's teaching regarding gender were ultimately self-defeating.

[15]Patricia Gundry, *Woman Be Free! The Clear Message of Scripture* (Grand Rapids, Mich.: Zondervan, 1977).

[16]Ibid., pp. 29-39.

[17]E.g., see the collection of materials edited by Roberta Hestenes and Lois Curley in *Women and the Ministries of Christ* (Pasadena, Calif.: Fuller Theological Seminary, 1979).

Dialogue and Division Within Evangelicalism: The 1980s

The next decade can be divided by the annual ETS meeting in the winter of 1986 in Atlanta. Prior to that, the dynamics of the debate seemed to be leading toward a dialogue between the opposing camps; after this meeting, face-to-face dialogue and debate began to diminish, although forceful written debate continued.

Moving toward dialogue: 1980-1986. With the 1980s came a conservative backlash to feminism in the culture at large,[18] which also took its toll on evangelical egalitarians toward the end of the decade. By 1980 Jewett had written his second book, *The Ordination of Women,*[19] as had Gundry with *Heirs Together.*[20] In her work Gundry developed and refined her methodology and applied it to the subject of marriage. During the same year Susan Foh responded to the emerging "biblical feminist threat" with *Women and the Word of God,*[21] as did Stephen B. Clark with *Man and Woman in Christ.*[22] James Hurley followed in 1981 with *Man and Woman in Biblical Perspective.*[23] The debate was clearly under way.

At the 1981 national meeting, Frank Gaebelein challenged the ETS when he said, "Another piece of unfinished business relates . . . to the place of women in our society. . . . There are areas in which they need greater freedom and more support and recognition. An attitude of male domination rather than mutual submission in Christ still persists among us, and we need to do more about it."[24]

Meanwhile a steady stream of books signaled the emerging civil war within evangelicalism. A few seemed committed to reconciliation,[25] but most saw no way through the impasse.

In 1982 Margaret Howe published *Women in Church Leadership,*[26] in which she examined the pertinent texts, distinguishing between "scriptural principles" and "cultural influences," and provided a historical analysis of Orthodox, Catholic and

---

[18]See the penetrating analysis by Susan Faludi in *Backlash: The Undeclared War Against American Women* (New York: Crown, 1991).

[19]Paul K. Jewett, *The Ordination of Women* (Grand Rapids, Mich.: Eerdmans, 1980).

[20]Patricia Gundry, *Heirs Together: Mutual Submission in Marriage* (Grand Rapids, Mich.: Zondervan, 1980).

[21]Susan Foh, *Women and the Word of God: A Response to Biblical Feminism* (Phillipsburg, N.J.: Presbyterian & Reformed, 1980).

[22]Stephen B. Clark, *Man and Woman in Christ* (Ann Arbor, Mich.:, Servant, 1980).

[23]James B. Hurley, *Man and Woman in Biblical Perspective* (Grand Rapids, Mich.: Zondervan, 1981).

[24]Quoted on the dedication page of Alvera Mickelsen, ed., *Women, Authority and the Bible* (Downers Grove, Ill.: InterVarsity Press, 1986).

[25]Such as Kari Torjesen Malcolm, *Women at the Crossroads: A Path Beyond Feminism and Traditionalism* (Downers Grove, Ill.: InterVarsity Press, 1982).

[26]E. Margaret Howe, *Women in Church Leadership* (Grand Rapids, Mich.: Zondervan, 1982).

Protestant traditions. She also exposed the difficulties of women in evangelical seminaries and church ministries, thus drawing attention to an important phase in the movement as the number of women seeking "higher levels" of ministry increased.

In the following year a British contribution appeared: Mary Evans's *Woman in the Bible*,[27] which addressed a more comprehensive list of texts, including the Mosaic law. Her work called evangelicals to reexamine the Bible—not to alter or ignore it, nor to fit it into modern ideas, but to make sure the ideas and practices of biblical equality were indeed biblical.[28] Evans understood the Scripture to teach "diversity, unity and complementarity"[29] without hierarchy. She also provided extensive footnotes and bibliography that were important to the movement at this stage.

Also during this year Willard Swartley published *Slavery, Sabbath, War and Women*.[30] Although his section on the gender question was relatively short (forty pages), it was important by virtue of his objective critiques of the hermeneutics employed by both sides. This would lay a foundation for what would become a major emphasis two decades later.

Twenty-six evangelical leaders gathered to discuss the matter in the Evangelical Colloquium on Women and the Bible in Oak Brook, Illinois, in 1984. As J. I. Packer observed, the colloquium suffered from the "awkwardness of a double-barreled agenda" that included (1) helping women who had been hurt by the "restrictions and put-downs of pseudo-Christian legalism" and (2) exploring critically the biblical passages and issues. However, Packer also correctly acknowledged that after this colloquium "the burden of proof regarding the exclusion of women from the office of teaching and ruling within the congregation now lies on those who maintain the exclusion rather than on those who challenge it."[31] Such an observation from a leading evangelical supporter of male leadership bespoke a significant turn-

---

[27]Mary J. Evans, *Woman in the Bible: An Overview of All the Crucial Passages on Women's Roles* (Exeter, U.K.: Paternoster, 1983; published in the U.S. in 1984 by InterVarsity Press).

[28]Ibid., p. 10.

[29]Ibid., p. 132. The concept of "complementarity" carries with it a wide range of connotations. It sometimes simply conveys the idea of "beneficial difference" (without implying male authority), as in this instance; at other times it is used as a euphemism for a very traditional view of male authority; and in yet other writings it represents a significantly softened male-leadership position that is quite similar in practice to an egalitarian model.

[30]Willard M. Swartley, *Slavery, Sabbath, War and Women: Cases in Biblical Interpretation* (Scottdale, Penn.: Herald, 1983).

[31]J. I. Packer, "Understanding the Differences," in *Women, Authority and the Bible*, ed. Alvera Mickelsen (Downers Grove, Ill.: InterVarsity Press, 1986), p. 298.

ing of the tide in the gender debate in the mid-1980s (although the tide would later turn back again).

In 1985 Aída Besançon Spencer's *Beyond the Curse*[32] and Gilbert Bilezikian's *Beyond Sex Roles*[33] also provided thorough treatments of the texts and extensive bibliographies reflecting the formative years of the movement. Spencer included a discussion of background material from first-century rabbinical sources, as well as a consideration of the feminine images of God, two topics not well explored until this time. She argued from Genesis that the design at creation was distorted by sin and the curse. God's responses both in Eden and at the cross were "models and effective agents to show and empower us to go *beyond the curse*, to live lives affected by redemption."[34]

Bilezikian's book was laid out in a Bible study format emphasizing the direct involvement of his readers with the "authoritative text." He dedicated it "to men and women in quest of obedience to Holy Writ" who are "desirous of complying with the dictates of the Word of God."[35] He too gave careful attention to Old Testament law and provided a lengthy treatment of "head" (Greek *kephalē*) as conveying the notion of "source." His paradigm was God's design in creation corrupted by sin, followed by an "Old Covenant Compromise" leading to "New Covenant Redemption."[36]

Ronald and Beverly Allen's *Liberated Traditionalism: Men and Women in Balance* also appeared during this year.[37] It marked a softening of the traditional position, reflecting the inroads made by egalitarians. Appearing at the height of the civil war within evangelicalism, it was a way out for many traditionalists.

The following year Alvera Mickelsen's *Women, Authority and the Bible* and Janette Hassey's *No Time for Silence*[38] came to press. In Mickelsen's edited volume the essays from the 1984 colloquium were made available as the first published collection of evangelical egalitarian writings. Critics had contended that one could not hold to

---

[32]Aída Besançon Spencer, *Beyond the Curse: Women Called to Ministry* (Nashville: Thomas Nelson, 1985; reprint Peabody, Mass.: Hendrickson, 1989).

[33]Gilbert Bilezikian, *Beyond Sex Roles: A Guide for the Study of Female Roles in the Bible* (Grand Rapids, Mich.: Baker, 1985).

[34]Spencer, *Beyond the Curse*, p. 133 (italics mine).

[35]Bilezikian, *Beyond Sex Roles*, pp. 5, 207.

[36]Ibid., pp. 15-18.

[37]Ronald and Beverly Allen, *Liberated Traditionalism: Men and Women in Balance* (Portland, Ore.: Multnomah, 1985).

[38]Janette Hassey, *No Time for Silence: Evangelical Women in Public Ministry Around the Turn of the Century* (Grand Rapids, Mich.: Zondervan/Academie, 1986; reprint Minneapolis: Christians for Biblical Equality, n.d.).

the authority of Scripture and at the same time argue for a functional equality of the sexes. This publication insisted with many unified voices that "the crux is not biblical authority but rather biblical interpretation and application."[39]

Hassey's analysis of the turn-of-the-century women's movement brought historical perspective to the debate by showing that its roots were in the early Bible institutes and ecclesiastical organizations, thus dispelling the myth that evangelical feminism was simply "a misguided effort to emulate the secular feminism which [had] gained ground since the 1950s."[40]

Formalizing the division: 1986-1989. By 1986 the time had come to address the "unfinished business" identified earlier by Gaebelein. In October a *Christianity Today* "institute" called "Women in Leadership" put the debate before the church, with Walter Kaiser and Bruce Waltke presenting the opposing views as "Shared Leadership vs. Male Headship."[41] Shortly thereafter the ETS came together for its national meeting in Atlanta with the theme of the entire conference being "Men and Women in Biblical and Theological Perspective." This historic event marked a milestone in the development of evangelical egalitarian thinking: the society was not merely allowing a presentation on the question, but was sponsoring the largest dialogue and debate among evangelicals in the history of the movement. Presentations representing both sides were published the following spring in the ETS journal.[42]

As noted above, face-to-face dialogue seemed to diminish after the Atlanta ETS conference, though the reasons for this are not entirely clear. The conference itself may have contributed to the quenching of productive academic exchange. The ETS dialogue made it clear that egalitarianism was taking root in rich evangelical soil and was here to stay. Traditionalists discovered (as Packer had noted) that the tables had turned and the burden of proof was now resting on them.[43] Both sides seemed painfully aware that their opponents would not be easily swayed by their respective arguments. Each side became more firmly entrenched in its own position.

As the evangelical public was responding to the ETS conference, more books

---

[39]From the back cover of Mickelsen, ed., *Women, Authority and the Bible.* Main contributors were Patricia Gundry, Robert K. Johnston, Roger Nicole, Clark H. Pinnock, Richard N. Longenecker, Berkeley and Alvera Mickelsen, Walter L. Liefeld, Klyne R. Snodgrass, David M. Scholer, Catherine Clark Kroeger, Joan D. Flikkema, Nicholas Wolterstorff, J. I. Packer and Jeannette F. Scholer.

[40]Roger Nicole's endorsement on the back cover of Hassey, *No Time for Silence.*

[41]*Christianity Today,* October 3, 1986.

[42]*JETS* 30, no. 1 (March 1987).

[43]J. I. Packer, "Understanding the Differences," in *Women, Authority and the Bible,* ed. Alvera Mickelsen (Downers Grove, Ill.: InterVarsity Press, 1986), p. 298.

advocating biblical equality were going to press. In 1987 Patricia Gundry added a third title to her list with *Neither Slave nor Free*,[44] and Gretchen Gaebelein Hull joined the discussion with *Equal to Serve*.[45] Hull's work was in part an autobiography of her journey in thinking and writing on the gender question. In addition, it provided two important appendices on the meaning of "head" by Catherine Clark Kroeger and an outline of views and sources on the debate by Sanford Douglas Hull.[46]

Ruth Tucker and Walter Liefeld's *Daughters of the Church* also appeared that year,[47] presenting little-known facts regarding women in church history. Though their investigation sought to be objective, the impact of their findings regarding the number and significance of women in leadership and the differing and changing attitudes toward women could be read only as an apologetic for gender equality.

Also appearing in 1987 was an anthology edited by Kathy Keay titled *Men, Women and God*,[48] which represented the developing discussion among British evangelicals on the gender issue. Its contributors addressed questions of men and women in both church and society as well as related topics such as family, breadwinning, singleness, abuse, homosexuality and the image of God.

In 1988 John Bristow's *What Paul Really Said About Women*[49] appeared as an important treatise for anyone who "reveres Scripture but who struggles with traditional interpretations . . . and who fears that a desire for equality between the sexes is a violation of biblical principles."[50]

---

[44]Patricia Gundry, *Neither Slave nor Free: Helping Women Answer the Call to Church Leadership* (San Francisco: Harper & Row, 1987).

[45]Gretchen Gaebelein Hull, *Equal to Serve: Women and Men in the Church and Home* (Old Tappan, N.J.: Fleming H. Revell, 1987).

[46]Other contributions in 1987 include Linda Raney Wright, *A Cord of Three Strands: Exploring Women's and Men's Roles in Marriage, Family and Church* (Old Tappan, N.J.: Fleming H. Revell, 1987); Mary Hayter, *The New Eve in Christ: The Use and Abuse of the Bible in the Debate About Women in the Church* (Grand Rapids, Mich.: Eerdmans, 1987); and Miriam Adeney, *A Time for Risking: Priorities for Women* (Portland, Ore.: Multnomah Press, 1987).

[47]Ruth A. Tucker and Walter L. Liefeld, *Daughters of the Church: Women and Ministry from New Testament Times to the Present* (Grand Rapids, Mich.: Zondervan/Academie, 1987). On pp. 410-34 in the final chapter they offer a review of people and publications influential in the gender debate from the 1970s through the mid-1980s.

[48]Kathy Keay, ed., *Men, Women and God: Evangelicals on Feminism* (London: Marshall Pickering, 1987). Contributors include Elaine Storkey, Andrew Kirk, Faith and Roger Forster, Dave Tomlinson, Valerie Griffiths, Veronica Zundel, Roger Hurding.

[49]John T. Bristow, *What Paul Really Said About Women: The Apostle's Liberating Views on Equality in Marriage, Leadership and Love* (San Francisco: Harper, 1988).

[50]Back-cover endorsement by Letha Dawson Scanzoni, ibid.

In the midst of these heated debates evangelicals began to realize that much of the church was not being addressed at a personal, practical level. Faith McBurney Martin answered this challenge in *Call Me Blessed* (1988).[51] Although clearly advocating biblical equality, her work was done in a spirit of reconciliation, expressing both "fulfillment and yearning." It wove a tapestry of personal narrative with discussions of biblical texts and theology and thus served as a bridge for those who shared the author's pain, as well as her hope.

Unfortunately, the time for reconciliation had not come. Instead a deeper entrenchment took place in 1987 with the founding of both Christians for Biblical Equality (CBE) and the Council on Biblical Manhood and Womanhood (CBMW). In its Danvers Statement the CBMW argued for "equality in personhood and value, but difference in roles."[52] Though the newly termed "complementarians" shunned the older terminology of "traditionalism" and "hierarchy," their defense of male authority in marriage and ministry was as adamant as ever, even if it was now being applied with greater levels of respect and fairness for women.[53] In response, CBE's 1989 "Statement on Men, Women and Biblical Equality" insisted on the full "biblical equality of men and women of all races, ages, and economic classes."[54]

As the chasm widened, Bonnidell and Robert Clouse's edited volume *Women in Ministry: Four Views* (1989)[55] sought to present a one-volume literary dialogue between the two sides. Although tending to obfuscate the issues by forcing the debate into a predetermined structure of *"four views,"* the book did represent a change that was taking place within the traditionalist camp by distinguishing the older "traditional" view from the newer "male leadership" view. The former (espoused by Robert Culver) emphasized church tradition expressed in long-established stereotypical roles; the latter (espoused by Susan Foh) allowed for greater ministry and decision-making opportunities for women but retained ultimate male leadership. The distinction was less clear between the two views on the biblical equality side (Walter Liefeld, Alvera Mickelsen). Unfortunately, as the next

---

[51]Faith McBurney Martin, *Call Me Blessed: The Emerging Christian Woman* (Grand Rapids, Mich.: Eerdmans, 1988).

[52]Danvers Statement, published in *Christianity Today*, January 13, 1989.

[53]<www.cbmw.org>.

[54]<www.cbeinternational.org>.

[55]Bonnidell Clouse and Robert G. Clouse, eds., *Women in Ministry: Four Views* (Downers Grove, Ill.: InterVarsity Press, 1989).

decade began even the appearance of this sort of friendly debate faded. It became a dialogue of the deaf.

By the end of the 1980s the matter had come strongly before the evangelical public. Some were hopeful that this promised a time of "open conversation" leading to an increasing awareness of the reasons and research behind the differing viewpoints.[56] Others sensed a growing polarization between the two sides. By consensus, there was a realization that the biblical equality movement was not going away.

Refining the Biblical Equality Position: The 1990s to the Present

Having established the credibility of their view in the 1980s, biblical egalitarians seemed to be working toward three goals in the 1990s and on into the twenty-first century: (1) deepening the research supporting their arguments, (2) exploring related topics and (3) taking their message to the church.

On the other side, John Piper and Wayne Grudem's edited volume *Recovering Biblical Manhood and Womanhood* appeared early in the decade (1991)[57] as an important restatement of the traditional view couched in the euphemistic language of "complementarity."[58] As such, it exemplified a growing inconsistency in the application of the hierarchical model. In theory its proponents argued for male authority, while in practice many of them bore a striking resemblance to their egalitarian counterparts. In other words, while "authority" was theoretically at the center of their argument, in actual practice it was often at the margins. At the beginning of the next decade a collection of essays edited by Robert Saucy and Judith TenElshof, *Women and Men in Ministry*, took this important change of emphasis even further, underscoring what a woman *could* do within the bounds of male leadership.[59]

Deepening the research. In 1992 Richard and Catherine Clark Kroeger's *I Suffer Not*

---

[56]Tucker and Liefeld, *Daughters of the Church*, p. 433.

[57]John Piper and Wayne Grudem, eds., *Recovering Biblical Manhood and Womanhood: A Response to Evangelical Feminism* (Wheaton, Ill.: Crossway, 1991). Wayne Grudem later edited a similar collection, *Biblical Foundations for Manhood and Womanhood* (Wheaton, Ill.: Crossway, 2002), and more recently published a monograph, *Evangelical Feminism and Biblical Truth* (Sisters, Ore.: Multnomah, 2004).

[58]The present volume seeks to clarify this important point by insisting that to the extent dialogue is possible, complementarity *without* hierarchy must be distinguished from complementarity *meaning* hierarchy.

[59]Robert L. Saucy and Judith K. TenElshof, eds., *Women and Men in Ministry: A Complementary Perspective* (Chicago: Moody Press, 2001).

a Woman[60] and Craig Keener's *Paul, Women and Wives*[61] were published. The Kroegers' examination of the life and language of the Greco-Roman world provided a useful resource for the interpretation of 1 Timothy 2.[62] Keener likewise made a valuable contribution with his examination of ancient sources, especially regarding the household codes for wives, children and slaves. In addition, he addressed the restrictive texts in Paul's letters and included a comprehensive bibliography and literature review that helped bring the discussion up to date.

In 1995 Stanley Grenz and Denise Kjesbo published *Women in the Church*,[63] also including an extensive bibliography. They surveyed the key theological issues and biblical passages, along with the state of affairs regarding the debate, in a more irenic and dialogical tone than many earlier works had done.

In the same year Elaine Storkey's *Contributions to Christian Feminism*[64] brought together a collection of talks given and articles written over a ten-year period. Storkey addressed what she perceived to be a serious imbalance in the way God's "masculine" authority has been emphasized through the centuries, rather than the relational aspects of the Trinity.

These works were followed in 1997 by Rebecca Merrill Groothuis's *Good News for Women*,[65] which set forth the case for gender equality from the perspectives of sound logic, theology and biblical exegesis. She argued against the traditionalist claim that men and women are "equal in being but unequal in function."[66] An extensive annotated bibliography was included.

In an insightful study that appeared in 1998 in Great Britain, titled *Speaking of*

---

[60]Richard Clark Kroeger and Catherine Clark Kroeger, *I Suffer Not a Woman: Rethinking 1 Timothy 2:11-15 in Light of Ancient Evidence* (Grand Rapids, Mich.: Baker, 1992). An important response to this came in Andreas J. Köstenberger, Thomas R. Schreiner and H. Scott Baldwin, eds., *Women in the Church: A Fresh Analysis of 1 Timothy 2:9-15* (Grand Rapids, Mich.: Baker, 1995).

[61]Craig S. Keener, *Paul, Women and Wives: Marriage and Women's Ministry in the Letters of Paul* (Peabody, Mass.: Hendrickson, 1992).

[62]Whether the Kroegers' translation of these verses emphasizing the Gnostic heresy at Ephesus is correct has been debated by many evangelical egalitarians. Regardless, their study was quickly recognized as an important contribution to the debate.

[63]Stanley J. Grenz with Denise Muir Kjesbo, *Women in the Church: A Biblical Theology of Women in Ministry* (Downers Grove, Ill.: InterVarsity Press, 1995).

[64]Elaine Storkey, *Contributions to Christian Feminism* (London: Christian Impact, 1995). See also her *What's Right with Feminism* (Grand Rapids, Mich.: Eerdmans, 1985), which is being updated in a new edition.

[65]Rebecca Merrill Groothuis, *Good News for Women: A Biblical Picture of Gender Equality* (Grand Rapids, Mich.: Baker, 1997).

[66]See Groothuis's further development of this argument in chapter eighteen below.

Women,[67] Andrew Perriman sought to move the debate toward what he believed could be a biblical consensus between the two sides. Following the work of Richard Cervin,[68] he argued for "prominence" or "pre-eminence" as the meaning of male "headship," rather than "authority" or "source." Though he presented a fair treatment of the traditional view, in the end his conclusions fit clearly within the egalitarian camp.

Linda Belleville's *Women Leaders and the Church* (2000)[69] responded to three key issues in the debate: (1) In which ministries can women be involved? (2) What roles can women assume in the family and society? (3) What if any positions of authority can women hold in the church? She concluded that (1) God gifts and calls women and men equally, (2) God intends the male-female relationship to be mutual, and (3) in the church "there is not . . . male and female."[70] Her work combined significant exegetical skill with an extensive knowledge of the cultural background to Paul's time and writings.

In 2001 another important contribution appeared by British scholar Elaine Storkey. In a concise but thorough treatment titled *Origins of Difference,*[71] she revisited the gender debate from the academic disciplines of sociology, philosophy, psychology and theology, in relation to the cultural shift from premodernism to modernism to postmodernism.

Also this year a second literary dialogue[72] was offered in *Two Views on Women in Ministry,* edited by James Beck and Craig Blomberg,[73] with contributions by Linda Belleville and Craig Keener (egalitarians), Ann Bowman and Thomas Schreiner (complementarians). The book included interaction and observations by the editors, as well as an appendix by Blomberg.

An Australian contribution by Kevin Giles appeared the next year. *The Trinity and Subordinationism*[74] delves deeply into historical theology to refute the claim of today's

---

[67]Andrew Perriman, *Speaking of Women: Interpreting Paul* (Leicester, U.K.: Inter-Varsity Press/Apollos, 1998).

[68]Richard S. Cervin, "Does *Kephalē* Mean 'Source' or 'Authority Over' in Greek Literature? A Rebuttal," *TrinJ* 10 (1989): 85-112.

[69]Linda L. Belleville, *Women Leaders and the Church: Three Crucial Questions* (Grand Rapids, Mich.: Baker, 2000).

[70]Ibid., p. 181.

[71]Elaine Storkey, *Origins of Difference: The Gender Debate Revisited* (Grand Rapids, Mich.: Baker, 2001).

[72]See note 55.

[73]James R. Beck and Craig L. Blomberg, eds., *Two Views on Women in Ministry,* Counterpoint, gen. ed. Stanley N. Gundry (Grand Rapids, Mich.: Zondervan, 2001).

[74]Kevin Giles, *The Trinity and Subordinationism: The Doctrine of God and the Contemporary Gender Debate*

patriarchalists that God the Son is eternally subordinate to God the Father and that this is analogous to the subordination of women. The book is unusual in being primarily theological rather than exegetical in approach. Moreover, it reflects a developing trend toward some common ground in that it (like the present volume) insists that the notion of "complementarity" should be applied to both sides of the debate—hierarchical and egalitarian. It also addressed related issues of slavery and homosexuality (though not in detail).

In this same year (2002) a book of a quite different kind appeared, *The IVP Women's Bible Commentary.*[75] Written almost entirely by women scholars, this volume has commentary on each biblical book that seeks to engage the concerns and experiences of women. Also included are some important essays on various theological and practical issues.

Exploring related areas. The 1990s began with the appearance of Mary Stewart Van Leeuwen's *Gender and Grace* (1990),[76] written by a psychologist in consultation with scholars in theology, history, biology and sociology. In her section on "nature versus nurture" she contended that regarding "genes, hormones and hemispheres . . . the differences [between male and female], when they occur, are both smaller and more complex than we thought. In most cases they are impossible to separate from the effects of learning."[77] In short, her book argued that a God-given "complementarity," to the extent that it can be objectively defined, does not necessarily predetermine "gender roles."[78]

In 1993 Van Leeuwen joined with a team of scholars, students and staff who lived together for one year while writing and editing *After Eden.*[79] This volume ad-

---

(Downers Grove, Ill.: InterVarsity Press, 2002). See a version of Giles's argument in chapter nineteen below.

[75]Catherine Clark Kroeger and Mary J. Evans, eds., *The IVP Women's Bible Commentary* (Downers Grove, Ill.: InterVarsity Press, 2002). Also to be noted in this regard is the earlier *Study Bible for Women: The New Testament*, ed. Catherine Clark Kroeger, Mary Evans and Elaine Storkey (Grand Rapids, Mich.: Baker, 1995).

[76]Mary Stewart Van Leeuwen, *Gender and Grace: Love, Work and Parenting in a Changing World* (Downers Grove, Ill.: InterVarsity Press, 1990). Also appearing in the same year was June Steffensen Hagen's edited volume *Gender Matters: Women's Studies for the Christian Community* (Grand Rapids, Mich.: Zondervan, 1990).

[77]Ibid., p. 105.

[78]Her section "Parents and Partners" is also helpful, as well as the chapters "Gender, Work and Christian Vocation" and "Sexual Values in a Secular Age."

[79]Mary Stewart Van Leeuwen, ed., *After Eden: Facing the Challenge of Gender Reconciliation* (Grand Rapids, Mich.: Eerdmans, 1993). Other contributors included Annelies Knoppers, Margaret L. Koch, Douglas J. Schuurman and Helen M. Sterk.

dressed historical, crosscultural, theological and rhetorical issues. It showed that evangelical egalitarians were able to critically examine the growth of the movement in the broader context of the world around them.

Also during this time Rebecca Merrill Groothuis's *Women Caught in the Conflict* (1994)[80] focused on the "culture war between traditionalism and feminism." While developing strategies for an egalitarian hermeneutic, she analyzed the historical and contemporary cultural influences on both sides of the debate.[81]

In the wake of the 1993 conference of the World Council of Churches called "Re-imagining God, Community and the Church," *The Goddess Revival* (1995)[82] was published. This collaborative work by Aída and William Spencer, Donna Hailson and Catherine Kroeger critiqued the burgeoning goddess spirituality by comparing and contrasting the God of the Bible with the gods and goddesses of pagan religions, both past and present.

Since the publication of Jewett's *Man as Male and Female*, the question had been raised whether the same arguments used for gender equality extend to "other gender questions," especially that of homosexual practice. The turn of the millennium saw two important contributions to this issue. In 1998 Stanley Grenz faced the growing challenge of alternative sexual lifestyles in *Welcoming but Not Affirming*.[83] He reasserted the historic Christian position with exegetical support but did so with more love and compassion than the church was accustomed to doing.

In 2001 William Webb's *Slaves, Women and Homosexuals*[84] built on the earlier work

---

[80]Rebecca Merrill Groothuis, *Women Caught in the Conflict: The Culture War Between Traditionalism and Feminism* (Grand Rapids, Mich.: Baker, 1994; reprint Eugene, Ore.: Wipf & Stock, 1997).

[81]In the same year John Stratton Hawley published his edited volume *Fundamentalism and Gender* (New York: Oxford University Press, 1994). Though Hawley is not an evangelical, his conclusions strongly supported those published for the previous two decades by evangelical feminists. While it is a valuable assessment of fundamentalism's place in the history of the movement, no mention is made of the fact that evangelical feminism survived and thrived past 1930.

[82]Aída Besançon Spencer, Donna F. G. Hailson, Catherine Clark Kroeger and William David Spencer, *The Goddess Revival* (Grand Rapids, Mich.: Baker, 1995). Also addressing the "gender" of God during this time was Paul R. Smith, *Is It Okay to Call God "Mother"? Considering the Feminine Face of God* (Peabody, Mass.: Hendrickson, 1993), which advocated going beyond the biblical language by calling God "Mother" as well as "Father."

[83]Stanley J. Grenz, *Welcoming but Not Affirming: An Evangelical Response to Homosexuality* (Louisville, Ky.: Westminster John Knox, 1998). The most valuable endorsement of this book came from James B. Nelson, who, though strongly opposing Grenz's "non-inclusive" conclusions, viewed it as "the clearest, fairest presentation of the non-affirming position" (back cover).

[84]William J. Webb, *Slaves, Women and Homosexuals: Exploring the Hermeneutics of Cultural Analysis* (Downers Grove, Ill.: InterVarsity Press, 2001).

of Swartley[85] and at the same time began an important contemporary discussion on the issue of what Webb has labeled a "redemptive hermeneutic."[86] This hermeneutic is illustrated by the church's rejection of slavery and is then applied to the issues of women and homosexuals to show that women's subordination is not transcultural but the biblical ban on homosexual practice is. Though sometimes controversial, his original, fair and well-crafted argument should continue to influence the gender debate for the foreseeable future.

Taking the message to the church. Having focused on the academy in the 1980s, advocates of biblical equality expanded their influence in the 1990s by taking their message to the street with a number of academically sound yet intentionally practical books. Three of these spanned the decade in the writings of Alice Mathews. Her first volume, *A Woman God Can Use,*[87] was published in 1990, followed the next year with *A Woman Jesus Can Teach*[88] and a third in 1998, *A Woman God Can Lead.*[89] In these Mathews explored a host of themes in the Old and New Testaments regarding prominent women, presenting them as didactic models for women in the modern world. She addressed such topics as decision making, difficult marriages, modern culture, depression, leadership, spirituality, priorities and evangelism.[90]

In Ruth Tucker's second volume on the gender issue, *Women in the Maze* (1992),[91] she condensed the exhaustive work done earlier with Liefeld in *Daughters of the Church,* making it more accessible for the average reader. She also added her own analysis of the texts and addressed contemporary issues such as inclusive language, ordination, feminism's effect on men, the status of women in the church, family life and reconciliation within evangelicalism.

Cheryl Sanders's *Ministry at the Margins* (1997)[92] widened the scope of evangelical egalitarianism. Writing as a pastor, professor, spouse and parent, she proposed a

---

[85]See note 30.

[86]See his chapters twenty-two and twenty-three below.

[87]Alice P. Mathews, *A Woman God Can Use: Lessons from Old Testament Women Help You Make Today's Choices* (Grand Rapids, Mich.: Discovery House, 1990).

[88]Alice P. Mathews, *A Woman Jesus Can Teach: Lessons from New Testament Women Help You Make Today's Choices* (Grand Rapids, Mich.: Discovery House, 1991).

[89]Alice P. Mathews, *A Woman God Can Lead: Lessons from Women of the Bible Help You Make Today's Choices* (Grand Rapids, Mich.: Discovery House, 1998).

[90]A similar contribution was made by Mary Ellen Ashcroft's *Balancing Act: How Women Can Lose Their Roles and Find Their Callings* (Downers Grove, Ill.: InterVarsity Press, 1996).

[91]Ruth A. Tucker, *Women in the Maze: Questions and Answers on Biblical Equality* (Downers Grove, Ill.: InterVarsity Press, 1992).

[92]Cheryl J. Sanders, *Ministry at the Margins* (Downers Grove, Ill.: InterVarsity Press, 1997).

model for ministry that included not only women but also ethnic minorities, youth and the poor. In 1999 Sanders was a plenary speaker for the CBE international conference in San Diego, California, where she called for, and symbolized, a renewed commitment by CBE to counter the pervasive effects of racism, sexism and elitism.[93]

In a similar manner, Ruth Haley Barton's 1998 publication *Equal to the Task*[94] took the message for the Christian woman beyond the church. Arguing in an egalitarian yet "complementary" fashion, she asserted that God created men and women for life together, "a mutuality in teamwork" that enables them to work together in the office and in marriage, parenting and friendship. Her work was informed by interviews with others in ministry and personal experiences in Willow Creek Community Church in South Barrington, Illinois.

Published by Youth with a Mission (YWAM), Loren Cunningham and David Hamilton's *Why Not Women?* (2000)[95] brought the message of biblical equality to the mission field. Although women in missionary leadership had long been a reality (though an inconsistency in the traditionalist view), YWAM now endorsed this practice with a strong biblical argument.

Two books by Lee Grady, *Ten Lies the Church Tells Women* (2000)[96] and *Twenty-five Tough Questions About Women and the Church* (2003),[97] have also had a significant impact at the popular level. Grady, a keynote speaker at the 2003 international CBE conference in Orlando, Florida, has a straightforward, charismatic style that wins many converts at the lay level but sometimes tends to minimize the complexity of the issues.

Also during 2003 a lay-oriented series titled Think Again[98] appeared, dividing

---

[93]See her comments on how she views her ministry in ibid., p. 18.

[94]Ruth Haley Barton, *Equal to the Task: Men and Women in Partnership* (Downers Grove, Ill.: InterVarsity Press, 1998).

[95]Loren Cunningham and David J. Hamilton, *Why Not Women? A Biblical Study of Women in Missions, Ministry and Leadership* (Seattle: YWAM, 2000).

[96]J. Lee Grady, *Ten Lies the Church Tells Women: How the Bible Has Been Misused to Keep Women in Spiritual Bondage* (Lake Mary, Fla.: Charisma House, 2000).

[97]J. Lee Grady, *Twenty-five Tough Questions About Women and the Church* (Lake Mary, Fla.: Charisma House, 2003).

[98]Joy Elasky Fleming, *Think Again About Eve (Genesis 3:16); Think Again About Adam and the Tempter (Genesis 3:17-19);* Bruce C. E. Fleming, *Think Again About Church Leaders (1 Timothy 2:8-3:16); Think Again About the Weaker Spouse (1 Peter 3:1-7); Think Again About Submission (Ephesians 5:15-6:9); Think Again About Women and Authority (1 Corinthians 11:2-16); Think Again About Women and Silence (1 Corinthians 14:34-40);* and *Think Again About the Bible (the Four Principles).* The entire series, totaling 461 pp., appeared at the same time (Minneapolis: Think Again, 2003).

a discussion of the key texts among eight booklets, two by Joy Elasky Fleming and six by Bruce Fleming. Each is designed to present an exegetical argument for biblical equality to the layperson in a popular format.

Sarah Sumner's *Men and Women in the Church* (2003)[99] is a difficult work to place in the present survey for two reasons. First, as it interweaves her theology of women with the narrative of her personal journey, its style vacillates between the academic and the personal. Second, and more important, she attempts to avoid taking sides on the issue while seeking to encourage dialogue and build a consensus among evangelicals. While her goal is admirable, the reader is left somewhat in the dark as to the substance of and basis for her conclusions.[100]

In summary, the 1990s into the beginning of the twenty-first century found biblical equality advocates functioning as a mature force within evangelicalism rather than fighting for a right to survive as in the preceding decades. Their literature reinforced their theological heritage, while at the same time developing it and expanding its influence in both theoretical and practical terms.

Concluding Observations

The following observations are warranted by a representative survey of evangelical egalitarian literature over the past thirty years. First, a theology of gender equality has been recovered from its nineteenth-century roots. Though undoubtedly influenced by the modern feminist movement, it was not the result of it; rather, the secular served as a catalyst to awaken the sacred.

Second, the struggles within evangelicalism in the 1980s had the long-term effect of strengthening the resolve of biblical egalitarians, forcing them to move to a greater level of maturity as the result of a vigorous self-defense.

Third, although the initial backlash of the late 1980s is past, the resultant polarity of the two sides presents an ongoing challenge for evangelicals. The need to get beyond this impasse in order to demonstrate unity with diversity in the body of Christ is greater than ever. Thus another matter of unfinished business is resuming dialogue with a spirit of reconciliation.

Fourth, the rise of the biblical equality movement has effected a change of prac-

---

[99]Sarah Sumner, *Men and Women in the Church: Building a Consensus on Christian Leadership* (Downers Grove, Ill.: InterVarsity Press, 2003).

[100]E.g., through four chapters (ibid., pp. 139-90) she asserts that "head" in I Corinthians II and Ephesians 5 does not mean "authority," "source" or "covering" (she does not acknowledge the "preeminence" view) but should simply be left as a "mystery" and a "picture."

tice, if not of mind, for many traditionalists. Not only have scores changed to an egalitarian position,[101] but many others have modified their traditionalism into a position that ends up being virtually egalitarian in practice. The result is that things seem to be generally better for evangelical women in marriage and ministry at the beginning of the twenty-first century, even in many so-called complementarian circles.

Fifth, a high view of Scripture has been an explicit part of evangelical egalitarian theology from the beginning. Despite some accusations to the contrary, these conservatives have not dismissed the teaching of the Bible as "merely cultural," nor have they developed a special hermeneutic to get around it, nor have they simply refused to submit to its authority. The evidence for this can be found in the chapters that follow in this volume.

---

[101]E.g., my own journey, recounted in Ronald W. Pierce, "Evangelicals and Gender Roles in the 1990's: I Timothy 2:8-15, a Test Case," *JETS* 36 (1993): 343-56.

PART II

LOOKING TO SCRIPTURE

The Biblical Texts

4

EQUALITY WITH AND WITHOUT INNOCENCE

Genesis 1–3

Richard S. Hess

The accounts of creation, the Garden of Eden and the Fall in Genesis 1–3 may contain more doctrinal teaching concerning the nature of humanity as male and female, as well as the state of the fallen world, than any other single text in the Bible. Their position at the beginning of the Torah, and thus of Scripture as a whole, makes them an important starting point for the study of the biblical teaching on gender equality.

From the outset it may be affirmed that the record of Genesis 1–3 is a matter of God's revealed will for his people so that they might live in communion with him. Its readership was ancient Israel, the people who emerged in the hill country of Canaan in the latter part of the Late Bronze Age (1550-1200 B.C.) and those generations who followed them in building a society that struggled with their covenantal life before God.

Genesis 1: Creation in God's Image

Genesis 1:26-28 describes God's creation of the man and the woman. As is clear from the parallel lines of Genesis 1:27, both are subsumed under the general rubric *'adam,* which describes the species as "humanity."

> God created the *'adam* in his image;
> > in the image of God he created him.
> Male and female he created them.

In Genesis 1–3 *'adam* has two different uses. It refers to "humanity" in Genesis I and to "the man" in the Garden of Eden in Genesis 2–3. The first clearly attested usage of *'adam* to denote the personal name Adam occurs in Genesis 4:25.[1] It should be pointed out that Old Testament Hebrew has no common term for "humanity" other than *'adam*.[2] The generic *'adam* was part of the West Semitic lexicon before Genesis 1–3 was revealed and written in the form in which it occurs. Therefore it is somewhat inaccurate to suggest that there was a conscious divine decision to use a masculine term to describe the human race. No other term was available, and there is no evidence that the writer of Genesis invented new words. It should also be noted that Hebrew has only two genders, masculine and feminine; there is no neuter. Moreover, the choice of gender for any noun is not predictable. And in any case, the evolution of a word from a common noun ("humanity" in Gen 1) to a title ("the man" in Gen 2–3) and finally to a personal name ("Adam" in Gen 4:25) is not unique to *'adam*. It is a linguistic phenomenon shared by many languages.[3] In short, the nature of revelation, Hebrew language and vocabulary, the semantic range of *'adam*, and the common linguistic development of words all argue against the presumption that "God's naming of the race 'man' whispers male headship."[4]

In verse 26, "Let us make *'adam* in our image," the pronouns may simply be the plural of majesty, used in the Bible to refer to human masters (e.g., Judg 3:25; 13:8; 19:11-12, 26-27; 1 Sam 20:38; 25:10). Yet the absence of a plural reference to God elsewhere in Genesis 1–10 suggests that something special is intended here. As God is somehow plural in relationship, so the created *'adam* is to enjoy the relationships that come from plurality. Although this is potentially true of all creatures, with *'adam* it becomes especially significant. In this way the reference anticipates the story of Genesis 2 and the harmony between the man and the woman.

---

[1]Richard S. Hess, "Splitting the Adam: The Usage of *'adam* in Genesis i-v," in *Studies in the Pentateuch*, ed. J. A. Emerton, *VT*Sup 41 (Leiden, Netherlands: Brill, 1991), pp. 1-15.

[2]A term such as *'am*, "people," denotes a smaller group within the larger class of humanity, often referring to a group related by kinship or to residents of a particular geographical area. As a collective (like the other terms in Gen 1), this often refers to a group related by kinship or to residents of a particular geographical area (*HALOT*, 2:837-39).

[3]Hess, "Splitting the Adam," pp. 7-10; John Lyons, *Semantics II* (Cambridge: Cambridge University Press, 1977), pp. 179-81.

[4]Raymond C. Ortlund Jr., "Male-Female Equality and Male Headship: Genesis 1-3," in *RBMW*, p. 98. This is also why Ortlund's statement referring to God's revelation makes little sense: "He does not even devise a neutral term like 'persons.'" Since there is no neuter gender in Hebrew, no term could satisfy the demand that it be neither masculine nor feminine. Masculine nouns do not "whisper" of male headship any more than feminine nouns "whisper" of female subordination.

However, it is equally important that while the text affirms ʾ*adam*ʹs creation by God who holds plurality (and thus relationship) as a part of his nature, it does not explicitly identify this as part of the image of God that all people possess. Therefore one cannot assume that marriage or even social activity is somehow essential to the image of God.

What then is the meaning of the terms *image (tselem)* and *likeness (demuth)*, used here to describe the image of God? It is best illustrated in the practice of ancient Near East kings of erecting or carving out images in order to represent their power and rulership over far-reaching areas of their empires.[5] These represented the dominion of the ruler when the sovereign was not present in the region (see Dan 3:1).

The emphasis in Genesis is on rulership of creation through stewardship. Phyllis Bird argues that gender distinction does not belong to the image of God, or to dominion, but to the theme of fertility that is found in the first chapter of Genesis.[6] Fruitfulness and reproduction are part of the plant and animal world (Gen 1:12, 22-25) and thus are not unique to the image of God in ʾ*adam*. Whereas the term *image of God* in the surrounding culture applies only to royalty, Genesis 1 emphasizes the role all of humanity has in dominion over creation. Bird also suggests that the command to be fruitful and multiply is a polemic against Canaanite fertility rituals.[7]

The only divine statement regarding the creation of ʾ*adam* that can apply to the image of God is the command to have dominion over the earth. Thus ʾ*adam* is different from creation (as possessing the image of God and the role of dominion), though part of creation (as sexually differentiated and capable of reproduction; cf. Ps 8).

Dominion is set in the context of the ideal world of Genesis 1 and is not altered with the sins of the following chapters (Gen 5:1-3; 9:1-6). Rather its original context suggests a harmony. As the sun and moon rule over day and night, so through its multiplication humanity rules over the earth by its presence throughout the world.[8] Thus the verbs *to rule (kabash)* and *to dominate (radah)* suggest the taking of

---

[5]Hans W. Wolff, *Anthropology of the Old Testament*, trans. Margaret Kohl (London: SCM Press, 1974), p. 160.

[6]Phyllis A. Bird, "Male and Female He Created Them: Gen. 1:27b in the Context of the Priestly Account of Creation," *HTR* 74 (1981): 134.

[7]"The power of created life to replenish itself is a power given to each species at its creation and therefore is not dependent upon subsequent rites or petitions for its effect" (ibid., p. 147).

[8]Bernard W. Anderson, *Creation in the Old Testament*, Issues in Religion and Theology 6, ed. B. W. Anderson (London: SPCK, 1984), p. 159; H. P. Santmire, "The Genesis Creation Narratives Revisited, Themes for a Global Age," *Interpretation* 45 (1991): 374-75.

the land and its stewardship (*kabash* is used in Josh 18:1).[9] Such stewardship is given to humanity as "male and female" in God's command for "them" to "rule over" creation (Gen 1:26-27) and is exemplified by the way the man "works and takes care of" (see NIV) the Garden (Gen 2:15) and names the animals (Gen 2:19-20). However, its ramifications go beyond gardening and zoology to include the ongoing activity of God's ordering and creating in the world and in civilization.

Does Genesis 1:26-28 address the question of the relationship between male and female? David Clines maintains that the reference to "male and female" (Gen 1:27) says nothing of their equality but reflects the two kinds of human beings, just as all other creatures are made "according to their kind."[10] However, this interpretation seems forced. Clines fails to demonstrate that male and female are ever understood as the *kinds (min)* used of different species in Genesis 1:21 and 24. Nowhere in Genesis is *'adam* so described; rather, other references to *'adam* connote the species as a whole. There is nothing in this first chapter to suggest anything other than an equality of male and female created together in the image of God.

Genesis 2: The Home, Work and Partner of the Man

The second account of creation beginning in the middle of Genesis 2:4 does not contradict the first but provides a different emphasis. Whereas Genesis 1 describes God as Creator of the cosmos and all of life, Genesis 2 focuses on the creation of the man along with his home, work and companion.[11] The two accounts of creation, a literary doublet, anticipate the use of this style in the structure of Genesis 1–11 and of the book as a whole.[12]

The creation of the man in this account occurs in a context of the divine planting of the Garden of Eden. Further, the term *man (*'adam*)* here always occurs with a definite article, "the man."[13] In Hebrew a definite article is never used with a per-

---

[9]Richard J. Clifford, review of Udo Rüterswörden, *Dominium Terrae: Studien zur Genese einer alttestamentlichen Vorstellung, JBL* 113 (1994): 701-2.

[10]David J. A. Clines, "What Does Eve Do to Help? and Other Irredeemably Androcentric Orientations in Genesis 1-3," in *What Does Eve Do to Help? and Other Readerly Questions to the Old Testament, JSOT*-Sup 94 (Sheffield, U.K.: Sheffield Academic, 1990), pp. 25-48.

[11]There have been other attempts to understand these two accounts. The traditional critical approach, in which Genesis 1:1–2:4a represents the P (priestly) source and Genesis 2:4bff. represents the J (Yahwist) source, is exemplified by Carol L. Meyers, *Discovering Eve: Ancient Israelite Women in Context* (Oxford: Clarendon, 1988).

[12]Richard S. Hess, "Genesis 1-2 in Its Literary Context," *TynBul* 41 (1990): 143-53.

[13]Or with the possibility for a definite article in the consonantal Hebrew text.

sonal name. Therefore *'adam* in this context is a title, not a name. But to what does the title refer? In Genesis 2:5 the *'adam* is created from the *'adamah*, "the ground." The wordplay between these two terms is intentional. On the one hand it affirms *'adam's* intimate association with the dust of the earth and thereby humanity's physical and carnal nature. On the other hand, it prepares the reader for the man's responsibility in taking care of the Garden, an earthy task. Hence "the *'adam*" designation is an appropriate one to describe this responsibility of "the man."[14]

In the ancient Near East a leader of a city or region often was designated by a similar title, such as "the men of Tob" (2 Sam 10:6-8) who appear in parallel with "the king of Maacah." Thus the term in Genesis 2 does not merely designate the first created person. It also describes the governorship of the man over the Garden, a responsibility anticipated in the injunction of dominion in Genesis 1 and now realized in Genesis 2. The command "to work it and take care of it" (Gen 2:15 NIV) addresses "the man" as one who cultivates the soil of Eden.[15] Thus the title which becomes a personal name in Genesis 4:25 describes the man's task and anticipates the name of the woman in Genesis 3:20 as Eve *(havvah)*, which will also describe a task of hers.

Genesis 2:16-17 form an interlude that anticipates the events of Genesis 3. God commands the man not to eat of the tree of the knowledge of good and evil but does not command the woman because she has not yet been created.[16] Genesis 2:18-25 serve to further themes already introduced. First, naming the creatures continues the theme of reflecting the image of God through ordering creation, just as God had ordered the major areas of the world in the first three days of creation. Second, this naming identifies the ideal harmony that the world enjoys. God, the

---

[14]See Hess, "Splitting the Adam."

[15]Eleanor F. Beach and Frederic L. Pryor, "How Did Adam and Eve Make a Living?" *Bible Review* 11, no. 2 (April 1995): 38-42, argue that this phrase means that the first man was a "servant guardian" and not involved in tilling the garden. However, this requires the original omission of the feminine suffixes on the verbs (translated "it"), which would have been added later. These suffixes refer either to Eden or to the soil (Gordon J. Wenham, *Genesis 1-15*, WBC I [Waco, Tex.: Word, 1987], p. 47). The natural sense of the text is that the man's role involved taking care of the Garden in its various aspects, cultivating as well as guarding.

[16]Some assert that because God spoke to the man here rather than the woman, this is proof that the man was given responsibility for leadership. See, e.g., Thomas R. Schreiner, "Women in Ministry," in *Two Views on Women in Ministry*, ed. James R. Beck and Craig L. Blomberg (Grand Rapids, Mich.: Zondervan, 2001), p. 203, who then argues that "God likely commissioned Adam to instruct Eve about this command." Not only is this lacking in the text, its absence is a key point in the narrative. See later in this chapter under "The Fall Narrative."

man and the world continue in perfect relationship. Third, the process of encountering each animal that God has created accentuates the man's loneliness and need for a helper like him.[17] Thus the man and the woman were created sequentially in Genesis 2 in order to demonstrate the need they have for each other, not to justify an implicit hierarchy.[18]

Male leadership advocates, however, often cite 1 Timothy 2:13 as evidence that Paul understood the sequential creation of humanity to imply an intended hierarchy of man over woman, especially in light of conventions of ancient Near Eastern culture regarding the rights of the firstborn son—primogeniture.[19]

Such an argument is problematic for several reasons. First, no rights of the firstborn found in Scripture provide a logical connection to creation order as establishing authority. Second, the norm among the patriarchs is *not* primogeniture but God's blessing on the second or third born (e.g., Isaac over Ishmael, Jacob over Esau, Joseph over his brothers, Ephraim over Manasseh, etc.). Third, in the biblical laws only Deuteronomy 21:15-17 mentions this principle in the context of the firstborn son of an unloved wife. There the basis for the right of the firstborn is found in the statement because he "is the first sign of his father's strength" (NIV). This is the only biblical text that could be construed as a rationale for primogeniture (there are no parallel texts that speak to this issue).

But, one must ask, what does God's creation of the man before the woman in Genesis 2 have to do with being "the first sign of his father's strength"? Is this God's strength? If so, could not the creation of the rest of the world before the creation of man and woman be seen as the first sign of God's strength? Further, "the first sign of his father's strength" establishes rights of inheritance in a family context, which has nothing to do with God's creation order. God does not beget the man or woman, nor is the question of authority in human society part of any "inheritance" that God gives to the man. Moreover, God does not give his inheritance, because he does not die.

Having argued that primogeniture is an illegitimate model on which to ground man's supposed authority over woman in the context of the creation order, I need

---

[17]This is the purpose of the woman's "help": to overcome loneliness. If it were, as Schreiner suggests, "to help Adam with the task of ruling over creation" (ibid., p. 204), then logic would require that she be created before the naming of the animals. The goal of overcoming loneliness is stressed in Genesis 2:23-24, not the woman's assistance in ruling over creation (though this is clear in Gen 1:26).

[18]Rebecca Merrill Groothuis, *Good News for Women: A Biblical Picture of Gender Equality* (Grand Rapids, Mich.: Baker, 1997), p. 137.

[19]Schreiner, "Women," pp. 201-3.

to consider whether there is in the text of Genesis 1–3, or in ancient Near Eastern parallels outside the Bible, any basis for the assumption that creation order establishes authority.

In its narrative, Genesis 1 declares that God (and no other deity) created the universe, the world and everything therein, while Genesis 2 explains humanity's special relationship with God by focusing on "the man" and exploring the harmonious relationships that he enjoyed with his God, his work, his world and his partner. In Genesis 2 the man is given responsibility over the Garden, a responsibility already given to both man and woman in Genesis 1, but he is not given authority over the woman. Genesis 2 nowhere suggests a hierarchical relationship between the man and the woman, and certainly not because of the "order of creation." Moreover, chapter 1 explicitly declares that the man and the woman share in God's image and bear the same responsibilities.

Some have argued that the sequence of creation reflects the patriarchal nature of ancient society. Regarding this it is worthwhile to compare the Mesopotamian creation story of Atrahasis (the copy we have comes from about the seventeenth century B.C., roughly the same culture and time as the production of the laws of Hammurabi), which provides parallel references to the creation of humanity in a paradise as well as a subsequent rebellion and a flood.[20] Though much of the text speaks of humanity without distinctive emphasis on gender, this is not the case at the point of humanity's creation and the discussion of marriage. There the woman is described before the man.[21] Likewise, whenever there is mention of the two genders, the woman is mentioned first.[22] No one would deny that legal texts, contracts and other sources for understanding the society of ancient Mesopotamia witness to a patriarchal society that exceeded ancient Israel in its value of the husband and subservience of his wife.[23] Yet in Atrahasis the woman is mentioned first. This indicates that the *sequence* of man's and woman's creation has no significance for im-

---

[20]Including many parallels with Genesis 6–9; see Alan R. Millard, "A New Babylonian Genesis Story," *TynBul* 18 (1967): 3-18; reprinted in *"I Studied Inscriptions from Before the Flood": Ancient Near Eastern, Literary and Linguistic Approaches to Genesis 1-11*, ed. Richard S. Hess and David T. Tsumura, Sources for Biblical and Theological Study 4 (Winona Lake, Ind.: Eisenbrauns, 1994).

[21]Bernard F. Batto, "The Institution of Marriage in Genesis 2 and in *Atrahasis*," *CBQ* 62 (2000): 627; his lines 271-76 of tablet I.

[22]E.g., *li-iḫ-ti-[ru aš-ša]-tum ù mu-sá* "let a wife and her husband choose one another," in line 300 of tablet I; see also line 301; following Batto, ibid.

[23]On the general subject, see Sophie Lafont, *Femmes, droit et justice dans l'antiquité orientale: Contributions à l'étude du droit pénal au Proche-Orient ancien*, OBO 165 (Göttingen, Germany: Vandenhoeck & Ruprecht, 1999).

plications of the society's view of or assumptions regarding hierarchy.

In sum, the view that the man's creation before the woman's implies his authority over her cannot be sustained by study of the text of Genesis 2, the context of Genesis 1–3, the comparative literature of the ancient Near East or the invocation of putative customs of primogeniture in ancient Israel.

The designation of the woman as a "helper corresponding to" (*'ezer kenegdo*) the man in Genesis 2 has also evoked much discussion. Clines represents traditional thinking when he argues that the word (*'ezer*) must refer to someone who is in a subordinate position.[24] However, he dismisses the evidence of the many occurrences in the Bible in which God is the "helper" for Israel or for an individual who appeals to him.[25] Such examples leave no doubt that *'ezer* can refer to anyone who provides assistance, whatever their relationship to the one whom they aid.[26]

The solution to the man's aloneness comes when God builds the woman from his side. "Rib" (*tsela'*) actually refers to the side of the man, a part of the body that is neither above nor below him.[27] The term is also used for the sides of the ark and

---

[24]See Clines, "What Does Eve Do?"

[25]E.g., Genesis 49:25 (the only text in Genesis, other than 2:18, 20); Exodus 18:4; Deuteronomy 33:7, 26, 29. See the affirmation of this argument in Linda L. Belleville, "Women in Ministry," in *Two Views on Women in Ministry*, ed. James R. Beck and Craig L. Blomberg (Grand Rapids, Mich.: Zondervan, 2001), pp. 142-43.

[26]Further, Clines's argument—that the patriarchal author's view on how Eve is a "helper" is that she is subordinate and serving the purely biological purpose of procreation—overlooks the main point of the text, which is overcoming loneliness or aloneness (pp. 27-37; also Ian Hart, "Genesis 1:1-2:3 as a Prologue to the Book of Genesis," *TynBul* 46 [1995]: 315-36, esp. 333). Ortlund, "Equality," pp. 102-4, introduces here the categories of ontological equivalence but functional hierarchy, but these are alien to Genesis 1–3, where hierarchy is explicitly ontological and functional between God, people and creation. See Genesis 1:26-28; Psalm 8; cf. Groothuis, *Good News*, p. 126.

[27]While her view that *'adam* was originally a sexually undifferentiated creature lacks explicit evidence (Hess, "Splitting the Adam," pp. 13-15), Phyllis Trible (*God and the Rhetoric of Sexuality* [Philadelphia: Fortress, 1978], p. 90) is correct when she writes that woman is "a companion, one who is neither subordinate nor superior; one who alleviates isolation through identity." For other attempts at identifying "the man" of Genesis 2 as a hybrid, see Mary Phil Korshak, "Genesis: A New Look," in *A Feminist Companion to Genesis*, The Feminist Companion to the Bible 2, ed. Athalya Brenner (Sheffield, U.K.: JSOT, 1993), pp. 39-52, who proposes the translation "groundling." Azila Talit Reisenberger ("The Creation of Adam as Hermaphrodite and Its Implications for Feminist Theology," *Judaism* 42 [1993]: 447-52) goes further by suggesting a hermaphrodite. Ellen van Wolde (*Words Become Worlds: Semantic Studies of Genesis 1-11*, Biblical Interpretations Series 6 [Leiden, Netherlands: Brill, 1994]), pp. 13-31, proposes a similar theory (though for different reasons) but extends it to all references to *'adam* in Genesis 2–3. This is even more difficult to accept, given the distinction between *'adam* and the woman in Genesis 3:19 and 21, in addition to the lack of any difference in *'adam* before and after the woman's creation in Genesis 2.

of the tabernacle (Ex 25:12, 14 et al.). Thus this represents a constituent part of the man that is used for the woman, a basic building pattern that can be drawn from the man and used to create a second person like the first.[28]

The man's exclamation and designation of the woman are, following G. W. Ramsey, "a cry of discovery, of recognition."[29] The only figure in the narrative who perceives what has happened (other than God, who does no naming after his creative work) is the man, making it logical and necessary that he call his new partner "woman." This is not a statement of power or authority. Rather, the man recognizes the woman as one taken from him (and thus "corresponding to him") by choosing terms for "man" (*'ish*) and "woman" (*'ishah*) that are so closely related that the only difference in their pronunciation is the characteristic feminine ending *-ah*.[30] These are the customary terms to differentiate man and woman. Though the other word for "man" (used until Gen 2:23) is *'adam,* its feminine form would be *'adamah,* which means "ground," a concept that has already been played upon in the creation of the *'adam* from the *'adamah.* Thus it is not used to designate the female; instead there is a corresponding wordplay between *'ish* and *'ishah.*

Schreiner argues that when the man named the animals he exercised authority over them, and thus when he named the woman he exercised authority over her.[31] This is unconvincing for several reasons. First, the text nowhere states that the man exercised authority over the animals by naming them. Rather, he classified them and thereby continued the work of the first three days of creation in chapter 1, where God divided the elements of matter. Second, there is no obvious way in which the man exercised any authority over either the animals or the woman. Third, Genesis 2:23, where the man designates the woman, begins with an affirmation of equality, "bone of my bones and flesh of my flesh."[32] Fourth, the second part of Genesis 2:23 is a chiasm (concentric structure) in which the words for "woman" and "man" are positioned at

---

[28]The verb *made* in the phrase "made a woman" of Genesis 2:22 (NIV) is *banah,* "to build."

[29]G. W. Ramsey, "Is Name-Giving an Act of Domination in Genesis 2:23 and Elsewhere?" *CBQ* 50 (1988): 24-35, esp. 35. Ilana Pardes ("Beyond Genesis 3: The Politics of Maternal Naming," *A Feminist Companion to Genesis,* The Feminist Companion to the Bible 2, ed. Athalya Brenner [Sheffield, U.K.: JSOT, 1993], pp. 173-93, esp. 175 n. 1), cites seventeen cases in the Hebrew Bible where a male names a child and twenty-seven cases where a female names a child.

[30]Linguistically, *'ish* and *'ishah* probably have two separate and unrelated origins. It is linguistically accidental that they come to appear similar in Hebrew. However, that is not relevant, because the Bible does not argue a linguistic association. The similar sound of the words provides a wordplay designed to relate them, just as the narrative explicitly connects the two.

[31]Schreiner, "Women," pp. 206-8.

[32]See Belleville, "Women," p. 143.

the center, suggesting a corresponding and equal relationship to one another.[33]

The point of Genesis 2:24 about the man's leaving his father and mother and cleaving to his wife is not to indicate that ancient Israel was originally matriarchal, nor to justify the institution of marriage (which is assumed in the Bible), nor to suggest patriarchy in view of the man's initiating the process. Rather, it is to observe that marriage achieves a reunion of what God had divided in the creation of the woman. That is, by using the flesh of the man to create the woman, God created a division that is restored when the two become one flesh again. Thus the woman was taken from the man's body when God created her and the man reunites the two when he joins with her in marriage. This certainly involved more than physical union, for Hebrew concepts of the person do not recognize a distinction between the physical and the spiritual before sin and death, but it says nothing about a hierarchy between man and woman.

Finally, in Genesis 2:25 the couple is described as being "naked" and "not ashamed." These themes are introduced in order to prepare the reader for what is to come in Genesis 3, where this harmonious unity would know corruption and distortion due to humanity's sin. A relationship that was once equally shared in a uniquely complementary design would become burdened with a struggle for authority from which the man would emerge the ruler.

Genesis 3:1-13: The Fall Narrative

The snake, who initiates the dialogue, approaches the woman.[34] Why not the man? Is this evidence of the snake's subversion of God's intended hierarchy? Should the serpent have given deference to the man before addressing the woman?[35]

Several points should be made in response to such an assumption. First, if name giving is intended to symbolize not domination but a kind of discernment and wisdom in determining the nature of a creature, then the man's task as caretaker of the Garden in 2:19-20 would have included the naming of the snake.[36] This would have implied the wisdom to see in the snake the characteristic of shrewdness. How this information was obtained we are not told, but there is no indication that the

---

[33]See J. P. Fokkelman, *Narrative Art in Genesis: Specimens of Stylistic and Structural Analysis,* 2nd ed., Biblical Seminar 12 (Sheffield, U.K.: JSOT, 1991), p. 37.

[34]See Richard S. Hess, "The Roles of the Woman and the Man in Genesis 3," *Themelios* 18 (April 1993): 15-19.

[35]Ortlund, "Equality," pp. 107-8; Schreiner, "Women," p. 209.

[36]See Ramsey, "Is Name-Giving an Act?"

woman was party to it or that the man informed her. Therefore she may have been more susceptible to the snake's persuasive powers.

Second, the reader never learns how the woman received the information that she cites to the snake. Yet is is clear from her words to the serpent that she knew God had forbidden them to eat from the tree. If the serpent and the man had dialogued and sin followed, there would never be certainty as to the guilt of the woman. The text wishes to make clear that both the woman and the man "who was with her" (Gen 3:6) participated in the guilt and both suffered the results, for both knew that eating the fruit was forbidden.[37]

Third, the text nowhere suggests that the snake approached the woman in order to subvert the man's authority over her. There is no mention by any of the characters of any such authority having been given. The challenge of the snake is not directed against the man's authority. It is against God's authority.

Following the dialogue between the woman and the serpent, the narrative resumes in a series of actions (Gen 3:6-8). The passive attitude of the man in contrast to the woman is evident in the initial verbs and their subjects. The fact that he is "with her" suggests the harmonious relationship that these partners shared and for which both were created; and it implies that the man knew what had happened in the preceding verses and thus fully shared in the guilt. In order for this to suggest that the man's leadership over the woman was here subverted, it is necessary to ask whence came that leadership. It is not in the text, nor is it necessary to the narrative.[38] The expression "who was with her" serves a completely different purpose.[39]

The couple's listening to the snake rather than to God is one irony. Another irony is that the trees, designed as a context for God's meeting the couple, are now used as a means of separating the two parties. These ironies enhance the effect the rebellion creates. This sin begins the alienation and breakdown of the harmony that God had so effectively created in Genesis 2. There is no longer an ideal relationship of trust and love. Everything takes a downward slide to suspicion and isolation.

The argument that God approached the man and addressed him first because he was the responsible party for the two has little merit.[40] It is derived from a pre-

---

[37]On gaps or omissions, see, e.g., David M. Gunn and Danna Nolan Fewell, *Narrative in the Hebrew Bible*, Oxford Bible Series (Oxford: Oxford University Press, 1993), pp. 14-17, 20-21, 27, 91, 185, 203-4.

[38]Contra Ortlund, "Equality," pp. 107-8.

[39]The reader does not know how the woman presented the fruit to the man. A traditional view that she enticed the man to sin is not clear from the text.

[40]Ortlund, "Equality," pp. 107-8; Schreiner, "Women," p. 209.

disposition to see hierarchy in the text rather than from a study of the text itself.
In fact God questions the man first and separately for three reasons. First, the man
had first received the injunction not to eat. Second, the interrogation of Genesis
3:9-13 reverses the sequence in which the characters are introduced in Genesis 3:1-
8. Such concentric or chiastic constructions are prominent in Hebrew narrative and
especially in Genesis.[41] The chiasm is completed in Genesis 3:9-13 with the reverse
appearance in sequence of the man, woman and snake. In the center of this chiasm
is the figure of God, on whom the narrative and subsequent interrogation hinge.
Third, God must question the man and the woman separately in order for them to
demonstrate the degree to which their sin has caused a loss of harmony in their
partnership. In the order of the Hebrew text, the first word of both responses of
the man and of the woman is the person or animal they want to blame (the woman!
the snake!). Thus sin's breakdown of the creation order was not an abdication of
divinely instituted hierarchy but the loss of loving harmony between the man and
the woman.

Genesis 3:14-20: Judgments, Not Curses

Though the snake (Gen 3:14-15) and the earth (Gen 3:17) are "cursed" because
of humanity's sin, the man and the woman are not. Most relevant is Genesis 3:16,
which describes the judgment that God gives to the woman. Traditional understandings of this passage have suggested that it describes the origin of pain in childbirth and a subordinate status for women in relation to men (or at least to their
husbands).

Regarding the first point, an alternative interpretation has been advanced by
Carol Meyers, who argues that "toil" ('itsabon) in Genesis 3:16 is not the labor of
childbirth but rather the increased effort involved in assisting the man in the cul-
tivation of the land.[42] The rationale for this interpretation lies in the judgment on
the man in Genesis 3:17, where the same Hebrew word ('itsabon) describes the
"painful toil" (NIV) now required of him to extract nourishment from the cursed
earth. Moreover, this form of the word is not used elsewhere to connote pain, including pain connected to childbirth. Thus Meyers's translation of the first clause
of Genesis 3:16 ("I will greatly multiply your efforts and your childbearing")

---

[41]See Fokkelman, Narrative Art in Genesis.

[42]Carol L. Meyers, "Gender Roles and Genesis 3:16 Revisited," in The Word of the Lord Shall Go Forth:
Essays in Honor of David Noel Freedman, ed. Carol L. Meyers and M. O'Connor (Winona Lake, Ind.:
Eisenbrauns, 1983), pp. 337-54. See also Meyers, Discovering Eve.

makes better sense of its syntax, as well as the meaning of *'itsabon.* This meaning would then carry over to the second clause in this part of the woman's judgment: "with [in the sense of 'in addition to'] *toil* you will bear children." It could also be legitimately translated "with *pain* you will bear children." Though taken from the same Semitic root, this form of the word (*'etsev;* Gen 3:16) is slightly different and is open to either the idea of "pain" or "toil" in a way that the previous form (*'itsabon;* Gen 3:16-17) is not. Thus the woman is required both to work with her husband *and* to bear children, perhaps now with additional pain.

This is why Adam now names his wife Eve: God has revealed to her that she will be the "mother of all living" (Gen 3:20). Thus the first clause of Genesis 3:16 has nothing to do with pain in childbirth but describes (agricultural) work alongside the conception of children. The second clause may repeat these two ideas, or it may describe pain in bearing children. No matter which option is chosen, the woman is required both to work with her husband and to bear children. The giving of the name reflects an awareness of this role for the woman.[43] Eve in Hebrew is *havvah,* which is associated with *hay* (living, alive),[44] denoting her function of giving and nurturing life.[45] Like *'adam* (which becomes a personal name only in Gen 4:20), *havvah* may have first functioned as a title. It first appears after the judgments and refers to the one aspect of woman's judgment that differs from that of man, the bearing of children.[46] The name occurs elsewhere only in Genesis 4:1-2 in the context of the conception and birth of her first son, Cain, followed immediately by that of his brother Abel.

In the second part of the woman's judgment, the translation "to rule over" or "master"[47] preserves a meaning that is clear and should not be altered. Comparing the usage of the words *desire (teshuqah)* and *rule (mashal),* which occur together only

---

[43]Meyers, "Gender Roles," pp. 344-49.

[44]Richard S. Hess, *Studies in the Personal Names of Genesis 1-11,* AOAT 234 (Kevelaer, Germany: Butzon and Bercker; Neukirchen-Vluyn, Germany: Neukirchener, 1993), pp. 19-24; Hess, "Roles of the Woman and the Man"; Scott C. Layton, "Remarks on the Canaanite Origin of Eve," *CBQ* 59 (1997): 22-32.

[45]The nominal form is best understood as designating occupation or profession.

[46]Lyn M. Bechtel, "Rethinking the Interpretation of Genesis 2.4b-3.24," in *A Feminist Companion to Genesis,* The Feminist Companion to the Bible 2, ed. Athalya Brenner (Sheffield, U.K.: JSOT, 1993), pp. 77-117, esp. 110, suggests that this name giving is evidence of Eve's maturity before the man's, whose name is not given until Genesis 4. This seems correct in terms of her acceptance of life's responsibilities. See also Lyn M. Bechtel, "Genesis 2.4b-3.24: A Myth About Human Maturation," *JSOT* 67 (1995): 3-26.

[47]Susan Foh, "What Is the Woman's Desire?" *WTJ* 37 (1975): 376-83.

here and in Genesis 4:7, Susan Foh suggests that woman's desire here is not a sexual desire but a desire to dominate, just as sin has a "desire" to "rule over" Cain (Gen 4:7).[48] Applying the basic hermeneutical principle of translating an expression in one context by the same expression in a nearby and related context, the text then depicts a struggle of the wills between men and women.[49] On this point Foh seems to have gotten it right and to have made an important contribution.

But she goes on to address the question whether the final statement of this verse is a statement of fact ("you will want to dominate your husband but your husband *will* rule over you"), or one implying a determined order on God's part ("you will want to dominate your husband but your husband *should* rule over you"), and she sides with the latter. However, the parallel with Genesis 4:7 and Cain's receiving advice to "rule over" sin is not decisive for solving this question (contrary to Foh), because of the nature of the judgments given the man and the woman. Rather, Genesis 3:16-17 is best understood as a description of the new order of things, of how life *will* be lived as the result of the Fall, rather than how it *should* be lived. It is not a command for one sex to rule over the other any more than Genesis 3:17-19 is a command for all Israelite men to be farmers or a prohibition of the use of weed-killer. These are not God's decisions on how things must be, such that violation of them would be sin.

Thus an additional burden of childbearing is placed on women, and there will

---

[48]The word *desire* occurs elsewhere only in Song of Songs 7:10. There it refers to the lover's desire for his beloved. Only in Genesis 3:16 and 4:7 do the verbs for "desire" and "rule over" appear in close proximity. Adrian Janis Bledstein ("Are Women Cursed in Genesis 3.16?" in *A Feminist Companion to Genesis,* The Feminist Companion to the Bible 2, ed. Athalya Brenner [Sheffield, U.K.: JSOT, 1993], pp. 142-45) attempts to identify the word *desire* with Akkadian *kuzbu,* "sexual allurement," used of goddesses. However, there is no reason to connect these words as cognates, nor is it easy to understand how sin in Genesis 4:7 can be sexually alluring to Cain.

[49]Meyers, *Discovering Eve,* associates the reference to the man's ruling over the woman with the agricultural work. She suggests that it means an additional task for the woman, that is, the man would "predominate" over her in labors in the field by doing more work while she was bearing children. Moreover, he would be able to insist on sexual relations because of social and economic necessities for continuation of the tribe. While her interpretation is possible, the evidence of the parallel text (Gen 4:7) and the context of Genesis 1–3 (God's creation of harmony and the subsequent loss of that harmony) points toward a different understanding of the conflict of wills.

   Adrian Janis Bledstein, "Was Eve Cursed? (or Did a Woman Write Genesis?)," *Bible Review* 9, no. 1 (February 1993): 42-45, translates the phrase as "you are attractive to your man, yet he can rule over you," suggesting, "the verse is concerned with men's arrogant abuse of power with regard to exploiting another person sexually." This is possible but not probable, as the parallel use of this expression (Gen 4:7) is best understood as "its [sin's] desire is for you" rather than "it is attractive to you."

be a power struggle between the wills of the husband and wife. The man's predominance over the woman may have to do with the greater physical strength that a husband would often possess in relation to his wife and the sad situation of the exertion of physical force to establish the husband's will against that of his wife.

The result of these judgments is loss of harmony in relationships. The earth does not function in conjunction with the humans. Thus the woman and the man must work against the tendency of the land to produce thorns and thistles. The woman and man, as well, now possess a natural inclination to fight one another, each seeking to exercise their own will against the will of their companion. That this too easily degenerates into violence anticipates the fratricide of Genesis 4.

Genesis 3:21-24: The Punishment of Expulsion

The expulsion from Eden in Genesis 3:21-23 can best be seen in light of sanctuary imagery.[50] The tunics of skin are God's means of providing for the sin of the couple by an animal sacrifice, perhaps anticipating the sacrifices of the tabernacle and temple. It literally covers them, thereby hiding their shame. The use of animal skins introduces physical death for the first time and suggests a barrier between God and his people,[51] between people and nature, and even between the man and the woman.

The expulsion from the Garden meant the cessation of the man's distinctive role as its caretaker (Gen 2:15); no longer would he cultivate it. Cast out from the presence of God and the opportunity to worship God at all times, man and woman would now have to fill their time with labor to meet life's basic needs and to raise a family. Worship of God, while still possible, would take on new meaning, requiring a separate and additional time of rest before God.

How does this fulfill God's promise of death to those who eat the fruit?[52] Death is a metaphor for personal decay, as can be found in a similar usage of the word

---

[50]See Gordon J. Wenham, "Sanctuary Symbolism in the Garden of Eden Story," *Proceedings of the Ninth World Congress of Jewish Studies*, Division A, Jerusalem, 1986, pp. 19-25; Terje Stordalen, *Echoes of Eden: Genesis 2-3 and Symbolism of the Eden Garden in Biblical Hebrew Literature* (Louvain, Belgium: Peeters, 2000).

[51]Robert J. Ratner, "Garments of Skin (Genesis 3:21)," *Dor le Dor* 18 (1989-1990): 74-80.

[52]Ortlund, "Equality," p. 110, writes, "God told Adam alone that he would die. But Eve died, too. Why then did God pronounce the death sentence on Adam alone? Because, as the head goes, so goes the member." Although the man was alone when God warned of a death sentence, the second-person common singular, *you*, in Hebrew regularly appears with a collective sense. In this case it was intended from the beginning to denote the entire human race. As noted, "shall surely die" is a legal term that regularly appears in the singular in laws that are intended as universal; e.g., Exodus 21:12, 15-18. The woman was correct to understand the punishment as applicable to her in Genesis 3:3.

death in the warnings of Deuteronomy 30:15, 19.[53] Thus death for the man and woman is primarily seen in their separation and alienation from Eden, from each other (blaming one another, the coats of animal skin) and now also from God.[54]

This is the real punishment for the sin of eating the fruit. It is not simply the creation of a hierarchy between the man and the woman. It is much worse. It is the collapse of the ordered and harmonious world of the Garden of Eden, the loss of worship with God, the demands of a struggle for existence in the world, and the emergence of disharmony and conflict between the man and the woman.

Conclusion

The relationship between man and woman in Genesis 1–3 has been examined with regard to several points. First, they were created equally in God's image, though clearly in different ways and sequentially, one after the other. Thus one might speak of a "creation order," though not in the sense of a hierarchy of the man over the woman. Second, they were commanded to share dominion over the rest of creation. This is the only authority given before the Fall. Third, the woman was formed from the man as his "corresponding helper" or partner, with no implication of inferiority or subordination. Fourth, the man described her as "woman," reflecting unity in personhood and diversity in their gender. Later he names her Eve, describing the function she would have in bearing children as the "mother of all living" (hence one could speak of a "procreation order" that counterbalances the creation order; cf. 1 Cor 11:12). But the text does not mention anything about authority in the giving of names. Finally, after the Fall, God's judgment included for the woman hard work alongside her husband in addition to bearing children. She would also have a desire to rule him, though he would end up ruling her.

In short, both unity and gender diversity are clear themes in the creation accounts. God created the woman and the man to be one in unity and love. There is neither explicit nor implicit mention of any authority or leadership role of the man

---

[53]R. W. Moberly, "Did the Serpent Get It Right?" *Journal of Theological Studies* 39.

[54]Alan J. Hauser, "Genesis 2-3: The Theme of Intimacy and Alienation," in *Art and Meaning: Rhetoric in Biblical Literature*, ed. David J. A. Clines, D. M. Gunn and A. J. Hauser, *JSOT*Sup 19 (Sheffield, U.K.: JSOT, 1982), pp. 20-36. The view that the expression can mean "you deserve to die" rather than "you will die" (so V. P. Hamilton, *The Book of Genesis Chapters 1-17*, NICOT [Grand Rapids, Mich.: Eerdmans, 1990]) is not supported by similar examples such as 1 Samuel 14:44 and Jeremiah 26:8. In these cases the statement is made by individuals whose threat is stronger than their ability to carry it through. Further, it is not clear that the Bible makes a decision between deserving to die and dying in terms of punishment.

over the woman, except as the sad result of their sin in the Fall and their ensuing judgments. Even then, such hierarchy is not presented as an ideal, but rather as a reality of human history like that of the weeds that spring from the earth. The resolution of this conflict in equality and harmony cannot be found in these chapters but looks forward to a future redemption.

5

FROM OLD TESTAMENT LAW
TO NEW TESTAMENT GOSPEL

Ronald W. Pierce

Because the law of Moses reflects a male-centered social environment, many view its statements regarding women as morally offensive.[1] For example, critics argue that women frequently appear in the Torah[2] as dependent on or even inferior to men and that legal rulings either ignore women or are negative toward them. Women are normally subject to the authority of a father, husband or brother, except when widowed or divorced—a precarious type of independence in ancient times.[3] Further, a woman's legal rights are usually stated in terms of her relation to a man (or lack thereof).[4] Even though such laws do not compose a large portion of the Pentateuch, they remain troubling to many evangelicals today.

In an effort to seek understanding of these passages in the broader context of the Bible's teaching regarding men and women, this chapter has a twofold emphasis.[5] First, it will highlight the positive, regulatory character of the law, given that it was designed (in part) to expose and restrain sinful behavior. In other words, the

---

[1]An attitude criticized by Walter C. Kaiser Jr., *Toward Old Testament Ethics* (Grand Rapids, Mich.: Zondervan, 1983), pp. 284-88.

[2]Unless otherwise explained, the Hebrew term Torah ("law" or "instructions") is used to refer to the legal sections of the five books of Moses, the Pentateuch.

[3]Rosemary Radford Ruether, ed., *Religion and Sexism: Images of Woman in the Jewish and Christian Traditions* (New York: Simon & Schuster, 1974), pp. 56-57.

[4]Phyllis Bird, "'To Play the Harlot': An Inquiry into an Old Testament Metaphor," in *Gender and Difference in Ancient Israel*, ed. Peggy L. Day (Minneapolis: Fortress, 1989), p. 77; Inger Lyung, *Silence or Suppression: Attitudes Towards Women in the Old Testament* (Stockholm: Almqvist & Wiksell, 1989), p. 40.

[5]The two aspects of this chapter may be illustrated by a comparison between "reading glasses" (for close viewing) and "driving glasses" (for distance viewing). In the first part we use "reading glasses" to examine the Old Testament in its own context; in the second, we use "driving glasses" to see more clearly the long-range implications for the gospel.

law not only showed us our need for redemption but also functioned as a guardian and disciplinarian until that redemption was more fully realized.[6]

Second, this essay will demonstrate a redemptive process,[7] of which the Law is but one stage. This process begins with (1) God's good *creation*, which is (2) marred by humanity's *sin*, which in turn is (3) regulated by the Mosaic *law*, a structure that is transcended in (4) the *gospel*. Thus just as the law took humanity beyond the judgments of Genesis 3:14-19, the New Testament believer is called to go beyond the law to the fullness of the gospel. This process is confirmed by comments of Jesus (Mt 5:17-48; 19:1-20) and Paul (Gal 3:19, 23; 4:4). Jesus explains the implications already inherent in the law yet adds his own countertheses that contrast a traditional understanding of the Torah with the fuller revelation of the gospel.[8] Likewise, Paul argues that the law "was added because of transgressions," guarding those under its care, while serving as their "disciplinarian" *until* "the fullness of time" when a Redeemer would appear, "born of a woman . . . under the law." In both contexts the law is honored yet understood as part of a redemptive *process* that led to something better.

The Law as Guardian and Disciplinarian

Because there are relatively few Old Testament laws regarding women, this chapter will address each one of them in turn under the following headings: (1) adultery and divorce, (2) slaves, daughters and prisoners of war, (3) levirate responsibility and a breach of modesty, (4) vows, purification and ceremonial participation, and (5) priests and firstborns.

Adultery and divorce. Adultery in the Old Testament and other ancient societies appears to have been understood as a sin or crime against the adulteress's husband (Ex

---

[6]In regard to the Deuteronomic materials discussed below, see Carolyn Pressler, *The View of Women Found in the Deuteronomic Family Laws*, BZAW (Berlin: Walter de Gruyter, 1993), p. 216. Her study reveals a careful, thorough exegesis and provides an extensive bibliography on the broader topic of woman's status in the Hebrew Scriptures. In addition, an excellent collection of essays has appeared on the topic: Victor H. Matthews, Bernard M. Levinson and Tikva Frymer-Kensky, eds., *Gender and Law in the Hebrew Bible and the Ancient Near East*, JSOTSup 262 (Sheffield, U.K.: Sheffield Academic, 1998).

[7]This is quite similar to William J. Webb's redemptive-movement model, emphasizing the "redemptive spirit" of the biblical text, developed in his chapter "A Redemptive-Movement Hermeneutic: The Slavery Analogy" in this volume; see also Webb's *Slaves, Women and Homosexuals: Exploring the Hermeneutics of Cultural Analysis* (Downers Grove, Ill.: InterVarsity Press, 2001).

[8]W. D. Davies and D. C. Allison Jr., *A Critical and Exegetical Commentary on the Gospel According to Saint Matthew* (Edinburgh: T & T Clark, 1988), 1:506, 508; quoted by Stephen Westerholm, "The Law in the Sermon on the Mount: Matt 5:17-48," *Criswell Theological Review* 6, no. 1 (1992): 52-53.

20:14; Deut 5:18), but not as a sin or crime against the adulterer's wife (or wives). Thus the consequences were less serious for a married man in having sexual relations with an unmarried (or unbetrothed) woman than with a married (or betrothed) woman. Here it seems Old Testament law implicitly agrees with or assumes the premise of polygamy,[9] namely, that a wife does not have exclusive sexual rights to her husband, though a husband has exclusive sexual rights to his wife (or wives).[10] However, it must be noted that in ancient Near Eastern culture polygamy also served to protect women, who would be at risk without a father or husband, and to insure the continuation of the family line, as in the case of levirate responsibility (discussed below).[11] Likewise, the Mosaic laws regarding adultery and divorce had a beneficial social value for guarding and protecting the institution of marriage at that time. Herein lies the *positive* value of the law as it functioned within this cultural framework.

Both men and women were held accountable under the law, though in different ways. This is demonstrated in injunctions such as those found in Numbers 5:11-31, Leviticus 20:10, and Deuteronomy 22:13-29 and 24:1-4. In Numbers 5:11-31 a man suspects his wife of infidelity and subjects her to a trial by ordeal in which she must drink "bitter water." If she is found guilty, she will never again bear children. Otherwise she suffers no further punishment and is vindicated. Here the law allows the husband to put his wife through the ordeal, but within a legal framework, preventing him from taking the matter into his own hands without her having the benefit of a trial. Thus though Torah does not reverse the judgment of male dominance (Gen 3:16), it guards and protects the woman within the situation.[12]

A litany of injunctions appears in Leviticus 20:10-21 against a variety of illicit

---

[9]There was no need for the Torah to address the hypothetical question of polyandry (multiple husbands) since the practice could not have existed in a patriarchal culture.

[10]See the discussion of this thorny problem in Gordon J. Wenham, *Leviticus*, NICOT (Grand Rapids, Mich.: Eerdmans, 1979), p. 258. Also, on Leviticus, see the massive three-volume commentary by Jacob Milgrom, *Leviticus 1-16*, *Leviticus 17-22* and *Leviticus 23-27*, Anchor Bible 3, 3A, 3B (New York: Doubleday, 1991-2001).

[11]When practiced to a modest extent, polygamy is neither condoned nor condemned in the Old Testament. Examples include Lamech (Gen 4:19), Jacob (Gen 29:14-30), Ashhur (1 Chron 4:5), Shaharaim (1 Chron 8:8), Gideon (Judg 8:30), Elkanah (1 Sam 1:1-2), David (1 Sam 27:3; 2 Sam 5:13), and several of the kings of Israel and Judah, especially Joash for whom Jehoiada the priest obtained two wives (2 Chron 24:3). To be clear, the injunction in Deut 17:14-20 against a king multiplying wives, silver and horses addresses the problems of royal abuse of power and self-reliance, not polygamy. Of course, Solomon is the famous example of breaking this law (1 Kings 11:3-8).

[12]This is not to say that a woman could call for a formal trial if she suspected her husband of adultery, as he could for her. On this the text is silent, and the patriarchal culture suggests that she most likely could not.

sexual relations, such as adultery, incest, homosexuality and bestiality. The relevant text is Leviticus 20:10, where the penalty for a man's committing adultery with his neighbor's wife is the death of both the adulterer and the adulteress. Here the law is expressed in male-oriented language but applies to both men and women.

Deuteronomy 22:13-29 links together several similar cases. First, in Deuteronomy 22:13-21 a man who is not satisfied with his new bride accuses her of engaging in sexual promiscuity prior to their marriage in order to divorce her. If her parents show proof that she was a virgin when they married, the man must pay a fine for disgracing the woman and may not divorce her in the future. However, if she is guilty, then she must die for disgracing her father's house. Again, the law works within its patriarchal context but regulates the husband's control over his wife through the involvement of her parents.

Second, in Deuteronomy 22:22-24 a married or betrothed woman has sex with another man "in the town" (Deut 22:23). If caught, they both must die. The man and the woman bear the responsibility together because the act was consensual: she could have cried out and been heard "in the town" but did not.

Third, Deuteronomy 22:25-29 considers the same case in the "open country," where the woman could not be heard if she cried out. Here a presumption of innocence is given to the woman. If she is married or betrothed, her assailant must die while she incurs no penalty. If she is an unbetrothed virgin, the man must pay the bride price (a valuable marriage present) to her parents and marry her without the option of divorce in the future. Or, according to Exodus 22:16-17, her father may deny the marriage, in which case the man must pay the monetary equivalent of the bride price in silver.[13] Again, this reflects the patriarchal culture: the woman is protected within the society either in the context of her family of origin or within an indissoluble marriage (the husband may never shirk his responsibility to provide for her). Though this concern for the victim seems minimal compared to modern standards, the arrangement is better than letting rape go unchecked.

Finally, in Deuteronomy 24:1-4 one finds a situation where a man divorces his wife because he believes she has been indecent in her conduct. Later a second man marries her but either dislikes her and divorces her or dies and leaves her a widow. In either case the first husband may not take her back, because she has been defiled and would bring guilt upon the land. Strictly speaking, the only legislation here is

---

[13]Although the reason for linking the three laws in Deuteronomy 22:13-29 is not entirely clear, it may be that the editor meant to carry forward the theme of an unsatisfied husband who initiates extramarital sex (consensual or not).

that a man may not remarry a woman whom he has divorced, if she has since married another.[14] By focusing on the issue in this manner, the rule served to allow for divorce under certain circumstances[15] but also to keep divorce and remarriage from being abused and turned into a form of legal adultery.[16]

In summary, the law's guardianship and discipline are discernible with respect to both women and men in the adultery and divorce regulations, despite the strong patriarchal influence of the ancient culture. The law's limitation of male authority allowed a woman to function (to an extent) as an active agent in the legal process, distinguishable from a husband and his status. In this sense such laws were an improvement of woman's status at that time, though in this form they remained less than ideal.

Divorce was neither instituted nor encouraged by Moses, although the law recognizes and allows for its existence. But at the same time Moses did not allow a husband to divorce his wife for just any reason; thus the law gives women a greater sense of dignity[17] and emphasizes the Lawgiver's concern for justice on their behalf.[18] Moreover, the law limited the practice of divorce and precluded some of its abuses,[19] thus protecting women from irresponsible accusations by their husbands and the resultant social risk. Finally, it defended the honor of the household and ensured the ceremonial purity of the land.[20]

Slaves, daughters and prisoners of war. Exodus 21:2-11 addresses two situations regarding Hebrew women as slaves,[21] which are discussed together because of their

---

[14]See William A. Heth and Gordon J. Wenham, *Jesus and Divorce* (London: Hodder & Stoughton, 1984), pp. 106-10, 121-22; also Bruce Kaye and Gordon J. Wenham, *Law, Morality and the Bible* (Downers Grove, Ill.: InterVarsity Press, 1978), pp. 36-37. Both studies interpret the second remarriage as incest, in that the wife "became like a sister" to her first husband.

[15]Since this is the only text in which Moses implicitly permits divorce, it seems reasonable to conclude that Jesus is alluding to Deuteronomy 24:1-4 in Matthew 19:3-9, where he states that Moses *permitted* the issuing of a certificate of divorce as an accommodation to humanity's hardness of heart.

[16]Peter C. Craigie, *Deuteronomy*, NICOT (Grand Rapids, Mich.: Eerdmans, 1976), pp. 304-5.

[17]See Eckart Otto, "False Weights in the Scales of Biblical Justice? Different Views of Women from Patriarchal Hierarchy to Religious Equality in the Book of Deuteronomy," in *Gender and Law in the Hebrew Bible and the Ancient Near East*, ed. Victor H. Matthews, Bernard M. Levinson and Tikva Frymer-Kensky, JSOTSup 262 (Sheffield, U.K.: Sheffield Academic, 1998) pp. 133-38.

[18]Jacob J. Finkelstein, "Sex Offenses in Sumerian Laws," *JAOS* 86 (1966): 367.

[19]S. R. Driver, *A Critical and Exegetical Commentary on Deuteronomy*, 3rd ed., ICC (Edinburgh: T & T Clark, 1895), p. 272. See also Kaiser's response, *Toward Old Testament Ethics*, p. 200.

[20]Pressler, *View of Women*, p. 15.

[21]It is important to note that slavery between Israelites (Ex 21:2-11) was debt servitude; that is, what was bought and sold was the labor of the slave, not the person. This was not the case, however, with slaves taken as prisoners of war (Deut 21:10-14). For the latter there was less protection.

similarity of status. In Exodus 21:2-6 two slaves are married and have children while in the service of their master. If the husband is set free at a later time, his wife and children must remain with the master as slaves. If the marriage took place before they were acquired as slaves, however, the wife and children may go with the husband. Linked to this in Exodus 21:7-11 is the sad case of a man who sells his daughter as a slave (presumably due to economic hardship) and she does not please her new owner. When this happens, the woman's owner may sell her to another or give her to his son and treat her like a daughter-in-law (i.e., not having sexual relations with her). If he[22] takes another wife, he must continue to provide for the first (the slave) or release her without receiving the normal remuneration (i.e., he cannot sell her). In addition to the strong patriarchal background to these two laws, the cultural rights of ownership and disposal of slaves are evident.

In Deuteronomy 21:10-14 the legislation allows an Israelite man to take a non-Israelite female prisoner of war as his wife, though he must first permit her a month of mourning for her father and mother, from whom she would have been separated. After consummating the marriage, if the Israelite husband is not satisfied with her, he may release her, but he may not sell her as a slave, since he has taken her as his wife and now divorced her.

The law of Moses does not endorse slavery (economic or personal) any more than it does patriarchy, but works within these frameworks and regulates them, providing a degree of care and protection for slaves and women. Further, neither Exodus 21:7-11 nor Deuteronomy 21:10-14 addresses the uncertain future for a woman who has been "released" into a patriarchal society. In short, these two passages reveal the harsh reality of the right of a father to dispose of his daughter's virginity and that of a husband to possess his wife's sexuality. Nevertheless, they indicate that even women of lower status had certain rights above being a mere possession. Though women did not have a reciprocal claim in most cases, the rights of husbands were to a degree limited,[23] even in the case of Gentile women acquired as spoils of battle. Thus such laws relating to Gentiles, slaves and women show a redemptive movement toward the ideal expressed in Paul's liberating words regarding these same three groups: "There is neither Jew nor Greek, neither slave nor free, neither male nor female, for you are all one in Christ Jesus" (Gal 3:28).

---

[22]It is not clear whether this refers to the father or the son.
[23]Pressler, *View of Women*, pp. 41-42.

Levirate responsibility and a breach of modesty. In Deuteronomy 25:5-12 two seemingly unrelated laws are joined. The first (Deut 25:5-10) involves the well-known case where a woman's husband has died without their having had children. In this case the law required the husband's brother[24] to marry the widow and father a child on his behalf in order to establish a memorial for the man and his family, protect the widow and guard the orderly succession of property.[25] Although the man remains the primary actor, concern for the widow leads to a limitation of his authority and prerogatives.[26] The *duty* of the man is emphasized, and the *desire* of the woman to remarry and have a child in memory of her deceased husband is assumed.

Because widows occupied a vulnerable position in Israel, legislation is solicitous on their behalf (Ex 22:22-24; Deut 14:29; 24:17).[27] In fact, if the brother of the deceased is reluctant to marry the widow, she becomes "the plaintiff in the local court," carrying out "the symbolic legal acts against the obstinate *levir*."[28] In addition, the solidarity of the family guarantees the continuation of the tribe, as well as that of the nation in the land.[29]

This regulation is linked to a law regarding a wife who attempts to rescue her husband from a fight by seizing the genitals of his opponent (Deut 25:11-12).[30] In such an unlikely event, the penalty is the loss of her hand. In contrast to the preceding law, this one contains no apparent protection for the woman. Because she intervened in this way on behalf of her husband she must lose a hand, regardless of whether an injury has occurred or how severe the results may be.

Though this seems harsh, one might argue that in cases like this the prerogative of the "victim" to determine a penalty for the woman could have been left unrestricted. And since "an eye for an eye" was literally impossible, another punishment was prescribed that might be seen as a relatively more equitable solution, in contrast

---

[24]The term *levirate* derives from the Hebrew *levir*, the brother who is to marry his deceased brother's widow. He is sometimes referred to as the "kinsman redeemer," as in the story of Ruth and Boaz.

[25]For a discussion of the management of property in the Old Testament, see Raymond Westbrook, *Property and the Family in Biblical Law*, JSOTSup 113 (Sheffield, U.K.: Sheffield, 1991).

[26]Pressler provides a useful discussion of the literary features of this text (*View of Women*, pp. 63-73).

[27]Cf. Susan T. Foh, *Women and the Word of God: A Response to Biblical Feminism* (Grand Rapids, Mich.: Baker, 1979), p. 73.

[28]Otto, "False Weights," p. 140.

[29]Lyung, *Silence or Suppression*, p. 47.

[30]This case law is probably connected to Deuteronomy 25:5-10 because of the importance of perpetuating the family line (cf. Gen 1:26-28), which a man might not be able to do if he were injured in this manner.

to more violent penalties in other societies contemporary to Moses'.[31]

Vows, purification and ceremonial participation. The list of participants called to attend Moses' speech (Deut 29:9-18) makes it clear that women were viewed as responsible members of the covenant community.[32] Similarly, examples of women singers at the temple can be cited (Ezra 2:65; Neh 7:67; 2 Kings 22:14; 1 Chron 25; 2 Chron 34:22).[33] However, this general principle of including women has exceptions. Though daughters, female slaves and widows were exhorted to "*rejoice* in the festival of booths," only males were required to *attend* it in Jerusalem (Deut 16:14-16; see also Ex 23:16-17). Indeed, men in that culture were considered representatives of the household. But this fact does not account for the inclusion of the women called for by Moses. Perhaps the *requirement* to travel as much as one hundred miles or more to the temple should be linked with problems of ritual impurity due to menstruation (e.g., Lev 15:19),[34] which would bar women from participating in religious ceremonies for the equivalent of several months each year.[35] It should be noted, however, that there is no restriction on women's attending otherwise (e.g., Hannah and Peninnah in 1 Sam 1:1-8).

Leviticus 27:1-8 gives the regulations regarding payments due to the sanctuary when a vow is made, which vary according to gender and age. Table 5.1 shows the comparison.

Table 5.1. Payment of vows

AGE (YEARS)	MALE (SHEKELS)	FEMALE (SHEKELS)
1 month-5	5	3
5-20	20	10
20-60	50	30
60+	15	10

---

[31]For a discussion of the relationship of Old Testament Law to other societies, see Shalom M. Paul, *Studies in the Book of the Covenant in the Light of Cuneiform and Biblical Law*, *VT*Sup 18 (Leiden, Netherlands: E. J. Brill, 1970); Raymond Westbrook, *Studies in Biblical and Cuneiform Law* (Paris: J. Gabalda, 1988); James R. Baker, *Women's Rights in Old Testament Times* (Salt Lake City: Signature, 1992); and Karel van der Toorn, *Family Religion in Babylonia, Syria and Israel* (New York: E. J. Brill, 1996).

[32]Mary J. Evans, *Woman in the Bible* (Downers Grove, Ill.: InterVarsity Press, 1983), p. 32.

[33]Kaiser, *Toward Old Testament Ethics*, p. 207.

[34]See the discussion of this text by Denise Lardner Carmody, *Biblical Woman: Contemporary Reflections on Scriptural Texts* (New York: Crossroad, 1988), pp. 15-21.

[35]Lyung, *Silence or Suppression*, p. 41.

The closing caveat in the passage regarding a person's ability to make the payment reveals the rationale behind this law. Men aged twenty to sixty were the most financially self-sufficient, while women and those older or younger were less so.[36] This may also explain why the time of purification after childbirth (Lev 12:2-5) was doubled when the child was female; that is, the regulations reflected the economic realities of patriarchal culture. It is important to note, however, that women *could* make vows and that they were "an indispensable part of the labor force, nearly equivalent [by economic standards] to that of the male."[37]

In Numbers 30:3-15 one finds a situation where a woman makes a vow while under the household authority of either a father or husband. In the first instance (Num 30:3-5) the woman is young and living at home. When her father hears of her vow, he may either condone it (even by his silence) or disapprove of it in a timely fashion. In the second case (Num 30:6-8) the woman makes the vow while unmarried but carries its obligations with her into marriage. In this context, the husband must remake the same decision that the father had made previously, since the vow will now affect him. In the third situation (Num 30:9) the woman is widowed or divorced when making the vow. Hence the vow is her choice alone. Last (Num 30:10-15), the vow is made while the woman is married, in which case the husband must approve or disapprove in a timely fashion and may not change his mind later without incurring guilt. It is noteworthy that the emphasis of the text is on the father or husband making a *timely* decision regarding the vow and being responsible for the decision made. Once again, the patriarchal framework of the household is reflected, though regulated. That is, it is assumed that the father or husband has authority in the household, but he must exercise that authority in a responsible manner.

Priests and firstborns. The *sons* of Aaron were chosen to exercise religious leadership as priests, offering sacrifices in the sanctuary (Num 17:1-13), thus representing the people to God. Even though Exodus 19:6 declares all of Israel "a kingdom of priests" (in that as a nation they mediated between the world and God), women were excluded from functioning as Aaronic priests within the nation, along with males with "physical defects" (Lev 21:1-24). Perhaps the exclusion of women priests may be traced to the ceremonial uncleanness of menstruation that would prevent them from officiating for a portion of each month.

---

[36]Foh, *Women and the Word*, p. 82.
[37]Milgrom, *Leviticus 23-27*, p. 2371.

In addition, the patriarchal culture (not biblical law) generally granted prestige and privilege to firstborn *sons* within a family, though there are notable exceptions (e.g., Isaac, Jacob, Joseph, Ephraim). When the first male child was born, the mother's esteem in the eyes of her peers immediately increased.[38] Following this, the child was honored over his brothers (and sisters) while the father was alive and received a double portion of inheritance, as well as leadership over the clan, after the father's death (Ex 13:13; Deut 21:17). In contrast, a daughter could receive an inheritance only if she had no brothers (Zelophehad's daughters, Num 26–27; 36) or if her father chose to override this patriarchal tradition (Job's daughters, Job 42:15).[39]

The texts regarding the priesthood and firstborn are relevant to a discussion of gender issues in view of the change that came when Jesus became the ultimate high priest over a priesthood of believers (Heb 9:7, 11, 25; 1 Pet 2:5, 9) and the firstborn of a larger family (Rom 8:29), both of which include women. Religious privileges of male descendants of Aaron without physical defect and the cultural privileges of firstborn males were erased within the New Testament community. Race, gender, economic status and physical defect were rendered inconsequential as divisions within the church.

Summary. It has been argued that the intention of the Torah was "neither to create nor to perpetuate patriarchy."[40] In contrast, it sometimes even disciplined the man and guarded the woman. Moreover, the family laws had a relatively progressive and protective attitude toward the legal status of women, exhibiting concern for limiting male dominance. Critics may judge the law's success in overcoming "the patrilineal and patriarchal pattern" of Hebrew society as being "too little and by no means enough." But for women living at that time, it was at the least beneficial.[41] It meant the difference between an ordered society and a chaotic anarchy with unrestrained male dominance.

Moving from Law to Gospel

It would be wrong to confuse the Mosaic law with an exhaustive statement of

---

[38]Roland de Vaux, *Ancient Israel: Its Life and Institutions* (New York: McGraw-Hill, 1961), p. 39.

[39]Other examples of this practice are presented by S. Joy Osgood, "Women and the Inheritance of Land in Early Israel," in *Women in the Biblical Tradition*, ed. George J. Brooke, Studies in Women and Religion 31 (Lewiston, N.Y.: Edwin Mellen, 1992): 37-52.

[40]Phyllis Trible, "Depatriarchalizing in Biblical Interpretation," *Journal of the American Academy of Religions* 41 (1973): 31.

[41]Otto, "False Weights," p. 140.

God's will for humanity or to assume that mere compliance with it could satisfy the righteousness God requires.[42] When Jesus declared that he came to fulfill the law without abolishing it (Mt 5:17), he called his disciples to move beyond traditional understandings of Torah observance to a way of life that embodies the will of God more perfectly. Moreover, he defended and illustrated this call with six antithetical rulings regarding adultery, divorce, murder, swearing falsely and keeping a vow, retaliation and hatred (Mt 5:21-48).[43]

Though Aída Besançon Spencer's thesis of moving "beyond the curse"[44] provides a helpful starting point for the discussion of gender equality in the Bible, Jesus' teaching suggests that one must also move *beyond the law*. His response to the question on divorce (Mt 19:1-12) and his treatment of the same subject in the legal rulings found in Matthew 5:21-48 (specifically Mt 5:27-32) speak directly to this point.

Adultery and divorce. Divorce was not instituted or encouraged by the law of Moses, although the Torah recognized and tolerated its existence, accommodating humanity's hardness of heart by providing for the orderly dissolution of a marriage when it is the lesser of the evils.[45] This is why Jesus could both underscore the sanctity of marriage and allow for divorce (though only in extreme cases such as adultery; Mt 5:31-32; 19:3-9).

But consider also the words of Malachi and Ezra (the latter "a scribe skilled in the law of Moses," Ezra 7:6). While Malachi was *criticizing* the returned Judeans for divorcing their Jewish wives "by covenant" (Mal 2:14-16), Ezra was *commanding* them to divorce the pagan wives they had taken in Babylon (Ezra 10:11). Both easy divorce and pagan religion threatened family purity within the covenant community. What Ezra commanded and what Jesus permitted reveal the same essential principle, though neither reflected an ideal situation.

However, Jesus goes beyond mere regulation of behavior by calling his disciples not only to avoid adultery but also to address the lustful desires that lead to the act (Mt 5:27-30). Passionately, and in contrast to the outward regulatory character of the law, Jesus places the intent of the heart in sharper focus (a concept already inherent in the giving of the law; cf. Deut 30:11-14). Viewing others as opportunities

---

[42]Westerholm, "Law in the Sermon on the Mount," p. 49.

[43]Ibid., p. 44-47.

[44]Aída Besançon Spencer, *Beyond the Curse: Women Called to Ministry* (Peabody, Mass.: Hendrickson, 1985).

[45]Westerholm, "Law in the Sermon on the Mount," p. 53.

for one's own gratification deeply offends the love that respects and delights in their otherness. The point is that love (in contrast to lust) transcends the law without dismissing it.[46]

In Matthew 19:1-12 the rationale for Jesus' treatment of the law becomes even clearer, revealing a paradigm similar to that discussed by the apostle Paul, who declares that the law was "added because of transgressions" and guarded us until the Messiah had come (Gal 3:19, 23; 4:4-5). Jesus' position on divorce (allowing it because of the people's "hardness of heart," even though "from the beginning it was not so," Mt 19:8) reveals the progression: creation —> judgment —> law —> gospel. The way it was "from the beginning" (creation) is contrasted with "hardness of heart" (sin and the resultant judgment). One of the functions of the law was to regulate human behavior while facing the harsh reality of the fallen state, which included a dominating, patriarchal culture. Finally, the fulfillment of the law in the redemptive era of the Messiah goes beyond the law by focusing on the attitude of the heart. In this, however, the law is neither changed nor abolished (i.e., it was still a good thing to be orderly about divorce when it occurred). Rather the emphasis shifted from a negative restriction to a positive initiative, carrying forward the divine intention that was present from the beginning.

Applying the paradigm to other issues. This principle can also be seen in the other statements of Jesus in Matthew 5. For example, murder was prohibited in the Decalogue (Ex 20:13), with serious penalties attached. However, in Matthew 5:21-26 Jesus goes beyond the restrictive commandment by calling his followers to seek reconciliation with one another instead of merely avoiding angry insults and injury.

Similarly, the Old Testament law taught that one should honor vows sworn by an oath (Num 30:2), even if keeping it would bring harm to oneself (Ps 15:4). In contrast, Jesus emphasizes a simple fidelity to one's word. Having to go further than this and swear an oath, or make a vow, might be seen as representing "society's inevitable compromises with human sin, the tolerance of the lesser evil, to avoid the consequences of the greater." Jesus did not set aside the restrictive law but exhorted believers to go beyond it.[47]

In the last two rulings (Mt 5:38-48) Jesus sharply contrasts retaliation and hatred with forgiveness and love. In the well-known injunction regarding "an eye for an eye" (Mt 5:38-42; Ex 21:24, 27; Lev 24:20; Deut 19:21), his method is most

---

[46]Ibid.
[47]Ibid., p. 54.

clearly revealed. The law was given to guard against uncontrolled anger expressed in disproportionate measures (our sinful nature might cause us to seek the death of another person for their having blinded us).[48] In response the law guards and disciplines us, limiting our revenge to justice and no more—"an eye for an eye." In its wording it allows for a proportionate response but does not encourage it.[49] Jesus goes beyond the law yet in a sense returns to its essential core—that is, the ideal that existed from the beginning. Thus he calls for no retaliation at all. Rather, his followers are to return forgiveness and love, leaving their fear of injustice in the hands of God (cf. Rom 12:19).

In the second ruling regarding loving one's neighbor and hating one's enemies (Mt 5:43-48), Jesus refers to a popular notion nowhere attested in the Hebrew Scriptures. Certainly the idea of loving one's neighbor is clearly commanded in Leviticus 19:18 and can be deduced from the last six of the Ten Commandments, which refer to treating one's neighbor fairly (cf. Mt 22:39). However, the Torah never commanded the hatred of Israel's enemies. This assumption is an example of misunderstanding a law by assuming that the converse is true. Beyond merely correcting the error, Jesus calls his listeners to go beyond the "second greatest commandment," to love one's neighbor, by showing love to and praying for an enemy.

Summary. The Gospels make it clear that many religious leaders in Jesus' time misunderstood the law's intention to restrain the sinful tendencies of humanity. Although Moses had already stated that keeping the law was primarily a matter of the heart (Deut 30:11-14), the people had fallen into believing that outward observance was mostly what God expected from humankind (cf. Hos 6:4-6; Amos 5:21-24; Mic 6:6-8). In contrast, Jesus' words point to "the moral equivalence"[50] of the Mosaic sanctions—the inward intention that should lead to the outward behavior. While doing so, he both demonstrated the original intention of the law to restrict sinful behavior and contrasted a way of living that exceeds the law's restrictive demands.

Conclusion

The situation in which women found themselves under the Old Testament law was

---

[48]For example, see the slaughter of the Shechemites by Simeon and Levi in response to Dinah's rape (Gen 34), which was appropriately condemned by Jacob (Gen 49:5-7).

[49]It may be argued that Deuteronomy 19:21 points in the opposite direction by adding the phrase "show no pity." However, there is sometimes a fine distinction between justice and revenge. Pity should not prevent a society from exacting justice, but this should not lead to getting revenge.

[50]Westerholm, "Law in the Sermon on the Mount," p. 52.

less than perfect. Clearly they continued to suffer under the heavy hand of male dominance as a result of the Fall and judgment. Nevertheless, the law regulated, to an extent, the severity of their plight. Adultery was forbidden to both men and women. A woman accused of sexual promiscuity or infidelity by her husband had the benefit of a trial. A man who raped a woman was held responsible for his actions. Divorce and remarriage were discouraged. The assumed rights of disposal of children, slaves and prisoners of war were also regulated. Widowed women were to be cared for by near relatives. Punishment of women was proportionate to their offenses. Women could participate in the covenant life of the community, including festivals and the making of vows. And fathers could override the custom of the time and bless their daughters alongside their sons with equal inheritance. Thus it can be argued that the law neither created nor perpetuated patriarchy but rather reflected a progressive and protective attitude toward women. It was beneficial to women in its time, bringing order to the society in which they lived.

However, the gospel transcended the law, going beyond mere restriction of sinful behavior, as illustrated in Jesus' treatment of the laws regarding adultery, divorce, murder, swearing falsely, keeping a vow, and traditional understandings of retaliation and hatred. It demonstrated the next step in the progression from creation marred by sin (and resultant judgment), by temporary way of the law, to the redemption inaugurated by the Messiah in the gospel.

But to a degree even the New Testament situation is incomplete: creation still waits for the *full* redemption found in the contrast of our "here and now" with the "then and there" of New Testament eschatology.

In applying this to the gender question, one may find peace in knowing that the Old Testament law improved the status of women from the judgment of sin, and the gospel went beyond that. The apostle Paul paradigmatically describes the new era as one in which there will no longer be the discrimination of Jew over Gentile, free over slave or male over female—for all believers will be one in the Messiah, Jesus (Gal 3:28). Jesus treated women with dignity and respect. Women, as part of the priesthood of believers, were permitted to learn (1 Tim 2:11), teach (Acts 18:26), lead in worship (1 Cor 11:4-16) and even serve as apostles (Junia, Rom 16:7). Husbands were called to mutually love and serve their wives, who, along with their children and slaves, were no longer to be treated as property (Eph 5:21-28). Thus believers have the joyful privilege of implementing this redemptive message while living in hope of the full redemption that is to come at the Messiah's return.

6

WOMEN LEADERS IN THE BIBLE

Linda L. Belleville

Studies of women leaders in the Bible can be readily found. Yet three research tools are now in hand that make revisiting the topic both prudent and worthwhile. First, there are recently published Qumran papyri and Greco-Roman inscriptions, which challenge considerably the common stereotype of women in both Jewish[1] and Greco-Roman[2] circles as little more than chattel. Second, there are current sociohistorical studies that show that there were more women leaders in antiquity, particularly in formerly male-dominated arenas,[3] than has commonly been acknowledged.[4] Third, Greek computer databases[5] permit a more informed and accurate understanding of

---

[1] The Babata documents from Qumran, in particular, show the legal capabilities of women in the most religiously conservative Judean circles. Here is a woman who inherits the properties of two husbands, buys and sells properties and supervises her holdings. The number of legal transactions that Babata handled is remarkable even by modern standards. Thirty-five legal documents were found in her possession. This accords with what is found in early mishnaic legal materials. A woman of independent means could bring suit for damages (*Mishnah Bava Qamma* 1.3), sell property in her possession (*Mishnah Ketubbot* 11.2), testify in court (*Mishnah Ketubbot* 2.5-6), swear an oath (*Mishnah Shevu'ot* 5.1; *Mishnah Ketubbot* 9.4; *Nedarim* 11.9), manage her earnings (*Mishnah Bava Metzi'a* 1.5) and arrange her own marriage (*Mishnah Qiddushin* 2.1).

[2] Greco-Roman inscriptions show that women under Roman law enjoyed more freedoms and privileges than has traditionally been supposed. These privileges included ownership and disposal of property, terminating a marriage, suing for child support and custody, making a will, holding office, swearing an oath and giving testimony. For further discussion of women's roles in Jewish and Greco-Roman first-century society, see Linda L. Belleville, *Women Leaders and the Church* (Grand Rapids, Mich.: Baker, 2000), pp. 71-96.

[3] Literature on women in antiquity has mushroomed since the 1960s. For an overview and bibliography, see ibid.

[4] For example, the decision whether the Greek name Junia(s) in Romans 16:7 is the masculine Junias or the feminine "Junia . . . outstanding among the apostles" can now be determined with relative ease and confidence. See the second section of this chapter, "Women Leaders in the New Testament."

[5] E.g., Thesaurus Linguae Graecae (TLG, ancient literary works), the Packard Humanities Institute (PHI, ancient papyri and inscriptions), and the Perseus Project (archaic and classical texts and artifacts).

women's roles in Scripture than has been attainable previously.

Women Leaders in the Old Testament

Few today contest the fact that women appear in a variety of ministry roles in the Old Testament. The key questions are, Were these *leadership* roles? Did the community of faith affirm women in such positions? The biblical record yields a yes on both accounts.

From early on, women were affirmed as leaders. Miriam is a good example. She is portrayed in the Exodus narratives as a leader in and of her own right and is accorded a level of respect similar to that of Aaron and Moses. The congregation of Israel viewed her role as essential to its mission, refusing to move ahead on one occasion until she was restored to leadership after her criticism of Moses (Num 12:15).

Her impact can be gauged by the affirmation she received from subsequent generations. Tradition commends her as a *prophet* sent by God to join her brothers in *leading* Israel out of Egypt and *redeeming* them from the land of slavery. Her memory is celebrated by the community of faith for the leadership she provided at this crucial juncture in Israel's history (Mic 6:4; cf. Ex 15:20).

Women proved to be capable leaders during Israel's subsequent history. During the period of the judges, Deborah particularly comes to mind. She assumed a variety of leadership roles, including "prophet" (Judg 4:4, 6-7), "judge" (Judg 4:5) and "mother of Israel" (Judg 5:7). In the role of prophet, her leadership was accepted without dispute as from "the LORD, the God of Israel," indicated by Barak's response to her summons (Judg 4:6).[6] This is due, in part, to cultural familiarity.

---

[6]Barak's submission to a woman has sometimes been construed as a sign of weakness for two reasons: his insistence on her presence in battle and Deborah's reply (Judg 4:8-9). In response to the first issue, it should be noted that Barak's demand that Deborah go with him most likely meant that he valued her leadership as a prophet so greatly that he would not fight without her. In response to the second, it should be noted that the NIV's "*Very well* . . . I will go with you" (changed to "*Certainly* I will" in TNIV) and the TEV's "*All right* . . ." (Judg 4:9) are misleading. The Hebrew participle used along with a finite form of the same verb serves to intensify rather than suggest a grudging agreement: "*Surely* [or 'Indeed'] I will go with you" (most translations). The LXX translator reflects this understanding by rendering it with the intensive: *poreuomenē poreusomai*. See Bruce K. Waltke and M. O'Connor, *An Introduction to Biblical Hebrew Syntax* (Winona Lake, Ind.: Eisenbrauns, 1990), 35.3.1-2; E. Kautzsche, *Gesenius' Hebrew Grammar*, trans. A. E. Cowley (Oxford: Oxford University Press, 1910), no. 133L; and F. C. Conybeare and St. George Stock, *A Grammar of Septuagint Greek* (Boston: Ginn, 1905; reprint Grand Rapids, Mich.: Zondervan, 1980), no. 81.

The NIV's "*but because* of the way you are going about this, the honor will not be yours" is also questionable (Judg 4:9). '*Efes* with a noun clause introduced by *ki* is restrictive, not causative: "*How-*

Archaeological finds show that female prophets, both professional and lay, were well known in antiquity.[7]

Deborah's stature as a judge is confirmed by the types of cases she handled. Intertribal disputes too difficult for the local judges fell to her (Deut 17:8).[8] She held court in the hill country of Ephraim between Ramah and Bethel, where men and women alike came to her to have their disputes settled (Judg 4:4-5; a similar itinerant route to that of the prophet Samuel, 1 Sam 7:16).[9]

Deborah's ability as a commander-in-chief is also clear. When the tribes were incapable of standing together against their oppressors, Deborah not only united them but led them to victory. This is underscored by the placement of her name ahead of that of Israel's general: "Deborah and Barak . . . sang [a victory song] on that day" (Judg 5:1).

Deborah's overall leadership skills are highlighted in several ways. Her gender is placed first for emphasis: "Now Deborah, a woman prophet" (Judg 4:4 BBE). Her judicial role is expressed in the participial form ("judging Israel"), thereby emphasizing her ongoing activity (Judg 4:4). Her posture ("she used to sit under the palm," Judg 4:5) is that of an official exercising her duties. As a judge, she made a profound difference. Before her tenure "the roads were abandoned; travelers took to winding paths. Village life in Israel ceased" (Judg 5:6-7 NIV). With Deborah's ascendancy came a return of security in the countryside.

In her honor, the site was named "the palm of Deborah" (Judg 4:5) and the title

---

ever, you will have no glory on the enterprise" (most translations). See Ronald J. Williams, *Hebrew Syntax,* 2nd ed. (Toronto: University of Toronto, 1976), nos. 427, 558, "a restrictive clause"; cf. Waltke and O'Connor, *Hebrew Syntax,* 35.3.5e: "but [contrary to your expectations], there will be no glory for you."

[7]For instance, there were a large number of female prophets (lay and professional) at Mari, Syria, during the third and second millennia B.C., who were contemporaries of Israel's patriarchs and judges. This included King Zimrilim's own daughter. See Abraham Malamat, "A Forerunner of Biblical Prophecy: The Mari Documents," in *Ancient Israelite Religion,* ed. P. D. Miller, P. D. Hanson and S. D. McBride (Philadelphia: Fortress, 1987), pp. 33-47.

[8]"If a judicial decision is too difficult for you to make between one kind of bloodshed and another, one kind of legal right and another, or one kind of assault and another—any such matters of dispute in your towns—then you shall immediately go up to the place the LORD your God will choose" (Deut 17:8). Deborah's legal role is sometimes disputed (e.g., Paul R. House, *1, 2 Kings,* NAC 8 [Nashville: Broadman, 1995], p. 197). This, however, overlooks legal language such as *ham-mishpat,* which has to do with "decisions" made in response to particular legal inquiries. See Robert Boling, *Judges,* Anchor Bible 6a (New York: Doubleday, 1975), p. 95, n. 5

[9]The political involvement of female prophets in antiquity is well documented. See Herbert Huffmon, "Prophecy in the Mari Letters," *BA* 31 (1968): 101-24.

"mother in Israel" was bestowed on her (Judg 5:7). The phrase "in Israel" commends her as a national leader. "Mother in Israel" is comparable today to an honorary doctorate bestowed in recognition of national leadership contributions.[10]

Similarly, the prophet Huldah provided leadership during the time that prophets of the stature of Jeremiah (Jer 1:2), Zephaniah (Zeph 1:1), Nahum (Nah 3:8-10) and Habakkuk (Hab 1:6) were active. Huldah was related by marriage to a court official, which placed her at the center of public affairs (along with Zephaniah). Her renown as a religious counselor was such that when King Josiah commanded his advisers to "go, inquire of the LORD . . . concerning the words of this book that has been found [the book of the law]," they sought out Huldah (2 Kings 22:13-14).

The size and prestige of the embassy that sought her counsel indicates something about not only the seriousness of the situation but also Huldah's professional stature: the high priest (Hilkiah), the father of a future governor (Ahikam), the son of a prophet (Achbor), the secretary of state (Shaphan) and the king's officer (Asaiah). Huldah's counsel was immediately heeded, and sweeping religious reforms resulted (2 Kings 22:8-20; 23:1-25).

Some speculate that the king's advisers picked Huldah because she was a political insider. Yet the prophet Zephaniah was more closely identified with the ruling class as a descendant of King Hezekiah (715-686 B.C.; Zeph 1:1). More likely Huldah was approached because of her track record of prophetic leadership and expert counsel. The narrator calls attention to the fact that the whole people of God (including "the prophets") pledged themselves afresh to the covenant as a result of her counsel (2 Kings 23:1-3). Indeed Huldah's role in Josiah's reforms may have helped elevate all the true prophets to their rightful place in Judah's religious community.

It is sometimes remarked that God permitted women to lead at times when Israel lacked adequate male leadership. But the examples of Miriam, Deborah and Huldah, who ministered in the context of other renowned male figures (Moses, Barak, Josiah, Jeremiah, etc.), demonstrate the opposite. Others plead exceptional circumstances. They argue that Israel's nomadic existence during the wilderness years and a leadership vacuum after years of slavery in Egypt called for exceptional measures. The period of the judges, they point out, was a unique time when everyone did whatever was deemed right in their own eyes. Yet if there was any time when

---

[10]See Roman codes such as the Theodosian Code 16.8.4.

wise spiritual counsel was in evidence, strong leadership was in place and the nation was on an even keel, it was during King Josiah's reign—and Huldah's tenure. The prophet Jeremiah speaks highly of Josiah (Jer 22:15-16), as does the author of 2 Kings (2 Kings 22:2).

Why, though, were there so few women leaders? The lack of a comprehensive history of the period makes it difficult to know actual percentages. Matter-of-fact references to female prophets may indicate that women such as Miriam, Deborah and Huldah were only the tip of the leadership iceberg. There are a number of un-named women that suggest as much: the female prophet whom Isaiah was in-structed to marry (Is 8:3), the female prophets Ezekiel spoke against (Ezek 13:17-23) and Noadiah, mentioned by Nehemiah (Neh 6:14). Some, like their male counterparts, were lured by fame and fortune. The prophet Ezekiel pronounced judgment against both the sons of Israel and the daughters of Judah, who prophe-sied "out of their own imagination" (Ezek 13:2, 17; cf. Jer 28:1-17).

There were women who served as advisers to heads of state. One example is the "wise woman" from Tekoa during David's reign, who advised the king regarding Absalom (2 Sam 14:1-33). Another example is the "wise woman" of Abel-beth-maacah who saved her city from destruction at the hand of David's troops by giving expert counsel (2 Sam 20:16-22). Such would not have been the case had these women not had significant standing and authority within their local setting.[11]

Women leaders are also well attested in the political arena. City records and in-scriptions give ample evidence of their civic-mindedness. Women's names appear in connection with the underwriting of temples, theaters, gymnasiums, public baths and other civic projects.[12] From time to time women even served as heads of state. Athaliah ruled Judah 842-836 B.C., albeit unwisely (2 Kings 11:1-3; 2 Chron 22:10-12); Salome Alexandra, honored queen of the Hasmonean Dynasty, reigned 76-67 B.C.; and Cleopatra was the effective ruler of Egypt from 51 to 31 B.C.

Though there appear to have been more men than women in the political spot-light, it was not due to a lack of intelligence, temperament or political savvy. Nor

---

[11]See Claudia Camp, "The Wise Women of 2 Samuel: A Role Model for Women in Early Israel?" *CBQ* 43 (1981): 14-29.

[12]For example, Phile, the first woman magistrate in Priene, Asia Minor, dedicated at her own expense a cistern and the water pipes (1st-century B.C. *Epigraphica* 2.5.G). Another woman, Eumachia, was public priestess of Pompeii, Italy, and patron of the guild of fullers, one of the most influential trade guilds of the city (*Corpus Inscriptionum Latinarum* 10.810, 1st century A.D.). See H. W. Pleket, *Epigraph-ica II: Texts on the Social History of the Greek World* (Leiden, Netherlands: E. J. Brill, 1969).

is there any notion in the Old Testament that women leaders were inappropriate. The only exception is the Levitical priesthood, where purity laws precluded Jewish women's serving in certain ceremonial roles due to uncleanness related to childbirth and menstruation. Men too were excluded but for different reasons (e.g., not being a Levite, sexual uncleanness or physical defect). Other roles, however, show women and men serving side by side. Women were involved in building and furnishing the tabernacle (Ex 35:22-26) and standing watch at its entrance (Ex 38:8; 1 Sam 2:22).[13] They played musical instruments in public processions (Ps 68:25), danced and sang at communal and national festivals (Judg 21:19-23), and chanted at victory celebrations (1 Sam 18:7). Women brought offerings, performed rituals prescribed for purification and pardon, performed vows (Lev 12:1-8; 13:29-39; 15:19-29; 1 Sam 1:11, 24-28), and were recipients of divine communication (Judg 13:2-7; 8-20).[14] There is also every indication that women and men worshiped and ministered side by side. Together they sang in the choir (2 Chron 35:25; Ezra 2:65; Neh 7:67) and offered sacrifices (1 Sam 1:24-25).

Women Leaders in the New Testament

Women leaders come to the fore with the advent of the apostolic period. Several factors explain this. One is the Spirit's empowerment of both women and men for ministry. The outpouring of the Spirit at Pentecost was an equal opportunity event. The women among Jesus' disciples were enabled for witness just as the men were (Acts 1:8, 14-15; 2:17-18). The result was a major paradigm shift from the male priesthood of the Jewish cult to the charismatic worship format and gender-inclusive leadership of the early church.[15] "When you assemble," Paul states, "each one has a psalm, has a teaching, has a revelation, has a tongue, has an interpretation" (1 Cor 14:26 NASB).

Another factor was the involvement of women in leadership positions in Greco-Roman religion and politics.[16] Recent sociohistorical studies have shown that offi-

---

[13] The Hebrew *tsaba'* ("to serve") is used elsewhere of the Levites to describe their role in the tabernacle (Num 4:23; 8:24) and of Israel's warriors (Num 31:7, 42).

[14] In these respects they functioned in a parallel fashion to women in the pagan cults. See Phyllis Bird, "The Place of Women in the Israelite Cultus," in *Ancient Israelite Religion*, ed. P. D. Miller, P. D. Hanson and S. D. McBride (Philadelphia: Fortress, 1987), pp. 397-411.

[15] See chapter sixteen in this volume.

[16] There were some political exclusions. Women were not present in the Roman assemblies and did not hold positions of command in the military. Public speaking roles were also scarce. Although this restriction was increasingly a formality, women continued to need a male guardian for perform-

cial religion in the Roman Empire was gender inclusive and women leaders were a known phenomenon. For example, while Paul was planting the Ephesian church, Iuliane served as high priestess of the imperial cult in Magnesia, a city fifteen miles southeast of Ephesus.[17] Also, because religion and society were inseparable, to lead in one arena was often to lead in the other. Mendora, for example, served at one time or another during Paul's tenure as magistrate, priestess and chief financial officer of Sillyon, a town in Pisidia, Asia.[18]

Women in the Roman church. The more Romanized the area, the more visible were women leaders. Since Paul's missionary efforts focused on the urban areas of the Roman Empire, it should come as no surprise that most of the women named as church leaders in the New Testament surface in his letters.

This is especially true of his letter to the Roman church. The letter carrier was a woman (Rom 16:1-2), and at least five of the nine women Paul greets were ministry colleagues ("co-workers," Rom 16:3, 6-7, 12). English translations stemming from the 1940s to the 1980s tend to obscure this fact. A hierarchical, noninclusive understanding of leadership during this period is partly to blame: women can't be leaders, so the language of leadership must be eliminated. Phoebe becomes a "servant" and Paul's "helper" (instead of a church deacon and Paul's patron; Rom 16:1-2),[19] and the esteemed apostle Junia becomes the masculine "Junias" (Rom 16:7).

Junia is especially to be noted. Among the leaders recognized at Rome, she receives highest marks. Paul greets her and a coworker named Andronicus as "my fellow Jews who have been in prison with me. They are outstanding among the apostles" (Rom 16:7 TNIV). Andronicus and Junia could have been among "all the apostles" (beyond the Twelve) or among the five hundred to whom Christ appeared (1 Cor 15:6-7).[20] But the facts better fit their having been among the "visitors from Rome" who responded to Peter's preaching at Pentecost (Acts 2). Both were Jewish, both had Greek (Hellenized) names, and both preceded Paul "in Christ"

---

ing important transactions such as making a will, selling a piece of land, freeing a slave, entering into a contract or accepting an inheritance.

[17]*Die Inschriften von Magnesia am Maeander* 158.

[18]Inscriptiones Graecae ad res Romanas pertinentes 3.800-902.

[19]The translation "deaconess" in Rom 16:1 (RSV, JB, NJB, Phillips) is anachronistic, for the feminine *diakonissa* was not in use during the apostolic period. The first clear instance is about the time of the Nicaean Council in A.D. 325 (canon 19).

[20]Paul uses *apostolos* more broadly than "the Twelve." James, Andronicus, Junia, Barnabas, Silas, Timothy and Apollos are all called apostles (Rom 16:7; 1 Cor 4:6, 9; 9:5-6; Gal 1:19; 2:9; 1 Thess 1:1; 2:7).

(Rom 16:7). This would place them most naturally during the early years of the church's outreach in Jerusalem (Acts 2–7).

Some try to circumvent the attribution of apostleship to a woman by changing the gender. The majority of English translations done from the 1940s to the early 1970s translate *Iounian* as the masculine name Junias.[21] On the other hand, older translations (e.g., Wycliffe Bible, Tyndale New Testament, Geneva Bible, KJV, Weymouth), more recent revisions (NKJV, NRSV, NABr, REB, TNIV) and newer translations (e.g., God's Word, NLT, Holman Christian Standard, NET, ESV) render *Iounian* as the feminine Junia. They do so for good reasons. The masculine name Junias does not occur in any inscription, letterhead, piece of writing, epitaph or literary work of the New Testament period. The feminine Junia, however, appears widely and frequently. Perhaps the best-known Junia is the half-sister of the famed Roman general Brutus.[22] The name Junia also appears in first-century inscriptions from such familiar New Testament locales as Ephesus, Didyma, Lydia, Troas and Bithynia.[23] "Junia" is found as well on tombstones—especially in and around Rome.[24]

Others attempt to get around Paul's apostolic acknowledgment by translating the Greek prepositional phrase as "esteemed *by*" or "*in the sight of* the apostles"

---

[21]This requires that *Iounias* be understood as a contraction of the masculine name *Iounianus*. In this case, the masculine accusative ending of *Iounias* would be the same as the feminine accusative ending of *Iounia*—except for the accent. The contracted (or shortened) form would have a circumflex. The feminine would have an acute accent. Ancient manuscripts typically did not contain accents, so the Greek technically can go either way.

Even so, from the time accents were added to the text until the early decades of the twentieth century, editions of the Greek New Testament printed the acute accent and not the circumflex. The reasons for this are clear. The shortened form of Junianus would be Junas, not "Junias." Also, while it is true that Greek nicknames were abbreviations of longer names, Latin nicknames were typically formed by lengthening the name, not shortening it—hence Priscilla for Prisca (Acts 18:2, 18, 26; cf. Rom 16:3; 1 Cor 16:19; 2 Tim 4:19). See John Thorley, "Junia a Woman Apostle," *NovT* 38 (1996): 24-26.

[22]Plutarch *Marcus Brutus* 7.1.4.

[23]The inscription evidence includes *Ephesos Ionia* 627.1; 788.1; 822.1; 2373.1; *Didyma Ionia* 225.1; *Tituli Asiae Minoris* V.1403.5; *Kyzikene Propontiskueste Mysia/Troas* 2077.11; *Die Inschriften von Prusias ad Hypium* 93.1.

[24]E.g., "Here lie infants [Anu]nia Iounia Noeta," *Corpus inscriptionum Judaicarum* 10.1; cf. 303.1. For additional primary sources, see Peter Lampe, *Die stadtrömischen Christen in den ersten beiden Jahrhunderten*, WUNT 2, no. 18 (Tübingen: Mohr, 1987), pp. 156-64. The evidence for "Junia" is so compelling that even the most traditional scholars are now conceding that *Iounian* in Rom 16:7 is feminine. See, for example, Thomas Schreiner, "Women in Ministry," in *Two Views on Women in Ministry*, ed. James R. Beck and Craig L. Blumberg (Grand Rapids, Mich.: Zondervan, 2001), p. 198.

rather than "outstanding *among* the apostles." To do this, however, is to introduce a strange thought for Paul. In Paul's writings there are *"us* apostles" (I Cor 4:9), *"Christ's* apostles" (I Thess 2:6-7), *"his [God's]* holy apostles" (Eph 3:5), *"the other* of the apostles" (I Cor 9:5), those "who were *already apostles"* (Gal 1:17) and *"other of* the apostles" (Gal 1:19). There are also the "pillars" (Gal 2:9) and the "super-apostles" (2 Cor 12:11), but not *"the* apostles." The terminology appears in the kerygma that preceded Paul. Paul states in I Corinthians 15:3-7 that he was faithful in transmitting to his converts and church plants "as of first importance" what he himself had received—"that he [Christ] appeared . . . to all the apostles." But "the apostles" is not native to Paul's own thinking or speaking.

To say that Junia was "esteemed *by"* or "prominent *in the sight of* the apostles" is to ignore early Greek translations and commentaries. For example, the Vulgate, the standard Latin translation of the Western church, has "Junia . . . notable *among* the apostles" *(nobiles in apostolis).* John Chrysostom, bishop of Constantinople in the fourth century, states, "To be even *amongst these of note,* just consider what a great enconium this is! . . . Oh how great is the devotion of this woman [Junia] that she should be even counted worthy of the appellation of apostle!" (*Homilies on Romans* 31 [on Romans 16:7]).[25]

More recently the translation "outstanding among the apostles" has been challenged on the basis of usage outside the Bible. It is argued that every known instance of the adjective *episēmos* with the preposition *en* and the personal dative bears the exclusive sense of "well-known *to"* rather than the inclusive "notable *among."*[26] The first implies that Junia was outside the group of apostles but esteemed *by* them; the second implies that she was honored *as one of* them.

But all considerations support the latter. For one, *episēmos* is the adjective "notable" and not the passive verb "well known to."[27] Two, it is a compound of *epi*

[25]Subsequent Greek commentators echo the attribution (Theodoret *Epistles* 82.2 [4th century]; *Catena on the Epistle to the Romans* 519.32 [5th century]; *Chronicon Paschale* [7th century]; John of Damascus *Epistles* 95.565 [7th century]).

[26]E.g., Michael Burer and Daniel B. Wallace, "Was Junia Really an Apostle? A Re-examination of Rom 16.7," *NTS* 47 (2001): 76-91.

[27]None of the standard Greek lexicons support such a meaning. Johannes P. Louw and Eugene A. Nida, *Greek-English Lexicon of the New Testament Based on Semantic Domains,* 2 vols., 2nd ed. (New York: United Bible Societies, 1988-1989), no. 28.31, has "pertaining to being well known or outstanding, either because of positive or negative characteristics—'outstanding,' 'famous,' 'notorious,' 'infamous.'" Indeed, Louw and Nida render Romans 16:7 as "they are outstanding among the apostles" (contra Burer and Wallace, "Was Junia Really an Apostle?" p. 84 n. 39).

(upon) and *sēma* (mark), yielding the literal sense "having a mark, inscription," "bearing the marks of," and the metaphorical sense "remarkable, notable" (LSJ s.v.). This would make Junia a "distinguished" or "remarkable" *member of* (not simply *known to*) the apostles. Three, overwhelming usage of the preposition *en* and the personal dative (inside and outside the New Testament) bears the local meaning "in/among."[28] While dative personal nouns often designate the recipients (to/for), this is not the case for the preposition *en*. In fact, the standard grammars and lexicons lack salient examples of its bearing the sense "to."[29] On the other hand, *episēmos en* with either a personal or impersonal object in each case yields the meaning "notable *among*," not "well known *to*."

- Additions to Esther 16:22 (NRSV): "Therefore, you shall observe this with all good cheer as *a notable day among* your commemorative festivals."

- Josephus *Jewish Wars* 2.418: "So the men of power . . . sent ambassadors; some to Florus . . . and others to Agrippa, *eminent among* whom were Saul, Antipas, and Costobarus."

---

[28] A. T. Robertson lists numerous examples of an adjective followed by *en* plus the personal plural dative as "inclusive" (i.e., a member of the larger group; *A Grammar of the Greek New Testament in the Light of Historical Research* [Nashville: Broadman, 1934], p. 587). See, for example, Matthew 2:6, "But you, Bethlehem, . . . are by no means least among the rulers of Judah *[en tois hēgemosin Iouda]*"; Acts 4:34, "There were no needy persons among them *[en autois]*."

[29] Burer and Wallace's study ("Was Junia Really an Apostle?") assumes a conclusion not found in the evidence. Despite their assertions to the contrary, they fail to offer one clear biblical or extrabiblical parallel to support their position that in this idiom the *en* phrase is "exclusive," not "inclusive." First, it should be noted that evidence for this construction *(episēmos* as an adjective modified by *en)* is exceedingly rare, much too rare to support their sweeping conclusions. They do concede, somewhat grudgingly, that the one certain instance (Lucian *On Salaried Posts* 28) in fact supports the traditional view of Romans 16:7. On the other hand, what *they* perceive as the closest parallel to Romans 16:7 becomes so only because it is not cited accurately. When citing *Psalms of Solomon* 2.6, which reads *en episēmō en tois ethnesin*, they drop the preposition *en*, permitting *episēmos* to be read as a straight adjective modifying the preceding "seal" (thus "with a seal, a spectacle among the Gentiles"). But that strains the plain sense of the grammar in every way; much more likely it is a neuter noun ("with a mark," "brand"). Thus: "Their [captive Jews'] neck was *with* a seal *[en sphragidi]*, *with* a slave-brand *[en episēmō]* among the Gentiles *[en tois ethnesin]*" (i.e., describing what made "their captivity" in Babylon "grievous"). "Aphrodite, glorious to mortals" (Euripides *Hippolytus* 103) looks to be an "exclusive" example. But translators (e.g., Rex Warner, 1949; Michael R. Halleran, 1995) and scholars on this text typically define *episēmos* as "renowned, notorious among" and not "glorious to." See Richard Hamilton, *Euripides' Hippolytus: Commentary* (Bryn Mawr, Penn.: Bryn Mawr Greek Commentaries, 1980-1982), p. 8, line 103. Moreover, the Greek of Euripides predates Paul's by five centuries, when the adjective had not yet acquired a comparative sense, and thus does not offer a contemporary parallel.

- Lucian *On Salaried Posts* 28: "So you must raise your thirsty voice like a stranded frog, taking pains to be *conspicuous among* those who praise [the mistress' page]."

- Lucian *Dialogues of the Dead* 438: "We had quite a crowd with us on our way down, *most distinguished among whom* were our rich countryman Ismenodorus [and others]."

Thus the clearest reading of this reference to Junia yields an example of a woman not only functioning as an "apostle" in the New Testament church but being highly esteemed as such by Paul and his apostolic colleagues. This flies in the face of arguments that Jesus excluded women from the Twelve because their gender precluded their functioning as apostles.[30]

Women in the Philippian church. Euodia and Syntyche are singled out as leaders of the Philippian church. That Paul does this is significant. It is not his practice to name names in letters to his churches. In part, the public nature of his letters precluded it. They were written to be read aloud and concerned matters that affected the whole church (Col 4:16). When Paul does mention someone by name, it is with decided intentionality.

Paul's initial evangelistic foray in Philippi took place among a group of Jewish women during sabbath prayers (Acts 16:13-15). Some, such as Euodia and Syntyche, then partnered with Paul in the preaching of the gospel, as well as in leading the congregation. Paul's public appeal to a "loyal companion" to "help these women" to "be of the same mind in the Lord" says something about their stature within the Christian community (Phil 4:23).

Euodia's and Syntyche's differences were not of a petty or personal nature. Paul speaks to the issue of conflict in the church, spending significant time exhorting the church to stand firm in *one spirit* (Phil 1:27), to be of the *same mind* (Phil 2:2, 5; 3:15), *striving side by side* for *the faith of the gospel* and in no way intimidated by their opponents (Phil 1:27-28). Much of this same language is used of Euodia and Syntyche. They too are called to be of *the same mind*, having *struggled beside* Paul in *the work of the gospel* (Phil 4:2-3). Their role so clearly involves leadership that their disagreement put the unity of the church in jeopardy.

There is no hint that these or any other women should not be in leadership roles. If this had been so, Paul would have said as much. He is not shy to do so elsewhere (e.g., 1 Tim 1:19-20). Nor is the disagreement an indication that women

---

[30]Contra Michael J. Wilkins, "Women in the Teaching and Example of Jesus," in *Women and Men in Ministry: A Complementary Perspective*, ed. R. L. Saucy and Judith TenElshof (Chicago: Moody Press, 2001) pp. 91-112, esp. 105-6; on this matter see chapter seven in this volume.

are not well suited for leadership. Paul himself sharply disagreed with a colleague on at least one occasion (Acts 15:36-41). At issue is simply two leaders not seeing things the same way in the context of outside opposition to the church.

Women in the Cenchrean church. Phoebe is commended as "a deacon of the church in Cenchrea" (Rom 16:1). Some translations obscure this fact by rendering *diakonos* as "servant" (e.g., NKJV, NASU, NIV). To do so is to miss the official character of Paul's commendation. Phoebe was Paul's designated letter carrier to the Roman church (Rom 16:2).

A church's welcome was based on the presentation of credentials. This is why Paul routinely provided credentials for his letter carriers (e.g., 2 Cor 8:16-24; Eph 6:21-22; Phil 2:25-30; Col 4:7-9). Since Phoebe was a virtual unknown, strong credentials would have been critical in her case. "Servant" would hardly have sufficed in the imperial capital. "A *deacon* of the church in Cenchrea" is what was needed (TNIV, NRSV; cf. NLT, NEB, CEV).

Here we do well to take our cue from the early church fathers. "Deacon" is how they universally understood Phoebe's role. Origen cites Romans 16:7 as an example of the fact that "even women are instituted deacons in the church."[31] John Chrysostom understands *diakonos* to be a term of "rank."[32]

Paul instructs the Roman church to "receive [Phoebe] in the Lord" and to "give her any help she may need" (Rom 16:2). Elsewhere this is technical language for an itinerant missionary (e.g., 1 Cor 16:10-11; 2 Cor 7:15). In Phoebe's case it indicates that Paul entrusted her with a mission beyond carrying his letter. This was certainly within the scope of a deacon's job description. Ignatius, bishop of Rome at the turn of the century, twice refers to a deacon of one church serving as an ambassador to another church.[33]

Women in the Lycus Valley churches. Priscilla and Aquila are twice greeted by Paul as "co-workers" (Rom 16:3-5; 2 Tim 4:19). It is a common misconception within evangelical circles that Greco-Roman women rarely left their house and that when they did go out they did not speak to members of the opposite sex. There was no stratum of Roman society where this was the case. Even the wives of Roman artisans worked side by side with their husbands (Acts 18:3). Priscilla and Aquila were no exception. They are recognized throughout the New Testament as a team.

The language Paul uses of both Priscilla and Aquila points to the equivalent of

---

[31]Origen *Homilies on Romans* 10.17 (third century).
[32]John Chrysostom *Homilies on Romans* 31 (on Rom 16:1; late 4th century).
[33]Ignatius *Letter to the Philadelphians* 10.1; *Letter to the Ephesians* 2.1.

today's church planter, a role very much like his own. They are Paul's "co-workers in Christ Jesus," "they risked their lives" for him, and "all the churches of the Gentiles are grateful to them" (Rom 16:3-4).

What is unusual is the order of their names. As in our "Mr. and Mrs." nomenclature, the Roman husband's name typically appeared first. When New Testament writers refer to their occupation of tentmakers and to "their house," the order is "Aquila and Priscilla" (Acts 18:2; 1 Cor 16:19). But when ministry is in view, the order is "Priscilla and Aquila" (Acts 18:18; Rom 16:3; cf. 2 Tim 4:19). This is also the case with the instruction of Apollos (Acts 18:26), suggesting that Priscilla possessed the dominant ministry and leadership skills of the duo.[34]

Women were also among the ranks of deacons in the Ephesian church: "Women [deacons], likewise, are to be worthy of respect, not slanderers, temperate, and trustworthy in everything" (1 Tim 3:11, my trans.). That Paul is speaking of women in a recognized leadership role is apparent not only from the listing of credentials but also from the fact that these credentials are duplicates of those listed for male deacons in 1 Timothy 3:8-10. Also, the Greek word order of 1 Timothy 3:8 and 11 is identical: "[Male] deacons likewise *[diakonous hōsautōs]* must be serious, not double-tongued, not indulging in much wine. . . . Women likewise *[gynaikas hōsautōs]* must be serious, not slanderers, but temperate" (1 Tim 3:8, 11 NRSV).

Postapostolic writers understood Paul to be speaking of women deacons. Clement of Alexandria (second-third centuries), for instance, says, "For we know what the honorable Paul in one of his letters to Timothy prescribed regarding women deacons."[35] And John Chrysostom (fourth century) talks of women who held the rank of deacon in the apostolic church.[36]

Among the Lycus Valley churches, Nympha surfaces as another woman leader. Paul greets her at the close of Colossians: "Give my greetings to the brothers and

---

[34]Luke is precise throughout Acts about the order of names in ministry teams. For example, when the famous missionaries are commissioned by the church at Antioch, the order is "Barnabas and Saul" (Acts 11:30; 12:25; 13:2-7). But when Saul takes the lead, the order becomes "Paul and Barnabas" (Acts 13:9-12, 43; 14:12, 20; 15:2, 22, 35). The two exceptions are Acts 15:12 and 15:25, where political diplomacy and expediency dictated the order. Andreas Köstenberger ("Book Review," *JETS* 44 [2001]: 346) claims that 1 Corinthians 16:19 proves otherwise: "Aquila and Prisca, together with the church that meets in their house, greet you warmly." But "their house" is a statement of ownership, not ministry, thus warranting the order.

[35]Clement of Alexandria *Stromateis* 3.6.53.

[36]John Chrysostom *Homilies on Timothy* 11 (on 1 Tim 3:11).

sisters in Laodicea, and to Nympha and the church in her house" (Col 4:15). While the reference is brief, the implications are noteworthy. Patronage of a house church was an authoritative role. The householder in Greco-Roman times was automatically in charge of any group that met in his or her domicile. Households in the first century included not only the immediate family and relatives but also slaves, freedmen and freedwomen, hired workers, and even tenants and partners in a trade or craft. This meant that the female head of household had to have good administrative and management skills (see *oikodespotein*, "to rule one's household," in I Tim 5:14). Paul thus places great emphasis on a person's track record as a family leader, as it is a definite indicator of church-leadership potential (I Tim 3:4-5; 5:14).

Women in the Caesarean church. Luke commends Philip's four daughters as prophets in the Caesarean church (Acts 21:9). They belong to a tradition of women prophets stretching back to Mosaic times. In fact, if there was one gift that women consistently possessed and exercised throughout the history of God's people, it is this one. (Anna also continued this tradition in New Testament times; Lk 2:36-38.)

Luke's reference to Philip's daughters is brief. No further commentary was necessary, undoubtedly because women prophets were well established as church leaders. Postapostolic authors confirm this. Papias tells how he heard a wonderful story from the lips of Philip's prophetic daughters (Eusebius *Ecclesiastical History* 3.39). Proclus (third-century leader of the Phrygian Montanists) places their later prophetic ministry in Hierapolis, Asia. Eusebius ranks them "among the first stage in the apostolic succession" (*Ecclesiastical History* 3.37.1).

Philip's daughters were not lone exceptions. A woman named Ammia in the Philadelphian church is also said to have prophesied during New Testament times (Eusebius *Ecclesiastical History* 5.17.2-4). In fact, the second-century Montanists Priscilla and Maximilla used women like Ammia to justify their own prophetic office (Eusebius *Ecclesiastical History* 5.17.4).

Some argue that early church prophecy was merely an impromptu movement of the Spirit and not a recognized leadership role in the church. Yet Luke makes it clear that the prophet was just such, when he identifies the leaders of the church at Antioch as "prophets and teachers" (Acts 13:1-3). Nor was prophecy, as some would claim, an activity valued less than other forms of ministry. This is evident from Paul's identification of prophetic speaking with "revelation" (*apokalyphthē*, I Cor 14:29-30) and his naming apostles and prophets together as the "foundation" of the church, when speaking of it metaphorically (Eph 2:20). He even goes further and puts apostles and prophets in a category by themselves. It is to "God's holy apostles and prophets" that "the mystery of Christ . . . has now been revealed by the Spirit" (Eph 3:4-5). In a very real sense, therefore, the New Testament prophet carries on the "Thus saith the Lord" task of the Old Testament prophet.

Conclusion

Recent studies have focused appropriately on Paul's language for male and female leaders. The uniform conclusion is that Paul uses exactly the same language of colleagues in ministry be they male or female. The men are "fellow prisoners," "fellow workers" and "hard workers" who "risked their necks" for Paul and "labored side by side" with him "in the gospel" (Rom 16:3, 7, 9, 21; 1 Cor 3:9; 4:12; 16:16-17; 2 Cor 8:23; Phil 2:25; 4:3; Col 4:10-11; 1 Thess 3:2; 5:12; Philem 1:1, 24). The women are equally "fellow prisoners, "fellow workers" and "hard workers" who "risked their necks" for Paul and "labored side by side" with him "in the gospel" (Rom 16:3-4, 6, 12; Phil 4:2-3).

Parallel language reveals the same pattern in Greco-Roman society. Epigraphical data shows that terms such as *magistrate, chief officer, prophet, priest/priestess, patron/protectress, overseer* and the like are used equally of women and men in the religious cults and civic associations of the day.

What is too often overlooked is the fact that women as well as men are named without qualification or geographical boundaries, and in commensurate numbers for each leadership role. Junia was "outstanding *among the apostles*" at Rome (Rom 16:7). Phoebe was a *deacon* of the Cenchrean church (Rom 16:1-2). Syntyche and Euodia were leaders of the Philippian church and *evangelists* alongside Paul himself (Phil 4:3; cf. 1:1). Philip's four daughters were *prophets* at Caesarea (Acts 21:9). Priscilla was a *church planter* alongside Paul (Rom 16:3-4) and a *teacher* at Ephesus, who expounded "the way of God" to a man in exactly the same way Paul expounded the gospel to men and women in Rome (*exethento* from *ektithēmi*, Acts 18:26; cf 28:23). Under Roman law, Nympha had legal responsibility for and hence *authority over* the church that met in her house (Col 4:15).

These are facts hardly open to debate—although some remain eager and willing to attempt to circumvent them. To do so, however, one must dismiss the evidence of women leaders in the culture at large, deny the impact of the union of religion and life on the church, or impose on the biblical women the image of a cloistered, domestic female that did not exist in the Greco-Roman world of antiquity. If anything, the matter-of-fact mention and listing of women in ministry permits us to conclude there was a substantially wider and well-established early Christian praxis of women leaders.[37]

There is no indication that men and women functioned within any hierarchical leadership framework in the New Testament church. Indeed, the fact that Paul called women "laborers" and "fellow workers" means that what is said of other leaders must apply also to them. Paul urges the Corinthian church to "submit to such as these [who have devoted themselves to the service of God's people] and to *everyone* who joins in the work and labors at it" (I Cor 16:16). And he asks the Thessalonians "to acknowledge those who work hard among you, who care for you in the Lord and admonish you. Hold them in the highest regard in love because of their work" (I Thess 5:12-13). It follows that Paul would presume such respect and esteem should also be shown toward the women who work and labor in the Lord—proclaiming, admonishing, teaching and leading.[38]

---

[37]Stefan Schreiber, "Arbeit mit der Gemeinde (Röm 16.6, 12): Zur versunkenen Möglichkeit der Gemeindeleitung durch Frauen," *NTS* 46 (2000): 204-26.

[38]Keith A. Gerberding, "Women Who Toil in Ministry, Even as Paul," *Currents in Theology and Mission* 18 (1991): 285-91.

7

JESUS' TREATMENT OF WOMEN IN THE GOSPELS

Aída Besançon Spencer

In 1667 Quaker Margaret Fell declared that "women's speaking" was "justified, proved and allowed of by the Scriptures" because "women were the first that preached the tidings of the Resurrection of Jesus, and were sent by Christ's own command, before He ascended to the Father, John 20:17."[1] In this she was echoing Chrysostom's (fourth-century) sentiments that women carried on the race that "apostles and evangelists ran." About Andronicus and Junia he wrote:

> Indeed to be apostles at all is a great thing. But to be even amongst these of note, just consider what a great encomium this is! But they were of note owing to their works, to their achievements. Oh! How great is the devotion of this woman, that she should be even counted worthy of the appellation of apostle![2]

Christian writers have long marveled at the impact of Jesus' words and deeds on the status of women, even when they have differed on the roles women and men were to have in the later church.

The purpose of this chapter is to look at the data in the Gospels once again, because even though many scholars view positively Jesus' affirmations of women, some are reluctant to see this as having bearing on women's possible leadership roles in the church.[3] After an overview of what is generally accepted by all, that

---

[1]Margaret Fell (Fox), *Women's Speaking Justified* (1667; reprint, Los Angeles: University of California Press, 1979). See also Ruth A. Tucker and Walter L. Liefeld, *Daughters of the Church: Women and Ministry from New Testament Times to the Present* (Grand Rapids, Mich.: Zondervan, 1987), pp. 230-31.
[2]John Chrysostom *Epistle to the Romans* 31.
[3]See, e.g., Michael J. Wilkins, "Women in the Teaching and Example of Jesus," in *Women and Men in Ministry: A Complementary Perspective*, ed. Robert L. Saucy and Judith K. TenElshof (Chicago: Moody Press, 2001), pp. 91-112.

Jesus both affirmed and elevated women, I will examine more closely how Jesus' actions affect the priorities in women's lives. The chapter will conclude with a reexamination of the key point of disagreement: the significance of Jesus' choosing twelve males to form the so-called inner circle of his disciples.

Jesus Affirms Women

Recognizing that Jesus both affirmed and elevated the status of women has now become commonplace on both sides of the "women in leadership" divide. Among those opposed to women in senior leadership roles in the church, Michael Wilkins states that

> Jesus restored and affirmed the worth and dignity of women. . . . [He] did not make a distinction between women and men in this ministry of restoration. . . . Women were called to be Jesus' disciples. . . . As disciples of Jesus, women have restored to them the full dignity that was theirs in the creation, when men and women were both created in the image of God. . . . Women received instruction and nurture as Jesus' disciples.[4]

He adds, "Jesus restored and affirmed women to his ministry team" as "colaborers with men."[5]

Wilkins follows the positive tone set earlier by James Borland: "Christ placed a high value on women" by "recognizing their intrinsic value as persons," by "ministering to women" and by "according them dignity in his ministry."[6] Wayne House agrees: "Jesus treated women with kindness and respect and considered them equal before God," and he assumed women were "of equal intelligence, equal spiritual discernment, and equal religious acumen."[7] Samuele Bacchiocchi further reiterates this perspective. Jesus was unique in contrast to first-century Judaism. He viewed women as *persons* for whom He had come . . . not in terms of sex, age or marital status." He appreciated their "intelligence and faith," accepted women as "treasured members of the human family," admitted them "into His fellowship" and took "time to teach them the truths of the Kingdom of God."[8]

---

[4] Ibid., pp. 95, 97-98.

[5] Ibid., p. 100.

[6] James A. Borland, "Women in the Life and Teachings of Jesus," in *RBMW,* pp. 113-115, 117. See also James B. Hurley, *Man and Woman in Biblical Perspective* (Grand Rapids, Mich.: Zondervan, 1981), pp. 82-111.

[7] H. Wayne House, *The Role of Women in Ministry Today* (Grand Rapids, Mich.: Baker, 1995), pp. 21, 82.

[8] Samuele Bacchiocchi, *Women in the Church: A Biblical Study on the Role of Women in the Church* (Berrien Springs, Mich.: Biblical Perspectives, 1987), pp. 47-50.

The ways Jesus affirmed women can be summarized under four broad categories. First, Jesus' conversations with women indicate his esteem for them. Jesus
openly conversed with women despite the ancient practice of discouraging men
from speaking with women in public.[9] For example, in John's Gospel Jesus has a
deep theological discussion with a man, Nicodemus (Jn 3:1-21), followed by a
deep theological discussion with a woman, a Samaritan, at Jacob's well (Jn 4:4-42).
She is the first person to whom Jesus discloses that he is the Messiah (Jn 4:25-26),
and she becomes an evangelist to her people (Jn 4:28-29, 39-42). Later in the same
Gospel, Martha affirms the key doctrines about Jesus: Jesus is "the Messiah, the
Son of God, who was to come into the world" (Jn 11:27).[10]

Second, Jesus' teachings are favorable to women. Jesus is firm that marriage entails commitment between one man and one woman for life,[11] whereas rabbinic
teaching allowed polygamy and divorce for many reasons other than adultery.[12] As
well, women, like men, were to place obedience to God as most important (Mt
12:46-50; Mk 3:31-35; Lk 8:19-21; 11:27-28).

Third, women form an important part of Jesus' ministry, helping usher in the
time of God's rule. Five women are included in his messianic pedigree: Tamar, Ra-
hab, Ruth, Bathsheba and of course Mary (Mt 1:3-16). Many women serve as positive models of faith. Mary's role, as a virgin who conceived by the Holy Spirit, is
highlighted. She is presented as a thinker of great faith (Mt 1:18; Lk 1:26-56;

---

[9]We are explicitly told that Jesus' disciples were "surprised" that he spoke "with a woman" (Jn 4:27).
According to rabbinic teaching, if a woman spoke with a man in public she could be divorced without having her dowry repaid (*Mishnah Ketubbot* 1:8; 7:6). Earlier ben Sirach asserted, "Do not let
[your daughter] parade her beauty before any man" (Ecclesiasticus 42:12).

[10]For extended descriptions of Jesus' special treatment of women, see Gilbert Bilezikian, *Beyond Sex
Roles: A Guide for the Study of Female Roles in the Bible* (Grand Rapids, Mich.: Baker, 1985), chap. 4; Leonard Swidler, *Biblical Affirmations of Woman* (Philadelphia: Westminster Press, 1979), pp. 164-290;
Linda L. Belleville, *Women Leaders and the Church* (Grand Rapids, Mich.: Baker, 2000), pp. 48-60, 109-
111.

[11]See, e.g., Matthew 5:31-32; note that this is preceded by his extending adultery to include even
looking at another woman lustfully (Mt 5:27-30). See further Matthew 19:3-9; Mark 10:2-12;
Luke 16:18.

[12]For polygamy see *Mishnah Sanhedrin* 2:4. The schools of Hillel and Shammai debated the allowable
grounds for divorce on the basis of the phrase "something objectionable about her" (Deut 24:1).
The Hillelites took the extreme view (see esp. *Mishnah Gittin* 9:10), which allowed divorce even for a
spoiled dish or a facial blemish (*Babylonian Talmud Ketubbot* 75a) or if the husband found someone
more attractive. See also *Mishnah Yevamot* 14:1; *Mishnah Ketubbot* 7:1-10; *Mishnah Qiddushin* 2:5. On the
Greek side, even though Epictetus argues for monogamy, he begins with the presupposition that
"women by nature" are "common property" (*Discourses* 2.4.8-10).

2:19, 34-35, 51). A Canaanite woman is also extolled for her great faith (Mt 15:28; cf. Lk 4:25-26), similar to the way a Roman soldier is praised (Mt 8:10). Likewise a restored prostitute who is allowed to touch Jesus is commended for her faith, greater than that of the rude Simon and his Pharisee friends (Lk 7:36-50). A healed woman is called "a daughter of Abraham" (Lk 13:16) in the same way as a male tax collector is called a restored "son of Abraham" (Lk 19:9-10); thus both women and men are included in the newly formed people of God that Christ himself both represents and gathers. And Mary of Bethany is commended for her insight into Jesus' coming crucifixion—insight that went far beyond that of the Twelve (Jn 12:1-8).

Besides these, Luke singles out Elizabeth who names John (Lk 1:60), the prophet Anna (Lk 2:36-38), the named women who are among his disciples (8:1-3), an only daughter whom Jesus heals (Lk 8:40-42, 49-56), a woman with constant bleeding who by touching Jesus' cloak makes him "unclean" (Lk 8:43-48), Martha and Mary (Lk 10:38-42), the women who mourn his impending death (Lk 23:27-28), and the women who come to anoint the buried Jesus but instead are the first to hear and tell of the resurrection (Lk 23:55–24:12).

Fourth, Jesus' teachings and comments often take into consideration a woman's perspective. He uses female images for himself—a hen desiring to gather her chicks under her wings (Mt 23:37; Lk 13:34). Similarly God's care for the lost exemplified in Jesus' eating with sinners is pictured not only as a father with lost sons (Lk 15:11-32) but also as a woman with a lost coin (Lk 15:8-9). Humanity is described as those "born of women" (Mt 11:11). Both father and mother are to be honored (Mk 7:10-11).

In his analogies Jesus uses household activities common to women, such as sewing (Lk 5:36) and cooking (Lk 6:38; 13:21). Household service is a key to understanding genuine obedience to God: feeding and clothing the hungry, the stranger, the ill, the inmate, the wounded (Mt 25:37-39, 42-43; Lk 10:34). The church becomes a loving family (Mt 23:8; Jn 19:25-27). Jesus shows special concern for pregnant and nursing women and widows (Mt 24:19; Mk 12:40; 13:17; Lk 7:12-17; 18:3; 20:47; 21:2-4, 23; 23:29; Jn 16:21). Pressure against Christ's followers will come from both male and female relatives (Mt 10:35-37; 19:29; Mk 10:29-30; Lk 12:53; 14:26; 18:29; 21:16). And of course marriage has a significant place in representing God's reign (Mt 25:1; Mk 2:19; Lk 5:34-35; Jn 2:1).

Thus most scholars would agree that Jesus' teachings and actions are favorable to women and that women are an important part of his ministry. Nonetheless, advocates of male-only leadership do not always develop the implications of Jesus' actions toward women—actions that stood in remarkable contrast to his own culture and society.

Jesus' Actions Affect Women's Priorities

Rather than simply reassert, as many continue to do, that "the woman's place is in the home"—as though that were a *biblical* (and not merely cultural) viewpoint—one needs to ask such questions as: Why were first-century Jewish women discouraged from having formal higher education in biblical law? Why were women not required to pursue religious training at all or given merit if they did study? Why was no one required or encouraged to teach them?[13] Why were women not admitted into Jewish schools? Why even in the synagogue service were they not to "study fully"?

These restrictions for women were made for two reasons: (1) women were primarily to be homemakers, and (2) they were to be protected against unchastity. Philo of Alexandria, a slightly older contemporary of Jesus, described what was considered the ideal for Jewish women in the Diaspora:

> Market-places and council-halls and law-courts and gatherings and meetings, where a large number of people are assembled, and open-air life with full scope for discussion and action—all these are suitable to men in both war and peace. The women are best suited to the indoor life which never strays from the house, within which the middle door is taken by the maidens as their boundary, and the outer door by those who have reached full womanhood. Organized communities are of two sorts, the greater which we call cities and the smaller which we call households. Both of these have their governors; the government of the greater is assigned to men under the name of statesmanship, that of the lesser, known as household management, to women.[14]

Similarly, rabbinic laws were constructed to ensure that women were not encouraged to leave their homes. As in Philo, the location of women seems to be the

---

[13]Wilkins ("Women," p. 351 n. 18) suggests that *Mishnah Nedarim* 4:3 implies that a father could teach his sons *and* daughters Scripture. But this is not referring to formal training in Torah but to the training a husband/father was expected to give to his whole household so that they all might walk in the ways of the Lord. See further Aída Besançon Spencer, *Beyond the Curse: Women Called to Ministry* (Peabody, Mass.: Hendrickson, 1985), pp. 47-56.

[14]Philo of Alexandria *On the Special Laws* 3.169-70 (LCL 7:583-85). Cf. *Flaccus* 89 (LCL 9:51), where this is expressed in a more abbreviated form.

underlying concern.[15] Indeed Jewish law consistently assumed the necessity for women to be centered on their household. If women spent time in study of the law, it was feared, their care of the household would suffer.

Wives were required to sustain a household's economy, unless they had servants to direct. For instance in the Mishnah a wife is required to grind flour, bake bread, wash clothes, cook food, nurse her child, make ready her husband's bed, oversee sabbath celebrations and spin wool.[16] Women were so integrally associated with the house and homemaking that Rabbi Judah said that "his house" (in Lev 16:6) is a synonym for "his wife."[17] Rabbi Jose, commenting on *Yoma* 1:1, proudly adds: "Never have I called my wife by that word ['my wife'], but always 'my home.'" Even a woman's body came to be perceived as constructed for homemaking. Rabbi Hisda thus interprets Genesis 2:22, wherein God takes Adam's rib and "builds (it) into a woman": "This teaches that the Holy One, blessed be He, built Eve in the shape of a storehouse. As a storehouse is [made] wide below and narrow above so that it may contain the produce, so was [the womb of] a woman [made] wide below and narrow above so that it may contain the embryo."[18]

However, this emphasis on women's remaining in the household as much as economically possible does not flow from any clear teaching in the Old Testament. (According to Deuteronomy 31:12 and Joshua 8:35 all people—Hebrew men, women, children and foreigners—were exhorted to attend regularly the reading of the Law.) Rather, it reflects an inculturation from the larger pagan society that goes far back in time. For instance, Xenophon (fourth century B.C.) creates an ideal gentleman, Ischomachus, who explains to his wife that God

---

[15]Women were exempt from leaving the home for any period of time. Thus they were exempt from attending synagogue school as well as traveling to Jerusalem for the feasts of Passover, Pentecost and Tabernacles (*Mishnah Qiddushin* 1:7, *Hagigah* 1:1, *Sukkah* 2:8). The rabbis concluded that the Torah was applicable to men who traveled about daily since they considered the Torah comparable to phylacteries (small leather boxes) worn on the head and left arm during prayer by men only. A woman instead had a *mezuzah* on her doorpost (*Mishnah Berakhot* 3:3; *Babylonian Talmud Qiddushin* 34a-35a). At a later time, Rabbi Jeremiah upheld an ancient tradition when he said, "A woman generally stays at home, whereas a man goes out into the streets and learns understanding from men" (*Midrash Rabbah Genesis* I, 18.1).

[16]*Mishnah Ketubbot* 5:5, 9.

[17]*Mishnah Yoma* 1:1.

[18]*Babylonian Talmud Eruvin* 18a-b; see Spencer, *Beyond the Curse*, pp. 47-57. *The Constitutions of the Holy Apostles* (which is semi-Arian) also relegates women to indoor tasks: "Let the widow therefore own herself to be the 'altar of God,' and let her sit in her house, and not enter into the houses of the faithful, under any pretence, to receive anything; for the altar of God never runs about, but is fixed in one place" (3.1.6).

from the first adapted the woman's nature, I think, to the indoor and man's to the outdoor tasks and cares. For he made the man's body and mind more capable of enduring cold and heat, and journeys and campaigns; and therefore imposed on him the outdoor tasks. To the woman, since he has made her body less capable of such endurance, I take it that God has assigned the indoor tasks. And knowing that he had created in the woman and had imposed on her the nourishment of the infants, he meted out to her a larger portion of affection for new-born babes than to the man. And since he imposed on the woman the protection of the stores also, knowing that for protection a fearful disposition is no disadvantage, God meted out a larger share of fear to the woman than to the man; and knowing that he who deals with the outdoor tasks will have to be their defender against any wrong-doer, he meted out to him again a larger share of courage. . . . Thus, to the woman it is more honorable to stay indoors than to abide in the fields, but to the man it is unseemly rather to stay indoors than to attend to the work outside.[19]

Jesus, in contrast, does not treat women primarily as homemakers. A woman called out in Jesus' hearing: "Blessed is the woman who gave you birth and nursed you!" Here we see this principle of woman primarily as mother voiced before Jesus. And what is his reply? "Blessed rather are those who hear the word of God and obey it!" (Lk 11:27-28). What Jesus states here explicitly, he models earlier in his actions. Thus when Mary sits as a pupil in rabbinic fashion before Jesus (Lk 10:38-42) while Martha follows the cultural mandate to serve as homemaker, Jesus declares that Mary is the one who has selected the good share—to sit at a rabbi's feet in learning. She has made the right choice, and he will not allow anyone to take learning away from those who sit at his feet.[20]

Despite all this, many evangelicals today still see homemaking as women's primary role. For instance, Thomas R. Schreiner writes that childbearing "represents the fulfillment of the woman's domestic role as a mother in distinction from the man. Childbearing, then, is probably selected by synecdoche [in 1 Tim 2:15] as representing the appropriate role for women."[21] James Hurley agrees: "Women in general (and most women in [Paul's] day) will be kept safe from seizing men's roles by participating in marital life (symbolized by childbirth)." Similarly, Dorothy

---

[19]Xenophon *Oeconomicus* 7.22-25, 30.

[20]See Spencer, *Beyond the Curse*, pp. 57-63; Hurley, *Man and Woman*, pp. 88-89; and most contemporary commentaries on Luke.

[21]Thomas R. Schreiner, "An Interpretation of 1 Timothy 2:9-15: A Dialogue with Scholarship," in *Women in the Church: A Fresh Analysis of 1 Timothy 2:9-15*, ed. Andreas J. Köstenberger, Thomas R. Schreiner and H. Scott Baldwin (Grand Rapids, Mich.: Baker, 1995), pp. 150-51.

Patterson asserts: "Keeping the home is God's assignment to the wife."[22]

I am by no means suggesting that bearing and rearing children are not essential and honorable tasks. Rather, obeying and learning from God have a *higher* priority for men as well as for women. Moreover, rearing children is a significant ministry for men as well as women. Godly overseers and deacons need to govern well their own household before becoming church leaders (I Tim 3:4-5, 12), just as godly widows do (I Tim 5:10). Indeed, how can they say they love God if they do not love, and therefore care for, their neighbors and family (e.g., I Jn 4:8)?

Jesus' Apostles Affirm the Jewish Foundation of His Covenant

Despite noting Jesus' affirmation of women as people, many supporters of male-only leadership today use the same "evidence" to restrict women's roles as did the fourth-century *Constitutions of the Holy Apostles*, which declared:

> We do not permit our "women to teach in the Church," but only to pray and hear those that teach; for our Master and Lord, Jesus Himself, when He sent us the twelve to make disciples of the people and of the nations, did nowhere send out women to preach, although He did not want such.[23]

This argument has several levels. First, it assumes that gender is the abiding precedent but does not extend this precedent to race or political state; thereby it selectively eliminates "male and female" from the basis for equality in Christ established in Galatians 3:28. The same argumentative strategy could be used to exclude all Gentiles from leadership. Second, it assumes that what the biblical model does not establish it thereby prohibits. Yet although the biblical model establishes that men *can* be apostles, it does not establish that women *cannot* be. The hermeneutical presupposition of the *Constitutions*, and that of some contemporary evangelicals, seems to be that the Bible's teaching is limited to whatever is explicitly stated. In effect, if the text does not specifically say you *may* do something, then you may not. Thus House, for example, states: "The biblical record says nothing at all about Christ considering a woman's role in ministry leadership or spiritual headship indistinguishable from a man's. There is no evidence that any woman was commissioned as one of the seventy-two or the Twelve."[24] Silence on this matter means that

---

[22]Hurley, *Man and Woman*, p. 223; Dorothy Patterson, "The High Calling of Wife and Mother in Biblical Perspective," in *RBMW,* p. 366.

[23]*Constitutions* 3.1.6.

[24]House, *Role of Women*, p. 21.

women may not be ordained as overseers.

What makes this hermeneutical stance more valid than its opposite, except assertion pure and simple? Why not take a less limited view of the text? If the text does not actually prohibit something, either explicitly or in principle, one may well choose to do it—especially given the way Jesus explicitly affirms women. Nowhere does Jesus ever say—or even imply in anything he says—that only men can be leaders in the church. Similarly, neither of the two ecumenical councils at Nicaea and Chalcedon (A.D. 325 and 451) limits church leadership to men.[25]

Wilkins takes the male-only argument a step further by mapping out concentric circles to locate the various followers of Jesus: the "large number of disciples who believed in Jesus"; the Seventy(-two) who were "sent out on a preaching tour" (Lk 10:1-17); the women (not included in the Seventy[-two]) who "traveled with Jesus and the Twelve to support Jesus' missionary tour (Luke 8:1-3)"; the Twelve "who were called to be trained as apostles"; and the inner circle of "Peter, James, John, and sometimes Andrew (e.g., Mark 13:3)."[26] Under this scenario, women can be among the disciples "who have believed on Jesus" and are "called into ministry with and to Him." But their absence from the two inner circles means that they were not among those being trained "to be the leadership of the church."[27]

In order to evaluate this recent reconstruction of the *Constitutions'* argument, we need to reconsider what may appear obvious but is often neglected: the emphasis in Jesus' own teachings. He does not teach that we will advance God's reign by maintaining male-female distinctions in leadership. For example, in Mark's Gospel we learn that Jesus has authority on earth to forgive (Mk 2:10, 17) and is Lord of the sabbath (Mk 2:27; 3:3-5); his family is composed of those who do God's will (Mk 3:31-35); he is merciful and compassionate (Mk 5:19; 6:34), the Messiah, the crucified one, God's beloved Son who will return (Mk 8:29, 31; 9:7, 31; 14:61-62). Explicit teachings such as these, which have the same meaning for both men and

---

[25]It was the Synod of Laodicea in Phrygia (A.D. 343-81) that began a process of restricting women, deacons, laity, artists and Messianic Jews. For example, female elders are not to be appointed in the church (canon 11), women may not approach the altar (canon 44), a deacon may not sit in the presence of an elder (canon 20), only the canonical singers may sing in the church (canon 15), and Christians may not rest but must work on the sabbath so as not to "judaize" (canon 29). Ironically, as the church became more anti-Semitic, it also became more legalistic! The Council of Trullo explains one reason women could not speak during the divine liturgy: their monthly flux of blood was polluting (canon 70)—a total collapsing of new covenant ministry into that of the old.

[26]See Wilkins, "Women," pp. 96-99.

[27]Ibid., pp. 101-2.

women, are the focus of the Gospels. Jesus' teachings do not focus on gender or race for Christian leaders.

In the same vein, the authority given to the apostles by Jesus was not over other people but rather over demons or unclean spirits (to drive them out) and over illness and death—that is, against nonhuman enemies of God's reign (Mt 10:1, 8; Mk 3:14-15; 6:7-30; Lk 9:1).[28] Thus Jesus' apostles were to be distinct from false apostles who, like Gentile leaders, take authority to dominate others (Mk 10:42-45; 2 Cor 11:20-21). When some argue today that only men are to have authority in the church, they appear still to be arguing in this pagan vein of "who is the greatest?" (Mk 9:34)—in this case, men or women. When the truly "greatest" welcomes the little child in Jesus' name, leadership no longer is a question of power but rather of service.[29] These instructions to the Twelve are important for all Christians, especially leaders, setting forth the Christlike character traits they should have. Leaders are to be like Jesus, who came to serve and to give his life as a ransom for many, not like the Gentiles who "lord it over" others.[30]

Furthermore, apostleship is not synonymous with church leadership as such. At a very early stage in the church "apostles" and "elders" were distinguishable categories (Acts 15:2, 4, 6, 22, 23; 16:4). A little later (1 Cor 12:28), along with "apostle," Paul lists other gifts such as "prophet" (one who confronts and builds up the church, cf. 1 Cor. 14:4), "teacher" (one who leads by instructing) and "leadership" (*kybernēsis* = "guidance"). Moreover, "apostle" is never linked directly to "overseer" (e.g., 1 Tim 3:1).

So why did Jesus choose twelve Jewish men as the first apostles? First, he chose twelve Jews to serve as a synecdoche, representing the twelve tribes of Israel (Mt 19:28; Lk 22:30; Rev 21:12). Jesus' call to ministry was focused on reaching Israel[31] because the earlier covenant was made with Israel (e.g., Gen 35:10-12; 1 Kings 18:31). Jesus' choice of the Twelve indicates the importance of the new covenant's being founded on the old covenant. That is why at the end of the New Testament the two covenant peoples are symbolically joined in the New Jerusalem, on

---

[28]See the discussion in chapter fifteen below.

[29]Leadership established according to the principles of a crucified Messiah is the difficult lesson Paul tries to explain to the Corinthians (in both letters).

[30]Mark 10:42-45. See also Matthew 18:1-5; 19:14; 20:20-27; 21:15-16; Mark 9:35-37; 10:13-16; 12:14,38-40; Luke 9:46-48; 10:21; 18:16-17; 20:21; 22:24-27; John 13:12-17. Cf. Gilbert Bilezikian, "Biblical Community Versus Gender-Based Hierarchy," *Priscilla Papers* 16 (2002): 3-10.

[31]Matthew 10:5-6; 15:24; Luke 7:9; John 1:11; Romans 15:8; 13:1; Eusebius *Ecclesiastical History* 6.14.

whose twelve foundations are the names of the twelve apostles of the Lamb and whose twelve gates bear the names of the twelve tribes of Israel (Rev 21:12-14). Gentile inclusion in God's household rests on the earlier witness of Jewish apostles and prophets (Eph 2:20). Many of the original twelve focused their ministries in Jerusalem and to the Jews (Acts 8:1,14; cf. Gal 1:17; 2:8).

The Twelve, who represent the twelve tribes, do so because they also represent the twelve patriarchs.[32] Thus the Twelve could not have been other than Jewish free males. If there had been Gentiles or women or slaves among them, the deliberate reconstitution of Israel in Jesus himself, signaled by the Father at his baptism (Mt 3:13-17), simply would not have worked.[33] As an integral part of the ministry of Jesus, the Twelve represented not only the twelve patriarchs/tribes of Israel but also the newly constituted Israel under the new covenant in Christ. Consequently, the Twelve cannot serve as precedents for *Gentile* leadership, which is what prevails in the church today.[34]

---

[32]Richard Bauckham cites Numbers 1:4-16 as important because it shows the Twelve are the symbolic heads of the new Israel, corresponding to the twelve patriarchs of Israel's founding generation (*Gospel Women: Studies of the Named Women in the Gospels* [Grand Rapids, Mich.: Eerdmans, 2002], p. 188). Scot McKnight also notes the importance of the Twelve as a symbol of the leadership characteristics of Jesus' new "nation," so that the land could be reclaimed for God's covenant ("Jesus and the Twelve," *BBR* 11 (2001): 229-31.

[33]I am indebted to Gordon Fee for some of these observations. Fee further notes that during the whole of his ministry Jesus himself symbolically steps into the role of Israel, from his baptism (= Red Sea) and forty days in the desert to be tested (he overcame precisely where Israel failed), to his assuming the role both of Israel's King-Messiah (Son of God; Ps 2:7) and of Isaiah's Suffering Servant, articulated for him in the voice from heaven at his baptism. And at the end he symbolically "cleanses" the temple and offers his own resurrection as the new locus of God's presence among his people (Jn 2:22). With the Twelve about him at the final meal, he reconstitutes the bread and wine of Passover to become a meal in which they will recall his death as effecting the new covenant. At the same time, the one certain "instruction" he gave to the Twelve is about their eschatological role in "judging" Israel (Lk 22:13-30).

[34]Some evangelicals (e.g., Borland, "Women in the Life," p. 122) have observed that even after the resurrection Peter specified that Judas's replacement had to be male. However, Acts 1:21-22 literally reads: "Therefore, it is necessary that of those having accompanied us, one of these men, who all the time that the Lord Jesus went in and out among us—beginning from John's baptism until the day he was taken up from us—one of these should become a witness of his resurrection with us" (my trans.). The emphasis of the text is on someone who had been with the Twelve throughout Jesus' ministry ("of those who accompanied us"). The sentence structure highlights not the candidate's gender but rather the candidate's function as an eyewitness to Jesus' life, resurrection and ascension.

In addition, even though Peter uses the plural of *anēr* ("men") in Acts 1:21, he also employs this term when speaking to a crowd including men and women. At Pentecost women are present (Acts 1:14) and spoken about ("your sons and daughters will prophesy," Acts 2:17); nevertheless Peter

Nevertheless, the first set of twelve apostles had certain other defining criteria in common with the rest of the apostles. First, an apostle by definition is a messenger, someone "sent off" with orders. What makes Christ's apostles distinct from other apostles is that they were sent by and represented Jesus himself (Mt 10:5; Mk 3:14). Paul also was sent by Christ (Acts 26:16-18) and preached a gospel not of human origin (Gal 1:11-12). By way of contrast, Epaphroditus was an apostle/messenger "sent off" from and representing the church at Philippi to Paul (Phil 2:25), and the "brothers" who carried the monetary gift to Corinth were "apostles [messengers] from the churches" (2 Cor 8:16-24).

Second, the first apostles had to have been "with" Jesus. Indeed, the first reason for his appointing the Twelve was for them "to be with" him (Mk 3:14; cf. Lk 8:1; Acts 1:21-22). Being with Jesus was a key component of their training.

Third, an apostle is an eyewitness of the resurrected Christ. When Paul exclaims to the Corinthians, "Am I not an apostle?" he first follows that rhetorical question with the defense, "Have I not seen Jesus our Lord?" (I Cor 9:1). Having seen the risen Lord is crucial in the Gospels (Mt 28:18-20; Jn 20:21-22), in Acts (1:21-22; 4:33) and in the letters (I Cor 15:5-8; Gal 1:11-12). As eyewitnesses to the resurrection, apostles are listed first among God's gifts to the church (I Cor 12:28-29).[35]

Fourth, an apostle is commissioned to preach God's reign: "As you go, proclaim this message: 'The kingdom of heaven has come near'" (Mt 10:7; Mk 3:14; Lk 9:2). Preaching *(kēryssō)* is never an action prohibited to women.

Thus *apostolos* in the Gospels clearly includes the twelve who were chosen from a larger group of disciples for the first commission (Mt 10:1-2; Lk 6:13). After Jesus' death and resurrection, *apostle* was broadened to refer to other disciples who had been with Jesus and now were sent off as witnesses to the resurrection. And in the new covenant era the apostolic witness includes both women and men.

This larger group of apostles explicitly includes Paul (Rom 1:1; I Cor 1:1; 2

---

addresses the crowd with the plural of *anēr*, "fellow Jews" (Acts 2:14; see also Acts 17:22, 34; 25:23-24). Moreover, even if Peter were being gender-specific in Acts 1:21-22 but not in Acts 2:14, the Twelve were not replaced at all after their deaths (e.g., James in Acts 12:2), which suggests that by then they had served their purpose of symbolically representing Israel at the start of the new covenant.

[35]It is doubtful that today's church planter is a New Testament "apostle" of Jesus Christ, since being a witness of the resurrection is a key aspect of the latter. It is also doubtful whether Timothy should be included as an "apostle," despite the "we" in I Thessalonians 2:6-7; he is called an "evangelist" in 2 Timothy 4:5.

Cor 1:1; Eph 1:1; Col 1:1; I Tim 1:1; 2:7; 2 Tim 1:1; Tit 1:1),[36] Barnabas (Acts 14:4, 14), James (Gal 1:1, 12-19), and Andronicus and Junia (Rom 16:7).[37] Paul and James the brother of Jesus are included in the list of apostles because they were eyewitnesses to the Messiah's resurrection (1 Cor 15:7-8). Then how might Junia, Barnabas and Andronicus have been included? They may have been among the "more than five hundred of the brothers and sisters" who witnessed the risen Lord (1 Cor 15:6-7).[38] Or being part of the larger group of "all the apostles," perhaps they had been among the Seventy-two (Lk 10:1).[39] Clement of Rome calls Apollos an apostle.[40] Eusebius suggests that Barnabas, Sosthenes, Matthias and Justus were part of the Seventy(-two) and that the more than five hundred witnesses and James the Lord's brother were apostles as well. Eusebius explains that these other apostles were "patterned on the Twelve."[41]

This understanding of the New Testament data means that the female disciples, like the males, had spent time with Jesus and were sent out to preach God's reign. They were *with* Jesus, learning from his teachings to seek God's reign, selling their possessions and giving all to the Lord's ministry, as they were taught by Jesus (Lk 12:31-34; 18:22). The women from Galilee may not have been part of the Twelve, but they certainly were part of an inner circle that was trained in all ways as the twelve men were. They had been with Jesus since Galilee (Mt 4:23; 27:55; Mk 15:40-41; Lk 23:49, 55). Since the angels reminded the women that in Galilee Jesus had told them he would suffer, be crucified and be raised (Lk 24:6-8), this suggests they were present in Matthew 17:22, Mark 9:31 and Luke 9:18-22. Mark tells us Jesus wanted to be separated from the crowds because "he

---

[36]In Galatians 1:17 he also refers to "those who were apostles before I was," presumably the Twelve and James.

[37]Junia is "outstanding among the apostles" (Rom 16:7); see the discussion of this matter in chapter six above.

[38]"Brothers and sisters" is an accurate translation of the plural of *adelphos*. See LSJ, p. 20. See also Aída Besançon Spencer, "Exclusive Language—Is It Accurate?" *RevExp* 95 (1998): 388-89. Women are included clearly in the plural of *adelphos* in Acts 16:40 and Philippians 4:1-2.

[39]The seventy-two disciples most likely are a deliberate echo of the seventy-two elders who helped Moses (Num 11:16-17, 26-29). They model the premise that all the Lord's people can be filled with God's Spirit and prophesy, as would happen at Pentecost (Acts 2:17-18). On the textual question favoring seventy-two over seventy (as in the TNIV), see Kurt Aland's argument in *A Textual Commentary on the Greek New Testament*, ed. Bruce M. Metzger, 2nd ed. (Stuttgart: United Bible Societies, 2002), p. 127.

[40]*1 Clement* 47:3-4.

[41]Eusebius *Ecclesiastical History* 1.12; 3.5,7.

was teaching his disciples" (Mk 9:30). These women would have heard Jesus' teaching to "deny themselves and take up their cross daily" (Lk 9:18-25); thus they denied themselves by giving generously to Jesus' mission (Lk 8:2-3; Mt 27:55). They recognized, accepted and honored the forthcoming suffering of the Messiah by anointing Jesus before the crucifixion and being present at the crucifixion (Mt 26:6-13; 27:61; Mk 14:3-9; Lk 23:55; Jn 11:2; 12:3-8). Mary anointed Jesus' feet, having understood that the Messiah would be crucified (Jn 12:3-7), a lesson Peter did not understand until later (Mt 16:21-23; Lk 24:33-49; cf. 1 Pet 2:19-24).

The women did not understand everything perfectly. They too were surprised by the empty tomb, the angelic messengers and the resurrected Messiah (Mk 16:8). Nevertheless, as the eleven male disciples were in Jerusalem to hear Jesus' final revelations, so too very likely were some early women disciples (Mk 8:31-33; Lk 24:33).[42]

As witnesses of the resurrection, women were *sent* by Jesus to proclaim the good news. Jesus sends Mary Magdalene to "go" to "my brothers [and sisters] and tell them, 'I am ascending to my Father and your Father'" (Jn 20:17).[43] Similarly, in the Synoptic accounts the angel first tells the women (Mary Magdalene, the "other Mary," Salome), "Go quickly and tell [Jesus'] disciples: 'He has risen from the dead and is going ahead of you into Galilee. There you will see him'" (Mt 28:7; cf. Mk 16:1, 7; Lk 24:1-10). Then Jesus himself appears to the two Marys and commissions them: "Do not be afraid. Go and tell my brothers [and sisters] to go to Galilee; there they will see me" (Mt 28:10).

Jesus certainly broke convention by choosing women as the first witnesses for the greatest event of all times, the resurrection, even though women were not considered valid witnesses in court. Roman law treated women as "weak" and "light-

---

[42]It is possible that Cleopas's companion was his wife—after all, the two travelers invite Jesus into their home to stay with them (two single men living alone in a village dwelling seems most highly unlikely). Almost certainly Luke intends women to be included in his statement "They found the eleven *and those with them.*" See Bauckham, *Gospel Women,* pp. 112-15, 165-94, 282, who explains exhaustively how the Galilean women were discipled by Jesus and present at Jesus' preascension teachings, as well as part of the seventy-two disciples. The women might also be included in "apostles" in Acts 1:2, 14. See also Lee Anna Starr, *The Bible Status of Women* (1926; reprint, New York: Garland, 1987), pp. 172-73.

[43]Some in the early church regarded Mary Magdalene as "an apostle to the apostles" (Swidler, *Biblical Affirmations,* pp. 209-10; Esther de Boer, *Mary Magdalene* [Harrisburg, Penn.: Trinity Press International, 1996], pp. 60-61).

minded."[44] First-century Jewish thinkers repeat this perspective. For instance, Philo declares that "the judgments of women as a rule are weaker."[45] Josephus proclaims that Jewish law states, "Let no evidence be accepted" from women because of their "levity and temerity."[46] Rabbinic law stated that women did not have to testify (*Mishnah Shevu'ot* 4:1, 3); they were ineligible to declare the new year and to speak for ownerless property (*Mishnah Sanhedrin* 3:3). Women as witnesses were in the same class as dice players, usurers, pigeon flyers, traffickers in seventh-year produce and slaves (*Mishnah Rosh HaShanah* 1:8). Generally, rabbinic tradition disqualified women as witnesses.[47] Even some of the male disciples reflected such views when they did not at first believe the women who gave witness to the resurrection (Lk 24:11).

In contrast, for Jesus faith is the key determiner of one's place in the new covenant—as it originally was of the old covenant. Thus women functioned as witnesses or "apostles" who had been with Jesus, were eyewitnesses of the resurrection and were sent by Jesus to proclaim the good news.[48] As apostles sent by God, the twelve Jewish men looked back to the old covenant, whereas the multinumbered women and men looked forward, beyond the resurrection to the new covenant.

When scholars disqualify women from church leadership by using the twelve male apostles as precedents, they ignore the significance both of their number (twelve) and of their Jewishness, and they dismiss the importance of women's functioning as "apostles" and of Junia's being titled an "apostle." Why choose the Twelve and not, for example, the loyal Galilean women as paradigmatic of all leadership, since after Pentecost the rest of the Twelve (after Judas) are not replaced after their deaths in Acts (e.g., Acts 12:2)? If their particular ministry was not perpetuated, how can the Twelve serve as a precedent for church leadership today?

We do, however, have the precedents of men *and* women who were commissioned to preach the gospel. Therefore we should emphasize what Jesus emphasized in his teachings: humble mutual service, not male-female distinctions in leadership.

---

[44]Spencer, *Beyond the Curse*, p. 62. Sarah B. Pomeroy, *Goddesses, Whores, Wives and Slaves: Women in Classical Antiquity* (New York: Schocken, 1975), p. 150. In contrast, when Peter calls wives a "weaker partner" (referring most likely to physical strength), his call is for husbands to bestow "honor" on "heirs with you of the gracious gift of life" (1 Pet 3:7).

[45]Philo *Embassy* 40.319.

[46]Josephus *Antiquities of the Jews* 4.8.15.219.

[47]For an explanation of the general rules and the exceptions, see Tal Ilan, *Jewish Women in Greco-Roman Palestine* (Peabody, Mass.: Hendrickson, 1996), pp. 163-66.

[48]Similarly, Philip's four daughters "were prophesying" (Acts 21:9). The early church had no hesitation in calling them prophets (Eusebius *Ecclesiastical History* 3.31).

In our applications we need to keep in mind what Jesus commanded and modeled and explicitly prohibited, not what we *assume* he implied by his actions.

Finally, we must remember that the new covenant is no longer focused on the nation of Israel—as the rest of the New Testament makes clear.

Conclusion

Jesus was "the light of *all* people" that "through him *all* might believe" (Jn 1:4, 7). Scholars agree that Jesus' ministry of salvation, restoration and transformation included men and women, without distinction. As their Creator, Jesus treated women as intrinsically valuable; he respected them as intelligent and faithful, and as disciples and laborers along with men.

Since we are agreed on these points, why are some churches not following the example of Jesus? Sometimes today the church and academia are not instructing women as disciples, not listening to their spiritual discernment and not treating them equally as colaborers.

Instead some still separate women for the indoor tasks of homemaking and men for the outdoor tasks of worldmaking. Jesus' practice undermined this scheme when he talked with women, instructed them along with men and sent them out on mission. If the Bible and ecumenical councils did not hold back women who wanted to lead others in serving Christ, why should we? We should act out of grace, not from an unwritten law. Maintaining male-leadership role distinctions is not the best way to save, restore and transform our church families and society.

John's heavenly vision is of "a great multitude that no one could count, from every nation, tribe, people and language" (Rev 7:9). In the postresurrection, post-Pentecost new covenant, apostles are no longer limited to twelve but are multinumbered, because Jesus' ministry has refocused from the Jewish people (the twelve tribes, the old covenant) to the Gentiles (the nations, the many tribes, the new covenant). At Pentecost the Holy Spirit equipped every believer to be a priest and proclaimer before God. As Jesus had reminded the disciples earlier, Spirit-gifted leaders must be servants enabling *all* other new covenant priests to function fully.

8

PRAYING AND PROPHESYING
IN THE ASSEMBLIES

1 Corinthians 11:2-16

Gordon D. Fee

The interpretation of I Corinthians 11:2-16 has long been a major crux in the study of Paul's letters.[1] This is mostly because several key aspects of the passage are shrouded in mystery, including the specific nature of the sociocultural issue Paul is addressing, what the Corinthian women (presumably) were doing that called forth this response, how Paul's response works as an argument and especially the meaning of several crucial terms.[2] At the same time, the argumentation as a whole is especially uncharacteristic of Paul, both in terms of his generally relaxed attitude to the presenting issue itself and of his arguing primarily on the basis of cultural shame

---

[1]This is illustrated in part by the considerable differences of interpretation to be found in three recent major commentaries in English: Gordon D. Fee, *The First Epistle to the Corinthians*, NICNT (Grand Rapids, Mich.: Eerdmans, 1987); R. F. Collins, *First Corinthians*, SP (Collegeville, Minn.: Liturgical Press, 1999); Anthony C. Thiselton, *The First Epistle to the Corinthians*, NIGTC (Grand Rapids, Mich.: Eerdmans, 2000). Necessary limitations of space for each chapter in this book prohibit lengthy interaction with the wide range of options available. I apologize in advance to some scholars who will feel slighted by what I have done—but this is written as an essay rather than an academic piece that would give proper recognition to the work of others.

[2]Including (1) the meaning of *head*, which seems to fluctuate between the literal physical head on one's body and the (not totally clear) metaphorical use posited in I Corinthians 11:3; (2) the phrase in I Corinthians 11:4-5 translated "head covered" in most English versions, literally "having down the head"; (3) the word for "uncovered" in I Corinthians 11:5 and 13; (4) the phrase "authority over her head" in I Corinthians 11:10; (5) the prepositional phrase "because of the angels" in I Corinthians 11:10; (6) the preposition *anti* in I Corinthians 11:15, which ordinarily means "in place of"; and (7) the clause "we have no such custom" in I Corinthians 11:16, which most English translations (illegitimately?) render "we have no *other* custom."

rather than from the person and work of Christ. And finally, the basic datum in verse 5, that women are here assumed to pray and prophesy in the gathered community, stands in stark contrast to the requirement of absolute silence "in church" in I Corinthians 14:34-35.[3]

Yet despite these many uncertainties, acknowledged in part by almost everyone who has written on this passage, one may still find some who are bold to assert that this passage teaches "that women should pray and prophesy in a manner that makes it clear that they submit to male leadership."[4] In light of what Paul actually says—or does not say—such an assertion is made with a great deal more confidence than a straightforward exegesis of the passage would seem to allow.

Limitations of space do not permit me to deal with all the issues raised above. For our present purposes five matters will be addressed: (1) the nature of the issue that called forth this response, (2) the structure of Paul's argument as a whole, (3) the significance of "praying and prophesying," (4) the meaning of the metaphorical use of *head* in I Corinthians 11:3 and (5) the meaning of I Corinthians 11:10 in the argument of I Corinthians 11:7-12.

The Presenting Issue in Corinth

In I Corinthians Paul is responding both to issues reported to him (I Cor 1:11; cf. 5:1) and to the Corinthians' letter to him (I Cor 7:1). With the formula "now concerning the matters you wrote about" in I Corinthians 7:1,[5] he begins to pick up a series of items from their letter. This formula recurs in I Corinthians 7:25 and then at the beginning of the extended argument of I Corinthians 8:1–11:1.[6] Since the latter deals with matters of "worship"—pagan worship in this case—it appears that Paul moves on next to deal with three matters of worship within the believing community itself. The final one of these (I Cor 12–14) again picks up the formula "now about" and therefore most likely emerges from their letter. But the source of the two items addressed in I Corinthians 11 is much less certain.

---

[3]This, of course, is a problem only for those who consider I Corinthians 14:34-35 authentic. For an argument against its authenticity, with some rejoinder to those who have objected to this view as presented in my commentary, see Gordon D. Fee, *God's Empowering Presence: The Holy Spirit in the Letters of Paul* (Peabody, Mass.: Hendrickson, 1994), pp. 272-81.

[4]Thomas R. Schreiner, "Head Coverings, Prophecies and the Trinity: I Corinthians 11:2-16," in *RBMW,* p. 138.

[5]Translations of I Corinthians in this chapter are my own.

[6]In some of these instances he is clearly quoting from their letter itself (I Cor 7:1; 8:1, 4); see Fee, *First Epistle,* 275-77, 362.

They are tied together by intentionally contrasting introductions in I Corinthians 11:2 and 17, the first as commendatory as the second is confrontational. The second matter at least has surely been reported to him.[7] It probably sits in its present context—between items from their letter rather than in I Corinthians 1–6—because of the overarching theme of "worship matters" in I Corinthians 8–14.

The placement of our section in the letter is thus easily explained. It too takes up a matter of worship; at the same time it is not a problem of such serious consequence as is the potential destruction of the community when the rich abuse the poor at the Lord's Table (see I Cor 11:20-22). Most likely the present issue (I Cor 11:2-16) has been reported to Paul as well; and although he feels strongly enough about it to speak to it, his repeated, basically cultural appeals[8] make it clear that even though the Corinthian believers are not being commended with respect to the head-covering issue, neither are they being scolded as they were in I Corinthians 1:10–4:21, 5:1-13, 6:1-11, 6:12-20 and 8:1–10:22 and will be in I Corinthians 11:17-34 and 14:36-38. Thus the passage serves as a useful, contrasting lead-in to the major issue to be taken up next.

But what exactly is the issue in our text? Here there is a division of the house—in four ways: whether both men and women are involved in the behavior Paul seeks to correct;[9] what exactly the women were doing, whether they were discarding an (assumed) external head covering or simply letting down their hair in this semipublic setting;[10] whether the covering was always to be in place or only when they prayed or prophesied (no clear decision can be made here, but at least it included the latter); and whether the men and women involved are (only) husbands and

---

[7]This is indicated both by the clear "I hear" statement in verse 18 and the confrontational nature of the whole.

[8]Although there are theological and biblical moments expressed in verses 3 and 7-9, all the rest is based on "shame" (vv. 5-6), what is "fitting/proper" (v. 13), "nature" (v. 14) and "custom" (v. 16), none of which is implied as bringing "shame" on Christ!

[9]It is sometimes argued (most recently by Collins and Thiselton) that the issue is with the behavior of both. While the passage most certainly has to do with both, in terms of relationships within the community, the structure of the three parts to the argument (I Cor 11:3-6, 7-12, 13-15) makes a double-sided behavioral issue highly improbable. In the first two cases Paul starts with the man but shows interest primarily in the woman (note esp. the "therefore" regarding the woman in I Cor 11:10), while in the final section he starts with, and deals mostly with, the woman (the man is mentioned in I Cor 1:14 merely to serve as a contrast to the woman in I Cor 11:15).

[10]See the helpful summary discussions in Thiselton, *First Epistle*, pp. 823-26, 828-33. Although most scholars continue to believe that it involves some kind of external head covering on the women, deciding this issue is ultimately irrelevant for our present purposes.

wives or all women in relation to all men (it is usually assumed that Paul is dealing with husband-wife relationships because of I Corinthians 11:3-4, but in fact everything that is said could be addressed generically to all women in relationship to all men).

In any case, even though much of this discussion is fraught with uncertainty regarding details, determining the precise nature of the presenting problem does not seem to be absolutely essential to an understanding of Paul's argumentation as a whole, nor will it greatly affect how one views the relational issues involved—except at one crucial point, which will be taken up at the end: *Why* were they doing whatever they were doing, so that Paul addresses the issue in terms of male-female *relationships?*

Paul's Response: An Overview

The place to begin one's discussion of any of the details is to have some sense of how Paul's argument works and how its various parts relate to each other. Thus after the commendation in I Corinthians 11:2, Paul sets out to correct a matter regarding appropriate head apparel/appearance, which, even though not especially disturbing to him, apparently still had the potential of causing a measure of distress within the community.

The complexity of the argument begins with I Corinthians 11:3, where Paul anticipates what he will say about their heads *literally*, by using "head" (Greek *kephalē*) *metaphorically* with regard to three sets of relationships: "Christ" and "every man," "man" and "woman," and "Christ" and "God." Although the meaning of this metaphor is hotly debated, the concern here is to point out how this statement works in the argument itself. For the very next thing Paul says in I Corinthians 11:4 picks up the first set of relationships in I Corinthians 11:3: "every man praying or prophesying 'having down the head' brings shame to *[kataischynei]* his 'head.'" This seems to refer at least to bringing shame on his metaphorical "head" (Christ) in I Corinthians 11:3.[11]

A similar thing is then said about the woman, that if she does the opposite of the man ("prays or prophesies *uncovered* as to the head"), she brings shame to her head. But in her case Paul elaborates on the theme of shame. An uncovered head when prophesying is equal to her being "shaved" or "shorn"; and if these are

---

[11]Those who see the problem as having to do with the behavior of both men and women also argue that the "head" referred to in this instance is first of all the man's own head (see, e.g., Thiselton, *First Epistle*, pp. 827-28); but this seems to put verse 3 on the back burner altogether.

shameful—and the supposition is that they are indeed[12]—then let her be covered. The unexpected turn in the argument is that the shame is now her own,[13] with no mention of the relationship to the man. The upshot is that the meaning of the crucial phrase in 1 Corinthians 11:5 ("shame on her head") now seems to be a toss-up: is "her head" "the man" of 1 Corinthians 11:3-4 or her own head? The most likely resolution lies in a form of double-entendre; that is, by shaming her *own* "head" in this way, she also brings shame on "her head = man" in some way.

The next two parts of the argument seem intended to elaborate on the man-woman relationship. The first (1 Cor 11:7-12) is full of intrigue. Here is a case where the structure of the argument and the reason for it are clear enough, while the content and intent of the two key sentences (1 Cor 11:7, 10) are filled with mystery. Paul begins with the man, initially simply repeating the point of 1 Corinthians 11:4: "A man ought not to cover his head."[14] This is then qualified by a participial phrase that seems to require a causal or explanatory sense: "since he is the image and glory of God." But here we face further difficulties.

That Paul is appealing to Genesis 1–2 can scarcely be doubted, especially in light of the double explanation given in 1 Corinthians 11:8-9: that woman is "from the man" and was "created for his sake." But because Paul is alluding to the Genesis creation narrative, he does two things. First, he abandons the relationship expressed in 1 Corinthians 11:3 for the one narrated in Genesis 1–2 (that is, between "man" and "God," not "man" and "Christ"), thereby suggesting that the relationships expressed in 1 Corinthians 11:3 probably do not control the whole passage. At the same time he restates the nature of the relationship between "man" and "woman" in terms of her being his "glory."[15] His point

---

[12]Although one cannot be sure precisely why this would be so. There is some evidence for the use of verbs to refer to a woman who wanted to appear "mannish." See Fee, *First Epistle*, p. 511 n. 81. An older view, which has no support from the literature, suggested that "shorn" women were prostitutes.

[13]The Greek text makes this quite clear: *ei de aischron gynaiki*, "if it is shameful to/for a woman to . . ."

[14]These are the two sentences (1 Cor 11:4, 7) that have led some to see the problem as dealing as much with the man as the woman. But in fact, things are not equal. Paul offers no elaboration to these sentences, nor does he make a further point of them. Indeed, in the present instance (1 Cor 11:7) he concludes by saying something about the woman's relationship to the man, and that is what is elaborated in the rest of the section.

[15]After all, the Old Testament narrative is clear that man and woman together were created in God's image, which is why Paul adds the phrase not found in Genesis, that man, who is indeed "in the image of God," is at the same time "God's glory," a phrase that Paul will pick up in 2 Corinthians 4:4-6 to refer to Christ in his humanity as being in both the "image" and "glory" of God.

seems to be that she who was created to be man's "glory" is behaving in a way that is causing "shame." And with this turn in the argument the metaphorical use of "head" now disappears altogether—at least in terms of actual usage.

The real puzzle comes with I Corinthians 11:10. The "for this reason" with which the new sentence begins probably[16] picks up what is said about the "man-woman" relationship in I Corinthians 11:7-9. But after that we get neither what we would expect, given the way the argument has unfolded to this point, nor what is in any way clear. What we expect, in light of the argument of I Corinthians 11:4-5 and to correspond fully with I Corinthians 11:7, is "Therefore the woman ought to have her head covered." What we get instead is the most obscure clause in the whole passage: "[She] ought to have authority over her head because of the angels." This sentence in turn is followed by an adversative "nonetheless" (or "in any case")[17] which introduces two sentences intended (at least) to modify in reverse order the relational statements based on creation in I Corinthians 11:8-9, while at the same time also modifying I Corinthians 11:10 in some way.

As the woman was created for the man's sake (I Cor 11:9), so now "in the Lord" neither is to live without the other (I Cor 11:11); and as the woman originally came from the man (I Cor 11:8), the man subsequently is born "through the woman," so that "all things come from God" (I Cor 11:12).

The final section (I Cor 11:13-15) appeals only to what is "fitting" and to "nature itself." In another very complex set of sentences Paul urges that the very fact that "nature"[18] has given a man short hair and a woman long hair argues for her need to keep with the traditional covering.[19] And then the whole is wrapped up in I Corinthians 11:16 with a final appeal: "Anyone who might appear to be contentious" over this matter should acknowledge that "we have no

---

[16]"Probably" because this inferential conjunction (*dia touto*) functions in Paul's letters either backward or forward, or in many cases, as is most likely the case here, simultaneously in both directions.

[17]Greek *plēn*, a "marker of someth[ing] that is contrastingly added for consideration" (BDAG). It seems highly probable that it has a double function: to limit the degree of "authority over her head" a woman possesses (if that is in fact the meaning of this verse—see below) and to sharply qualify I Corinthians 11:8-9 so that they will *not* be understood in the subordinating fashion that so many are prone to read into them.

[18]Meaning, as the TNIV rightly has it, "the very nature of things." After all, "nature" in the case of the man comes about by an *un*natural act, namely a haircut.

[19]This is too easy an answer to a very complex issue, offering a conclusion without argumentation; but settling this exegetical issue is not crucial for the purposes of this paper and is a rat's nest for people on all sides of the sociocultural issue (for a fuller argument, see Fee, *First Epistle*, pp. 526-29).

such[20] custom, nor do the churches of God." In this way Paul appeals to what is true of his own churches as well as of the church universal.

In the end, it is plain that Paul wants the woman to maintain the tradition (whatever it is) and to do so primarily for reasons of "shame" and "honor" in a culture where this is the primary sociological value.[21] He is prepared to base this argument also on some basic matters regarding the relationship between men and women that goes back to creation, but he is equally prepared to qualify the latter by appealing to what it means for both to be "in the Lord" and to the fact that subsequent to creation the "order of creation" is reversed. But that still leaves us with several unresolved matters, which will be spoken to in the rest of this essay.

It is of interest to note that the metaphorical use of "head" in I Corinthians 11:3 simply disappears from the argument after I Corinthians 11:5. And while the relational dimension of the argument regarding men and women continues through I Corinthians 11:7-12, it is not found at all at the end, nor is it picked up in any way at the conclusion.

On Women Praying and Prophesying

Despite an occasional demurral,[22] the text is quite clear that women were regular participants in the "praying and prophesying" that were part of the worship in churches under Paul's oversight. This is fully in keeping with what we meet later in I Corinthians 14, where Paul variously says that "*all* speak in tongues" (I Cor 14:23), that "*all* may prophesy, one by one" (I Cor 14:29), and that when they assemble, "*each one* of you has [some participatory role]" (I Cor 14:26). No distinction is made between men and women in these matters, and our present text makes it certain that the *all* means what we should expect it to mean: that women and men alike participated in verbalized expressions of worship in the early house churches.

It is also likely that our present passage anticipates the argument of I Corin-

---

[20]The Greek adjective *toiautēn* means "of such a kind, such as this" (BDAG); to stretch it, as most English translations tend to do, to equal *allos*, "other," is to make it conform to what one thinks Paul ought to have said. Most likely he is referring back to what the women are doing, as indicated in I Corinthians 11:5 and 13. That is, the churches have no such custom as the women are promoting by their behavior—although earlier commentators thought the "custom" referred to was to be contentious itself (so also Collins, *First Corinthians*, p. 414).

[21]See, e.g., David A. deSilva, *Honor, Patronage, Kinship and Purity: Unlocking New Testament Culture* (Downers Grove, Ill.: InterVarsity Press, 2000), pp. 23-93, and the literature cited in his notes.

[22]See Fee, *First Epistle*, p. 497 n. 22.

thians 14 in yet another way: in the distinction Paul will make there between "speaking in tongues" and "prophesying." What is certain in I Corinthians 14 is that Paul is trying to cool the Corinthians' ardor for "tongues." To do this he sets it in a context of "edification" in the gathered assembly. Thus he argues, first, that only intelligible utterances can edify the community (I Cor 14:1-19) or bear witness to outsiders (I Cor 14:20-25), and second, that everything must be orderly, since God is a God of "shalom," not chaos (I Cor 14:26-33). In the process he clearly denominates "tongues speaking" a form of prayer (I Cor 14:2, 14, 28), while "prophecy" represents all forms of Spirit-inspired intelligible speech, capable of edifying the whole community (I Cor 14:6). Thus "tongues" equals speech that is God-directed (prayer) and "prophecy" equals speech that is community-directed.

In light of this later distinction, it seems altogether likely that Paul intends "praying and prophesying" to be not exclusive of other forms of ministry but representative of ministry in general. And since "prophets" precedes "teachers" in the ranking in I Corinthians 12:28 and prophesying is grouped with teaching, revelation and knowledge in I Corinthians 14:6, one may legitimately assume that women and men together shared in all these expressions of Spirit gifting, including teaching, in the gathered assembly.[23]

The Probable Meaning of "Head" as a Metaphor

Kephalē in 1 Corinthians 11:3. Paul's metaphorical use of "head" in verse 3 has set off an unfortunate, but massive, debate[24] that has often produced as much heat as light. Without rehashing that debate, we may safely isolate several things about Paul's usage here.

1. This is both its first occurrence in Paul's writings and its only appearance in a context where "the body" is not mentioned or assumed. Later when Paul speaks of Christ as "head" in relationship to the church (Eph 4:15-16; Col 2:19), it is a metaphor not for "lordship" but for the supporting, life-giving role that in ancient Greek thought the (literal) head was understood to have in relationship to the physical body.

2. In this passage it is not Christ's relationship to the church that is in view but specifically his relationship to the man (= male human being). And whatever the

---

[23]See Fee, *God's Empowering Presence*, pp. 144-46.
[24]See the especially helpful overview, with bibliography, in Thiselton, *First Epistle*, pp. 812-22.

relationship of Christ to the man envisioned by the metaphor in this context, it must be viewed in a way that is similar to Paul's understanding of the relationship of God the Father to Christ. That is, it is highly unlikely that Paul has set up the whole argument with a relational metaphor that would change meaning from pair to pair. So at issue, finally, in this whole passage is the nature of the relationship perceived between God and Christ.[25]

3. What we also know from the evidence is that when the Jewish community used this metaphor, as they did frequently in the Old Testament, it most often referred to a leader or clan chieftain. On the other hand, although something close to this sense can be found among Greeks,[26] they had a broader range of uses,[27] all of which can be shown to arise out of their anatomical understanding of the relationship of the head to the body (its most prominent or important part; the "source" of the body's working systems, etc.).[28]

---

[25]It should perhaps be noted that John Chrysostom, who assumed the metaphor in the case of man and woman to express a hierarchical relationship based on the Fall, felt compelled to argue against the "heretics" (Arians) that of necessity it had to have a different sense in the God-Christ pair (*Homilies on the Epistles of Paul to the Corinthians*, Homily 26 on I Cor 11:2-16). But in either case he utterly rejects that the metaphor includes the notion of "rule and subjection"; otherwise Paul would "not have brought forward the instance of a wife, but rather of a slave and master." With regard to Christ and man, and God and Christ, he resorts to the language "authors of their being." His reason for abandoning that meaning for the man-woman relationship (which he understands as husband-wife) is that he imports here his understanding of Ephesians 5:22 as supporting a hierarchical relationship.

[26]There is no known instance where *kephalē* is used as a metaphor for the husband and wife relationship; this seems to be unique to Paul. The closest thing to metaphorical *kephalē* = "lord over" is found in Aristotle (*Politics* 1255b): "The rule of the household is a monarchy; for every house is under one head." But here *head* does not mean "male human being," since Aristotle's observations would apply, e.g., to Lydia (Acts 16:15) and Nympha (Col 4:15), as well as to Philemon (Philem 1). There is a similar usage (apparently) in Plutarch (*Pelopidas* 2.1; *Galba* 4.3), in both cases to refer to a general and his troops. But in the second instance, one of the rare instances where "head" and "body" occur together, he refers to the army as "a vigorous body [= the Gallic provinces with 100,000 men in arms] in need of a head." While this certainly refers to their need of a commander, the metaphor in this case seems more to call for someone with brains to lead them.

[27]Note, e.g., Thiselton's caption for his excursus "*Kephalē* and Its Multiple Meanings" (*First Epistle*, p. 812).

[28]Thus Chrysostom (see n. 24), with regard to the two pairs Christ-man and God-Christ, understands the metaphor in a very anatomical way: "the head is of like passions with the body, and liable to the same things."

The clearest evidence for the real differences between the Jewish and Greek metaphorical uses is to be found in the Septuagint (LXX). In the hundreds of places where the Hebrew *rosh* is used for the literal head on a body, the translators invariably used the only word in Greek that means the same thing, *kephalē*. But in the approximately 180 times it appears as a metaphor for leader or chieftain, they almost always eliminate the metaphor altogether and translate it *archē* ("leader"), which

4. The earliest extant consistent interpretation of the metaphor in this passage is to be found in a younger contemporary of Chrysostom, Cyril of Alexandria (d. 444?), who explicitly interprets in terms of the Greek metaphor: "Thus we can say that 'the head of every man is Christ.' For he was made by *[dia]* him . . . as God; 'but the head of the woman is the man,' because she was taken out of his flesh. . . . Likewise 'the head of Christ is God,' because he is of him *[ex autou]* by nature" (*Ad Arcadiam et Marinam* 5.6). That is, as with Chrysostom's understanding of the two pairs (God-Christ, Christ-man), Cyril is ready to go this way with all three pairs because of what is said in verse 8: that the woman was created from the man. Not only was the idea that the head is the source of supply and support for all the body's systems a natural metaphor in the Greek world, but in this case it also supported Cyril's christological concern (not to have Christ "under" God in a hierarchy), just as it did for Chrysostom.

The question for us, then, is whether Paul was speaking out of his Jewish heritage or whether in speaking into the Corinthians' Greek setting he used a metaphor that would have been more familiar to them.[29] At issue, of course, is what kind of relationship between the man and the woman is envisaged in verse 3 and how this plays out in the discussion that follows. For several reasons, it seems most likely that something very much like Cyril's understanding was in Paul's mind.

1. Despite repeated assertions to the contrary, nothing that is said following this verse hints at an authority-subordination relationship. Most often those who advocate this view have either a husband-wife or a "church order" relationship in view. But the latter is to read something into the text that simply is not there, and while it is possible that the former may be intended, nothing inherent in the discussion that follows requires such a view. The final wrapup in I Corinthinas 11:13-15 is about men and women in general and therefore offers no further help for understanding the metaphor.

2. In the one instance in our passage where Paul might be picking up some dimension of the metaphor (I Cor 11:8-9), the relationship envisaged is clearly not one of subordination to the man as "leader." Paul is setting out to explain his as-

---

is evidence that they were uncomfortable with (unfamiliar with?) the Jewish metaphor and simply translated it out. The few instances (six in all) where they do not do this (Judg 11:11; 2 Sam 22:44; Ps 18:43; Is 7:8-9; Lam 1:5) are simply the exceptions that prove the rule.

[29] And, of course, one cannot appeal to the Old Testament usage as a place of familiarity for them, since they would not know Hebrew and their Greek Bible already had the metaphorical usage basically translated out.

sertion that "the woman is the *glory* of man." The answer lies in the Genesis narrative: she came from man (in the sense that she was taken from his side) and was created for his sake; this is what makes her the man's "glory." If this is an extension of the metaphor in I Corinthians 11:3, then it clearly points to "man" as metaphorical head in the sense Cyril maintains. Moreover, there is no usage of "glory" anywhere in Scripture that would suggest that Paul is here advocating a subordinating relationship by means of this word.[30] On the other hand, in a context where women are bringing shame on themselves and thus on their husbands, this appeal makes perfectly good sense. She who is to be his "glory" is behaving in a way that turns that glory into shame.

3. One of the ongoing puzzles for all interpreters is why Paul should include the third member in his opening sentence, since "God as the head of Christ" is not picked up again in any way. Most likely this is because the saying had prior existence and Paul is simply appealing to it. But if so, what was its point? Although one cannot be certain here, most likely it was a useful metaphor to express something of a chronology of "salvation history." According to I Corinthians 8:6, all things (including Adam) were created "through Christ"; the man then became the "source" of the woman's being, while God was the "source" of Christ's incarnation. In any case, this view of the saying can make sense of all three members, in a way that seeing the metaphor as expressing subordination does not seem to—unless one wants to embrace a heterodox Christology.[31]

Kephalē elsewhere in Paul. Nonetheless it is common to appeal to Paul's later use of this metaphor in Colossians and Ephesians, as Chrysostom did, and then to import here a hierarchical meaning from there.[32] But much confusion seems to be at

---

[30]See Fee, *First Epistle*, p. 571: "Paul is really reflecting the sense of the Old Testament text to which he is alluding. Man by himself is not complete; he is alone, without a companion or helper suitable to him. The animals will not do; he needs one who is bone of his bone, one who is like him but different from him, one who is uniquely his own 'glory.' In fact, when the man in the Old Testament narrative sees the woman he 'glories' in her by bursting into song. . . . She is not thereby subordinate to him, but necessary for him. She exists to his honor as the one who having come from man is the one companion suitable to him, so that he might be complete and that together they might form humanity."

[31]See chapter nineteen in this volume.

[32]One of the problems with much of the debate regarding the metaphorical use of *kephalē* in Paul is the tacit assumption that the resolution lies in deciding once and for all what the metaphor meant in Greek sources outside the New Testament. This seems especially evident in the debate between Wayne Grudem and Richard Cervin, carried on first in the *Trinity Journal* (Grudem, 6 [1985]: 38-59; Cervin, 10 [1989]: 85-112; Grudem, 11 [1990]: 3-72) and in a final rejoinder by Cervin that

work here, since in these two later (companion) letters the metaphor is used in three distinct ways: to point to (a) Christ's relationship with the church (Eph 4:15-16; 5:23; Col 1:18; 2:19), (b) Christ's relationship to "the powers" (Eph 1:22; Col 2:10) and (c) a householder's relationship to his wife (Eph 5:23).[33]

The imagery in its first instance (Col 1:18; 2:19) seems to stem ultimately from Paul's view of the church as the "body of Christ," celebrated at every Lord's Supper according to I Corinthians 10:16-17 and 11:29. What is at issue in Colossians are some people who are moving in clearly heretical directions, who are "not holding fast to the head" (Col 2:19) but are cutting themselves off from the "body" altogether and, by implication, being "joined" to the "powers" to whom they now give undue significance. This concern is anticipated in the earlier occurrence of the metaphor in Colossians 1:18, where it appears in a clause that serves as the "janus" between the two stanzas of the hymn in Colossians 1:15-20: "And he [the Son of God] is the head of the body, the church."[34] This otherwise unnecessary insertion into the hymn/poem of Colossians 1:15-20 seems clearly intended—as does the whole hymn/poem itself—to set the stage for some things that will be said later about Christ's relationship both to the powers

---

was distributed as an unpublished paper (c. 1991) by Christians for Biblical Equality. But what Cervin has especially demonstrated in his survey of the literature is the diversity of options to be found there—even though he wants finally to narrow it to a primary meaning of "prominent" or "topmost." The problem with this narrowing of things is that while there can be no question that Christ as "head" of the church is the most prominent part of the body, this can hardly be Paul's point. Rather, Paul's meaning is the Greek anatomical one, that the body is sustained by its relationship to its most "prominent" part.

[33]I use the term *householder* here because the entire passage in Ephesians (5:21-6:9) assumes the Greco-Roman villa, not relationships within other settings. After all, Colossians (a companion letter to Ephesians) was written at the same time as Philemon and assumes the reading of both letters in the context of that household. For example, if there were a married slave couple in the household, Philemon would be the "head" of the slave wife in the same way he would be of Apphia. Paul's point in using the metaphor in Ephesians is that the householder is the "savior" of his wife, in the sense of being the one on whom the entire household is dependent for their well-being. See further Gordon D. Fee, "The Cultural Context of Ephesians 5:18-6:9," *Priscilla Papers* 16 (Winter 2002): 3-8.

[34]I say "janus" here because this clause is otherwise unrelated to the content of the first stanza (Col 1:15-17), where the emphasis is on the Son as the "firstborn" over the whole created order; in him all things, including the powers, were created; indeed, they were created by him and for him; and in him all things hold together. The balancing second stanza begins in the second part of Colossians 1:18—"he [the Son] is the beginning, the firstborn from the dead"—and moves on to speak of his redemptive work that makes him so. The beginning of Colossians 1:18, "the Son is the head of the body, the church," joins these two stanzas. Thus with Paul's later use of this metaphor, the church is dependent on its life-giving, life-sustaining "head" (Col 2:19); at the same time Christ is head over "the powers" (Col 2:10).

and to the church in the main argument of Colossians 2:6-19.

First, Paul claims that Christ is "head of [= over] every power and authority" (Col 2:10), and is so, he adds in Ephesians 1:22, *for the sake of* the church. These two instances are in fact the only certain places where Paul uses the imagery in this more specifically Jewish way. Although he will go on to speak of Christ as head of the body, here the metaphor stands alone without connection to a "body" and clearly refers to Christ's authority over all the powers. Thus Paul appears in this usage to be making a play on the metaphorical options. Christ is "head over the powers"— whom he has conquered through his death, resurrection and ascension.

Second, when the imagery is used in relationship to the church, the key to its intended meaning is the elaboration in Colossians 2:19, where the false teachers have lost connection with the head. This is obviously not a metaphor for subordination or "lordship" but for the maintenance of life, as the rest of the sentence makes plain. To lose connection with the head means to lose life itself, since the church functions as Christ's body only as it maintains connection with the head. This is also how the head/body imagery is elaborated in Ephesians 4:15-16. Now in a positive context, the imagery encourages the life and growth of the church as a unity, which is why in Colossians those who cease to "hold fast" to the head cease to live—and in fact are moving the church itself toward death.

This relationship between head and body seems also to be the point of the analogical use of the metaphor in Ephesians 5:22-24.[35] Precisely because Paul is deliberately using an analogy, not offering a literal description of reality,[36] the point of the analogy takes us back to Ephesians 4:15-16, *not* to the relationship of Christ to "the powers." And this point is the apt one: just as the church is totally dependent on Christ for life and growth, so the wife in the first-century household was totally dependent on her husband as her "savior," in the sense of being dependent on him for her life in the world.

In view of all this, the importation into 1 Corinthians of *any* of Paul's later uses of the imagery is probably suspect at best. That is, Paul surely does not intend here

---

[35]It should be pointed out that the metaphor is *not* used for the other two relationships with the householder (children and slaves), where "lordship" is plainly expressed. The change of verbs from *hypotassō* (where the middle suggests a form of volunteerism that is expected of all, but in a special way of wives) to *hypakouō* for children and slaves (in both Colossians and Ephesians) suggests that Paul simply would never have used the latter for wives and that there is therefore a basic difference between them, despite occasional semantic overlap.

[36]That is, the husband is *not* the savior of his wife in the same way as Christ is of the church!

that the first member of each pair is "head over" the other in the same sense in which Paul asserts that Christ is "head over the powers," having disarmed and triumphed over them (Col 2:10, 15). Moreover, since there is no "head-body" relationship expressed in our passage, neither does it seem appropriate to think of the second member as "sustained and built up by" its relationship to the first (as in Eph 4:15-16; 5:22-33; Col 2:19). That leaves us, then, with Cyril's view—the first member as the source/ground of the other's being—as the most likely meaning here. This, after all, is the one relationship actually spelled out in our passage (the woman coming from the man, I Cor 11:8; the man now coming from the woman, I Cor 11:12).

The Meaning of 1 Corinthians 11:10

First Corinthians 11:10 is the most puzzling sentence in the entire passage—for three reasons: (1) what is said is not what we would expect on the basis of I Corinthians 11:7, (2) the sudden use of the word *authority* in relation to the woman's head is both unexpected and seemingly unrelated to anything that has been said heretofore, and (3) the second reason offered, "because of the angels," is shrouded in obscurity.

1. The unexpected nature of this sentence is in part due to what is actually said; but in part it is also due to the way it begins, "for this reason." If the connector in this case points both backward and forward, then the forward look would probably be anticipating the phrase "because of the angels"; thus, "for this reason, namely because of the angels."

But a backward look is more likely the primary intent. If so, then even though it would embrace the content of I Corinthians 11:8-9, Paul most likely intends to draw an inference from the end of I Corinthians 11:7: "but the woman is the glory of man." This, after all, is what I Corinthians 11:8-9 are setting out to justify. But it is this very reality that makes the *content* of I Corinthians 11:10 so puzzling, since not a single word that follows has any immediately apparent relationship to what has been said up to this point.

2. The most puzzling moment in the entire passage is Paul's use of the word *exousia* ("authority/right to act") at the very place where I Corinthians 11:7 has set us up to expect "ought to have *her head covered.*" It is for this reason that the church has historically assumed, and many continue to assert, that what Paul does write should in fact be understood as standing in for what we are led to expect. But this historic position is full of difficulties, bluntly expressed a century ago by Robertson

and Plummer: "The difficulty is to see why Paul has expressed himself in this extraordinary manner. That 'authority' *(exousia)* has been put for 'sign of authority' is not difficult; but why does St Paul say 'authority' when he means 'subjection'?"[37] Precisely! But the problems are far more substantial than his simply "saying one thing when he meant another."

First, the only way one can come to this view is by a particular reading of the context. If we were to come across this sentence in a free-standing setting, no one would interpret it in this "passive" sense. This construction (subject, the verb *echein* ["has/have"], with *exousia* as the object followed by the preposition *epi*) would be read in the only way it is known to occur in the language: the subject has the authority "over" the object of the preposition. This does not mean that in context a passive sense could not occur; but in fact such an occurrence is otherwise unknown.

Second, this is simply not a case of one word's standing for another. Because a passive relationship of the subject (woman) to the object *(exousia)* is required, one must make two jumps to get to the assumed meaning (as Robertson and Plummer clearly recognized). That is, the word *exousia* would stand in for the covering itself (a "veil"—so some early versions and English translations), which in turn stands in for a "sign of" the authority a man presumably has over her (see NRSV, NEB). But this double jump is not easy to come to from a straight reading of the text.

Third, the word *exousia* has already occurred several times in I Corinthians, most of them in the immediately preceding argument, where it is used in a strictly pejorative way. It emerges first in I Corinthians 8:9 (surprisingly, but absolutely straightforwardly), where Paul warns that those who are acting on the basis of "this *exousia* of yours" are thereby putting a stumbling block in the way of others. The word is then picked up again in the extended defense of Paul's apostolic "rights" to the Corinthians' material support (I Cor 9:1-23), where the context indicates that they are rejecting his apostleship precisely because he does not make use of his rightful *exousia* (see 2 Cor 12:13)! He argues in defense (see I Cor 9:1-3) that he has the *exousia* all right but has freely curtailed it (I Cor 9:12-19) for the sake of the gospel ("so that by all possible means I might save some," I Cor 9:22). His ultimate point is that the Corinthians themselves should act accordingly. It is precisely this faulty/arrogant use of their *exousia* that is the cause of the warnings in

---

[37]Archibald Robertson and Alfred Plummer, *A Critical and Exegetical Commentary on the First Epistle of St Paul to the Corinthians*, 2nd ed., ICC (Edinburgh: T & T Clark, 1914), p. 232.

I Corinthians 10:1-13. Given this immediate context to our passage, it would seem likely that this is also how we should understand the present sentence in context: that the women do indeed have *exousia*, but at issue again is the use they would make of it.

3. The equally puzzling "because of the angels" has been the bane of all interpreters, and any number of suggestions have been brought forward.[38] A good case can made for at least starting with the evidence from I Corinthians itself, where, besides this passage, angels are mentioned three other times (I Cor 4:9; 6:2-3; 13:1). There is good reason to believe that the Corinthians understood "speaking in tongues" to be speaking the language of the angels (I Cor 13:1) and thus to be evidence of a superior spirituality.[39] If so, then the earlier two occurrences make sense in terms of Paul's trying to help the Corinthians gain perspective on this matter: he designates the angels as witnesses to his apostolic weaknesses (I Cor 4:9), and he asserts that the Corinthians themselves will be involved in the eschatological judgment of angels (I Cor 6:2-3). In keeping with this suggestion, "because of the angels" in this passage may thus reflect the Corinthians' own positive view of being like the angels.

Within this scenario, our sentence could be yet another instance in the letter where Paul is reflecting their own point of view—in this case, of some Corinthian women.[40] As elsewhere, Paul would be agreeing with them in principle, but then he sets out qualifications so that his agreement ends up being in principle only. If this is the case, then Paul is here momentarily allowing the rightness of the Corinthian women's perspective: that because of their "angelic" status they have the right to put what they please (or not) on their own heads.

But this also means the *plēn* ("nevertheless") that immediately follows is a very important qualifier. First, Paul is not backing down from what he has affirmed in I Corinthians 11:8-9 on the basis of the Genesis story, which explains how the woman is man's glory. But neither will he allow that to be taken in a subordinating way. The first set of realities is not reversed "in the Lord," but neither is it to be understood wrongly. At the same time, if I Corinthians 11:10 is his (ostensible)

---

[38]For example, that the angels were understood to be the guardians (or "overseers" or "assistants") of Christian worship and would be offended by impropriety, or that the angels would lust after women who were uncovered. See further Fee, *First Epistle*, pp. 521-22; Thiselton, *First Epistle*, pp. 839-41.

[39]See the discussion in Fee, *First Epistle*, pp. 630-31.

[40]As would also be true of I Corinthians 7:1 (cf. I Cor 6:12-13 for the perspective of some men, and I Cor 8:1, 4, 8 for the perspective of those "in the know").

agreement with the reasons the women are discarding the normal covering, then I Corinthians 11:11-12 also functions as a rejoinder to their position. Being "in the Lord" does not mean *exousia* to be as the angels now, where distinctions between male and female are understood no longer to exist; rather it means that in the present age neither man nor woman can exist without the other, and gender distinctions are part of the "all things [that] are from God."

A Possible Explanation

That leads to a final suggestion as to *what* was going on in the church gatherings in Corinth and *why* some women had both abandoned the cultural norm and perhaps argued for the right to do so. The most common answer to this question, either expressed or assumed, is that it was an act of insubordination on the part of some wives toward their husbands. The problem with this answer, of course, is that nothing else in I Corinthians seems to support it. But by gathering up all the evidence in the letter, including what Paul says here, one may reconstruct a fairly consistent point of view that covers most of the letter.

Beginning at the end (I Cor 12–14), we find a community that has put a considerable emphasis on "speaking in tongues," and Paul's reference to "speaking the language of angels" (I Cor 13:1) probably has direct bearing on their reasons for it.[41] Speaking in an angelic tongue gave these new believers, the majority of whom were not among the Corinthian elite (I Cor 1:26-28), a new sense of status. And with that also came a sense that they had begun to move in a "spirituality" that resembled the existence of the angels themselves. Moreover, such a viewpoint could have been attributed in part to Paul himself, since whatever else is true, he had a thoroughly eschatological view of being in Christ—that the basic moments of the future (resurrection and the outpoured Spirit) have already taken place, even though their final expression was yet to be.

If this understanding of "spirituality" prevailed in Corinth, and especially if some of the women were deeply into it, then one can account for several other matters in our letter, including the church's basically negative attitude toward the apostle (I Cor 1:10-12; 4:1-21; 9:1-19). His bodily weaknesses, combined with his not using his *exousia* regarding their support,[42] serve as evidence for the Corinthians that Paul lacks true *exousia*—the right to choose one's behavior for oneself. But

---

[41]See Fee, *First Epistle*, pp. 630-31.

[42]This is such an obvious source of contention between them that Paul picks it up again very sarcastically in 2 Corinthians 11:7-9 and 12:13.

even more important, such a view can especially account for some women's (apparent) rejection of the marriage bed (I Cor 7:1-7; because they are already as the angels), so much so that they could even argue for divorce if need be (I Cor 7:10-16). It also accounts for their (possibly) discouraging some "virgins" already promised in marriage from following through (I Cor 7:25-38) and for some men's resorting to prostitutes as a result (I Cor 6:12-20). This also explains in part the denial of a future bodily existence on the part of some (I Cor 15:12, 35) and very likely lies behind their fascination with "wisdom" (I Cor 1–4) and "knowledge" (I Cor 8–10). These views are generally shared by both men and women in the community; but they especially find expression in the behavior of the women in I Corinthians 7 and 11:2-16.

If this is a reasonable explanation for the women's behavior in this passage, then what lies behind it is not so much an act of insubordination as a deliberate casting aside of an external marker that distinguished women from men.[43] That is, the issue in Corinth is very likely a subtle movement toward androgyny, where distinctions between men and women are of little value "because of the angels"; they have already experienced a form of angelic life where there is neither marrying nor giving in marriage (Lk 20:35-36).[44]

For Paul this is not only a betrayal of the gospel but also a denial of the "not yet" dimension of our present eschatological existence. And above all, it puts considerable strain on present relationships between men and women. Paul begins his answer with a metaphorical appeal to one's "head" because the problem lies squarely on the head. In a culture where the vast majority of women are dependent on a man for life in the world, a woman who brings shame on her own head by getting rid of one of the cultural markers of distinction also brings shame on her metaphorical head, the one on whom the woman is primarily dependent and to whom she is responsible in the Greco-Roman household (which also serves as the nucleus expression of the house church that meets in the household).

While none of this is certain, it does offer a view of I Corinthians 11:2-16 that

---

[43]This at least explains the one moment of vigor in the whole argument, I Corinthians 11:5-6, where Paul expostulates that if they are going to remove the external marking of gender difference then they might as well go all the way and have their hair cut in a mannish style. For the evidence for this meaning of these verbs, see Fee, *First Epistle*, p. 511 n. 81.

[44]The significance of Luke's expression of this pericope is that Luke's Gospel most likely gave written form to the Jesus tradition as it circulated in Paul's churches, for which their common tradition of the words of institution (I Cor 11:24-25/Lk 22:19-20) serves as ample evidence.

can make sense of all its parts and at the same time fits well into the larger perspective of the letter. Paul's intent therefore is not to put women in their place, as it
were, but to maintain a cultural tradition that has the effect of serving as a gender
distinctive, even while "in the Lord" neither is independent of the other (I Cor
11:11).

9

LEARNING IN THE ASSEMBLIES

1 Corinthians 14:34-35

Craig S. Keener

Very few churches today take 1 Corinthians 14:34-35 to mean all that it could possibly mean. Indeed, any church that permits women to participate in congregational singing recognizes that Paul was not demanding what a face-value reading of his words seems to imply: complete silence as a sign of women's subordination. Thus almost *everyone* has a problem with pressing this text literally, and interpreters must explain the divergence between what it states and what they believe it means. But beyond this near consensus, church traditions and interpreters diverge: just how silent must women be?

Various Interpretations

Interpretations vary considerably. Some scholars, for example, argue that Paul cites a Corinthian position here which he then refutes, as he sometimes did earlier in the letter (e.g., 1 Cor 6:12-14). First Corinthians 14:36 does not, however, read easily like a refutation of preceding verses.[1] Others propose that, following synagogue practice, husbands and wives met in different parts of the church, so that women who asked questions could not avoid disrupting the worship. This proposal fails on two counts. First, synagogues were probably not segregated in this period.[2] Second, although the Corinthian church started in a synagogue (Acts 18:4) it now met in homes (Acts 18:7)—which would hardly

---

[1] I cite documentation for all these positions in Craig S. Keener, *Paul, Women and Wives* (Peabody, Mass.: Hendrickson, 1993), pp. 74-80; for the sake of space I omit most documentation here.

[2] Shemuel Safrai, "The Synagogue," in *The Jewish People in the First Century*, 2 vols., ed. Shemuel Safrai and M. Stern (Philadelphia: Fortress, 1974-76), p. 939; Bernadette J. Brooten, *Women Leaders in the Ancient Synagogue* (Chico, Calif.: Scholars Press, 1982), pp. 103-38.

afford the space for such gender segregation!

Some scholars question whether Paul even wrote the passage, noting both textual evidence and its contrast with its context and Paul's usual teaching.[3] There is no question that it sounds intrusive. For example, the opening "or" of I Corinthians 14:36, in light of Paul's usage elsewhere in I Corinthians, most naturally follows "as in all the churches of the saints" in I Corinthians 14:33 (which itself naturally reads as concluding what precedes it, as in the similar appeal of I Cor 11:16).[4] The early Western textual tradition has I Corinthians 14:34 and 35 in a different location, which may mean that early scribes were still debating the best place in Paul's writings to insert them. These scholars point out that such relocation in ancient texts usually suggests an interpolation and that this is the only passage in Paul's writings where scribes changed the sequence of his argument. The earliest evidence, including from the church fathers, treats 14:34-35 as a unit distinct from the context.

But though the passage certainly does interrupt the context, none of the ancient manuscripts lack these verses. That the verses do not seem to fit the context could explain why scribes struggled with where to locate them. Brief digressions were common both in Paul and other ancient writers.[5] It is thus possible that Paul himself inserted this brief digression into a context involving order in church meetings to address a problem with some Corinthian women's behavior, of which he had been informed.

Still, trying to fit the passage into the immediate context is not simple, as the variety of context-based interpretations suggests. Some suppose that Paul is silencing women's practice of spiritual gifts such as prophecy or prayer in tongues. While this proposal does pay attention to the context (which regulates public use of the gifts), it is difficult to square with Paul's acceptance of women's praying and prophesying in church earlier in the same letter (I Cor 11:5).

Some readers interpret this passage as prohibiting women's teaching the Bible

---

[3] Argued by F. F. Bruce, Wayne Meeks and others; but the most persuasive exponent of this position is Gordon D. Fee, *The First Epistle to the Corinthians*, NICNT (Grand Rapids, Mich.: Eerdmans, 1987), pp. 699-705; most fully, Gordon D. Fee, *God's Empowering Presence* (Peabody, Mass.: Hendrickson, 1994), pp. 272-81. In a series of articles P. Barton Payne has also argued the likelihood that some earlier manuscripts omitted these verses, though this evidence remains disputed.

[4] Translations of I Corinthians are my own.

[5] Cf. D. A. Carson, "'Silent in the Churches': On the Role of Women in I Corinthians 14:33b-36," in *RBMW*, p. 142. For digressions, see e.g., Josephus *Against Apion* 1.57; *Life of Flavius Josephus* 336-67; Livy *History of Rome* 9.17.1–9.19.17; Cicero *Finibus* 2.32.104; *De Oratore* 43.148; *Ad Atticus* 7.2; Arrian *Indica* 6.1; Sallust *Bellum Catilinae* 5.9–13.5.

publicly, based on their understanding of 1 Timothy 2:11-12. Unfortunately, the Corinthians could not simply flip in their Bibles to 1 Timothy (which had not been written yet) to figure out what Paul meant, and unlike prophecy and tongues, teaching is not even mentioned directly in the present context! Of course, if Paul enjoins complete silence on women, that silence would necessarily preclude teaching; but it would also preclude public prophecy and prayer (contradicting Paul's earlier remarks) as well as modern congregational singing.

One proposal that is no more persuasive, yet has gained a wide hearing, is that Paul simply prohibits women from *judging* prophecy (1 Cor 14:29).[6] Most of the supporters of this proposal are nonegalitarians, though even if the proposal were correct, one is hard-pressed to see why restricting women from judging prophecies in Corinth would thereby restrict women from teaching (yet not prophesying or praying) then or today. Judging prophecy is a task assigned to all who prophesy (1 Cor 14:29), perhaps (given the use of the cognate term) part of the gift of discerning spirits (1 Cor 12:10); and again, women can prophesy (1 Cor 11:5). The only kind of speech specifically mentioned here (asking questions) seems little related to evaluating prophecies' accuracy.[7] Perhaps the greatest weakness of the position is that there is nothing in the text that specifically leads us to suppose that "judging prophecies" is the particular sort of speech in view; if the previous proposal about limiting women's involvement in spiritual gifts fails because it contradicts 1 Corinthians 11:4-5, at least it was a specific *emphasis* in the preceding context (and not simply one activity among many others in the context, like evaluating prophecies in 1 Cor 14:29).[8] What in 1 Corinthians 14:34-35 specifies "judging" prophecies? And where does the text suggest that "judging prophecies" reveals a higher degree of authority than prophesying God's message itself? That many nonegalitarians support this reading (rather than a more explicit argument against teaching) shows how difficult it is to target Bible teaching or pastoral ministry without eliminating prophecy or prayer, and ultimately suggests that this is a difficult text for all modern interpreters, including nonegalitarians.

---

[6]E.g., Carson, "Silent," p. 152; James B. Hurley, "Did Paul Require Veils or the Silence of Women? A Consideration of I Cor. 11:2-16 and I Cor. 14:33b-36," *WTJ* 35 (1973): 217; also some egalitarians (Walter L. Liefeld, "Women, Submission and Ministry in 1 Corinthians," in *Women, Authority and the Bible*, ed. Alvera Mickelsen [Downers Grove, Ill.: InterVarsity Press, 1986], p. 150).

[7]Although people asked questions of oracles (*Oxyrhynchus Papyri* 1148-49, 1477; Maximus of Tyre *Orations* 8.3) or "inquired of the Lord" (e.g., 1 Sam 9:9), this was not a method of *evaluating* prophecy.

[8]D. A. Carson, *Exegetical Fallacies* (Grand Rapids, Mich.: Baker, 1984), p. 115, offers one of the classic warnings against the danger of interpretive overspecification.

What Situation Was Paul Addressing?

When Paul named various people in the church in Corinth, he did not have to explain to his readers who these people were (e.g., 1 Cor 1:11, 14, 16; 16:17). The Corinthian Christians already knew them. Likewise, he could refer to practices like food offered to idols and women wearing head coverings with no concern that twenty-first-century readers might struggle to reconstruct the situation. After all, the verse that tells us that Paul was writing to the Corinthians (1 Cor 1:2) is just as inspired as more popular parts of the letter, and the letter genre itself invites us to consider his readers' situation.

Some readers today reject any interpretation of a passage that requires us to take the particular situation into account. Such readers are never consistent, however: few, for example, provide offerings for the Jerusalem church every Sunday (1 Cor 16:1-4). Likewise, many do not require head coverings or holy kisses (1 Cor 11:2-16; 16:20), recognizing that these practices meant something different to first-century readers from what they would mean to us today.[9] We cannot simply cite the present passage and claim that it applies to all situations without begging the question. In any case, the first task of the reader of Scripture is the exegetical one: understanding the text on its own terms in its own context. Only after we have understood it contextually can we apply it appropriately.

Paul can hardly mean that all women in all churches must be completely silent all the time; that would contradict Paul's earlier words in the same letter (1 Cor 11:5), not to mention his valuing of women laborers in the gospel (Rom 16:1-7, 12). As mentioned above, it would also contradict the practice of the majority of even the most conservative churches today. Since those who allow women to participate in congregational singing do not apply this text any more literally than egalitarians do, all could benefit from further discussion of the background. Tongues speakers (1 Cor 14:30) also were to remain silent, but only under particular circumstances. What clues does Paul offer us in the text itself concerning the reasons for the silence? The context addresses not simply spiritual gifts but order and propriety in house church meetings (1 Cor 14:27-33).

Two things are absolutely central to a proper understanding of this passage. First,

---

[9]For the cultural practices involved here, see Craig S. Keener, "Head Coverings," "Kissing," in *Dictionary of New Testament Background*, ed. C. A. Evans and S. E. Porter, pp. 442-47, 628-29 (Downers Grove, Ill.: InterVarsity Press, 2000). For further examples of the need for cultural sensitivity in interpreting these passages, see Craig S. Keener, "Women in Ministry," in *Two Views on Women in Ministry*, ed. James R. Beck and Craig L. Blomberg (Grand Rapids, Mich.: Zondervan, 2001), pp. 46-49, 55-57.

and most important, our verses themselves *specify only one particular kind of speech* that we can be certain Paul addresses here. Unless Paul changes the subject from women's submissive silence (I Cor 14:34) to asking questions privately (I Cor 14:35) and back again to silence (I Cor 14:35), asking questions is at least a primary example of the sort of speech he seeks to forbid. In fact, Paul explicitly bases his injunction to ask questions privately on his demand for silence (I Cor 14:35, "for"). Second, and related to the first, Paul explicitly ties the women's speech in this case to shame. And since honor and shame are areas in which cultures differ considerably, it is worth our while to determine the source of "shame" in this particular instance.

Why would women have been tempted to ask questions during the service? And what problems would these interruptions have posed? Here it is helpful to note that questions were standard fare in all ancient lecture settings—except when asked by those insufficiently learned, who were expected to keep quiet, at least so long as they remained novices. There is good reason to suppose that most of the women in the Corinthian church—even those raised in the synagogue—were insufficiently learned. Further, their gender itself would have rendered their outspokenness offensive to conservative Roman and Greek men, probably even in the familial setting of a Corinthian house church.

Women's Silence and Questions in Public Settings

Reading our passage on its own terms, I had always found most plausible the view that women were interrupting the service with questions.[10] But I never could imagine what circumstances provoked these public questions until I read Plutarch's essay *On Lectures.* Then I realized that listeners regularly interrupted lectures with questions, whether to learn more about the subject or to compete intellectually with an inadequately prepared lecturer. I quickly realized that questions were common in Jewish settings as well and were a regular part of ancient Mediterranean lecture settings in general.[11] House churches were undoubtedly less formal than larger settings but apparently included, when possible, a teaching element that would prob-

---

[10]Also, e.g., Don Williams, *The Apostle Paul and Women in the Church* (Glendale, Calif.: Gospel Light, 1977), p. 70; Kevin Giles, *Created Woman: A Fresh Study of the Biblical Teaching* (Canberra, Australia: Acorn, 1985), p. 56.

[11]See, e.g., Plutarch *Lectures* 11, *Moralia* 43B; Aulus Gellius *Attic Nights* 1.26.2; 8.10; 12.5.4; 16.6.1-12; 18.13.7-8; 20.10.1-6; Seneca *Epistles to Lucilius* 108.3; *Tosefta Sanhedrin* 7:10; *Avot de Rabbi Nathan* 6A; Martin Goodman, *State and Society in Roman Galilee* (Totowa, N.J.: Rowman & Allanheld, 1983), p. 79; also intellectual conversation, e.g., Polybius *Histories* 31.23.9; Plutarch *Table-Talk* 2.1.2, *Moralia* 630BC.

ably follow many practices familiar from similarly sized learning gatherings in the culture (cf. 1 Cor 12:28-29; 14:6, 26; Rom 12:7).

But why would Paul have restricted questions coming specifically from women? The questions could be an example of a broader kind of speech in the assembly prohibited to women; but then why does Paul permit the women to pray and prophesy in 11:5? Two possibilities make good sense.

The first is that ancient Mediterranean protocol would disapprove of an otherwise honorable woman addressing unrelated men.[12] Thus, for example, in one novel a noble woman protests that it is proper only for a man to speak when men are present, explaining that she speaks only under duress.[13] Speech to "their own husbands" here may thus contrast with speaking to other men—a practice Greek men permitted for "inspired" speech but rejected as shameful for casual conversation. This sort of situation could easily arise in the ambiguous boundaries between private and public spheres experienced in a house church.[14]

In current Western society it is nearly impossible for anyone who engages in any activity in public—working, attending university, shopping—to avoid some casual cross-gender conversation, but this was not the case in the first century. Although many men considered women prone to gossip, social convention particularly respected women who were socially retiring and did not talk much with men outside their household.[15] Many men questioned women's judgment.[16] Women who con-

---

[12]E.g., Valerius Maximus *Memorable Doings and Sayings* 3.8.6; cf. 8.3.2. This principle is often acknowledged here; e.g., Christopher Forbes, *Prophecy and Inspired Speech in Early Christianity and Its Hellenistic Environment* (Peabody, Mass.: Hendrickson, 1997), pp. 274, 277; cf. James D. G. Dunn, *The Theology of Paul the Apostle* (Grand Rapids, Mich.: Eerdmans, 1998), pp. 589, 592.

[13]Heliodorus *Ethiopica* 1.21-22, especially 1.22 (probably third century A.D.).

[14]See especially Terence Paige, "The Social Matrix of Women's Speech at Corinth: The Context and Meaning of the Command to Silence in 1 Corinthians 14:33b-36," *BBR* 12 (2002): 217-42, published during the editing of this essay. Although we cite some of the same ancient texts, his work shows no awareness of my earlier work (nor was I aware of his article when I completed the final draft of this essay or cited these texts), suggesting that ancient literature led us to very similar conclusions independently.

[15]See Plutarch *Bride* 31-32, *Moralia* 142CD; Heliodorus *Ethiopica* 1.21. Later rabbis felt Jewish men should avoid unnecessary conversation with women (*Mishnah Avot* 1:5; *Tosefta Shabbat* 1:14; *Babylonian Talmud Berakhot* 43b, bar.; *Eruvin* 53b), and the strictest felt that a wife who spoke with a man in the street could be divorced with no marriage settlement (*Mishnah Ketubbot* 7:6). Some felt that such verbal intercourse could ultimately lead to sin (Ecclesiasticus 9:9; 42:12; *Testament of Reuben* 6:1-2). Traditional Middle Eastern societies still view social intercourse as nearly the moral equivalent of sexual infidelity (Carol Delaney, "Seeds of Honor, Fields of Shame," in *Honor and Shame and the Unity of the Mediterranean*, ed. D. D. Gilmore [Washington, D.C.: American Anthropological Association, 1987], p. 43).

[16]See Cicero *Pro Murena* 12.27; Philo *Qui Omnis Probus Liber Sit* 117; *Hypothetica* 11.14-17; Josephus

versed with men laid themselves open to gossipers' complaints about their morality.[17] Traditional Romans regarded wives' speaking publicly with others' husbands as horrible behavior, reflecting possible flirtatious designs and subverting the moral order of the state.[18] By contrast, meekness and shyness in women were considered honorable.[19] First-century Romans, including many in Corinth, had generally become more tolerant, but enough traditional sentiments remained to create tension in the house-church setting, especially with various cultures present. (Corinth was officially Roman in this period, but Paul's writing in Greek and presupposing Jewish customs suggests a mixed church.)

Because women's public speech was sometimes shameful in Corinth, one cannot simply assume that Paul's claim that it is "shameful" for a woman to speak in the assembly (I Cor 14:35) is meant to be transcultural, any more than his earlier injunction to cover their heads (related to shame in I Cor 11:5-6) or his later one to greet with a holy kiss.[20] When applied to gender relations, "shameful" often involved a woman's reputation in sexual matters.[21] Conservative Greek culture, for example, regarded a wife's talking with a young man as "shameful" (the same Greek term).[22] While Paul challenges some social conventions of his day, he supports oth-

---

Antiquities of the Jews 1.49; 4.219; Craig S. Keener, "Marriage," in Dictionary of New Testament Background, ed. C. A. Evans and S. E. Porter (Downers Grove, Ill.: InterVarsity Press, 2000), p. 688.

[17]Theophrastus *Characters* 28.3—also if they (rather than a husband or porter) answer the door (this suggests they have a paramour; see Tibullus 1.2.7, 15-24, 41, 55-56).

[18]Livy *History of Rome* 34.2.9; 34.4.18. A more progressive speaker argues that this behavior is acceptable under some circumstances (34.5.7-10).

[19]E.g., Sophocles *Ajax* 293; Demosthenes *Against Meidias* 79; Valerius Maximus *Memorable Doings and Sayings* 7.1.1; Ecclesiasticus 22:5; 26:14; see further Keener, "Marriage," pp. 687-90.

[20]Liefeld ("Submission," pp. 140-42) finds here the idea of glory and disgrace, as in 11:7, related to decorum or "order" (cf. 12:23; 11:34; 14:40); he rightly notes that unnecessary social criticism could hinder the spread of Christianity. Speaking was "shameful" when inappropriate (e.g., in the case of a shameful speaker; Aeschines *Timarchus* 28-29).

[21]The designation *shameful* often applied to sexual immorality (e.g., Dionysius of Halicarnassus *Roman Antiquities* 1.78.5; Diodorus Siculus *Library of History* 5.55.6-7; 10.31.1; 12.15.2; 12.21.2; 32.10.9; 33.15.2; Christians would agree here), which was the opposite of appropriate womanly meekness (Arrian *Indica* 17.3), or to women being in male company (Diodorus Siculus *Library of History* 4.4.1; on women's relative seclusion in earlier traditional Greek society, see further Keener, "Head Coverings," p. 443). But some observed that not all cultures shared the same sense of shame on such matters (Arrian *Indica* 17.3; Diodorus Siculus *Library of History* 5.32.7). See further Paige, "Matrix," pp. 223-24 (also noting that Paul never applies such a designation to abuse of gifts, evaluating prophecy or other traditional proposals).

[22]E.g., Euripides *Electra* 343-44 (though there are two men). Liefeld, "Submission," p. 142, points out that Plutarch and Livy viewed it as disgraceful for women to "express themselves visually or vocally in public."

ers (including gender-related conventions like head coverings). Presumably he often does this for strategic reasons (especially where different passages in his writings offer different approaches, as they clearly do on women's roles; see e.g., Rom 16:1-2; I Cor 11:5; Phil 4:2-3).[23] A wife's behavior reflected on her husband's status, and certainly neither spouse should risk shaming the other (cf. I Cor 11:3-9; Prov 12:4; 31:23, 28).

Paul also has reason to be concerned for the church's reputation in the larger society (I Cor 6:6; 14:23), a concern that, incidentally, becomes all the more prominent in his later writings, often specifically concerning household relationships (I Tim 3:7; 5:14; 6:1; Tit 2:5, 10).[24] It seems likely that in I Corinthians 14:34-35 he supports the cultural expectation of honorable matrons' verbal self-restraint. Exceptions could be made, as they were even in pagan religion, for divinely inspired utterances, and perhaps Paul regarded freedom to pray in house church meetings as a nonnegotiable right of all believers (I Cor 11:4-5; cf. Judg 4:4).[25] But the general cultural expectation was dominant, and Paul is usually reticent to divide Christians over cultural or personal issues (cf. Rom 14:15; I Cor 8:9, 13; 9:12).

Ancient culture reflects this general expectation of women's restraint far more pervasively than the suggestion to which I now turn. Indeed, even on its own this general expectation in antiquity could explain Paul's prohibition. Nevertheless, the specific circumstances probably implied in the text suggest an additional problem (for which I argued in *Paul, Women and Wives*). The second possibility, therefore, is that some kinds of questions were considered inappropriate, particularly questions that revealed that the questioner had failed to master the topic sufficiently.[26] I sometimes compare this to students whose questions reveal that

---

[23]For Paul's strategic approach, see e.g., Craig S. Keener, "Paul: Subversive Conservative," *Christian History* 14, no. 3 (1995): 35-37.

[24]See Keener, *Paul, Women and Wives*, pp. 139-48; Alan Padgett, "The Pauline Rationale for Submission: Biblical Feminism and the *Hina* Clauses of Titus 2:1-10," *EvQ* 59 (1987): 39-52.

[25]Pagan Greco-Roman society also respected the speech of prophetesses. Most abundant are references to the inspiration of the mythical Sibyl (e.g., Ovid *Metamorphoses* 14.129-53; Virgil *Aeneid* 6.77-102; Juvenal *Satirae* 3.3; Heraclitus *Epistulae* 8; throughout *Sibylline Oracles*, and also in her historic successors in Diodorus Siculus *Bibliotheca historica* 4.66.6) and the historic Delphic priestess (e.g., Longinus *Sublime* 13.2; Callimachus *Hymn* 4.89-90; Valerius Maximus *Memorable Doings and Sayings* 1.8.10; Cicero *Divinatione* 1.36.79; Plutarch *Oracles at Delphi* 21, *Moralia* 404E; *Dialogue on Love* 16, *Moralia* 759B; Dio Chrysostom *Personal Appearance* 12; Pausanias *Description of Greece* 2.2.7).

[26]See e.g., Plutarch *Lectures* 18, *Moralia* 48AB; Diogenes Laertius *Lives of Eminent Philosophers* 7.1.19.

they have not done the assigned reading before class.

This suggestion, however, raises an issue: why would women be less likely to ask learned questions than men would? One could argue that this unlearned behavior reflects a transcultural, genetic limitation in women's ability to interpret Scripture. I have been a Bible professor of enough students of both genders over the years, however, to state unequivocally that such a claim is by empirical standards demonstrably false.[27]

More reasonably, women on average were less educated than men, an assertion that no one genuinely conversant with ancient literature would doubt. To be sure, one can collect examples of many educated women in antiquity (normally from wealthier families), but on average women were far less likely to be educated than men.[28] More to the point, even among the Jews and God-fearers who constituted the initial nucleus of the Corinthian congregation (Acts 18:4-5), women would have less opportunities than men for training in Scripture. Although they would learn alongside men in the synagogues, they lacked the special training that some of the men would have. More critically here, whereas most Jewish boys were taught to recite Torah growing up, the same was not true for Jewish girls.[29] Teachers and primary questioners in the house churches probably were mostly men who had been part of the synagogue.[30]

That Paul appeals to the law as confirming his case raises the question of what statement in biblical law he may have in mind (1 Cor 14:34). Paul cites the law as teaching that women or wives should submit themselves (presumably to their husbands) and possibly also that it enjoins their silence. Josephus seems to have understood the law in the same way, though as part of his apologetic appeal to the

---

Plutarch's essay is the best source for the conduct of lectures in this period. Distracting others from a lecture by one's conversation was also considered rude (Plutarch *Lectures* 13, *Moralia* 45D). Concerning silence for novices, see e.g., the extreme example of the Pythagoreans in Seneca *Epistles to Lucilius* 52:10; Aulus Gellius *Attic Nights* 1.9.3-4; Philostratus *Vita Apollonii* 1.1.

[27]Scientific studies would also undermine this claim; see Mary Stewart Van Leeuwen, *Gender and Grace: Love, Work and Parenting in a Changing World* (Downers Grove, Ill.: InterVarsity Press, 1990), pp. 75-105; also note the averages in Gregg Johnson, "The Biological Basis for Gender-Specific Behavior," in *RBMW*, p. 290.

[28]See e.g., Forbes, *Prophecy*, p. 277; James S. Jeffers, *The Greco-Roman World of the New Testament* (Downers Grove, Ill.: InterVarsity Press, 1999), pp. 249, 255-56.

[29]See e.g., Keener, *Paul, Women and Wives*, pp. 83-84; for women and the law in general, cf., e.g., Josephus *Antiquities of the Jews* 4.219; *Mishnah Avot* 5:21; *Hagigah* 1:1; *Sukkah* 2:8; *Tosefta Berakhot* 6:18; *Babylonian Talmud Qiddushin* 34a.

[30]Ancient writers could state general rules with the understanding that these sometimes permitted specific exceptions (see Quintilian *The Orator's Education* 7.6.5; Craig S. Keener, *And Marries Another* [Peabody, Mass.: Hendrickson, 1991], pp. 24-28).

broader Greco-Roman world.[31] What is surprising in light of this—problematic for all interpretations except the view that Paul did not write it—is that the law nowhere specifically commands either women's silence or their submission! Interpreters differ as to whether Paul appeals to a particular passage in the law, perhaps to the verdict at the Fall (Gen 3:16), or to the general status of women in the period treated in the Pentateuch (cf. 1 Pet 3:5). In either case, the texts *describe* women's subordination rather than prescribe it, and Paul could uphold the law to avoid offense (1 Cor 9:20).

Though inspired, biblical law worked within a broader cultural milieu and, like any civil law, limited sin rather than creating the kingdom ideal. Because it often represents concessions to human weakness enshrined in existing culture, very few would argue that it represents God's highest ideal (cf., e.g., Ex 21:21; Lev 19:20; Mk 10:5).[32]

Paul might well appeal to the creation order, as in 1 Corinthians 11:8-9 (though only those who press transculturally Paul's mandate concerning head coverings in this earlier chapter should press transculturally the claims of 1 Cor 14:34). But the creation narrative itself does not teach women's subordination, and when Paul appeals to the creation narrative, his appeals do not force us to read it this way, especially given his application of Scripture (including some texts related to the creation of man and woman) elsewhere in his writings.[33]

Assuming (as I do) that Paul would have known this, it seems easier to believe that he appeals to the law as allowing rather than mandating this situation. God challenged some aspects of ancient Near Eastern patriarchal tradition but nevertheless worked within patriarchal societies (cf. also 1 Pet 3:5-6), including the modified Greco-Roman patriarchalism of Paul's day. This hardly mandates the continuance of such structures today when the spirit of Paul's teaching militates against them, any more than we would maintain slavery today (e.g., Eph 6:5-9).

Paul's Solution

Rather than let the women learn by asking questions in the church, Paul admon-

---

[31]Josephus *Against Apion* 2.201.

[32]Cf. Keener, *Paul, Women and Wives*, pp. 188-93. All students of the Old Testament are familiar with the repetition of many of the categories of casuistic law found in earlier Mesopotamian legal collections.

[33]See in much more detail in Keener, "Women in Ministry," pp. 58-63; Joy Elasky Fleming, "A Rhetorical Analysis of Genesis 2-3 with Implications for a Theology of Man and Woman," Ph.D. diss., University of Strasbourg, 1987. See also chapter four in this volume.

ishes them to ask their husbands at home. From what we know of the culture, most of the women would have been married, and most such statements can address the general group without denying the existence of exceptions.[34]

To most modern ears this proposal sounds sexist, but if we read Paul less anachronistically, in his own social context it would have helped the women as well as establishing order. Paul implicitly makes husbands responsible for their wives' tutoring, but Plutarch tells us that most men did not believe that their wives could learn anything. (This would be especially true of Greek men, who on average were a decade or more older than their wives.) Plutarch regards himself as one of the most progressive voices of his day because he instructs a young man to take an interest in his wife's education—though Plutarch goes on to note that this is necessary because if left to themselves women produce only base passions and folly.[35] Happily, Paul's concern for women's private tutoring does not cite such grounds!

Paul avoids social impropriety by advising the women to avoid questioning other men during the Christian education component of the gathering, but he is not against their learning. Yet as noted above, their lack of learning may have been precisely part of the problem. With greater understanding, they might become better able to articulate themselves intellectually in the same assemblies in which they could pray and prophesy. Viewed in this light, the real issues are not gender but propriety and learning—neither of which need restrain women's voices in the church today.

Conclusion

Scholars have read this passage from various angles. Most likely the passage addresses disruptive questions in an environment where silence was expected of new learners—which most women were. It also addresses a broader social context in which women were expected not to speak much with men to whom they were not related, as a matter of propriety. Paul thus upholds church order and avoids appearances of social impropriety; he also supports learning before speaking. None of these principles prohibit women in very different cultural settings from speaking God's word.

---

[34]For the married status of most women, see Keener, *And Marries Another,* pp. 68-74, and "Marriage," 680-81; for general statements allowing exceptions, see *And Marries Another,* pp. 24-28.

[35]Plutarch *Advice to Bride and Groom* 48, *Moralia* 145BE. Earlier, cf. similarly Xenophon *Oeconomicus* 3.10-16; 7.4-5, 10-22; 9.1.

10

MALE AND FEMALE
IN THE NEW CREATION

Galatians 3:26-29

Gordon D. Fee

Toward the end of his argument that Jew and Gentile form one people of God
on the common ground of "faith in Christ Jesus,"[1] Paul applies what he has argued
thus far to the present circumstances of the Galatian believers:

> So in Christ Jesus you are all children of God through faith, for all of you who were
> baptized into Christ have clothed yourselves with Christ. There is neither Jew nor
> Greek, neither slave nor free, neither male nor female, for you are all one in Christ
> Jesus. If you belong to Christ, then you are Abraham's seed, and heirs according to
> the promise. (Gal 3:26-29)

At issue in the debate about gender equality in this passage[2] is the scope of the
unexpected elaboration in Galatians 3:28 of the "all of you" in Galatians 3:27. Is
the equality, or oneness, of the three pairs—Jew and Greek, slave and free, male and
female—to be limited to the justifying work of Christ alone, or does it include
other aspects of life in the believing community as well? Or is it possible that put-

---

[1]My reasons for following the historic tradition regarding this phrase can be found in Gordon D. Fee,
Paul's Letter to the Philippians (Grand Rapids, Mich.: Eerdmans, 1995), p. 325. In any case, the ultimate
predicate is God's grace, not our faith (see Eph 2:8).

[2]Since I was raised in a home and church where gifting took precedence over roles, I find the present
debate over equality, complementarity and hierarchy to be something of a retrogression. My father
was a pastor and also gave general leadership to the home; yet it was clear that he and my gifted
mother were always in it together. Moreover, gifted women preached and taught in our church, and
no one objected. Thus it is difficult for me to engage a passage like this from the perspective of an
ideological controversy. Nevertheless, what Paul is saying about the people of God has much broader
implications that need to be explored. Getting at Paul's own purposes is the key exegetical issue.

ting the question this way already exhibits prejudice toward the text one way or the other, since this question does not seem to rise immediately out of the text of Galatians itself?

But a key exegetical question, seldom noted, does beg to be answered: Why does Paul add the second and third pair at all in an argument that otherwise has to do only with Jew and Gentile? And especially, why the addition of the third pair—with its formulation "male and female," not "man and woman" (which could mean "husband and wife")—since in similar moments elsewhere (1 Cor 12:13 [cf. 7:17-24]; Col 3:10) this pairing is not included?

The pursuit of this basic exegetical question should give us some insight into the nature and scope of the "newness" Paul sees as available in the new creation. But to get there, we must first examine the argument of Galatians as a whole and of Galatians 3:1–4:7 in particular.

At Issue in Galatians: Jew and Gentile as One People of God

Most agree on the nature of the crisis in Galatia: that Jewish Christian "agitators" (Gal 1:7; 5:10) had infiltrated these Gentile churches insisting that the men be circumcised (see Gal 6:12; cf. 2:3-5; 5:2-3)—the crucial item of a larger agenda of Torah observance that would have included the sabbath and food laws as well (Gal 4:10-11; 2:11-14). Galatians is Paul's response to this crisis.

But there is less agreement regarding a strategy for reading Paul's response. Traditionally it has been to read it through the eyes of Martin Luther.[3] The starting point here is the so-called *propositio* of Galatians 2:15-16, where three times in one sentence Paul asserts negatively that justification is not "by works of law," and three times positively, "but by faith in Christ Jesus." So what drives Galatians is framed in terms of whether people are justified by faith or by works.

But this appears to be a slightly skewed reading strategy. Not only does it leave too much of Galatians unaccounted for—especially the central role the Spirit plays in the argument—but it also tends to focus on the individual believer's relationship with God rather than on Paul's primary concern: *the people of God* as such. This is not to negate the central role of "justification by faith"; rather this phrase simply does not provide an adequate strategy for reading Galatians as a whole. After all, this terminology is missing altogether from Paul's "defense" with which the letter be-

---

[3]Advocated, for example, by R. Y. K. Fung, *The Epistle to the Galatians* (Grand Rapids, Mich.: Eerdmans, 1988); cf. S. L. Johnson Jr., "Role Distinctions in the Church: Galatians 3:28," in *RBMW,* pp. 154-64.

gins (Gal 1:10–2:14) and from Galatians 4, where the first biblical-theological argument is brought to conclusion (Gal 4:1-7) and the second one is given *in toto* (Gal 4:21-31).

At issue, rather, for Paul is the passion of his life and calling: Jew and Gentile as one people of God in Christ Jesus. For him the crisis has to do with whether Gentiles get in on the promise to Abraham (Gen 12:2-3; cf. Gal 3:14) without also taking on Jewish identity, especially those marks of identity that specifically distinguished Jews from Gentiles in the Diaspora (circumcision, sabbath and food laws[4]). To put that in a more theological way, the driving issue in Galatians is not first of all soteriology but ecclesiology:[5] who constitute the people of God in the new creation brought about by the "scandal of the cross" (Gal 6:11-16)?

Here is where the crucial issue of "justification by faith" comes into the picture. It is through the work of Christ and the gift of the Spirit that the ground has been leveled, so that Jews have no advantage over Gentiles or vice versa. Thus the argument of the letter finally concludes on this very important note based on the "scandal of the cross": that "neither circumcision [= being Jewish] nor uncircumcision [= being Gentile] means anything; what counts is a new creation" (Gal 6:15).[6]

That *Jew and Gentile as one people of God* is the driving issue in Galatians is made clear by the way the several arguments are worked out, especially Paul's "defense" (Gal 1:10–2:14) and the two central arguments from Scripture in Galatians 3:1–4:7 and 4:21-31.

What emerge in Paul's defense regarding the "truth of the gospel" (Gal 2:5, 14) are not terms like *justification, faith* or *works of law.* Rather the overriding concern is for Gentile inclusion in the people of God. Thus in part one of Paul's defense (Gal 1:13-24), where he asserts his nondependence on Jerusalem for his gospel and apostleship, he refers to his calling in terms of God's revealing "his Son *in me* so that I might *preach him among the Gentiles*" (Gal 1:16). In part two (Gal 2:1-10), where he relates his first visit to Jerusalem for the purpose of discussing his understanding of the gospel, the narrative focuses on his role in the Gentile mission (Gal 2:2-9),

---

[4]Circumcision was the chief distinguishing mark and the chief reason for Gentile men remaining "God-fearers" without becoming full proselytes. See Galatians 2:3-5; 5:3-5, 11; 6:12-15; for the "observance of days" see Galatians 4:8-11; for food laws see Galatians 2:11-14.

[5]In its proper sense, referring to our understanding of the people of God as such, not church order and function.

[6]Cf. the earlier expression of this dictum in Galatians 5:6, where the concern was ethical ("faith expressing itself through love"), and the still earlier 1 Corinthians 7:19, where Paul negates change of status as a value for those who live in the new creation.

not on the content of the gospel as such. And so also in part three (Gal 2:11-14), where he recounts the disagreement in Antioch over table fellowship, which has altogether to do with the inclusion of Gentiles as full and equal members of the people of God (see especially Gal 2:14).

In the same way, the argument that justification is "by faith" and therefore "law-free" (Gal 3:1–4:7) focuses on the place of the Gentiles in God's new economy. Paul begins with the Galatians' (as uncircumcised Gentiles) own past and present experience of the Spirit (Gal 3:1-6), since the Spirit is the new identity marker over against circumcision or any other form of Torah observance. Here is where "by faith" comes into the argument: their new constitution as the people of the Spirit came as a gift, by "faith" and not by "observing the law." Paul concludes (Gal 3:6) by appealing to Abraham as both the paradigm and the "father" of all who live by faith.[7]

The rest of this argument (Gal 3:7–4:7) then takes up the question, who are Abraham's true "seed" and thus "heirs" of the promise? Paul's answer begins with the assertion that "Scripture foresaw that God would justify the Gentiles by faith" (Gal 3:8), which is immediately picked up in terms of the Abrahamic covenant (Gen 12:3) that "all nations [Gentiles] will be blessed through you." He then contrasts life based on faith, like Abraham's (Gal 3:7-9), with life based on works of law (Gal 3:10-12), pointing out on the basis of two Old Testament texts (Hab 2:4; Lev 18:5) that these are incompatible options (that is, one cannot just *add* circumcision to faith). Those who would "live" must do so by faith alone; those who would keep the law must "live" by "observing the law," which thus excludes living by faith. This part of the argument is then brought to a momentary conclusion in Galatians 3:14: "He redeemed us in order that the blessing given to Abraham might *come to the Gentiles* through Christ Jesus [Abraham's true 'seed'], so that by faith we might receive *the promise of the Spirit*."[8]

After arguing in two different ways for the temporary, thus secondary, nature of the law (Gal 3:15-18, 19-22), Paul wraps up this first biblical-theological argu-

---

[7] Because Paul never starts an independent clause with the comparative *kathōs*, the TNIV rightly has included Galatians 3:6 as the conclusion of Galatians 3:1-5. Thus the argument from the Galatians' *experience* of the Spirit, expressed in a series of rhetorical questions (Galatians 3:2-5), concludes with this intertextual appeal to Genesis 15:6, setting the next part of the argument in motion.

[8] The "we" in this concluding sentence refers to Jew and Gentile alike, since Christ died to remove the curse of having to live by law (an especially Jewish reality), when in fact life comes only through faith (Gal 3:10-14).

ment with two concluding paragraphs (Gal 3:23-29; 4:1-7), which together focus on the primary question, who are Abraham's true heirs? His answer: those who are God's "sons" through God's Son, both Jew and Gentile alike. Our text is the main point of the first of these two conclusions. Appealing to the believers' common baptism (reflecting the new creation theology of Romans 6:1-11), in which they have "clothed themselves with Christ," Abraham's true "seed" (Gal 3:15-18), Paul points out the logical result: since *all* are now "children of God through faith" and *all* who have been baptized are thus clothed with Christ, there is therefore "neither Jew nor Greek, . . . for you are *all one in Christ Jesus*" (Gal 3:28). This, at least, is where the argument has been heading and where it will go from here.[9]

But in fact Paul says more than this, and it is the "more than" that should catch our attention; for what is at stake is not simply the soteriological question of *how* people are saved, whether it is by faith or by works of law. The final clause in Galatians 3:28 makes this clear. Paul's explanatory "for" does not elaborate that all are *equally justified* in God's sight through faith in Christ Jesus but rather that all *constitute one people* (form one body) by their equal standing in Christ. After all, those involved in the struggle in Galatia are already "saved." What is at stake is ecclesiology: who constitute the *people of God* under the new covenant of Christ and the Spirit, and *on what grounds* are they constituted? Paul's answer: (1) Jew and Gentile together form the one people of God, (2) on the grounds of their common trust in Christ and reception of the Spirit.[10]

This is precisely why here alone in Galatians Paul adds the otherwise extraneous "neither slave nor free, neither male nor female." These pairs are *not* inherent in an argument about "justification by faith," but they are crucial to Paul's understanding of the people of God as being newly constituted by Christ and the Spirit. For these three pairs represent the primary ways people were divided/separated from each other in the structures of the present age that was now passing away (1 Cor 7:31; cf. 1 Cor 2:6): on the basis of race, social standing and gender. But "in Christ Jesus," Paul asserts, these categories have lost their structural significance and rele-

---

[9]It is instructive that the final conclusion (Gal 4:1-7) does not mention faith at all; rather it concludes on the matter of "sonship" and "heirs" (= Abraham's true seed as God's children).

[10]The second biblical-theological argument (Gal 4:21-31) further supports this reading strategy, where again there is no mention of "justification by faith." At issue now is the identity of the true children of Sarah, that is, "children of promise" (Gal 4:23, 28). The answer: those who are "born by the power of the Spirit" (Gal 4:29), which again has to do with Gentile inclusion, as the whole argument makes clear.

vance;[11] that is, these very things that keep people distanced from or at odds with each other in a fallen world have been relativized in the body of Christ, where not only Jew and Greek but also masters and slaves, men and women, all form that one body together.

Therefore the ultimate exegetical question that arises in Galatians 3:26-29 is, where did Paul come by this radically new understanding of equality "in Christ"?

Galatians 3:28 and New Creation Theology

Another surprising moment in this passage is Paul's use of baptismal language in Galatians 3:27, language belonging to a much larger theological framework. For at the heart of Paul's own calling and mission is a conviction that Christ and the Spirit have ushered in God's promised "new creation," which is now awaiting its final eschatological consummation (Gal 6:15). Deeply embedded in this perspective is the inclusion of Gentiles, which goes back to the Abrahamic covenant, and in the prophetic tradition came to be associated with the eschatological "new order" that God would someday establish.[12] Paul understood his role as apostle to the Gentiles to be in keeping with this eschatological hope that was in process of fulfillment.[13] Gentile inclusion in the one people of God was now made possible through the death of Christ and the gift of the eschatological Spirit. Thus Jew and Gentile are mutually related to God on the same grounds with a mutual identity in God's new creation.

New creation theology is articulated in two ways by Paul. First, in the key passage (2 Cor 5:14-17) Paul is arguing again (cf. 1 Cor 1:18–4:21) for both his gos-

---

[11]There are some inherent tensions regarding the three pairs, in that over against ethnicity and social standing, gender belongs to the created order as something ordained by God and therefore good. To be human is to be either male or female. So while it is true that value and identity based on gender, especially with regard to societal structures and roles, are now a thing of the past for the people of God, that is not true of ontological essence. In ways that one will not always be "Jew or Gentile, slave or free," one will always be male or female. The new humanity, after all, is grounded in the humanity of Jesus Christ, so that the distinctions between male and female remain just that—distinctions, diverse yet essential ways of being human. Our present unity in diversity as human beings is not lost, precisely because this diversity is essential to our being human; thus at one and the same time it equally matters and does not matter in terms of final reality. What Paul is therefore leveling here are the values and structural norms imposed on these distinctions.

[12]E.g., see Isaiah 2:1-5; 25:6-8; 51:4; 66:19-21; Micah 4:2-5; Zechariah 14:16.

[13]E.g., see how the argument of Romans ends with the eschatological inclusion of the Gentiles with Jews as one people of God as its main point (Rom 15:1-13), which is immediately followed by an explanation of Paul's role in this reality (Rom 15:14-21).

pel of a crucified Messiah and his own cruciform apostleship. He asserts that the new creation brought about by Christ's death and resurrection nullifies viewing anyone/anything from the "old age" perspective (Greek *kata sarka*, "according to the flesh"). Why? Because Christ's death has brought the whole human race under the sentence of death (2 Cor 5:14), so that those who live in God's new order do so for the One who died for them and was raised again (2 Cor 5:15). Thus being "in Christ" means belonging to the new creation: the old has gone, the new has come (2 Cor 5:17). This radical, new-order point of view—resurrection life marked by the cross—lies at the heart of everything Paul thinks and does (cf. Phil 3:4-14).

Second, this leads to a series of texts in which Paul picks up "second exodus" imagery from Isaiah 40–66: God is about to do a "new thing" (Is 43:18-19) and in the end will establish a "new heavens and a new earth" (Is 65:17; 66:22-23). In Paul's writings this theme is applied to believers, who through association with Christ's death and resurrection have themselves experienced death and being raised to newness of life (Rom 6:1-14; 7:4-6; Eph 4:20-24; Col 3:1-11). Common to these texts, either explicitly (Rom 6:1-14) or implicitly (e.g., cf. Col 3:1-11 with 2:9-12), is an association with Christian baptism. Colossians 3:1-11 is especially noteworthy, since it concludes: "Here there is no Greek or Jew, circumcised or uncircumcised, barbarian, Scythian, slave or free, but Christ is all, and is in all." That is, in the new order already set in motion through Christ's death and resurrection the value-based distinctions between people—ethnicity and status—no longer maintain.

The thematic resonance of Galatians 3:26-29 with these texts—especially the baptismal presuppositions of Romans 6:1-14—seems unmistakable. Thus Paul concludes Galatians by deliberately negating both circumcision (= being Jewish) and uncircumcision (= being Gentile) as having value because "the new creation" is now in place (Rom 6:15). This does not refer to a "new creature" at the individual level, true as that might be, but to a world made new as promised in Isaiah 65–66. After all, it is the corporate nature of the new creation that is emphasized in our text ("for you are all one in Christ Jesus").

Thus what is in view here is not the individual believer's being "justified by faith in Christ Jesus" but that those who have had such faith, and have expressed it in Christian baptism, have been joined to one another as a new body that is to live the life of the future in their present circumstances, whether Jew or Greek, slave or free, male or female. It is this all-encompassing eschatological reality of "the new order," in which all these diverse expressions of being human are made one, that lies behind the remarkable addition of "slave nor free, . . . male nor female" to "Jew nor Greek."

The Implications of New Creation Theology

Our difficulty with this text in relation to the "gender question" is how we are to understand some inherent ambiguities in the way Paul addresses issues in his churches where God's diverse, but one, people live out their "already/not yet" eschatological existence in a social context. The key lies in two places.

I. One must begin by taking Paul seriously with regard to ethnicity, status and gender no longer being relevant for constituting value and social identity in the new creation—especially in light of his thrice-repeated "neither circumcision nor uncircumcision has any value" (Gal 5:6; 6:15; cf. I Cor 7:19). That is, even though the categories themselves still function in the present, their significance in terms of old-age values has been abolished by Christ and the Spirit. Each of Paul's readers would have been some combination of the three (e.g., a Jewish free woman or a Gentile male slave). But in the new creation none of this counts in terms of significance or value; so even though they continue to live in old age sociological contexts, they do so under a new set of rules. The Jewish free woman is now "Christ's slave," the Gentile male slave is "Christ's freedman" (I Cor 7:19-24). The sociological categories count for nothing; how one lives within the categories counts for everything.

The difficulty for most contemporary Christians is in understanding the truly radical nature of Paul's assertion in Galatians 3:28, a difficulty that has two dimensions. First, Paul's eschatological, new creation framework (the future as "already but not yet"), which was the *primary* way the earliest believers understood their existence, is quite foreign to us. Second, the culture of the Westernized world is equally foreign to that of these early believers at fundamental points. For them position and status prevailed in every way,[14] identifying and circumscribing their existence, giving advantage to some over others with little chance that the disadvantaged might change their status.

Thus Gentiles had all the advantages over Jews, so Jews took refuge in their relationship with God, which they believed advantaged them before God over the Gentiles. Hatred was deep and mutual. Likewise, masters and slaves were consigned

---

[14]Regretfully, this is still true for some in the West, especially for many nonwhite males and many women.

to roles where power and authority went to masters.[15] The same was true for men and women, especially in the household, where women were subordinated in every way to their husbands as "master of the household." A typical marriage was established by contract, not based on love, and was usually between a man of about thirty and a teenage girl who went straight from her father's household to his and therefore came under his protection and instruction. A householder's wife existed primarily for two purposes: providing a legitimate heir and managing certain aspects of the household. So unenviable was her station (and therefore her person) that according to Diogenes Laertius, Socrates used to say every day that "there were three blessings for which he was grateful to Fortune: first, that I was born a human being, and not one of the brutes; next that I was born a man and not a woman; thirdly, a Greek and not a barbarian."[16] This obviously influenced the famous rabbinical prayer "Blessed are you, O God, . . . that I'm not a brute creature, nor a Gentile, nor a woman."[17]

It is difficult for us to imagine the effect of Paul's words in Galatians 3:28 in a culture where position and status preserved order through basically uncrossable boundaries, and where attempting to cross those boundaries brought shame instead of honor (the one core value of the culture).[18] Paul asserts that in the fellowship of Christ Jesus significance and status no longer lie with being Jew or Greek, slave or free, male or female. The all-embracing nature of this affirmation, its countercultural significance, the fact that it equally *disadvantages* all by equally *advantaging* all—these stab at the very heart of a culture sustained by people's maintaining the right position and status. But in Christ Jesus, the One whose death and resurrection inaugurated the new creation, all things have become new; the new era has dawned.[19]

2. But precisely because Paul still lived eschatologically in a world in which

---

[15]This is one place, it should be pointed out, where change could take place in that culture, because slavery was not based on race as in the tragic history of the United States. Because it was based primarily on war or economics, people could change status: people could sell themselves into slavery, and masters often manumitted slaves. Paul himself addresses this matter in I Corinthians 7:20-24.

[16]Diogenes Laertius *Lives of Eminent Philosophers* 1.33 (LCL). It should not surprise us therefore that female babies were often "exposed," thrown away on trash heaps.

[17]*Menahot* 43b (Epstein translation).

[18]See David A. deSilva, *Honor, Patronage, Kinship and Purity: Unlocking New Testament Culture* (Downers Grove, Ill.: InterVarsity Press, 2000), pp. 23-42.

[19]It should also be pointed out, however, that the consummation of the new era inaugurated by Christ, which will bring an end to "Jew and Gentile, slave and free," will not do the same for male and female. See note 11 above.

honor and shame were the primary values, he also reflects a degree of ambivalence toward cultural structures and norms. On the one hand, the fact that early believers followed a "crucified Messiah" (the ultimate oxymoron for both Jew and Greek) meant they aligned themselves with a religious sect whose founder had experienced ultimate shame (hence Paul's saying to the basically Gentile congregations at the heart of the empire that the gospel is not a matter of shame for him [Rom 1:16]). To follow Christ and thus experience cultural shame and isolation were not negotiables for Paul; this is the way God had chosen (through the foolish things of the world) to bring the present order to an end (the point of the argument in I Cor 1:18–2:5).

On the other hand, precisely because the present age is in the process of passing away, and because cultural shame was at the very heart of the Christian gospel, Paul was quite ready to yield on certain cultural matters so as not to predicate the shame on lesser things.[20] Thus one should hardly expect him to tinker with roles and structures in a world that is on its way out. Though he recognizes their existence, he does not argue (except in the case of government in general, Rom 13:1-7) that they are divinely ordained. Rather, since Christ and the Spirit have already pronounced death on the old order, one can live as Christ's servant regardless of ethnicity or status (I Cor 7:17-24). But Paul will not give *significance* to these fundamental irrelevancies, in either direction.

This relativizing of old age structures is why Paul can say in another setting, "Stay as you are" (I Cor 7). Where the Corinthians were making change itself a matter of religious value, Paul insists that status neither advantages nor disadvantages one in the body of Christ.[21] At the same time, he runs roughshod over cultural norms by insisting that the sexual union between husband and wife was no longer a matter of the husband's having it his way. To the contrary, in Christian marriage the wife has "mastery/authority" over her husband's body in a way that is equal to his (I Cor 7:3-4). Indeed, the mutuality argued for in I Corinthians 7:1-16 stands all by itself in the literature of the ancient world. For Paul the structures as such are irrelevant because "this world in its present form is passing away" (I Cor 7:31).

Thus regarding the societal implications of his new creation theology, it looks as if Paul were full of ambiguity; but I think not. Rather, he is altogether consistent

---

[20]Cf. Paul's argument on the basis of cultural shame over the matter of head coverings in the assembly in I Corinthians 11:2-16, esp. I Corinthians 11:4-6 and 13. See chapter eight in this book.

[21]On this whole question see Gordon D. Fee, *Commentary on Paul's First Letter to the Corinthians*, NICNT (Grand Rapids, Mich.: Eerdmans, 1987), pp. 307-9.

with his dictum that "neither circumcision nor uncircumcision counts for a thing, but the new creation." Always for him the issue itself (circumcision or food, for example) is irrelevant: Jews and Gentiles may do as they wish. But when someone makes a religious issue of it one way or the other, then he comes out fighting.

The easiest place to see this at work is at table, a matter addressed first in I Corinthians[22] and deeply embedded in the argument of Galatians. Indeed, besides circumcision this is the only specific issue related to "justification by faith for Jew and Gentile alike" that is discussed in Galatians (Gal 2:11-14)—a sure indication that the focus of this letter is primarily ecclesiological. It seems clear on the basis of Galatians 2:14 that in the (house) churches in Antioch, Jews and Gentiles shared community meals where Jewish dietary laws were not observed. But after "certain people came from James," Peter and Barnabas "began to draw back and separate" themselves from such Gentile tables, incurring condemnation and public disgrace from Paul for their actions.

But might they not have argued that they were following Paul's own example? After all, in I Corinthians 9:19-23 he affirms that when eating with Jews, he is *as* a Jew, and when with Gentiles, *as* a Gentile—all of this in order that he "might win some." So what makes Peter's action in Antioch bring forth fighting words? The answer lies with Paul's deeply embedded new creation worldview. Kosher means nothing in the new creation; therefore Jews may continue to live as Jews and Gentiles as Gentiles in the privacy of their own homes. But when Jewish believers insist on kosher meals in the setting of the community of faith, they are giving *significance* to kosher, which is precisely what has been abrogated through Christ and the Spirit.

This is also how Paul views the wealthy Corinthian householders who abuse others at the Lord's Table (I Cor 11:17-34). "Don't you have homes to eat and drink in?" he asks, assuming that old practices may remain in private meals (from which slaves and [usually] wives and daughters were excluded). "Or do you despise the church of God by humiliating those who have nothing?" he goes on, making it clear that in the gathered community only "new creation" practices are welcome: thus husbands and wives, masters and slaves, Jew and Gentile all feast together in anticipation of the great final eschatological banquet.

---

[22]See I Corinthians 5:6-13, where the incestuous man is excluded from the table; I Corinthians 8:1-13 and 10:1-22, where believers are excluded from eating meals in the pagan temples; I Corinthians 9:19-23 and 10:23-31, where he establishes his own attitude toward eating meals in various settings; and I Corinthians 11:17-34, where he condemns the maintaining of distinctions based on status at the Lord's Table.

The reason for what may appear as duplicity in Paul is that in the ongoing expression of life in the old age such matters count for nothing—because Christ has changed the rules so drastically. But that is also why in the community of faith the old rules cannot be maintained; to do so would be to give them significance that in fact they no longer have.

This relaxed attitude toward roles and structures comes out equally clearly in Paul's use of family and household images for the church. Thus Paul urges that all are "brothers and sisters" because the Spirit of the Son has been sent into our hearts so that we now call God "Abba" in the language of the Son (Gal 4:6-7). So when Onesimus is returned to his owner Philemon, Paul delicately urges Philemon to take him back into the household to reassume his role as a slave. But with consummate spiritual wisdom he says far more, by adding: "no longer as a slave, but better than a slave, as a *dear brother*" (Philem 16). This does not abolish the system, but carried through by Philemon, it dismantles the significance given to it (and in this indirect way, of course, heads toward the dismantling of the system itself!).[23] But one should also note Onesimus's vulnerability in this matter. He could not secure a change of status or relationship; this depended on the grace of the gospel's having penetrated Philemon so that the slave could in practice become Christ's freedman and Philemon's "brother."

So where does that leave us with regard to "male and female"? In much the same place. The household codes in Colossians 3 and Ephesians 5 assume the structural norm (of the privileged few who had large households), where the husband, father and master are the same person—the patron (hopefully benevolent) of his wife, children and slaves.[24] But Paul radicalizes this norm in a countercultural way, by insisting that the believing husband *love* his wife—which had very little to do with marriage in that culture. Not only so, he further insists that he love her "as Christ loved the church and gave himself up for her" (Eph 5:25), putting the significance attached to the structures into jeopardy. In the new order husband and wife are first

---

[23]This Onesimus is very likely the same who became bishop of Ephesus; and even if this is not the case, we are not wrong as to the possibility of it. See Ignatius *Ephesians* 1.1-3: "In God's name, therefore, I received your large congregation in the person of Onesimus, your bishop in this world, a man whose love is beyond words. My prayer is that you should love him in the Spirit of Jesus Christ and all be like him. Blessed is he who gave you such a bishop. You deserved it."

[24]Benevolence was the more common reality, in part because it was in the householder's self-interest, in that the Greco-Roman household was not a haven of retreat but primarily a place of production (see Carolyn Osiek and David L. Balch, *Families in the New Testament World: Households and House Churches* [Louisville, Ky.: Westminster John Knox, 1997], p. 54).

of all brother and sister in Christ, thus radically altering the perspective, so that she is not simply a member of his household but is in *relationship* to him; they are members together of "one body."[25] As such, either may prophesy or teach (1 Cor 14:26)—which are matters of Spirit gifting, not gender—as long as some cultural norms that distinguish male and female were maintained (1 Cor 11:2-16).

At the same time the church itself is God's household; and in the practical outworking of the community of faith their corporate life was expressed in the context of individual households. It is reasonable to assume that the patron of a household gave leadership to the church that functioned in the context of that household; indeed, it is impossible to imagine that it could have been otherwise in Greco-Roman culture. So when the householder was a woman (e.g., Lydia, Nympha), we may rightly assume that, as in all other matters in her own household, she gave some measure of leadership to her house church. To think otherwise is to impose modern ideas on the Greco-Roman household, on the basis of a prior commitment to her (unprovable) subservient "role" in the church.

All of this to say that Paul was not overly concerned about roles and structures as such. The new creation had abolished eschatological significance for them, so that one could live cruciform in whatever structural role one was found. Paul did not sanctify the structures and roles, as though they had meaning in themselves; for the death and resurrection of Christ and the gift of the Spirit had brought an end to that possibility in terms of what it means to be in *God's* family/household.

Conclusions

So where does this bring us in conclusion to a discussion of Galatians 3:28—with its eye-catching addition of slave and free, male and female to the primary issue of Jew and Gentile? The answer lies first with the fact that both the argument of Galatians as a whole and the specifics of this passage itself indicate that this text has to do with Paul's ecclesiology: what it means to be the people of God under the new covenant brought about through Christ's death and the gift of the Spirit. Second, it lies with Paul's new creation theology embedded in this text, which sounds the death knell to the old order, even though its structures remained in the surrounding culture.

Paul's concerns regarding structures may appear ambiguous, but that is precisely

---

[25]To conclude otherwise forces one logically into the position of justifying slavery as a God-ordained structure for the present age, since the two household codes (Eph 5:21–6:9; Col 3:18–4:1) assume both realities in the same structure: the Greco-Roman household of the privileged. Those who advocate the continuation of male authority today have failed to address this problem adequately.

because of their ultimate irrelevance. Cultural structures simply exist—as the ways sociological groups maintain their identity and live within their comfort zones. In Paul's view, one can serve Christ well within such limits. What he disallows is giving *significance* to structures and roles as such. Because when one does this, the Jew will demand that the Gentile be circumcised, the husband will want his wife to be his servant, and Philemon can take Onesimus back only as a slave, not as a brother.

It seems arguable, therefore, that even though our text does not explicitly mention roles and structures, its new creation theological setting calls these into question in a most profound way. There is no biblical culture (in the sociological sense) that belongs to all human societies. And to give continuing *significance* to a male-authority viewpoint for men and women, whether at home or in the church, is to reject the new creation in favor of the norms of a fallen world.[26] It is to give a significance to being male that in the end usurps the work of the Spirit not only in the wife and her relationship to God but also in the church—the expression of the new order and new humanity that is already present, even while it is yet to be.

Indeed, on the basis of this text and its place in the argument of Galatians—where socialized distinctions between people in their relationship to God have been overcome by Christ and the Spirit—one must argue that the new creation has brought in the time when the Spirit's gifting (the Spirit who is responsible for ushering in the new order) should precede roles and structures, which are only a carryover from the old order that is passing away.[27]

And in the end, if it appears that too much is being made of ecclesiology beyond the obvious soteriological dimension of our text, one must remember that for Paul these cannot be easily separated. To be saved meant to become a member of Christ's body/family/household. It is therefore not without significance that the one specific illustration in Galatians of the distinction between Jew and Gentile besides circumcision had to do with eating together at a common meal (Gal 2:11-14). If the gospel does not take root here (with cultural forces against it on both sides, as they were with the place of slaves and women at table) then individualistic salvation would seem to count for little, if it counts for anything at all.

---

[26]This is especially true of the hierarchical position that the wife is dependent on her husband for her spiritual well-being, including a hierarchy of spiritual communication: Christ —> husband —> wife. In sharp contrast, Paul insists here that to be "one in Christ" (because in Christ there is neither Jew nor Greek, slave nor free, male nor female) means that each is individually baptized into the one body of Christ, so that all are mutually interdependent for life in the new order.

[27]See chapter fourteen in this volume.

11

MUTUAL LOVE AND
SUBMISSION IN MARRIAGE

Colossians 3:18-19 and Ephesians 5:21-33

I. Howard Marshall

Colossians and Ephesians both have a fairly clear division between the doctrinal and the practical. Colossians 3–4 expounds the conduct expected of those who have been "raised with Christ," and Ephesians 4–6 describes the "life worthy of the calling you have received" (Eph 4:1). Both conclude by addressing each of the two parties in the three main relationships in the ancient household: wives and husbands, children and fathers, slaves and masters (Col 3:18–4:1; Eph 5:21-6:9). In all cases Paul is dealing with Christian behavior, emphasizing both what is expected of Christians in their life "in the Lord" and what they are capable of doing through the power of the Spirit in their risen life with Christ. We shall place the two passages in their context and then consider each in turn.

The Household Tables and Their Interpretation Today

Greco-Roman "household tables" offer no precise parallels to the New Testament material, although the general pattern of giving teachings structured according to household roles, addressed to the same three pairs of people and inculcating recip-rocal duties, can be traced back to Aristotle.[1] The teaching requires wives, children and slaves to be submissive to, or to obey, husbands, parents and masters respectively; the latter are essentially told not to abuse their position of authority.

In Colossians, social duties appropriate in the first-century context are given a

---

[1]The secular forms do not include direct address to the "inferior" parties. For Paul, however, children and slaves are part of the household church and take their place alongside the other members.

Christian motivation.[2] The Christocentricity of the teaching to wives, children and slaves is notable (seven of the fourteen references to "the Lord" in Colossians appear in these nine verses). The behavior of husbands and fathers is motivated more pragmatically, although masters are reminded that they are answerable to their heavenly Lord. Their position of authority is simply assumed, because it was authorized by Roman law and social custom.[3] Thus they are not instructed to exercise authority; rather in so doing they are to show love[4] and not to treat wives harshly, to refrain from provoking children and to treat slaves justly and fairly.

Ephesians gives a considerably expanded form of the same teaching, with fuller biblical and theological backing. Wives are to be submissive to their husbands in the same way as the church is submissive to Christ; an analogy is drawn between the relation of the husband as head to the wife and the relation of Christ as head (and savior) to the church. The very brief "Husbands, love your wives and do not be harsh with them" in Colossians is expanded by an analogy with the love of Christ for the church, expressed in his self-giving for the church so as to sanctify it. Paul draws on the body metaphor already used in Ephesians 5:23 and develops it in a fresh way: as Christ loves his body, the church, so husbands should love their wives *as* their own bodies. A concluding summary reminds the husband to love his wife and the wife to respect her husband.

There is a concealed hermeneutical trap for readers of this instruction. Since much of it can be seen as still appropriate in the modern world, it is tempting to assume that whatever Paul says here should be applied without significant modification to our situation. In fact, adjustment to changed circumstances is required, as can be seen by a consideration of the material about children and slaves.

Children and parents. The instructions to parents and children appear to be commonsensical and Christian. The only practical way for responsible parents to cope with some of the problems of children as they progress through childhood and adolescence to adulthood and independence is to expect obedience; young children must do what parents require without always understanding why it makes sense to do it. They must also do what parents want rather than what they want where there is a clash of interests.

---

[2] The mention of masters and slaves indicates that the texts are concerned with wealthier households where the congregations would have met, rather than those of the poorer classes.

[3] Cf. P. T. O'Brien, *The Letter to the Ephesians*, PNTC (Grand Rapids, Mich.: Eerdmans, 1999), p. 419.

[4] If the command to love within the marriage relationship is not unique to Christianity, it is certainly not common in non-Christian writings.

Nevertheless, despite the appearance of following the letter of Scripture on this matter, we do in fact behave somewhat differently. One important question concerns the age at which children cease to be under the strict authority of their parents. In the modern world there is an ill-defined "coming of age" at which this happens. But in the ancient world this subordination continued to a more advanced age than would be natural for us. Today we would regard it as essential to teach children to develop independence of their parents and learn to make their own decisions wisely and "in the Lord."

Further, the father as patriarch had a much greater authority over sons and daughters than is the case today. A modern son or daughter can claim independence of parents in a way that is not contemplated in Paul's commandment, understood in its contemporary social setting.[5]

Most significant, there is no mention here of love between parents and children.

Slaves and masters. The instructions to slaves and masters similarly contain advice that could well be given to modern employees and employers or managers. Justice, fairness and avoidance of violence are self-evidently right. Doing one's work well and putting it in the context of work done for the Lord is appropriate whether one is working under contract for a wage or fee or working for a slave owner.

In this case, however, there is an even clearer shift in the modern setup. The way authority over workers is exercised was radically altered in the shift from slavery to employment. There are limits to the authority of employers and managers and to the ways their authority may be exercised. Strict legal codes must be observed, whereas the ancient slavemaster was in many (but not all) respects a law to himself.

There is also the development of trade unions and industrial tribunals; these institutions are not provided for or foreseen in the New Testament but are appropriate and necessary ways of settling disputes and safeguarding rights. A blanket command to "obey your earthly masters in everything" is emphatically not the complete solution to employment problems, even if it is balanced by "provide your slaves with what is right and fair." Something more is needed, in order that the meaning of "right and fair" may be correctly spelled out and so that proper practices may be enforced on sinful employers. Christians today would feel it a part of their Christian duty to help set up arbitration and conciliation procedures and to take part in them.

---

[5] P. T. O'Brien, *Colossians,* WBC (Waco, Tex.: Word, 1982), p. 224 (cf. *Letter to the Ephesians,* pp. 440-41), states that Paul here is probably addressing young children rather than those who are already grown up, but he offers no evidence for this assumption. For detail on children in the ancient world, see especially A. T. Lincoln, *Ephesians,* WBC (Dallas: Word, 1990), pp. 398-403.

Behind these changes lies a significant shift in the status of workers which is not spelled out in the New Testament.[6] Today Christian theologians recognize that slavery is not an acceptable form of relationship; it is rejected on the basis of larger biblical considerations having to do with the facts that all human beings are created in the image of God and that all human beings are potentially objects of redemption since Christ died for all.[7] All human beings may be regarded as brothers and sisters one to another, a relationship that is actualized (however imperfectly it may be realized) in the church and is potential for those outside the church. Such brotherhood clearly allows for contractual obligations being drawn up where one brother or sister may employ another, but it excludes the absolute power of one brother or sister over another that occurs in slavery.

Consequently, what is said here about masters and slaves is not the last word on the matter. A modern system of industrial relationships must draw its principles and practice from a wider consideration of scriptural teaching than simply these two (and other related) passages. The abolition of slavery has radically altered the way employment relationships are expressed; thus while the spirit of the instructions here can inspire our relationships, the actual practice of them will be very different.

Subjects and rulers. In related teaching in Romans, I Peter and elsewhere, people are commanded to obey their rulers as those authorized by God himself to rule in human society. This teaching presupposes what was in fact the normal situation for most people in New Testament times, the existence of an imposed monarchical or aristocratic system of one kind or another.[8] The New Testament teaching recognizes the realities of this situation and urges people to behave appropriately as obedient citizens: granted that the system may not be ideal and cannot be changed, make the best of it, and commend the gospel by the way you behave in fulfilling the obligations laid upon you.

However, most (Westernized) countries today have political systems in which, within the structures of democracy, we can vote out our rulers if they turn out to be incompetent or unjust or even if we simply want to see a change of personnel. In these new situations we put the New Testament passages about political subor-

---

[6] We can ignore here the category of the freedperson and the relationships between patrons and clients in the New Testament world.

[7] This point is valid whether Christ died literally "for all people" or "for all kinds of people."

[8] Although classical Greece thought of itself as "democratic," a huge proportion of the populace was permanently disfranchised.

dination and obedience into a wider perspective and recognize that the key elements in Romans 13 and elsewhere may be expressed differently in the different
conditions that now exist, and that political thinking can go beyond the parameters
that appear to exist there.

Implications. These three examples have shown that the specific biblical teaching
about behavior in these relationships contains much that can and should be practiced in the very different situations of today, where strict parental authority is limited to younger children,[9] there is no slavery, and democracy has replaced dictator-
ship. Yet we have also seen that (1) we modify in practice the specific ways we
follow out the principles in the teaching; (2) important aspects of behavior within
the relationships are not discussed here or elsewhere in specific terms in Scripture;
(3) the social structures assumed in these teachings may need to be changed and
replaced by something different.

In short, these passages do not tell the whole story about these sets of relationships;
they deal purely with limited aspects of them. In the cases of the family, employment
and politics, Paul assumes the existence of particular structures. But these structures
are not sacrosanct, and few would doubt that the changes to them have on the whole
been for the better. More important, absolutism and slavery are now recognized to be
forms of power/authority that sit uncomfortably with biblical teaching; and total authority of parents over older children would not be acceptable to Christians today. In
all three cases we live within different structures and recognize a need for change from
the first-century structures as a result of our continuing evaluation of society in the
light of the gospel. With changes in structures and relationships, there naturally come
changes in the kinds of behavior required of Christians in them. It would be very
strange if similar considerations did not apply in the case of marriage.

Wives and Husbands in Colossians

At first sight there is no problem in applying to modern readers the injunction to
husbands to love their wives and not to treat them harshly.[10] But what about the
requirement that wives be "submissive" to their husbands? Significantly, the term
obey (used for children and slaves) is not used here; nevertheless, for Paul's audience

---

[9]Older sons and daughters should respect their parents but are not expected to obey them "in everything."

[10]No specifically Christian backing is provided for this injunction, beyond the fact that it appears
within the context of a Christian ethic that inculcates love, forbearance and forgiveness to be shown
by all to all (Col 3:12-15).

there may not have been a lot of difference in practice between being submissive and being obedient.[11] The statement is "christianized" by the comment that this "is fitting in the Lord." In other words, this command flows out of the situation in which Christians stand under the authority of Christ as Lord and follow out his commands.[12] It is thus like the statements about subjection to the state (although, as we have seen, they do not necessarily legitimate absolute despotism as the only form of rule appropriate in the modern world).

The marital setup in the various societies in the ancient world was complex, and it is dangerous to generalize. There was certainly a tendency for a wife to be understood as her husband's "chattel," his possession, although this term was not actually used.[13] For example, a Jewish wife was guilty of adultery against her husband if she allowed another man to usurp her husband's marital rights over her, but if a husband had sexual relations with another woman he was not guilty of adultery against his wife. This one-sidedness arose because the wife was thought of as her husband's possession.

Jesus radically overturned this situation by his declaration that a husband who has relations with another woman commits adultery *against his own wife* (Mk 10:11). Furthermore, Paul states that husband and wife have sexual obligations to one another (1 Cor 7:3-4), not merely the wife to the husband. Peter puts the point even more strongly by talking of husband and wife as joint heirs of the grace of life (1 Pet 3:7). We have, then, in the New Testament the beginnings of the development of a different understanding of marriage in which a wife is not her husband's chattel, but they are mutually responsible partners.[14]

---

[11] Although Lincoln, *Ephesians,* pp. 367-68, 402, and Ernest Best, *A Critical and Exegetical Commentary on Ephesians* (Edinburgh: T & T Clark, 1998), p. 533, think that there is little or no difference between the verbs, it seems to me that there is a distinction. *Be submissive* is broader and conveys more than simply obeying specific commands; *obey* could have the effect of reducing the husband-wife relationship to a purely authoritarian one. *Obey* is used in this connection only in 1 Peter 3:6, and there only with reference to Sarah's relationship to Abraham.

[12] O'Brien, *Letter to the Ephesians,* p. 437, states that submission was called for "not because it was conventional for wives in Greco-Roman society, but because it was part and parcel of the way in which they were to serve their Lord." But this ignores the fact that the particular way they were to serve the Lord was constrained at least to some extent by social convention.

[13] L. W. Countryman, *Dirt, Greed and Sex* (London: SCM Press, 1989), pp. 147-67. See the carefully nuanced discussion in David A. deSilva, *Honor, Patronage, Kinship and Purity* (Downers Grove, Ill.: InterVarsity Press, 2000), pp. 178-93, 229-37.

[14] O'Brien is right to affirm that Paul's injunctions are given to wives as "ethically responsible partners" (*Colossians,* p. 220).

According to O'Brien, the language of "subordination" was not especially characteristic of Greek literature concerning marriage.[15] He seems to want to regard it as being rather a specifically Christian virtue here. Paul's teaching, we are told, does not rest on natural inferiority of any kind but is a call to voluntary assumption of a position grounded in a hierarchy laid down in the order of creation: "The Christian wife should recognize and accept her subordinate place in this hierarchy."[16] What O'Brien seems to be doing here (and throughout his expositions of both letters) is to try to base Paul's teaching here on a creation ordinance laid down in Genesis and to argue that Paul is inculcating Christian virtues that would be valid and appropriate even if they did not happen to fit in with the social conventions of his time. In this way O'Brien can maintain that Paul's teaching is not culture-bound but rests on theological principles. But there are problems!

Nowhere does O'Brien indicate precisely what such "submission" would entail in practice.[17] The reader is left with no guidance as to what the Christian wife today should actually do. Suppose, for example, that the wife has a husband who does not treat her with honor as the weaker sex (I Pet 3:7) and insists on intercourse when she is not disposed to it: is she to be submissive to his will if he forces himself on her? Or suppose that the husband is guilty of domestic violence: does she meekly forgive and put up with it? It would seem that there must be some limits set to wifely submission. It is obviously inadequate to say that the husband for his part must behave lovingly: what is the wife to do when he is *not* behaving lovingly?

Submission, then and now. Social conventions of the time, both Greco-Roman and Jewish, expected subordination from the wife.[18] The same husbandly attitudes would continue after conversion to Christian faith, and the same structures of marriage would be assumed.[19] An insubordinate wife was a bad witness for the gospel in a situation where non-Christian husbands expected subordination.

It may also be the case that some Christian wives were carrying their new freedom in Christ too far. Elsewhere Paul had affirmed that there is no longer "slave

---

[15]O'Brien, *Colossians*, pp. 221-22, holds that this motif is in fact rare in the secular literature. But although the actual term is only found in two passages, the motif is more widespread and was certainly found in Judaism (Lincoln, *Ephesians*, p. 367).

[16]O'Brien, *Colossians*, p. 222.

[17]See, however, G. W. Knight III, "The Family and the Church," in *RBMW,* pp. 345-57.

[18]Roman law upheld husbandly authority.

[19]Paul here (and especially in Ephesians) assumes a situation in which both husband and wife are believers, although he would presumably have given the same advice to partners in mixed marriages. See especially Best, *Critical and Exegetical Commentary*, pp. 525-27.

nor free, neither male nor female, for you are all one in Christ Jesus" (Gal 3:28),[20] and they may have been claiming a carry-over from their position in the congregation into the household.[21] This would have accentuated the problem faced by husbands who felt that the gospel was too radical in its social effects.

But in the Western world today expectations have changed. Many husbands and wives see one another as equal partners, and one-sided subordination of the wife to the husband is seen as inappropriate and is not demanded. Does Christian teaching to new converts require the imposition of a relationship of subordination that was previously not present?[22]

Here we must note the quite remarkable stress on wives being submissive "in everything" to their husbands which is found in the parallel passage in Ephesians (Eph 5:24; cf. Col 3:20 of children; 3:22, of slaves).[23] This would suggest that no area of a wife's life is outside the jurisdiction of her husband.[24] It is hard to believe that any modern Christian husband would take this in such a comprehensive manner so that he could (at least in theory) interfere in any aspect of her life.

All this suggests that adherence to the literal sense of what Paul says would produce a very odd understanding of what marriage is: a relationship in which a wife is basically a person controlled by her husband in every respect in the same way as children and slaves.

Indications that we must move beyond the "letter" of Paul's instructions. If we put together the instructions given by Paul to Christian wives and husbands, we have a combination of teachings that points us forward to a deeper understanding of marriage. The wife is submissive to her husband in that she has to follow out all the decisions that he makes; he for his part loves his wife and does nothing that could be regarded as harsh, which must surely mean that he will not make decisions that cause her pain or discomfort unless there is mutual agreement between them. This structure might be labeled "love-patriarchy." But once love is taken as seriously as that, it

---

[20] In Colossians 3:11, however, this crucial pairing is omitted.

[21] Some such emancipatory tendencies were probably an element in the situation faced in 1 Corinthians and in 1 Timothy 2; B. W. Winter, *After Paul Left Corinth: The Influence of Ethics and Social Change* (Grand Rapids, Mich.: Eerdmans, 2001), pp. 121-41; I. H. Marshall, *A Critical and Exegetical Commentary on the Pastoral Epistles* (Edinburgh: T & T Clark, 1999), p. 441.

[22] Presumably the contributors to *RBMW* wish to see this happen.

[23] Paul would certainly have excepted obedience that would clash with obedience to the Lord; cf. F. F. Bruce, *The Epistles to the Colossians, to Philemon and to the Ephesians* (Grand Rapids, Mich.: Eerdmans, 1984), p. 386 n. 89.

[24] Cf. Best, *Critical and Exegetical Commentary*, p. 538.

would seem to follow that the wife is, in fact, being treated as an equal partner, with her husband's decision being, in effect, hers as well.

Such a marriage relationship is different from the master-slave or the employer-employee relationship. An employer may discuss tasks with employees to get their points of view, but if there is a difference of opinion, the employer's decision is the determinative one. The contract lays down that in the last resort the employer decides what is to be done, and if the workers don't like it, in theory at least they can resign. Yet this is how hierarchicalists must see marriage: when the rubber hits the road, the husband must overrule the wife.[25]

But does this apply in areas where the wife may have expertise or insight that the husband lacks? Does it apply in areas where the wife will be put to considerable inconvenience or even self-sacrifice? The hierarchicalist will presumably say that the loving husband will take his wife's desires into consideration. But in the end he has the authority to command, and even if he is not a loving, considerate husband, the wife must still obey.

It is actually very difficult to see where a loving contemporary hierarchical husband would in practice insist on his way over against the will of his wife. I suspect that in fact many husbands who are hierarchicalists in theory are virtually egalitarians in practice.

What I have been arguing is that the actual *nature* of "submission" is not explained or dictated by the passage and that there are probably differences among different ages, cultures and individual situations. But above all, the command to husbands to love their wives and the fact that a wife is not a slave or a child indicate that something is silently happening to the nature of the relationship. From patriarchalism we have moved to love-patriarchalism, and the road is open to mutual love between brothers and sisters in Christ. This final step was not taken by Paul, any more than he took the step from accepting slavery to recognizing that his own teaching contained the seeds of its inevitable abolition, but this is the direction in which the evidence clearly points. Mutual love transcends submission.

Summing up so far. Several conclusions about the Colossians teachings can be stated briefly.

The teaching in Colossians is given in a situation where the wife was expected to be submissive to her husband. Paul sees, as he often does, the first line of Chris-

---

[25]Knight, "Family and the Church," pp. 349-50. This remains the case, although a loving Christian husband must show consideration for his wife (Wayne Grudem, "Wives like Sarah, and the Husbands Who Honor Them. 1 Peter 3:1-7," in *RBMW*, pp. 205-8).

tian duty to lie in doing what is expected within an existing setup: that the wife should be submissive.[26]

He balances this with a reminder to husbands that they must act in love—and that will certainly affect the way they express their authority. Paul assumes the structure of patriarchalism but qualifies it by propounding a love-patriarchalism.

Here he gives no theological foundation for this understanding of authority and submission in marriage.[27] We can therefore say that the basic qualities of loving and seeking to please one's partner upheld here can be carried over into a different structure of marriage and that in itself the passage does not require that Christians move back to a hierarchical view of marriage.[28] Love that cares for the partner, does not make unreasonable demands and is willing to endure sacrifice for the sake of the partner is paramount.[29]

The concept of marriage between equal partners is just beginning to be perceived in the New Testament, and Paul should not be expected to step outside his time and see the consequences of his teaching any more than he is to be faulted for not commanding the abolition of slavery or the development of universal suffrage.

Wives and Husbands in Ephesians

The argument is incomplete, however, until we also bring in the evidence of Ephesians. Does the fuller use of theological argument here strengthen my case, or does it constitute an objection to it? Does Paul's teaching not only require that people fulfill the requirements of the social structures in which they find themselves but also mandate these structures themselves? Or does Scripture itself lead us to adopt different structures from those prevalent in the first century—just as we have seen to be the case with children, slavery and government?

Mutual submission. Ephesians 5:18 contains an injunction to be filled with the

---

[26]The presupposition of these texts in Paul is that the householder is a believer (quite the opposite of the situation in I Peter 2:18–3:7). He would surely not countenance a believing wife's submitting to her husband's demands that she continue to honor the household gods.

[27]O'Brien (*Colossians*, pp. 222-23) does think that the wife's submission is "fitting in the Lord" because of the hierarchy established by the Lord at creation. But "fearing the Lord" is also brought in as a sanction in the case of the master-slave relationship, which is not a creation ordinance.

[28]To say this is emphatically not to imply that our contemporary structures of marriage (and equivalent relationships) should be taken over without a Christian critique. I am arguing for a *Christian* view of marriage here, not a secular one.

[29]Thus the duty of caring, at considerable personal cost, for a severely ill or handicapped spouse would be understood as an integral part of Christian marriage "in sickness and in health," even if Scripture does not explicitly say so.

Spirit, to which is attached a set of participial phrases, the last of which is "submitting to one another out of reverence for Christ" (see Eph 5:21). This in turn is expanded with a more particular reference to wives submitting to their husbands as to the Lord,[30] on the analogy of the church's submission to Christ, and to the obedience of children and slaves. The general command to submission is not particularized with reference to husbands, parents and masters. So the question arises whether the opening command is to be taken generally, of all Christians being mutually submissive to all other Christians,[31] or whether it simply means that some Christians—that is, all wives, children and slaves—should be actually submissive to those to whom they ought to be submissive.[32]

O'Brien argues for a purely one-directional submission in this verse.[33] He states that *hypotassomai* is used in the New Testament only of submission within ordered relationships, that is, only of persons being submissive to those who are over them in some recognized hierarchical relationship (citizens-government, church members-leaders, Christ-God the Father, servants-masters) and therefore it cannot be used of mutual relationships or weakened to refer simply to deference and courtesy to others.[34]

---

[30]Both the NRSV and TNIV treat this last participle as if it were a separate imperative introducing the new section. This obscures the fact that the verb is closely tied to what precedes so as to indicate a further aspect of the new behavior that is associated with being filled with the Spirit. In order to make the flow of thought smoother in English, they then repeat the verb in the specific injunction to wives.

[31]Bruce, *Epistles*, p. 384 n. 79.

[32]Clearly the specific submission required of wives is only to their own husbands; there is no suggestion of submission to other men. Accordingly, there is no prohibition here of a woman's exercising authority in the world at large, whether as a political ruler or in business. But this point was probably outside Paul's horizon.

[33]O'Brien, *Letter to the Ephesians*, pp. 398-405. There is some anticipation of these arguments and a response to them in Walter L. Liefeld, *Ephesians* (Downers Grove, Ill.: InterVarsity Press, 1997), pp. 140-41.

[34]He further argues that the reciprocal pronoun *allēlous* is not always used for "one another" but can simply mean "others." A careful examination of all the references that he cites does not establish the point. For example, Galatians 6:2 refers to bearing the burdens of each other as is appropriate, and 1 Corinthians 11:33 surely means loosely "you wait for me and I wait for you, whichever of us is there first."

Admittedly, the pronoun is regularly used of people's doing things to others who are also doing the same things to them, but without specifying that literally everybody does it to literally everybody else. "We talked to each other" clearly means "I said something to you and you said something to me." "They said to one another" suggests more loosely that an unspecified number of people in the group said something to others in the group, with the result that at least some people were both

Elsewhere, however, reciprocal duties are laid down for believers. The key passage in Paul is Galatians 5:13, where believers are to be *slaves* to one another (even stronger than "being submissive"!) in love. Similarly, in Philippians 2:3-4 they are to consider others better than themselves and to look to the interests of others (cf. Rom 12:10). If this is to be true of Christian relationships in general, it must surely include the marriage relationship. In John 13:14 the disciples are to wash one another's feet, and Jesus as Lord sets an example by doing this to his disciples. The collocation of a command to the younger to be submissive to the older members/ elders with a command that all are to put on humility toward one another in I Peter 5:5 indicates that it was possible to combine the general and the specific and offers a parallel to what is done here.

It follows that all believers should place themselves under other believers in this spirit of mutual humility, even if this is the only place where the verb *hypotassomai* is so used. Ephesians itself provides a context that inclines toward this interpretation in this particular verse: Paul uses the pronoun *allēlous* in Ephesians 4:2, 25, 32, thus establishing a presumption in favor of its use here for church members in general.[35]

What Paul is doing, then, is to teach the need for a concern for one another's interests and for a mutual submission in the church which provides a new context for the one-sided submission that was expected within certain relationships at that time.[36] He is doing something new, even startling, with the language here.

As in his teaching on the new relationship between Philemon and Onesimus as brothers both in the Lord and in the flesh, Paul has here enunciated a principle that calls into question the structures of the ancient world, although he himself proba-

---

speakers and hearers. But there is nothing in the usage to suggest that the people can be divided into distinct groups of those who spoke and heard. Similarly, it is highly unlikely that on hearing "Be subject to one another," some members of the congregation said, "But of course that doesn't apply to me, since I am a husband/father/master/church leader."

O'Brien also appeals to the flow of the argument, in which the general command to be submissive (to appropriate authorities) is then unpacked with specific reference to wives and husbands. This simply begs the question.

[35]Best, *Critical and Exegetical Commentary*, pp. 515-16. Cf. also in the immediate context Ephesians 5:19, where *heautous* is equivalent to the reciprocal pronoun. Reciprocity is also prominent in Colossians 3:9, 13, 16.

[36]J. P. Sampley's view that the writer uses Ephesians 5:22 to relativize what follows is incorrect (*"And the Two Shall Become One Flesh": A Study of Traditions in Eph 5:21-33* [Cambridge: Cambridge University Press, 1971], pp. 116-17); cf. Lincoln, *Ephesians*, p. 366. Nevertheless, Ephesians 5:22 remains part of the scriptural context within which we must interpret the passage.

bly did not perceive its full implications.[37]

Head as metaphor. The instruction is backed up with the statement that the husband is the "head" of the wife (cf. I Cor II:3), and an analogy is drawn with Jesus as "head" of the church.[38] Attempts to weaken the sense of *head* to mean nothing more than "source" are not persuasive, although notions of the head as "prominent, outstanding or determinative" and thus possessing "preeminence" or functioning as "ground of being" are well founded.[39] But attempts to show that the term must virtually always carry up front the nuance of "authority" also need careful scrutiny.

Gordon Fee has rightly argued that the usage here needs to be understood in the light of the usage elsewhere in this letter and in Paul.[40] In Colossians and Ephesians the term is used of Christ as the supplier of guidance and power to the body; the body must hold fast to the head from which it grows (Col 2:19) and must grow up into the head (Eph 4:15-16). In Ephesians I:22 Christ as head over all things is given to the church, the clear implication being that the church shares in his headship over the other powers in the universe. Fee then argues that the point of the analogy here is that the husband is the person on whom the wife depends just as the church depends on Christ, and therefore submission is appropriate. The statement that Christ is the Savior of the body favors such an understanding of the husband as essentially the provider, the one who cares for his wife.[41] There is nothing

---

[37]We may compare this to the way Peter directs his readers to honor all people as well as to honor the emperor, and bids Christian husbands honor their wives as joint heirs of the grace of life.

[38]On the origins of this motif see I. H. Marshall, "'For the Husband Is Head of the Wife': Paul's Use of Head and Body Language," in *The New Testament in Its First Century Setting: Essays on Context and Background in Honour of B. W. Winter on His 65th Birthday,* ed. P. J. Williams, Andrew D. Clarke, Peter M. Head and David Instone-Brewer (Grand Rapids, Mich.: 2004), pp. 165-77.

[39]Cf. Heinrich Schlier, "κεφαλή," in *TDNT* 3:674, 679; cf. Richard S. Cervin, "Does *Kephalē* Mean 'Source' or 'Authority Over' in Greek Literature? A Rebuttal," *TrinJ* 10 (1989): 85-112. Linda Belleville argues that nuances of "source" are present in the usage here (see her "Women in Ministry," in *Two Views on Women in Ministry,* ed. James R. Beck and Craig L. Blomberg [Grand Rapids, Mich.: Zondervan, 2001], pp. 137-39). The debate has not been closed by the work of Wayne Grudem, "The Meaning of *Kephalē* ('Head'): An Evaluation of New Evidence, Real and Alleged," *JETS* 44 (2001): 25-66. See the careful study by Anthony C. Thiselton, *The First Epistle to the Corinthians,* NIGTC (Grand Rapids, Mich.: Eerdmans, 2000), pp. 812-22, who argues for multiple meanings. Grudem deals mainly with the external evidence, but as Fee, Belleville and others insist, Paul's usage must be understood by considering how he uses the word in its various contexts.

[40]Especially in this section I am grateful to Gordon Fee for his helpful editorial comments. See also his "The Cultural Context of Ephesians 5:18–6:9," *Priscilla Papers* 16, no. I (2002): 3-8, and chapter eight in this volume.

[41]Thus rather than the mention of Christ as Savior of the church having no counterpart in the analogy

more to the analogy than that. The wife is not her husband's body (as Eph 5:28 makes clear), and the Christ-church relationship is an analogy or pattern, not a ground for the wife's submission.

Submission would be naturally expected in this relationship in the ancient world, especially as the wife could have been as much as twelve to fifteen years younger than her husband and the marriage would have been arranged. Consequently, in the first-century context submission can be seen as appropriate, but the element of authority is not inherent for all time. What Paul is doing is to indicate the way wives should be submissive within a society where such submission was expected, just as he can also tell slaves how they are to be obedient in the slave-master relationship; in both cases he bases it in the relationship to Christ.

The injunction to husbands is *not* that they exercise their proper authority; rather it has a quite extraordinary emphasis on the total love and devotion that the husband must show to the wife. This is developed by the use of two "natural" analogies: the love that one has for one's own body and the love that one has for oneself. The second of these is the criterion for supreme human love, in that love of neighbor is to be as intense as love of oneself. The biblical command to love one's neighbor as oneself is here transmuted and focused into love for one's wife as for oneself.

These motifs are taken to an even higher level by being placed in the context of the love of Christ that extended to self-giving in death for the church. This is followed by a statement of the purpose of Christ's love: that he might have a completely pure and blameless bride. The concept of the church as the body of Christ is also taken up. The correspondence in the analogy is partial in that the wife is not the body of the husband, and therefore the command is that the husband love his wife and care for her in the same way he cares for his actual body.[42] The husband's love thus is expressed in care and respect. Not only is this instruction to husbands to love their wives unusual and unconventional in the world of the New Testament,[43] but the sheer intensity of the love demanded is extraordinary.

Like Colossians 3, this passage teaches a requirement for a husband to love and

---

(as is often assumed), there is some correspondence with the role of the husband as the provider for his wife. The thought of the husband's acting as "savior" by leading his wife to Christian conversion would be contrary to Paul's usage of this noun, with its rich LXX background of God as Savior. He uses the verb *save* in this way, but with the sense of "winning" (1 Cor 7:16; 9:22).

[42]In the succeeding elaboration it is recognized that the husband and wife form one flesh through marriage, and therefore it would seem that in loving his wife the husband does love himself.

[43]Lincoln, *Ephesians*, p. 374.

care for a wife, which was certainly compatible in the first-century context with a position of authority over her (just as parents love their children). What we have here, then, is another example of "love-patriarchalism," in which the traditional element of submission by the wife to her husband is required, but with a remarkable development of the motif of self-giving love as the dominant characteristic of the Christian husband. The tensions that we found in Colossians are here in an even stronger form.

"To have fulfilled one's role and carried out one's duties under the guidelines of mutual submission, and as a wife to have subordinated oneself voluntarily to a husband who cherishes one with a self-sacrificial love, would have been to experience a very different reality than that suggested by the traditional discussions of household management."[44] There is thus something distinctly new in the Christian understanding of marriage, even though Paul's teaching here assumes a patriarchal structure of marriage. Does it, however, *require* this structure? Interpretation is not complete until we have asked what it has to say to contemporary readers.

Evangelical Hermeneutics

The typical conservative evangelical method of dealing with Scripture, particularly its ethical injunctions, is to derive from any specific passage the underlying, "timeless" principles or injunctions that are expressed in the cultural, specific setting of the time, and then to ask how these are to be reexpressed in a manner appropriate to a modern setting.[45] Despite criticisms that have been offered of it, this approach must remain an essential part of our hermeneutics. The problems lie in determining what is culturally or situationally bound and what is of universal relevance. Problems arise where something that might be thought to be time bound is apparently justified in Scripture by a theological principle. Probably many Christians would thankfully recognize the command to women to learn in silence in I Timothy 2 as specific to a situation were it not for the apparent appeal to fundamental truths in the following verses; fortunately, the passage should be interpreted otherwise.[46] Here in Ephesians the problem is the apparent theological rooting of one-sided submission by the wife, with the husband as her head and holding a position analogous to Christ's.

I have argued above that the "head" metaphor can be seen in Paul's cultural con-

---

[44]Ibid., pp. 390-92.
[45]See William J. Webb, *Slaves, Women and Homosexuals* (Downers Grove, Ill.: InterVarsity Press, 2001).
[46]See chapter twelve in this volume.

text in terms of a relationship in which submission is appropriate. But there is more to be said. A currently popular approach attributes to Scripture a broader type of authority—that of a story or metanarrative.[47] On this view the fundamental thing in Scripture is the interpretation of history and existence in terms of the (true and valid) story of God as Creator and Redeemer who acts in history to save people, with consequences for how they are to behave. On this view the Bible does not so much give detailed instructions for conduct as set the patterns that should mold our behavior.

If this approach is taken on its own, its weaknesses are obvious. But if we combine it with the first approach, its strength is to emphasize that instructions for conduct must be seen and understood in light of the overarching story; Scripture must be interpreted by Scripture. All statements in Scripture are to be interpreted in light of the total context provided by the scriptural story. This approach takes seriously the need to recognize the "center" or "climax" of the biblical revelation and to evaluate the continuing significance of the parts in light of the center. It is precisely because of this principle that much of the legal teaching in the Old Testament is recognized to have reached its fulfillment and its end in Christ and is no longer applicable to Christians.

A further principle recognizes that growth and development are possible both in doctrine and in ethical requirements beyond the explicit letter of the scriptural revelation. The recognition that slavery is incompatible with Christian faith goes beyond the explicit teaching of Scripture while being fully scriptural: we now recognize (as the biblical writers were not yet able to do) that slavery is inconsistent with the biblical understanding of humanity in creation and redemption.[48] The biblical assumption that the "powers that be" are ordained by God has not prevented Christians from defending democracy, including universal suffrage.[49]

We must go beyond the letter of Scripture when the trajectory of scriptural teaching takes us further than what Scripture explicitly says and requires us to recognize that some culturally specific scriptural teachings and commands are no

---

[47]See Richard B. Hays, *The Moral Vision of the New Testament* (New York: HarperCollins, 1996), with the discussion by Douglas J. Moo, Judith Gundry-Volf and Richard B. Hays in *BBR* 9 (1999): 271-96.

[48]Thus taking the authority of Scripture seriously may require us to introduce some fresh commands that go beyond the letter of Scripture as such.

[49]This is not the place to illustrate how Christian doctrine builds on scriptural material to produce understandings, e.g., of the Trinity, the atonement or ecology, that were not envisaged by the biblical writers.

longer mandatory. All recognize that the Christian revelation takes us well beyond the Old Testament revelation (and renders some aspects of it obsolete). By analogy, the growth in understanding of Christian revelation under the continuing guidance of the Spirit may lead us to apply some culturally specific parts of the New Testament in a way that does not compromise its supreme authority for us.

This procedure is emphatically not a means of getting rid of scriptural passages that contemporary readers may happen not to like. The combination of (1) searching for basic theological and ethical principles, (2) interpreting individual passages in the light of Scripture as a whole and (3) recognizing that there is progress in revelation is a method of interpretation that is based on the Bible itself.[50]

Application to wives and husbands. That there is a general trajectory in Scripture toward a recognition of the equality of men and women in salvation is incontestable.

It is appropriate to look again at slavery. The obedience of the slave to the master is seen as an aspect of service to Christ, which seems to imply that the individual master is to be treated in the same way as Christ and possesses a similar authority. Yet the authority of the master is relativized by his being submissive to Christ. Once it is said that slaves and masters have the same Master and are both answerable to him, the absolute rights of the master over the slave are relativized. Later, even where legal slavery had ceased to exist, the position of many employers was tantamount to that of masters in that employees had no option but to obey them. It took the development of unions to change that situation. There can thus be a move from master to employer in which the apparently divinely permitted structure of slavery is transformed into something else that is no longer slavery. A similar development with regard to marriage is both appropriate and necessary.

The de facto patriarchal authority of the husband is so transformed by the command to love his wife that it ceases to be exercised in the old way. Thus not only are abuses of power recognized to be wrong but the power relationship itself is also seen to be inappropriate. When this husbandly duty of love is undertaken consistently and fully, a one-sided submission becomes impossible, for Christian love by the husband requires him also to respect and submit to his wife. This insight could not be expected to develop immediately, and the New Testament writers should not

---

[50]See I. Howard Marshall, *Beyond the Bible: Moving from Scripture to Theology* (Grand Rapids, Mich.: Baker Academic, 2004).

be faulted for not spelling this out explicitly. The implications of Ephesians 5:21 and other passages noted above must be allowed to have their proper force.

The wife's submission ceases to be one-sided in that she is recognized by her husband as a joint heir of grace and as a full person, not as a chattel. It is impossible to see how taking joint heirship seriously can allow a husband to expect one-sided submission "in everything" from his wife; her relationship with him is different from that of a child or servant.

Only by interpreting Paul in this way are we in fact upholding the authority of Scripture. Paul's teaching remains authoritative for today, but it is authoritative, just as he himself would insist, as an expression of the gospel. And it is the authority of the gospel that compels us to move forward into an understanding of how the *structure* of marriage is no longer to be understood in patriarchal terms. To repeat: the thesis of this study is that we do not reach this insight into mutual partnership in marriage through ignoring Scripture or imposing anachronistic interpretations on it; rather, Scripture itself as a whole and in the light of its central revelation of the gospel compels us to a deeper understanding of human relationships. The raw materials for this deeper understanding are there in Scripture, but their full significance was not yet realized, just as we recognize that the doctrines of the Trinity and Christology were formulated only at a later point.

So Christian employees do seek to serve their employers willingly and honestly and with commitment, but they also know that they have rights and they are not slaves. Christian children will obey their parents as is appropriate in those who are not yet adult and mature. A Christian wife recognizes that in the relationship of marriage she is summoned to practice self-denial and prefer the interests of her husband, but she is also aware that she is in a relationship of love with a fellow heir of the grace of life and that her attitude to her husband is balanced by his calling to self-denial and preferring of *her* interests. Although these passages say nothing whatever about wives' specifically loving their husbands (!), in light of the gospel they cannot do less than show their husbands the kind of love their husbands are here told to show them.

A recognition of the fully egalitarian implications of scriptural teaching thus takes place at the level of the application of Scripture to the contemporary reader, rather than solely at the level of what individual texts were saying specifically to the original readers. But the deeper application is made in light of the gospel and in recognition that the gospel pushes us on to a fuller understanding, while the new situations in which we live require us to seek in Scripture answers to questions that lie beyond the horizons of the original readers and writers alike.[51]

The positive elements in Ephesians are to be characteristic of both partners: a mood of subordination in which each partner subordinates their own interests to their spouse's, the motivation of sacrificial love in which each partner strives to help the other achieve the sanctification that is God's will for them, and the consciousness that this loving relationship is the nearest thing on earth to the relationship between Christ and the church.

These elements are possible within an egalitarian relationship. Indeed, they are *more* attainable within such a relationship, since the roles of both husband and wife are more fully spelled out than in the patriarchal setting. For what is being done is not to deny that wives should submit to their husbands as to the Lord but to add that husbands also must submit to their wives as to the Lord. And whereas Paul tells only husbands to show love and only wives to show respect, now both realize that they are called to love each other with the kind of love Christ has shown to the church. Within this context of total submission flowing out of love on both sides, there can develop a freedom for each to be what Christ wants them to be in their high calling as his people.

Conclusion

Paul wrote as he did about marriage because in his world he did not know any other form than the patriarchal. As he did with other relationships, he worked within the structures of his time and gave directions for Christian behavior within them. The danger is to think that this validates the setup for all time. Christians have rightly seen that slavery and unrepresentative government are inconsistent with the implications of the gospel. They have also recognized that the relation of children to parents can take different forms in different cultures and times. They have been less certain about marriage and the place of women in leadership and teaching in the church, because many have thought that the New Testament sanctioned a patriarchal, subordinationist structure.

My contention is that in the passages we have examined, when rightly understood, patriarchalism is not given a theological grounding as the only possible structure, and that the gospel itself leads us out of patriarchalism into a different kind of relationship that mirrors more adequately the mutual love and respect that is God's purpose for his redeemed people.

---

[51]Thus it is appropriate to look for answers that will be in accordance with Scripture to questions such as the status of the unborn child and people in a so-called vegetative state.

12

TEACHING AND
USURPING AUTHORITY

1 Timothy 2:11-15

Linda L. Belleville

T he battle over women leaders in the church continues to rage unabated in evangelical circles. At the center of the tempest sits I Timothy 2:11-15. Despite a broad spectrum of biblical and extrabiblical texts that highlight female leaders, I Timothy 2:11-15 continues to be perceived and treated as the Great Divide in the debate. Indeed, a hierarchical interpretation of this passage has become for some a litmus test for the label *evangelical* and even a necessity for the salvation of unbelievers.[1]

The complexities of I Timothy 2:11-15 are many. There is barely a word or phrase that has not been keenly scrutinized. The focus here will be on the key interpretive issues (context, translation, the Greek infinitive *authentein*, grammar, cultural backdrop) and some common concerns regarding what this text says about men and women in positions of leadership and authority. This analysis will make use of a wide array of tools and databases now available with the advent of computer technology that can shed light on what all concede to be the truly abstruse, head-scratching aspects of the passage.

Context

In getting a handle on I Timothy 2:12, we must be clear about where the verse sits in the letter as a whole. Paul begins by instructing his stand-in, Timothy, to stay

---

[1]A case in point is Andreas Köstenberger's rationale for *Women in the Church: A Fresh Analysis of 1 Timothy 2:9-15*, ed. Andreas Köstenberger, Thomas Schreiner and H. Scott Baldwin (Grand Rapids, Mich.: Baker, 1995), pp. 11-12. He argues that a hierarchical view of men and women is necessary for "a world estranged from God" to "believe that God was in Christ reconciling the world to himself."

put in Ephesus so that he can command certain persons "not to teach false doctrines any longer" (1:3). That false teaching is Paul's overriding concern can be seen from the fact that he bypasses normal letter-writing conventions (such as a thanksgiving section and closing greetings) and gets right down to business (cf. Galatians). It is also obvious from the roughly 50 percent of the letter's contents that Paul devotes to the topic of false teaching.

Some believe that false teaching is a minor concern compared with that of "church order." To be sure, Paul does remind Timothy of "how people ought to conduct themselves in God's household" (1 Tim 3:15). It is critical mass, however, that determines the overriding concern.[2] Also, a lack of details about leadership roles and an absence of offices steer us away from viewing church order as the primary matter.[3] Paul's posture throughout is corrective rather than didactic. For example, we learn very little about what various leaders do, and what we do learn, we learn incidentally. Yet there is quite a bit about how not to choose church leaders (1 Tim 5:21-22) and what to do with those who stumble (1 Tim 5:19-20). There is also little interest in the professional qualifications of church leaders. Instead we find a concern for character, family life and commitment to sound teaching (1 Tim 3:1-13). This is perfectly understandable against a background of false teaching. Then there are the explicit statements. Two church leaders have been expelled (1 Tim 1:20). Some elders need to be publicly rebuked due to continuing sin, while the rest take note (1 Tim 5:20).[4] There are malicious talk, malevolent suspicions and constant friction (1 Tim 6:4-5). Some, Paul says, have in fact wandered from the faith (1 Tim 5:15; 6:20-21).

Were women specifically involved? Women receive a great deal of attention in 1 Timothy. Indeed there is no other New Testament letter in which they figure so prominently. Behavior befitting women in worship (1 Tim 2:10-15), qualifications for women deacons (1 Tim 3:11), appropriate pastoral behavior toward older and younger women (1 Tim 5:2), support of widows in service of the church (1 Tim 5:9-10), correction of younger widows (1 Tim 5:11-15) and familial responsibil-

---

[2]For further discussion, see Gordon D. Fee, 1 and 2 Timothy, Titus, NIBC (Peabody, Mass.: Hendrickson, 1988), pp. 20-23.

[3]Qualifications for leaders are outlined in 1 Timothy 3:1-13 and 5:9-10, but there is no instruction as to who they are or what roles they fill.

[4]Since the tense and mood are present indicative, Paul is dealing with a present reality not a hypothetical possibility. Thus TNIV reads: "But those who are sinning you are to reprove before everyone" (cf. NRSV, "As for those who persist in sin, rebuke them in the presence of all"), replacing the NIV's "Those who sin are to be rebuked publicly so that the others may take warning."

ities toward destitute widows (1 Tim 5:3-8, 16) are all concerns of Paul. Moreover, Paul speaks of widows who were going from house to house speaking things they ought not (1 Tim 5:13). That something more than nosiness or gossiping is involved is clear from Paul's evaluation that "some have in fact already turned away to follow Satan" (1 Tim 5:15).

Some are quick to point out that there are no explicit examples of female false teachers in 1 Timothy, and they are correct. No women (teachers or otherwise) are specifically named. Yet this overlooks the standard principles that come into play when we are interpreting the genre of "letter." The occasional nature of Paul's letters always demands reconstruction of one sort or another, and this from only half of the conversation. The cumulative picture, then, becomes that which meets the burden of proof. All told, Paul's attention to false teaching and women occupies about 60 percent of the letter. It would therefore be foolish—not to mention misleading—to neglect considering 1 Timothy 2 against this backdrop. "They [the false teachers] forbid people to marry" (1 Tim 4:3) alone goes a long way toward explaining Paul's otherwise obscure comment "Women will be saved [or 'kept safe'] through childbearing" (1 Tim 2:15), as well as his command in 1 Timothy 5:14 that younger widows marry and raise a family (which is different from his teaching elsewhere, e.g., 1 Cor 7:8-9, 39-40).

The grammar and language of 1 Timothy 2 also dictate such a backdrop. The opening "I exhort, *therefore*" (1 Tim 2:1 NASB, *parakalō oun*) ties what follows in chapter 2 with the false teaching of the previous chapter and its divisive influence (1 Tim 1:3-7, 18-20). The subsequent "*therefore* I want" (NASB, *boulomai oun*) eight verses later does the same (1 Tim 2:8). Congregational contention is the keynote of 1 Timothy 2. A command for peace (instead of disputing) is found four times in the space of fifteen verses. Prayers for governing authorities are urged "that we may lead peaceful and quiet lives" (1 Tim 2:2). The men of the church are enjoined to lift up hands that are "without anger or disputing" (1 Tim 2:8). The women are commanded to show sound judgment (1 Tim 2:9, 15, *sōphrosynēs*), to learn in a peaceful (not quarrelsome) fashion (1 Tim 2:11; see below) and to avoid Eve's example of deception and transgression (1 Tim 2:13-14). The language of deception, in particular, calls to mind the activities of the false teachers. A similar warning was given to the Corinthian congregation. "I am afraid," Paul says, "that just as Eve was deceived by the serpent's cunning, your minds may somehow be led astray from your sincere and pure devotion to Christ" (2 Cor 11:3).

In Corinth the false teaching involved preaching a Jesus, Spirit and gospel different from what Paul had preached (2 Cor 11:4-5). What was it in Ephesus? One pointer is Paul's command that women learn "quietly" (1 Tim 2:11) and behave "quietly" (1 Tim 2:12 Phillips, NEB, REB, NLT). Some translations render the Greek phrase *en hēsychia* as "in silence," and Paul is understood to be setting forth public protocols for women. In public, women are to learn "in silence" and be "silent" (KJV, NKJV, RSV, NSRV, CEV, NIV, JB; cf. "keep quiet" TEV; "remain [or be] quiet" BBE, NAB, NJB, TNIV). But does this make sense? Silence is not compatible with the Socratic dialogical approach to learning in Paul's day.[5] Also, Paul does not use the Greek term *hēsychion* this way nine verses earlier: "I urge . . . that petitions, prayers, intercession and thanksgiving be made . . . for kings and all in authority, so that we may lead peaceful and quiet *[hēsychion]* lives in all godliness and holiness" (1 Tim 2:1-2).[6]

Yet all too often it is assumed that Paul is commanding women not to speak or teach in a congregational setting as a sign of "full submission" to their husbands. On what grounds, though? "A woman should learn . . ." does not suggest anything of the sort (1 Tim 2:11). In a learning context, it is logical to think in terms of submission either to teachers or to oneself (cf. "the spirits of prophets are subject to the control of prophets," 1 Cor 14:32). Submission to a teacher well suits a learning context, but so does self-control. A calm, submissive spirit was a necessary prerequisite for learning back then (as now).

Some translations seek a way out by narrowing "women" and "men" to "wives" and "husbands" (e.g., Knox, Young, Williams). Lexically this is certainly possible. *Gynē* can mean either "woman" or "wife," and *anēr* can mean "man" or "husband" (see BDAG s.v.): "I permit no *wife* to teach or to have authority over *her husband.*" Yet context determines usage, and "husband" and "wife" do not fit. "I want the men everywhere to pray" (1 Tim 2:8) and "I also want women . . ." (1 Tim 2:9-10) simply cannot be limited to husbands and wives. Nor can the verses that follow be read in this way. Paul does refer to Adam and Eve in 1 Tim 2:13-14; but it is to Adam and Eve as the prototypical male and female, not as

---

[5]See chapter nine in this volume.

[6]Nor does Paul use the term *hēsychia* to mean "silence" elsewhere. When he has absence of speech in mind, he uses *sigaō* (Rom 16:25; 1 Cor 14:28, 30, 34). When he has "calmness" in view, he uses *hēsychia* and its cognate forms (1 Thess 4:11; 2 Thess 3:12; 1 Tim 2:2). This is also the case for the other New Testament authors. See *sigaō* in Luke 9:36; 18:39; 20:26; Acts 12:17; 15:12-13; and *sigē* in Acts 21:40 and Revelation 8:1. For *hēsychia* (and related forms) meaning "calm" or "restful," see Luke 23:56; Acts 11:18; 21:14; 1 Thessalonians 4:11; 2 Thessalonians 3:12; 1 Peter 3:4. For the sense "not speak," see Luke 14:4 and, perhaps, Acts 22:2.

a married couple ("formed first," "deceived and became a sinner").

Paul's commands for peaceable and submissive behavior suggest that women were disrupting worship. The men were too. They were praying in an angry and contentious way (I Tim 2:8). Since Paul targets women who teach men (I Tim 2:12) and uses the example of Adam and Eve as a corrective, it would be a fair assumption that a bit of a battle of the sexes was being waged in the congregation.

Translation

Without a doubt, the most difficult clause to unpack is *didaskein de gynaiki ouk epitrepō oude authentein andros*—although the average person in the pew wouldn't know it. English translations stemming from the 1940s to the early 1980s tend to gloss over the difficulties. A hierarchical, noninclusive understanding of leadership is partly to blame. Women aren't supposed to be leaders, so the language of leadership, where women are involved, tends to be manipulated. One of the primary places where this sort of bias surfaces is I Timothy 2:12. Post-World War II translations routinely render the clause as "I do not permit a woman to teach or to have [or *exercise*] authority over a man" (e.g., RSV, NRSV, NAB, NABr, TEV, NASB/U, JB/NJB, NKJV, NCV, God's Word, NLT, Holman Christian Standard, ESV, TNIV)—although some, such as the BBE, qualify it with "in my [Paul's] opinion."

Earlier translations were not so quick to do so. This was largely owing to dependence on ancient Greek lexicographers and grammarians. In fact, there is a virtually unbroken tradition, stemming from the oldest versions and running down to the twenty-first century, that translates *authentein* as "to dominate" rather than "to exercise authority over":[7]

- Old Latin (2nd-4th cent. A.D.): "I permit not a woman to teach, neither to *dominate* a man [*neque dominari viro*]."

- Vulgate (4th-5th): "I permit not a woman to teach, neither to *domineer over* a man [*neque dominari in virum*]."

---

[7]There are two notable exceptions. (1) Martin Luther (1522): "Einem Weibe aber gestatte ich nicht, dass sie lehre, auch nicht, dass sie des Mannes Herr sei." Luther, in turn, influenced William Tyndale (1525-1526): "I suffre not a woman to teache nether to have auctoritie over a man." (2) Rheims (1582): "But to teach I permit not vnto a woman, nor to haue dominion ouer the man." Rheims, in turn, influenced the ASV ("nor to have dominion over a man") and subsequent revisions of Casiodoro de Reina's Santa Biblia. See, for example, the 1602 Valera revision: "ni ejercer dominio sobre" ("neither to exercise dominion over").

- Geneva (1560 edition): "I permit not a woman to teache, nether to *vfurpe* authoritie ouer the man."

- Casiodoro de Reina (1569): "I do not permit the woman to teach, neither to *take [tomar]* authority over the man." *No permito á la mujer enseñar, ni tomar autoridad sobre el hombre.*[8]

- Bishops (1589): "I suffer not a woman to teach, neither to *usurpe* authoritie over the man."

- KJV (1611): "I suffer not a woman to teach nor *usurp* authority over a man."

A wide range of modern translations follow the same tradition:[9]

- L. Segond (1910): "I do not permit the woman to teach, neither to *take [prendre]* authority over the man." *Je ne permets pas à la femme d'enseigner, ni de prendre autorité sur l'homme.*

- Goodspeed (1923): "I do not allow women to teach or to *domineer over* men."

- La Sainte (1938): "I do not permit the woman to teach, neither to *take [prendre]* authority over the man." *Je ne permets pas à la femme d'enseigner, ni de prendre de l'autorité sur l'homme.*

- NEB (1961): "I do not permit a woman to be a teacher, nor must woman *domineer over* man."

- JBCerf (1973): "I do not permit the woman to teach, neither to *lay down the law for* the man." *Je ne permets pas à la femme d'enseigner ni de faire la loi à l'homme.*

- REB (1989): "I do not permit women to teach or *dictate to* the men."

- New Translation (1990): "I do not permit a woman to teach or *dominate* men."

- CEV (1991): "They should . . . not be allowed to teach or *to tell* men *what to do.*"

- *The Message* (1993): "I don't let women *take over and tell* the men *what to do.*"

There are good reasons for translating *authentein* this way. It cannot be stressed

---

[8]Compare this with "exercise authority" (*ejerza autoridad*—*La Biblia de las Américas* 1986) and "exercise dominion" (*ejercer dominio*—Reina-Valera 1960, 1995).

[9]Technically, *vir* in Latin and *Weibe* in German (like *gynē* in Greek) can mean either "woman" or "wife." Consequently, some translations opt for "wife." See, for example, Charles B. Williams's 1937 translation: "I do not permit a married woman to practice teaching or domineering over a husband."

enough that in *authentein* Paul picked a term that occurs only here in the New Testament. Its cognates are found merely twice elsewhere in the Greek Bible. In the Wisdom of Solomon 12:6 it is the noun *authentēs* (murderer) used with reference to indigenous peoples' practice of child sacrifice:

> Those [the Canaanites] who lived long ago in your holy land, you hated for their detestable practices, their works of sorcery and unholy rites . . . these parents *who murder [authentas]* helpless lives. (NRSV)

In 3 Maccabees 2:28-29 it is the noun *authentia* ("original," "authentic"). The author recounts the hostile measures taken by the Ptolemies against Alexandrian Jews toward the end of the third century B.C., including the need to register according to their original status as Egyptian slaves and to be branded with the ivy-leaf symbol in honor of the deity Dionysus.[10]

> All Jews [in Alexandria] shall be subjected to a registration *[laographian]*[11] involving poll tax and to the status of slaves. . . . Those who are registered are to be branded on their bodies by fire with the ivy-leaf symbol of Dionysus and to register *[katachōrisai]* in accordance with their [Egyptian] *origin [authentian]* of record *[prosynestalmenēn]*.[12]

These two uses in the Greek Bible should give us pause in opting for a translation such as "to have [or exercise] authority over." If Paul had wanted to speak of an ordinary exercise of authority, he could have picked any number of words. Within the semantic domain of "exercise authority," biblical lexicographers J. P. Louw and Eugene Nida have twelve entries and of "rule," "govern" forty-seven entries.[13] Yet Paul picked none of these. Why not? The obvious reason is that *authentein* carried a nuance (other than "rule" or "have authority") that was particularly suited to the Ephesian situation.

---

[10]Branding in honor of a deity was a common practice in antiquity. See Bruce Metzger and Roland Murphy, eds., *The New Oxford Annotated Apocrypha* (New York: Oxford University Press, 1991), p. 289 n. 28.

[11]*Laographia* (registration) is a rare word found in the Greek papyri from Egypt with reference to the registration of people of the lower classes and slaves. See ibid.

[12]R. H. Charles's "they shall also be registered according to their former *restricted status*" does not fit the lexical range of possibilities for *authentia* (*The Apocrypha and the Pseudepigrapha of the Old Testament*, 2 vols. [London: Oxford University Press, 1913]).

[13]Johannes P. Louw and Eugene A. Nida, *Greek-English Lexicon of the New Testament Based on Semantic Domains*, 2 vols., 2nd ed. (New York: United Bible Societies, 1988-1989), 37.35-47, 37.48-95. *Authentein* is noticeably absent from both of these domains.

Nouns: Greek literary materials. So what is the nuance? Lexicographers, for the most part, agree that the root of *authentēs* is *auto* + *entēs,* meaning "to do or to originate something with one's own hand" (LSJ *autoentēs*). Usage confirms this. An *authentēs* is someone who originates or carries out an action. During the sixth to second centuries B.C., the Greek tragedies used it exclusively of murdering oneself (suicide) or another person(s).[14] The rhetoricians and orators during this period did the same.[15] The word is rare in the historians and epic writers of the time, but in all instances it too is used of a "murderer" or "slayer."[16]

During the Hellenistic period the primary meaning of *authentēs* was still "murderer,"[17] but the semantic range widened to include "perpetrator,"[18] "sponsor,"[19] "author"[20] and "mastermind"[21] of a crime or act of violence. This is the case regardless of geographical location, ethnicity or religious orientation. For instance, the Jewish historian Josephus speaks of the *author (authentēn)* of a poisonous draught (*Jewish War* 1.582; 2.240). Diodorus of Sicily uses it of (1) the sponsors *(authentas)* of some daring plans (*Bibliotheca historica* 35.25.1), (2) the perpetrators *(authentais)* of a sacrilege (*Bibliotheca historica* 16.61) and (3) the mastermind *(authentas)* of a crime (*Bibliotheca historica* 17.5.4.5). By the first century A.D., lexicographers

---

[14] Aeschylus (2x) *Agamemnon* 1573, *Eumenides* 212; Euripides (8x) *Fragmenta* 20.645, *Andromacha* 39.172, 614, *Hercules* 43.839, 43.47post11312, *Troades* 44.660, *Iphigenia aulidensis* 51.1190, *Rhesus* 52.873. For a detailed study of the nominal forms of *authentein,* see Leland Wilshire, "The TLG Computer and Further Reference to ΑΥΘΕΝΤΕΩ in I Timothy 2.12," *NTS* 34 (1988): 120-34, and "I Timothy 2:12 Revisited: A Reply to Paul W. Barnett and Timothy J. Harris," *EvQ* 65 (1993): 43-55.

There is a disputed reading of *authentēs* in Euripides' *Suppliant Women* 442. Arthur Way (*Euripides: Suppliants* [Cambridge, Mass.: Harvard University Press, 1971], p. 534) emends the text to read *euthyntēs* ("when people *pilot* the land"), instead of *authentēs.* David Kovacs (*Euripides: Suppliant Women, Electra, Heracles* [Cambridge, Mass.: Harvard University Press, 1998], p. 57) deletes lines 442-55 as not original. Thus Carroll Osburn erroneously cites this text as "establishing a fifth century BC usage of the term *[authentēs]* meaning 'to exercise authority'" and mistakenly faults Catherine Clark Kroeger for not dealing with it ("ΑΥΘΕΝΤΕΩ" [I Timothy 2:12]—Word Study," *RestQ,* 1982, p. 2 n. 5).

[15] Antiphon (6x) *Tetralogies* 23.4.6, 23.11.4, 24.4.3, 24.9.7, 24.10.1, *On the Murder of Herod* 11.6; Lysias (1x) *Orations* 36.348.13.

[16] Thucydides (1x) *History of the Peloponnesian War* 3.58.5.4; Herodotus (1x) *Historia* 1.117.12; Apollonius (2x) *Argonautica* 2.754, 4.479.

[17] Appian (5x) *Mithridatic Wars* 90.1, *Civil Wars* 1.7.61.7, 1.13.115.17, 3.2.16.13, 4.17.134.40; Philo (1x) *Quod Deterius Potiori Insidiari Soleat* 78.7.

[18] Josephus (1x) *Jewish Wars* 1.582.1; Diodorus (1x) *Bibliotheca historica* 1.16.61.1.3.

[19] Posidonius (1x) *Fragmenta* 165.7 (= Diodorus *Bibliotheca historica* 3.3435.25.1.4).

[20] Cf. Josephus (1x) *Jewish Wars* 2.240.4; Diodorus (1x) *Bibliotheca historica* 17.5.

[21] E.g., Diodorus *Bibliotheca historica* 17.5.4.5.

defined *authentēs* as the perpetrator of a murder committed by others (not the actual murderer himself or herself).[22]

Was there a meaning that approached anything like the ESV's "exercise authority over" and the NIV's "have authority over"? "Master" can be found, but it is in the sense of the "mastermind" of a crime rather than one who exercises authority over another. For example, in the first and second centuries B.C. historians used it of those who masterminded and carried out such exploits as the massacre of the Thracians at Maronea[23] and the robbing of the sacred shrine at Delphi.[24]

Greek nonliterary materials. A search of the nonliterary databases (Duke papyri, ostraca, tablets and inscriptions of the Packard Humanities Institute [PHI]) produces quite different results. While *authent-* appears quite regularly in Greek literature from the sixth century B.C. on, it first appears in nonliterary materials in the first century B.C.[25] The popular form is *authentikos* (from which we derive our English word *authentic*) and not *authentēs* (murderer). Numerous examples of *authentikos* can be found in Greek inscriptions and papyri of the Hellenistic period.[26]

Verbs. Verb forms contemporary with or prior to Paul (including the verbal noun [infinitive] and verbal adjective [participle]) are rare to nonexistent in Greek literary and nonliterary materials. There are a mere handful in the TLG (Thesaurus Linguae Graecae) and PHI (Packard Humanities Institute) databases. But these are of critical importance for shedding light on the verbal noun *authentein* in I Timothy 2:12.

---

[22]See, for example, Harpocration *Lexicon* 66.7 (1st cent. A.D.): "*Authentēs:* Those who commit murder *[tous phonous]* through others. For the perpetrator *[ho authentēs]* always makes evident the one whose hand committed the deed."

[23]Polybius *Historicus* 22.14.2.3 (2nd cent. B.C.).

[24]Diodorus of Sicily *Bibliotheca historica* 17.5.4.5 (1st cent. B.C.). In the patristic writers the noun *authentēs* does not appear until the mid to late second century A.D. and then in Origen in the third century—far too late to provide a linguistic context for Paul. Predominant usage is still "murderer" (Clement 3x), but one also finds divine "authority" (Irenaeus 3x; Clement 2x; Origen 1x) and "master" (*Shepherd of Hermas* 1x; for the second-century dating of the *Shepherd* 5.82, see Michael Holmes, *Apostolic Fathers*, 2nd ed. [Grand Rapids, Mich.: Baker, 1992], p. 331). The rest—the vast majority— are uses of the adjective ("authentic," "genuine"). The verb does not occur until well into the third century A.D. (Hippolytus *Short Exegetical and Homiletical Writings* 29.7.5).

[25]The root *authent-* appears six times in first-century A.D. inscriptions, ostraca and tablets: (1) *authenteia/authentia* ("power," "sway," "mastery"; *Scythia* I[2]5); *Mylasa* 10), (2) *authentikos* (*Mylasa* 2, 6) and (3) *authentēs* (*Tituli Asiae Minoris* V 23; *Ephesos* 109). It surfaces in the first-century B.C. papyri only once (see above). It picks up steam in the first century A.D., but virtually all are the term *authentikos* ("genuine," "authentic"; 22x).

[26]See, for example, *Oxyrhynchus Papyrus* 2.260.20 (A.D. 59): "I, Theon, son of Onophrios, assistant, have checked this authentic *[authentikei]* bond."

The first is found in the fifth to first centuries B.C. *Scholia* (or explanatory remarks) on a passage from Aeschylus's tragedy *Eumenides:* "His [Orestes'] hands were dripping with blood; he held a sword just drawn [from avenging the death of his father by killing his mother]" (42). The commentator uses the perfect participial form of *authenteō* to capture the intentional character of the deed: "Were dripping" is explained as "The murderer *[ho phoneutēs],* who just now *has committed an act of violence [authentēkota] . . ."*

The second use of *authenteō* is found in the first-century B.C. grammarian Aristonicus. Commenting on a portion of Homer's *Iliad* ("So he [Odysseus] spoke and they [King Agamemnon and his people] all became hushed in silence, marveling at his words; for so masterfully did he address their gathering"), he states, "This line, which appears in other places, does not fit well here; for it usually is spoken, where *the author [ho authentēn]* of the message delivered something striking. But now, however, he [the author] would speak for Odysseus, who relates the things which had been spoken by Achilles."[27]

The third use of *authenteō* is found in a 27/26 B.C. letter in which Tryphon recounts to his brother Asklepiades the resolution of a dispute between himself and another individual regarding the amount to be paid a ferryman for shipping a load of cattle: "And I had my way with him *[authentēkotos pros auton]* and he agreed to provide Calatytis the boatman with the full fare within the hour" (BGU IV 1208). Evangelical scholarship has been largely dependent for its understanding of *authentein* on George Knight III's 1984 study and his translation of *authentēkotos pros auton* as "I exercised authority over him."[28] Yet this hardly fits the mundane details of the text—payment of a boat fare. Nor can *pros auton* be understood as *"over* him." The preposition plus the accusative does not bear this sense in Greek. "To/toward," "against" and "with" (and less frequently "at," "for," "with reference to," "on" and "on account of") are the range of possible meanings.[29] Here it likely means something like "I had my way *with* him" or perhaps "I took a firm stand *with* him."[30] This certainly fits what we know of the Asklepiades archive. As John White notes, this part of the archive (BGU IV 1203-9) is a series of seven letters written between family members—three brothers, Asklepiades, Paniskos

---

[27]Aristonicus *De signis Iliadis* 9.694 (1st cent. B.C.).
[28]George Knight III, "ΑΥΘΕΝΤΕΩ in Reference to Women in I Timothy 2.12," *NTS* 30 (1984): 145.
[29]See LSJ, 1497 C. *with the accusative.*
[30]See Friedrich Preisigke, *Wörterbuch der griechischen Papyrusurkunden* (Berlin: Papyrusurkunden Berlin, 1925), s.v. *fest auftreten* (to stand firm).

and Tryphon, and one sister, Isidora. Although various business matters are discussed in the correspondence, it is evident that these are private letters, written for the most part by Isidora, who is representing her family's interests abroad.[31]

The fourth use of *authenteō* occurs in Philodemus, the first-century B.C. Greek poet and Epicurean philosopher from Gadara, Syria. Philodemus wrote against the rhetoricians of his day and their penetration into Epicurean circles. Rhetors were the villains; philosophers were the heroes of the Roman Republic. He states, "Rhetors harm a great number of people in many ways—'those shot through with dreadful desires.' They [rhetors] fight every chance they get with prominent people—'with powerful lords *[syn authent[ou]sin anaxin].' . . .* Philosophers, on the other hand, gain the favor of public figures . . . not having them as enemies but friends . . . on account of their endearing qualities" (*Rhetorica* 2 Fragmenta Libri [5] fr. 4 line 14).

Once again Knight's analysis falls short. He states that "the key term is *authent[ou]sin*" and claims that the rendition offered by Yale classicist Harry Hubbell is "they [orators] are men who incur the enmity of those in authority."[32] But Hubbell actually renders *authent[ou]sin* rightly as an adjective meaning "powerful" and modifying the noun *lords:* "they [rhetors] fight with powerful lords *[diamachontai kai syn authentousin anaxin].*"[33]

The fifth use of *authenteō* is found in influential late-first- and early-second-century astrological poet Dorotheus. He states that "if Jupiter aspects the Moon from trine . . . it makes them [the natives] leaders or chiefs [some of civilians and others of soldiers] especially if the Moon is increasing; but if the moon decreases, it does not make them *dominant [authentas]* but subservient *[hyperetoumenous]*" (346). Along similar lines, second-century mathematician Ptolemy states: "Therefore, if Saturn alone takes planetary control *[tēn oikodespotian]* of the soul and *dominates [authentesas]* Mercury and the moon [who govern the soul] [and] if Saturn has a dignified position toward both the solar system and its angles *[ta ken-*

---

[31]John White, *Light from Ancient Letters* (Philadelphia: Fortress, 1986), p. 103.

[32]Knight, "ΑΥΘΕΝΤΕΩ," p. 145. Knight also overlooks the fact that *syn authent[ou]sin anaxin* is actually a quote from an unknown source, not Philodemus's own words. Fallacies have the tendency to perpetuate themselves. See, for example, H. Scott Baldwin, who cites Knight's inaccuracy (instead of checking the primary sources firsthand), "Appendix 2: *Authenteō* in Ancient Greek Literature," in *Women in the Church: A Fresh Analysis of 1 Timothy 2:9-15,* ed. Andreas Köstenberger, Thomas Schreiner and H. Scott Baldwin (Grand Rapids, Mich.: Baker, 1995), p. 275).

[33]Harry Hubbell, trans. and commentary, "The Rhetorica of Philodemus," *Connecticut Academy of Arts and Sciences* 23 (1920): 306.

tra],[34] then he [Saturn] makes [them] lovers of the body . . . *dictatorial, ready to punish.*
. . . But Saturn allied with Jupiter . . . makes his subjects good, respectful to elders,
sedate, noble-minded . . . (*Tetrabiblos* 3.13 [no. 157]). Although Dorotheus and
Ptolemy postdate Paul, they provide an important witness to the continuing use of
authenteō to mean "to hold sway over, to dominate."

Ancient Greek grammarians and lexicographers suggest that the meaning "to
dominate, hold sway" finds its origin in first-century popular ("vulgar" versus literary) usage. That is why second-century lexicographer Moeris states that the Attic
autodiken, "to have independent jurisdiction, self-determination," is to be preferred to the Hellenistic (or Koine) *authentēs.*[35] Modern lexicographers agree.
Those who have studied Hellenistic letters argue that *authenteō* originated in the
popular Greek vocabulary as a synonym for "to dominate someone" *(kratein tinos).*[36] Biblical lexicographers J. P. Louw and Eugene Nida put *authenteō* into the
semantic domain "to control, restrain, domineer" and define the verb as "to control in a domineering manner": "I do not allow women . . . to dominate men" (1
Tim 2:12).[37] Other meanings do not appear until well into the third and fourth
centuries A.D.[38]

So there is no first-century warrant for translating *authentein* as "to exercise
authority" and for understanding Paul in 1 Timothy 2:12 to be speaking of the
carrying out of one's official duties. Rather the sense is the Koine "to dominate,
to get one's way." The NIV'S "to have authority over" therefore must be under-

---

[34]Knight misreads (or perhaps mistypes) F. E. Robbins's (transl., LCL) "angles" as "angels" ("AY-
ΘΕΝΤΕΩ," p. 145.). Baldwin once again quotes Knight's inaccuracy rather than doing a fresh analysis
as the book's title claims ("Appendix 2: *Authenteō,*" p. 275).

[35]Moeris, *Attic Lexicon,* ed. J. Pierson (Leiden, 1759), p. 58. Cf. thirteenth- to fourteenth-century At-
ticist Thomas Magister, who warns his pupils to use *autodikein* because *authentein* is vulgar (*Grammar*
18.8).

[36]See, for example, Theodor Nageli, *Der Wörtschatz des Apostels Paulus* (Göttingen, Germany: Vandenhoeck und Ruprecht, 1905), pp. 49-50; cf. James Hope Moulton and George Milligan, *The Vocabulary
of the Greek Testament* (London: Hodder and Stoughton, 1930), s.v., and the Perseus Project, *Greek-
English Lexicon,* s.v. "to have full power over *tinos.*" <http://www.perseus.tufts.edu>

[37]Louw and Nida also note that "to control in a domineering manner" is often expressed idiomati-
cally as "to shout orders at," "to act like a chief toward" or "to bark at." The use of the verb in 1
Timothy 2:12 comes quite naturally out of the word "master, autocrat" (*Greek-English Lexicon,* p. 91);
cf. BDAG, which defines *authenteō* as "to assume a stance of independent authority, give orders to,
dictate to."

[38]The noun *authentēs* used of an "owner" or "master" appears a bit earlier. See, for example, the
second-century *Shepherd of Hermas* 9.5.6, "Let us go to the tower, for the *owner* of the tower is coming
to inspect it."

stood in the sense of holding sway or mastery over another. This is supported by the grammar of the verse. If Paul had a routine exercise of authority in view, he would have put it first, followed by teaching as a specific example. Instead he starts with teaching, followed by *authentein* as a specific example. Given this word order, *authentein* meaning "to dominate" or "gain the upper hand" provides the best fit in the context.

Grammar

So how did "to exercise authority over" find its way into the majority of modern translations of 1 Timothy 2:12? Andreas Köstenberger claims that it is the correlative that forces translators in this direction. He argues that the Greek correlative pairs synonyms or parallel words and not antonyms. Since "to teach" is positive, *authentein* must also be positive. To demonstrate his point, Köstenberger analyzes "neither" + verb 1 + "nor" + verb 2 constructions in biblical and extrabiblical literature.[39]

Yet there is a grammatical flaw intrinsic to this approach. It is limited to *formally* equivalent constructions, excluding *functionally* equivalent ones, and so the investigation includes only correlated verbs. Thus it overlooks the fact that the infinitives ("to teach," *authentein*) are functioning grammatically not as verbs but as nouns in the sentence structure (as one would expect a verbal *noun* to do). The Greek infinitive may have tense and voice like a verb, but it functions predominantly as a noun or adjective.[40] The verb in 1 Timothy 2:12 is actually "I permit." "Neither to teach nor *authentein*" modifies the noun "a woman,"[41] which makes the *authentein* clause the second of two direct objects. Use of the infinitive as a direct object after a verb that already has a direct object has been amply demonstrated by biblical and extrabiblical grammarians.[42] In such cases the infinitive re-

---

[39]Andreas Köstenberger, "A Complex Sentence Structure in 1 Timothy 2:12," in *Women in the Church: A Fresh Analysis of 1 Timothy 2:9-15*, ed. Andreas Köstenberger, Thomas Schreiner and H. Scott Baldwin (Grand Rapids, Mich.: Baker, 1995), pp. 81-103.

[40]See, for example, Nigel Turner, *Syntax*, vol. 3 of *Grammar of New Testament Greek*, ed. Nigel Turner (Edinburgh: T & T Clark, 1963), p. 134, who classifies infinitives as "noun forms."

[41]See, for instance, James A. Brooks and Carlton L. Winbery, *Syntax of New Testament Greek* (Lanham, Md.: University Press of America, 1979), especially "The Infinitive as a Modifier of Substantives," pp. 141-42. Köstenberger overlooks the role of the infinitive as a verbal *noun* ("Complex Sentence Structure," pp. 81-103).

[42]E.g., Edwin Mayser (*Grammatik der Griechischen Papyri aus der Ptolemaer-Zeit* [Berlin/Leipzig: Walterr Gruyter, 1926, 1970], 2:187), BDF §392), Ernest Dewitt Burton (*Syntax of the Moods and Tenses in New Testament Greek* [Chicago: University of Chicago Press, 1900], nos. 378, 387), Turner (*Syntax*, pp. 137-38). Of particular relevance is Nigel Turner's observation in his volume on Greek syntax

stricts the already present object. Following this paradigm, the I Timothy 2:12 correlative *neither to teach nor authentein* functions as a noun that restricts the direct object "a woman" *(gynaiki)*.

It behooves us, therefore, to correlate nouns and noun substitutes in addition to verbs. This greatly expands the possibilities. "Neither-nor" constructions in the New Testament are then found to pair synonyms (e.g., "neither despised nor scorned," Gal 4:14), closely related ideas (e.g., "neither of the night nor of the dark," I Thess 5:5) and antonyms (e.g., "neither Jew nor Greek, neither slave nor free," Gal 3:28). They also function to move from the general to the particular (e.g., "wisdom neither of this age nor of the rulers of this age," I Cor 2:6), to define a natural progression of related ideas (e.g., "they neither sow, nor reap, nor gather into barns," Mt 6:26), and to define a related purpose or a goal (e.g., "where thieves neither break in nor steal" [i.e., break in to steal], Mt 6:20).[43]

Of the options listed above, it is clear that "teach" and "dominate" are not synonyms, closely related ideas or antonyms. If *authentein* did mean "to exercise authority," we might have a movement from general to particular. But we would expect the word order to be the reverse of what we have in I Timothy 2:12, that

---

that the infinitive as a direct object with *verba putandi* (e.g., "permit," "allow" and "want") is peculiar to Luke, Paul and Hebrews in the New Testament. In such cases, he argues, the infinitive restricts the already present object.

Daniel Wallace (*Greek Grammar Beyond the Basics* [Grand Rapids, Mich.: Zondervan, 1996], pp. 182-89) identifies *authentein* as a verb complement ("I do not *permit* to teach . . .") instead of the direct object complement that it is (ibid., pp. 598-99). It is not that Paul does not *permit to teach* a woman, but that he does not permit *a woman* to teach. Cf. Romans 3:28; 6:11; 14:14; I Corinthians 11:23; 12:23; 2 Corinthians 11:5; Philippians 3:8.

[43]Here are other examples. (I) *Synonyms:* "neither labors nor spins" (Mt 6:28), "neither quarreled nor cried out" (Mt 12:19), "neither abandoned nor given up" (Acts 2:27), "neither leave nor forsake" (Heb 13:5), "neither run in vain nor labor in vain" (Phil 2:16). (2) *Closely related ideas:* "neither the desire nor the effort" (Rom 9:16), "neither the sun nor the moon" (Rev 21:23). (3) *Antonyms:* "neither a good tree . . . nor a bad tree" (Mt 7:18), "neither the one who did harm nor the one who was harmed" (2 Cor 7:12). (4) *General to particular:* "you know neither the day nor the hour" (Mt 25:13), "I neither consulted with flesh and blood nor went up to Jerusalem" (Gal 1:16-17). (5) *A natural progression of closely related ideas:* "born neither of blood, nor of the human will, nor of the will of man" (Jn 1:13), "neither the Christ, nor Elijah, nor the Prophet" (Jn 1:25), "neither from man nor through man" (Gal 1:1). (6) *Goal or purpose:* "neither hears nor understands" (i.e., hearing with the intent to understand; Mt 13:13), "neither dwells in temples made with human hands nor is served by human hands" (i.e., dwells with a view to being served; Acts 17:24). See Linda L. Belleville, *Women Leaders and the Church* (Grand Rapids, Mich.: Baker, 2000), pp. 176-77.

is, "neither to exercise authority [general] nor to teach [particular]." They do not form a natural progression of related ideas either ("first teach, then dominate"). On the other hand, to define a purpose or goal actually provides a good fit: "I do not permit a woman to teach so as to gain mastery over a man," or "I do not permit a woman to teach with a view to dominating a man."[44] It also fits the contrast with the second part of the verse: "I do not permit a woman to teach a man in a dominating way *but* to have a quiet demeanor [literally, 'to be in calmness']."

Culture

Why were the Ephesian women doing this? One explanation is that they were influenced by the cult of Artemis, in which the female was exalted and considered superior to the male. Its importance to the citizens of Ephesus in Paul's day is evident from Luke's record of the two-hour long chant, "Great is Artemis of the Ephesians" (Acts 19:28-37). It was believed that Artemis (and brother Apollo) was the child of Zeus and Leto (or Latin *Latona*). Instead of seeking fellowship among her own kind, she spurned the attentions of the male gods and sought instead the company of a human male consort. This made Artemis and all her female adherents superior to men. This was played out at the feast of the Lord of Streets, when the priestess of Artemis pursued a man, pretending she was Artemis herself pursuing Leimon.[45]

An Artemis influence would help explain Paul's correctives in 1 Timothy 2:13-14. While some may have believed that Artemis appeared first and then her male consort, the true story was just the opposite. For Adam was formed first, then Eve (1 Tim 2:13). And Eve was deceived to boot (1 Tim 2:14)—hardly a basis on which to claim superiority. It would also shed light on Paul's statement that Christian "women will be kept safe [or 'saved'] through childbirth" (1 Tim 2:15 NIV [1973 and 1978 editions]), presumably by faith in Christ. Thus they need not look to Artemis as the protector of women, as did other Ephesian women who turned

---

[44]Cf. Philip Payne (*"Authentein* in 1 Timothy 2:12," Evangelical Theological Society Seminar Paper (Rehoboam Baptist Church, Atlanta, Georgia, November 21, 1986). His own position is that "neither-nor" in this verse forms a closely associated couplet (like "hit 'n' run": "teach 'n' domineer").

[45]Pausanias *Guide to Greece* 2.27.4; 8.53.3. For further details, see Sharon Gritz, *Paul, Women Teachers and the Mother Goddess at Ephesus: A Study of 1 Timothy 2:9-15 in Light of the Religious and Cultural Milieu of the First Century* (Lanham, Md.: University Press of America, 1991), pp. 31-41, and "Artemis," in *The Encyclopaedia Britannica*, Netscape Navigator, Netscape Communications, 1997.

to her for safe travel through the childbearing process.[46]

The impact of the cults on the female population of Ephesus and its environs has been challenged by S. M. Baugh, who contends that the lack of any first-century Ephesian high priestess runs counter to an Artemis impact on the church.[47] Although Baugh is correct in saying that urban Ephesus lacked a high priestess during Paul's day, he overlooks the fact that suburban Ephesus did. While Paul was planting the Ephesian church, Iuliane served as high priestess of the imperial cult in Magnesia, a city fifteen miles southeast of Ephesus. She is honored in a decree of the mid-first century.[48] There were others as well. Inscriptions dating from the first century until the mid-third century place women as high priestesses in Ephesus, Cyzicus, Thyatira, Aphrodisias, Magnesia and elsewhere.[49]

Baugh also argues that female high priestesses of Asia did not serve in and of their own right. They were simply riding on the coattails of a husband, male relative or wealthy male patron.[50] This simply is not true. Many inscriptions naming a woman as high priestess do not name a husband, father or male patron. In the case of those that do, prestige was attached to being a relative of a high priestess and not vice versa. Iuliane's position, for example, was hardly honorary. While it is true that her husband served as a high priest of the imperial cult, Iuliane held her position long before her husband held his. Nor was her position nominal. Priests and priestesses were responsible for the sanctuary's maintenance, its rituals and ceremonies, and the protection of its treasures and gifts. Liturgical functions included ritual

---

[46]As the mother goddess, Artemis was the source of life, the one who nourished all creatures and the power of fertility in nature. Maidens turned to her as the protector of their virginity, barren women sought her aid, and women in labor turned to her for help. See "Artemis," *Encyclopaedia Britannica*.

S. M. Baugh takes issue with the premise that Artemis worship was a fusion of a fertility cult of the mother goddess of Asia Minor and the Greek virgin goddess of the hunt ("A Foreign World: Ephesus in the First Century," in *Women in the Church: A Fresh Analysis of 1 Timothy 2:9-15*, ed. Andreas Köstenberger, Thomas Schreiner and H. Scott Baldwin [Grand Rapids, Mich.: Baker, 1995], pp. 28-33). But fourth-century B.C. "Rituals for Brides and Pregnant Women in the Worship of Artemis" and other literary sources support the fusion. See Franciszek Sokolowski, *Lois sacrées de l'Asie Mineure*, Travaux et mémoires 9 (Paris: E. de Boccard 1955); idem, *Lois sacrées des cités grecques. Supplément.* Travaux et mémoires 11 (Paris: E. de Boccard 1962); idem, *Lois sacrées des cités grecques*, Travaux et mémoires 18 (Paris: E. de Boccard 1969).

[47]See Baugh, "Foreign World," pp. 43-44.

[48]*Die Inschriften von Magnesia am Maeander* 158.

[49]See R. A. Kearsley, "Asiarchs, Archiereis and the Archiereiai of Asia," *Greek, Roman and Byzantine Studies* 27 (1986): 183-92.

[50]Baugh, "Foreign World," pp. 43-44.

sacrifice, pronouncing the invocation and presiding at the festivals of the deity.[51]

Baugh further maintains that Asian high priestesses were young girls whose position was analogous to the private priestesses of Hellenistic queens. Theirs was a nominal position of no real substance, given to daughters and wives of the municipal elite.[52] This too runs counter to Greco-Roman evidence. The majority of women who served as high priestesses were hardly young girls.[53] Vestal virgins were the exception. Delphic priestesses, on the other hand, were required to be at least fifty years old, came from all social classes and served a male god and his adherents.

The primary flaw of Baugh's study is that it is not broad based enough to accurately reflect the religious and civic roles of first-century women in either Asia or the Greco-Roman Empire as a whole. Because Roman religion and government were inseparable, to lead in one arena was often to lead in the other. Mendora, for example, served at one time or another during Paul's tenure as magistrate, priestess and chief financial officer of Sillyon, a town in Pisidia, Asia.[54]

Common Concerns

What about the prohibition in I Timothy 2:12: "I do not permit a woman to teach . . ."? There are several aspects of I Timothy 2:12 that make the plain sense difficult to determine. The exact wording of Paul's restriction needs careful scrutiny. What kind of teaching is Paul prohibiting at this point? Some are quick to assume he means a teaching office or other position of authority. But teaching in the New Testament period was an activity and not an office (Mt 28:19-20), a gift and not a position of authority (Rom 12:7; I Cor 12:28; 14:26; Eph 4:11).

There is also the assumption that authority resides in the act of teaching (or in the person who teaches). In point of fact, it resides in the deposit of truth—"the deep truths of the faith" (I Tim 3:9; 4:6), "the faith" (I Tim 4:1; 5:8; 6:10, 12, 21), the trust (I Tim 6:20) that Jesus passed on to his disciples and that they in turn passed on to their disciples (2 Tim 2:2). Teaching is subject to evaluation just like any other ministry. This is why Paul instructed Timothy to publicly rebuke (I Tim 5:20) anyone who departed from "the sound instruction of our Lord Jesus Christ" (I Tim 6:3).

---

[51]Kearsley, "Asiarchs," pp. 183-92.

[52]Baugh, "Foreign World," p. 43.

[53]See Riet van Bremen, "Women and Wealth," in *Images of Women in Antiquity*, ed. Averil Cameron and Amélie Kuhrt (Detroit: Wayne State University Press, 1987), pp. 231-41.

[54]*Inscriptiones Graecae ad res Romanas pertinentes* 3.800-902.

It is often countered that teaching in 1 Timothy takes on the more official sense of doctrine and that teaching doctrine is something women can't do. Yet doctrine as a system of thought (i.e., dogma) is foreign to 1 Timothy. Traditions, yes; doctrines, no. While Paul urged Timothy to "command and teach these things" (1 Tim 4:11; 6:2), the "things" are not strictly doctrines. They included matters like avoiding godless myths and old wives' tales (1 Tim 4:7), godly training (1 Tim 4:7-8), God as the Savior of all (1 Tim 4:9-10) and slaves treating their masters with full respect (1 Tim 6:1-2). The flaw therefore lies in translating the Greek phrase *tē hygiainousē didaskalia* as "sound doctrine" instead of "sound teaching" (1 Tim 1:10; 4:6; cf. 1 Tim 6:1, 3; 2 Tim 4:3; Tit 1:9; 2:1).

What about Paul's naming Adam as first in the creation process? Isn't Paul saying something thereby about male leadership? "For Adam was formed *first*, then Eve" (1 Tim 2:13). Yet if one looks closely at the immediate context, "first-then" (*prōtos . . . eita*) language does nothing more than define a sequence of events or ideas. Ten verses later Paul states that deacons "must first [*prōton*] be tested; and then [*eita*] . . . let them serve" (1 Tim 3:10). This, in fact, is the case throughout Paul's letters (and the New Testament, for that matter). "First-then" defines a temporal sequence, without implying either ontological or functional priority. "The dead in Christ will rise *first. After that* we who are still alive and are left will be caught up together with them in the clouds to meet the Lord in the air" is a case in point (1 Thess 4:16-17). "The dead in Christ" gain neither personal nor functional advantage over the living as a result of being raised "first" (cf. Mk 4:28; 1 Cor 15:46; Jas 3:17).

But doesn't *gar* at the start of 1 Timothy 2:13 introduce a creation order dictum? Women must not teach men *because* God created men to lead (following the creation order of male, then female); Eve's proneness to deception while taking the lead demonstrates this. This reading of the text is problematic for a number of reasons. First, there is nothing in the context to support it. Paul simply does not identify Eve's transgression as taking the lead in the relationship or Adam's fault as abdicating that leadership. Second, the conjunction *gar* ("for") typically introduces an *explanation* for what precedes, not a cause.[55] If the sense of 1 Timothy 2:12 is that women are not permitted to teach men in a domineering fashion, then 1 Timothy 2:13 would provide the *explanation*: that Eve was created as Adam's partner (Gen 2:24) and not his boss. By contrast, *effect* ("women are not permitted to teach men

---

[55]The principal Greek causal conjunction is *hoti* (or *dioti*). See BDF 456.

in a domineering fashion") and then *cause* ("Adam was created to be Eve's boss" [i.e., first]) surely makes no sense. Third, those who argue for creation-fall dictums in I Timothy 2:13-14 stop short of including "women will be saved (or kept safe) through childbearing" in I Timothy 2:15. To do so, though, lacks hermeneutical integrity. Either all three statements are normative or all three are not.

What about Eve's seniority in transgression? Isn't Paul using Eve as an example of what can go wrong when women usurp the male's created leadership role? "And Adam was not the one deceived; it was the woman . . ." (I Tim 2:14). This view is without scriptural support. Eve was not deceived by the serpent into taking the lead in the male-female relationship. She was deceived into disobeying a command of God, namely, not to eat the fruit from the tree of the knowledge of good and evil. She listened to the voice of false teaching and was deceived by it. Paul's warning to the Corinthian congregation confirms this: "I am afraid that just as Eve was deceived by the serpent's cunning, your minds may somehow be led astray from your sincere and pure devotion to Christ" (2 Cor 11:3).

The language of deception calls to mind the activities of the false teachers at Ephesus. If the Ephesian women were being encouraged as the superior sex to assume the role of teacher over men, this would go a long way toward explaining I Timothy 2:13-14. The relationship between the sexes was not intended to involve female domination and male subordination. But neither was it intended to involve male domination and female subordination. Such thinking is native to a fallen creation order (Gen 3:16).

Summary

A reasonable reconstruction of I Timothy 2:11-15 would be as follows: The women at Ephesus (perhaps encouraged by the false teachers) were trying to gain an advantage over the men in the congregation by teaching in a dictatorial fashion. The men in response became angry and disputed what the women were doing.

This interpretation fits the broader context of I Timothy 2:8-15, where Paul aims to correct inappropriate behavior on the part of both men and women (I Tim 2:8, 11). It also fits the grammatical flow of I Timothy 2:11-12: "Let a woman learn in a quiet and submissive fashion. I do not, however, permit her to teach with the intent to dominate a man. She must be gentle in her demeanor." Paul would then be prohibiting teaching that tries to get the upper hand—not teaching per se.

13

A SILENT WITNESS IN MARRIAGE

1 Peter 3:1-7

Peter H. Davids

First Peter 3:1-7 has often been read as a text instructing Christian wives in subordination. Thus Wayne Grudem writes that 1 Peter 3:1 "means willingly to submit to your husband's authority or leadership in marriage,"[1] including submission "to good or harsh . . . husbands."[2] Though he makes an exception in cases of "spousal abuse" or a "*morally objectionable* behavior pattern,"[3] some evangelicals, such as James Hurley, do not.[4] While others, on the basis of 1 Peter 3:3, argue that this text prohibits women from wearing jewelry and anything other than plain clothing (as such is defined by the reference group), many evangelical scholars see this verse as cultural but still argue that the text as a whole teaches female subordination within marriage.

Evangelicals who emphasize gender equality take a different approach. Rebecca Merrill Groothuis states that 1 Peter 3 is directed to women with unbelieving husbands, arguing that it should be read within its cultural context, thus entailing quite different behavior today.[5] Craig S. Keener sees here a strategy for life within the

---

[1] Wayne Grudem, *1 Peter,* TNTC (Grand Rapids, Mich.: Eerdmans, 1988), p. 135.

[2] Wayne Grudem, "Wives like Sarah and the Husbands Who Honor Them: 1 Peter 3:1-7," in *RBMW,* p. 201, and n. 13 on p. 501.

[3] Ibid., p. 203 (emphasis his).

[4] James B. Hurley asserts, "She is to continue to live a godly life even with an abusive pagan husband who can in no way be considered to demonstrate Christ's love for the church. . . . Her willing suffering love for her husband . . . shows the willing suffering and love of Christ" (*Man and Woman in Biblical Perspective* [Grand Rapids, Mich.: Zondervan, 1981], p. 154). For examination of this issue in the context of both pastoral care and this passage, see Maxine O'Dell Gernert, "Pentecost Confronts Abuse," *JPT* 17 (2000): 117-30.

[5] Rebecca Merrill Groothuis, *Good News for Women: A Biblical Picture of Gender Equality* (Grand Rapids, Mich.: Baker, 1997), pp. 172-76.

Greco-Roman world, aimed at witness and reducing grounds for the charge that Christianity was subversive.[6] Such authors would not see this passage as teaching unilateral submission of wives within the *contemporary* context. Who is right?

Christian Wives with Non-Christian Husbands (1 Pet 3:1-6)

Wives within the Greco-Roman world. Language is an expression of a given culture existing in space and time. It takes its meaning from the definitions that culture gives to certain sounds and their associated graphic symbols. It is a truism that any given word, or its associated sound, in one culture may have a different meaning from the same word or sound in another. Furthermore, words in all languages change their meanings over time. In I Peter we have language (Greek) from a particular part of the first-century Mediterranean world. In interpreting it we are trying to understand what it meant as an expression of a given historical culture or social world. With this in mind, it is important that we see how the wives addressed in I Peter might have heard this instruction within their own social context.[7]

First, it is clear that I Peter is addressed to a largely Gentile Christian audience. In fact, a number of expressions (I Pet 1:14, 18; 2:9-10, 25; 4:3-4) indicate they were largely, if not exclusively, converts from paganism.[8] Their earlier state was "ignorance," and they had "futile ways inherited from [their] ancestors."[9] They were once "not a people" and had "already spent enough time in doing what the Gentiles like to do." These descriptions would not have fit Jewish Christians. Thus I Peter is not addressed to Christians with a Jewish upbringing but to those with a pagan or Gentile past. This helps us understand both the background of the wives and the nature of their husbands.

Second, while it is clear that the wives in I Peter 3:1-6 are Christians, this is not evident regarding their husbands, who appear to be a separate group from the believing husbands addressed in I Peter 3:7. We can be certain that at least some of the husbands in I Peter 3:1-6 are not Christians, since verse I reads "al-

---

[6]Craig S. Keener, *The IVP Bible Background Commentary: New Testament* (Downers Grove, Ill.: InterVarsity Press, 1993), p. 715.

[7]For a valuable discussion of the hermeneutics of this passage and others dealing with marriage and family, see Stephen C. Barton, *Life Together: Family, Sexuality and Community in the New Testament and Today* (Edinburgh: T & T Clark, 2001), pp. 3-55. In Barton's terms, what I am attempting to achieve in this chapter is to lay the exegetical framework for a more rounded theological approach to our topic, one which will be found throughout the other chapters in this volume.

[8]Peter H. Davids, *The First Epistle of Peter*, NICNT (Grand Rapids, Mich.: Eerdmans, 1990), pp. 8-9.

[9]Translations of I Peter are my own unless otherwise noted.

though some of them do not obey the word," where the grammar implies a condition of fact.[10] The primary reason for advocating wives' appropriate domestic behavior is "so that . . . [unbelieving husbands] may be won over without a word by their wives' conduct." Therefore the focus of the passage (1 Pet 3:1-6) is on women living with non-Christian husbands in the area of the Greco-Roman world to which the letter is addressed.[11] And even if women with Christian husbands were also intended, their behavior would likewise be conditioned by the evangelistic motive of this text.

Although we do not have an abundance of information about the specific social world of the women to whom this passage is addressed—the northwestern quadrant of modern-day Turkey—we do know that certain moral literature circulated throughout the Greco-Roman world at this time. In any case, Peter appears at times to reflect this literature—or perhaps he is drawing from the Roman situation where his letter originated.[12] One thing of which we can be most certain about the Greco-Roman world in general is that a woman was expected to follow the religious choices of her father and, after marriage, her husband. Plutarch, a Roman moralist of the era, held that

> a wife ought not to make friends of her own, but to enjoy her husband's friends in common with him. The gods are the first and most important friends. Wherefore it is becoming for a wife to worship and to know only the gods that her husband believes in, and to shut the front door right upon all queer rituals and outlandish superstitions.[13]

To the Roman mind, all beliefs other than traditional Roman religions were "outlandish superstitions." This included Judaism and, along with Judaism, Christianity. When a woman became a Christian independent of her husband's decision, she was immediately suspect as a rebel against the social order.

Related to this was the normal expectation that the husband should rule the

---

[10]The NRSV "even if" may be read as implying doubt; yet this is a real condition, not one implying doubt. Thus my translation "although." See Linda L. Belleville, *Women Leaders and the Church* (Grand Rapids, Mich.: Baker, 2000), p. 119.

[11]Since the evangelistic strategy is the expressed purpose, it is quite possible that the "some" indicates the situation of most of the women. This fits with the general theme of this section: minimizing conflict with the non-Christian culture. See further Paul J. Achtemeier, *1 Peter*, Hermeneia (Minneapolis: Fortress, 1996), p. 208, and the next section of this chapter.

[12]See Davids, *First Epistle of Peter*, pp. 5-7.

[13]Plutarch *Advice to Bride and Groom* 19, *Moralia* 140D (LCL). And Plutarch, it should be noted, was among the most egalitarian writers of his time. Cf. Achtemeier, *1 Peter*, p. 207.

wife. This was true for Plato,[14] Aristotle[15] and their followers. While David Balch has shown that household management was a common topic of discussion in the ancient world,[16] his evidence also indicates a virtually universal perception that women were to be ruled by men, usually with the assumption that they were inferior to men.[17] In this context, the teaching "wives, . . . submit to your own husbands"[18] would sound quite normal to the women being addressed. It was what their pagan society had always taught. The unusual part of our passage is the assumption that there is a reason for this behavior that goes beyond its fitting "women's nature."

A strategy for a Christian wife's witness in first-century Rome. Our passage is part of a letter. The letter form was well known in antiquity, for letter writing was an art as well as a means of communication. A letter may be of two types. It may be a *published* document, more a piece of literature than a missive sent to an actual recipient (or recipients). Or it may be an *occasional* document, intended to communicate in a specific way to a particular person or group. First Peter fits into this second category. As a result, we have only half of a two-way communication. That is, Peter has somehow received information about a group of churches in northwest Asia Minor, which stimulated him to write this letter. The topics he chooses and how he selects them are an expression of both his own cultural background and his perception of the situation of the recipients. The interpretation of any such letter involves at least a partial reconstruction of this dialogue.

Our text is located in the second main section of the letter, the "table of household duties" (I Pet 2:11–3:22),[19] and must be read as part of this wider context.

---

[14]E.g., Plato *Republic* 4.431C.

[15]E.g., Aristotle *Politics* 3.1260a; *Nicomachean Ethics* 8.1160b-61a.

[16]David L. Balch, *Let Wives Be Submissive: The Domestic Code in 1 Peter*, SBLMS 26 (Chico, Calif.: Scholars Press, 1981), pp. 27-29, 44-45.

[17]E.g., the Stoic Epictetus makes no positive references to women; his teaching is addressed entirely to men. Women are often described as "silly." See further Peter Lampe and Ulrich Luz, "Nachpaulinisches Christentum und pagane Gesellschaft," in *Die Anfänge des Christentums: Alte Welt und neue Hoffnung*, ed. Jürgen Becker et al. (Stuttgart: W. Kohlhammer, 1987), pp. 185-216.

[18]Literal translation. Although the NRSV's "accept the authority of" correctly assumes the expectations of a first-century Roman household, it implies stronger terminology than does the Greek text.

[19]This is marked out by the *inclusio* (framing device) created by two forms of *hypotagē* = "be in submission" in I Peter 2:13 and 3:22. Dorothy I. Sly, "I Peter 3:6b in the Light of Philo and Josephus," *JBL* 110 (1991): 126, notes the *inclusio*; the rhetorical analysis of Barth L. Campbell, *Honor, Shame and the Rhetoric of 1 Peter*, SBLDS 160 (Atlanta: Scholars Press, 1998), pp. 99-171, ends the section in I Peter 3:12. Certainly at least a subunit ends in I Peter 3:12, for by then the book has come to

First Peter 3:1 begins with "submit to your husbands," language that has already been used in I Peter 2:13, 18. This is an attitude that Christian subjects are to show to rulers and Christian slaves to masters. But in each case it is a qualified submission, since believers in Christ know themselves in reality to be "resident aliens" (I Pet 2:11); thus they are not really part of the structures of the present age, whether governmental or familial (including slavery and marriage), which are "human creations" (I Pet 2:13).[20] They are "free" (I Pet 2:16) and submit to others because God is their true Master and this is God's desire. They behave as they do, not because of the intrinsic authority of the other human being but to silence the criticism of unbelievers through doing what is right (I Pet 2:15).

Having addressed the issue of submission to "governing structures" in general (I Pet 2:13-17), Peter turns to two special cases, both addressed by pagan moralists.[21] In the first (I Pet 2:18-25), believing slaves are to submit to their (pagan) masters in imitation of the suffering of Christ. In one sense they could do nothing else, for should they rebel they would receive a beating or worse. As in the case of wives, the general Greco-Roman position was that slaves by nature were created to be ruled by masters, and therefore no choice was given to them in this matter.[22] Where Peter knows slaves could exercise the power of choice is in their acceptance of unjust suffering based on their identification with Christ.[23] There is here no admission that their master is just or is exercising his rights. The point is that Christ did indeed die unjustly (I Pet 2:22). Because of this, one who is suffering unjustly need not announce this to the world but can choose to identify with Christ and his silent acceptance of injustice. This is not a slave's recognition of the authority of the earthly master but a slave's identifying with her or his true master—the One

---

a basic resolution of the issue of suffering for doing good. For our purposes it is the beginning of the section rather than the end that is more critical.

[20]The Greek *(pasē anthrōpinē ktise)* puts the emphasis not on "authority" as such (TNIV) but on its being an "institution" (see NRSV) created either by or for human beings. Since this is a heading sentence for the whole section, it may rightly be assumed to cover both government (I Pet 2:13-17) and the household (I Pet 2:18–3:7).

[21]See, e.g., Balch, *Let Wives,* p. 43. It should be noted that the chapter break at I Peter 3:1 is especially unfortunate, since it may cause the ordinary reader to miss Peter's clear connections.

[22]Indeed, it was as much part of household management to rule slaves as it was to rule one's wife. Hence Plato and Aristotle and those coming after them discuss the management of slaves in the same places as the management of wives and children.

[23]In I Peter 4:16 the text speaks of suffering "as a Christian," while our section is silent on the cause of suffering, perhaps for apologetic reasons; one reason for unjust suffering was surely a slave's stubborn insistence on remaining a practicing Christian.

who died for the sins of others—and thus seeing value in unjust suffering and recognizing that God will set all things right.

The second special situation is that of a believing woman married to a pagan householder. Although, in contrast to slavery, the Bible clearly sanctions marriage as divinely ordained, it is nonetheless also a temporal, human institution—that is, it belongs to this age, not the age to come.[24] Thus it is introduced here with "likewise" or "in the same way," as an intentional parallel with slavery. Also parallel with slavery is the way the authority of the "master" is undermined even as it is affirmed to a certain degree. To be sure, the woman accepts her husband's authority, but not because she recognizes it as justified (as Plato and Aristotle would have it) or as a universal divine structure (as some pagan moralists and the Hellenized Jews Josephus and Philo taught). Rather she is to do so in order to evangelize him and to keep Christian teaching in good repute (1 Pet 2:16). Her husband had sole authority to decide if her babies lived, whether she would remain his wife and how she would be treated physically. Here she is given a way of reframing a situation that she cannot avoid, in order to have a strategic purpose within God's inbreaking rule in the world.

Yet what she is to do is also subversive in a sense. There is no hint that she should reject the worship of her Lord to worship her husband's gods. Indeed, she is expected to willfully hold on to her "superstition" despite the disapproval of her culture and her husband. However, in other culturally defined areas she is to show appropriate "female virtue," for like the slave's quiet acceptance of unjust treatment, this expresses Christian values and undermines criticism of Christianity.

Such virtue is described as "purity in fear" (1 Pet 3:2). "Fear" here, as elsewhere in this letter (1 Pet 1:17; 2:18; cf. 3:16 and the related verb in 1 Pet 2:17), most likely means "reverent fear [of God]" (see TNIV of 1 Pet 1:17 and 2:18). Indeed, Peter specifically *rejects* fearing/reverencing human beings or what they normally fear (1 Pet 3:6, 14). Thus the address to women begins with encouraging the fear of God and ends with rejecting the fear of human beings (including husbands).

"Purity" includes, as well as transcends, sexual purity, as seen elsewhere in the New Testament (Phil 4:8; 1 Tim 5:22; Jas 3:17; 1 Jn 3:3).[25] Sexual purity can be

---

[24]Peter does not cite Matthew 22:30, although there is evidence that he knew the Matthean tradition (see Rainer Metzner, *Die Rezeption des Matthäusevangeliums im 1. Petrusbrief,* WUNT 2/74 [Tübingen, Germany: Mohr, 1995]), but like Jesus in Matthew and Paul in 1 Corinthians 7, he views marriage as part of this age and not the age to come.

[25]Friedrich Hauck, "ἁγνός," in *TDNT* 1:122; Heinrich Baltensweiler, "Pure, Clean," in *DNTT* 3:100-102.

seen in the instruction to reject the use of outward adornment. Epictetus said, "When [women after puberty] see that they have nothing else but only to be the bedfellows of men, they begin to beautify themselves, and put all their hopes in that."[26] And pagan (especially Stoic) moralists frequently described outward adornment as an indication of sexual seductiveness.[27] This is understandable, since, as Epictetus notes, sexual attractiveness was the one power women were able to exert within their society. Moreover, such dress was also a mark of many cults, which were viewed as making women lascivious.[28] Thus Christian women are being exhorted to avoid appearing morally improper by the standards of their culture.[29]

In contrast to women displaying their sexuality, "a gentle and quiet [peaceful] spirit" characterized the pure way of life. The virtue of gentleness is not limited to women, since Jesus uses the word to describe himself (Mt 11:29). And Paul speaks of himself as coming "with a spirit of gentleness" (1 Cor 4:21) and includes "gentleness" as a "fruit of the Spirit" (Gal 5:22; cf. Col 3:12), which is to be exercised when restoring a sinning brother or sister (Gal 6:1). Likewise, the virtue of quietness or peacefulness (not primarily silence but remaining quiet rather than protesting) is applied to both men and women (1 Thess 4:11; 2 Thess 3:12; 1 Tim 2:2), and only in one other passage specifically to women (1 Tim 2:11-12).[30] While these were considered virtues for both men and women in the Greek world, they were viewed as particularly important for women.[31]

---

[26]Epictetus *Encheiridion* 40. He goes on to instruct, "It is worth while for us to take pains, therefore, to make them understand that they are honored for nothing else but only for appearing modest and self-respecting" (LCL 2, p. 525/27).

[27]Cf. Plutarch *Moralia* 1, 141; Seneca *De Beneficiis* 7.9; Perictione *On the Harmony of a Woman* 143. Among Jewish writers, see *Testament of Reuben* 5.5; Philo *De Virtibus* 39; *Vita Mosis* 2.243.

[28]See Balch, *Let Wives*, p. 101.

[29]It is not clear whether Peter is trying to curtail the actual behavior of some Christian women, since the language is so traditional in terms of Greco-Roman morality. If this is a literal reference, it would be addressed to middle- or upper-class women, for female slaves and peasant women would have had only one or two sets of everyday clothing. More likely this is a traditional denunciation of dress as a symbol of sexual seductiveness, thus especially to be avoided by Christian wives.

[30]Seen clearly in Philo *De Abrahamo* 27: "The opposite quality to rest is unnatural agitation, the cause of confusion, and tumults, and seditions, and wars, which the wicked pursue; while those who pay due honor to excellence cultivate a tranquil, and quiet, and stable, and peaceful life." Cf. Gerhard Delling, "ἄτακτος κτλ.," in *TDNT* 8:47-48.

[31]The two terms are also paired in *1 Clement* 13:4 and *Epistle of Barnabas* 19:4. See Friedrich Hauck and Siegfried Schulz, "πραΰς, πραΰτης," in *TDNT* 6:646: "It is one of the chief virtues in a woman." See Plutarch *Praecepta Conjugalia* 45 and *Consolatio ad Uxorem* 2. Hauck and Schulz add, "One finds it in feminine deities," including Artemis (*Anthologia Palatina* 6, 271; cf. also 9, 525, 17) and Leto (Plato *Cratylus* 406a).

Clearly, Christianity had subverted the authority of the Greek husband to determine the religion of his family. But rather than disturb the peace of the household further, Christian wives were to show that they were not sexually provocative (avoiding the charge that Christianity produced loose sexuality) and to contribute to the general peace of the household (rather than being harsh or rebellious). Since these were Christian virtues valued in both men and women, the women were not being asked to behave in any way other than a fully Christian manner. Since these were also Greco-Roman virtues especially admired in women, they showed that Christianity did not totally undermine the order of the family.

Peter goes on to attribute these virtues to unnamed "holy women who hoped in God" and "clothed themselves" with these virtues in submission to their husbands. This is a general statement, just as Luke 1:70, Acts 3:21 and 2 Peter 3:2 refer in general to the "holy prophets." That they "hoped in God" means they expected to receive their vindication at the consummation of the age, rather than in the present world order.[32]

At this point Sarah is used as a specific example of the "holy women" who "hoped in God." The terminology changes from "submitting" *(hypotassō)* to "obeying" *(hypakouō)*, and it is specifically said that she called Abraham "lord" (Hebrew *'adonai*, Greek *kyrios* = "lord/master," "husband" or "sir"). Only once in canonical Scripture does Sarah use this term regarding Abraham: "So Sarah laughed to herself, saying, 'After I have grown old, and *my husband* is old, shall I have pleasure?'" (Gen 18:12).[33] This statement is a disbelieving response to God and indicates no particular submission to Abraham.[34] While Sarah agrees to several re-

---

[32]Hebrews 11:13-16 also expresses this attitude well, using some of the language found in 1 Peter: "All these people were still living by faith when they died. They did not receive the things promised; they only saw them and welcomed them from a distance, admitting that they were foreigners and strangers on earth. People who say such things show that they are looking for a country of their own. . . . Therefore God is not ashamed to be called their God, for he has prepared a city for them." Cf. also the virtues of patient endurance expressed in James 5:7-8.

[33]Bible translations divide over whether to translate this term according to its use in 1 Peter or within the context of Genesis. Like the NRSV, the NAB translates the term contextually as "my husband." The NKJV follows the traditional AV rendering of "my lord." The NIV has "my master" with the alternative "husband" in a note. The NLT compromises with "my master—my husband."

[34]This fact leads Mark Kiley ("Like Sara: The Tale of Terror Behind 1 Peter 3:6," *JBL* 106 [1987]: 689-92), as well as Grudem (*1 Peter*, pp. 141-42), to argue that the reference is to her *implicit* obedience in Genesis 12 and 20. If this is the referent, then Kiley is correct when he states that it refers to what we would call an abusive situation. That is, to require one's wife to make herself available for marriage to someone else in a foreign land away from all support and protection, and to do so

quests from Abraham outside of Genesis 18:12 (see Gen 12:13; 20:5, 13), she does not use the term *lord* on these occasions, nor is her *obedience* to Abraham mentioned anywhere in the Genesis narrative.[35] On the other hand, Abraham is explicitly said to agree to[36] Sarah's requests in Genesis 16:2 and 21:10-12.[37] In the end, therefore, the information in Genesis, both Hebrew and Greek, does not appear to support the behavior Peter is commending in Sarah, making it unlikely that he is referring directly to Genesis 18:12.

But we do find Sarah frequently using *kyrios* when referring to, or addressing, Abraham in extracanonical Jewish works such as the *Testament of Abraham* (roughly contemporary with 1 Peter).[38] In this work especially, *kyrios* is used by Sarah to address Abraham (usually "my *kyrios* Abraham"), although only in casual or solemn discourse, not in contexts of "obedience."[39] This reinterpretation of Genesis accords

---

in order to preserve one's own life, without there being an explicit threat to it, in our present understanding be read only as abusive. However, Achtemeier, *1 Peter*, pp. 215-16, especially n. 141, points out that a "lack of evidence" of other references makes even Kiley agree that Genesis 18:12 is the focal passage.

[35]In fact, while the narrative often refers to her as Abraham's wife, it only once refers to him as her husband (Gen 20:3), using the word *ba'al* rather than the more generic *'adoni* used in Genesis 18:12. The latter is used in addressing God and men of equal or superior status to the speaker but is not otherwise used in speaking about another individual in the way it appears in Genesis 18:12.

[36]Indeed, the word translated "obey" *(hypakouō)* in 1 Peter 3:6 is actually used in the LXX in Genesis 18:6, to refer to Abraham's "listening to, heeding" Sarah. So while the Greek Bible used by Peter and these churches never speaks of Sarah's "obeying" Abraham, it does refer to his "obeying" her!

[37]The former instance fit his cultural values and thus gave him permission to do what he would have felt was right. The latter violated his cultural values, but divine intervention informed him that his wife was right, so he obeyed. The only other recorded interaction between Sarah and Abraham is his rushed but normal request in Genesis 18:6, making a total of only five interactions between them in the Old Testament.

[38]In a summary of the evidence, James R. Mueller ("Abraham, Testament of," in *ABD*) states, "Most scholars regard the 1st century B.C.E. or 1st century C.E. as the most likely [date for the work]." Though the *Testament of Abraham* may be as late as the late first century, as argued by Troy W. Martin ("The TestAbr and the Background of 1 Pet 3:6," *ZAW* 90 [1999]: 139-46), even that could make it in a sense contemporary with 1 Peter, for surely the legends contained in it were recited long before the book was composed. But the verbal overlap is significant enough that there could be actual dependence.

[39]This work, which probably originated in Egypt sometime in the first Christian century, was (also probably) composed originally in Greek. It comes to us in two distinct but related recensions, Recension A being about twice as long as B. In Recension A Sarah addresses Abraham this way seven times (5:13 [2x]; 6:2, 4, 5, 8; 15:4), in B two times (4:1; 6:5), while Isaac addresses his father once this way as well (7:2). But it should also be noted that Isaac addresses his mother with this expression (A 3:5, my *kyria* mother), and on one occasion the archangel Michael addresses Abraham this way (A 2:10).

with other Hellenistic Jewish literature from this period. For instance, Philo "indicates that Sarah's obedience to Abraham (or vice versa) was a matter of some discussion among biblical commentators in the first century."[40] Philo looks on instances where men listened to their wives as bringing a curse, using Genesis 3:7 as his prototype.[41] Josephus argues in one place, "A woman is inferior to her husband in all things. Let her, therefore, be obedient to him; not so that he should abuse her, but that she may acknowledge her duty to her husband; for God has given the authority to the husband."[42] Influenced by their culture, these authors developed creative ways of dealing with texts in which women (Sarah in particular) gave instructions that their husbands heeded. They might allegorize the woman so that the man would be heeding virtue rather than a woman,[43] or minimize the woman's (Sarah's) role altogether,[44] or alter the passage by inserting elements on which the text is silent.[45]

In light of these contemporary ways of presenting the Genesis texts,[46] and given

---

[40]Sly, "I Peter 3:6b," p. 126; cf. her discussion on pp. 127-29.

[41]Philo *Legum Allegoriae* 3.222.

[42]Josephus *Against Apion* 2.25.

[43]Philo *De Congressu Eruditionis Gratia* 63-68. Cf. *De Cherubim* 9: "The name of the woman was still Sarai; the symbol of my authority, for she is called my authority . . . [being] classed among things particular and things in species . . . such as the prudence which is in me, the temperance which is in me, the courage, the justice, and so on in the same manner." This builds on the picture in *De Congressu Eruditionis Gratia* 2: "The name Sarah, being interpreted, means 'my princedom.' And the wisdom which is in me, and the temperance which is in me, and the particular justice, and each of the other virtues which belong to me alone, are the princedom of me alone."

[44]See Sly, "I Peter 3:6b," p. 128: "Philo . . . devotes the treatise *On the Migration of Abraham* to commentary on the first six verses of Genesis 12 but skips over v. 5 which deals with Sarah. In the treatise he mentions Sarah in only three sections (126, 140, 142). In his other treatise on Abraham, he again disregards Gen 12:5, turning Abraham from a family man into a solitary traveler: 'But Abraham, the moment he was bidden, departed with a few or even alone' (*Abr.* 66). When he finally does bring Sarah to the fore (245-46), he changes her into a proper Hellenistic wife, an uncomplaining partner in life's wanderings, privations, and mishaps, whose distinguishing feature is wifely love *(philandria)*" (*De Abrahamo* 245-46, 253).

[45]For instance, Josephus (*Antiquities of the Jews* 1.10.4) writes, "Now Abram . . . being uneasy at his wife's barrenness, . . . entreated God to grant that he might have male issue; and God required of him to be of good courage, and said that he would add to all the rest of the benefits that he had bestowed upon him . . . the gift of children. Accordingly Sarai, at God's command, brought to his bed one of her handmaidens, a woman of Egyptian descent, in order to obtain children by her."

[46]I have not discussed rabbinic developments of traditions about Sarah. There is a parallel to the Hellenistic enlargements on the Sarah tradition in *Tanjuma*. See Giuseppe Ghiberti, "Le 'sante donne' di una volta (I Pt 3:5)," *Rivista Biblica* 36 (1988): 287-97. However, *Tanjuma* is from the fourth century B.C. (Tanjuma bar Abba) or later. Furthermore, I Peter does not demonstrate significant contact with rabbinic traditions. Interestingly, *Genesis Rabbah*, when commenting on Genesis 18, does not mention Sarah's obedience or her calling Abraham "lord."

that what Peter does say does not fit the Genesis narrative well, it seems most likely that in his reference to Sarah he is utilizing material known to his readers from these contemporary Jewish sources. Here Sarah is depicted in terms of an ideal Hellenistic wife, an illustration that serves Peter's purpose. Christian wives will be Sarah's "daughters" (i.e., among the holy women) if they are also good Hellenistic wives and emulate her (Greco-Roman) virtue (that is, do good and refuse to fear).[47] The refusal to fear would apply specifically to the displeasure—and the consequences it would bring—of their non-Christian husbands and Greek society regarding their involvement in the Christian faith.

Contemporary application. One of Peter's strategies is to minimize the tension between Christians and the surrounding society. He wants to make Jesus the issue, not unnecessarily divisive behaviors. In particular, he seeks to defend Christians against the charge that they are subverting the social order, since at the very core of things (religious devotion) they are already doing that very thing! This leads to his general statements in 1 Peter 2:12-13, 15 and to more specific discussions of the behavior of slaves and wives in 1 Peter 2:18-25 and 3:1-6 respectively.

In the latter two cases, the attempt to present Christianity as nonsubversive is complicated by the fact that Peter will not compromise on a central point: both slaves and wives must be free to commit themselves to the Christian faith regardless of the wishes of their masters or husbands. While not every slave would have a non-Christian master, or every wife a non-Christian husband, the tendency of the passage in each case is to assume that they do. This makes the best sense of the apologetic tone. In the case of the wives the apologetic defense was particularly important, for their refusal of the family religion determined by their husband would be more public, as well as more intimate,[48] and more influential in that typically wives were responsible for raising children for the first period of the children's lives.

The strategy was to advise wives not to talk about their religion but to model culturally appropriate behavior. This dictated that they not be sexually provocative

---

[47]Exactly how "doing good" and "refusing to fear" (participles) fit with being a daughter of Sarah is debated. I have chosen to understand them as circumstantial. For a fuller discussion see Martin, "TestAbr," pp. 143-44.

[48]Slaves might indeed be intimate with the master in that many masters used both male and female slaves sexually, but their intimacy was less official. Furthermore, slaves had quarters to withdraw to, so their devotional practice was less public. Also, they were not as involved in the family religious practices as were the wives.

outside of the home,[49] that their words be few, that they show gentleness and that they not foment "revolution" within the household.

Two encouragements are given to support such behavior. First, this kind of behavior can lead to the conversion of an unbelieving husband. Second, it puts the wife in a class with the "holy women" of Judaism whose behavior brought divine approval. Peter's example is Sarah, especially as portrayed in the *Testament of Abraham*. If Christian wives follow this model, they will likewise be considered holy women, approved by God, for they will fit the virtues of their culture, insofar as those virtues are consistent with Christian virtues.

However, unless we assume that first-century Greco-Roman society is the only form of society upholding virtues approved by God (an unlikely assumption), we may find that a direct application of Peter's teaching in modern and postmodern societies would subvert his original intentions. Language and behavior have particular meaning within a cultural context. This has generally been recognized when it comes to the application of the passage about slaves, women's dress in church (I Cor II), and braided hair, gold ornaments or fine[50] clothing (I Pet 3:3). Today hairstyle is—within limits—generally viewed as indifferent with respect to Christian virtue. Braiding is often regarded as a conservative hairstyle rather than being sexually provocative. Women in most churches can be seen wearing gold jewelry, and the use of decorative clothing (rather than purely functional clothing) is often characteristic of "going to church." This is because in Western culture the wearing of decorative clothing and gold jewelry is not considered seductive or dishonorable. Indeed, in some cases it might be viewed as dishonoring (even to the husband) if a woman dressed in an unstylish or plain manner. Groups that insist on a literal application of this text—forbidding all decorative clothing and jewelry (although not normally braided hair)—are usually viewed by the culture as making Christianity

---

[49]In the case of at least upper-class wives in some parts of the Roman Empire, this would also be true within the home. The ideal wife was sexual enough to get pregnant and bear three or so children but would give up sexual relations altogether by her mid-twenties and even before that would expect her husband to get his main sexual needs met elsewhere. See Aline Rousselle, "Body Politics in Ancient Rome," in *A History of Women*, ed. Pauline Schmitt Pantel (Cambridge, Mass.: Harvard University Press, 1992), pp. 313-24. Cf. Reay Tannahill, *Sex in History* (New York: Stein and Day, 1982), pp. 132-35.

[50]The adjective *kosmos*, translated "fine" in the NRSV, in this context carries the meaning "to beautify or adorn." Thus the accurate translation "You should not use outward adornment to make yourselves beautiful as in the way you fix your hair or in the jewelry you put on or in the dresses you wear," in Johannes P. Louw and Eugene A. Nida, *Greek-English Lexicon of the New Testament Based on Semantic Domains* 2 vols., 2nd ed. (New York: United Bible Societies, 1988-1989), no. 6.188; cf. 79.12.

less attractive rather than as upholding and supporting the social order. This would be contrary to Peter's strategy.

So how should we apply the silent witness of 1 Peter 3? Unlike the Greco-Roman society, modern societies generally do not give exclusive authority to husbands. Nor would it be regarded favorably for a wife to call her husband "my lord" (though women in the Victorian era did). This is because, unlike Greco-Roman society, our society expects marriage to be a partnership with a significant degree of intimacy. The removal of the husband's unilateral authority—a concept illustrated but not prescribed in Scripture—has greatly increased such intimacy. At the same time, marital intimacy is not enhanced by a barrage of criticism or a constant harping on the theme of religious beliefs. While wives are expected to be sexual within the boundaries of the marital relationship, faithfulness and a lack of seductiveness outside of that relationship are appropriate Christian virtues and would certainly constitute appropriate purity today.

Women are expected to be assertive in contemporary culture, but there is a difference between harshness and gentle assertiveness. The latter is entirely in keeping with Christian virtue for both men and women. The idea of "being at peace" entails not trying to rebel against or overthrow societal structures. Within the context of marriage this would at least include a commitment to the marital relationship.

Ironically, interpretations that focus on the unilateral obedience or submission of wives to husbands, regardless of cultural context, achieve the opposite of Peter's intention. Rather than promoting harmony with culture, they set Christian marriage partners at odds with culture and thus heighten the tension, and Christianity is perceived as undermining culture in a retrogressive way. This is precisely what 1 Peter is seeking to minimize.

Thus if we want to preserve 1 Peter's strategy and intention within Western culture, we might appropriately paraphrase its teachings this way:

> Wives, embrace your marital relationship, so that even if your husband is not a believer he may be won without a word by your behavior when he observes that your sexuality is for the marriage alone and your piety is genuine. So don't be sexually provocative in your dress outside the home. Instead let your "dress" be a gentle assertiveness and a commitment to the marital relationship, which are precious in God's sight. That's how the holy women of long ago lived. They were committed to their marriages. Sarah was committed to Abraham and behaved accordingly within her culture. You are her daughters if you do what is good and do not let threats from your husband turn you from your faith.

Christian Husbands with Christian Wives (1 Peter 3:7)

A Christian husband's treatment of his wife in first-century Rome. The address to the believing husbands completes the section on wives and husbands. A brief treatment is appropriate in view of the brevity of the instruction.[51]

First, although the behavior of the wives is not explicitly described in this verse, the majority of scholars have argued that the husbands in question are married to Christian wives. This is certainly true if the women are "fellow heirs of the grace of life," which is the most natural reading of the sentence.[52] Thus we are dealing with women who have come to faith, either on their own or following their husbands (as would be natural in a Greco-Roman setting).

Second, there is no main verb in this sentence. The husbands are "likewise" to do something (parallel to I Pet 3:1, which picks up on I Pet 2:13, 18) by means of the two following participial clauses (i.e., showing consideration for and paying honor to their wives). Is the implied verb "be submissive to" (cf. I Pet 3:1, 2:18, and 2:13)? Likely so, in which case the reference is to I Peter 2:13—the authority of human institutions, in this case marriage. Whatever the exact referent, the implication is that the husband is experiencing a limitation on his freedom parallel to that which the wife and slave have previously experienced.

Third, the husband needs to live with his wife recognizing that she is "weaker." How she is weaker is not specified. Evidence from the Greco-Roman worldview could support an assumption of physical weakness, social weakness, intellectual weakness or moral weakness.[53] The point is that the husband is in some respect "stronger" and needs to recognize this fact in his life with his wife, so that he does not exploit this disparity in strength, consciously or unconsciously. Rather, he is to treat her as an equal, a "fellow heir of the grace of life"—a complementary equality. His words and actions are to accord her this status, *honor* being a key status term in Greco-Roman culture.

Fourth, the reason for the husband's need to do this is so that "your" prayers

---

[51]For a more extensive treatment, see Davids, *1 Peter*, pp. 122-23.

[52]For a contrary opinion based on the fact that the "weaker vessel" of I Peter 3:7 is singular and the "fellow heirs" is plural, see Carl D. Gross, "Are the Wives of I Peter 3:7 Christians?" *JSNT* 35 (1989): 89-96. He translates the phrase "giving her honor as you also do to your fellow heirs of the grace of life," i.e., treat her as honorably as you do your Christian brothers and sisters. This is, however, a minority position and overlooks (1) that this verse seems almost an afterthought rather than part of the larger structure and (2) the verse's beginning with "husbands" (plural) would make the shift from singular to plural for the wives quite natural.

[53]Gross, "Are the Wives of I Peter 3:7 Christians?" p. 123.

may not be hindered (either those of the husband—which is more likely since he is being addressed—or those of the couple). In other words, a failure to treat his wife as an equal will, by implication, result in divine displeasure and a damaged relationship in which prayers are not answered.

Here Peter follows the general New Testament strategy of requesting that those with power give up their power. When addressing those without power (slaves and wives), he does not call for revolution but upholds the values of the culture insofar as they do not conflict with commitment to Christ. He then reframes their behavior by removing it from the realm of necessity and giving it a dignity, either that of identification with Christ or of identification with the "holy women" of Jewish antiquity. When speaking to the ones with power, however, he asks them not to use their power but to treat those they could dominate as their equals—for in fact they are. In this he is acting analogously to Paul's strategy in Philemon on the subject of slavery.

Contemporary application. The question for today is: Will men/husbands try to hold on to an authority over their wives that once was given them by the surrounding culture but now for the most part they no longer have?[54] Or will they gladly drop power, as well as the pretense to power, and treat their wives as equals, reaping not only a more intimate marriage relationship but also divine pleasure?

---

[54]Naturally the average man is in some respects physically stronger than the average woman. Also, women are economically and socially disadvantaged even in Western culture. However, Western culture, which is the context of this study, no longer sanctions such differences, nor does it sanction the use of male physical strength against women, even if everyday life has not caught up with moral theory.

PART III

THINKING IT THROUGH

Logical and Theological Perspectives

14

THE PRIORITY OF
SPIRIT GIFTING
FOR CHURCH MINISTRY

Gordon D. Fee

This chapter will explore how the gifting of the Spirit affects our understanding of people's ministries and areas of service in the church. I begin with a disclaimer about the concept of "equality." What is at stake is not whether all people are equally gifted; they are not. What is at stake is whether God the Holy Spirit, in his gifting the people of God, ever makes gender a prior requirement for certain kinds of gifting. I will argue that on this point what biblical data we do have seems clear: the Spirit does not.

But in order to get there, we need to cover some much-covered ground yet again, regarding (1) the nature of biblical revelation and authority, including the hermeneutics of ad hoc documents that do not speak to a given concern as a matter of advocacy, and (2) the complex nature of early church "structures" that are reflected in our documents, which do not address those structures as a primary concern. At issue in the use of such texts is the question, what does the Bible teach?—and what does one mean by "teach," when the "teaching" is not explicit? Then there is our constant use of *biblical* in our rhetoric: what do we mean by this term?—that something is "biblical" only when it is prescriptive? And if we include what is otherwise merely descriptive, on what grounds do we move from description to prescription?

So what I hope to do in this chapter is threefold: (1) to point out the ambiguity of the biblical texts with regard to church structures and ministries, and thus (2) to define a hermeneutical starting point from which our quest might legitimately be carried forward, and (3) to look at a variety of texts that state or imply that Spirit gifting precedes all questions of structures and gender.

The Bible's Ambiguity Regarding Church Structure and Ministries

One thing that should perhaps strike the serious reader of Scripture is the general lack of concern in the New Testament about the way the church ordered its corporate life, whether in its structures ("offices," etc.) or its gatherings for worship.[1] So much is this so that every present form of church government appeals to New Testament texts in support of its particular organizational flow chart.[2] This is true from the ultimate hierarchical understanding of church in Roman Catholicism to the much more subtle hierarchy of the Plymouth Brethren, not to mention Baptists and Presbyterians in between. The New Testament documents simply show no interest in defining these matters; their ecclesiological interest rather is on the who and how of the composition of the people of God under the new covenant effected through Christ and evidenced by the Spirit.[3]

It is precisely the opposite, however, with regard to the former covenant ratified at Sinai between Yahweh and Israel. Here there are specific, intentional instructions about how Israel would function both as a people and in its worship of Yahweh. Although women like Deborah functioned as both "prophet" and "judge/leader" (Judg 4) and Huldah as a "prophet" (2 Kings 22:14), there was no place for women in the priesthood, whose rules were very explicitly laid out in terms of men only. Such instruction is completely missing from the New Testament, where the Old Testament priesthood has been made obsolete through the crucifixion of Christ and the subsequent new covenant gifting of the Holy Spirit (in fulfillment of Joel 2:28-29)—a gifting that comes upon men and women, old and young, slave and free alike.

The net result is that we know very little about the "organization" of the early church, either as a whole or in its local expressions. And what we do learn, we gather from "gleanings" of texts, not from intentional instruction. The closest

---

[1] Take the longstanding difficulty of determining the relationship between the meal and the Lord's Table that arises in Paul's heated response in 1 Corinthians 11:17-34 and how this (these?) is (are) further related to the spontaneous Spirit utterances in 1 Corinthians 14:26-33.

[2] See Gordon D. Fee, "Reflections on Church Order in the Pastoral Epistles, with Further Reflection on the Hermeneutics of Ad Hoc Documents," *JETS* 28 (1985): 141-51.

[3] The "how" of course is by faith in Christ and the gift of the Spirit; the "who" is Jew and Gentile, slave and free, male and female (Gal 3:28; cf. 1 Cor 12:13; Col 3:10); see chapter ten in this book. So much is this so that I have considerable difficulty with the theological rubric *ecclesiology*, which should refer to discussion about the people of God but has been generally co-opted to refer to structures, ministry and function. Perhaps we need a word like "laiology" in order to talk about the real issues: what it means for the church to be the people of God.

thing to the latter appears in I Timothy 3:1-13 and Titus 1:5-9; but here, to our dismay, we learn only about the qualifications for certain positions of leadership; we learn next to nothing about who they were and what role they played. And the concept of "office," in the sense that there were offices in the church that needed to be filled with persons, is just barely a possibility in I Timothy 3:1 and appears nowhere else in the New Testament. Rather, there were persons who *functioned* in certain capacities, whose function eventually was expressed in a more titular way. That is, before there were "prophets," individuals prophesied, and they were sometimes called "prophets"; and "elders" (a term with roots in the synagogue) gave oversight to the community and eventually came to be called *episkopoi* (overseers), a term derived from the Greco-Roman world.

Even here we get just enough information to whet our appetites for more, but nothing bordering on certainty. Thus when one asks on the basis of Paul's use of "elders" and "overseers" in I Timothy 3 and 5 and Titus 1, how these people might be distinguished from one another, we get an amazing spread of answers, precisely because of the *ambiguity of our texts.* For example, I have argued that the best solution is to see *elder* as the broad term that included both "overseers" and "deacons"[4]; but I also recognize how foolish it would be to press that or to make "church order" based on it, because such an opinion is the result of exegetical decision making, not of clear intentional revelation from the Holy Spirit.

Thus what is totally lacking in our documents is any instruction intentionally stipulating who, what, how many and the duties of these various people. At the "church universal" level we get tantalizing glimpses, but scarcely anything on which all can agree. The role of the Twelve is especially ambiguous. What seems certain from the data is the significance of the number twelve, precisely because Jesus was deliberately offering himself as the new expression of Israel in the coming rule of God. This seems to be made certain by Luke's narrative in Acts 1 about the filling out of that number. But when one gets into the rest of the narrative of Acts, the role of the Twelve becomes more and more ambiguous: they never appear again as a group, and when the church gathers in a semi-official way in Acts 15 it is James, not one of the Twelve, who leads the deliberations.[5]

This is likewise the case with Paul. A comparison of a passage like Acts 15 with a variety of passages in Paul's letters leaves us with several impressions but with

---

[4]See Gordon D. Fee, *1 and 2 Timothy, Titus,* NIBC (Peabody, Mass.: Hendrickson, 1988), p. 78.

[5]In fact one of the mysteries of early church history is how and when this happened, not to mention the mystery of "whatever happened to the Twelve?"

nothing in sharp focus. It seems, for example, that Paul did not think of "apostle-ship" as an office in the church charged with oversight of the whole; in fact, it is quite the opposite. He mentions "the Twelve" (even when they were only eleven!) only in their historic role as eyewitnesses to the resurrection of Jesus (1 Cor 15:5). But there is no sense in which he defers to them. Rather, when he refers to James and two of the Twelve in Galatians 2:1-10, he speaks in terms of their being "es-teemed" as leaders, not in terms of their official, God-given authority.

Similarly, Paul's own authority as an apostle had to do with the churches he had founded,[6] not with the church universal. Thus he is as prepared to resist any form of outside interference with "his" churches (see Gal and 2 Cor 10–12) as he is def-erential when writing to a church that he did not found (see Rom 1:8-15).

When we look at the church at the local level, it is even more the case that we do not know enough to be certain about very much—even at the purely descriptive level, let alone at any prescriptive level. We can make an educated guess, if the ma-jority opinion is correct about the letter of James, that the local communities in Palestine were patterned after the Jewish synagogue (see Jas 2:2, where that lan-guage occurs).[7] Likewise, even though we can be sure that the communities founded by Paul in the Greco-Roman world took the form of house churches, what we cannot be sure of is whether they were also patterned after the Greco-Roman household. Many of us think so, especially since Paul uses this very language at times as an image for the church (see "God's household" in 1 Tim 3:15). But others would argue that the synagogue still functioned as the pattern for the household church. And even though I think that is most highly unlikely,[8] in the end I too must admit that the reason one can so argue is that the evidence itself is not clear.

Moreover, if I am right about the structure of the house(hold) church, then it would follow naturally (or so it could be argued) that the householder functioned

---

[6]On the basis that he had seen, and had been commissioned by, the risen Lord (1 Cor 9:1; cf. 15:7-11). See Gordon D. Fee, *The First Epistle to the Corinthians*, NICNT (Grand Rapids, Mich.: Eerdmans, 1987), p. 395 n. 16.

[7]This may also be true of Hebrews 13; in any case, the difference between Hebrews 13:17 ("have confidence in your leaders and submit to their authority") and 1 Thessalonians 5:12 ("acknowledge those who work hard among you, who care for you in the Lord and who admonish you") is consid-erable and probably reflects two different kinds of "church."

[8]Where in the synagogue, for example, would there be a place for something like "the Lord's Table," which fits the household extremely well, or for spontaneous utterances from the Spirit as envisioned in 1 Corinthians 14:26-33, which fits better the *symposium* of the Jewish mystical group described by Philo (*On the Contemplative Life* 64-90) in the context of a meal?

in the same way in the household church as in the household as such. If so, then women like Lydia (Acts 16:13-15) and Nympha (Col 4:15) would have ordinarily functioned that way in their households. But many think otherwise, precisely because the texts are ambiguous, and in such cases we tend to bring some prior hermeneutical or religious commitments to our reading of them.

Ordinarily, having come this far in such an argument, one would go on and try to ferret out from our various snippets of data what we *can* have a degree of certainty about—for example, that the churches did have leadership and that leadership was important, even if we do not know what it looked like. But my concern here is simply to point out the high degree of uncertainty all of us face when asking questions about this dimension of "church" on the basis of the New Testament evidence. We have enough information to offer descriptive guesses with varying degrees of certainty. But what we lack is the one essential thing: intentional instruction about the church: its structures, the nature of its leadership, both local and beyond, and its worship—the various aspects of it, who led it and its "order."

And that leads to my second concern: what degree of hermeneutical certainty should we impose on texts that are not intentional in their instruction, and from which we learn only by bringing our questions to the text and ferreting out the evidence?

A Hermeneutical Starting Point

One of the greatest difficulties that "biblical Christians" have is to come to terms with the term *biblical* in that formula. At issue here is how prescriptive we make biblical texts that only narrate what is and do not say explicitly that this is also the way things *must be*. Do analogies and examples carry the same "for all times in all places" freight as explicit instruction? And if so, how so? What is the guiding hermeneutic that makes some merely descriptive matters like church order and the relationship of gender to ministry and gifts become *prescriptive*, while at the same time among many who hold such a view, a very prescriptive word by Paul, "Be eager to prophesy, and do not forbid speaking in tongues" (1 Cor 14:39), is consistently, sometimes cavalierly, disobeyed? The answer, of course, is a hermeneutic that is culturally conditioned and unrelated to the biblical data! And since the texts themselves do not prescribe, on what grounds do some believers develop a "hierarchy of hermeneutics" that argues for the eternal validity of 1 Timothy 3:1-11 (and includes the *duties* of overseers, even though the texts do not speak to this question), while instruction about the care for and remarriage of widows in 1 Timothy 5:1-16 carries no weight at all?

Some years ago, in searching for some hermeneutical solid ground regarding our use of biblical narratives for what is normative[9] in the church, I argued that normativity must finally lie with authorial intentionality. In that piece I pointed out that doctrinal statements tend to be of three kinds: Christian theology (what Christians believe), Christian ethics (how Christians ought to live in relation to others) and Christian praxis (what Christians do as "religious" people). Moreover, within these three kinds of statements there are some that are primary and nonnegotiable (e.g., the deity of Christ), while others are secondary (e.g., the two natures and how they cohere). The difference between these two is that the first are always explicitly taught in Scripture, the second are derivative from what is explicit. It seems to be a plain fact of church history that most of the differences between Christians lie in two places: (1) with the secondary-level statements in the first two categories (theology and ethics)[10] and (2) with both levels of statements in the third category (praxis).

For example, now picking up only on the third category of Christian praxis, most Christian communions believe that the celebration of the Lord's Table is explicitly taught in Scripture,[11] but the church is unfortunately deeply divided over almost everything else about the Table: the "meaning" of the bread and wine, the frequency of participation, who are the legitimate participants, who can administer and so forth. And it will take very little by way of observation to note that all these differences are predicated on *different readings of texts that give no explicit instruction;* everything is implied.

This is precisely what lies behind our differences pointed to above in the area of church order and ministry as well. *That* the church has some form of recognizable

---

[9]See Gordon D. Fee, "Hermeneutics and Historical Precedent: A Major Problem in Pentecostal Hermeneutics," in *Perspectives on the New Pentecostalism,* ed. Russell P. Spittler (Grand Rapids, Mich.: Baker, 1976), pp. 118-32. This material was then recast for a larger Christian audience in chap. 6 of Gordon D. Fee and Douglas Stuart, *How to Read the Bible for All Its Worth* (Grand Rapids, Mich.: Zondervan, 1982), pp. 94-112. These two pieces set off a flurry of activity over my use of the word *normative,* which I took—and still take—to mean "that which is required practice for the church in all times and all places, so that not to do so is to disobey." In any case some clarification was needed, which was incorporated into the second edition of the book (Zondervan, 1993), pp. 105-12.

[10]That is, all would agree that the sovereignty of God is taught throughout Scripture, both explicitly and implicitly, but churches are deeply divided over the implications of this reality on the matter of the "freedom of the will"—a matter, I am quick to point out, that is less certainly addressed in the biblical texts. And so also with Christian ethics; consider the command "keep yourselves pure" and how that is worked out in many different Christian communions, and often in very divisive ways.

[11]As commanded by our Lord himself, "Do this in remembrance of me" (Lk 22:19; I Cor 11:24-25).

organization, we may well assume on the basis of our many scattered data; but *what form* that structure took can be derived only from the reading of texts by implication, not from gathering explicit statements intended to guide us in these matters.

And the same is especially true with regard to the matter of gender as it relates to structures and ministry. The texts simply do not have explicit teaching on these matters.[12] Therefore advocates on both sides are left with sharply contrasting readings of the biblical texts, precisely because the biblical texts themselves do not have an agenda on this question. Rather, they speak into a wide variety of ad hoc situations that reflect a wide variety of scenarios, which, when they are all put side by side, seem to show evidence of a wide variety of practices.

But what they do *not* do in an intentionally instructive way is to speak to the question whether women may or may not be in leadership; and except for I Timothy 2:11-12, they do not otherwise speak to the issue of women's participation in some, but not other, activities of ministry. The obvious difficulty with the I Timothy passage is that it stands in unrelieved tension with passages that either narrate (Acts 18:26) or imply (I Cor 14:26, 29-31) that women were involved in some form of teaching. And it will simply do no good here to go through a series of circuitous exegetical hoops to argue that "teaching" implies an office of "teacher," and therefore there are different kinds and levels of teaching, some of which women can be excluded from.[13] What is derived only from a series of exegetical jumps can scarcely be regarded as either "the plain teaching of Scripture" or a norm for the contemporary church.

Finally, it should be noted that our hermeneutical difficulties here are exacer-

---

[12]Many will demur on this point, pointing to I Timothy 2:11-12; but here the issue is, explicit about what? It is extremely tenuous to derive church office from this text! Those who do so bring a carload of presuppositional baggage to their reading of the text. The immediate context has to do with "prayers for all people" because God wants all people to be saved (I Tim 2:1-7) and proper *demeanor* in prayer, with instruction/correction first to the men (I Tim 2:8) and then to the women (I Tim 2:9-15). To argue that I Timothy 2:13 has to do with church order is to throw a red herring about structures into an otherwise clearly corrective admonition—most likely based on the ad hoc situation of this letter. After all, the final resolution in I Timothy 2:15 sounds like I Timothy 5:14: the fact that some younger widows have "already turned away to follow Satan" (I Tim 5:15) is what lies behind the correction given in I Timothy 5:14.

[13]See, e.g., Wayne Grudem, "Prophecy, Yes, but Teaching, No: Paul's Consistent Affirmations of Women's Participation Without Governing Authority," *JETS* 30 (1987): 11-23, a marvelous example of a prior hermeneutical agenda's preceding the reading of texts—so much so that the plain reading of I Corinthians 12:28 is subjected to, and thus rejected because of, language that is not biblical at all ("governing authority"!).

bated by the fact that our only experience of church, even for those who have broad intercommunion experience, is of a later development of church that looks almost nothing like the house churches of the first-century Greco-Roman world. This is not a criticism of us; it is simply a statement of reality. But our hermeneutical difficulty here is seldom addressed, and that is, how do these first-century texts apply when we cannot be sure how our own reality is related to theirs? For example, Paul regularly puts the activities of apostles and prophets together in the church (1 Cor 12:28; Eph 2:20; 3:5; 4:11), but for a variety of reasons, historical and otherwise, very few contemporary expressions of the church are comfortable with these designations for church offices of any kind. On the other hand, Paul in one place (Eph 4:11) and Peter in another (1 Pet 5:1) refer to some who are called "shepherds" (often brought into English as "pastors"). The single article controlling the two final nouns in the Ephesians passage indicates that the "shepherds" were also "teachers." Together these passages could be understood to refer to the "elders" who gave leadership to a local assembly.[14] But what is not clear at all is that there is a true correspondence between this biblical designation and the contemporary Protestant use of the term *pastor* to refer to the chief administrative officer and preacher of a local congregation!

In light of the ambiguities and consequent difficulties, therefore, I would argue that a proper hermeneutic for such matters would be similar to the one I suggested for biblical precedent regarding the narratives of Scripture.[15] In matters of Christian practice, a biblical precedent that comes to us by way of narration or implication alone may often be regarded as a repeatable pattern for the later church; but nothing that is merely narrated or described, even if narrated more than once, should be understood to be normative for the church in all places at all times. And I use *normative* here in the sense that we are disobedient if we do not follow the norm.

Thus regarding church order, the ambiguity between the synagogue model and the household model should probably leave plenty of room for variety within the ongoing life of the church. And since the New Testament does *not* teach explicitly that only men may lead or serve in certain ways, and in fact seems to leave the door open on this matter (in the case of women as householders), the issue should more

---

[14]This is rather explicit in 1 Peter 5:1; one gets there in Paul by noting his use of "apostle and prophet" elsewhere in Ephesians to refer to those who founded churches, thus perhaps reflecting itinerant ministries, while the "shepherd-teachers" would be the local elders. But this is only a (reasoned) exegetical guess.

[15]See note 9 above.

likely be giftedness, not gender. Indeed, I for one have as much resistance to the notion that women *ought to be* in leadership along with men as to the notion that *only* males are gifted to lead. The former notion also assumes a gender-based, not gift-based, model for leadership; and both Scripture and common experience give the lie to the second notion.

On the other hand, those who have been recognized by the community as a whole to be gifted for ministry and leadership should receive "the laying on of hands" on that basis alone, whether male or female. And that leads to my final point. Does this view hold up under the scrutiny of the biblical evidence?

Verbal Ministries in the New Testament Church

When we come to questions about "gift-based ministry," there are two kinds of issues that need to be looked at. (1) What does "ministry" mean? Can one make a legitimate distinction between ministry as "office" in the church and ministry as serving the church in other capacities? (2) What is the evidence that women were involved in ministry that included teaching, especially instructing others in Scripture? The place to begin is with the biblical evidence for the latter concern: gift-based ministry on the part of women.

First Corinthians 11:4-5. Although some have denied it,[16] there can be little question that this passage implies that women prayed and prophesied in the gathered community. At issue here is whether a woman should do so "uncovered as to her head." Because of the somewhat (apparently, at least) offhand way this is said, it is very likely that these two words represent all such activity in the assembly. Prayer is the primary form of speech directed toward God in such settings, and thus it probably stands for all speech directed to God (and would therefore also include speaking in tongues, 1 Cor 14:2, 28). Likewise "prophecy" is Paul's preferred form of speech addressed to the rest of the community and as such probably stands for all such forms of speech (teaching, revelation, word of knowledge, word of wisdom, etc.; see 1 Cor 14:6). The point is that "prophecy" at least is Spirit-inspired speech, and the clear implication of this text is that it was practiced by women and men alike.

First Corinthians 14:23-33. This passage should be read in light of the preceding one. Here Paul says twice, "All prophesy" (1 Cor 14:24 and 31). Even though the first of these is stated with hypothetical all-inclusiveness, that very fact indicates that prophecy in the gathered community *potentially* included everyone, male and fe-

---

[16]See Fee, *1 Corinthians*, p. 497 n. 22.

male alike. This is even more the case in I Corinthians 14:31, where he gives explicit instruction: "You can all prophesy in turn." What is important about this sentence is that it gives the purpose of such prophesying as "so that everyone may *be instructed* and *encouraged* [or *exhorted*]." These latter two verbs are most often associated, first, with receiving instruction through teaching and, second, with proclamation—which suggests that Paul did not have neat categories for these various verbal expressions prompted by the Spirit.

It should be pointed out further that up to I Corinthians 14:29-33 in the argument of I Corinthians 14 Paul refers to prophecy and tongues mostly with verbs. His emphasis is clearly on the *activity* of prophesying, not on the content of the speech[17] or the person of the prophet. But at I Corinthians 14:29 he begins with the designation "prophets," about whom he speaks in terms of "receiving a revelation," and finally comes back to their activity of "prophesying." This seems to indicate that "prophet" is not used to refer to a specific group in the church who are known as prophets but simply to those who engage at times in the activity of prophesying.

It is important to note that I Corinthians 14:26 is a *corrective* text; that is, it is Paul's way of resolving the apparent fact that when they gather "everyone speaks in tongues" (I Cor 14:23), which most likely included the women as well as the men. In this corrective he explicitly says, "When you come together, each of you has a hymn, or a word of instruction, a revelation, a tongue or an interpretation." Even though this text gives rather explicit directives, most subsequent Christians who look at I Corinthians as sacred Scripture see this ad hoc listing not as normative (as what *must* happen in all churches at all times) but as representative of the variety of ways the Spirit can speak through people, again both men and women, so that the whole community might be built up.

Ephesians 5:18-20/Colossians 3:16. These two texts must be looked at together, because they have so much in common and because both assume the context of the household. There are three significant points to make here. First, the worship that is depicted is, as in I Corinthians 11:4-5, double-focused; very much like the Psalter, the singing involves praise and thanksgiving to God while at the same time it instructs and admonishes the people (indeed the verb in Ephesians is "*speak* to one another [through song]"). Second, the singing itself is Spirit-inspired; they are

---

[17]Indeed, when he does refer to the speech itself, he mentions both "prophecy" and "revelation" in I Corinthians 14:6; but then in I Corinthians 14:30 he seems to merge the two, while in I Corinthians 14:26 "revelation" almost certainly stands in for "prophecy." Precision in language is obviously not Paul's concern.

to sing in this praising and instructional way as they are "filled with the Spirit." Third, the focus as they "teach and admonish one another . . . through psalms" is "the message of Christ" (Col 3:16).[18]

Summary of the biblical data. When we put all of this evidence together, several generalizations can be made. First, one finds a general lack of precision in Paul when it comes to describing verbal ministries within the community of faith. Both prophesying and singing, for example, are addressed at times in the language of teaching or instruction. Second, in no instance in Paul's letters does he mention leader(s) who are to be in charge of what takes place;[19] for him the Spirit is the obvious leader of the community in its worship. Third, there is no distinction of any kind between men and women when it comes to the actual verbal activities involved; indeed, a straightforward reading of all the texts together seems to imply that "all" means both men and women.

If there are not more data than these, that should not surprise us, because for the most part what we do learn is in the context of correcting an abuse of some kind in the church. Worship for these believers was like eating; it is something one did all the time. It would simply never have occurred to any of the early Christians that they should either describe their worship in full or lay down rules for it for a later time.

At the same time, it is this collection of evidence that makes the two well-known and much-debated texts, I Corinthians 14:34-35 and I Timothy 2:11-12, seem to stand in open contradiction to the rest of the evidence.[20] Despite protests from some, I continue to believe on text-critical grounds that the first of these is not a part of Paul's inspired letter.[21] Those who take issue with me on this score have yet

---

[18]For a more complete discussion, including the basis for this translation, see Gordon D. Fee, *God's Empowering Presence: The Holy Spirit in the Letters of Paul* (Peabody, Mass.: Hendrickson, 1994), pp. 648-57.

[19]The possible exception to this is Philippians 4:3, where he addresses a trusted friend and companion to lead the way in bringing reconciliation between Euodia and Syntyche.

[20]Despite a number of ploys used to get around the plain sense of the I Corinthians passage, the plain sense must prevail: In an argument based on "the law" (in Paul, of all things), women are forbidden *absolutely* to speak in the assembly. Even for learning they must ask their husbands at home. To make this refer to speaking in tongues or to the discerning of prophecies (so that they are not "judging" utterances from their own husbands) is a form of special pleading that does injustice to both the language and the structure of the two sentences and Paul's argument, and exists only because the text stands in such unrelieved contradiction to the rest of Paul's writings. For a different view, see chapter nine in this volume.

[21]See my response to some critiques in the excursus on these verses in Fee, *God's Empowering Presence*, pp. 273-81.

to offer an adequately historical answer to the *textual* question that drove me to this view many years ago. If it is original with Paul, then how does one explain that in one whole sector of the church it is known only at another place in the text? There is simply no comparable instance of such a radical displacement of an argument in Paul's letters on the part of copyists, and I do not find "for reasons unknown to us" to be a satisfactory answer when a well-attested *historical* explanation lies at hand: a marginal gloss that was placed into the text at two different places.

Similarly, within a deluge of literature that has appeared on I Timothy 2:11-12 since my commentary on these letters, I have yet to find one that has given convincing arguments (for me, at least) demonstrating that this is *not* an ad hoc word to a very case-specific issue in the churches of Ephesus.[22] In any case, there is still more that we don't know than that we do about this one text that stands in tension with the rest of the New Testament evidence. Whatever else, it does not seem to be dealing with "offices" in the church; at least that certainly cannot be demonstrated, even if one were to wish desperately for it to be so.

Implications for Women in Church Offices: Giving the Spirit Priority

It is one thing to allow, as many do, the priority of Spirit gifting for the verbal ministries as outlined here. It is quite another, they would argue, for women to hold offices in the church. So some final words need to be added about this matter. Our problems here are especially complicated by the ambiguities outlined in the first section of this essay. And it must be said again with all candor that the biblical record simply does not express the same level of urgency about this matter that one can find in many quarters in the contemporary church—not to mention the history of the church in general.

Since the biblical data are either nonexistent or ambiguous at best, there are generally three ways to go on this matter: try to muster the evidence in such a way as to negate women in leadership offices; or try the opposite of mustering the evidence so as to support them; or admit that the New Testament simply does not

---

[22] The appeal to the order of creation in I Timothy 2:13 as a theological statement is surely in the eye of the beholder, since Paul's concern in I Timothy 2:9-15 is *not* with the men but with the women; and he immediately follows I Timothy 2:13 with the analogy that he is really after: the man was created first, but the woman was first to be deceived and thus to fall into transgression. There is not a hint in the Genesis narrative that the sequence of their creation has theological meaning, nor that the woman fell because she did not follow the lead of her husband, nor of countless other imaginative ways of trying to make a point that Paul is not making at all.

explicitly teach on this matter and let Spirit gifting have the priority. I obviously opt for the last. In support of this view I would make just a few observations.

First, the very fact that the biblical revelation does not show concern about the nature and structures of church order should catch our attention. This does not mean that there is not some evidence for certain kinds of structures, although the concept of "offices" per se is surely a debatable one. Nor does it deny that the leadership that does emerge in the New Testament documents was primarily male; it was indeed. But it does mean, to repeat, that its writers did not show sufficient interest in these matters as to offer explicit, intentional instruction on them.

In this regard, there is an often overlooked bit of evidence from Paul's writings that should strike us but apparently rarely does: Paul never addresses the leaders of the churches when he writes to them,[23] either to take charge of a situation that has gone awry or to commend them for work well done. Even in the Pastoral Epistles (1 and 2 Timothy and Titus), Paul writes to the churches of Ephesus and Crete through Timothy and Titus because these younger colleagues were there in *his* place, not because they were the permanent leaders. In both cases, the letters make it clear that he wants them to leave in due time (2 Tim 4:9; Tit 3:12), and in neither case is there any instruction for them to hand over to local leaders the task of correction.

The reason for this seems ready enough at hand; most of Paul's letters were addressed to his own churches, where he understood himself to have the primary role of leadership. But even so, it is remarkable indeed that he never speaks to the leaders, or addresses his letters to the leaders, as those responsible for carrying out the directives. He does at times tell the community to "recognize" its leaders, but the language is in the form of verbs describing their activities rather than nouns that indicate their "offices" (see 1 Thess 5:12-13). Moreover, this is still the case in the one certain letter to a church (Romans) that he did *not* found and over which he apparently felt no sense of jurisdiction.

My point is a simple one. Concern over these matters seems to arise at a later time in the church (see, e.g., 3 Jn) and can be found in full bloom in the letters of Ignatius from the second decade of the second Christian century. But they are not

---

[23] The puzzling apparent exception in Philippians 1:1 is actually a case in point. He addresses the whole church "together with the overseers," perhaps in this case because two of them were women who were not seeing eye to eye on things; and when he does address someone in the second person singular to oversee this matter (Phil 4:3), he is most likely speaking to one of his trusted itinerant companions, perhaps Luke. See Gordon D. Fee, *Paul's Letter to the Philippians*, NICNT (Grand Rapids, Mich.: Eerdmans, 1995), pp. 66-69, 393-95.

part of Paul's writings. How is it, one wonders, that the later church can exercise so much energy in "getting it right" with regard to leadership, when the New Testament itself shows so little interest in this?

The reason finally for urging Spirit gifting as the key both to ministry and to leadership is that it recognizes the priority of gifting over gender; and that is certainly one biblical way of looking at things. It is not that Spirit gifting does not need to be discerned; indeed it does. That, after all, is said in a very prescriptive way in 1 Thessalonians 5:19-22. But in the end there are three advantages to going this way biblically, rather than going the route of gathering a load of implicit information and making it normative for all times and places.

First, it is less authority driven and more ministry driven. The priority of Spirit gifting does not usually lead to asking, "Who's in charge around here?" Rather, it sets the whole community free to discern and encourage the giftings within the body, so that all may grow and be built up. Perhaps such a priority might lead to a more important question: Are we all ministering and being ministered to in love by the Spirit of Christ? (Rom 12; 1 Cor 12–14).

Second, it alleviates an age-old problem that often emerges in seminaries, where many male students assume they are gifted for ministry precisely because they meet the assumed first requirement: being male. To begin with gender rather than gifts and calling simply puts the emphasis at the wrong place, especially for the new covenant people of God, where there is no longer any priesthood (at least not as part of biblical revelation!). Further, God explicitly announced that he would pour out his Spirit on *all* people for prophetic ministry (Joel 2:28-29), where "all" is explicitly defined in categories of men/women, slave/free and young/old.

Third, and most important, it opens the door to the possibility that ministry is a two-way street. It seems a sad commentary on the church and on its understanding of the Holy Spirit that "official" leadership and ministry is allowed to come from only one half of the community of faith. The New Testament evidence is that the Holy Spirit is gender inclusive, gifting both men and women, and thus potentially setting the whole body free for all the many parts to minister and in various ways to give leadership to the others.

Thus my issue in the end is not a feminist agenda—an advocacy of women in ministry. Rather, it is a Spirit agenda, a plea for the releasing of the Spirit from our strictures and structures so that the church might minister to itself and to the world more effectively.

15

THE NATURE OF AUTHORITY
IN THE NEW TESTAMENT

Walter L. Liefeld

An understanding of authority in the New Testament is crucial to decisions regarding the ministry of women in the contemporary church. It is important to consider not only what kinds of authority existed in the New Testament churches but also the varieties of church government, styles of ministry and forms of authority in contemporary churches so we can correctly apply the relevant Scriptures. Therefore, after a few brief observations on the present situation, I will deal with the biblical evidence and then return to the contemporary scene for proposed application.

Initial Observations on the Issues

Many Christians today seem overly concerned with the question, "Who's in charge here?" Others, more concerned with the involvement of all believers in ministry, easily overlook the importance of order. The rapid growth of "independent" churches today makes the problem more difficult to solve, because lines of authority are even less uniform from church to church. Also the variety of books, articles and seminars on leadership over the past several decades has resulted in a diversity of terms and goals.

We may distinguish authority from leadership on the one hand and from raw power on the other.[1] *Leadership* is used here as a general term to describe personal influence that generates a positive response among followers. It is earned, it may be invited, and it is voluntarily accepted. *Authority*, in the sense under consideration, is

---

[1]This is not an attempt to deal with the more precise vocabulary sociologists employ. A frequently quoted and useful treatment of such matters is Bengt Holmberg, *Paul and Power: The Structure of Authority in the Primitive Church as Reflected in the Pauline Epistles* (Philadelphia: Fortress, 1978).

a narrower term used to describe the right to command others and to enforce obedience. It is usually conferred, through appointment or election, on someone having a position in an organizational setting. *Power* is usually thought of as influence and authority that are seized rather than earned or voluntarily conferred. Often what begins as welcomed leadership or acknowledged authority is later transformed by an ambitious person into power or even tyranny.

Such power can be identified as existing in one or another form in some churches today, and Scripture condemns it.[2] The difference between leadership and authority is more difficult to assess. For example, a church might debate inviting a woman to teach an adult class of men and women under the assumption that 1 Timothy 2:12 forbids "teaching authority." But what they need to decide is whether a person who does that kind of teaching is thereby assuming a position of authority or simply exercising a spiritual ministry of leadership. Such an example, of course, could be multiplied, but it serves to indicate something of the gray area between these two words.

Instances of Authority in the New Testament

Examples of authority in the New Testament are numerous. The following are chosen because they involve "authority" language, background, principles or instructions important for decisions in contemporary circumstances, especially where the authority of women is in question.

The authority of Jesus. Jesus taught, healed and cast out demons with unique authority (Mt 7:29; Mk 1:22, 27; Lk 4:32, 36). Unlike the rabbis, Jesus did not cite the teachings of his predecessors for support. The Sermon on the Mount shows that Jesus interpreted the Old Testament Scriptures on his *own* authority. His authority to teach was backed up by his power to cast out demons and to heal people.[3] Jesus also had authority to forgive sins. Indeed, when his authority to do so for a paralyzed man was called into question, Jesus responded by healing the man (Mt 9:2-8; Mk 2:3-12; Lk 5:18-26).

The leaders in Jerusalem challenged Jesus' authority during the week preceding his crucifixion, and he refused to answer them on their terms but tested their re-

---

[2] Third John 9 criticizes Diotrephes, "who loves to be first" and would "have nothing to do" with John.

[3] This is especially striking in Luke 4:32, 36. It is noteworthy that of over twenty occurrences of the term *authority* in Luke-Acts, this is the only one that is connected with teaching (see R. H. Stein, *Luke*, NAC [Nashville: Broadman, 1992], pp. 162-63).

sponse to the authority of John the Baptist (Mt 21:23-27; Mk 11:27-33; Lk 20:1-8). Prior to his ascension Jesus issued the "great commission," which was based on the fact that "all authority in heaven and on earth" had been given to him (Mt 28:18). At issue for us is what dimension of his unique authority, if any, was passed on to his followers.

The authority of the Twelve. It is common, when considering apostolic authority, to think of preaching and teaching. Yet in the instructions of the Lord Jesus to the Twelve, the only mention of *exousia* ("authority") relates to authority over demons. This is clear in the word order: "He appointed twelve that they might be with him and that he might send them out to preach and to have *authority to drive out demons*" (Mk 3:14-15). Clearly the authority was not connected with preaching but with exorcism.

Similarly, in the sending of the Twelve in Matthew's account (Mt 10:1), Jesus gave them "*authority to drive out evil spirits* and to heal every disease and sickness." Instructions about preaching do not occur until Matthew 10:7, and authority is not mentioned in that verse. The same connections and emphases occur also in Luke 9:1-2 and Mark 6:7. In all these narratives the evidence is uniform that authority applies not to preaching but to exorcism and healing, and one rarely hears arguments about whether women should perform the latter.[4]

True, Peter was given the "keys" of the kingdom so as to "bind" or "loose" (Mt 16:19; 18:18); and there is implied authority here, even though the actual word is not used.[5] But in neither case is there a reference to teaching and preaching. The context of its use in Matthew 18 is church discipline, which has led to a wide variety of interpretations. Evangelicals tend to see the keys as opening the way to forgiveness and the kingdom by the proclamation of the gospel (see also Jn 20:22-23, regarding Jesus' bestowal of the Holy Spirit in connection with forgiving sins).[6]

---

[4]The significance of this should not be overlooked. Along with our insistence on the Reformation elevation of the authority of Scripture, we have tended also to elevate the authority of *the preacher*. But the preacher, whose responsibility is to interpret the Word correctly, stands *under* the authority of that Word as it is being preached, along with those who hear.

[5]It should be noted that terminology of "binding and loosing" was used in rabbinic circles, though it was not until a later time that teaching authority was connected with it.

[6]Another ongoing issue is whether this authority given to the disciples in these passages (especially regarding forgiveness) is now the province of clergy only or whether it is extended to all believers who proclaim the gospel of forgiveness. While an important question in its own right, it is not a part of contemporary discussion among evangelicals about the role of women, and therefore it is not pursued here. For a useful introduction, see D. A. Carson, *Matthew,* in *The Expositor's Bible Commentary,* vol. 8 (Grand Rapids, Mich.: Zondervan, 1984), pp. 370-74.

Important for the current discussion is that near the conclusion of his ministry Jesus specifically prohibited his disciples from adopting the authoritarian, domineering attitudes of Gentile rulers (Mt 20:25-28; Mk 10:42-45; Lk 22:25-26). The two verbs used to describe the forbidden attitude are *katexousiazō* ("have the right of control"; a verbal form of *exousia*) and *katakyrieuō* ("bring into subjection," "have mastery"). The authority given to the Twelve was over evil powers, not over the Lord's people.

We have seen thus far that there *are* aspects of Jesus' authority that were given to the Twelve, notably authority over demons, authority to heal diseases and authority to proclaim forgiveness of sins (though not the same as Jesus' divine authority actually to forgive sins). By contrast, it is noteworthy that the Gospels do *not* say that Jesus' teaching authority was transferred to the Twelve.

Paul's apostolic authority. Paul's paternal authority over the churches he founded shows itself throughout his epistles and hardly needs illustration. But several things deserve special notice. First, he exercised authority over his coworkers[7] (e.g., 2 Cor 8:16-24; Phil 2:19-30) and churches he himself had founded.[8] Second, he primarily uses *exousia* ("authority") language in a struggle with the Corinthians over "rights" (I Cor 8:9; 9:1-18).[9] Third, with the exception of urgent and emotional cases, he was usually gentle in his authority, "urging" rather than commanding Timothy and Titus (I Tim 1:3; 2 Cor 8:6) and not issuing a "command" to the Corinthians (2 Cor 8:8).[10] I shall mention below the extension of his apostolic authority to Timothy and Titus in the Pastoral Epistles. Apart from that extension it is questionable whether a pastor can rightly assume such individual authority today.

The question of authority and "church government." While there is clear evidence for the *fact* of early church governance, there is no express teaching on the subject in the New Testament. Nonetheless, several important passages need to be studied. One is Hebrews 13:17, "Obey your leaders and submit to them" (NRSV). Here the Greek word rendered "obey" (*peithō*) is quite fluid in meaning. In the active voice

---

[7]At least those who were his traveling companions; he obviously did not have authority over a coworker like Apollos (I Cor 16:12).

[8]Cf. his more deferential attitude toward Roman believers (Rom 1:8-13; 15:14-16).

[9]He also uses it of his apostolic authority in 2 Thessalonians 3:9 and 2 Corinthians 10:8 and 13:10.

[10]Of course the volatility of Paul's emotions in his relations with the Corinthians and Galatians is well known. But in fact his mood fluctuates dramatically in these letters between such volatility and tender appeal.

it carries the sense of "persuasion" and related connotations, but in the middle and passive voices the meanings flow from "being persuaded" to "believing" and "trusting," and finally to the less common sense of "being won over as the result of persuasion" (BDAG), hence "obeying."

This last meaning is the one most translations choose for this verse, but it has been called into question. The reason is that there are very few texts where it appears to have that meaning. The rest of the New Testament evidence for the sense of "obey" for this verb is problematic,[11] and there are only a few classical texts where the verb can be translated "obey."[12] The most we can say is that "obey" is only an *available* meaning *if* the context requires or strongly suggests it. For these reasons the TNIV has rendered the imperative "Have confidence in your leaders and submit to their authority."

But attention must also be given to the *object* of this verb, "your leaders" (literally "those who lead"). In Matthew 2:6 the corresponding noun form clearly means "ruler" ("out of you will come a ruler"), as it does in Acts 7:10, where it refers to Joseph as a ruler of Egypt. In nineteen occurrences of the noun form it can be rendered "governor."

All of this means that Hebrews 13:17 can certainly be offered as evidence of "governing authority" in the early church, bringing into question any idea that there is no authority in the church. However, it would also be improper to ignore its very moderate tone, with words that are clearly temperate in comparison to stronger terms in the same semantic domain. One needs only to consider the stronger terms for the authoritarian ways of worldly rulers used in Matthew 20:25 and Luke 22:25 to see the contrast between their kind of rule and the temperate authority of Christian leaders. This is consistent with the quality of gentleness required of overseers in 1 Timothy 3:4 (cf. Tit 1:7-8).

This discussion must also take into consideration Paul's use of *proistēmi*, a verb whose eight New Testament occurrences are all in his letters, six of them in the Pastoral Epistles. By the Hellenistic period this verb was used in two distinct ways: "to

---

[11]The most probable instance where "obey" is a proper rendering of *peithesthai* is James 3:3 ("we put bits into the mouths of horses to make them obey us"). Less certain is Galatians 5:7 ("who cut in on you to keep you from obeying the truth?"), where the NLT has "following the truth," since the plain sense of the question has to do with no longer *being persuaded by* the truth. So also in Romans 2:8, where the NRSV has "obey not the truth," the TNIV has "reject the truth and follow evil." This is in contrast to the use of the verb *hypakouō*, used, e.g., of the required "obedience" of children and slaves (but not wives) in Ephesians 6:1, 5 (cf. Col 3:20, 22).

[12]See LSJ, p. 1354.

show concern/care for/devote oneself to" and "to be at the head of" (thus to exercise leadership). Its use in Titus 3:8, 14 unambiguously carries the former meaning. But its usage elsewhere is more ambiguous.[13]

Its two appearances outside the Pastoral Epistles (Rom 12:8; 1 Thess 5:12) occur in settings describing people who minister in some way. In 1 Thessalonians it sits between "those who work hard among you" and "who admonish you." Together the three phrases clearly refer to people in leadership roles. While most translations have something like "who are over you in the Lord" (NIV), the TNIV has opted for "who care for you in the Lord" (cf. Louw and Nida, "who guide you"). In any case, the verb lacks any connotation of authority in this passage.

In Romans 12:8 it occurs sixth in an ad hoc list of seven *charismata* ("spiritual gifts"). Even though it is often translated as having to do with "leadership" as such (NIV, NRSV, etc.), two factors suggest that here it also carries the sense of "providing care for": (1) it occurs sixth in a list whose first four items are prophesying, serving, teaching and exhorting/encouraging, and (2) it rests at the end of the list between "giving generously" and "showing mercy." Hence the TNIV alternate reading is probably the correct one: "if it is to provide for others, do it diligently."[14]

Authority in the Pastoral Epistles. That leads, then, to the four other occurrences of *proistēmi* in the Pastoral Epistles. Three of these (1 Tim 3:4-5, 12) relate to an elder's or deacon's relationship to his family: he must "manage/guide/care for his own family and see that his children obey him, and he must do so in a manner worthy of full respect" (1 Tim 3:4). When this idea is elaborated in 1 Timothy 3:5, Paul repeats the verb in the first clause, having to do with the family ("if anyone does not know how [to] *prostēnai* his own family"). But in the second clause, where it is applied to the church, Paul switches to a verb whose only meaning is "to care for" ("how can he take care of [*epimelēsetai*] God's

---

[13]It is of some importance to note here that in Johannes P. Louw and Eugene A. Nida, *Greek-English Lexicon of the New Testament Based on Semantic Domains*, 2 vols., 2nd ed. (New York: United Bible Societies, 1988-1989), this verb appears under three domains ("guide," "be active in helping," "strive to") but not at all under "exercise authority," "rule" or "govern." For the clear distinctions between this verb and a verb of "ruling," see Josephus *Antiquities of the Jews* 14.196 (citing a letter from Julius Caesar regarding Hyrcanus): "That his children shall rule over [*archē*] the Jewish nation . . . and that the high priest, being also an ethnarch, shall be the protector [*proistetai*] of those Jews who are unjustly treated."

[14]In any case it is difficult to justify the NIV's "if it is leadership, let him govern diligently."

church?").[15] This suggests that this is also the nuance of the verb *proistēmi* in these verses.

The final instance of *proistēmi* is in I Timothy 5:17, which does have a stronger image of elders as leaders in the church. But it is especially problematic whether one can rightly translate this verb "rule" (as do NRSV, NASU, ESV, all following the KJV), since that strong nuance would be exceptional given the verb's normal semantic domain.[16] The NIV and TNIV move in the direction of "guide" ("direct the affairs of the church"), which better fits both the established meaning of the verb and its other uses in I Timothy.

Such leaders are also "worthy of double honor," especially[17] those whose ministry is preaching and teaching. What was noted above as to the meaning of *proistēmi* applies here as well. These persons brought the authoritative *Scriptures* to bear on the life of the church and in that sense their words carried "authority." As with I Thessalonians 5:12, this description shows evidence of a plurality of leadership, a group who are to be respected, esteemed, loved and honored (probably with financial support).

The result of our biblical inquiry so far, therefore, is to discover that church leadership is described more in terms of guidance and caring for than of exercising authority, an important point when considering whether women should or should not be church leaders.

It should also be noted, however, that in other places in the Pastoral Epistles the tone is somewhat different. In I Timothy 1:3 Paul tells Timothy to *command* (not just urge) certain people to stop teaching false doctrines. But it is equally clear that Timothy is *not* functioning as an "elder" or "local pastor" but as Paul's own apostolic representative, carrying Paul's full authority in the church. The verb Paul uses for "command," *parangellō*, occurs thirty-two times in the New Testament (mainly in the Gospels and Acts), five of which are in I Timothy. This letter also has two out of five New Testament occurrences of the noun form of that verb. And while

---

[15]This verb occurs only two other times in the New Testament, both in the parable of the good Samaritan (Lk 10:34-35), where the Samaritan "took care of" the victim and then paid the innkeeper to "take care of" him.

[16]BDAG, which includes the usage in this verse under the general heading "to exercise a position of leadership, *rule, direct, be at the head (of)*," does not distinguish readily between "leadership" and "ruling," a distinction Louw and Nida think is necessary (*Greek-English Lexicon*, 1:466, par. 36.1).

[17]The word translated "especially" in I Timothy 5:17 can also be translated "I mean," in which case it indicates that all the leaders in mind preached and taught, not only a select group who are chosen to receive the benefit indicated.

the verbal form of another word that means "command" *(epitassō)* is not used at all in the Pastoral Letters, three of seven occurrences of the *noun* form *(epitagē)* do occur in these epistles. The first occurrence is in 1 Timothy 1:1, where it refers to Paul's apostleship as being "by the command of God." This indicates how important the idea of authority is in the Pastoral Letters; but the authority to command is vested in the apostle Paul, not in the local leaders.

Thus Timothy and Titus were responsible to transmit Paul's authoritative commands to those churches. But nowhere are they told to transfer or transmit the "commanding" to others in the church. Indeed, the idea of transmission occurs only in 2 Timothy 2:2, and here Timothy is told to "entrust" the *content* of what Paul has taught to persons "who will also be qualified to teach others." Today the appropriate equivalent of these younger delegates representing the apostle Paul in the churches is not a local pastor but the canonical New Testament containing Paul's own words.

Specifically gender-related passages. There are two passages regarding the relationship between men and women in the New Testament that contain a word in the *exousia* ("authority") word group. One is 1 Corinthians 7:1-5, which deals with the sexual relationship between husband and wife. This is a significant passage for those advocating exclusively male leadership, given that they argue the male-female relationship *in marriage* is basic to the proper role relationship of men and women *in the church.* First Corinthians 7:4 begins, "The wife does not have authority over *[exou siazei]* her own body but yields it to her husband." Then it continues, "In the same way, the husband does not have authority [same verb] over his own body but yields it to his wife." Thus in the most intimate aspect of marriage the authority of husband and wife is equal.

The other gender-related passage containing the word *exousia* is 1 Corinthians 11:11-12. In this passage about women's head coverings, scholars disagree about the exegesis and the nature of authority in view. Does the woman have authority (the right) to pray and prophesy, or authority (control) over her head? One thing is less debatable; the use of a head covering is *not* a "sign" that the woman is *under* authority.[18] For our present purposes it is sufficient to note that however the head-covering issue may be decided, this passage assumes not silence but vocal partici-

---

[18]Among useful recent discussions of this are Linda L. Belleville, "Women in Ministry," in *Two Views on Women in Ministry,* ed. James R. Beck and Craig L. Blomberg (Grand Rapids, Mich.: Zondervan, 2001), p. 105 n. 54; and Craig Blomberg, *1 Corinthians,* NIV Application Commentary (Grand Rapids, Mich.: Zondervan, 1994), p. 212. See also chapter eight in this volume.

pation of women in prayer and prophesying in public worship.

On the much-discussed 1 Timothy 2:12, see chapter twelve in this book. Here I simply note the following. This sentence does not contain *exousia* or *exousiazō* but rather *authenteō*, a word that occurs only here in the New Testament. In BDAG this verb is defined as "to assume a stance of independent authority, give orders to, dictate to." Research on this word continues. Church decisions concerning the extent of authority to be granted women are often made on the assumption that 1 Timothy 2:12 forbids women from ever having *any* authority. But the BDAG definition of the verb, in addition to sound exegetical reasons, warns us to question that assumption. These considerations, to say nothing of the whole context of 1 Timothy, including chapter 2, are so complex that a broad application of that term to forbid any kind of authority is highly questionable. As many have rightly concluded, Paul's instructions (or his *practice* at that time, since no command is given) most likely had a specific and limited objective in the circumstances existing at that time.

Our task, then, is to determine what, if any, circumstances today correspond sufficiently to those in Ephesus at the time 1 Timothy was written to justify forbidding authority to women now. Although quests for a background to 1 Timothy 2:12 have yielded different results, a consideration of the doctrinal concerns of the Pastorals, as well as of Paul's teachings and missionary concerns expressed elsewhere, show us that *our* ecclesiastical practices ought not stand against the ministry of all believers, including the leadership of women.

Order and Structure in New Testament Churches

Discussion about authority in today's church can easily move in the wrong direction. It often starts with one's own church structure and with assumptions that are more characteristic of our times than of the first century. It then moves back to the New Testament, seeking to fit its teachings into our contemporary structures. However, the proper direction is the reverse, to start with the nature of churches and ministry and the instructions to churches in the New Testament, as far as that can be determined. Then we should submit our contemporary styles of worship and ministry to the New Testament for possible correction and reforming.

Organization, ministry and leadership. Churches in New Testament times met in homes, often with several congregations in a city. The homes were usually small, though not necessarily tiny, since rooms in larger homes could accommodate more people than the average living or family room today. Church organization probably differed somewhat from place to place, but as noted above, churches founded by

Paul, at least, had plural leadership by elders. The early church had no equivalent to the Old Testament priesthood,[19] nor is there evidence in the New Testament that one person with special authorization "presided" at the Lord's Supper.

Leadership roles were quite different from those of today. Apostles, prophets and teachers are given pride of place (NIV "first of all") in I Corinthians 12:28. But that is very likely primarily a temporal ordering, not structural,[20] and there is no firm dividing line between them and the workers of miracles, those with gifts of healing and so on. Interestingly, those with gifts of guidance (TNIV)[21] are not at the top. The point of the whole chapter, after all, is that each needs the other. Apostles unquestionably were acknowledged as the leading figures in the church; but no provision is made in the New Testament for their "succession." People designated as "pastors" (Eph 4:11) functioned *within* congregations, not above them. The upshot is that we are given ministry designations, which have been carefully scrutinized (especially in Eph 4:11), but no certain definitions of their role or rank.

With the exception of the Pastoral Epistles, addressed to Paul's apostolic delegates, Paul's letters are addressed to the churches themselves. None is addressed to a single leader, nor is one person ever spoken to as being "in charge" of the church. At Philippi the overseers and deacons (both plural) are also addressed, but not first (Phil 1:1). Eventually there was more than one congregation (house church) in a city, and it is not possible in such cases to know with certainty from the biblical references whether every congregation had more than one elder.

This is also the picture presented in Acts. Although Peter is the early spokesman for the church in Jerusalem, he is clearly presented as one among equals (Acts 2:14; 3:3-4; 4:13). The first group decision (Acts 6:1-6) is by the Twelve, with the specifics left to others. Similarly in Acts 15, James "leads" the council toward a decision, but the decision itself is by "the apostles and elders, with the whole church" (Acts 15:22, 25), and the letter that was circulated adds that the Holy Spirit was in accord with the decision. At the local level we are told (Acts 14:23) that Paul

---

[19]Both I Peter 2:5, 9 and Revelation 1:6 and 5:10 echo Exodus 19:5-6, where Israel (and now the church) is to function as God's priesthood for the nations.

[20]That is, this is the chronological order of the church's founding and its subsequent growth (see Gordon D. Fee, *The First Epistle to the Corinthians*, NICNT [Grand Rapids, Mich.: Eerdmans, 1987], pp. 619-20; cf. Blomberg, *1 Corinthians*, p. 247). This also best explains why, in using "building" imagery (household/temple) for the church in Ephesians 2:19-22, Paul speaks of apostles and prophets as "the foundation."

[21]The NIV's "administration" seems to be an anachronism. See Fee, *First Epistle*, p. 622; cf. Ben Witherington, *Conflict and Community in Corinth* (Grand Rapids, Mich.: Eerdmans, 1995), p. 261.

and Barnabas appointed elders (plural) in *each* church *(kat' ekklēsian)*.

The letters to the seven churches in Revelation 2–3 are a special case, and the significance of the "angels" of the churches is debated, some thinking they are pastors—but the evidence for this is especially slender. Some think the "lady" addressed in 2 John was the host and therefore the leader of the church in her home, but her position is unclear. Third John is addressed to Gaius precisely because Diotrephes wanted to be prominent; but Gaius's own role is not described.

The role of teachers. Because the modern term *teaching authority* is prevalent in discussions of women's role in the church, we need to look briefly at teaching in the New Testament church. Most relevant to the issue of authority is the mention of teachers as recognized church leaders in Romans 12:7, I Corinthians 12:28 and Ephesians 4:11; but in each list they appear no higher than third. Furthermore, there is no verbal connection in the New Testament between the word *teacher* and the vocabulary of *authority.* Hence the very term *teaching authority*, as though authority were vested in the teacher rather than in what is taught, is an anachronism when we are discussing teaching/teachers in the New Testament.

What is often overlooked in these discussions is that women traditionally were not welcomed as teachers in either Greek or Jewish society.[22] To restrict the ministry of teaching to men would not have been surprising in the world of the New Testament. If missionaries, like Paul, were to be all things to all people to win them to Christ (I Cor 9:22), public proclamation of Christian teachings would ideally be done by men.

The case of Priscilla is debated, but it seems specious and unreasonable to argue that hers was not legitimate teaching because she instructed Apollos in her home and not in a church service or because she is said to have "explained" the "way of God" rather than to have "taught" the "Scriptures" (Acts 18:26). After all, the church *met* in her home (Rom 16:3-5), and in any case, how does one explain something without teaching? "The way of God" was a recognizable phrase for God's truth and the gospel in those early days when the New Testament Scriptures were not yet completed.

The limitations on a woman's teaching and promoting Christianity in New Tes-

---

[22]James G. Sigountos and Myron Shank, "Public Roles for Women in the Pauline Church: A Reappraisal of the Evidence," *JETS* 26 (1983): 283-95. Of course the Romans were not as uniform and restrictive regarding women, and actually the aggressive enterprise of some women became a threat to the men. However, I believe the evidence of restriction in the ancient world is broad and strong enough to be factored into our hermeneutics.

tament times can be understood better when we notice that although the Gospels show that women were the first at the empty tomb, Paul does not cite them as witnesses to the resurrection. This reflects the historical situation in which a woman's testimony was not considered reliable.

In summary, teaching was a widespread ministry in the early church, often carried on mutually but with a clearly distinguished group of leaders at the forefront. The Word was their authority, but in the earliest days before that Word was available it was the word of the witnesses and teachers that had to be relied on as authoritative. This is probably relevant to I Timothy 2:12.[23]

The role of elders. Although Acts 14:23 tells us that at the beginning Paul and Barnabas appointed elders in each church, this language does not emerge in Paul's letters until the very end (I Tim 4:14; 5:17; Tit 1:5). The fact that they were appointed (Tit 1:5) shows that they were a clearly delineated group. In a context like this the verb *appointed (kathistēmi)* can indicate the conferring of a position, status or responsibility (cf. Mt 24:45, 47; 25:21, 23; Lk 12:14, 42, 44; Acts 6:3; 7:10, 27, 35; Heb 5:1; 7:28; 8:3).

It thus seems clear that eldership was a position with a degree of authority exceeding that of just leadership, but with two caveats. First, there is no evidence of an individual elder who acted with autonomous authority. Eldership was plural, whether in a church or in a town. This should be a pertinent consideration for those who believe the Bible prohibits a woman from having authority in the church. For if elders act in concert on administrative matters, the presence of a woman among the elders would not grant her individual authority any more than it would a man. Second, elders were shepherds, not a board of directors.[24]

---

[23]It may be noted in connection with the topic of teaching that the Catholic Church has a clear position on teaching authority. Their theologians deal with the theological contours of the faith, but it is the pastoral wing of the church (bishops and the pope) that declares what must be believed. It is in this connection that Catholics employ such terms as "teaching authority" or "magisterium." Thus, for example, although Sister Agnes Cunningham holds the honor of having been the first female president of the Catholic Theological Society of America, she could never become a bishop or priest and thereby have authority to declare what the church must believe. This comparison, made respectfully, illustrates the importance of teaching authority in the Catholic Church. Protestant pastors who claim an office and a teaching authority that others do not have are conforming in part to the Catholic position.

[24]Historically (as well as biblically) elders and "bishops" have correctly been designated as "shepherds" (Greek *poimēn*, Latin *pastor*). According to Paul's charge to the Ephesian elders, that is their commission ("keep watch over yourselves and over all the flock of which the Holy Spirit has made you overseers," Acts 20:28). Cf. I Peter 5:2-3: "Be shepherds of God's flock that is under your care,

On the other hand, nowhere does Paul say that individuals or groups possessing an ongoing authority made the decisions. In his earlier letters the local church as a whole was to carry out Paul's instructions (1 Cor 5:4-5). The rhetoric in 1 Corinthians 6:1-6 allows for the possibility of one person acting as "judge," but the whole church is being brought to task for failure to handle this problem from within.[25] Apparently whatever role the elders played, it would be to lead the whole church in the decision-making process.

Ordination. It is increasingly recognized that while ordination is significant, it is not found in its usual modern sense in the New Testament or in early Christianity. The practice as we know it developed toward the third Christian century. Although the laying of hands on Timothy (1 Tim 4:14; 2 Tim 1:6) is sometimes cited as an ordination, several facts militate against this: (1) what is conferred on Timothy is a "gift" (*charisma*), not a status; (2) that gift is not an "office"—the gift is "in" him and can be "fan[ned] into flame" (2 Tim 1:6); (3) it is not a Christian counterpart to rabbinic ordination because, among other reasons, that did not involve the laying on of hands.[26]

Whatever else, the laying on of hands was not an appointment to an "office" but corporate recognition of a ministry already in progress, which is the point of 1 Timothy 5:22. It is equally so in Acts 13:3 in the case of Barnabas and Paul, who were already engaged in Christian ministry. Theirs was not a lifetime empowerment to an "office" but a commissioning for a specific missionary trip that was declared "completed" in Acts 14:26.

The fact that the New Testament church did not practice ordination as commonly understood today is significant, because spiritual authority has long been

---

watching over them—not because you must, but because you are willing, as God wants you to be; not pursuing dishonest gain, but eager to serve; not lording it over those entrusted to you, but being examples to the flock." Being a shepherd certainly implies the feeding of the sheep with the authoritative Word of God; equally, it expressly excludes "lording it over" them. Leadership is commanded; domination is forbidden. This surely accords with Jesus' words, referred to earlier, prohibiting the disciples from dominating other believers in a worldly way.

[25]The NIV et al. suggest that the church is to "appoint judges" to handle this matter; but it is altogether unlikely that *kathizete* is an imperative here, coming at the end of Paul's sentence as it does. Therefore its more likely sense is "to seek for a ruling" from someone (as in Josephus *Antiquities of the Jews* 13.75). See Fee, *First Epistle*, p. 236; cf. Blomberg, *1 Corinthians*, p. 117 n. 3.

[26]There are various instances of the laying on of hands in Scripture. They are connected with the identification of one's successor (such as Joshua, Num 27:23), the setting apart of the Levites (Num 8:10), the establishment of the group to distribute food to the Grecian widows (Acts 6:6), numerous acts of healing and other acts that are not liturgical or official.

connected with ordination.[27] In summary, the issues surrounding ordination are complex, but it is extremely doubtful that a woman's ordination or nonordination should determine the bounds of her ministry and authority.

The use of titles and the term "office." The use of titles has always been a means of portraying superiority and authority. Jesus said,

> But you are not to be called "Rabbi," for you have only one Master and you are all brothers. And do not call anyone on earth "father," for you have one Father, and he is in heaven. Nor are you to be called "teacher," for you have one Teacher, the Messiah. The greatest among you will be your servant. For those who exalt themselves will be humbled, and those who humble themselves will be exalted. (Mt 23:8)

Along with titles, a perception of authority can be conveyed by the use of the term *office*, as in "pastoral office" or "teaching office." But *office* is not a New Testament church term. The concept of "office" can be traced to the use of this English word in the KJV, which gave the impression that it is in the Greek text; but in none of the passages in which the KJV has the word *office* (except concerning the Jewish priesthood) does any word meaning "office" occur in the Greek.[28]

Considerable debate has taken place during the past few decades over the difference between office and function. That debate is beyond the focus of this chapter; the point to be made is that our common use of the nonbiblical term *office* enhances perceived authority. To be sure, it can be argued that the terms used in the New Testament to describe leadership in the early church together form a mosaic that could be described by the general term *office*. However, such a term is ours, not the biblical authors', and it can be misleading. Function is more important than office.[29]

---

[27]While much of the contemporary discussion over what authority women may or may not have centers on eldership, teaching, preaching and the pastorate (especially the senior pastorate), historically the issues of authority included such functions as presiding at Communion and performing baptisms. Early in Christian history it was argued by some that women could not be ordained because for a woman to be at a raised altar presiding over the sacrament of Communion during her period was unthinkable.

[28]The KJV "I magnify mine office" (Rom 11:13) represents *diakonia*, "service." "All members have not the same office" (Rom 12:4) renders *praxis*, "function or work." "Office of a bishop" (1 Tim 3:1) is *episkopē*, "superintendence." "Use the office of a deacon" (1 Tim 3:10) renders the verb *diakonei*, "serve" (also in 1 Tim 3:13). Two instances where the word *office* actually *is* appropriate are "priest's office" (Lk 1:8-9) and "office of the priesthood" (Heb 7:5), which are renderings of the verb *hierateuō*, meaning to serve as a priest, and *hierateia*, which refers to service, office or position of a priest.

[29]Two of the studies that deserve consideration regarding office are R. Y. K. Fung, "Function or Office? A Survey of the New Testament Evidence," *Evangelical Review of Theology* 8, no. 1 (1984): 16-39; and Holmberg, *Paul and Power* (n. 1 above).

Contemporary Expressions of Authority

De jure, de facto and de senso authority. If decisions regarding authority in the contemporary church are to be considered biblically legitimate (= *de jure*) for the church, they must derive from biblical principles and precedents such as those discussed above. Yet it would be unrealistic to ignore the fact that often individuals have an actual *(de facto)* rule over others in a setting where Scripture does not grant them *de jure* authority. An aura of *de facto* authority, for example, sometimes marks the founders of the congregation. Their status is such that others would not make major decisions without consulting them even if they do not hold an elected or appointed position at the time. Status in the church is also often granted to people with advanced degrees, community leaders, business leaders, the wealthy and others with social standing.

Further, the *perception* of authority has changed in recent years. The past half-century has seen the growth of lay-centered and lay-empowered movements. Paradoxically, however, the prominence of today's senior pastor and preacher has tended to increase the perceived (or what we might call *de senso*) authority of the person in the pulpit over those in the congregation. In some cases the pastor builds on that perceived authority even to the point of exercising veto power over all church board or congregational decisions. One pastor recently asserted that to oppose him was to oppose God. If one views megachurches as "apostolic,"[30] it is just a short step to considering the pastor an apostle with authority like the New Testament apostles.

It is extremely difficult for many to imagine a woman in such an authoritative role. It must be said, however, that strong leadership is important and necessary in such churches, and it is due to such leadership that those churches exist. The questionable perception of authority I speak of is not inevitable but depends on the attitude of the pastor.

Further practical issues. I have already noted the different types of authority that can exist in religious contexts. The sociological literature on power would open up even further ways to examine the subject. But there are other issues that confront Christians who think it is necessary to limit the authority of women.

Given the biblical evidence, is there actually any clear locus of authority in the church? Our survey has shown that the answer must be positive. Without clear, wise and gentle authority there can be no guarding of doctrine, shepherding of the flock

---

[30]See C. Peter Wagner, *The New Apostolic Churches* (Ventura, Calif.: Gospel Light, 1998). This seems to be new jargon in some charismatic circles for those who have founded megachurches; but such usage has its obvious downside.

or exercise of discipline.[31] But churches and denominations differ as to where authority resides, and the possible role of women will differ in each structure, if women's authority is deemed limited by those churches.

If authority is in the church itself as a "committee of the whole," do women have a vote? Theoretically, in a church with a majority of women they could make the difference in hiring or firing a pastor, thereby having ultimate authority over the pastor.

If authority resides in a leadership group such as a church board, the scenario could be the same in voting if women are in the majority on that board. (We lack biblical evidence that an individual elder has personal authority. The authority seems to lie in the group as a whole, and the authority is therefore always plural.)

It is increasingly common, especially in Baptist and independent churches, for the senior pastor to have ultimate, perhaps absolute, authority, especially if that person is the founding pastor. A woman is rarely found in that position.

Sometimes the circumstances and questions are even more complex. What about the paradox that sometimes exists when a church forbids women to become elders but includes female deacons on a church board that has veto power over the elders' proposals? And, concerning the role of a senior pastor, how far does the pastor's *de jure* leadership actually *enforce* compliance of staff or congregation? Another issue is whether the preaching of a sermon is an authoritative act, because that logically carries the implication that the congregation *must* obey the imperatives *in the sermon*, not just those in the Scripture being quoted. Further, churches may differ as to whether baptism and "presiding" at the Lord's Supper are acts of authority that should be restricted to ordained clergy. This is *de jure* in some denominations but undocumented and therefore *de facto* in some churches.

It is understood, of course, that a church or denomination in a democratic society has the right to decide on its own organizational arrangement, but it also has the responsibility to be open to the question of scriptural precedence. A further complexity exists regarding spiritual authority outside of the local church. This can exist in several forms, including within denominational, missionary and parachurch organizations, but these will not be examined here.

---

[31]The assertion that "it is the church that possesses authority and not particular individuals (or positions, for that matter)" (Belleville, "Women in Ministry," p. 106 n. 20) is certainly true with regard to the church's authority over external forces of evil, and it is realized with greater or less success in congregational-type churches that practice government by a simple majority of the whole. But government by the whole is hard to imagine as being functional in a church of any size. Some kind of internal authority seems not only biblical but also necessary to prevent chaos.

Concluding Observations: Four Distortions

There are four instances of distortion that emerge from the picture of the contemporary church as we compare it with the church in the New Testament. Women are usually excluded from leadership on the basis of these distortions, not on the basis of New Testament teaching itself.

Formalization. The legitimate and functionally efficient roles of leaders prescribed and portrayed in the New Testament, such as those of pastor, teacher and elder, have been formalized through an overstressing of their authority. Thus we have developed the artificial and exclusive "office of pastor," "teaching office" and "office of elder." We have also changed the legitimate and necessary recognition of leaders and missionaries, often expressed by the laying on of hands in ordination, into a ceremony that elevates the individual and bestows privileges not envisioned in the New Testament.

Normalization. The distinctive and indeed extraordinary authority of New Testament apostles has sometimes been assumed by pastors as *their* normal right and as the legitimatization of their control over the church. But such a transfer has no biblical basis of any kind.

Generalization. The particular kind of authority described by the word *authenteō* and the kind of teaching that would have been shameful and offensive if done by women in the New Testament world has been generalized in our churches to cover all authoritative roles and all teaching of men by women. They are therefore excluded from ministries in a way Paul would probably not have intended for his churches.

Minimalization. Along with the above distortions is the tendency to view the ministries in which women served in the New Testament as less important than they were. Thus the teaching of Priscilla and her husband Aquila is reduced in its significance. Likewise minimized are the ministries of Phoebe as a deacon and as Paul's benefactor and of Junia as an apostle (Rom 16:1, 7).[32]

Finally, we do well to remember that all church authority is under Christ, under the Scriptures and under the leading of the Holy Spirit. The purpose of authority is to glorify the Lord and to facilitate his mission in the world. Elders and pastors are primarily shepherds, not bosses. Leadership is a form of servanthood. When we become obsessed with the question, Who's in charge? we may obscure the more important question, Who is a servant?

---

[32]On these passages see chapter six in this volume.

16

BIBLICAL PRIESTHOOD
AND WOMEN IN MINISTRY

Stanley J. Grenz

Since the 1970s, the propriety of women serving in the pastoral office in the church has been a contentious issue.[1] The controversy has increasingly polarized evangelical participants in the discussion into two basic positions. On the one side stand those who support gender equality, who assert that the Holy Spirit may call both men and women to all leadership roles in the church. Their position is opposed by male-leadership advocates, who aver that certain ecclesiastical positions (or functions) are for men only.

Advocates of male leadership are united in the conviction that some restrictions are to be placed on the service of women in the church. Nevertheless, they do not speak with one voice as to what specific offices are off limits. Hence some would bar women from any position that places men under their authority, whereas others reserve only the "role of authoritative pastoral leadership"[2] embodied in the office of sole pastor or senior pastor. Whatever the degree of restriction they may advocate, those arguing for male leadership build their theological case for limiting the role of women from the fundamental belief they all share that God has placed within creation itself an ordering of the sexes that delegates to men the prerogative of leading, initiating and taking responsibility for the well-being of women, and entrusts to women the role of following male leadership, as well as supporting, enabling and helping men. Because the pastoral office (or function) entails by its very nature authoritative oversight, male-leadership proponents conclude that this role

---

[1]This essay is adapted from Stanley J. Grenz and Denise Muir Kjesbo, *Women in the Church: A Biblical Theology of Women in Ministry* (Downers Grove, Ill.: InterVarsity Press, 1995), pp. 173-230.

[2]J. I. Packer, "Let's Stop Making Women Presbyters," *Christianity Today*, February 11, 1991, p. 20.

is—as J. I. Packer so tersely put it—"for manly men rather than womanly women."[3]

A corollary to the claim that the pastoral office is authoritative, and hence off-limits to women, is the idea that the pastoral role is priestly in character. Because women could not serve as priests in the Old Testament, the argument runs, the pastoral office (or function) is properly filled by men only. The view that the pastorate is priestly in character is widely assumed among opponents of women's ordination in the more liturgical traditions—the Orthodox,[4] Roman Catholic[5] and Anglican[6] communions. But it has found its way into the thinking of partisans in free churches as well.[7]

The goal of this essay is to interact with the thesis set forth by those who would restrict pastoral leadership to males regarding the priestly character of the pastoral office. In what follows, I explore the relationship between the concept of priesthood and the propriety of women in the pastorate. More specifically, I tackle the question: Does whatever priestly character that may be predicated of the pastoral office (or function) necessitate an all-male pastorate? To this end, I engage first with the idea of a connection between the Old Testament priesthood and the pastorate and relate this to the New Testament doctrine of the priesthood of all believers. Then I tackle the question of the representational character of the pastorate. Finally, I indicate the implications of the New Testament focus on the priesthood of gifted persons for our understanding of the pastorate. In this manner, I will argue that whereas an all-male pastorate might logically follow from the link between priest and pastor (erroneously) forged by theologians in liturgical traditions, the understanding of the church most widely espoused in evangelical circles leads to viewing the pastorate as a gifted leadership serving within a gifted people.

The Levitical Priesthood and the Pastorate

Many opponents of women in ministry claim that the pastorate is to be understood in a priestly manner and that this office (or function) is the ecclesiastical in-

---

[3]Ibid. Packer's article provides a succinct articulation of this widely propagated view.

[4]Patrick Henry Reardon, "Women Priests: History and Theology," *Touchstone* 6, no. 1 (Winter 1993): 26-27.

[5]E.g., Michael Novak, "Women, Ordination and Angels," *First Things*, no. 32 (April 1993): 25-32.

[6]See the summary of the position of Canon Geddes MacGregor in Paul K. Jewett, *The Ordination of Women* (Grand Rapids, Mich.: Eerdmans, 1980), pp. 15-16.

[7]See, for example, Bernard E. Seton, "Should Our Church Ordain Women? No," *Ministry* 58, no. 3 (March 1985): 16. Seton is a former associate secretary of the General Council of the Seventh-day Adventists.

stantiation of the general biblical principle of male priesthood. Bernard Seton, for example, offers this sweeping statement: "The Bible establishes an all-male priesthood or ministry, both within and outside the family."[8]

At first glance, the correctness of the contention that God intends that the priestly role be limited to males appears almost self-evident. Male-leadership advocates find what they see as God's intention displayed throughout salvation history. In the Old Testament, priestly functions were performed by men, not women. These functions included representing the people to God, accepting the people's offerings and presenting the offerings to God in sacrifice. Later, the priestly function was more formally codified when God established Israel as his people and selected the sons of Levi—specifically, Aaron and his male descendants—for this role.

Rather than overturning the Old Testament precedent, male-leadership proponents add, the New Testament reaffirms it. They find the foundation for its continuation in Jesus' selection of twelve male apostles, for in so doing our Lord maintained the older principle of the male priestly ministry, even while he himself superseded the priestly order. Seton explains: "The days of the Levitical priesthood had passed; the apostolic age was about to dawn. But in each age men filled the priestly roles."[9] The church, in turn, followed Jesus' lead by replacing Judas with a male successor and later by ordaining men such as Paul and Timothy to leadership roles and by establishing an all-male presbytery. The presbytery (that is, the pastorate), it is concluded, is the ecclesiastical analogue to the ancient priesthood. Hence Thomas Schreiner, who only cautiously endorses the argument from the all-male priesthood in the Old Testament, remains true to the basic male-leadership line when he writes, "There is a suggestive pattern in that women functioned as prophets in both the OT and the NT, but they do not serve as priests in the OT nor as elders in the NT."[10]

Several considerations indicate that it is unwarranted to extend the Old Testament priesthood to the New Testament pastorate in a manner that bars women from the latter. Let me mention only one. The male-leadership apologetic builds from the assumption that the priesthood in ancient Israel exemplifies a divinely instituted pattern incumbent upon God's people in all ages and that the pastorate parallels, by divine design, this Old Testament structure. The argument runs

---

[8]Seton, "Should Our Church Ordain Women?" p. 16.
[9]Ibid.
[10]Thomas Schreiner, "Review of Stanley J. Grenz and Denise Muir Kjesbo, *Women in the Church*," *TrinJ* 17, no. 1 (Spring 1996): 121.

aground, I maintain, on the great theological principle known as the priesthood of all believers.

Believer priesthood and the leadership of women. The book of Hebrews asserts that the great high priest toward whom Old Testament worship pointed is Jesus himself (Heb 4:14–10:18). Because of Christ's work, all believers may now confidently approach "the throne of grace" and receive mercy (Heb 4:15-16). All may enter the "Most Holy Place" (which in the temple had been the prerogative solely of the high priest) and "draw near to God" (Heb 10:19-22). Indeed, Christ has made all believers priests of God (Rev 1:6; 5:10; 20:6). Consequently, together they constitute "a holy priesthood, offering spiritual sacrifices acceptable to God through Jesus Christ," including "the praises of him who called you out of darkness into his wonderful light" (1 Pet 2:5, 9; cf. Rom 12:1; Heb 13:5). And all share in the privilege of interceding for one another before God (2 Thess 3:1; 1 Tim 2:1-2; Jas 5:16). With a view toward the new status all believers now share, Jesus repeatedly warned his disciples against adopting the attitude of the Pharisees, who elevated themselves as teachers and masters over the people (Mt 23:8-12; see also Mk 10:42-44; 1 Tim 2:5). In short, the New Testament presents the church as a fellowship of believer priests.

The New Testament portrayal of the church as a priesthood of believers implies that the parallel to the Levitical priesthood is not the ordained office (or leadership function) but the church as a whole. If the people—and not merely church leaders—are God's holy priesthood, then the exclusion of women from the pastorate on the basis of the all-male nature of the Old Testament priesthood is unwarranted. Moreover, appeals to the priestly character of the pastorate risks losing the glorious truth of the gospel that the prerogative of serving as priests before God and toward one another—a prerogative once reserved for a small, select group among the people of God—has now been given to all through the work of Christ and by the outpouring of the Spirit.

Concern for this was one factor that triggered the Reformation rediscovery of the universal priesthood. Luther's quest for a gracious God led him to the theological issue of access to divine grace. According to the theology of the Middle Ages, the faithful become recipients of this grace through the sacraments of the church. The clergy are crucial in this process, according to medieval theology. Clergy act as priestly mediators between God and the people, serving as God's instruments in dispensing divine grace and forgiveness and acting as representatives of the people in bringing their offerings and prayers to God. Against the medieval understanding, Luther asserted that believers enjoy direct access to God apart from any human mediators (except Christ). They receive God's grace directly through faith, and they have the privilege of coming to God themselves.

Although the principle of the priesthood of all believers has gained nearly universal acknowledgment among evangelicals, those advocating male leadership aver that the principle does not necessarily entail that the pastorate is open to all believers regardless of gender. Denying that the priesthood of all believers opens the door to women in ministry requires, however, that this doctrine be deemed irrelevant to the issue of pastoral leadership.

Susan T. Foh makes this argument by first rejecting any connection between the Levitical priesthood and the ordained office: "There is no continuity between the office of priest, which ceased when Christ sacrificed himself once for all (Heb 7:11–10:25), and the office of elder or pastor-teacher."[11] According to Foh, the priesthood of all believers involves our offering of ourselves as spiritual sacrifices to God and our access to God through Christ. "Women are priests in these senses just as men," she affirms. Yet "this status does not qualify anyone for any church office."[12]

Foh's approach is a marked departure from the arguments of those male-leadership proponents who appeal to male Levitical priesthood as a model for the church's ordained office. In fact, her disjoining of the Old Testament priest and the New Testament pastor—which when viewed from the perspective of actual mediatory function is technically correct—serves to knock a prop out from under the case for an all-male pastorate. Foh likewise correctly interprets the New Testament priesthood as universal. She acknowledges that as priests all believers enjoy direct access to God and offer spiritual sacrifices to him. Yet at one point she is quite mistaken. Rather than not qualifying anyone for any church office, as she concludes, the status of priest is exactly what forms the basic qualification for all church offices.[13] Because Christ has qualified all believers to stand in God's presence, regardless of race, social status or gender, we are all ministers within the fellowship. As priests of God—and only because we are priests—we are called by the Spirit to ministries among Christ's people, and some of these ministries include positions of leadership.

---

[11]Susan T. Foh, "A Male Leadership View," in *Women in Ministry: Four Views*, ed. Bonnidell Clouse and Robert G. Clouse (Downers Grove, Ill.: InterVarsity Press, 1989), p. 93.

[12]Ibid., pp. 93-94.

[13]This position has enjoyed adherents throughout church history. See Ida Raming, "The Twelve Apostles Were Men," *Theology Digest* 40, no. 1 (Spring 1993): 24.

Evangelical ecclesiology and the leadership of women. Although the principle of believer priesthood has gained acceptance in nearly all Christian traditions, historically evangelicals have been at the forefront of emphasizing the concept and drawing out its implications. Commitment to the priesthood of all believers is connected with the evangelical understanding of the church as consisting ultimately in the people themselves and not in the ordained clergy. In short, evangelicals view the church as a community of reconciled sinners rather than as a dispenser of divine grace.

Evangelicals have understood believer priesthood to mean as well that the task of the church belongs to the people as a whole. This has provided the impetus among evangelicals for promoting the inclusion of all believers in the life of the church and for elevating the importance of every believer's contribution to the work of the ministry. In other words, the evangelical emphasis on the shared responsibility of all the people of God for the work of the congregation leads quite naturally to an egalitarian view of the pastorate. Evangelicals typically do not see clergy as mediators between God and the people. Pastors are not a special class of Christians who mediate God's grace to the people. Nor do clergy mediate Christ's authority to the church; they are to assist the people in determining the will of the risen Lord for his church. Simply stated, ordained ministers are persons chosen by God and acknowledged by the church, who have been charged with the responsibility of leading the people as a whole in fulfilling the mandate Christ has given to the entire church.

The centrality of these themes means that the evangelical understanding of the church not only poses no inherent roadblocks to women serving in leadership capacities but demands the full partnership of male and female within church life. A church in which all participate in the mandate they share is one in which women and men work side by side in the varied ministries of the community. They learn from each other, uphold one another and contribute their personal strengths to the common mission without being prejudiced by gender distinctions. In such a church, how could the partnership suddenly dissolve at the leadership level, with only men being viewed as qualified to serve in teaching and leadership? Why would a church of believer priests that otherwise focuses on the activity of all persons in the common ministry suddenly erect an ordained office (or foster a leadership role) characterized by a hierarchy of male over female?

The extension of the Old Testament structure of male priesthood to the New Testament church fails to understand that the priesthood has been radically transformed by the new covenant, which our Lord inaugurated. No longer do believers look to a special priestly class to whom God has entrusted the central responsibility for carrying out the religious vocation of his covenant people. Rather, all are participants in the one mandate to be ministers of God, and to this end all serve together. The role of the pastorate arises solely out of the ministry of the entire fellowship of believers. The pastoral office (or function) is an extension of the universal ministry of Christ's body, the church. This dimension of the church's ministry, as well as the church's ministry in general, is best fulfilled as women and men work together.[14]

Evangelicals agree that the sovereign Spirit calls different persons to differing functions in the church, including oversight responsibilities. The principle of the universal priesthood implies that the Spirit's call of some to the pastorate arises fundamentally out of his call to all believers to be ministers of Christ. Within this fellowship of believer priests, race, social status and gender cannot be overriding factors that disqualify a believer priest for selection to leadership among God's people, for service in the pastorate is based on the Spirit's sovereign call and gifting of certain persons for this particular ministry.

Before arguing this point explicitly, however, I must address another supposed priestly dimension of the pastorate that carries implications for the ministry of women: its representative character.

The Representative Priesthood and the Pastorate

In his defense of an all-male pastorate, C. S. Lewis asserts that the central issue that divides him from proponents of women in ministry is the meaning of the word *priest.* Lewis claims that his opponents forget that the basic role of a priest is representational, that a priest "represents us to God and God to us."[15] According to Lewis, the second aspect is the crucial consideration, for in his estimation a woman cannot fully represent God. Patrick Henry Reardon presses the point even further. He asserts that "ordaining the male sex to minister at the Eucharist has to do with the 'correct appearance' ('orthodoxy' in Greek), the proper iconography," and that altering the icon eventually will lead to the worship of "a different god." Consequently, Reardon concludes, ordaining women is "a grave act of disobedience and a first, but firm, step toward apostasy."[16]

The gravity of these charges requires a careful appraisal of a second dimension of the argument put forth by some male-leadership advocates, the representational

---

[14]Paul King Jewett, "Why I Favor the Ordination of Women," *Christianity Today,* June 6, 1975, p. 9.

[15]C. S. Lewis, *God in the Dock* (Grand Rapids, Mich.: Eerdmans, 1970), p. 236.

[16]Reardon, "Women Priests," p. 27.

aspect of the pastorate, especially the supposed role of the pastor in representing Christ. Putting the issue in the form of a question, Are pastors priests who represent Christ? And if so, in what sense?

Eucharistic representation. Those who would bar women from the pastorate on the basis of the representational character of the ordained office claim that pastors are priests who represent or "image" Christ.[17] For example, J. I. Packer declares, "Since the Son of God was incarnate as a male, it will always be easier, other things being equal, to realize and remember that Christ is ministering in person if his human agent and representative is also male."[18] Those who follow this line of reasoning generally find this representational function most readily displayed as ordained ministers represent Christ at the Eucharist.

In the West, the idea of the priest as Christ's representative at the Eucharist developed out of the commonplace designation of the officiator as acting "in the person of Christ" *(in persona Christi)*. Although the theological use of this idea may have arisen with Thomas Aquinas, since the Second Vatican Council it has been used widely in Roman Catholic circles to describe the priest as impersonating our Lord. According to official church teaching, in pronouncing the words of consecration at the Eucharist, the priest takes the role of Christ to the point of being his very image. Because those who take Christ's role must have a natural resemblance to him,[19] women cannot be ordained to the priesthood.

Protestants generally reject the Roman Catholic theology of the Mass, of course. Yet the idea of eucharistic representation remains embedded in the widely held perception that the Communion service is a reenactment of the Last Supper, in which the officiating pastor plays the part of Jesus. As a consequence, in the eyes of many Christians only a man can officiate at the Communion observance.

The officiant at the Lord's Supper does fulfill a certain representational function. But this representation is fundamentally vocal rather than visual.[20] In the eu-

---

[17]This argument is cited in Madeleine Boucher, "Ecumenical Documents: Authority-in-Community," *Midstream* 21, no. 3 (July 1982): 412.

[18]Packer, "Let's Stop," p. 20.

[19]Congregation for the Doctrine of the Faith, "Declaration on the Admission of Women to the Ministerial Priesthood," quoted in Kenneth Untener, "Forum: The Ordination of Women—Can the Horizons Widen?" *Worship* 65, no. 1 (January 1991): 52.

[20]Mark C. Chapman, "The Ordination of Women: Evangelical and Catholic," *Dialog* 28 (Spring 1989): 135. Cf. Martin Luther, *Book of Concord*, ed. Theodore G. Tappert (Philadelphia: Fortress, 1959), p. 448. Hull hints at a similar position. Gretchen Gaebelein Hull, *Equal to Serve* (Old Tappan, N.J.: Revell, 1987), p. 220.

charistic celebration, the presider announces Christ's words of invitation, thereby serving as the mouthpiece for the risen Lord, who is the true host. Nothing inherent in this representational function would bar someone from officiating at the table on the basis of gender. On the contrary, the church's eucharistic doctrine might actually be enhanced by women's presiding at the Lord's Table. As theologians of various denominations have concluded, an all-male clergy perpetuates the erroneous ideas that the Eucharist is a mass in which the priest acts as Christ, offering our Lord's body and blood to God, or that it is simply a reenactment of the Last Supper in which the pastor acts the part of Jesus.[21] Evangelical theologians are quick to point out that the Lord's Supper is not a reinstitution of Calvary. And although it is in a sense a reenactment of the Upper Room events, it is not merely an artistic drama. If limiting the officiators to men tends to perpetuate inaccurate and limited understandings of the Eucharist, then permitting both women and men to officiate could enhance the church's experience of this significant ordinance.[22]

Ontological representation. The representative function of those who officiate at the Eucharist is understood by some traditions to be an *ontological* representation of Christ; that is, the pastor is believed to embody in some symbolic manner the actual nature of our Lord. As the earlier quotation from J. I. Packer indicates, the idea of ontological representation provides a powerful rationale for the exclusion of women from the ordained office. Because the incarnate and exalted Lord is male,[23] and insofar as Jesus' maleness is not inconsequential but is of timeless, cosmic significance,[24] those who represent Christ must likewise be male.

Despite its seemingly unassailable logic, this argument has been questioned by a long list of Protestant and Roman Catholic scholars.[25] Critics do not necessarily reject the representative function of the ordained office. Rather, they aver that clergy represent Christ in his humanness, not in his maleness,[26] a point that finds

---

[21]John Austin Baker, "Eucharistic Presidency and Women's Ordination," *Theology* 88, no. 725 (September 1985): 357.

[22]This point is argued in ibid.

[23]E.g., Sara Butler, "Forum: Some Second Thoughts on Ordaining Women," *Worship* 63, no. 2 (March 1989): 165.

[24]S. M. Hutchens, for example, sees Jesus' maleness as indicating a cosmic priority of the male. See S. M. Hutchens, "God, Gender and the Pastoral Office," *Touchstone* 5, no. 4 (Fall 1992): 16-17.

[25]Constance F. Parvey, "Where Are We Going? The Threefold Ministry and the Ordination of Women," *Word and World* 5, no. 1 (Winter 1985): 9.

[26]Stephen C. Barton, "Impatient for Justice: Five Reasons Why the Church of England Should Ordain Women to the Priesthood," *Theology* 92, no. 749 (September 1989): 404.

support in both the biblical documents and the church fathers. The great declarations of the incarnation in the New Testament emphasize that Christ became human, not that he became male. John announces that "the Word became flesh" (Jn 1:14). And in speaking of Jesus Christ as "being made in human likeness" (Phil 2:7), Paul uses the general Greek word *anthrōpos* ("human") rather than the gender-specific *anēr* ("man"). Following the lead of the New Testament, the Nicene Creed declares that our Lord became a human being *(enanthrōpēsanta)*, thereby taking to himself the likeness of all who are included within the scope of his saving work. For the church fathers, the focus on the inclusiveness of Jesus' humanity was a theological necessity based on an important theological principle: what the Son did not assume in the incarnation he could not redeem.[27]

Advocates of gender equality find in Jesus' inclusive humanness important implications for the ordination of women. They argue that to elevate maleness as an essential requirement for ministry is to stand in opposition to the inclusive significance of Christ's saving work.[28] Thus, rather than barring women from ordination, classical Christology demands their inclusion in the ordained office. Madeleine Boucher explains concisely: "It may be argued that a priestly ministry of women and men would better image and represent the universality of Christ and redemption."[29]

But what about the undeniable maleness of Jesus? Certainly we do not wish to discount Jesus' gender any more than his Jewishness or his socioeconomic status.[30] What is at issue is the *soteriological* or saving significance of these aspects of our Lord's earthly existence. Boucher speaks for many when she explains, "We affirm—and affirm properly—that Christ redeems us *as* a man, as a Jew, as a poor person, and so on. The difficulty arises when it is implied that Christ redeems us

---

[27]This principle dates at least to Irenaeus. See Irenaeus *Adversus Haereses* 5.14, in The Ante-Nicene Fathers, ed. Alexander Roberts and James Donaldson (Grand Rapids, Mich.: Eerdmans, 1975), I:541. It formed an important consideration in the christological controversies. Against Apollinarius, for example, Gregory of Nazianzus asserted: "If any one has put his trust in him as a man without a human mind, he is himself devoid of mind and unworthy of salvation. For what he has not assumed he has not healed; it is what is united to his Deity that is saved" (Gregory of Nazianzus, "An Examination of Apollinarianism," in *Documents of the Christian Church*, ed. Henry Bettenson, 2nd ed. [London: Oxford University Press, 1963], p. 45). See also J. N. D. Kelly, *Early Christian Doctrines*, 5th rev. ed. (London: Adam and Charles Black, 1977), p. 297.

[28]Barton, "Impatient for Justice," p. 404. See also Untener, "Forum: The Ordination of Women," p. 57.

[29]Boucher, "Ecumenical Documents," p. 413.

[30]Ibid., p. 412. (Boucher then cites John Macquarrie, *Principles of Christian Theology*, p. 278.)

by virtue of the fact that he is a man, as though his maleness were a necessary condition for God's saving work in him."[31] Hence although the incarnation in the form of a male may have been historically and culturally necessary, attaching soteriological necessity to this would undercut Christ's status as representing all humans—male and female—in salvation.[32]

If clergy do represent Christ, then this demands that women and men serve together within the ordained office. Restricting the ordained office to males can cloud the symbolism of Christ's inclusive humanity. Moreover, whatever representative function ordained ministers fulfill is indirect, arising from their role within the church. Pastors function as ontological representatives of our Lord only insofar as they represent the church, which is Christ's body[33]—and hence is, in this sense, the ontological representation of Christ. Because Christ is creating one new human reality (Eph 2:15) in which distinctions of race, class and gender are overcome (Gal 3:28), the church—and consequently Christ—is best represented by an ordained ministry consisting of persons from various races, from all social classes and from both genders.

Yet I must voice a slight caveat here. I do not believe that these considerations necessitate denying all soteriological significance to Jesus' maleness. In fact, to do so is to reduce the importance of our sexuality,[34] which is an indispensable dimension of embodied human existence. Because Jesus was a particular historical person, his maleness was integral to the completion of his task. More particularly, being male facilitated Jesus in revealing the radical difference between God's ideal and the social structures of his day. Only a male could have offered an authoritative critique of those power structures.[35] Coming to this earth as a man, Jesus liberated both men and women from their bondage to the social orders that violate God's intention for human life-in-community. Jesus freed males from their slavery to the role of domination that belongs to the fallen world, in order that they can be truly male. On behalf of women Jesus acted as the paradigmatic human standing against the patriarchal system, bringing women to participate in the new order where sex distinctions no longer determine rank and worth.

---

[31]Ibid., p. 413.
[32]Parvey, "Where Are We Going?" p. 9.
[33]E. J. Kilmartin, "Apostolic Office: Sacrament of Christ," *Theological Studies* 36, no. 2 (1975): 263.
[34]Butler, "Forum: Some Second Thoughts," p. 165.
[35]Suzanne Heine, *Matriarchs, Goddesses and Images of God*, trans. John Bowden (Minneapolis: Augsburg, 1989), pp. 137-45.

But notice the implication: the church, in turn, best reflects, embodies and announces the liberating significance of Jesus' incarnation as a male by following the principle of mutuality he pioneered. This mutuality emerges as women and men work together in all dimensions of church life, including the ordained ministry.

The Priesthood of Gifted Persons and the Pastorate

Marianne Meye Thompson offers a helpful appraisal of the current state of the debate over the role of women in the church:

> Both those who favor women in ministry and those who oppose women in ministry can find suitable proof texts and suitable rationalizations to explain those texts. But if our discussion is ever to move beyond proof texting, we must integrate these texts into a theology of ministry. I suggest that the starting point for such a theology of ministry lies in the God who gives gifts for ministry and in the God who is no respecter of persons.[36]

In keeping with this insight, I want now to move to the positive side of my argument: to draw out the implications of the great evangelical acknowledgment that the Spirit's gifting is the basis for church leadership. This focus on the Spirit means that rather than being the New Testament counterpart to the Old Testament priesthood, the pastoral office (or role) is charismatic in character. It is to be filled by persons gifted for the pastorate, whether male or female, serving among the gifted people of God, who as a whole constitute the ecclesiastical counterpart to the Levitical priesthood.

The New Testament presents a gender-inclusive conception of spiritual gifts (or *charismata*). Paul indicates that lying behind all gifts, regardless of who receives them, is a common source—God (1 Cor 12:6, 28). Gifts are given not on the basis of human merit but by the will of the sovereign Holy Spirit (1 Cor 12:7-11) and the risen Christ (Eph 4:7, 11). The Spirit's endowments are bestowed on each believer, not merely a select few. The Lord of the church accords these gifts for the good of the church as a whole (1 Cor 12:7) and the completion of the common task of Christ's people (Eph 4:12). The egalitarian perspective of the New Testament raises two crucial questions for the pastoral office (or role) and the matter of who may serve in it.

First, what is the relationship of spiritual gifts to the pastoral office? Regarding

---

[36]Marianne Meye Thompson, "Response to Richard Longenecker," in *Women, Authority and the Bible*, ed. Alvera Mickelson (Downers Grove, Ill.: InterVarsity Press, 1986), p. 94.

this question, the New Testament witness to the practices of the early church suggests certain guiding principles. First, because pastors are to engage in certain specific activities, including preaching, teaching and leading, only those entrusted with the *charismata* that facilitate these aspects of ministry are appropriate candidates for the pastorate. Second, because some gifts are intended to be used only intermittently and in specific individual contexts, whereas others are designed for regular, constant use within the ongoing structure of wider community life, only those persons whom the Spirit has gifted for the regular public ministry of the community as a whole are likely to function in the pastorate. Third, insofar as leaders are to be involved in overseeing the ministry of the community, the church is to set in leadership those whom the Spirit has endowed with the appropriate gifts (such as administration) for leading the whole people of God in "works of service" (Eph 4:12).

Lying behind these principles is the assumption that spiritual gifts are foundational to office. For this reason, as the male-leadership Bible scholar Ronald Fung notes, "the charismata are the wherewithal, the tools, the means of the ministry. . . . It is by the endowment of charismata that its ministers are made sufficient."[37] In short, giftedness for the functions of the ordained ministry is the indispensable prerequisite for setting someone apart for such a ministry. The integral relation between gifts and ministry leads to the general principle that the church must give place for the giftedness of all persons, whether male or female. Men and women are to serve together, using whatever gifts the Spirit bestows on them.

This raises a second crucial question: does the Spirit endow women with the gifts essential for the pastorate? On this matter there seems to be little disagreement. Alvera Mickelsen's concise remark summarizes what most scholars would admit: "In Paul's lengthy discussions about spiritual gifts, he never indicates that some gifts are for men and other gifts for women."[38] This conclusion is exactly what we would expect from the observation made previously that the Holy Spirit is ultimately sovereign in endowing God's people with gifts for ministry. Because this task is the prerogative of the Spirit, it is not ours to decide on whom he can and cannot bestow certain gifts. On the contrary, the Old Testament prophets, who

---

[37]Ronald Y. K. Fung, "Ministry in the New Testament," in *The Church in the Bible and the World*, ed. D. A. Carson (Grand Rapids, Mich.: Baker, 1987), p. 178.

[38]Alvera Mickelsen, "An Egalitarian View: There Is Neither Male nor Female in Christ," in *Women in Ministry: Four Views*, ed. Bonnidell Clouse and Robert G. Clouse (Downers Grove, Ill.: InterVarsity Press, 1989), p. 191.

lived during the days of the all-male priesthood, anticipated a time when the Spirit would work through both women and men (e.g., Joel 2:28-29). According to Luke, the promised era dawned with Pentecost (Acts 2:14-18). Consequently, the Spirit is now at work freely in the church endowing whomever he chooses—both male and female—with whatever gifts he wills.

This point of agreement has important implications for the ministry of gifted persons—including women—in the church. To accomplish the mandate Christ has entrusted to the community of faith, our Lord has poured out the Spirit, who endows believers with spiritual gifts. These are distributed throughout the community according to the Spirit's will. The New Testament offers no hint that the Spirit restricts to men the gifts that equip a person to function in the ordained office (e.g., teaching, preaching, leadership), while distributing without distinction the gifts necessary for other ministries. Margaret Howe raises the obvious rhetorical question: if gifts equipping for pastoral ministry "are distributed by *God* to women, what higher authority does the Church have for denying the women their expression?"[39]

Those who would restrict pastoral leadership to males, however, are quick to respond: important as they are, the *charismata* do not constitute the only factor in determining the role of women in the church. Rather, as Fung declares, "Paul's practice and his teaching with regard to women in ministry also need to be taken into account."[40] He and his colleagues are convinced that in this matter Paul follows the principle of male leadership and female subordination. Hence Fung concludes from his study of the New Testament that "a woman who has received the gift of teaching (or leadership, or any other charisma) may exercise it to the fullest extent possible—in any role which does not involve her in a position of doctrinal or ecclesiastical authority over men."[41]

But notice what Fung is saying. To skirt the ecclesiological implications of the New Testament teaching on spiritual gifts, he must drive a sharp wedge between *charismata* and the ordained office. Fung finds no contradiction between "Paul's teaching concerning the indiscriminate distribution of spiritual gifts to men and women alike" and the restrictions he claims "Paul imposes on women's ministry by

---

[39]E. Margaret Howe, "The Positive Case for the Ordination of Women," in *Perspectives on Evangelical Theology*, ed. Kenneth S. Kantzer and Stanley N. Gundry (Grand Rapids, Mich.: Zondervan, 1979), p. 275.

[40]Fung, "Ministry in the New Testament," p. 179.

[41]Ibid., p. 209.

reason of woman's subordination to man." But to harmonize these two principles, Fung must declare unequivocally that "*gift* and *role* are to be distinguished."[42] In other words, to salvage their interpretation of Paul's approach to women in ministry, male-leadership proponents impose what appears to be an artificial dichotomy between the Spirit's gifting and the exercise of the ordained office.

This move evidences an even deeper problem with the male-leadership position. The limitation on a woman's use of the gift of teaching to those roles that do not place her in authority over men subsumes ecclesiology (the doctrine of the church) under anthropology (our understanding of what it means to be human). In the end, the case against women in the pastorate rests on a supposed divinely intended hierarchical ordering present within creation. Yet even if God had so ordered the sexes from the beginning (which he did not), this would not necessarily require that the church continue to be governed by structures that perpetuate male leadership and female subordination. Christ established the church not merely to be a mirror of original creation but to be the eschatological new community, living in accordance with the principles of God's new creation and thereby reflecting the mutuality that lies at the heart of the triune God.

Conclusion

The controversy over women in ministry hinges on the deeper question of what kind of church Christ came to inaugurate and, in turn, what kind of pastoral office advances our Lord's intention. Male-leadership advocates envision a church in which men lead and women—regardless of their spiritual gifts—follow male leadership. To this end, they view the pastorate as the ecclesiastical instantiation of an all-male priesthood. Egalitarians, in contrast, contend that Christ intends the church to be a fellowship in which all serve as they are gifted and called by the Spirit, which requires that pastoral leadership be open to those whom the Spirit has gifted for this role.

I am convinced that the impulses born in the Reformation and advanced through the evangelical awakenings lead directly to the second of these two visions. I believe that the evangelical model of the church is one in which gifted leaders serve within a gifted people. In this church, pastors—both male and female—serve together as instruments of the Spirit in the glorious task of empowering the people of God for the work of the ministry.

---

[42]Ibid.

17

GOD, GENDER AND
BIBLICAL METAPHOR

Judy L. Brown

Underlying many Christians' view of the proper roles of men and women is a wrong view of God's nature and of God's image in humanity. For example, it is commonly assumed that men have the exclusive assignment of being leaders in the home and in the church because in these roles they act as God's representatives, and of course, God is male, or at least more male than female. Eve is viewed as having been created less in the image of God than Adam. Whether explicitly or implicitly, she is regarded as bearing God's image "via Adam's rib"—that is, in a secondary, indirect or partial way.

Is there any truth to such claims? Is God in any way male? Is God in some way more male than female? Does a man, a husband or a male minister have more in common with God than does a woman, a wife or a female minister? These questions must be addressed because this alleged affinity between maleness and godlikeness is not only one of the most frequently voiced arguments against the leadership fitness of women, it is present in many Christians' understanding and presentation of God. After all, God the Father, God the Son, and the Bible's vast array of masculine terms and pronouns referring to God seem to make for a compelling case in favor of God's maleness.

The Challenge of Revealing God
The true God is Spirit, which is difficult for humans to comprehend. How can such an identity be revealed? How can the infinite divine be conveyed to finite humanity? The Bible presents God largely through the use of figurative language. Humanlike titles and relationships are assigned to God, such as "Father" and "King." Humanlike characteristics are ascribed to God through personification and anthro-

pomorphism. However, these literary devices are not meant to be pressed beyond their intended revelation. For example, God is said to see, but a Spirit God doesn't have actual eyes; God is said to hear, but a Spirit God doesn't have actual ears. In addition, similes, metaphors and analogies—or controlled comparisons—are made. In each instance, comparing is different from equating: comparing always means "God is like this, but God is also not exactly or fully like this." It is imperative that our interpretation of the revelation of God be approached with the utmost care and without any self-serving preconceptions.

Masculine Pronouns

Throughout Scripture God is consistently referred to as *he.* This is not the choice of a translation team; it is the language of the original text. Does this mean that God is male? No, not necessarily. Hebrew, Greek, English and most other ancient and modern languages do not offer a generic (ungendered) personal pronoun. The generic personal pronoun *they* can be used if the reference is plural, but what if the reference is to an individual who is not necessarily a male or a female? Either by rule or by common usage, whether in modern English or the ancient biblical languages, *he* has two possible meanings: it can refer specifically to a male or generically to an individual person of undesignated gender. Both uses are frequent and equally legitimate.

The generic pronoun *it* cannot be used of God because it is not a personal pronoun. It would not reflect the personal character of God and would thereby invite the theological error of viewing God as an abstract principle or force. Inserting *he/she* or interspersing *she* throughout the text is an unacceptable approach because *she* unavoidably connotes gender, and any connotation of gender invites the theological error of imputing our human nature to God's nature. What about using *they* for the "three-in-one" God? In a world of multiple false gods, it evidently was and probably still is essential that God's unity be given particular emphasis.

The only pronoun, then, that can properly be used of God in Hebrew, Greek, English and many other languages is *he.* The point of using the word is not to convey that God has a sexual or gendered nature but to emphasize God's personal nature. When *he* is used for God in Scripture, it is used in its general sense as a generic personal pronoun, not in its gender-specific sense as a masculine pronoun.[1]

---

[1]See Carl F. H. Henry, *God, Revelation, and Authority* (Waco, Tex.: Word, 1982), 5:159.

The Error of Gender

To attach gender significance to any of the references to God, and thus to conclude that God has sexuality in some sense, is to assign to God qualities belonging to humanity and the created order. This is what the ancient pagan cults did, especially the fertility cults that are denounced throughout the Old Testament. Not knowing the truth about God, these people simply defined their deities according to what they understood about themselves. They were sexual beings, so their deities became sexual beings. And as sexual beings, their male gods and female goddesses had sex organs and were capable of sexual activity.

Knowing the truth about God, Israel was to do no such thing: "You saw no form of any kind the day the LORD spoke to you at Horeb out of the fire. Therefore watch yourselves very carefully, so that you do not become corrupt and make for yourselves an idol, an image of any shape, whether formed like a man or a woman" (Deut 4:15-16 NIV). It wasn't just the wood or stone statue that was wrong. The prohibition also denounces the wrong thinking underlying the wrong action. It is wrong to confuse God's nature with the nature of physical, created beings. And perhaps there is no characteristic more distinctly physical than sexuality. According to this passage, it is just as wrong to depict God as malelike as it is to depict God as femalelike.

The fact that humanity bears the image of God cannot be turned into the notion that God bears the image of humanity. God says, "I am God, and not man" (Hos 11:9 NIV). God transcends creation, which means God transcends attributes of physicality, such as sexuality. It is the height of heresy and heathenism to propose that God has the sexuality that constitutes either gender. What follows this type of thinking? Does a male deity require the presence of a female deity? As children of God, are we in some way sexually produced by God? Is Jesus the product of an actual sex act between divinity and humanity? Such suggestions are repulsive. But each of these perversions begins with the claim that God is somehow male or malelike. The Bible is clear: "God is spirit" (Jn 4:24).

Moreover, the prohibition against ascribing sexual characteristics to God cannot be circumvented by positing that God's masculinity is metaphysical (and not physical). While some pagan and Eastern religions spiritualize sexuality—casting masculinity and femininity as spiritual polar forces defining and pervading all of reality—such notions are utterly alien to biblical teaching. According to Scripture, God created sexuality when he created physical life on earth. The being and nature of God does not partake of or participate in sexuality in any way.[2]

The Predominance of Masculine Imagery

Once it is understood that the scriptural revelation of God uses human language and humanlike descriptions in an attempt to reveal an infinite being to finite humanity, and once it is understood that these expressions must be interpreted as meaning only what they are intended to mean and no more, the fact remains that the Bible uses more masculine word pictures to describe God than it uses feminine word pictures. Is there any explanation for this other than that God is more male than female? Because Scripture—especially the Old Testament—makes it clear that God does not possess the created human characteristic of sexuality, there must be some other explanation.

God is revealed through the vehicle of human language, which, in turn, reflects its cultural context. The cultures of biblical times were patriarchal. The man was the central figure in society, and the husband-father was the authority figure as the family's primary protector and provider. It is understandable, then, that masculine terms would be the common choice for describing a God who is the great protector, provider and authority figure—a God who is independent rather than dependent, strong and able rather than vulnerable, and entitled to utmost regard. In ancient times, all these traits were more characteristic of men than of women and were summed up in the traditional father role.

God is like a father relationally, not sexually. God's relationship to his children is in many ways like that of a loving father. God is called Father in the New Testament (where Christ is revealed as God's Son) much more frequently than in the Old Testament, because it is in the context of Jesus' relationship with his Father in heaven that God is most fully revealed as our Father. Jesus' disciples are to call God "Father" because the work of Christ has made the intimate personal relationship between God the Son and God the Father available (in a lesser sense) to all those who believe in his name. Biblically, God's fatherhood primarily expresses our family relationship with God through Christ. It is not intended to signify that God's essential nature is masculine, or more masculine than feminine, or gendered in any sense.

Even as Scripture likens God to various animals (Deut 32:10-12; Hos 5:14;

---

[2]See Faith Martin, "Mystical Masculinity," *Pricilla Papers* 6, no. 4 (Fall 1992); and Rebecca Merrill Groothuis, *Good News for Women: A Biblical Picture of Gender Equality* (Grand Rapids, Mich.: Baker, 1997), pp. 83-100.

11:10; 13:7)—certainly not because God is an animal but because some animals have characteristics that help humanity better understand God—so too Scripture depicts God in terms of roles or attributes associated with men. This is done not because God is male or essentially masculine in nature but because men in ancient cultures possessed characteristics, including authority, that help portray God's relationship to his people. In a similar manner, Scripture likens God to various inanimate objects or entities (e.g., rock, fortress, shield, gate, bread, light), not because God is inanimate but because such things have an identity or a quality that helps humanity grasp certain qualities that are true of God. Just as it is hermeneutically and theologically unsound to conclude that animal terminology means God is an animal or that inanimate terminology means God is inanimate, so it is wrong to conclude from masculine terminology that God is male or malelike.

Furthermore, the fact that Scripture frequently portrays God's authority (along with a number of his other attributes) by means of masculine titles and word pictures does not mean that authority is necessarily or exclusively a masculine attribute. It simply means that Scripture reveals God as a personal being who has the power to command obedience—an attribute that typically characterized male persons and not female persons during biblical times.

The Use of Feminine Imagery

Any argument for God's maleness that is built on the use of masculine imagery should be checked by the fact that Scripture also contains a significant amount of feminine imagery for God. In light of the patriarchal culture of Israel and surrounding peoples, this is rather remarkable. Evidently a God who is not male cannot be adequately described using only male terms and comparisons.

Moses, the author of the opening books of Scripture, was led by the Spirit to record God's words when the law was first given on Mount Sinai, and those notable words include the likening of God to a mother eagle (Ex 19:4). This same imagery is repeated on another momentous occasion, the end of Moses' ministry and his final preparation of Israel to enter Canaan. He assigned to God the activities of a mother eagle—stirring up the nest, hovering over the young and carrying the young in flight (Deut 32:11). The language is identical to that of Genesis 1:2, in which "hovering" is ascribed to God's Spirit. Moses described God as being the One who both fathered and birthed Israel (Deut 32:18; "formed" instead of "birthed" in KJV ignores the wording of the Hebrew text "writhe in pain" and the fact that this wording was used in reference to childbirth). The words of God to his special servant Job also speak of the Almighty's combination of fathering and mothering qualities (Job 38:28-30).

Feminine imagery is common in the poetical writings. God is depicted as a midwife, definitely a female activity (Ps 22:9-10 NIV). He is likened to both a male master and a female mistress (Ps 123:2) and to the mother of a young child who has been breastfed (Ps 131:2). He is said to have given birth to the earth and the world (Ps 90:2; "brought forth" in NIV translates the Hebrew expression for a woman's giving birth). The proverbs extol God's wisdom in feminine terminology, personifying this wisdom as a woman (Prov 1:20-21; 4:5-9; 8:1-11; 9:1-6). This, of course, stands in sharp contrast to any accusation that women are inherently less intelligent or perceptive than men. In Proverbs 8:22-36, wisdom—personified as a woman—is presented as an attribute of God involved in the creation of the world. Jesus is also described as the wisdom of God (1 Cor 1:24, 30; Col 2:3) and the creative Word of God (Jn 1:1-3).

The prophet Isaiah uses a considerable amount of female imagery in his references to God. He describes God as being like a woman in the pains of childbirth (Is 42:14), like a woman who has given birth (Is 49:14-15) and like a woman breastfeeding her baby (Is 49:14-15). He quotes God as saying Yahweh has acted toward Israel like a woman who conceives and carries a child (Is 46:3) and like a mother comforting a child (Is 66:13). The prophet Hosea compares God to a mother bear with her cubs (Hos 13:8; NIV wording lacks the feminine).

Female imagery is continued into the New Testament. In a series of three parables, Jesus likens a sinner to a lost sheep, a lost coin and a lost son (Lk 15:3-32). In the second parable, the character who portrays the role of God is a woman. Jesus describes himself as being like a mother hen longing to gather her children under her wings (Mt 23:37; Lk 13:34). He explains salvation as being the result of God the Spirit birthing someone into existence (Jn 3:1-8). Thus every time a Christian speaks of being "born again," he or she employs female imagery for God and God's salvation act, imagery supplied by Jesus. The metaphor of God giving us birth is repeated in James 1:18.

Of course, none of these analogies means that God is female, any more than the masculine imagery means that God is male. The Spirit God is neither male nor female and is certainly not bisexual. Again, it must be emphasized, the Spirit God transcends all characteristics of physical creatures, including sexuality. Adam and Eve, man and woman, were both equally made in God's image; but their characteristics, especially their sexual characteristics, are not to be forced back upon a definition of God. Defining the Creator according to the creation lowers the Creator to the level of the creation and produces serious theological errors.

Feminism's Extremes

Since both the Old Testament and the New Testament use female imagery of God, especially the imagery of a mother, are liberal feminist theologians right in calling for God's title to be changed from "Father God" to "Father-Mother God"? Some of the arguments in favor of doing so could be compelling, particularly to Christians who are sympathetic to the cause of gender inclusiveness. For instance, it could be argued that such a title for God serves to acknowledge the fact that both men and women fully bear God's image. It could be said that inserting "Father-Mother God" terminology into the church's liturgy presents a gospel that is less offensive and perhaps more attractive to modern cultural sensibilities. Still others favor this step as a means of counterbalancing years of sexist theology regarding the nature of God.

Noble as these motivations may appear, there is need for extreme caution. It is possible that some liberal theologians have hidden agendas and that their gender-balancing terminology would address a god other than the God of the Bible. Throughout Scripture God has reserved the right to name himself and to reveal his names; there is never the slightest suggestion that humanity is invited to name or rename God. In fact, God's self-disclosed names are presented as bearing particular integrity and constancy.

It is possible that the concept of a "Father-Mother God" would revert to ancient fertility cults in which maleness and femaleness were incorporated into the deity rather than transcended by the deity.[3] The title seems to establish the sexuality of God rather than neutralize or negate divine sexuality. It leaves room for the possibility of bisexuality in God, and consequently the acceptance of bisexuality in humans. In light of such serious concerns as these, it seems that taking even well-intentioned liberties with God's name has the potential of leading the church down a very slippery slope.

There can be one and only one completely safe approach to take. The church should function within the truths and the terminology that are explicitly present in Scripture, no more and no less. This would mean that the plethora of feminine imagery for God is acknowledged, embraced and celebrated—something that clas-

---

[3]Mary Hayter, *The New Eve in Christ* (Grand Rapids, Mich.: Eerdmans, 1987), p. 38.

sical Christianity has failed to do across its history. This would also require differentiating between the imagery used to describe God and the titles that are acceptable in addressing God. The Bible specifically designates God as "our Father" (Is 64:8) and nowhere designates God as "our Mother." Jesus taught his disciples to address prayers to "our Father in heaven" (Mt 6:9) but did not teach them to pray to a heavenly Mother.

Everything that is taught about God by the mix of masculine and feminine imagery should be kept in focus. Nonetheless, the title given to God by Scripture is not Mother or Father-Mother but Father. In our language for God we should use biblical terms, but with a biblically informed and theologically sound understanding of what these terms do and do not mean.

Traditionalism's Extremes

One more time it must be emphasized that God's fatherhood does not mean God's maleness. Just as it is wrong for feminists to impose female gender on God, so it is wrong for traditionalists to impose male gender on God. Both claims are contrary to Scripture, theologically dangerous and usually self-serving in motive.

Since God is without gender, there is no reason to hold the view that men resemble God more closely than do women and that men therefore are better fit to represent God in positions of spiritual leadership. But even if God were male or essentially masculine, this still would not warrant limiting spiritual leadership to the male gender. Spiritual leaders do serve in certain ways as God's representatives, as do all Christians (2 Cor 5:20). But they are like ambassadors who serve as representatives of presidents or prime ministers. Being a *representative* is quite different from being a *representation*. Ambassadors speak for whoever sends them and act on behalf of the one who commissions them, but they do not have to imitate or impersonate that individual. Indeed, female ambassadors have represented men, and male ambassadors have represented women.[4] Representing a person involves reflecting the wishes of a person, not embodying that individual's personal characteristics (such as gender).

Furthermore, Scripture speaks metaphorically of spiritual leadership as a feminine activity. Moses likened his leadership over Israel to the activities of a woman (Num 11:12). Paul spoke in the same way on more than one occasion (Gal 4:19; 1 Thess 2:7).

---

[4]Ibid., p. 53.

Jesus' Maleness

But wasn't Jesus a male? Yes, of course he was. But the important question is, *why* was Jesus male? Was he male because God is male, or because spiritual leaders must be male? Or was he male for entirely different reasons?

What was theologically significant in Jesus' birth and life was not that God became male but that God became flesh (Jn 1:14). This is central to New Testament teaching: "Every spirit that acknowledges that Jesus Christ has come in the flesh is from God" (1 Jn 4:2). Jesus' primary title for himself, "Son of Man," as well as most other New Testament references to Jesus' being a "man," use the Greek word for "human being" *(anthrōpos)* rather than the Greek word for "male" *(anēr* or *arsēn)*. If Jesus' maleness had the spiritual significance that some try to attach to it, then women would not be savable or would not be as savable as men, and, of course, neither is the case.[5]

In order to be a representative human being (albeit without sin), Jesus had to be either male or female.[6] The choice could not have been based on God's gender, for God is neither male nor female. Nor could the choice have been based on God's preference, for God does not favor men over women. What, then, determined Jesus' gender? The culture into which Jesus was born is the most likely possibility.

The culture of first-century Judaism made it virtually impossible for anyone other than a man to be recognized as a teacher of truth. Generally speaking, men were not to let women read or study the law, nor were men to speak to women in public. The testimony of a woman was not legally credible. A Jewish man would normally say a prayer of thanksgiving every day praising God for not making him a Gentile, a slave or a woman. The Messiah simply had to be a man. Although it probably was theologically possible to be otherwise, it was not culturally possible.

Interestingly, the human nature that Jesus had to embrace in order to be the Savior was derived one hundred percent from a woman.[7] The greatest miracle of history, God's becoming human flesh, was accomplished without the involvement of a man; but it was not without the intimate involvement of a woman. All the aspects of humanity that equipped Jesus to be the ideal spiritual leader—whom all other spiritual leaders should emulate—were derived entirely from a woman. It seems as

---

[5]Aída Besançon Spencer, *Beyond the Curse* (Nashville: Thomas Nelson, 1985), p. 22.
[6]Paul K. Jewett, *The Ordination of Women* (Grand Rapids, Mich.: Eerdmans, 1980), p. 30.
[7]Ibid., p. 32.

if the Savior's *gender* is very much balanced by the unique elements of the Savior's *birth*.

Theologically, then, it is indefensible to view the female gender as in any way inherently inferior to the male gender. It is equally incorrect to claim that the female gender is inherently disqualified for spiritual leadership. Whatever the mix of reasons for Jesus' being white, male, Jewish and working class, it is not biblically or theologically necessary to require all of these characteristics of spiritual leaders today. Therefore it is inconsistent to require just one of them—maleness.

Again, however, a word of caution is in order. Just as the Bible refers to the first member of the Trinity as God the Father and not God the Mother, the second member of the Trinity is said to be God the Son and not God the Daughter. No compromising of this truth should be entertained. First, it is a historical fact that Jesus was born into this world as a male child. Second, Jesus' maleness was appropriate for the culture of first-century Palestine, but there may be additional reasons for his maleness. Perhaps, for example, the "male dominance, female subordination" consequence of the Fall had to be overturned by the dominant gender rather than by the subordinate gender. Perhaps the first human, who was male, had to be "matched" and redeemed by a Savior who was male.

Regardless of any additional reasons, God's determination of Jesus' gender is not negotiable or changeable. It is not necessary to deny historical fact or disregard biblical authority in order to recognize that Jesus' gender does not dictate the gender of other spiritual leaders.

God's Image in Men and Women

The humanity that God became flesh to redeem is introduced in Genesis 1:26-27 as bearing God's image and likeness and as consisting of "male and female." From its first reference to men and women, God's Word proclaims that they both bear the same divine image. The biblical account does not differentiate in any way; in whatever way Adam bore the image of God, Eve bore the image of God. The text gives us no reason to think otherwise. Male and female together constitute the humanity that was made in God's image.

Genesis 1:26-27 also mentions the counsel that God took within himself regarding this climactic creation act. Eve was just as much in God's original plan as was Adam. Humanity, as God intended it, was incomplete when the man was alone. And if counsel within the triune God underscores the worth of humanity, as is typically taught, then the woman's worth is even more solidly established in that God again took counsel within himself before creating her specifically (Gen 2:18).[8]

The fact that Adam was made with dust from the ground and Eve was made with bone from Adam does not in any way support a claim that Adam was made primarily in God's image while Eve was made primarily in Adam's image and only secondarily in God's image. The logic of such an argument fails. If Eve was made in the image of Adam because of coming from his bone, then Adam was made in the image of the ground because of coming from its dust. The dust and bone were simply raw materials in the hands of the true source of life, the One from whom both Adam and Eve were given their existence and divine image.[9] The erroneous claim that Eve was inferior to Adam, or less reflective of God's image, must be read *into* Scripture, for it is contrary to the scriptural record. According to the Bible, a woman's participation in the image of God is not less than or different from that of a man.

Volumes have been written about the meaning of the "image of God." It is not within the scope of this essay to exhaust all of the possible meanings of the expression, but several suggestions merit some consideration.

"Man" (*'adam*) is simultaneously singular and plural in Genesis 1:27: "humankind" is one, but "male and female" are two. One cannot read this verse without reflecting on the preceding verse: "God [singular] said, 'Let us [plural] make humankind in our [plural] image.'" The God who is one speaks as if he were more than one. And then the triune God follows the reference to making humanity in his image with the explanation that he made humanity male and female. Is it possible that the "image of God" is fleshed out in humanity via maleness and femaleness? In other words, was the state of unity, fellowship, equality and interdependence enjoyed by the Persons of the Trinity meant to define male-female relationships? Is this at least part of what it means to be made in the image of God?

This would not mean that someone must be married to be fully human or fully reflective of God's image. Although not every human being does marry, every human being is either male or female and experiences male-female associations. As one author notes, gender is "the first observation announced at the birth of a baby" and "the first characteristic we notice in meeting other humans."[10] Gender is probably the single most defining characteristic of someone's personhood. And male-female dynamics constitute the foundation on which much social interchange is

---

[8]Paul K. Jewett, *Man as Male and Female* (Grand Rapids, Mich.: Eerdmans, 1975), p. 125.
[9]Hayter, *New Eve*, p. 100.
[10]Stanley J. Grenz, "Is God Sexual?" *Christian Scholar's Review* 28 (1998): 24-41.

built. Although various members of the animal kingdom experience considerable interrelatedness in their male-female roles, nothing of the mutuality and fellowship available to men and women is known to exist outside of humanity.[11]

If it is true that the fellowship between Adam and Eve, and consequently between men and women in general, is a means through which God's image is to be visible in humanity, then several compelling ramifications must be noted. Human sexuality would be at the very center of the Christian doctrine of "man."[12] Ideally, the equality and dignity of each member of the triune God and the complementarity and unity within the Godhead would be reflected in human male-female relationships. There should be no attempt—by either a man or a woman—to disregard one's own sexuality or to devalue or degrade the other's sexuality. Such posturing would distort rather than reflect the image of God.

In light of these considerations, it becomes quite clear that homosexuality is a blatant denial of the very means through which an individual is rightly to reflect God's image. Likewise, the male chauvinism that has been a blight on society since antiquity and the radical feminism that answers back with equal venom are *both* diametrically opposed to the will of God. Each so disrespects the other sex as to negate any possibility of men and women's reflecting the harmony that exists within the Godhead.

Instead of participating in these antihuman, sinful aberrations, we should make every effort to affirm our own sex and to affirm the other sex as well.[13] The more this affirmation is present, the more we are capable of reflecting the image of God. Men and women are different from each other but equal to and essential to each other. Without this admission, our humanness and our godliness remain deficient, whether we are male or female.[14]

Some go so far as to propose that a male or female alone would not have been capable of reflecting God's image because male and female together are necessary to reflect the interrelationship within the Godhead; thus both genders are needed to depict the fullest possible representation of God's nature.[15] If this is true, then

---

[11]Jewett, *Man as Male and Female*, p. 35.

[12]Ibid., p. 43.

[13]Ibid., p. 49.

[14]J. I. Packer, "Understanding the Differences," in *Women, Authority and the Bible*, ed. Alvera Mickelsen (Downers Grove, Ill.: InterVarsity Press, 1986), p. 297.

[15]Spencer, *Beyond the Curse*, p. 21, 122; Ruth A. Tucker, *Women in the Maze* (Downers Grove, Ill.: InterVarsity Press, 1992), p. 14.

it is all the more important for the church to exemplify proper relationships between men and women, including welcoming both into spiritual leadership.

With Paul's declaration in Galatians 3:28 that the barrier between male and female has been broken down, perhaps Christ's work on the cross restores more than is sometimes realized. Perhaps the *re*-creation that occurs at salvation makes available to the church what was originally present at creation: the capacity for men and women to reflect the harmonious relationship that exists within God. This may be one aspect of the unity among believers that is requested in Jesus' precross prayer (Jn 17:20-23). Its potential impact is most compelling: so that "the world will know that you sent me." The church need not think long or hard to realize that the world does not yet know the One who has been sent to inaugurate a new creation (2 Cor 5:17). One cannot help but wonder how much of this stems from a lack of re-creation unity between men and women within the body of believers.

Another plausible explanation of the image of God is that rather than being manifest relationally between men and women, God's image is seen in individual persons. Evidence of this possibility is found in Genesis 9:6, in which the death penalty is enacted for anyone who wrongfully takes an individual human life, because "in his own image God made humankind." Suggestions for the meaning of this individual reflection of the divine usually have to do with humankind's intellectual, volitional and spiritual capacities, such as the abilities to be reflective and self-determining and to have fellowship with God. In view of this explanation, it is important to remember that according to Genesis 1:27, Eve received whatever capacities were given to Adam.

Yet a third possibility is that humanity is capable of reflecting the image of God in both ways, individually and relationally.[16] Of course, none of these three options suggests that men and women replicate God. There is only one God, and human beings are *not* small duplicates of the divine. There is merely a correspondence—a mirroring or reflecting—between humanity's nature and God's nature. This hint of Godlikeness in human beings is necessary for a finite person to catch even a glimpse of what the infinite, triune God is like. Still, after we make every attempt to better understand the Trinity, it remains one of the greatest mysteries among Christian doctrines.

Regardless of which explanation of the image of God is deemed most desirable (individual, relational or both), two truths remain essential to the discussion of

---

[16]Mary J. Evans, *Woman in the Bible* (Downers Grove, Ill.: InterVarsity Press, 1983), p. 13.

women in spiritual leadership. First, whatever image of God was given to Adam was given in equal measure to Eve. Eve was not created in any way inferior to Adam due to having received God's image to some lesser or different degree. Whatever effect Eve's sin had on God's image in her, Adam's sin, of equal or greater magnitude (Rom 5:12; I Cor 15:21-22), must have had a comparable effect on God's image in him. Yet although sin may have marred the image of God, it could not abolish it. The image was still present after the Fall, as noted in Genesis 9:6, even after human sinfulness became so deep and pervasive that it led to a purging of the world. There is a spiritual capacity put within humanity by God; though people can ignore it, violate it and even desecrate it, they cannot destroy it.[17] It remains available, and Jesus Christ gave his life to redeem the image of God in humanity to its fullest potential for all of eternity.

Second, whatever the connection between the image of God and male-female relationships, human sexuality is presented by the creation account as both positive and fundamental to what it means to be human. The biblical account is without sexual stereotyping. God created male and female equally good and equally perfect. There is no hint of superiority or inferiority, no mention of domination or subordination.[18] According to creation, then, if men are called by God to serve as spiritual leaders, women should be expected to be called as well. The church should *expect* the calling of women, not reject it.

---

[17]Hayter, *New Eve*, p. 87.
[18]Ibid., p. 89.

18

"EQUAL IN BEING,
UNEQUAL IN ROLE"

Exploring the Logic of Woman's Subordination

Rebecca Merrill Groothuis

According to Aristotle, the male is "by nature fitter for command than the female."[1] According to John Piper and Wayne Grudem, male authority and female submission are integral to the "deeper differences," the "underlying nature" and the "true meaning" of manhood and womanhood.[2] Men have the inherent right and responsibility to direct the affairs of others. Women are meant to be in submission, to have their affairs directed by men.[3] It seems that in both Aristotelian thought and evangelical patriarchy, the subordination of women to male authority follows from what is understood to be the created nature of maleness and femaleness.[4] Authority is deemed natural and fitting for men, and submission is deemed natural and fitting for women.

Yet there is one respect in which evangelical patriarchy has departed from Aristotle—and from the Western theologians and philosophers who have followed in his intellectual footsteps.[5] Aristotle maintained that it is precisely *because* "the male

---

[1] Aristotle *Politics* 1259.b.3.
[2] John Piper and Wayne Grudem, "An Overview of Central Concerns: Questions and Answers," in *RBMW,* pp. 60, 87.
[3] Ibid., pp. 78-79; and John Piper, "A Vision of Biblical Complementarity: Manhood and Womanhood Defined According to the Bible," in *RBMW,* pp. 35-52.
[4] In this essay the *nature* of a thing is understood to mean its inherent character, intended purpose, defining qualities, essence or being.
[5] In *The Less Noble Sex* (Indianapolis: Indiana University Press, 1993), Nancy Tuana develops the thesis that "Aristotle's conception of [woman as] the misbegotten man held sway in science, philosophy, and theology at least until the nineteenth century" (p. ix).

is by nature superior, and the female inferior, [that] the one rules, and the other is ruled."[6] Historically, male superiority was assumed to inhere primarily in a natural male advantage in morality and rationality. But when evangelical patriarchalists today claim that male leadership is natural and fitting given the deeper differences of masculinity and femininity, they accompany this claim with protestations that women are not morally or rationally deficient with respect to men; rather, men and women are "equal in being" but "different" (that is, unequal) in "function" or "role."[7]

Aristotle's conclusion—that men are by nature fitter for command than women—has been retained. Aristotle's premise—that men are by nature morally and rationally superior to women—has been rejected (which leaves the rationale for the conclusion somewhat unclear). Today it is undeniable that many women *are* morally and intellectually qualified for leadership. Although some patriarchalists may wish to categorize such women as "exceptions," the ban on women assuming "male" leadership roles is without exception. No matter how stellar a woman's spiritual and intellectual qualifications, this can *never* overrule the unalterable fact of her female nature, which dictates that in church and home she must not have authority over a man but must support and submit to man's authority over her.

But notice that in evangelical patriarchy a woman's subordination still follows—necessarily and permanently—from what she necessarily and permanently *is* by nature (namely, female). Her personal being decides and determines her subordinate status. Piper and Grudem concur: "Scripture and nature teach that personal manhood and womanhood are indeed relevant in deciding . . . who gives primary leadership in the relationship."[8] Men's authority and women's subordination are integral to "what true manhood and womanhood *are*."[9] The essence of masculinity is

---

[6]Aristotle *Politics* 1254.b.10.

[7]I will refer to nonegalitarian evangelicals as *patriarchalists* or in some cases *subordinationists*, since these terms identify most clearly the key concepts—male rule and female subordination—that distinguish this view from that of evangelical egalitarians. For the use of the term *patriarchy* to identify the doctrine of male leadership, see Steven Tracy, "Headship with a Heart: How Biblical Patriarchy Actually Prevents Abuse," *Christianity Today*, February 2003, pp. 50-54. Tracy defines patriarchy as "the affirmation of male authority over females," which is the sense in which I use it here. The issue at stake in this debate is precisely the concept of patriarchy—and not of hierarchy or tradition or complementarity (all legitimate concepts in themselves). For further discussion of the terminology issue, see the introduction to this volume.

[8]Piper and Grudem, "Overview," p. 87. Conversely, they feel dismayed that "'manhood' and 'womanhood' as such are now often seen as irrelevant factors in determining fitness for leadership" (p. xiii).

[9]Piper, "Vision," p. 34, emphasis added.

a sense of leadership, and the essence of femininity is a disposition to submit to male leadership.[10] In other words, men are to lead because authority is a constitutive element of masculinity, and women are to submit to male leadership because submission is a constitutive element of femininity. A man is fit to lead by virtue of his male nature. A woman, by virtue of her female nature, is not.

Despite the rhetoric of "roles" and "equality," it seems that a fundamental similarity remains between Aristotle and the evangelical patriarchalists of today. Woman's subordinate status is—as it has always been—decided solely by woman's female being. Whether woman is deemed unable to rule because of her mental and moral inferiority (historic patriarchy) or whether just *being* female makes a woman unfit for authority or decision making (today's patriarchy), it appears to be on account of a prior assumption about the meaning and nature of womanhood that women are not expected or permitted to share authority equally with men. By virtue of her female being a woman is fit to be subject to man's will and unfit to exercise her own will with the freedom and authority accorded a man. Nothing she *does* either confirms or negates this state of affairs. Aristotle would have agreed.

Unpacking the Rhetoric of Roles

Although evangelical patriarchy is similar to traditional patriarchy in key respects, it also trades heavily on the distinctive and historically novel claim that women are "equal in being but unequal in role." In other words, women are the equals of men spiritually and in their "being," but when it comes to living out the meaning and purpose of manhood and womanhood, women must submit to male rule. This distinction between being and function—or ontology and role—is fundamental to the doctrine of male leadership today. The distinction between equal being and unequal role serves as the hermeneutical lens through which the biblical data are interpreted. It is the theoretical construct that permits evangelical patriarchalists to interpret the submission texts as universal statements on the creational "roles" of manhood and womanhood, while also acknowledging biblical teaching on the spiritual and ontological equality of man and woman.

The "role" relationship of woman's subordination to man's authority is typically presented as a matter of "complementarity," "mutual interdependence" and "beneficial differences" between the sexes, without any implication of woman's inferior-

---

[10]Ibid., pp. 35-36.

ity.[11] The carefully chosen terminology serves to make this position appear plausible and persuasive to modern ears. Who can deny that there must be different roles, functional distinctions and a certain order in any human society? Or that male and female are complementary? Given the choice of rhetoric, it all sounds quite sensible and acceptable. As a result, many evangelicals find themselves perplexed by two antithetical interpretations of biblical teaching on gender relations—egalitarianism and patriarchalism—both of which appear to be plausible in some respects and problematic in other respects. It can seem to be a toss-up.

But what if it is not logically possible for the same person to be at once spiritually and ontologically equal *and* permanently, comprehensively and necessarily subordinate? What if this sort of subordination cannot truthfully be described as merely a "role" or "function" that has no bearing on one's inherent being or essence?

I believe we can choose between the two biblical interpretations by assessing each one in light of two fundamental premises. The first premise is theological: according to Scripture, women and men are equal spiritually and ontologically—a point that is uncontested in the gender debate. The second premise is logical: the foundational and indisputable law of noncontradiction, which states that A and non-A cannot both be true at the same time in the same respect.[12] The law of noncontradiction is not a mere human construct that God's truth somehow transcends. Rather, it is necessary and fundamental to all meaningful discourse and communication—including God's revelation of his Word in Scripture. That is why biblical scholars who hold to the Bible's infallibility seek to resolve apparent contradictions in Scripture: it is axiomatic that if the Bible contradicts itself, then it cannot be true in all that it affirms.[13]

Evangelical patriarchalists contend that women are unequal in a different respect from the way they are equal. I will argue that given its nature and rationale, woman's unequal "role" entails woman's unequal being. Thus it contradicts woman's equality in being and so renders contradictory (and therefore untrue) the evangelical patriarchal interpretation of Scripture that sees woman as equal but subordinate. This leaves only two logically tenable options. Either (1) women are created by God for perpetual subordination to men and so are not equal to men in

---

[11]John Piper and Wayne Grudem, "Preface," in *RBMW,* p. xiv.

[12]Aristotle *Metaphysics* Gamma 3.1005b.

[13]See Ronald H. Nash, *Life's Ultimate Questions: An Introduction to Philosophy* (Grand Rapids, Mich.: Zondervan, 1999), pp. 194-201, 207.

their nature/being/essence, or (2) women are created equal with men and so cannot be permanently, comprehensively and necessarily subordinate to men. But option 1 contradicts premise 1. Since Scripture cannot contradict itself, option 2 is the only position that is both logically and biblically tenable.

In part one of the chapter it will be argued that the *equal being/unequal role* construct fails to defend the subordination of women against the implication of women's inferiority.[14] First, I will consider what is meant by spiritual equality and ontological equality (equality of being) and will show how evangelical patriarchalism fails to honor and acknowledge such equality. Although spiritual equality is entailed by ontological equality, it will be addressed separately because of its particular relevance to this debate. I will then consider the nature and significance of the "different roles" that patriarchalists assign to women and men and will argue that these "roles" are not just about function but are fundamentally a matter of ontology or being. The purpose of these considerations will be to show that evangelical patriarchy neither respects women's equality nor limits women's subordination to a merely functional role. Instead, the nature of women's inequality in "function" implies, by logical necessity, women's inequality in being.

In part two of the chapter I will respond to key counterarguments—ways in which proponents of patriarchy have attempted to defend the efficacy and validity of the *equal being/unequal role* construct against objections to it.[15] This will include a brief critique of the analogy that patriarchalists draw between women's subordination in "role" and what they see as the eternal "role subordination" in the Trinity. I will argue that even if there were an eternal subordination of the Son to the Father, the analogy fails fundamentally.

PART I

Equality in "Being"

A biblical understanding of human equality should begin with Genesis 1:26-28, where women and men together and without distinction are declared to be created in God's image and are given authority over all creation. In both their being (the divine image) and their calling (authority and dominion) men and women are cre-

---

[14]The material in this chapter will build on and develop ideas presented in Rebecca Merrill Groothuis, *Good News for Women: A Biblical Picture of Gender Equality* (Grand Rapids, Mich.: Baker Books, 1997), especially pp. 27-83. Hereafter *GNFW.*

[15]Less compelling counterarguments will be addressed in footnotes in part one.

ationally equal. On the basis of this foundational text, as well as the overall teaching of Scripture,[16] evangelical egalitarians affirm an equality of human worth and human rights between women and men; that is, whatever human rights there may be, they belong no less to women than to men (since women are no less human than men).[17] From this follows an equality of consideration, whereby women and men alike have opportunity to earn and attain the place in church and society that is appropriate for each individual's God-given abilities and calling.

While this understanding of human equality resembles that of classical (nineteenth and early twentieth century) liberal political philosophy, it is here grounded in and justified solely by the biblical revelation of God's creational design for male and female humanity. This happens to be one point at which secular culture got it right, doubtless due in large part to the West's Christian heritage (a more prevalent influence in earlier centuries than at present). A task of the biblical thinker is to agree with culture where it agrees with the Bible.[18]

---

[16]See chapters four through twenty-two in this volume; see also *GNFW,* especially chaps. 1, 4-8.

[17]Nineteenth-century American feminists believed women's rights were simply the basic human rights applied equally to women. (See chapter twenty-four in this volume for discussion of early feminist thought.) In the feminist and broader cultural ideologies of recent decades, the notion of "rights" has often been abused and overextended. This is not the sense in which I speak of "rights" here. Claiming one's right to something is not, in itself, an unbiblical concept. Paul, for example, occasionally spoke of having rights, such as the right to receive recompense for his labor or to take "a believing wife" along with him in Christian ministry (1 Cor 9:4-12). Another example is the Syrophoenician woman who argued her case with Jesus, claiming (in essence) her right to ask for healing for her daughter. Jesus applauded her response and granted her request (Mk 7:24-30).

[18]Some seem to have missed this point entirely, insisting—evidently on the basis of a similarity between the equality of biblical egalitarianism and the equality of classical liberalism—that biblical egalitarianism is invalid because it is not grounded primarily in Scripture but is dependent on extrabiblical political premises. See, for example, Thomas R. Schreiner, review of *Good News for Women, Themelios* 23, no. 1: 89-90; Thomas R. Schreiner, "Women in Ministry," in *Two Views on Women in Ministry,* ed. James R. Beck and Craig L. Blomberg (Grand Rapids, Mich.: Zondervan, 2001), pp. 187 n. 16, 200; and Sarah Sumner, *Men and Women in the Church* (Downers Grove, Ill.: InterVarsity Press, 2003), pp. 33, 277, 281, 291 n. 16. Both Schreiner and Sumner misconstrue my remarks in *GNFW,* pp. 46-47, where I simply describe the classical liberal understanding of equality (which nineteenth-century feminists put into practice) and note that this understanding of equality is the logical and ethically consistent outworking of fundamental *biblical* principles. Thus the political philosophy serves as an illustration of—*not* as a justification for—the sort of equality that is most consistent with the tenets of Scripture. At no point is biblical gender equality grounded in or morally justified on the basis of classical liberalism or feminism. For a historical and cultural analysis of the relationship between biblical equality and feminism, see Rebecca Merrill Groothuis, *Women Caught in the Conflict: The Culture War Between Traditionalism and Feminism* (Grand Rapids, Mich.: Baker, 1994; reprint Eugene, Ore.: Wipf & Stock, 1997).

Although there are variations in ability between individuals, the human equality between women (as a class) and men (as a class) assures that women are inherently able to participate equally with men in the various distinctively human activities.[19] Due to both cultural and biological factors, there are some generalizable differences in behavior between women and men, and these differences not only determine different sexual and reproduction functions but may also make certain social roles generally (although not universally) more suitable for one gender than the other. However, these differences do not warrant the traditional notion that women are deficient in rationality and so are suited to be subordinate to men. Rather, the generally different aptitudes and proclivities of male and female point to ways in which women and men can complement one another as they live and work together in the context of a full recognition of their essential equality in maturity, giftedness, and social and spiritual value.

It should be evident from these observations that egalitarians do not affirm an equality of identity or sameness between women and men. Male and female are not identical. Sexual differences exist, and these differences make a difference. Sexual roles, therefore, are not interchangeable between men and women.[20] Egalitarians and patriarchalists agree that women and men are not equal in the sense of being identical and that the differences between men and women are complementary and mutually beneficial. But there is considerable disagreement as to the nature, meaning and significance of these differences.

There are a number of different ways in which people, or groups of people, can be said to be equal.[21] It seems that evangelical patriarchalists reject all types of equality between men and women, except equality in "being" (essence, nature, ontology) and human value. The question before us is whether the patriarchal paradigm in fact acknowledges female humanity to be fully human, equal in value to male humanity.

If women and men are both fully human, then women (as a class) and men (as a class) share equally in the distinctively human capacities, and no woman can be deemed inferior to a man in any such area solely on account of her womanhood. Distinctively human capacities are those that distinguish humans from other creatures. For example, higher intellectual functions such as rationality, ethical reason-

---

[19]More on this below.

[20]A sexual role has to do with sexual functions (marriage, parenthood, etc.). Ministries such as teaching the Bible and shepherding a church are not sexual functions.

[21]See *GNFW,* pp. 45-49, where different kinds of equality are explained and delineated.

ing and the ability to analyze abstract concepts are unique to humans.[22] Therefore it cannot be said that any given woman is any more or less likely than any given man to be fully equipped—in her God-given being—for such higher functions of the mind. More specifically, if women and men are equal in essence or being, then female humanity does not, in and of itself, suffer from a net deficiency of the valuable qualities and inherent capacities distinctively characteristic of human nature and human behavior.[23]

Yet the doctrine of male rule presupposes that woman is uniquely designed by God *not* to perform certain distinctively human activities. In order to be true to her divine design and her God-given femininity, woman must not engage in these activities (which, per patriarchy, are no longer distinctively human but reclassified as distinctively masculine). By contrast, there are no uniquely human behaviors from which male humans must abstain in order to be true to their masculine being. No, masculinity is defined precisely in terms of certain distinctively human activities that only men are deemed fit to do—namely, the spiritual discernment and high-level cognitive/rational behaviors involved in making decisions and directing and taking final responsibility for one or more other human beings.[24]

According to the patriarchal paradigm, women do have their own uniquely fem-

---

[22]At least some angels are probably also endowed with such capabilities, but the comparison here is with earthly creatures. Some animals may have some rational function but certainly not at the level of which humans are capable.

[23]Of course some individuals, male or female, will be less gifted in certain distinctively human activities than other individuals, whether by difference in training or innate ability. But this is a matter of variation between individuals; the point at issue here is variation between womanhood and manhood. That is, is being female in and of itself sufficient to render a person inferior, or likely to be inferior, in uniquely human capacities?

[24]The question of women's inherent *ability* to perform these tasks can elicit considerable equivocation among patriarchalists. The historically traditional view—based (erroneously) on I Timothy 2:14—is that women are constitutionally unfit for leadership because they are more easily deceived. This rationale for women's subordination is largely rejected today; but see Thomas Schreiner and Daniel Doriani, who have proposed a rationale similar to the traditional one, in *Women in the Church: A Fresh Analysis of 1 Timothy 2:9-15*, ed. Andreas Köstenberger, Thomas R. Schreiner and H. Scott Baldwin (Grand Rapids, Mich.: Baker, 1995), pp. 145-46, 262-67. (For a response to their view, see Rebecca Merrill Groothuis, "Leading Him up the Garden Path: Further Thoughts on I Timothy 2:11-15," *Priscilla Papers*, Spring 2002, pp. 11-12.) More recently, Robert Saucy also offers an ontological basis for male leadership when he suggests that the implications of the difference in "spirit" between maleness and femaleness (a notion he takes from M. Scott Peck) could provide a rationale for women's subordination to men. Robert L. Saucy, "The 'Order' and 'Equality' of Galatians 3:28," in *Women and Men in Ministry*, ed. Robert L. Saucy and Judith K. TenElshof (Chicago: Moody Press, 2001), p. 154.

inine activities not shared by men—for example, bearing and rearing their young and being submissive and obedient to the master of the home. But note that these activities are not unique to human beings; rather, childbearing and nursing are shared with females of all mammal species, and submission to the household master is shared (albeit in a different sense!) with a wide array of household pets.[25] Certainly, it is a privilege and joy for women to bear and rear children. The point is not to diminish the value of motherhood but to note that while childbearing and nursing are distinctively female capabilities, they are not, in and of themselves, among the distinctively human capabilities (such as high-level rationality).

Patriarchal men, for their part, govern their homes and churches—making decisions, teaching the whole body of believers, ascertaining and making final determinations of God's will for their families—and women do not. Furthermore, women *could* bear authority and responsibility for these things equally with men, but they do not because they are not permitted to do so. Men, by contrast, do not bear or nurse children, simply because they are not *able* to do so. The one is the "can't" of permission denied; the other is the "can't" of personal inability. This is not a case of equally dividing different opportunities and abilities between the sexes.

Nonetheless, those who insist that the woman must submit her mind and will to that of the man who is the master of the household also insist that the woman is equal to the man in her humanity and human value. But the full humanity of womanhood is not honored or recognized when what is deemed constitutive of femininity is shared by the lower species while what is deemed constitutive of masculinity is unique to the human species. This delineation of male-female "difference" fails to acknowledge the full humanity of woman. This is not to say that people with less ability in any of the distinctively human functions are somehow less human. However, when all women—purely by virtue of their womanhood—are denied opportunity to fully engage all the uniquely human capacities (to the degree of their ability), this logically implies that womanhood per se is characterized by a deficit of certain distinctively human traits.

Always, with patriarchy, it is the female human's *being* that is the decisive factor; it alone is sufficient to consign her to being subordinate. Because her human being is female, she is subordinate. As Raymond Ortlund puts it, "A man, just by virtue

---

[25]If this analogy seems a bit strong, it should be noted that Piper and Grudem ("Overview," p. 87) draw a comparison between the woman and the animals in Genesis 2, arguing that just as the animals were to be submissive to the man, so was the woman.

of his manhood, is called to lead for God. A woman, just by virtue of her woman-hood, is called to help for God."[26] So while woman is said to be equal in her essential being, she is deemed subordinate precisely because of her essential being. Yet the notion that woman is equal *in* her being yet unequal *by virtue of* her being is incoherent.

Could this inconsistency be reconciled by asserting that woman is equal in her *human* being but not equal in her *female* being? It seems not. There is, after all, no generic humanity; human "being" is either male or female. If I am equal in my human being, then I am equal in my female human being, because female is what my human being is. Or, conversely, human is what my female being is. At all times and in every respect, my "being" is essentially and intrinsically female and human. If I am unequal as a *female* human being, then I am unequal as a human being.

Given the above considerations, it seems warranted to conclude that patriarchy cannot fully acknowledge woman's human equality in being but rather implies her inferiority in being. This is even further in evidence when we examine woman's *spiritual* place in the patriarchal scheme of things.

Spiritual Equality

The human spirit—that which enables us to know and communicate with God—is inherent in the divine image. This spiritual capacity is definitive of and unique to human beings, among all God's earthly creatures. Scripture is clear that women and men equally bear God's image and rule over God's creation (Gen 1:26-28). God, at creation, gave spirituality and authority to male and female alike. This is the divine, uncorrupted, creational design. Nowhere in the Genesis creation account is this qualified by any mention of different kinds of spirituality or different degrees of authority for man and for woman.[27]

If women and men are equal before God, then surely God desires the same sort of relationship with female believers that God desires with male believers. There is no reason to believe that God's treatment and expectations of women with respect to spiritual concerns should be significantly different from God's treatment and expectations of men. By extension, we in the church have no basis for treating women as somehow less fit for certain spiritual gifts and ministries. Nor should we expect any woman to have a more distantly removed or "different" sort of relationship

---

[26]Raymond C. Ortlund, "Male-Female Equality and Male Headship: Genesis 1-3," in *RBMW,* p. 102.
[27]The Fall did not normatively change the male-female equality established at creation; see *GNFW,* chap. 5. See also chapter four in this volume.

with God simply because she is a woman.[28] Equality before God means that every believer may approach God, and minister to God, on the same terms—through Jesus Christ alone, in submission to the Holy Spirit.

So let us consider how the truth of spiritual equality fares in the context of woman's subordination to man's authority. In evangelical patriarchy today, the authority reserved exclusively for men is largely a *spiritual* authority. That is, within the contexts of marriage and the church, the exposition of God's Word and the discernment of God's will (and the decision making that follows such discernment) are deemed the "final responsibility" of men alone. Although there occasionally appears some general expression of concern that women not appear too authoritative (i.e., masculine) in everyday interactions in society at large—Piper, for example, wants to ensure that if a woman gives a man directions to the freeway, she does so in a properly feminine (submissive) manner[29]—the primary concern appears to be the exercise of spiritual authority.

Evangelical patriarchy teaches that the man is divinely charged with responsibility and authority to discern God's will on behalf of himself and his wife and children. Whether or not he gives consideration to his wife's insights, interests and expertise (as patriarchal teaching typically urges him to do), his "final decision" concerning God's will for the family has binding authority.[30] As George Knight puts it, "Because the headship of the husband is established by God, the husband who fulfills that role does so as a servant of God, and the leadership given to him in this role expresses God's authority in the marriage." Given that the husband's authority over the wife represents the authority of God, a wife "should submit to her husband as she submits to the Lord." Such submission is analogous to "the godly submission a Christian renders to the Lord Jesus."[31]

Patriarchal doctrine requires, in both marriage and the larger believing community, that men obey and hear from God directly while women obey and hear from God by hearing from and obeying the man or men in spiritual authority over them. A woman does not have direct authority under God but is under the spiritual au-

---

[28]Individuals (both male and female) will, of course, have different kinds of relationships with God. But these differences will be due to a host of factors relating to the unique circumstances of each person; they will not be strictly on account of gender.

[29]Piper, "Vision," p. 50.

[30]See Wayne Grudem, "Wives Like Sarah, and the Husbands Who Honor Them: I Peter 3:1-7," in *RBMW*, p. 207. However, the wife is exempted from obeying a decision that is overtly immoral.

[31]George W. Knight III, "Husbands and Wives as Analogues of Christ and the Church," in *RBMW*, p. 174.

thority of man, who mediates to her the Word and the will of God for her life. Woman's traditionally subordinate place within the social relationships of church and home is largely a consequence of the subordinate place in which she is believed to stand in the spiritual order. But note that this arrangement is not, as is often claimed, spiritual equality plus social inequality.[32] It is, quite simply, spiritual inequality.

According to key representatives of evangelical patriarchy, God has invested the man with the spiritual authority "to decide, in the light of Holy Scripture, what courses of action will most glorify God" for his family.[33] The man is "finally responsible" for both his own and his wife's moral and spiritual condition.[34] The husband's authority "expresses God's authority in the marriage."[35] The man's role in the family has him "standing in the place of Christ,"[36] to "act as Christ" and "for Christ" with respect to his wife,[37] obligating him to "protect [his family] from the greatest enemies of all, Satan and sin."[38] But if these things be true—if, indeed, only a man and never a woman can be deemed fit to serve as a stand-in for Christ, and if every married woman actually needs a man to serve in this capacity for her (which must be the case if the man's "headship" is to be an act of love and service rather than presumption and condescension)—then it follows that men and women are not on the same spiritual level at all.

Nowhere does the Bible say that it is a man's job to discern the will of God, take responsibility for another person's spirituality and protect others from Satan and sin. If God has given responsibility and dominion to both male and female (Gen 1:26-28), if we all stand on equal ground before God (Gal 3:26-28), if women are

---

[32]However, a fair description of the situation in the New Testament church would be spiritual equality with social inequality (due to the cultural patriarchy of ancient times). Nothing in the New Testament stipulates that a man must have authority over and responsibility for his wife's spiritual condition, as many patriarchalists today advocate. The apostle Peter commended Christian women who refused to submit to their husbands' false religious beliefs, yet urged these women to be submissive to the social roles of the time (1 Pet 3:1-6). Evangelical patriarchalists today actually invert the New Testament situation by advocating, in essence, an inequality in spiritual rights and responsibilities for women in a cultural context in which women generally experience equality in social rights and responsibilities. See GNFW, pp. 36-39. See also chapter ten in this volume.

[33]Ortlund, "Male-Female Equality," p. 482 n. 50.

[34]Ibid., p. 110.

[35]Knight, "Husbands and Wives," p. 174.

[36]Piper, "Vision," p. 38. This is qualified by the comment that a husband "must not be Christ to his wife."

[37]Ibid., and Piper and Grudem, "Overview," RBMW, p. 64.

[38]Piper, "Vision," p. 37.

equal heirs of the grace of God (1 Pet 3:7) and if all believers together—both men and women—form God's new priesthood (1 Pet 2:5, 9; Rev 1:6; 5:10), then there is no reason for anyone to take this sort of spiritual responsibility for anyone else. If Jesus Christ is a female believer's Lord and Savior in the same way that he is a male believer's, then surely no Christian woman has need of a man to stand in the place of Christ for her.

Despite popular evangelical teaching, the New Testament never says the man authoritatively represents God as the priest of the home.[39] This teaching may derive from a misunderstanding of the analogy Paul draws in Ephesians 5:21-33 between a husband as "head" of his wife, and Christ as "head" of the church. Patriarchalists readily perceive that Paul did not mean that the husband is like Christ in redeeming his wife from her sins, for this would contradict biblical teaching elsewhere. Yet neither did Paul mean that the husband—like Christ—has the authority to serve as a priestly mediator between God and his wife; for this contradicts biblical teaching that Christ is the one mediator between God and humans (1 Tim 2:5, see also Mt 11:27; Jn 14:6). What Paul *was* saying by means of this analogy is evident from his description of the husband's Christlike ministry of life-giving, self-giving love for his wife (Eph 5:25-30).[40] As Christ loves, nurtures, provides for and sacrifices his own life and special (divine) prerogatives for the church, so should the husband for his wife; as the church submits to the ministry of Christ (and as believers submit to one another, Eph 5:21), so should the wife to her husband.[41]

Under the new covenant, every believer is a representative of God (2 Cor 5:20) with direct access to God through Christ our high priest (Heb 4:14-16). Designating masculinity as a condition for the authoritative discernment and mediation of God's will denies the equal access to God through Christ that the new covenant provides to all believers.[42]

A male hierarchy of spiritual communication and command also violates the status and identity that every believer has in Christ. The New Testament teaches that God gives all believers the responsibility and prerogative to use their gifts, to

---

[39]Some go even further, proclaiming "the husband as prophet, priest and king." See the workshop by this title at the conference cosponsored by the Council on Biblical Manhood and Womanhood held March 20-22, 2000, in Dallas.

[40]There is no implication in the text that the husband has *spiritual* authority over his wife, although the husband's *civil* authority was assumed, given the culture of Paul's day. On the "head" metaphor, see chapter eight in this volume.

[41]See *GNFW,* pp. 152-55, 164-70, 180-82.

[42]See discussion of Galatians 3:28 in *GNFW,* chap. 1.

preach the gospel, to teach other believers, to discern and obey the Word and will of God, to serve as priests unto God, to have the mind of Christ, to exercise spiritual authority in the name of Christ and to represent Christ to the world at large. Yet patriarchalists alter the teaching of God's Word by denying to women a measure of each one of these God-given privileges and responsibilities, allocating to men the lion's share of what the Bible speaks of as the status and calling of all believers.[43]

Patriarchalists consign women to a permanently inferior status in a hierarchy of spiritual authority, calling, responsibility and privilege, all the while insisting that women are not spiritually inferior to men but that women and men stand on equal ground before God. This position is logically incoherent and so cannot be true. Women do not stand on equal ground before God if God has permanently denied them spiritual opportunities and privileges to which every man has access.

Difference in "Role" or "Function"

To say that two people differ in function is not necessarily to say that one is personally superior to the other. Therefore when we are told that men and women are equal yet have different functions, we can readily agree with the face value of that statement. There are many instances in which equals have different roles—even roles of subordination and authority—yet with no entailment of personal inequality.[44]

We can affirm that there are role differences between men and women without necessarily affirming that spiritual authority belongs by divine right to men. The latter belief does not follow from the former, and to reject the latter is not to reject the former. This conceptual distinction was not missed by respondents to a *Christianity Today* readers' poll on gender issues. A significant number of people who agreed that men and women are "equal in personhood and value but different in roles" also rejected the idea that men should have primary leadership in churches and homes.[45] The existence of gender role differences neither entails nor justifies a permanent hierarchy of male authority.

---

[43] The spiritual authority that patriarchalists reserve exclusively for male believers actually goes beyond the biblical ministry of *all* believers in that the man's priestlike spiritual authority encroaches upon the unique mediatorial ministry of Christ. See *GNFW,* pp. 115-17.

[44] There has been persistent misrepresentation and misunderstanding on this matter. Schreiner, for example, asserts that "the basic point of Rebecca Merrill Groothuis's *Good News for Women* is that one cannot logically posit both equality of personhood and differences in role" (Schreiner, "Women in Ministry," p. 200). In fact, I affirm quite the opposite of this "basic point." See *GNFW,* pp. 49-52, where I show that many types of role differences *are* compatible with personal equality.

[45] Agnieszka Tennant, "Adam and Eve in the 21st Century," *Christianity Today,* March 11, 2002, p. 61.

Although functional differences often are compatible with personal equality, this is not always the case. Advocates of male authority seem to have difficulty acknowledging that the *reason* for the difference and the *nature* of the function determine whether such a difference can logically coexist with equality of being. As it happens, the reason for and the nature of woman's subordination logically exclude woman's equality.[46] The vocabulary of evangelical patriarchy reflects and reinforces this conceptual confusion. For example, woman's lifelong subordination to male authority is routinely referred to as merely a "role difference" or "functional distinction." Semantic strategies such as these subsume the disputed concept (woman's subordination) under a larger—and largely undisputed—conceptual category (role differences, functional distinctions), thereby appearing to legitimate the disputed concept ipso facto.[47]

By these and other means, patriarchalists implicitly present their *equal being/unequal function* defense of woman's subordination in the following form:

1. Different function does not necessarily entail personal inferiority or superiority.

2. Woman's subordination and man's authority involve different functions.

3. Therefore the subordination of woman to man's authority has nothing to do with female inferiority or male superiority; these are male-female role differences, pure and simple.

The argument is invalid. The premises are correct, but the conclusion does not follow logically from them. While the notion that equal beings may have different roles is certainly legitimate, it is not applicable to, or descriptive of, the male-female authority relations prescribed by evangelical patriarchalists. Patriarchy involves different functions, to be sure, but the different functions are grounded in supposed differences in the nature, meaning and purpose of manhood and womanhood. To describe as merely "roles" the different functions that follow from these ontological/teleological differences is to equivocate and obfuscate.

"Equal in being but subordinate in role" *can* accurately describe instances of functional subordination; however, it does not serve as a description of *every* rela-

---

[46]This will be argued below. Also, see *GNFW*, pp. 49-56, 60-63.

[47]On rhetorical strategies of patriarchalists, see Rebecca Merrill Groothuis, "Strange Bedfellows," *Priscilla Papers,* Fall 2000; see also Kevin Giles, *The Trinity and Subordinationism* (Downers Grove, Ill.: InterVarsity Press, 2002), pp. 187-90.

tionship of subordination to authority, and it cannot accurately be applied to woman's subordination. Female subordination is not functional subordination; therefore it cannot be justified on those grounds.

Functional subordination is typically determined either according to an individual's abilities (or lack thereof) or for the sake of expediency in accomplishing a specific task; therefore such subordination is limited in scope or duration. An example of functional subordination for the sake of expediency would be a person who serves on a committee under the direction of a coworker who is otherwise her equal in the organization; her subordination is limited to the task at hand, and it ends whenever the committee completes its work or she leaves the committee. An example of functional subordination based on unequal ability would be a student who is subordinated to his teacher—but only in the context and for the duration of the class.

Functional subordination is not necessarily limited in both scope and duration. If the subordinate's deficiency in ability is permanent (if he either cannot or will not overcome the deficiency), then his subordination in that area of deficiency will be permanent. If the unequal ability is innate, then the resulting subordination does reflect the person's inherently inferior ability in that particular area. But it need not indicate the subordinate's inferiority as a person, because the subordination remains limited in scope to the area of deficient ability; the person may far excel the average person in even more important areas of function.[48]

Female subordination differs from functional subordination in its scope, duration and criterion. The subordination of women is limited neither in scope nor in duration. It is not based on inferior ability or designed to accomplish a temporary task. It is comprehensive (encompassing all that a woman does), permanent (extending throughout the life of a woman and applying to all women at all times) and decided solely by an unchangeable aspect of a woman's personal being (femaleness). Although femaleness is, in fact, irrelevant to ascertaining a person's innate abilities in the higher human functions involved in leadership, decision making and self-governance, these are precisely the functions from which women are permanently excluded; thus the inferiority of female persons in these key areas is clearly implied.

When subordination follows necessarily *and justifiably* from the subordinate per-

---

[48]See *GNFW,* pp. 50-51. For an example of functional subordination with limited duration and unlimited scope, see section below entitled "False Analogies."

son's unalterable nature, the subordinate *is* inferior in at least some aspect of her being; in this case, the scope and duration of the person's subordination will reflect the extent and significance of the inferiority. Because the subordination that is demanded by women's unalterable (female) being is of comprehensive scope and permanent duration—excluding women from a wide range of high-level, distinctively human functions—it implies an extensive and significant personal inferiority. But in this case the subordination is *not* justifiable, because women are not, in fact, innately inferior in these distinctively human capabilities. Put more formally and succinctly:

1. If the permanent, comprehensive and ontologically grounded subordination of women is justified, then women are inferior persons.

2. Women are not inferior persons.

3. Therefore women's subordination is not justified.[49]

Another way to distinguish functional subordination from female subordination is in terms of the concepts of necessity and contingency. Something that is contingent obtains (is the case) only in certain contexts or under certain conditions. It is thus dependent, or contingent, on these contexts or conditions; it is not always and necessarily true. Unlike functional subordination, female subordination is not contingent. Because a woman is always and necessarily female, she is always and necessarily subordinate. No condition or context in this life nullifies her subordination to male authority.[50]

---

[49]See *GNFW,* pp. 44-45, 49-56, 60-63, 74-77, for further explanation of these issues. Robert Saucy ("'Order' and 'Equality,'" pp. 153-54) tries to debunk my claim that woman's permanent subordination implies woman's inferiority by arguing that if woman is rendered unequal because her subordination is permanent, then the mere passing of time must make a person unequal (which is nonsensical). However, I do not say that permanent subordination *necessarily* implies personal inequality. The issue is not simply permanence but whether the subordination is truly functional. Subordination can allow for equality of personhood *only* if it is a *functional* subordination—which female subordination is not; moreover, it *is* possible for functional subordination to be permanent (see *GNFW,* pp. 50, 74-75). Saucy ("'Order' and 'Equality,'" p. 154) appears to attempt another *reductio ad absurdum* argument when he claims that I say subordination renders a person inferior only if the subordination is *not* based on inferior abilities (also nonsensical). But my point is not that female subordination actually *renders* women inferior but that it logically *implies* women's inferiority, and that women's subordination is unjustified precisely because women are *not* inferior to men in leadership ability.

[50]Some patriarchalists believe the "pattern of male leadership" extends throughout the next life as well. See, for example, Wayne Grudem, *Systematic Theology* (Grand Rapids, Mich.: Zondervan, 1994), p. 940.

Given evangelical patriarchy's theological premise that God designed man and woman at creation for a (benevolent) male-rule relationship, it is necessary for a woman to be subordinate to male rule if she is to be true to the divinely designed meaning of womanhood. Not to submit would be unnatural and unfitting. Her subordination to male authority is thus a moral necessity, rooted in ontology—in the way God made man and woman to be from the beginning. Philosophically speaking, this is a hypothetical necessity, because it follows from a certain premise. *If* God created man to rule woman and woman to serve man, *then* a woman's submission to male authority obtains necessarily, solely by virtue of her womanhood. Her subordination is not contingent on her voluntarily taking on this "role."[51]

Functional subordination, on the other hand, is dependent on limited contexts or occasional conditions. A blind person submits to the authority of his seeing-eye dog in the context of negotiating a busy street. A student is subordinate to her teacher, given the student's inferior ability in the subject being taught. In these cases, subordination is limited in scope or duration because it is contingent on conditions that do not always and everywhere obtain. But because female subordination is necessary (context independent), it is both permanent (enduring throughout a woman's life) and comprehensive (including all that a woman does; in all things she must be submissive).[52]

It should be evident from these observations that woman's subordination does not fit the definition of a "role." A role is a part that is played or a particular function or office that is assumed for a specific purpose or period of time. Anyone with the requisite abilities can play the part. By definition a role is not synonymous with or inexorably tied to who a person is. Yet the "roles" of male authority and female subordination are deemed essential to God's creational design for true manhood

---

[51]Saucy objects to my depiction of woman's subordination as necessary and not voluntary, insisting that it is indeed voluntary because nobody can force a woman to submit to her husband's authority (Saucy, "'Order' and 'Equality,'" pp. 157-58). But this seems to equivocate on the meaning of *voluntary*. Normally an act is considered voluntary if one can choose either to do or not to do it without censure. But when something is the law—whether civil law or God's law—those who are under the law are obligated to obey it, and disobedience incurs some form of censure. (Referring to the biblical "command" for wives to submit, Grudem ["Wives Like Sarah," p. 207] notes that "submission to one's husband is not optional for Christian wives.") Even more to the point, woman's subordination is grounded in her female being, not in her will. The rationale for women's subordination is not that they choose of their own volition to be subordinate but that they are created to be subordinate.

[52]Some milder forms of patriarchy today allow women to have authority over men so long as it is not "final authority" or spiritual authority. Nonetheless, a married woman must be submissive to her husband's authority in every area of her life.

and womanhood. Indeed, Piper and Grudem state that their concern is not merely with "behavioral roles" but with the "true meaning" and "underlying nature of manhood and womanhood."[53]

A woman can have many roles in life—teacher, office administrator, physician, writer—but none of these roles is seen as *essential* to true womanhood. That is because these roles are truly roles—chosen or appropriate for some women but not for others. Submission to male authority is the only "role" that is deemed essential for every woman who would be truly feminine and fulfill the purpose for which God created womanhood. That is because this "role" serves the role of constituting the meaning of femininity, of identifying a woman as a *real* woman. Female submission to male authority, then, is a "function" only in the sense that it is a *necessary* function of a woman's true being.

That submission is considered to be inherent in what a woman is by nature (and authority inherent in what a man is by nature) is evident in the patriarchalists' slippery-slope argument that egalitarianism leads logically to acceptance of homosexuality.[54] Their thinking is that once we say gender is irrelevant for deciding who is to have "primary leadership," the next "logical" step is to say the gender of one's marriage partner is also irrelevant. Just as a woman is meant to marry a man and not another woman, so a woman is meant to be submissive to a man and not to share authority equally with a man. Patriarchalists believe that gender differences in status and authority are as natural and essential to manhood and womanhood as is heterosexuality. To eliminate the former entails eliminating the latter, because it consists of eliminating what is inherent and universally normative in the gender distinction. The elimination of a mere role would not evoke such comparisons and predicted consequences.

It should also be noted that although role theology has become central to evangelical patriarchy, nowhere does Scripture use the term *role* or any synonym for it with reference to the responsibilities of believers toward God or one another. At no point do we read that God designed us—and requires us—to "play a role." No, God's concern is for each of us to *be* a righteous person and to use whatever gifts of the Spirit we have been given for the good of the church and the glory of God. The Bible's focused exhortation is that we are *all* to be Christlike, to follow the example of Jesus' earthly life—in humility, faithfulness, submission to God and spir-

---

[53]Piper and Grudem, "Overview," p. 60.
[54]See ibid., pp. 82-84 and 85-87.

itual authority (in Christ's name) over all the powers of evil.

The consistency and clarity of this biblical message stands starkly against the notion that women do not have direct authority under God and so must submit spiritually to men, who are the primary wielders of spiritual authority in the body of Christ. This doctrine of spiritual inequality posing as "gender role difference" simply doesn't fit with the Bible's clear, core message.

When "Role" Plays the Role of "Being"

Regardless of how patriarchal gender relations may be explained or masculinity and femininity defined, the fact remains that woman's subordinate "role" is determined exclusively and necessarily by her personal nature; that is, *solely* on account of her *being* female she *must* be subordinate. Therefore woman's "role" designates not merely what she does (or doesn't do) but what she is. She is female; she is subordinate.

It may sound quite plausible to insist that woman's subordination and man's authority are merely roles assigned by God and so do not entail woman's personal inferiority. Roles, by definition, do not necessarily bespeak qualities of personal being. But patriarchal gender roles are not roles in accordance with the usual definition. These "roles" have a one-to-one correspondence with being. Where the "being" is, there the "role" is also. "Female being" corresponds precisely to "a role of subordination to male authority." The word *role* is used in a way that renders its meaning basically synonymous, or redundant, with *being*.

Female subordination and male authority may be semantically reduced to "roles" or "functions," but in reality they serve as modes of being—permanent personal identities, built into each one's personal makeup by the Creator himself. Thus when the man rules and the woman obeys, each is only doing what each is inherently designed to do.

As a blind person is not fit to negotiate unfamiliar territory on his own, so a woman is not fit to preach God's Word with authority or to discern God's will for her own life apart from her husband's spiritual authority over her. The female person and the blind person must each have someone do for them what they are not fit to do for themselves. However, the state of being blind does not bear the weight of ontological necessity or the implication of personal inferiority that woman's subordination does. Under patriarchy, a woman's deficiency in personal authority is regarded as ordained by God's creational decree. But a blind person—even if blind from birth—is not deficient in sight by virtue of God's creational design for humanity. His limitations are not intrinsic to and demanded by his essential, created nature. Nor are his limitations as deep or as wide as a woman's. He is deprived of a physical function; he is not denied a spiritual ministry or the governance of his own life under God. Moreover, blindness is not necessarily a life sentence; it can sometimes be reversed.

Could it then be accurate to say that a blind person's "role" is to be sightless? No, this is simply the way the person *is;* it is a mode of being, not a mode of behavior that is assumed for a specific purpose (as is a role). If a blind person's lack of sight cannot rightly be described as a role that has no bearing on his state of being or personal ability, then *(a fortiori)* neither can woman's creationally based lack of authority in key areas be accurately spoken of as a role that has no ontological entailment.

Thus the theoretical distinction between woman's being and woman's subordinate role evaporates under scrutiny. Woman's lifelong subordination to man's authority is not merely a role that is independent of and ontologically isolated from her being. Rather, the role is determined by the being and obtains solely because of the being. Where there is female being, there must of necessity be subordinate function. When one's "role" is grounded in one's essential being and obtains in all things and at all times, one's "role" defines one's personhood. Women are subordinate persons—by nature and definition. Their subordination is constitutive of and essential to their personhood.[55] But this is not ontological equality. Nor is it merely a matter of playing a role; rather, it is about *being* what one intrinsically *is* by virtue of the God-ordained nature and meaning of one's sex.

The basis for women's subordination (God's design and purpose for womanhood), as well as the "functions" in which women are subordinate (spiritual discernment, decision making and self-governance), is all about being. Woman's nature or ontology, her life purpose or teleology, her will, intellect and moral understanding, her spiritual responsibilities before God—these are matters as close to the heart of a person's being as anything ever could be. They define and characterize what a person *is.* The suppression of women (and not men) in these critical areas of personhood is not meaningfully described merely as women's "different role."

The nature of and rationale for female subordination, then, make it fundamentally unlike functional subordination. Its nature (necessary, permanent and com-

---

[55]See the excellent discussion of "role difference" in Giles, *Trinity and Subordinationism,* pp. 179-88.

prehensive) and its rationale (God's creational design) place woman's subordination foursquare in the realm of being. In woman's "equal being and unequal role," the "role" is as much about woman's being as is the "equality." Thus evangelical patriarchy does not have woman being unequal in a different respect from the way she is equal. Rather, a woman is unequal (subordinate) in the same respect that she is equal—by virtue of her being, as a constitutive element and necessary consequence of her being. Therefore woman's equality (as biblically defined) and woman's subordination (as defined by patriarchalists) cannot coexist without logical contradiction. Evangelical patriarchy's *equal being/unequal role* construct must be deemed internally incoherent.

PART 2

"But It's About God's Will, Not Gender"

Defenders of the *equal being/unequal role* distinction may insist that female subordination does not imply woman's inferiority because it is not determined by or grounded in a woman's female nature; rather, it is determined by and grounded in God's will alone. In other words, authority is not essential to manhood, nor is subordination essential to womanhood. Rather, women have a subordinate "role" and men have an authoritative "role" (or "office," the term of choice for some). And women and men are assigned permanently to their "roles" not because of their gender but simply because God, for reasons of his own, has commanded that women "function" in a "role" of subordination to men.[56]

But if God has commanded subordination of all women and only women—such that femaleness is the necessary and sufficient criterion that decides a person's permanent and comprehensive subordination—then God has indeed decreed a subordination that is determined by female gender. That is, God has set up an arrangement whereby the question "Who is to be in charge, and who is to be subordinate?" is answered solely according to gender.[57]

---

[56]Sarah Sumner offers an argument to this effect in *Men and Women in the Church*, p. 278. She calls this the "Scotist" view—that we cannot, nor need we, understand the reasons for God's commands. She claims Piper and Grudem hold this view; yet these men affirm that the nature, meaning and deeper differences of manhood and womanhood are relevant to deciding who submits and who has authority, thus affirming an ontological basis for gender "roles." But perhaps the Scotist perspective often serves more as an ad hoc argumentative strategy than as a principled conviction.

[57]This is precisely the case in determining authority in marriages. For church leadership, maleness is necessary but (unlike male rule in marriage) not sufficient; other qualifications must be met as well.

A crucial point at issue here is whether God has in fact decreed such a thing. If God's Word makes it clear that women are not ontologically inferior to men, and if—as has been argued above—the permanent, comprehensive and necessary subordination of women logically implies the ontological inferiority of the female gender, then we must conclude that God has *not* decreed such a thing and that biblical texts understood to convey such a decree have been wrongly interpreted.

Furthermore, the idea that woman's subordination is not in any sense determined by or grounded in what a woman *is* or what God designed her to *be* is contrary to the ways of God in that it separates God's will for creation from his design for creation. Ontology and teleology become detached, irrelevant to one another. In what other area of theology would this be asserted? Can the will of God be deemed to be at odds with the created nature of things? Would God require—has God ever required—of us anything for which he did not design us? God's decrees always tell us something about his character, our humanity, the very nature of things the way God created them. For example, God's ban on homosexual relationships tells us about—and is grounded in—the created nature of sexuality, its meaning, design and purpose. Surely if God has banned women from leadership in key areas and consigned women to be subordinate to male leadership, this tells us something about the created nature of womanhood and manhood.

The idea that what women may and may not do is ontologically disconnected from what women can and cannot do is also contrary to the whole tenor of New Testament teaching—that whatever one has been given one should use by investing it in and for the kingdom of God (e.g., 1 Pet 4:10-11). Being and function, fruit and gifts, personal character and public ministry are tandem expressions of faithful service and obedience to Christ. Biblically, one does not stop short of serving God's people in a way for which one has been divinely gifted and prepared, any more than one takes on a ministry role that one is not personally or spiritually equipped to handle.

At least one patriarchalist has a clear view of the fallacy of using role language to describe what it means to be a man or a woman. German theologian Werner Neuer writes:

> A person does not play the role of a man or a woman, but he is a man or she is a woman. Sex is no role, that can be changed at will like stage roles, but is a fundamental aspect of human existence from which no one can escape. It carries with it quite definite tasks and modes of conduct. And language must reflect this state of affairs. . . . Sex is concerned with being and not with roles. . . . In the cause of truth we

should therefore give up talking about the roles of the sexes.[58]

Neuer states the patriarchal position sans the role rhetoric: "The Christian view of the sexes starts from the premise that both men and women are in every respect God's creatures and of equal value, but that in their *being* they are fundamentally distinct. Consequently they have different tasks to fulfill."[59] That is, the different "functions" or "tasks" (male authority and female subordination) are grounded in and determined by the ontologically distinct male and female beings.

Indeed, it seems the typical patriarchal view is not just that God has *willed* that women and men have these "distinct functions" but that because God's creational design is for women to be subordinate to men, these "roles" are in some sense uniquely fitting expressions of personal manhood and womanhood. God has designed men and women such that true femininity inclines toward submissiveness and true masculinity inclines toward personal, directive leadership.[60] Few patriarchalists today consistently claim or believe that submissiveness does not in some sense "fit" with the nature of womanhood, or that men are not by virtue of their manhood more suited to be in authority than are women.

What many patriarchalists actually believe about the being (and not merely the "function") of women is reflected not only in their discussions of the subject but also in their day-to-day interactions with women and men in churches and Christian ministries. What, I wonder, would the church look like if people consistently believed—in both theory *and* practice—that superior male function does not bespeak superior male being (but only God's apparently arbitrary will)? It is difficult to imagine, but it seems certain that women would not be treated the way they now are. If women were truly regarded as no less than men in their intrinsic capacities and inbuilt resources for leadership, decision making and spiritual understanding, then men in leadership would routinely utilize women's abilities fully in such areas as financial and administrative management, ministry to both men and women, moral and theological reasoning, spiritual gifts and insights, and biblical exegesis and exposition. Furthermore, women would not be consistently interrupted, dismissed, patronized or ignored when they speak up in classrooms or staff/faculty/ board meetings of Christian organizations. Rather, men would listen to, respect,

---

[58]Werner Neuer, *Man and Woman in Christian Perspective* (Wheaton, Ill.: Crossway, 1991), pp. 29-30.

[59]Ibid., p. 23, emphasis added. Neuer apparently does not acknowledge that such a difference or inequality in being implies women's inferiority in being.

[60]As noted earlier in this chapter, this is the view of Piper and Grudem, who are representative of many, especially those of the Council on Biblical Manhood and Womanhood.

appreciate and seek out women's counsel and expertise in all the areas where gifted women stand to contribute to the important tasks of shepherding God's flock and sharing the gospel of Christ with the world at large.

People's actual treatment of women often belies their professed belief that only the role is inferior, not the person. It is, after all, not possible to live out an implausible belief. Role theology would have us believe that although the subordinate role is not demanded by the nature of the female person, a woman who is truly feminine will play the role of submission to male authority because God ordained at creation that this is to be the woman's permanent role, and only the woman who plays this role is fulfilling her purpose and true identity as a woman.

However, it is illogical to maintain that there is no basis for the role in the nature of the person when the role is one of moral necessity given the nature of the person, and when the role is perceived as defining one's personal gender identity and as having been established by God at creation. In what other area of life do we freight a mere *role* with such ontological significance? Creational design, personal nature, gender identity—this is the stuff of *being*, not of a mere role or function. The concept of "role" is simply playing the role of "being"!

The logical connection between woman's being and woman's subordinate "role" is attested not only by common sense but also by common experience—an experience all too common for countless women who have followed God's call into Christian ministry.

False Analogies

Many attempts to defend woman's subordination against the implication of woman's inferiority resort to some kind of argument by analogy: that is, if other instances of "role difference" are compatible with equality in being, then woman's subordination in "role" is compatible with her equality in being. But are such analogies valid, or are they comparing apples and oranges? We have already seen that not all differences in function or role logically permit personal equality. Many of these arguments attempt to justify woman's subordination (which is incompatible with personal equality) by likening it to a role that *is* compatible with personal equality. In order to refrain from falling into such logical errors, one must have a keen eye for the critical differences between female subordination and functional subordination. Subordination is necessarily personal and not merely functional when (as in female subordination) its scope is comprehensive, its duration is permanent, and the criterion for its determination is one's unalterable ontology.

One argument-by-analogy often put forth is that if a child's subordination to a parent does not imply the child's inferiority in being, then neither does a woman's subordination to her husband imply that the woman is inferior in being.[61] But this is a classic case of false analogy. The child's subordination is *like* female subordination in that it is comprehensive and ontologically based; however, it is *unlike* female subordination in that its ontological basis—childhood—is a temporary condition. It is also unlike female subordination in that the child's parental governance follows justifiably from the child's lack of experience and inferior skills in decision making. The child's subordination ends when its purpose has been accomplished and the child is sufficiently mature to make independent decisions.

Because the nature of childhood warrants the child's subordination, and childhood is a temporary condition that all humans undergo, the subordination of child to parent does not imply the child's inferiority in fundamental personhood. The child, for that matter, could grow up to hold a position of authority over her own parents. (A woman can never "grow up" to have authority over—or even equal with—a man.) Of course, the grown child will still owe respect and honor to her parents as a permanent obligation. However, the point at issue is not whether a woman should respect and honor her husband (as she certainly should) but whether she should submit to his rule.

Space does not permit a response to all such spurious arguments-by-analogy.[62] The rest of this chapter will address two key theological analogies that are often advanced in order to justify woman's subordination.

The Priests and the Levites

Some have argued that because God assigned the Levites, especially those in the Aaronic priesthood, to a special religious function from which other Israelites were excluded, this shows, by analogy, that the doctrine of male authority in marriage and ministry does not violate the essential equality of women and men.[63] This argument is flawed both analogically and theologically.

It is true that each arrangement grants to some people a religious status that is denied to others, based entirely on physical attributes of birth. However, the analogy fails at several key points. Unlike male authority and female subordination, the

---

[61]Ortlund argues along these lines in "Male-Female Equality," p. 104.

[62]See *GNFW,* pp. 49-52, 60-63, for additional examples and discussion.

[63]See, for example, James B. Hurley, *Man and Woman in Biblical Perspective* (Grand Rapids, Mich.: Zondervan, 1981), pp. 44-45; and Schreiner, "Women in Ministry," p. 201.

special role of the Levites did not meet all the characteristics of criteria, duration and scope, which together render a superior-subordinate order fundamentally ontological rather than merely functional.[64]

Although the Levitical priesthood is roughly analogous to male authority in terms of its lifelong duration and its basis in unalterable physical being, its scope is a different matter. The scope of female subordination to male authority is comprehensive. A married woman is subject to her husband's authority in every area of her life. There is no area in which a woman has any authority, privilege or opportunity that a man is denied.[65] The male is consistently advantaged with respect to the female, and the female is consistently disadvantaged with respect to the male. The Levites, however, were not consistently advantaged with respect to the people; they were denied the right of the other tribes to own and inherit land (Num 18:20). In patriarchal agrarian societies, land ownership was deemed supremely desirable and a mark of social status—a right generally denied the less privileged classes (such as women and slaves). It was also denied the Levites. Thus there remained a sense of equality or parity between the Levites and the other Israelites in that each group had its own advantages and disadvantages.

Furthermore, while God chose the Levites to perform a ministry of lifelong duration, it was not a permanent decree as is the (supposed) divine decree that women be subordinate to male authority. The authority/status difference between women and men is deemed an essential feature of God's creational design; thus it is permanent not only in the sense that it endures throughout a person's lifetime but also in that it pertains to all men and women everywhere for all time. The Levites' role, by contrast, was not permanent but provisional, in that it pertained only to a temporary religious system at a particular time and for a particular purpose in history.

It should also be noted that men in the Levitical priesthood did not have the sort of spiritual authority over the people that men today are given over women in the church and home. In the Old Testament, spiritual authority in this sense—whereby certain individuals spoke for God and made the will of God known to others—was exercised less by the priests than by the prophets (among whom were women).

Moreover, there was a discernible purpose and reason for God's choosing the Levites for a special spiritual status. Intrinsic to God's rationale was the fact that

---

[64] See previous section "Difference in 'Role' or 'Function'"; see also chart in *GNFW*, p. 45.

[65] As noted in the "Equality in Being" section above, this is not effectively countered by the claim that there is functional parity between male and female because only women can have babies.

this arrangement was *not* permanent or inherent in creational design but served a specific and limited function until the new covenant in Christ. The Bible characteristically does not reveal God's universal commands without also revealing the moral or theological reasons for the commands. Yet there is no discernible reason why God would have chosen men for permanently superior spiritual status. The only possible *logical* rationale would be that all men are spiritually superior to all women—a supposition for which no evidence exists, and which today's proponents of male authority deny.

God chose the Levites to serve on behalf of all the firstborn sons of Israel, who by right belonged to Yahweh. In lieu of demanding the firstborn of every family, God set aside the Levites as his own (Num 3:11-13, 40-51). In this sense the Levites were playing a role. It was for symbolic, illustrative and instructional purposes that God formally consecrated the priests and Levites for their special role of representing God's holiness to the people and representing Israel before God (Num 8). The Levitical priesthood was justified during the time of the old covenant, because God had ordained that certain individuals who possessed physical attributes and pedigrees deemed worthy by human standards should serve as an object lesson for the people, a visible picture of an invisible God who is utterly perfect and supremely worthy.[66] Furthermore, God's ultimate covenant purpose was for *all* his people to serve as his priesthood (Ex 19:6; Is 61:6). The representative ministry of the Levitical priesthood prevailed only until the new covenant instituted the high priesthood of Christ and the priesthood of all believers.

Everything that was prefigured in the Levitical priesthood has now been fulfilled forever in Jesus Christ, who is the firstborn of all creation (Col 1:15), the one Mediator between God and humans (1 Tim 2:5) and our high priest forever after the order of Melchizedek, which supersedes the order of Aaron (Heb 6:19-20; 7:11-28). The perfect representation of God has now been given once and for all in the life, ministry, death and resurrection of Jesus Christ (Jn 14:9; Col 1:15, 19; Heb 1:3), and this leaves no room for addition, development or duplication in the form of men who believe they stand in the authority of Christ vis-à-vis women.

In the new covenant, physical distinctions such as race and gender no longer demarcate unequal levels of religious privilege (Gal 3:26-28). No one in the body of Christ is excluded from the priestly responsibilities of representing God's holiness to the world, offering spiritual sacrifices to God, representing God before other be-

---

[66]See *GNFW*, pp. 31-36.

lievers and interceding for others before God. The failure to perceive and honor the pivotal difference between priesthood in the old covenant and priesthood in the new covenant is a fundamental theological flaw of evangelical patriarchy.[67] This point of confusion is reflected in the attempt to defend a special spiritual status for Christian men by comparing it to the Levitical priesthood of the old covenant.

The Subordination of the Son to the Father

Support for the claim that woman's unequal role does not bespeak woman's unequal being is often sought in the analogy of the relationship of God the Son to God the Father.[68] It is argued that the Father and the Son are "equal in being" yet in all things and through all eternity they relate to one another according to a hierarchy of authority and obedience; thus the analogy of the "eternal functional subordination" within the Trinity illustrates and vindicates woman's permanent and comprehensive subordination to man's authority. As with the Levitical argument, I believe the trinitarian argument fails to hold up either analogically or theologically.

False analogy. Christian orthodoxy affirms that God and Christ are of the same substance and nature; they are not just equal in being but *one* in being. There is no difference between the divine nature of the Father and the divine nature of the Son.[69] Thus human nature is not analogous to divine nature. God (three Persons sharing one divine nature) is a unitary being, while humanity (billions of persons sharing human nature) is a category consisting of a multiplicity of beings. There is a oneness in nature/essence/substance between the Father and the Son that is absent from any male-female relationship.

Therefore any subordination of Christ to God would necessarily be fundamentally dissimilar to the subordination of woman to man, which is decided by and deemed essential to the "deeper differences" of manhood and womanhood. Unlike woman's subordination to man, the Son's subordination to the Father cannot be grounded in or determined by his "different" nature. Although subordinationists consider Christ's eternal subordination to be an inherent, unchanging element of the Godhead, it evidently obtains by virtue of Christ's relationship as Son to the Father, not by virtue of his nature being different from the Father's. (Yet here, too,

---

[67]See *GNFW,* chaps. 1 and 4, especially pp. 31-36, 115-17. See also chapters ten and sixteen in this volume.

[68]See, for example, Grudem, *Systematic Theology,* pp. 459-60.

[69]See Millard J. Erickson, *Christian Theology* (Grand Rapids, Mich.: Baker, 1985), pp. 337, 339.

they assume a false analogy. A son is not permanently subordinate in all things to his father.)

It has often been stated that one purpose of male leadership in marriage is to determine who makes the decision when husband and wife cannot agree. The properly submissive wife will act against her own best judgment if the husband's "final decision" is contrary to her will. But the members of the Trinity are always completely one in will.[70] Unlike the subordination prescribed for women, there could be no subordination in the eternal Trinity that would involve one divine Person acting against his own preference or best judgment under orders issued from the contrary will of another divine Person. When the Father sent the Son, it was not along the lines of an earthly father who says, "Well, son, here's what I'm going to have you do," at which point the son learns what he had better do or else. Rather, with Father, Son and Holy Spirit of one mind on how to redeem sinful humans (as they always are on every matter), it was the Son's will to go as much as it was the Father's will to send him (Phil 2:5-11).

Moreover, in Christ's own description of his earthly ministry, he states that the Father has given him all judgment and authority (Mt 28:18; Jn 5:21-27; 17:2).[71] Even during his earthly incarnation, when Jesus did only the Father's will (Jn 5:30; 8:28-29), the relationship of Father and Son was not at all like that of husband and wife in a patriarchal marriage, where the husband holds final decision-making authority and is neither expected nor required to share this authority with his wife.

Even if there were an eternal subordination of the Son to the Father, it would fail to model the key elements of woman's lifelong subordination to man. What would female subordination to male authority look like if it were truly analogous to a subordination of the Son to the Father? First, the authority of the man and the submission of the woman would not be decided or demanded by their different male and female natures. Second, there would never be an occasion in which the

---

[70]Although Paul exhorts believers to be of one mind (Phil 2:2), this refers to unity and harmony in relationships, not to the complete and consistent oneness in will and desire that characterize the members of the Trinity.

[71]Patriarchalist Steven Tracy acknowledges this aspect of the Father-Son analogy and says this should challenge men to "exercise biblical headship by giving women authority in various spheres of life and ministry." Males, however, must still retain "final decision-making authority" over females (Tracy, "Headship with a Heart," p. 53). This sort of arrangement, however, falls short of the analogy of the Father's giving "all judgment" to the Son. Note also that even in Tracy's benevolent construal of patriarchy, the woman has no direct authority under God; she has only the authority her husband decides to give her.

man's will would or should overrule the woman's will; the man therefore would "send" the woman to do only what was in accordance with her own will. Third, every husband would willingly and consistently share all authority with his wife, acknowledging her full authority to make judgments and decisions on behalf of both of them. In short, the oneness in being of the divine Persons, which results in oneness of will, precludes invoking the Trinity as either illustrating or vindicating the doctrine of woman's subordination to man.

Theological problems. The oneness in nature and will of the divine Persons not only renders any "eternal functional subordination of the Son" disanalogous to female subordination but also brings into question the logical coherence of the doctrine itself. What could be the logic of one person always functioning subject to the authority of another person without some cause or ground for this continuous subordination in the respective natures of the two persons? And how could there be a permanent, unilateral "order" of authority and obedience between persons who are always of one mind and will, who have the same perfect knowledge and understanding, the same perfectly righteous desires, the same infinite and inexhaustible wisdom and love? How could there even be any sense or purpose in such an arrangement?

Philippians 2:5-11 states that during his time on earth in human flesh, Jesus put human limitations on his equality with God by choosing to take on the role of a servant. He "became obedient" (Phil 2:8 NRSV). The time of Christ's earthly incarnation was not business as usual for God the Son and God the Father; it was an epic—although temporally limited—change in their relationship. Hebrews 5:7-8 states, "Son though he was, he learned obedience" while he was on earth in the flesh, and God heard his prayers "because of his reverent submission." Since this was the first time the Son needed to be obedient to the Father, he had to learn how to do it. It was not until his earthly incarnation that the Son "*became* obedient" and "*learned* obedience." There is no indication of an *eternal* order of the Son's obedience to the Father's authority.[72]

Furthermore, when Christ humbled himself to become human in order to redeem fallen humanity, it was not so much a demonstration of the Son's submission to the Father as a demonstration of the nature and being of the Father. As F. F. Bruce notes, "Nowhere is God more fully or worthily revealed as God than when we see him 'in Christ reconciling the world to himself' (2 Cor 5:19)."[73]

---

[72]See Gilbert Bilezikian, "Hermeneutical Bungee-Jumping," *JETS* 40, no. 1 (March 1997): 65.
[73]F. F. Bruce, *The Epistle to the Hebrews*, rev. ed. (Grand Rapids, Mich.: Eerdmans, 1990), p. 80.

In the incarnation, the Son became functionally subordinate to the Father only with respect to his work as our Redeemer. Thus Christ's subordination is limited in both scope and duration, since the work of redemption has a beginning and end point in time. But if, as patriarchalists typically argue, Christ's subordination is not limited temporally and functionally but pertains in all things throughout all eternity, then it is not a functional subordination; it is a personal subordination. Subordinate is what he always is, what he always has been, what he always will be; it necessarily defines and characterizes the person and identity of the Son throughout all eternity.

The idea that Christ's subordination is eternal yet merely functional (and thereby compatible with ontological equality) is incongruent. An eternal subordination of Christ would seem logically to entail his ontological subordination.[74] As Millard Erickson concludes, "A temporal, functional subordination without inferiority of essence seems possible, but not an eternal subordination."[75]

The doctrine of an eternal "role" subordination of the Son to the Father not only is rife with logical and theological difficulties but utterly fails as an analogy to woman's subordination. Thus it serves neither to illustrate nor to vindicate the claim that woman's subordination and woman's equality can coexist without contradiction.[76]

In Conclusion

Whether within a marriage or within the Trinity, subordination is not functional but ontological when it defines and characterizes a person in all his or her aspects, in perpetuity—when subordination is thereby inherent in the very identity of a person. To attempt to legitimize such subordination by declaring it to be a "role" that has no bearing on the "equality in being" of the subordinated person is a rhetorical sleight of hand. Saying it doesn't make it so—or even logically possible.

Truly functional subordination *can* logically coexist with equality of being.

---

[74]Those who affirm the Son's "eternal functional subordination" deny that the Son's subordination is ontological. Thus my argument is not that these proponents of trinitarian subordination are heretical but that they fail to acknowledge this theological and philosophical entailment of their position. Robert Letham's ruminations illustrate how the notion of eternal functional subordination collapses into ontological subordination. See Letham, "The Man-Woman Debate," *WTJ* 52 (1990): 67-68. For a response, see *GNFW,* pp. 57-58.

[75]Millard J. Erickson, *God in Three Persons* (Grand Rapids, Mich.: Baker, 1995), p. 309.

[76]See chapter nineteen in this volume for a more detailed theological critique of the doctrine of Christ's subordination.

However, neither female subordination nor an eternal subordination of the Son to the Father fits the definition of functional subordination. Female subordination is not about performing a function as much as it is about being—*being* female, *being* submissive to male authority. Because women's subordination is not merely a function or a role but is fundamentally ontological, it contradicts the biblical teaching of the essential equality of women and men. Similarly, any eternal subordination of the Son would seem logically to entail the Son's ontologically inferior status and so to contradict biblical teaching on the oneness of God and the absolute equality in being of Father, Son and Holy Spirit.

Woman's inferior "role" cannot be defended by the claim that it is ontologically distinct from woman's equal being. In female subordination, being determines role and role defines being; thus there can be no real distinction between the two. If the one is inferior, so must be the other. If, on the other hand, woman is *not* less than man in her personal being, then neither can there be any biblical or theological warrant for woman's permanent, comprehensive and ontologically grounded subordination to man's authority.[77]

---

[77]I am grateful to Douglas Groothuis and a half-dozen other writers and scholars who critiqued earlier versions of this chapter.

19

THE SUBORDINATION
OF CHRIST AND
THE SUBORDINATION OF WOMEN

Kevin Giles

Contemporary conservative evangelical arguments for the permanent subordination of women frequently tell us that the Son is *eternally* subordinated to the Father.[1] This "truth" is taken to be both a rationale for women's permanent subordination to men (since the Trinity reflects the God-given ideal for male-female relationships) and an example of how subordination in role or function and equality in being/essence/person/dignity can coexist without contradiction. We are told that in the church and home, women are equal with men in their essential being yet are subordinated to men "in role."[2] Just as the divine Father-Son relationship is *hierarchically*[3] ordered, so too are the husband-wife relationship in the home and the man-woman relationship in the church.

---

[1] On all that follows, see in more detail Kevin Giles, *The Trinity and Subordinationism: The Doctrine of God and the Contemporary Gender Debate* (Downers Grove, Ill.: InterVarsity Press, 2002).

[2] See *RBMW*, pp. 103-4, 128-30, 394-96, 457, 462. See also, among others, George W. Knight, *The New Testament Teaching on The Role Relationship of Men and Women* (Grand Rapids, Mich.: Baker, 1977), pp. 33, 55-56; Michael Harper, *Equal and Different: Male and Female in Church and Family* (London: Hodder & Stoughton, 1999), pp. 4, 6, 14, 60, 153-63, 203-4; Wayne Grudem, *Systematic Theology: An Introduction to Biblical Doctrine* (Grand Rapids, Mich.: Zondervan, 1994), pp. 454-70; Robert Letham, "The Man-Woman Debate: Theological Comment," *WTJ* 52 (1990): 65-78; John Dahms, "The Subordination of the Son," *JETS* 37, no. 3 (1994): 351-64; Stephen D. Kovach and Peter R. Schemm, "A Defense of the Doctrine of the Eternal Subordination of the Son," *JETS* 42, no. 3 (1999): 461-76; Paul Barnett, *1 Corinthians* (Rosshire, U.K.: Christian Focus, 2000), p. 200.

[3] See index under "hierarchy" in *RBMW*, pp. xiv, 67, 83, 104, 130, 162, 163, 257, 282, 290, 293, 394, 396, 412, 414, 415, 418, 462, 481, 492, 494, 500, 533, 534. Harper, *Equal and Different*, stresses this throughout his book.

In the recent conservative evangelical literature advocating the *eternal* subordination of the Son, two differing approaches can be seen. Both agree that the Son is equal to the Father in divinity, but from this point on they part company. The most popular position is endorsed in *Recovering Biblical Manhood and Womanhood: A Response to Evangelical Feminism* and most fully spelled out in Wayne Grudem's *Systematic Theology: An Introduction to Biblical Doctrine* (1994).[4] He sums up this position in these words: "The Son is eternally subordinated to the Father in role or function," not in being.[5]

The alternative position is most fully articulated in the 1999 Diocese of Sydney (Anglican) Doctrine Commission Report, "The Doctrine of Trinity and Its Bearing on the Relationship of Men and Women."[6] This document reflects the theological commitments of the largest seminary in Australia, Moore Theological College Sydney, which is known for its conservative evangelical and Reformed stance and opposition to the ordination of women. This report asserts that speaking of the functional subordination of the Son is only "true as far as it goes."[7] The Son's functional subordination to the Father reflects "the essence of the *eternal* relationship between them."[8] Within the Godhead there are "differences in *being*."[9] The subordination of the Son and the Spirit "belongs to the *very persons themselves in their eternal natures*."[10] The Son's "obedience to the Father arises from the *very nature of his being* as Son."[11] On this view the eternal role subordination of the Son is based on his subordination in "person," "nature" or "being." Evangelicals who hold this position maintain that if the Son's subordination in role is eternal, it must imply his eternal subordination in essence/person/being. They think that eternal role subordination apart from a personal subordination in nature, essence or being is logically untenable.

In both approaches, those who argue for the eternal subordination of the Son in function or being claim that their theology of the Trinity is entirely orthodox. Grudem says that to reject eternal role subordination is to reject what all orthodox

---

[4]Grudem, *Systematic Theology*, pp. 454-70.

[5]Ibid., p. 245 n. 27.

[6]"The Doctrine of Trinity and Its Bearing on the Relationship of Men and Women," *Diocese of Sydney Doctrine Commission Report*, 1999, <www.anglicanmediasydney.asn.au/doc/trinity.html>. This document is published in full as an appendix in Giles, *Trinity and Subordinationism*. For similar views see Letham, "Man-Woman Debate," and Dahms, "Subordination."

[7]"Doctrine of Trinity," par. 32.

[8]Ibid.; I have added emphasis to key terms or phrases by putting them in italics.

[9]Ibid., par. 25. See also pars. 18, 21, 26, 32.

[10]Ibid., par. 33. See also pars. 17-18, 21-22, 32.

[11]Ibid., par. 18.

Christians have believed from the Council of Nicaea onward.[12] Likewise, the authors of the Sydney Doctrine Commission Report claim there is an orthodox subordinationism that stresses both the full divinity of the three Persons and subordination "in the very nature" of the Son.[13] This position, they tell us, is supported by "Calvin, and the Calvinists (Edwards, Berkhof, Hodge, Dabney, Packer, Knox),"[14] and the Nicene and Athanasian creeds.[15] Similarly, Stephen Kovach and Peter Schemm assert, "It cannot be legitimately denied that the eternal subordination of the Son is an orthodox doctrine believed from the history of the early church to the present day."[16] In support, they quote Athanasius, Augustine, Calvin and the Nicene Creed.

The claim that historic orthodoxy has always endorsed the eternal subordination of the Son, so long as his divinity is not questioned, catches the attention of all evangelicals. We want to believe that our theology is what the church has always taught. When this historic argument is reinforced by appeal to the Scriptures, the case seems conclusive. We are told that this doctrine is taught explicitly in John 14:28 and 17:3, 1 Corinthians 11:3 and 15:28, and Hebrews 3:2 and 5:8,[17] and that it is suggested in passages that speak of the Son as doing the Father's will and being sent by the Father.

Should we then accept the *eternal* subordination of the Son? I think not. I will argue that to teach the eternal subordination of the Son to the Father in being or role, person or function, is to teach contrary to the way the best theologians have interpreted the Bible across the centuries and to reject what the creeds and Reformation confessions of faith affirm.

---

[12]Grudem, *Systematic Theology*, p. 245 n. 27 and pp. 251-52. Similarly, Thomas R. Schreiner, "Head Coverings, Prophecy and the Trinity: 1 Corinthians 11:2-6," in *RBMW*, p. 129; Wayne Grudem, "The Meaning of *Kephalē* ('Head'): A Response to Recent Studies," in *RBMW*, p. 457; and Kovach and Schemm, "Defense."

[13]"Doctrine of Trinity," par. 18.

[14]Ibid., par. 26. See also pars. 14-15. This assertion is not correct. Charles Hodge was definitely a subordinationist, as was D. B. Knox, but Calvin certainly was not, nor was Jonathan Edwards. See Richard M. Weber, "The Trinitarian Theology of Jonathan Edwards: An Investigation of Charges Against Its Orthodoxy," *JETS* 44, no. 2 (June 2001): 297-318, esp. 312. Later in this essay I will show that most Calvinists have in fact rejected the eternal subordination of the Son. This seems to be Louis Berkhof's position, but in one line he does speak of the subordination of the Son. See Giles, *Trinity and Subordinationism*, p. 75, where I discuss Berkhof's orthodox trinitarianism.

[15]"Doctrine of Trinity," par. 25.

[16]Kovach and Schemm, "Defense," p. 464.

[17]Texts the Arians first highlighted.

The Alternative Positions

Virtually all Christians agree that in the incarnation the Son subordinated himself to the Father. He functionally assumed the role of a servant. But most Christians do not believe that the Son's subordination in the incarnation is definitive of the Father-Son relationship in the eternal or immanent Trinity.[18] In Philippians 2:5-11 Paul asserts that the Son had equality with the Father *before* he voluntarily emptied himself to become man and die on the cross, and that *afterward* he was exalted to reign as Lord. Before the incarnation the Son was the co-Creator, equal with the Father, and after the resurrection he was exalted to his former glory. In exalting the Son the Father gave to the Son preeminence. He is now the Lord, the head of all things, who sustains all things and exercises all authority in heaven and on earth (Eph 1:22; Col 2:10; Heb 1:2-3; Mt 28:18). On this view, the Son's subordination evident in the incarnation is restricted to the time when "he took the form of a servant" for our salvation. It is not eternal. Nevertheless, the Son's voluntary, temporal subordination is not something that sets apart the Father and the Son. The Father who is revealed in the Son is a God who gladly stoops to save. So Jesus says, "Anyone who has seen me has seen the Father" (Jn 14:9).

In contrast to the position just outlined, which I believe expresses historic orthodoxy, there have always been those who have argued that the subordination of the Son seen in the incarnation defines his relationship with the Father in the eternal or immanent Trinity. Across the centuries there have been many different expressions of this position known as "subordinationism." Usually it involves believing that while the Son is divine, he is subordinate in his person or being *and* in his works or functions. What distinguishes the most popular expression of subordinationism among evangelicals today is the claim that the Son is eternally subordinated to the Father in his work/role/functions yet is not in any way subordinated in his being or person.

This expression of subordinationism is entirely novel. For the first time in human history we find Christians arguing for eternal functional subordination apart from

---

[18]Modern theologians make a notional distinction between the immanent and the economic Trinity. The immanent Trinity is the triune God as he exists for all eternity; the economic Trinity is the Trinity revealed in God's unfolding work in history recorded in the Bible, which is far wider than the incarnation. Human beings do not have direct access to the immanent Trinity, and even if they did they could not fully comprehend God as he is. What is revealed is what can be known and comprehended, albeit imperfectly. Most orthodox theologians, past and present, insist that what is revealed in Scripture accurately, though not exhaustively, reveals the immanent Trinity. In other words, God's revelation of himself is to be completely trusted.

ontological or personal subordination. How did this idea emerge? Confronted by
the new reality of women's emancipation in the late 1960s, evangelical Christians began abandoning the historic or traditional understanding of women as "inferior" to
men.[19] Instead, some evangelicals began to argue that men and women are equals,
though God has given them differing *roles.* This seemingly innocuous argument has,
however, a sting in the tail. When unpacked, what is actually being argued is that
women have been assigned a *permanent,* subordinate role to men. Men are to lead in
the home and the church, and women are to obey. In other words, women—simply
because they are women—are the subordinate sex and this can never change. Surely
this suggests that women are inferior to men in some way.[20]

To substantiate the claim that personal or ontological equality and permanent
role or functional subordination are not contradictory ideas, appeal is made to the
doctrine of the Trinity. In the Trinity, we are told, ontological equality and functional subordination coexist without one canceling out the other. If this is how the
Trinity is ordered, the argument continues, then the Trinity justifies women's permanent functional subordination. Furthermore, it is claimed that the differences
between the sexes and the differences between the divine Persons can be preserved
only if role differentiation—understood in both instances as the subordination of
one party to another—is upheld.

This argument seems to have persuaded many, but at this point two things
should be noted. First, prior to the 1980s no theologian had ever spoken of the
Son's subordination in "role" only. This use of the term, as well as the idea of permanent role subordination apart from personal subordination, came from the
woman debate, where it appeared for the first time in the mid-1970s. The language
and reasoning that was invented to make an acceptable-sounding case for the permanent subordination of women was introduced into theological discourse about
the Trinity and, in turn, the newly devised doctrine of the Son's role subordination
was used to support the doctrine of the role subordination of women.

Second, this new doctrine of the Trinity, formulated by evangelicals opposed to
the full emancipation of women, undermines the complete unity of person and
work in the Godhead so clearly taught in Scripture. On this view, the works of the
Son do not indicate that he is fully equal with the Father in divinity, majesty, power
and authority. This novel doctrine of the Trinity makes the Son eternally subordi-

---

[19]On this change in thinking among evangelicals, see Giles, *Trinity and Subordinationism,* pp. 143-68.
[20]For more on this issue, see chapter eighteen in this volume.

nated to the Father in what he does. In his works he is less in power and authority.

The Bible clearly opposes such reasoning. In Scripture, what the triune God does is a revelation of who he is: person and work go hand in hand. As Jesus himself taught, "Whatever the Father does the Son also does" (Jn 5:19). Thus one key reason most Christians conclude that the Son is equal with the Father in divinity, majesty, power and authority is that Jesus does the works that only God can do—creates, saves, forgives, judges and rules over all. He functions as God because he is God.

The Historical Argument

Despite claims made by subordinationists, the eternal subordination of the Son (whether ontological or functional) does not have the historical endorsement of the Nicene and Athanasian creeds, the Reformation confessions of faith, or theological luminaries such as Athanasius, Augustine and Calvin.

Athanasius (c. 296-373). Athanasius was one of the greatest theologians of all time. In opposition first to Arius and then to the Arians, he pioneered a way of understanding the Trinity that modern-day scholars recognize for its brilliance. To answer the Arians, who quoted many texts to prove that their teaching was based squarely on Scripture, Athanasius had first to establish how the Bible should be correctly read.[21] He came to see that two passages offered the key to grasping what he called the "scope" of Scripture: the prologue to John's Gospel, especially John 1:1 and 14, and Philippians 2:5-11. The first passage teaches that "the Word was God" and "the Word became flesh," and the second that the Son "was equal with God but emptied himself." These two texts give what he calls "a double account of the savior"—one eternal and one temporal.[22] He gladly accepts that there are passages in Scripture that speak of the Son's frailty and of him seeking always to do the Father's will. These, he says, emphasize the reality of the incarnation, which involved the Son's voluntary and temporary subordination for our salvation.

In the Son's eternal being, however, there can be no subordination at all. Because the Father and the Son are "one in being" *(homoousios)*, they act as one. For Athanasius, ontological equality demanded functional equality. One implied the other.

---

[21]For Athanasius's teaching, see *St. Athanasius: Select Works and Letters*, A Select Library of the Nicene and Post-Nicene Fathers of the Christian Church, series 2, vol. 4, ed. Phillip Schaff and Henry Wace (Grand Rapids, Mich.: Eerdmans, 1971). All quotations from Athanasius are taken from this translation.

[22]Athanasius *Against the Arians* 3.26.29.

There could be no disjunction between being and work, essence and function, person and role, within the eternal Trinity. He writes, "For where the Father is, there is the Son . . . and what the Father works, he works through the Son."[23] This insight, and the teaching of John 14:11 ("I am in the Father and the Father is in me"), led Athanasius to speak of the mutual indwelling or coinherence of the Persons, which later would be called the doctrine of *perichoresis.* This implies that whatever the divine three do, they do cooperatively and conjointly. We thus never find Athanasius speaking of the Father commanding and the Son obeying.

Athanasius grounds the distinction between the Father and the Son on the unchanging relations between the divine Persons. He writes, "They are two, because the Father is the Father and is not the Son, and the Son is the Son and not the Father."[24] And to ensure that this distinction is not made a division, he says many times, "Everything that the Father is the Son is, except for being Father."[25] He never distinguishes the Father and the Son on the basis of differing works or functions or differing authority. Repeatedly he quotes John 10:30, "I and the Father are one," and John 14:9, "Anyone who has seen me has seen the Father."

In answer to the Arians who argued that a son is always less than his father, Athanasius replied that while it true that the Bible speaks of the Son as "begotten" of the Father, this in no way makes him subordinate or inferior to the Father.[26] A son is of the same nature as his father and one day assumes the same authority as his father. For Athanasius, the biblical term *begotten* differentiates the Father and the Son; it does not subordinate one to the other or mean that the Son was "created in time," as the Arians argued. To stress the profound oneness of the Father and the Son, Athanasius repeatedly appeals to the analogy of light and its radiance, which while distinguishable as two are yet the same.

In Athanasius we find a thorough repudiation of the idea that the Son is in any way eternally subordinated to the Father. Without any caveats, he insists that the Father and the Son and the Holy Spirit are one in being *and* action, person *and* function. Wolfhart Pannenberg rightly concludes, "Athanasius vanquished subordinationism."[27]

---

[23]Athanasius *Against the Arians* 2.18.41. See also 3.15.11, 14.

[24]Athanasius *Against the Arians* 3.23.4.

[25]Athanasius *Against the Arians* 3.23.4, 3.23.5; Athanasius *On the Councils of Ariminum and Seleucia* 3.49.3-4, 3.49.66-67; cf. *Against the Arians* 4.3; *On Luke 10:22* 3-4.

[26]In this paragraph I am following the wording and ideas in Athanasius *Against the Arians* 1.7.

[27]Wolfhart Pannenberg, *Systematic Theology*, trans. G. W. Bromiley (Grand Rapids, Mich.: Eerdmans, 1991), 1:275.

Augustine (354-430). Augustine wrote extensively on the Trinity, his most important work being *De Trinitate (The Trinity)*.[28] In book I of this work, Augustine seeks to prove by appeal to the Bible the complete equality of the divine Persons.[29] His approach is noteworthy. He begins with the Scriptures, which he believes affirm the full divinity of the Son and the Holy Spirit (Jn 1:1, 5:21; Rom 11:36; 1 Cor 1:24; 1 Tim 6:14-16, etc.). Then he turns to the passages that speak of the subordination of the Son to the Father. In dealing with these he makes it a "canonical rule"—what we would call today a hermeneutical principle—to interpret them as referring exclusively to the incarnate Son who took "the form of a servant." For Augustine, Philippians 2:5-11 is the one text through which all else in Scripture about the Son should be understood. Here Paul declares that the Son, "being in very nature God, did not consider equality with God something to be used to his own advantage; rather he made himself nothing by taking the very nature of a servant, being made in human likeness."

Another canonical rule Augustine lays down is that the biblical metaphorical language of "sending" the Son must not be taken to imply subordination.[30] He argues that when the Bible speaks of the Father's sending the Son, what is in mind is the Son's "mission" to become the incarnate mediator. The "begetting" of the Son and the "procession" of the Spirit are eternal, whereas the "mission" of the Son and the Spirit are temporal.

Having laid down these canonical rules for correctly interpreting the Scriptures, and having shown on this basis that Scripture insists on the unequivocal equality of the three divine Persons, Augustine proceeds to develop a theology that completely excludes subordination within the eternal Trinity. His starting point is not the Father as the *monarchē* ("sole source") of the Son (and the Spirit) but the one divine substance shared by the three Persons. With this as the starting point, there can be no question of the equality of the three, for they "share the inseparable equality of one substance present in a divine unity."[31] This unity of substance indicates "the supreme equality of Father, Son and Holy Spirit."[32]

---

[28]See particularly Augustine, *The Trinity*, with introduction, translation, notes by Edmund Hill, part I, vol. 5 of The Works of St. Augustine (Brooklyn, N.Y.: New City Press, 1991). All the references below are taken from this translation of *De Trinitate.*

[29]Augustine *The Trinity* 1.3.14.

[30]Augustine *The Trinity* 2.2.27.

[31]Augustine *The Trinity* 2.7.15.

[32]Augustine *The Trinity* 6.10.15.

For Augustine, the Persons of the Trinity are differentiated primarily by their
relations to one another. The terms *Father, Son* and *Holy Spirit* are names given to
three distinct subsistent relations within the Godhead, which Augustine reluctantly
concedes may be designated "Persons." The Father is distinguished as Father
because he "begets" the Son; the Son is distinguished because as the Son he is "begotten"; the Spirit is distinguished from the Father and the Son because he is "bestowed" by them.[33] Augustine does not distinguish the divine "Persons" on the
basis of their works or functions or supposed difference in authority.

Because the three share the same divine essence, they have one will and work as
one. Augustine writes, "The Father and the Son have but one will and are indivis-
ible in their workings."[34] "Just as Father, Son and Holy Spirit are inseparable, so
do they work inseparably."[35] This unity of action does not obliterate the distinctive
work of each of the Persons. The Father, Son and Holy Spirit are involved in every
operation of the Godhead in the world; nevertheless, the Scriptures "appropriate"
particular works or functions to particular Persons of the Godhead.[36]

By placing the unity of the Trinity "squarely in the foreground," says J. N. D.
Kelly, Augustine "rigorously excluded subordinationism of every kind."[37]

John Calvin (1508-1564). The first question Calvin poses in his discussion of the
Trinity in the *Institutes of the Christian Religion* is what to call the divine three. He allows the word *person* but carefully defines this term as a "subsistence in God's essence, which while related to the others, is distinguished by an incommunicable
quality."[38] What he is saying is that while God is one in being or substance, the
divine three "subsist," or as we might say, "exist as," Father, Son and Holy Spirit,
being distinguished "by an incommunicable quality." What this quality is he does
not attempt to explain. This definition of a divine Person does not allow for any
subordination whatsoever. Because for Calvin the Persons of the Godhead are one
in "being itself," they cannot be unequal ontologically or functionally when
thought of as "being-in-relation."[39]

Repeatedly Calvin warns against dividing the one Godhead. He allows only for

---

[33] Augustine *The Trinity* 5.1-8.

[34] Augustine *The Trinity* 2.9.

[35] Augustine *The Trinity* 1.7.

[36] Augustine *The Trinity* 6.1-7.

[37] J. N. D. Kelly, *Early Christian Doctrine* (London: A & C Black, 1977), p. 272.

[38] Calvin *Institutes of the Christian Religion* 1.13.6.

[39] Thomas F. Torrance, "Calvin's Doctrine of the Trinity," in *Trinitarian Perspectives: Towards Doctrinal Agreement* (Edinburgh: T & T Clark, 1994), p. 70.

"a distinction not a division" between the three. He writes, "Let us not then be led to imagine a Trinity of persons that keeps our thoughts distracted and does not at once lead them back to that unity."[40] With this emphasis on the unity of the Godhead, it is of no surprise to find that he endorses the doctrine of *perichoresis,* although he does not use this term. He writes, "The Father is wholly in the Son, the Son wholly in the Father, even as he himself declares: 'I am in the Father, and the Father is in me'" (Jn 14:10).[41] This unity and coinherence within the Trinity mean that the wills of the three are one and they work as one. Calvin never depicts the eternal Father-Son relationship in terms of differing authority.

Nevertheless, along with Athanasius, Augustine and virtually all other theologians, Calvin believes the three divine Persons work in an orderly way; differing contributions to the one work may be discerned. Thus he notes that, according to Scripture,

> to the Father is attributed the beginning of activity, and the fountainhead and well-spring of all things; to the Son, wisdom, counsel and the order and disposition of all things; but to the Spirit is assigned the power and efficiency of that activity.[42]

For Calvin, the Son is differentiated from the Father on a personal and relational basis: the Son is the Son *of* the Father; the Father is the Father *of* the Son. These relationships cannot be reversed. Calvin utterly rejects the idea that the Son *derives* his divinity from the Father. The Son is God from all eternity in his own right. "Christ in respect to himself is called God; with respect to the Father, Son."[43]

Furthermore, Calvin rejects any hierarchical ordering in the eternal Trinity, insisting that there can be *"in eternity* no before or after" within the Godhead.[44] He maintains that John 14:28, where Jesus says, "The Father is greater than I," is often "twisted in various ways"[45] by those who want to "prove" that the Son is subordinated to the Father. "Christ is here not drawing a comparison between the divinity of the Father and of himself, nor between his own human nature and the divine essence of the Father, but rather between *his present state and his heavenly glory* to which he was shortly to be received."[46]

---

[40]Calvin *Institutes* I.13.17.

[41]Calvin *Institutes* I.13.19.

[42]Calvin *Institutes* I.13.18.

[43]Calvin *Institutes* I.13.19; italics added. See also I.13.23; I.13.25.

[44]Calvin *Institutes* italics added.

[45]John Calvin, *The Gospel According to St. John,* trans. T. H. L. Parker (Edinburgh: Oliver and Boyd, 1959), p. 89.

[46]Ibid., p. 90; italics added.

In their scholarly studies of Calvin's doctrine of the Trinity, Benjamin B. War-field and Thomas F. Torrance both maintain that the great Reformer was opposed to subordinationism in any form. Warfield says that Calvin sought the "elimination of the last remnants of subordinationism"[47] and was consistently in "inexpugnable opposition to subordinationists of all types."[48] As far as Torrance is concerned, Calvin "leaves no room for any element of subordinationism."[49]

The creeds and confessions. At the Council of Constantinople in 381, the creed of Nicaea promulgated in 325 was reaffirmed, albeit with different wording at key points and with an additional clause spelling out the full divinity of the Holy Spirit. The Nicene Creed of 381 asserts that the Son is "true God from true God" of "one being with the Father," who "for us and our salvation came down from heaven." In other words, it teaches that the Son is eternally equal with God the Father, although in the incarnation for our salvation he temporally subordinated himself ("came down").

At the doctrinal level, the confession that the Father and the Son are "one in being" implicitly excludes the eternal subordination of the Son in function/role. If the Father and the Son are eternally one in being, then they must function or work as one.[50] At the hermeneutical level, what is concluded doctrinally in this confession prescribes how the Bible is to be interpreted. Scripture is not to be read to teach the Son's eternal subordination either in person/being or in function/role.

In about 500 the Athanasian Creed first appeared. Essentially it is a summary of Western trinitarian theology, reflecting the thought of Augustine more than anyone else. The creed begins by declaring that to be saved one must "hold the Catholic Faith," which is identified with the trinitarian and christological affirmations that follow. In regard to the Trinity, "the Catholic Faith is this: That we worship one God in Trinity, and Trinity in unity; neither confounding the persons: nor dividing the substance." The confession of the "unity" of the Trinity involves belief that the three Persons are identical in substance and have identical attributes and

---

[47]B. B. Warfield, "Calvin's Doctrine of the Trinity," in *Calvin and Augustine* (Philadelphia: Presbyterian & Reformed, 1956), p. 230.

[48]Ibid., p. 251.

[49]Torrance, *Trinitarian Perspectives*, p. 66.

[50]See Thomas F. Torrance, *The Christian Doctrine of God: One Being, Three Persons* (Edinburgh: T & T Clark, 1996). One of the central arguments of Torrance's magisterial study is that the Nicene faith insists on a unity of divine being and act, person and function. On this theme, see pp. 4, 6, 22, 24, 30, 95, 115, 149, 152, 194, 236, 243. I think this book is the best study on the Trinity available.

authority. The creed declares that "such as the Father is, such is the Son, and such is the Holy Spirit," and "none is afore, or after other; none is greater, or less than another; but the whole three Persons are co-eternal together and co-equal." The three divine Persons are distinguished by the differing relations they bear to each other. Works or functions do not distinguish the Persons, nor do differences in authority (all three are confessed as "almighty" and "Lord").

According to Leonard Hodgson, the Athanasian Creed "expresses rejection . . . of all subordinationism."[51] Similarly Kelly, in his definitive study of this creed, concludes that "the dominant idea [is] the perfect equality of the three persons."[52]

All of the Reformation confessions of faith seek to exclude subordinationism and modalism (another recurring heresy), but as these two errors were rejected by the Catholic Church and by the Nicene and Athanasian creeds, what is said on the Trinity is usually brief and to the point. The Reformation understanding of the Trinity is conceptually Western. God is one divine essence or substance in three Persons who are to be distinguished but not divided, being equal in divinity, majesty and authority. The longest discussion of the Trinity is found in the Second Helvetic Confession of 1566, "the most widely received among Reformed Confessions."[53] This confession opposes "all those who blaspheme" and heretics who teach that the Son and Holy Spirit are "created and subservient, or subordinate to another in the Trinity, and that there is something unequal in it, a greater or less . . . something different with respect to character or will." The term *subservient* points to those who teach that the Son must always obey the Father as a servant (i.e., that he is eternally subordinate in function or role), while the term *subordinate* points to those who teach that the Son is eternally subordinate in person/being.

The Modern Period

The late nineteenth and early twentieth centuries were a particularly bleak period for trinitarian theology. Many comments allowing or endorsing the eternal subordination of the Son can be found in Protestant theological textbooks published during this time. The doctrine of the triune God of Christian revelation was marginalized and deficiently expounded by many theologians. Nowhere is this truer than among conservative evangelicals.

This deficiency is seen most clearly in the writings of Charles Hodge (1797-

---

[51]Leonard Hodgson, *The Doctrine of the Trinity* (London: Nisbet, 1955), p. 102.
[52]J. N. D. Kelly, *The Athanasian Creed* (London: A & C Black, 1977), p. 79.
[53]A. C. Cochrane, *Reformed Confessions of the Sixteenth Century* (London: SCM Press, 1966), p. 220.

1878), professor of theology at Princeton Seminary for nearly fifty years. For him three "essential facts" sum up the doctrine of the Trinity, "unity of essence, distinction of persons and subordination."[54] Thirteen times in volume I of his *Systematic Theology* he speaks of the "principle of the subordination of the Son to the Father, and the Spirit to the Father and the Son."[55] He suggests that the Son (along with the Spirit) is subordinated to the Father because he derives his divinity from the Father.[56] This, then, results in a subordination in "the mode of subsistence and operations of the persons."[57] In the Western theological tradition, the term *subsistence* refers to the individual Persons of the Trinity. This is how Calvin uses the term. It is the equivalent of the Latin *persona* and the Greek *hypostasis*. Thus Hodge is asserting that the Son and the Holy Spirit are subordinated to the Father in their personal existence (subsistence), just as they are in their operations/works/functions. In other words, Hodge maintains that although the Son is fully divine, he is subordinate in *his being as the Son* as well as in *his work as the Son*. Hodge recognized that subordination in subsistence and in operations are inseparably connected. The former implies the latter and vice versa.

Although Grudem claims that his position is endorsed by Hodge, this is not true. For Hodge, it is impossible to think of the Son as eternally subordinated to the Father in his operations or role unless he is likewise eternally subordinated in his subsistence or person.[58] The Moore College theologians are of the same opinion.

Hodge's successor at Princeton, Benjamin B. Warfield, categorically rejected subordinationism. Warfield tells us he wrote on the Trinity in order to "vigorously reassert the principle of equalization."[59] He readily admits that there are passages in the Scriptures that speak of the subordination of the Son,[60] but he insists that it is "thoroughly illegitimate to press such passages to suggest any subordination for the Son or the Spirit" in either eternal "subsistence" or "operations."[61]

Warfield's interpretation of the Scriptures is convincing and perfectly captures

---

[54]Charles Hodge, *Systematic Theology* (Edinburgh: T & T Clark, 1960), I:467.

[55]Ibid., p. 460. See also pp. 445, 460-62, 464, 465, 467-68, 474.

[56]Ibid., p. 465.

[57]Ibid., p. 464.

[58]It should be also noted that Hodge's hierarchical understanding of the Trinity perfectly reflects his hierarchical understanding of society. He believed God had set men over women and whites over blacks. He is well known for his unambiguous support of slavery in the Old South.

[59]Benjamin B. Warfield, "The Biblical Doctrine of the Trinity," in *Biblical Foundations* (London: Tyndale, 1958), p. 116.

[60]See ibid., pp. 79-116.

[61]Ibid., p. 112.

the thinking of Calvin and most Calvinists. For example, in *The Doctrine of God* Herman Bavinck enumerates several forms of subordinationism besides Arianism and repudiates all of them.[62] It is his view that Augustine once and forever "banished all subordinationism."[63] Likewise, Herman Hoeksema opposes a hierarchical understanding of the Trinity. He says in *Reformed Dogmatics* that "there is no division, no separation, no subordination between the three persons"[64] and that "the most absolute equality exists between Father, Son and Holy Spirit."[65] Similarly, Cornelius Van Til says, "A consistently biblical doctrine of the Trinity would imply the complete rejection of all subordinationism."[66]

This same rejection of all forms of subordinationism is evident in the numerous books on the Trinity written in recent years. In *These Three Are One: The Practice of Trinitarian Theology*, David Cunningham speaks of "a radical, relational, co-equality" within the Trinity.[67] In *God as Trinity: Relationality and Temporality in Divine Life*, Ted Peters describes contemporary thinking about the Christian God as "antisubordinationist trinitarianism."[68] The respected conservative evangelical systematic theologian Millard Erickson is of the same opinion. In his 1995 book *God in Three Persons: A Contemporary Interpretation of the Trinity*, he says, "There is a mutual submission of each to each of the others and a mutual glorifying of one another. There is complete equality of the three."[69] Likewise Wayne House, a conservative evangelical and a contributor to *Recovering Biblical Manhood and Womanhood: A Response to Evangelical Feminism*,[70] says that orthodoxy "unhesitatingly sets forth Father, Son and Holy Spirit as co-equal and co-eternal in the Godhead with regard to both the divine essence and function."[71] Among contemporary conservative evangelicals, Christopher Kai-

---

[62]Herman Bavinck, *The Doctrine of God* (Grand Rapids, Mich.: Eerdmans, 1951), pp. 280-81, 283, 288, 314.

[63]Ibid., pp. 281, 283.

[64]Herman Hoeksema, *Reformed Dogmatics* (Grand Rapids, Mich.: Reformed Free, 1966), p. 151.

[65]Ibid., p. 152.

[66]Cornelius Van Til, *A Christian Theory of Knowledge* (Philadelphia: Presbyterian & Reformed, 1969), p. 104.

[67]David Cunningham, *These Three Are One: The Practice of Trinitarian Theology* (Oxford: Blackwell, 1998), p. 113.

[68]Ted Peters, *God as Trinity: Relationality and Temporality in Divine Life* (Louisville, Ky.: Westminster/ John Knox, 1993), p. 45.

[69]Millard Erickson, *God in Three Persons: A Contemporary Interpretation of the Trinity* (Grand Rapids, Mich.: Baker, 1995), p. 331.

[70]*RBMW,* pp. 358-63.

[71]Wayne House, *Charts of Christian Theology and Doctrine* (Grand Rapids, Mich.: Zondervan, 1992), p. 47.

ser,[72] Charles Sherlock[73] and Gerald Bray[74] also argue that the Bible and creedal orthodoxy disallow any suggestion that the Son (or the Spirit) is eternally subordinated to the Father in being or function.

It is of particular interest that Erickson regards as logically impossible the contemporary evangelical arguments for the ontological equality of the three divine Persons with an eternal role subordination of the Son:

> A temporal, functional subordination without inferiority of essence seems possible, but not an eternal subordination. And to speak of the superiority of the Father to the Son while denying the inferiority of the Son to the Father must be contradictory.[75]

Here Erickson captures one of the fundamental insights of historical orthodoxy. From the time of Athanasius, theologians have recognized that if the Son is eternally subordinate in his work, function or operations, it must mean he is eternally subordinated in being, essence, nature, person or subsistence. If the Son or any human being is a personal equal to another, they may choose to subordinate themselves to the other; but when subordination is both permanent and obligatory, the personal inferiority of the subordinate is implied. If one party is *always* and *necessarily* subordinate to the other, the subordinate person must lack something the superior person possesses.

Reading the Bible Theologically

When it comes to discussing what the Bible teaches about the Trinity, we face the same problem as we do in the debate about the status and ministry of women. Texts can be quoted and interpreted to "prove" contradictory positions. No one denies that there are texts that can be read to subordinate the Son to the Father and women to men; but the question is, how do these texts relate to the texts that speak of or imply the equality of the Father and the Son and of women and men?

Long ago Athanasius and Augustine saw this problem and addressed it. They both insisted that when deriving a doctrine from the Bible, the theologian must first establish what is theologically primary or fundamental in the teaching of Scripture on any question in view and then read the relevant texts in this light. Re-

---

[72]Christopher Kaiser, *The Doctrine of God* (London: Marshall, Morgan and Scott, 1982).
[73]Charles Sherlock, *God on the Inside* (Canberra, Australia: Acorn, 1991).
[74]Gerald Bray, *The Doctrine of God* (Leicester, U.K.: Inter-Varsity Press, 1993).
[75]Erickson, *God in Three Persons*, p. 309.

garding the Son, they believed his unequivocal equality in divinity, majesty and authority with the Father is primary in Scripture.[76] This conviction was eventually endorsed by the church, first in the East in the Nicene Creed and then in the West in differing wording in the Athanasian Creed. From this point on these creeds prescribed not only what was to be believed but also how the Bible was to be read and interpreted.

In declaring that the Son is "of one being with the Father" (the Nicene Creed) and all three divine Persons are "coequal" (the Athanasian Creed), these two creeds capture perfectly what is implied in the confession "Jesus is Lord" (Rom 10:9). Nothing in Scripture is more central and primary than this confession. To confess Jesus Christ as Lord is to recognize him as the God who saves and rules. Thus New Testament writers speak of Jesus as God (Jn 1:1; 20:28; Rom 9:5; Heb 1:8) and say that he is equal with God (Phil 2:6). Furthermore, Jesus himself said, "I and the Father are one" (Jn 10:30), and "Anyone who has seen me has seen the Father" (Jn 14:9). This teaching allows for no eternal subordination of the Son to the Father. After the resurrection, Jesus Christ is confessed not as the obedient Son but as the Lord of all. His subordination, Paul teaches, is limited to the incarnation (Phil 2:7).

Once agreement was reached in the creeds and the confessions as to what Scripture taught regarding the eternal Trinity, it was evident that isolated passages ought not be interpreted in any way that would call into question the perfect equality of the Father, Son and Holy Spirit. Thus in dealing with the biblical passages their opponents quoted to prove the eternal subordination of the Son, Athanasius, Augustine and Calvin argued that such texts allude only to the temporal and voluntary subordination of the Son in the incarnation. Orthodox exegetes today often give more nuanced interpretations of some of these verses, while maintaining that they neither negate the full divinity of the Son nor teach the eternal subordination of the Son in being or function.

In recent years conservative evangelicals who believe God's ideal is the permanent subordination of women have made much of I Corinthians 11:3, where Paul says, "The head of Christ is God," and of I Corinthians 15:28, where Paul speaks of the Son's being made subject to the Father at the end of time—texts they insist subordinate the Son to the Father eternally. None would deny these are difficult

---

[76] In Giles, *Trinity and Subordinationism*, I argue that the Bible's teaching on the equality of men and women is the primary revealed truth on the sexes given in Scripture. It is put first in the Bible (Gen 1:27-28), and we should put it first. Nothing in Scripture should be read to negate this truth.

texts, if for no other reason than that they seem to conflict with other scriptural teaching. For example, in Ephesians 1:22 (cf. Col 2:10) Paul says Christ is "head over everything." When it comes to the rule of the Son, other texts speak of this as continuing "forever" (Lk 1:33; Heb 10:12; 2 Pet 1:11; cf. 2 Sam 7:13; Is 9:7). In the book of Revelation in the age to come, God and "the Lamb" rule on the throne together (Rev 22:1, 3).

In the historical sources on the Trinity, 1 Corinthians 11:3 is seldom quoted or discussed. The following comment from *Against Eunomius* is perhaps the most interesting:

> If the head of the "man is Christ, and the head of Christ is God," and man is not of one substance with Christ, Who is God (for man is not God), but Christ is of one substance with God (for He is God) therefore God is not the head of Christ in the same sense as Christ is the head of man. The natures of the creature and the creative Godhead do not exactly coincide. God is head of Christ, as Father; Christ is head of us, as Maker.[77]

This interpretation makes the point that speaking of the Father as the head *(kephalē)* of the Son means something very different from speaking of Christ as the head *(kephalē)* of man. We may assume he would follow the same rule in the third pairing, "man is the head of woman." The other thing to be noted is that in neither pairing does the author think that the Greek word *kephalē* suggests "authority over." In the first pair mentioned he holds that the word *kephalē* implies the divine Father-Son relationship, in the second, the Creator-creature relationship. In discussing this text Augustine vacillates between concluding, on the one hand, that the word *God* here refers to the triune God and, on the other, that it serves as a reminder that while the Son was incarnate on earth the Father was "greater."[78] Calvin opts for the latter interpretation.[79]

In contrast, in the contemporary debate among evangelicals about the status and ministry of women, this text is frequently quoted and much discussed. Those ar-

---

[77]Quoted from "Prolegomena," *St. Basil: Letters and Selected Works,* trans. Blomfield Jackson, A Select Library of the Nicene and Post-Nicene Fathers of the Christian Church, series 2, vol. 8, ed. Philip Schaff and Henry Wace (Grand Rapids, Mich.: Eerdmans, 1968), p. xl. Though this quotation from book 4 of *Against Eunomius* is included in printed editions of Basil, most scholars do not believe he is its author. Nonetheless, it is fully consistent with fourth-century Cappadocian opposition to Eunomius's Arian views.

[78]Augustine *The Trinity* 6.2.10.

[79]John Calvin, *The First Epistle of Paul to the Corinthians,* trans. J. W. Fraser (Grand Rapids, Mich.: Eerdmans, 1960), p. 229.

guing for the permanent subordination of women and the eternal subordination of
the Son make I Corinthians 11:3 pivotal to their case on the basis that here the
two relationships are analogous (contra *Against Eunomius*). In both instances Grudem argues the word *kephalē* means "ruler, authority over."[80] So he concludes that
this text teaches that just as the Father is eternally set over the Son in authority,
husbands are permanently set over their wives in authority in the home and men
over women in the church.

In his persuasive reply to Grudem, Anthony Thiselton concludes that in this
context, whatever *kephalē* may mean, it does not "denote a relation of 'subordination,' or 'authority over.' "[81] It should also be noted that Paul does not speak in this
text of a fourfold hierarchical order, God-Christ-man-woman, but of three paired
relationships, Christ-man, man-woman, God-Christ. This suggests he is differentiating the persons paired, not subordinating one to another. He makes this comment in anticipation of the argument he is about to develop, namely, that men and
women alike may lead in prayer and prophecy in church so long as they are differentiated by what they have or do not have on their head.[82]

What exactly Paul had in mind when he penned I Corinthians 15:24-28 is difficult to know. Commentators and theologians continue to struggle with this text.[83]
Possibly the most profound insight is offered by Pannenberg, who finds here proof
of the mutual dependence of the Father on the Son and the Son on the Father. After the resurrection the Father makes the Son ruler over all, and on the Last Day
the Son voluntarily hands back the rule of all things to the Father.[84]

Conclusion

The evidence is compelling. Contemporary evangelicals who argue for the eternal
subordination of the Son in being or function have broken with historic orthodoxy,
both in what they believe and in how they interpret the Scriptures. They have mistakenly concluded that relations within the Trinity are ordered hierarchically, and
on this premise they have sought to justify the hierarchical ordering of male-female

---

[80]Grudem, "The Meaning of *Kephalē*," *RBMW,* p. 467.

[81]Anthony C. Thiselton, *The First Epistle to the Corinthians,* NIGTC (Grand Rapids, Mich.: Eerdmans,
2000), p. 816.

[82]For further discussion of the exegesis of I Cor 11:2-16, see chapter eight of this book.

[83]For a good discussion of the history of interpretation, see J. F. Jansen, "I Cor 15:24-28 and the
Future of Jesus Christ," *Scottish Journal of Theology* 40 (1987): 543-70. See also Thiselton, *First Epistle
to the Corinthians,* p. 1238.

[84]Pannenberg, *Systematic Theology,* 1:312-13.

relations. In doing so they have defined divine relations in terms of fallen human relations, where some rule and others obey and where people are differentiated according to the authority they exercise or are excluded from exercising.

The orthodox doctrine of the Trinity stands in opposition to such thinking. It speaks of divine Persons who are "coequal," differentiated by their personhood and relations to one another. They coexist in perfect harmony, working together as one. Because the orthodox doctrine of the Trinity categorically and unambiguously rejects the *eternal* subordination of the Son and the Spirit in being *and* work, it does not and cannot be used to support the subordination of women to men, nor to demonstrate that personal equality can be reconciled with permanent role subordination.

PART IV

ADDRESSING THE ISSUES

Hermeneutical and
Cultural Perspectives

20

BIBLICAL HERMENEUTICS

Basic Principles and Questions of Gender

Roger Nicole

Establishing and defining principles that help the interpreter understand accurately the meaning of the biblical text is critical to ascertaining properly the teaching of Scripture regarding gender relationships in Christ. This science is called *biblical hermeneutics*. The term is used here in the classical sense to speak of "principles that serve to ascertain the meaning of verbal statements."[1] Such principles should prevent us from reading into a passage what it does not contain, as well as ensure that a satisfactory approximation to its full meaning is attained.[2] In the classical view, *exegesis* is the term for applying hermeneutical principles to particular texts. Hermeneutics then relates to exegesis as rhetoric relates to the composition of a discourse or the art of cabinetmaking relates to the construction of wooden furniture. The task of this chapter is to show how following valid hermeneutical principles will aid in the proper understanding of the passages relevant to the gender discussion.

Before proceeding, it is of great importance to emphasize that we acknowledge God as the primary author of Scripture. The search for "authorial intent," which is paramount to hermeneutics in general, may not in biblical hermeneutics disre-

---

[1] Another understanding of the word *hermeneutics* made its appearance in the twentieth century. Here *exegesis* refers to the search for the meaning of a statement in the original setting, while *hermeneutics* attempts to evaluate its impact at the present time and in the circumstances of the reader or hearer. In that sense, exegesis would absorb a part of the hermeneutical task, and hermeneutics proper would involve an application of the text to a different time and location. While acknowledging that this too is part of the appropriate task of theology, I use the term *hermeneutics* in the classic sense.

[2] A similar effort is made in connection with a translation into another language, but interpretation does not entail the space limitation that a translation must observe (*hermēneuō* means "to translate" as well as "to interpret").

gard the divine intent. The divine intent of the text is at times elucidated in other Scriptures and always undergirds the human writers' intent. The use made of earlier Scripture by later Scripture, particularly the Old Testament by the New, bears witness that the meaning perceived by the human writers does not necessarily exhaust the full meaning of a text. The fact that the New Testament interpretation of the Old had its origin in the teaching of Jesus himself (Mt 5; Lk 24) strongly suggests the possibility that a divine meaning might transcend the evident intention of the human author.[3]

This chapter, then, will set forth six foundational hermeneutical principles—principles on which all evangelicals would agree—and will show by illustration how they might apply to texts in the contemporary gender debate.

Literal or Figurative Meanings

In a certain sense we need to take the Scripture "to the letter," for "not the smallest letter, not the least stroke of a pen, will by any means disappear" (Mt 5:18). This indicates that anything in Scripture is authoritative, but not that the writers have altogether avoided figures of speech, for in some respects even our ordinary vocabulary is constellated with figurative meaning.[4] For instance, etymologically the word *window* derives from a conflation of words for *wind* and *eye*. Or think of phrases such as "the eyes of your heart" (Eph 1:18). Likewise God is often represented in anthropomorphic form, as in the "the LORD's arm" (Num 11:23 NIV) or "the LORD came down to see the city" (Gen 11:5). Since the ultimate nature of God is incomprehensible to humans, God's being and actions are often represented by images drawn from human experience. This would include ascribing gender to God, who is "Spirit" (not having human flesh with sexuality). Of course when God the Son becomes incarnate, he takes on human male sexuality.

One particularly significant example is the representation of marriage as reflecting the union of God with his people. A key (figurative of course!) verse in this respect is Genesis 2:24, which applies in the first place to human wedlock but is quoted in Ephesians 5:31-32 as describing not only the unity of humans in the marriage commitment but also the climactic unity of Christ and the church (cf. "the wedding supper of the Lamb" in Rev 19:5-10; 21:9). In this respect, God's people are always viewed as the bride, whether it be Israel as married to Yahweh or

---

[3]Caiaphas's statement in John 11:50-52 illustrates the possible existence of a *sensus plenior.*
[4]For a conspectus of such passages in Scripture, see Walter Elwell, *Topical Analysis of the Bible* (Grand Rapids, Mich.: Baker, 1991), pp. 34-38.

the church as united with Christ. The city of Jerusalem (feminine in both Hebrew and Greek) becomes a symbol for God's people and is finally seen as the epitome of the elect (Gal 4:25-26; Rev 21:1-7). Here the use of the feminine, far from being demeaning, is a title of magnificence for women, since it lifts up humanity to a position of unity with God. Inversely, the gravity of adultery and prostitution accentuates the importance of the marriage union in God's eyes. The prostitute is typically depicted as female to contrast with the elect bride. As such, the prophets present her as the delinquent (though this is certainly not an accusation to which males are immune).

Prescriptive or Descriptive Texts

It is important in the hermeneutical process to distinguish what in Scripture is *prescriptive*, embodying God's commandment to us, and what is *descriptive*, relating events or attitudes that may or may not be desirable. It is true that at times what someone has done is presented as exemplary (e.g., Jn 13:15; 15:12; I Cor 11:1; Eph 5:1; Heb 13:7). Yet it is imperative to recognize that certain practices in both Testaments are merely *described*, or serve as the cultural background of the activity even of some who were God's children, without implying that we should conform to these practices.

Surely Lot's dedication to the custom of protecting his guests, while admirable in principle, took a form that can hardly be commended when he offered his virgin daughters to be ravished by strangers (Gen 19). Similarly, though the patriarchal society in the Old Testament serves as a background of much of Israel's history, this does not imply a divinely sanctioned order that must be observed universally for all time. Indeed, it should be noted in this regard, and over against many patriarchalists, that patriarchy is never *prescribed* in either Testament. Thus Paul's descriptive analogy between Adam's priority in creation and Eve's priority in sin in I Timothy 2:13-14— even though it is used to support the ad hoc prescription in I Timothy 2:12—seems to fall far short of being theologically prescriptive or determinative.[5]

In this respect, it is important to recognize that God's judgment on Eve and her

---

[5]Despite how often this is asserted in the literature, it has no other biblical support as a *theological dictum for all time*. The primary point of the analogy is that the woman, who was created second, was first to yield to the deception of Satan. And this seems to be happening again in Ephesus (cf. I Tim 4:1-3; 5:13-15). It is noteworthy that when Paul deals with the origin of sin in the human race, he does not mention Eve at all (Rom 5:12). One simply cannot make universal gender statements on the basis of ad hoc descriptions that are used to serve other points.

daughters ("and he [the man] shall rule over you [the woman]," Gen 3:16) is not
a prescriptive mandate that men ought to observe in order to do God's will. Rather,
the phrase is a description of what was going to occur in human history, a prophecy
fulfilled millions of times in the oppression of women throughout the world. Likewise, it is certainly appropriate to seek to ease the pain of childbirth and to lighten
the burden of male labor, which are also part of God's judgment on Adam and
Eve's sin (Gen 3:17-19).

This principle likewise applies to Ephesians 5:21-33, where Paul describes the
husband as "head" (kephalē). Although the wife's submission to her husband in the
Greco-Roman household was prescriptive within that cultural context, husbands
are never instructed in the Bible to "exercise authority over," "provide leadership
for" or "be responsible for" their wives. Paul's description of male authority in the
ancient Greco-Roman household does not attain to a prescription for all times.
And if some would argue that such is there by implication, it must be stated
strongly that implication is not prescription. However, the passage does clearly prescribe for the husband Christlike behavior of love and sacrifice toward his wife.[6]

Individual, Collective and Universal References

When we are in the presence of a clearly prescriptive passage, sound hermeneutics
demands that we ascertain to whom the prescription applies. Distinctions must be
made between *individual, collective* and *universal* references. For example, Jesus' healing
of the sick and demonized was both descriptive and prescriptive in the Gospel
records, in that the Twelve and Seventy-two were sent out to heal the sick as part
of Jesus' mission (Mt 10:8; Lk 10:9). But Jesus' command to the blind man, "Go,
wash in the Pool of Siloam" (Jn 9:6), does not constitute a *universal* mandate, not
even a mandate for all blind people who seek healing. Rather, it applies to a particular person in a particular context. By contrast, the commandment "You shall
not murder" (Ex 20:13) concerns every human being, as the context of the Ten
Commandments (Ex 20:1-17) makes clear, as does the relevant text in Genesis 9:1-
7, not to mention Jesus' own extension of it in Matthew 5:21-22.

A proper interpretation demands that the scope of reference be carefully ascertained. Concerning 1 Timothy 2:9-15, for example, there is a question whether
Paul is speaking to/about women in general or to married women specifically. The

---

[6]See further the exegetical and hermeneutical discussion of this passage in chapter eleven in this volume.

word *gynē* can mean "woman" or "wife." On the one hand, the context with its reference to Adam and Eve, as well as to the bearing of children (I Tim 2:15), appears to favor "wife." Yet the activities mentioned in I Timothy 2:8-11 could apply to men and women in general in a Christian assembly. Moreover, Paul seems to be writing with understanding of a specific background to a particular set of problems in the church of Ephesus.[7] So one must be careful not to jump to immediate conclusions about the nature and scope of the commands given here.

Peripheral Versus Central Doctrines

Some elements of our faith or duty are more basic to our understanding of our doctrine or life, while others are more peripheral. Jesus made this point in emphasizing the importance of spiritual purity over ceremonial cleanliness (Mk 7:1-21) and again in denouncing the scribes and Pharisees who insisted on minute tithing of spice but "neglected the more important matters of the law" (Mt 23:23).

Thus, for example, although certainly not peripheral, the doctrine of the virgin birth of Christ is less central in the Christian faith than that of his substitutionary atonement. The former surely has a strong foundation in Scripture: prophetically (Is 7:14), historically (Mt 1:18-24; Lk 1:26-38) and theologically (Gal 4:4; Heb 7:26-28). Moreover, it is affirmed in the great creeds of church history. But it does not have the *centrality* of the atonement, which is foreshadowed in the Old Testament sacrifices, reasserted by the prophets (Is 53), celebrated in the Psalms (Ps 40:6-9; cf. Heb 10:1-10), proclaimed as central in the teaching of Jesus (Mk 10:45; Jn 12:27) and in the apostolic presentation (Rom 3:21-26; 5:11; I Cor 2:2; Gal 6:14; Heb 2:14-18, etc.).

When this principle is applied to gender issues related to church leadership, it is of some interest that many patriarchalists affirm the gifting of women for ministry of various kinds but are resistant to women's holding positions of leadership in the official structures of the church. On this matter, one would think that Spirit gifting, which receives considerable attention in the New Testament with regard to the ministry of the body of Christ to itself and in the world (Rom 8:3-8; I Cor 12–14; etc.), would be more central than "church order." This is especially so since there is *no prescriptive passage* that dictates the structures or nature of church order.

---

[7]To the extent these can be ascertained, as well as the meaning and scope of his words; see the full discussion in chapter twelve in this volume.

Church order was undoubtedly assumed; but the lack of prescriptive instruction about it suggests that it is a more peripheral consideration than ministry itself.[8]

Fragmentary Versus Canonical Interpretations

Another major rule of hermeneutics is that a proper interpretation must be appropriate to the context in which the passage in question is found. This is a safeguard against what is called "prooftexting," that is, lifting a passage from its context and thus incurring the danger of misunderstanding and misapplying it.

The immediate context involves the nearest verses before and after the text, but regard must also be given to the chapter in question, and then to the book in which it is found, and to the observable position of the author of that book (when known). For the Bible, even when proper attention is given to the human author, this is not enough, for the ultimate author is the God who inspired the whole Scripture so as to constitute it the "Word of God." This means that no interpretation is truly acceptable which results in a contradiction between one part of Scripture and another part. Scripture is the best guide for interpreting any portion of it; or to put it differently, we interpret in keeping with the "analogy of faith." As Bruce Demarest puts it so well, "The exegete will . . . bear in mind that interpretation must not contravene what is taught elsewhere in Scripture and that, in unfolding the meaning of a text, other inspired Scripture may help clarify the specific intention of the biblical writer."[9]

This is another hermeneutical principle on which all would tend to agree. At issue again is *praxis*, both (1) the application of some texts in light of others when the evidence presents itself ambiguously and (2) the grounds for preferring one set of texts over against the others. Some, for example, forbid women to teach men on the basis of I Timothy 2:11-12 but in so doing are dismissive of the evidence that stands on the other side (see chapter six above). Others, on the basis of I Corinthians 14:34-35, either disallow women to speak at all in a church gathering or severely limit what speaking is allowed. But to do so they must reject not only the surrounding context of I Corinthians 14 but also the evidence of I Corinthians 11:4-5, not to mention much else in the New Testament.

The Situation of Those Being Addressed or Represented

It is important to recognize that the Scripture was addressed at first to people in

---

[8]For a fuller discussion of this issue, see chapter fourteen in this volume.
[9]Bruce Demarest, "Analogy of Faith," in *Evangelical Dictionary of Theology*, ed. Walter Elwell, 2nd ed. (Grand Rapids, Mich.: Baker, 2001), p. 58.

ancient Near Eastern (Old Testament) and Greco-Roman (New Testament) cultures with habits and needs that are not identical to those of believers today. We must understand scriptural statements in terms of the situation of the people addressed or represented. That some people would make "an opening in the roof" in order to lower a paralytic into the presence of Jesus (Mk 2:1-12) does not make good sense in terms of Western architecture. The repeated command to "greet one another with a holy kiss" reflects a culture in which that was the ordinary way of greeting family and friends.

The Old Testament commandments concerning pure and impure foods (Lev 11) were given to Israel as a religious discipline and undoubtedly had some benefits for hygiene given the climate of the ancient Near East and the cooking methods at that time. But they were superseded by divine mandate after the coming of Christ (Mk 7:19; Rom 14:13-17; 1 Tim 4:1-5). Cultural differences demand of us a double shift: we must ascertain the principles at the root of cultural mandates made in antiquity in order to perceive their significance in relation to our own time and place; and we must beware lest we present as divine mandate what may be only a cultural feature of some part of our own Christian environment (which has happened all too often in crosscultural witness).

The task of discerning what is simply cultural and what is perennially mandatory in the Christian ethos is undoubtedly very delicate, and mistakes have often been made in this domain. Similarly, it is not always easy to perceive the cultural aspect of some biblical injunctions. Too often well-meaning people have viewed as mandatory what was a culturally couched form of an ethical precept, while others have perhaps glibly eliminated as cultural some aspect of a commandment with deep moral significance.

This aspect of the discussion has a considerable impact in relation to the legitimate place and action of women in the home, in society at large and in the church. We need to recognize that the books of the Bible were written at times and in places where the oppression of women was especially grievous. We must also note that the biblical revelation was more generous to women than the practice of surrounding nations[10] (and, alas, often of Christian communities throughout church history!). The great problem for Christianity is not that biblical egalitarians have been carried away by their desire to emulate secular feminism. Rather, the problem appears to be that Bible-believing people have permitted themselves to fall below

---

[10]For details, see chapters five and twenty-two in this volume.

biblical standards because they were unduly influenced by surrounding societies in which oppression prevailed in spite of centuries of Christian witness.

First Corinthians 11:3-16 deals with the significance of a "head covering" for women while they are praying and prophesying in the gathered church. The significance of a head covering appears to be a cultural factor that is quite diverse in various times and places. Indeed, because of the diverse nature of Corinth itself—a Roman colony situated at the center of the Greek world—it is nearly impossible to know for certain what would have been normal for Corinthian culture as such. In the contemporary Western world such head coverings (whatever they were in fact) have little to no social significance. Thus this is rightly understood to be a cultural issue and a matter of personal choice for a believer today.

Moreover, this passage probably does not relate to a "headship"[11] of any man in relation to any woman but to the relationship of husband and wife within the home, in relation to the reputation of Christian women. It is therefore of some interest that evangelical patriarchalists almost to a person reject altogether the one clear *prescription* in this passage (1 Cor 11:6, that women must have their heads covered when praying and prophesying). Yet at the same time they wish to use the passage as theological evidence for the subordination of women to men in the church and home—to the point that some will even argue for eternal subordination within the ontological Trinity[12] in order to make this lesser point!

In I Corinthians 14:34-35 we have a case of a fairly evidential ad hoc prescription. If the passage is authentic, as most believe,[13] Paul surely did not intend to mandate total silence, since he permits women to pray and prophesy in church (I Cor 11), and congregational singing and response do not appear to be forbidden to women in this passage. Instead Paul seems to be forbidding an activity that carried cultural shame—women's speaking publicly to men other than their husbands—thus bringing disrepute on the gathering of believers for worship. In principle Paul's concern to avoid cultural disrepute would apply today to both men and women, though in Corinth at this time it was clearly specifically applicable to the women involved.

---

[11]In this book we do not use *headship* to mean "leadership" (as patriarchalists have trained people to do) but to refer to whatever meaning is intended in a given text.

[12]See note 2 in chapter nineteen in this volume and Kevin Giles's refutation of this perspective.

[13]See especially the discussion in chapter nine in this volume.

Conclusion

It appears to be a sad reality that most of the differences between patriarchalists and egalitarians in the present gender debate are hermeneutically based, if one includes exegesis as a dimension of hermeneutics. It is hoped that by the articulation of these basic hermeneutical principles—on which most people on both sides of the debate would agree—a more genuine dialogue might develop on both sides, with much less heat and acrimony. What I have tried to set forth in brief in this essay, then, are some fundamental principles of biblical hermeneutics, so that first of all we might recognize areas of basic agreement. At the same time, I have offered brief descriptions of how these basic principles might apply from an egalitarian perspective to various texts that hold central place in this ongoing debate. A fuller application of these principles to the basic texts and issues may be found in the biblical and theological chapters in this volume.

21

HERMENEUTICS AND THE
GENDER DEBATE

Gordon D. Fee

It is of some interest that the present gender debate is primarily an event taking place among evangelical Christians. For fundamentalists this is a closed issue. Their selective and literalistic approach to Scripture has won the day for eternal patriarchy. For more moderate or liberal Christians it is also a closed issue, with patriarchy dismissed as culturally outdated. At the end of the day, the primary differences among the three forms of Protestant faith are hermeneutical, having to do with both the meaning of texts (exegesis) and their application, but it is especially so among evangelicals involved in the debate over patriarchy and gender equality. Unfortunately, on this issue there is often a tendency on both sides to dismiss by name calling. But it is also common among patriarchalists to argue that egalitarian hermeneutics resort to a "special hermeneutic" to arrive at their conclusions. In some cases it has been further argued that this "special hermeneutic" opens the floodgates to an assortment of evils, such as rejection of biblical authority and acceptance of homosexual practices.[1]

This chapter[2] addresses these matters by examining some fundamental hermeneutical issues that divide the two sides, as well as by articulating a hermeneutic that leads to genuine obedience to Christ and is at the same time consonant with the gospel of grace and gifting—and with Paul's own rejection of law keeping. Such a hermeneutic is preferred to one that tends to turn questions of gender relationships into a form of law in which "roles" and "structures" are placed on the same

---

[1]This, of course, is not true at all and looks very much like a scare tactic rather than an honest interaction with hermeneutical issues as such. See also chapter twenty-three in this volume.

[2]Some of this material appeared in earlier form in Gordon D. Fee, *Gospel and Spirit: Issues in New Testament Hermeneutics* (Peabody, Mass.: Hendrickson, 1991), pp. 24-51.

level as the ethical obligation to love one's neighbor. In order to get there we need to go back to the beginning: why hermeneutics at all? And what does it mean for us to speak hermeneutically from a particular (in this case, evangelical) doctrine of Scripture?

Why Hermeneutics?

By its very nature, human speech—the use of symbols (words) to convey meaning—requires hermeneutics. When we speak we tend to think of it rather straightforwardly: *my* thoughts, expressed in words common to both of us, heard by *your* ears and recorded and deciphered by *your* mind. Unfortunately, however, between the mind of the speaker and that of the hearer are symbols—chiefly words, sometimes inflections or body language—so that what is intended as straightforward speech is commonly misunderstood.

Brief dialogue between two people who know each other well usually has a high degree of understanding, especially since dialogue allows for clarification. But the possibility of misunderstanding is increased as one is distanced from his or her hearer or reader—when, for example, monologue replaces dialogue, or the speaker is unknown to the hearer(s), or writing replaces speaking. When one adds other distancing factors—especially time, culture and a second language—the possibility of misunderstanding is heightened all the more, unless the writer has tried to be particularly sensitive to such distancing factors. But even then the degree of understanding is predicated very much on the degree of common experience.

It is this factor—our distance from the biblical writers in time and culture—that demands that we be good exegetes, if we are truly to hear Scripture as God's eternal Word. We must wrestle with *their* use of words, syntax and literary forms, which express *their* ideas, and we must hear those ideas within both the author's and the readers' cultural contexts and presuppositions, if ever we are adequately to understand what they intended by their words.

But that is only one part of the task, and it is one that we can engage in with a relative degree of objectivity—although it is also true that any interpreter always brings to a text a considerable amount of cultural baggage and personal bias. The other side of the task, however, and for the interpretation of Scripture the urgent one, is relevance. What does the biblical author's intended meaning, as expressed in these ancient texts, mean for us today? At this point very much depends on the presuppositions of the interpreter. Here is where evangelical and liberal divide, where Pentecostal and dispensationalist, or Baptist and Presbyterian, part company.

Many evangelicals, of course, tend to think the answer lies in finding the meaning of the text itself; and sometimes that is true. But very often it is not so. After all, there are a large number of evangelicals who claim to take Paul's prohibition regarding women's speaking in the assembly (I Cor 14:34-35) at face value, yet they reject altogether the prohibition six verses later in I Corinthians 14:39 ("do not forbid speaking in tongues"). By what kind of tortured hermeneutics does such a thing happen, one wonders.

What the text means as an eternal word for *us* is the crucial hermeneutical question. Since one's presuppositions determine so much at this point, we need to examine the basic presupposition common to all evangelicals that will distinguish us both from other expressions of Christianity and from other religious expressions: the nature of Scripture.

Scripture and Religious Authority

Evangelical Protestantism identifies itself by its adherence to the biblical documents as inspired Scripture and therefore as the basis of religious authority for its theology and life in the world. But what does it mean for us to name as Scripture these documents that were written in recognizable human language, in largely recoverable historical contexts of a roughly fifteen-hundred-year span some nineteen-hundred-plus years ago? To answer that requires us to articulate a few presuppositions about the nature of religious authority in general, before particularizing our understanding of religious authority.

Let's begin with three preliminary observations.

1. The question of religious authority is an ultimate one, and ultimately we are dealing with the triune God. The problems lie with the penultimates—how God communicates or reveals himself, or what authoritatively mediates God and God's will to humankind.

2. A person's basic authority is ultimately a matter of faith; that is, one makes a faith commitment of some kind that says "This plus this," or "This not that," has authority in my life or church. This is so even if one does not articulate it.

3. Related to this is the reality that one cannot finally *prove* one's authority to be the correct one. What one can hope to show is the reasonableness of it. Thus, for example, just as a historian cannot prove the resurrection of Jesus but can nonetheless show how the resurrection seems to make the best sense of all the available historical data, so we cannot prove the Bible to be God's Word, but we can show by a variety of evidence that it makes good sense to believe it to be so.

Religious authority itself is of two kinds: either (1) it is *external* to oneself (so-called objective authority), or (2) it is *internal* (so-called subjective). External authority is of three kinds: (a) a sacred book, (b) an authoritative person(s) (sometimes = the founder) or (c) a community of persons (sometimes = tradition). Internal authority is of two kinds: reason and experience.

Each of these has its problem areas. For external authority there is always the question of authentication: why this one and not another. The problem with internal authority is that it lacks any means of verification or absoluteness. People with similar religious experience or a common view of reason may find support in one another, but the ultimate authority lies with oneself—it is *my* experience, after all, or *my* reason—and the result is the autonomy of the individual. This idolatry, the autonomy of reason and the individual—which reflects a failure to take the Fall seriously enough—divides the Christian from most Western non-Christians as well as the evangelical from the liberal.

The evangelical stance on the question of religious authority is that our basic authority is external. This is predicated on the prior theological grounds (which we find eminently reasonable) of the nature of God and the reality of the Fall. We believe that our vision of God was distorted by the Fall and therefore that God cannot be *discovered* through our reason or experience; that is, God cannot be known from below, as it were. God must reveal himself if he is to be known at all. We further believe that God has so revealed himself: by deeds, in a Person and through a book that both reports and interprets those deeds and that Person. Because ultimately we know the Person, or hear the gospel, through the book, we take the book to be our primary penultimate authority. That is, we believe that this is the way God chose to reveal and to communicate. The other forms of authority (tradition, reason, experience) in various ways authenticate, verify or support, but all must themselves finally be authenticated by Scripture.

The church has traditionally tried to find ways to verbalize this conviction regarding the ultimate revelatory nature of Scripture so as to safeguard it from being watered down, either by one of the other kinds of authority on the one hand or by the drifts of culture or collective fallenness on the other. Out of such concern arose various attempts to articulate the doctrine of the inspiration of Scripture by the Holy Spirit. By this articulation we were first of all affirming that because Scripture is ultimately inspired by the Spirit of God, it is self-authenticating. In the final analysis, we believe that the authority is intrinsic. God has spoken—and will continue to speak—here. Let the lion out of the cage; it will defend itself. At the same time we were articulating our conviction that God himself is the ultimate source of the Christian faith, as it is revealed or defined in our sacred book.

The Nature of Evangelical Hermeneutics

It is *the doctrine of inspiration*—the tenet that God inspired not only the people who spoke but also the words they spoke—that distinguishes the evangelical view of Scripture and also forces us to wrestle with the issues of hermeneutics. Inspiration maintains that God indeed "spoke all these words and said . . ." But it does not maintain that God *dictated* all these words. To the contrary it recognizes, indeed argues, that *the Bible is God's Word spoken in human words in history.*[3] As God's Word it has eternal relevance; God addresses us. It is ours to hear and obey. But as human words in history the eternal Word has historical particularity. None of the words was spoken in a vacuum. Rather they were all addressed to, and conditioned by, the specific historical context in which they were spoken.

Evangelical hermeneutics therefore, by its very understanding of the nature of Scripture, must always be interacting with the intersection of the human and divine in these words that are believed also to be *the* Word. Thus we must struggle against the tendency to come down on either side (the human or the divine) in such a way as effectively to negate the other.

For example, though sympathetic, an evangelical rejects the fundamentalist's anxiety over the need for *absolute* authority, which tends thereby to replace the authority of the Word with the authority of the interpreter. To arrive at such an absolute the fundamentalist tends to see Scripture as a divine word *only*, and thus merely pays lip service to its human authors. As with Docetists or Apollinarians in Christology, the Word may appear to be human, but in reality the divine has been so superimposed on the human as to eliminate its genuine humanity almost altogether.

On the other hand, the evangelical also sympathizes with, but finally rejects, the liberal's fear of imposing on the church—in the name of God—rules that seem to be more arbitrary than loving, or dogmas that are difficult for moderns to swallow. Here, as with Arian Christology, the error lies in an affirmation of the human that diminishes—or negates altogether—the divine. All too often the emphasis on the human side of Scripture results in the hearing of *a human* word more than *the* Word

---

[3]This is adapted from George Eldon Ladd, *The New Testament and Criticism* (Grand Rapids, Mich.: Eerdmans, 1967), p. 12.

of God. Scripture is therefore primarily "God-talk" by us rather than "thus says the Lord."

Although not all of our fear on this side may be fair or well grounded, the evangelical response to such hermeneutics is still valid. Such an attitude toward Scripture tends to divest it of its divine authority. Rather than a powerful word from God that addresses us and sits in ultimate judgment on our impoverished human lives, what is left of Scripture is the meager results of Western rationalism with its pallid moralism and a historical criticism that sits in heavy judgment on the text itself. If we select only parts of Scripture as God's Word or listen only to what is compatible with contemporary broad-mindedness, how does the God who judged human wisdom as folly through the scandal of the cross speak his judgments on our fallenness and do it with any authority? In such case God speaks only what we think God should speak, only what is palatable to certain political or economic convictions, or finally only what *we* allow him to say. The final word and judgment are ours. That seems to us to be too great a price to pay to be contemporary or incarnational or "loving." The scriptural view is that one must speak the *truth* in love.

So evangelicals feel compelled to reject those hermeneutical stances that see Scripture either as a divine word in such a way as to divest it of its truly human character or as a human word in such a way as to blunt or negate its also being God's very Word. But to steer between these two polarities, to see Scripture as *both* human and divine, is not without its own difficulties and tensions.

First, the intersection of the eternal Word with historical particularity leaves us with far more ambiguities than some feel comfortable with. What do we do with the holy war and the slaughter of nations? How do we reconcile God's abundant mercy with the lament that speaks of dashing Babylonian children's heads against rocks? What do we do with the holy kiss, charismatic gifts, head coverings, the mode of baptism, the sovereignty of God and human freedom, to name but a few items where evangelicals who hold the *same* view of Scripture are deeply divided as to what it means for our lives at specific points?

The longing for absoluteness in all matters, which compels the fundamentalist mindset, is ever with the evangelical as well—precisely because of the conviction that Scripture is *God's* Word above all. Since God is unseen and known only by revelation and faith, and must finally be trusted, the need for certainty is often vested in the penultimate that leads us to God. Such a need drove the Pharisee to put a hedge around the law and the legalist to put a hedge around certain behaviors, in

order to keep people within the boundaries. For some, it is too much to trust in
God without absolute certainty, which of course is its own form of idolatry.

Hence there is always pressure from this side of our fallenness to eliminate ambiguity. If God himself is infallible, then the text of his Word must be infallible. If
the text is infallible, then there must be an infallible understanding of it. But that
is not an evangelical syllogism. The text itself in its intent is infallible, we would
argue, because of its character as God's Word. And we insist on this, because even
if we disagree on the meaning of the text, our hope lies in the text itself to have its
inherent power as God's Word to correct us.

But the buck stops there, at the text and its intent, as to what is infallible. God
did not choose to give us a series of timeless, non-culture-bound theological propositions to be believed and imperatives to be obeyed. Rather he chose to speak his
eternal Word *this* way, in historically particular circumstances and in every kind of
literary genre. By the very way God gave us this Word, he locked in the ambiguity.
So one should not fight God and insist that he give us his Word another way or, as
we are more apt to do, rework his Word along theological or cultural prejudgments
that turn it into a mine field of principles, propositions or imperatives but denude
it of its ad hoc character as truly human. The ambiguity is a part of what God did
in giving us his Word *this* way. Our task is to recognize and capitalize on what God
has done.

Second, Scripture's historical particularity—the fact that the eternal word was
expressed in specific historical and cultural contexts—brings with it a degree of *accommodation.* At issue here is whether the vessel (the cultural context) is also somehow vested with a dimension of the eternal. Here too is an area of evangelical anxiety, since what some see as part of the cultural trappings others would contend for
as having eternal value. That there is *some* accommodation is a matter on which all
agree—even the fundamentalist, albeit usually unwittingly. But how much, and of
what kind(s)—these are the burning questions. And here is where some sore spots
among evangelicals are openly festering, especially on gender issues.

Third, inherent in the conviction that Scripture is both human and divine is the
recognition that it has *diversity within an essential unity.* The diversity results from its
historical particularities, the unity from its ultimately divine origin. But how to articulate this unity and diversity is another area in which evangelicals are not all
agreed. The traditional hermeneutical principle here is the *analogy of Scripture*—
Scripture interprets Scripture, because God is its ultimate author and therefore
gives it unity. While I would argue vigorously for the validity of this principle, the

problem arises at the point of working it out in practice. Sometimes, in the name of this hermeneutical principle, what appears to be a highly improbable meaning is superimposed on a text in order to make it conform to other texts for the sake of unity—which is often the result of a prior commitment to the *shape* of that unity as much as to the unity itself. Unity is often understood to mean uniformity. That Scripture might reveal a diverse witness on some matters is summarily ruled out before one even looks at the texts.

While it is certainly true that one can make a beautiful quilt out of whole cloth, it is also true that one can do so out of patchwork. Any two pieces of patchwork lying side by side in isolation could indeed appear to be discordant. But when those two become part of a whole, with pattern and design, the glory of the quilt's unity lies precisely in the patterns of diversity.

Granted, to insist that the very nature of Scripture has locked into it a degree of ambiguity, accommodation and diversity causes some people to capitulate in despair—either toward the certainties of fundamentalism or toward the ambiguities of liberalism. Far better to opt for the radical middle. If God gave us his Word *this* way, then our task is to hold on to both realities—its eternality and historical particularity—with equal vigor. If we cannot always have absolute certainty as to meaning or application, we can certainly move toward a higher degree of common understanding.

The way toward that higher level of commonality, I would argue, is still to be found at the crucial point of authorial intentionality, which we would insist is also the Holy Spirit's intentionality.[4] After all, speech has intent; and if we are to hear God's Word rightly for ourselves, we must begin with that original intent. If God did not speak timeless aphorisms, he did speak an eternal Word. That Word had specific intent in its historically particular moments. Our task is to discover and hear that Word in terms of God's original intent as expressed by the biblical writer, and then hear that same Word again in our own historical setting, even when our particulars are quite different from those of the original setting.

But this does not mean we need to keep their historical particulars intact as well. For good or ill, history brings changes to culture, a fact that is especially so for

---

[4]This, of course, is a tacit rejection of postmodern assumptions, especially as expressed in reader-response criticism, where it is argued that meaning is to be found only with the reader and the reader's interaction with a text. For a critique of these assumptions, see the appendix in the third edition of Gordon D. Fee, *New Testament Exegesis: A Handbook for Students and Pastors* (Louisville, Ky.: Westminster John Knox, 2002), pp. 181-85.

Western culture. Instead of seeing this as a debility, we should recognize the greater glory of Scripture and praise God for it. That he would speak so directly to *their* contexts is what gives us hope that God will always through that same Word speak again and again to our own historical context as well as to all others.

Tension Points in Evangelical Hermeneutics

One can expect general agreement among evangelicals on most of what has been said to this point. Our differences result when all of us look at the same texts, all with a similar view of Scripture as the Word of God, yet either understand the *original meaning* of the texts in different ways or have different views as to how they do or do not apply. While this is true for all sorts of matters of theology, ethics and church practice,[5] it is especially true for the so-called gender debate.

At issue finally in this debate is the basis on which we construct our theological statements about what it means to be human, as both male and female, and then how this theological understanding works out in the practical areas of relationships between men and women in church and home. Our principal hope for greater consistency and larger agreement in these matters, it seems to me, lies still with the first task of hermeneutics—the careful exegesis of texts, which has the *original intent of the text* as its primary goal. This is why chapters four through thirteen of this volume are devoted to the original intent of the several "disputed" texts. Since God chose to communicate himself to us through human speech in historically particular circumstances, we are locked into a hermeneutical process that demands that we listen carefully first of all to what is intended; there alone lies our hope of hearing what God wants us to hear.[6]

But to argue for discerning the intention of texts as the *prior* hermeneutical task does not resolve all our difficulties. It is merely the way forward. Several hermeneutical tasks remain. The rest of this essay will explore two areas of application, re-

---

[5] On these distinctions see chapter fourteen, under the heading "A Hermeneutical Starting Point."

[6] Authorial intentionality also serves as a corrective, or sets some limits, as to what texts may *not* be made to mean. One need only think of how B. B. Warfield interpreted "the perfect" in I Corinthians 13:10 to refer to the canon of New Testament Scripture to recognize the cruciality of original intent. It must be a hermeneutical axiom for the straight prose of a letter that what neither the author nor his readers could have understood cannot possibly be the "meaning" of the text. On this matter Paul himself set the limits. In I Corinthians 5:9 he is quite upset with the Corinthian congregation because they have either misunderstood or, more likely, disregarded his instructions in an earlier letter. For him there is only one meaning to his words—*his* meaning; and they are quite blameworthy for having disregarded it.

lated to the two primary texts that divide us on gender issues (Eph 5:21-33; 1 Tim 2:11-12). The two areas of concern are tendencies on the part of some evangelicals (1) to create "theology by way of implication" rather than on the basis of clear and explicit statements in Scripture, and (2) to turn some ad hoc biblical imperatives into a form of Christian law requiring observance. In each case an alternative hermeneutical model is offered for consideration, which attempts to be true to the intent of the text of Scripture on the one hand and to the intent of the gospel on the other. At the same time it takes into consideration the realities of ambiguity, accommodation and diversity.

Theology by Way of Implication

It is an evangelical axiom that what is absolutely basic to Christian theology is clearly and explicitly taught by intention in Scripture.[7] The universal sinfulness of humankind, for example, is based on passages like Romans 3:23, where Paul by inspiration of the Spirit says plainly that "all [Jew and Gentile alike] have sinned and fall short of the glory of God." Furthermore, Scripture without ambiguity has a single witness on this matter and other matters like it.

On the other hand, this axiom does not mean that all Christian theology is so explicitly set forth. Many things that evangelical—and other—Christians believe to be true about God and the world are either derived from the primary texts or learned by way of implication. But most such theological statements are of a secondary nature, which does not mean that they are unimportant but that they do not have the same level of import as primary theological constructs.[8] For example, evangelicals believe that the material creation, including the human body, is good. This is based on Genesis 1 and Paul's affirmations about the body in such passages as 1 Corinthians 6:13-14 and 15:35-57. But there is considerable disagreement over the nature of the resurrected body and over how "the creation itself will be liberated from its bondage to decay" (Rom 8:21), precisely because of the ambiguity on these matters in the New Testament itself.[9]

---

[7] Some of what is said here is also covered by Roger Nicole in the preceding chapter, under the heading "Prescriptive and Descriptive Texts."

[8] On the distinction between the primary and secondary natures of our doctrinal statements, see chapter fourteen, under the heading "A Hermenutical Starting Point."

[9] Take the inherent tension created by the narrative in Luke 24:42 and Paul's statement that "flesh and blood cannot inherit the kingdom" but must undergo substantial change (1 Cor 15:50). On the question of the nature of the resurrected body, see the vigorous interchange between Norman Geisler and Murray Harris. In response to Harris's solid exegetical analysis of the biblical data (*Raised Immor-*

One can think of dozens of such matters. For example, the Pentecostal doctrine of tongues as "the initial physical evidence" of Spirit baptism is derived by implication from several passages in Acts that narrate such receptions of the Spirit. The baptistic mode of baptism by immersion is based on biblical narratives, plus the meaning of the verb *to baptize*, especially as it is assumed in Paul's letters (Rom 6:3-4; I Cor 12:13). Weekly (or daily) celebration of the Eucharist is based on narratives only. In all these cases, and many more like them, one can offer *theological* reasons for one's point of view. But in fact on such matters evangelical Christians are deeply divided, because the theological positions are derived by implication, not by explicit scriptural instruction.

And this is the reason for division among evangelicals when it comes to men and women's relationships or roles in both church and home—because there is no *explicit* teaching in the New Testament either about this relationship or about church order, structures or worship.[10] That is, one may derive a patriarchal view of church and home by way of implication from a certain understanding of a few texts, but nowhere does Scripture explicitly say, for example, that only men may hold certain church offices—especially since the idea of "offices" (as having priority and needing to be "filled" by someone) does not appear at all in the New Testament.

Paul thus assumes a Greco-Roman patriarchal culture when he instructs Christians on how to live within it in Ephesians 5:21–6:9, but he does not thereby bless the culture itself nor explicitly instruct men to exercise authority over their wives. Furthermore, there is far more ambiguity in the biblical evidence than patriarchalists seem ready to allow. For example, the two household codes in Colossians and Ephesians are especially "elitist," directed toward people like Philemon,[11] in whose villas some house churches would have met. But such households would also have been in the minority in terms of the overall number of believers; furthermore,

---

tal: Resurrection and Immortality in the New Testament [Grand Rapids, Mich.: Eerdmans, 1983]), Geisler wrote his The Battle for the Resurrection (Nashville: Thomas Nelson, 1987)—a clear example of trying to raise a secondary level matter to the first level and then to excommunicate those who disagree. See Harris's irenic response: From Grave to Glory: Resurrection in the New Testament (Grand Rapids, Mich.: Zondervan/Academie, 1990), pp. 337-463.

[10]On this matter see chapter fourteen above.

[11]It is surprising how seldom the connection between the two household codes in Colossians 3 and Ephesians 5 and the letter to Philemon is made in the literature. The certain evidence for the connection is the first expression of the "code" in Colossians 3:18–4:1, where the word to slaves is equal in quantity to the words to all the other relationships in the household. Should this surprise us, given the presence of Onesimus at the reading of both this letter (Col 4:9) and the letter to Philemon?

Paul's letter to the Ephesians assumes a full household, with husband and wife, children and slaves. One wonders, for example, how this passage would have been heard in Nympha's house church (Col 4:15). Not only was she the householder, and therefore most likely gave leadership to the church that met in her house, but there would have been no husband to submit to, and she would have assumed the man's role in the other relationships. Moreover, the word to wives has to do with the *householder's* wife, not the wife in a slave couple, who herself would be required to obey the householder, not her husband, because she was owned by the former.

Furthermore, the structures evident among the wealthy in the typical Roman villa seem to be less evident in the households found in a typical *insula.*[12] Thus it is of interest to note the differences between how Paul speaks of Philemon's household and the church that met there and how he speaks of that of Priscilla and Aquila in Romans 16:3-5. In the former case Paul greets both Philemon and his wife Apphia; but when greeting the church he uses the singular pronoun ("and the church that meets in *your* [Philemon's] home"). Priscilla and Aquila, on the other hand, were artisans (tentmakers), who would not have lived in a villa but (most likely) in an insula, where the house church would have met in a large room upstairs. In their case, and in contrast to Philemon, not only is Priscilla mentioned first,[13] but Paul sends greetings to the church that meets "at *their* house" (cf. I Cor 16:19).

Given both the ambiguity of the New Testament evidence and the lack of explicit teaching on patriarchy as the norm in the new creation, to derive a theology of patriarchy from the Ephesians passage would thus seem to be a dubious form of theologizing at best. There is no question that these texts *reflect* the patriarchal worldview of the Greco-Roman world, but they do not bless that worldview theologically. Rather, Paul's instructions (like Peter's in I Pet 2:18–3:7) have to do with how to live out the life of Christ in such a cultural setting. Christian theology that requires adherence from all believers in all times and places needs to be made of sterner stuff—derived from clear, explicit texts whose intent is specifically to instruct regarding what Christians are to believe.[14]

---

[12]This was often a large dwelling along a city or town street; business was carried on downstairs in rooms that opened onto the roadway, while the family primarily occupied rooms upstairs. See Carolyn Osiek and David L. Balch, *Families in the New Testament World: Households and House Churches* (Louisville, Ky.: Westminster John Knox, 1997), pp. 18-19.

[13]On the significance of this matter, see the discussion in chapter six of his volume.

[14]Cf. Nicole's principle regarding "peripheral and central doctrines" (in chapter twenty, "Peripheral Versus Central Doctrines" section). See also chapter eleven and the discussion of *kephalē* in chapter eight of this volume.

A key text used to derive patriarchy as a *theological* concept is I Timothy 2:11-15, where Paul appeals by way of analogy to the creation narrative.[15] Here Paul is addressing a situation in the Ephesian church where some elders had gone astray. These men in turn had apparently led some younger widows astray with them, probably using these women and their domiciles for the propagation of the false teaching.[16] It is the deceitful nature of this teaching that concerns Paul. After all, later he excoriates the men (and women) who are spreading the falsehoods as following "deceiving spirits and things taught by demons" (I Tim 4:1) and clearly says that some of the younger widows have "already turned away to follow Satan" (I Tim 5:15). Precisely for this reason he also urges (in contrast to his explicit advice given in I Cor 7:39-40) that these younger widows marry and have children (I Tim 5:14). The language in this latter passage echoes that of I Timothy 2:8-15, where Paul is addressing both the men (I Tim 2:8) and the women (I Tim 2:9-15) with regard to proper demeanor in worship. It should also be pointed out that after dealing with the younger widows in I Timothy 5:11-15, Paul goes on in I Timothy 5:17-25 to address how Timothy is to deal with the straying elders.

Paul appeals to the Genesis narrative to support his not permitting a woman to teach a man in order to domineer over him.[17] That Paul is using the Genesis narrative for ad hoc purposes seems plain in light of his first assertion in I Timothy 2:14, that "Adam was not the one deceived." Paul's interest in Genesis is with the language of "deception"—which does not come from the actual narrative of the Fall (Gen 3:1-7) but from the woman, who responded to God's "What is this that you have done?" by excusing herself and blaming the serpent, who "tricked me, and I ate." Paul's interest lies with the younger widows in Ephesus, whose deception by Satan is addressed in the rest of I Timothy 2:14-15, where he reflects the Genesis

---

[15]It is true, of course, that some use Ephesians 5:23 ("the husband is the head of the wife as Christ is the head of the church") to theologize regarding patriarchy, but that is full of dubious exegetical jumps, as is pointed out elsewhere in this volume. The only other texts where Paul uses this head-body imagery are Ephesians 4:15-16 and Colossians 2:19, and in both cases his point is neither leadership nor lordship. Rather his point is that the body (the church) is dependent on the head (Christ) for its ongoing life in the world—as the wife was dependent on her husband in this cultural setting.

[16]See I Timothy 5:13 and 2 Timothy 3:6-7. For a full exposition of this position, based on what is actually said in the Pastoral Epistles, see Gordon D. Fee, *1 and 2 Timothy, Titus*, NIBC (Peabody, Mass.: Hendrickson, 1988), pp. 5-10. Paul had already anticipated some of the elders' going astray in his "farewell speech" to them, recorded in Acts 20:30.

[17]Regarding this as the probable meaning of the much-debated word *authentein*, see the discussion by Linda Belleville in chapter twelve above.

narrative: "the woman . . . was deceived and became a sinner." But as he will urge later (I Tim 5:14), her salvation rests in her "childbearing" (cf. I Tim 2:15).

All of this to say that Paul's use of the Genesis narrative is scarcely explicit theological instruction on patriarchy with regard to ministry in the church.[18] His concern is *not* with establishing patriarchy (from man's priority in creation) but with the woman's deception by Satan (which is being repeated again in Ephesus). Paul prohibits a woman from teaching a man so as to dominate him because he does not want the women in Ephesus to replay the sin of Eve, who was deceived and led Adam into sin.

Thus this ad hoc reference to the Genesis narrative is simply not concerned with establishing a new-creation mandate based on a "creation order" that gives man authority in home and church. Furthermore, the Genesis narrative itself does not make Adam's priority in creation *a theological point*. Rather, a straightforward reading of that narrative makes two basic points: that humanity created in God's likeness is not complete with only the male, and that the two are made *for each other*—so that in the sexual union the man and the woman actually become "one flesh." Thus the concern is with (1) their differentiation, (2) their bearing God's image together and (3) their unity in the marriage union.

My point, then, is that no New Testament text explicitly teaches patriarchy as the divine order that is to prevail across the two biblical covenants. It is also highly questionable exegetically whether in these few texts Paul intends even by implication to set forth patriarchy as the divine order under the new covenant. And here is where the issues of ambiguity and diversity of witness come to the fore.

First, what Paul is said to be arguing here by way of analogy is not explicitly taught anywhere else in Scripture. In the Genesis narrative patriarchy in fact begins with the Fall and is expressly related to the woman's role in the Fall (Gen 3:16). But the analogy pointed to here—that man is to rule woman because he was created prior to woman—occurs nowhere else in all of Scripture.

Second, the ambiguity of using this analogy from the Genesis narrative for such a theological construct is that Paul appeals to this narrative in two earlier instances in his letters, where a rather different picture emerges. First, in 2 Corinthians 11:3 Paul also refers to Eve and her being "deceived by the serpent's cunning"; but in this case it has to do with the whole church in Corinth—including presumably

---

[18]By way of analogy, it is difficult to imagine the Protestant Reformation's ever having occurred if the doctrine of "justification by faith" were based on incidental evidence like this.

some male leaders—being deceived by false teachers. Second, and more significant, in Romans 5:12-21, precisely because Paul is contrasting the "original sin" in Eden with the work of Christ, it is Adam, not Eve, who is responsible for the sin that has fully infected the human race. This is also an ad hoc creation on Paul's part. But in this case a very clear theological point is being made regarding the universality of human sinfulness; and because Christ is put forward as the "second Adam," the universality of human sinfulness is not expressed in terms of Eve's deception and fall but as having come through the man.

Thus Paul uses the Genesis narrative in a variety of ways. The only place where *theological* points are drawn from the narrative is where he refers to Adam's sin. The two references to Eve have to do with her being deceived by Satan and his concern that such deception is being repeated in his churches.

All of this to suggest, then, that a theology that articulates what all Christians in all places and at all times should believe needs to be drawn from texts that teach such theology explicitly or from texts where the theology is implicitly embedded in what is being said. But in the latter instances, such theology should also reflect the universal perspective of Scripture, without ambiguity and diverse witness. Where there is ambiguity and diversity of witness, it would seem that what is being "taught" is Christian truth that is being accommodated to that culture and its structures.

A Hermeneutic of Gospel and Spirit

Related to the difficulties with establishing patriarchy as a divine order for all cultures is the necessity in an egalitarian culture to set boundaries as to what women may or may not do in the home and church. The net result is that patriarchy thus turns the gospel of grace and Spirit gifting into a set of laws to be adhered to.

Take the household code in Ephesians 5:21-33. Here we are often told that the man is under divine obligation to be the ruler of the household. But that does not appear as an imperative in this passage—even by implication. It was simply the cultural assumption that he would be, and *requiring* it by way of imperative would be outside of Paul's cultural frame of reference. In fact, the only two imperatives in this passage are for the wife to submit to her husband and for the husband to love his wife as Christ loved the church. The imperative to the wife would not have been seen as a heavy burden; after all, submission to one another is at the very heart of the Christian ethic (see especially Phil 2:3-4, where Christ becomes the paradigm).

The radical imperative is what was said to the husband, who by law had all the rights and privileges in the Greco-Roman household. In a situation that simply begged for abuse, Paul is calling on the Christian householder to love his wife— not meaning sexually in this case but by a constant giving of himself for her. This, of course, also lies at the very heart of the Christian ethic, in which the whole Torah is summed up in a single imperative from Leviticus 19:18: "Love your neighbor as yourself."[19] So radical is Paul's imperative within its Greco-Roman culture that he repeats it three times in this passage (Eph 5:25, 28, 33)—and then uses the example of Christ's giving himself redemptively in his death for us as the paradigm.

Thus what needs to be noted in the end is that there is no imperative regarding the structures of the household—these were simply assumed. The only imperatives are those that are fully in keeping with the gospel of grace and the Spirit.

One problem with turning this passage into a transcultural mandate for patriarchalism is what to do when the culture shifts as radically as it has in the West over the past century-plus. If current English-speaking North American culture is not fully egalitarian, by law it is now generally so in the public domain. Husbands and wives very often are equally educated; they often marry in part because they recognize complementary gifting in each other; and in a large number of cases both work outside the home, sometimes with the wife having a management position. It is common to hear some patriarchalists rail against this "demise of the family in Western culture"; but it is a cultural reality whether appreciated or not.

The issues for us have to do with how we live Christianly in this, or any other, culture. And here is where the hermeneutical issue comes to the fore. The contemporary Western home is a radically different thing from its Greco-Roman forebear. In order to uphold male rule in today's household, patriarchalists are regularly faced with the necessity of fine-tuning various rules and restrictions regarding "biblical gender roles." In the end, the gospel of grace and the Spirit is turned into a form of law, which gives rise to the pharisaic problem of needing to put a hedge around the law, deciding what is or is not "allowable" within its framework.

Peter's very pharisaic question "How many times must I forgive?" is now turned into "What constitutes wifely submission?" Or, "When husband and wife come to a stalemate in decision making, who has the last word?" One wonders whether Paul would laugh or cry! The gospel of grace and gifting leads to a different set of questions: How does one best serve the interests of the other? How does one en-

---

[19]This is across the board in the New Testament: see Matthew 22:34-40; Mark 12:28-34; Luke 10:25-28; Romans 13:8-10; Galatians 5:13-14.

courage the Spirit's gifting in the other? Questions like these cross all gender boundaries.

A similar kind of casuistry has had a long history in the evangelical church with regard to women's role in the church, especially with regard to "teaching men," based on an interpretation of 1 Timothy 2:12 as permanently subordinating women's ministry to men's authority. For example, with the advent of the modern missionary movement, single women regularly went abroad on the basis of their calling, whether sent out by the local church or not. After the women were successful in gaining converts and establishing growing churches, then the North American church stepped in and "ordered" the church under male leadership. Hypocritically (and with blatant racism) they "allowed" the woman missionary to teach the Bible to men in Africa or Asia but frequently forbade her to do so back home. The same kind of "putting a hedge around the law" has occurred more recently in patriarchal settings. For example, even though a woman who is a biblical scholar writes books that men read, and even though she is sometimes "allowed" to teach the Bible in a college classroom, she may not teach an adult Sunday school class in church when men are present—or if she may, it is still casuistry that makes it "allowable."

This kind of casuistic approach to law tends to prevail wherever patriarchalism is the "legal rule" of the church. The question is always framed in terms of legalistic boundaries rather than in terms of recognition of genuine giftedness by the Spirit. There would seem to be a much better way, and that is to read the two "limiting" texts as not making specific roles and structures obligatory for all times and places. Rather, since 1 Timothy 2 stands in tension with much else in Paul's letters, it is better understood as an ad hoc word intending to forbid some young widows from being carriers of the "diseased" teaching in Ephesus. Likewise, the household codes in Colossians and Ephesians are not intended at all to set boundaries but rather to encourage Christian deportment within an existing patriarchal culture. What the church should be encouraged to do is to recognize Spirit gifting wherever it is found and find ways of developing such gifting so that the whole church may benefit.

Conclusion

In the end, then, the hermeneutical questions raised by those who hold firmly to Scripture as God's eternal Word must take into account the nature of that Word as both human and divine. And because of this, we must be prepared to recognize and articulate the nature and kinds of ambiguity, accommodation and diversity that the double nature of Scripture forces on us. Within this hermeneutical framework our theology, ethics and church practice should be predicated on two firm foundational stones:

1. Only what is explicitly taught in Scripture by intention should be understood as obligatory for all believers, and what is merely implied in Scripture should accordingly be held in abeyance.

2. Our hermeneutics of imperatives should be driven by the gospel of grace and Spirit gifting, not by a new form of pharisaic legalism that tries to find ways to put a hedge around a form of Christian law.

22

A REDEMPTIVE-MOVEMENT
HERMENEUTIC

The Slavery Analogy

William J. Webb

The biblical texts regarding slaves have much to teach the church about how to understand and apply certain texts regarding women. In this essay I hope to show, by the use of a redemptive-movement hermeneutic, that an abolition of patriarchy is consistent with the abolition of slavery and is in keeping with the redemptive movement that pervades all of Scripture.

A Redemptive-Movement Model

There are two ways of approaching the Bible: (1) with a *redemptive-movement* or *redemptive-spirit* appropriation of Scripture, which encourages movement beyond the original application of the text in the ancient world, or (2) with a more static or stationary appropriation. A static approach understands the words of the text in isolation from their ancient historical-cultural context and with minimal—or no—emphasis on their underlying spirit. This restricts contemporary application to how the words of the text were applied in their original setting. But to do so actually can lead to a *mis*appropriation of the text, precisely because one has failed to apply the redemptive spirit of the text in a later cultural setting.

Figure 22.1 and the accompanying example illustrate a redemptive-movement approach I call the X⇒Y⇒Z principle.[1] Within the model, the *central position* (Y) represents particular words of the Bible at that stage of their development of a sub-

---

[1]This model and definitions section has been condensed from William J. Webb, *Slaves, Women and Homosexuals: Exploring the Hermeneutics of Cultural Analysis* (Downers Grove, Ill.: InterVarsity Press, 2001).

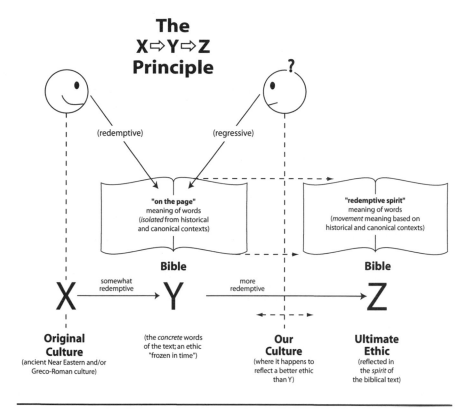

Figure 22.1. The X⇨Y⇨Z Principle

ject, if those words are understood in an isolated, "on the page" sense. On either side of the biblical text's words, one must ask the question of perspective. First, how is the text to be understood from the perspective of the *original culture* (X)? And then, what does the text look like in our culture, when our culture happens to reflect a more redemptive social ethic—closer to an *ultimate ethic* (Z)—than the ethic revealed in the culturally particularized words of the biblical text? From the one direction the biblical text appears redemptive; from the other direction it appears regressive.

The X⇒Y⇒Z principle illustrates how aspects of the biblical texts were *not* written to establish a utopian society with complete justice and equity.[2] They were

---

[2]While the X⇒Y⇒Z diagram here differs from an earlier one (see Webb, *Slaves, Women and Homosexuals*, p. 32), the changes simply represent an attempt to express the same ideas in a clearer way.

written within a cultural framework with limited, incremental moves toward an ultimate ethic.

To illustrate: Deuteronomy 23:15-16 instructs Israel to provide safety and refuge to slaves fleeing harsh treatment in a foreign country. Such a slave was to be given shelter, was permitted to live in any of Israel's cities and was not to be handed over to his or her master. The redemptive dimension of this slavery legislation sparkles brightly in comparison to that of the surrounding nations. Most ancient Near Eastern countries had extradition treaties and administered severe punishment to runaway slaves, their families and those who aided in their escape.

A static hermeneutic would apply this slavery-refuge text by staying strictly with the words on the page, read in isolation from their "movement" meaning. Rather than being led by the spirit-movement meaning of this text to cry out for the abolition of slavery, the static reader would permit slavery in our culture (because the Bible did)—although she or he might seek to show kindness toward runaway slaves within the church or to give refuge to slaves in abusive relationships. Such an approach to applying the Bible would emphasize the words of the text in a highly isolated sense, while missing the spirit of the text.

What we should live out in our modern culture is not the isolated or "on the page" words of the text but the *redemptive spirit* that the text reflects when read against its original culture. In applying the Bible to our era, we do not want to remain static with the isolated words of the text (Y). Rather, we need to move beyond the frozen-in-time, concrete specifics of the text and take the redemptive dimension of those words to a further redemptive level—toward an ultimate ethic, Z.

The Need for a Redemptive-Movement Hermeneutic

As various problematic components surface within the biblical texts on slaves and women, one strong impression emerges: a less-than-ultimate ethic in the treatment of slaves and women is reflected in various parts of Scripture. But rather than avoid these texts, we need to embrace them—even the difficult parts. After all, a good hermeneutic must be able to handle difficult texts as well as what we might deem to be easier.

Slavery texts: Falling short of an ultimate ethic. There exist a number of "not so pretty" components within the biblical slavery texts, where the treatment of slaves falls short of an ultimate ethic. We need to let the Bible's redemptive spirit take us beyond the original application of these texts.[3]

1. *Attitude/perspective of ownership/property.* The Bible accepts the treatment of human beings as property (e.g., Ex 12:44; 21:20-21, 32; Lev 22:11).

2. *Release of Hebrew slaves versus foreign slaves.* Foreign slaves in Israel did not experience the same humane treatment as did Israelite slaves with the seventh year of release (Lev 25:44-46; cf. 25:39-43).

3. *Using slaves for reproductive purposes.* Some Israelites struggling with infertility used their slaves to produce offspring (Gen 16:1-4; 30:3-4, 9-10).

4. *Sexual violation of a slave versus a free woman.* An Israelite man who raped a betrothed Israelite woman was to be put to death (Deut 22:25-27), whereas sexual violation of a betrothed slave woman resulted in a mere payment/offering of damages (Lev 19:20-22).

5. *Physical beating of a slave.* A slave owner could beat his slave severely without any penalty, provided the slave survived the beating by a couple of days (Ex 21:20-22).

6. *Value of a slave's life versus a free person's life.* The Torah legislation values a slave's life less than a free person's life (Ex 21:28-32).

We should note that within ancient Near Eastern culture, many of these texts were slightly to moderately redemptive. Nevertheless, the above practices cannot be said to reflect an ultimate ethic. One solution might be to legislate in our contemporary setting a much more humane treatment of slaves as persons, attempting to clean up these liabilities by allowing the redemptive spirit already in the slavery texts as a whole to be taken further. However, that would surely be a makeshift solution. What is really needed is a reworking of the sociological structure itself.

Women texts: Falling short of an ultimate ethic. As with the slavery texts, we need honestly to acknowledge numerous "not so pretty" biblical texts that illustrate a less-than-ultimate ethic in the treatment of women.[4] In these areas, better actions or dispositions toward human beings are both possible and desirable.

1. *Attitude/perspective of ownership/property.* Like slaves, women are often treated more as property than as people in the Old Testament. The wife is referred to as *be'ulath ba'al* ("a wife owned by her husband"; e.g., Deut 22:22), while her husband is sometimes referred to as her *ba'al* ("master") or *'adon* ("lord"; see Gen 18:12; Judg 19:26-27; Amos 4:1; 1 Pet 3:6).

2. *Less-than-adult, closer-to-a-child status.* Under biblical law, at marriage a woman

---

[3]For detailed bibliographic references for this and the next three biblical sketches, see ibid., pp. 73-82, 162-78.

[4]See the discussion in chapter five of this volume.

transferred from being under her father's authority to being under her husband's authority. The husband had the right to overturn his wife's religious vows with no less prerogative and authority than a father had in overturning the vows of his daughter.[5]

3. *Inheritance/ownership of property.* Property was generally inherited by sons, not daughters. Even though a daughter without a brother could inherit family property (Num 27:5-8), she was required to marry within her clan, since at marriage her property was assumed to transfer to her husband (Num 36).

4. *Virginity expectations.* The Bible expresses considerable concern for the virginity of females (e.g., Gen 24:16; Num 31:35; Esther 2:2, 17-19; Ps 45:14-15; Lk 1:27). The male, however, is never applauded for virginity. Furthermore, proof of virginity is required for females but not for males (Deut 22:13-19; see also Ezek 23:42-45; Mt 1:18-19), and a lack of virginity resulted in the stoning of females (but not males; Deut 22:20-21; see also Lev 21:9, 13-15).

5. *Adultery and extramarital sex legislation.* The Torah included an elaborate ritual for the wife suspected of adultery (Num 5:11-31) but no reciprocal ordeal for the husband. In the case of infidelity a wife was always to be stoned, whereas a husband was stoned only if his infidelity involved another man's wife (Lev 20:10; cf. Deut 22:22, 23-24).

6. *Divorce legislation.* Old Testament legislation assumes the right of the male to initiate divorce (Deut 21:14; 22:19, 29; 24:1-4); two of these texts (Deut 21:14; 24:1-4) imply that the male could initiate divorce if he simply found something displeasing in his wife. The lack of gender equity in divorce settlements along with these broad-based grounds for divorce left women in an extremely vulnerable position.

7. *Other features of biblical patriarchy.* The biblical portrait of women in society included many other components that would seem to benefit from a greater infusion of redemptive spirit: polygamy (e.g., Gen 4:19-24; 25:1-4; 26:34; 29:14-30; 35:23-24; 36:1-4; 46:10; 2 Sam 5:13; 12:11; 1 Kings 11:1-4; 2 Chron 11:18-21) and concubinage (e.g., Gen 16:1-4; 35:25-26; 2 Sam 5:13; 1 Kings 11:1-4; 2 Chron 11:18-21), levirate marriages (Deut 25:5-10; see also Gen 38:8; Ruth 4:5; Mt 22:24-28), unequal value of men and women in vow redemption (Lev 27:1-8), the double impurity for female offspring (compared to male offspring; Lev 12:4; see also 12:6-7), the passing on of tradition primarily to sons (Deut 4:9-10; 6:2,

---

[5]Numbers 30:1-16; notice that sons are not even mentioned in the discussion of daughters.

7, 20; 11:19, 21; 32:46), the treatment of women as trophies of war,[6] the treatment of women as spoils of battle (e.g., Num 31:25-32; Deut 21:10-14; see also 20:14), the husband's implied authority to physically discipline his wife (e.g., Jer 13:20-27; Ezek 16:32-42; 23:22-30; Hos 2:1-3, 10), the uneven focus in the book of Proverbs on contentious women,[7] the restriction of the old covenant sign of circumcision to males (Gen 17:14), along with the pejorative comparison of cowardly warriors with women (Is 19:16; Jer 50:37; 51:30; Nahum 3:13; cf. Judg 9:54).

To speak of this portrait of women as "sexist" would be anachronistic; indeed, relative to its culture the biblical treatment of women as a whole was redemptive. Yet it does not take a lot of imagination to figure out how one might improve on the treatment of women in these examples. As with the slavery texts, one solution might be to clean up some of these culture-based liabilities by permitting the redemptive spirit already within these texts as a whole to be taken much further, but still within the bounds of patriarchy. But again, such an approach seems to be only a makeshift solution. What is needed rather is a reworking of the sociological structure itself. At the very least, these texts point to the need for a redemptive-movement approach to applying the Bible.

To summarize several hermeneutical insights from this "not so pretty" section:

- A less-than-ultimate ethic in the treatment of slaves and women is a significant element in our Bible.

- We cannot assume that "just because something is in the Bible" it must reflect an ultimate ethic.

- A static or stationary (nonmovement) approach to Scripture does not resolve the problems presented in these "not so pretty" texts.

The Basis for a Redemptive-Movement Hermeneutic

Fortunately, these "not so pretty" texts are not the whole story. There exists a much more redemptive side to the biblical treatment of slaves and women. It is this positive side that supports the legitimacy of a redemptive-movement hermeneutic, whose key principle is this: Movement is a crucial component of meaning within the biblical text. In fact, an examination of biblical texts reveals various kinds of redemptive movement—*foreign* movement (in relation to the ancient culture), *domes-*

---

[6]Joshua 15:16 (Acsah); cf. 1 Samuel 18:12-19 (Merab); 18:20-27 (Michal).
[7]Proverbs 21:9; cf. 19:13; 21:19; 25:24 (a twice repeated proverb).

tic movement (in relation to existing traditions or social norms within the immediate covenant community[8]) and *canonical* movement (across large epochs in salvation history, primarily from the Old Testament to the New). These three streams of "movement meaning" within Scripture provide the basis for contemporary application of the text that can carry us beyond bound-in-time assumptions about Scripture. As before, let's begin with the slavery texts.

Slavery texts: Redemptive movement. Both Old and New Testaments make significant modifications to the institution of slavery relative to their broader cultures.

1. *Generous number of days off work.* Many ancient Near Eastern and Greco-Roman cultures gave slaves time off for festival holidays. By comparison, however, the extent of holidays for festivals (Deut 16:10-12) and for the weekly sabbath rest (Ex 23:12) in Israel was generous.

2. *Elevated status in worship setting.* Some ancient cultures restricted slaves from involvement in sacred rituals. The Roman Empire, for example, barred slaves from ceremonial aspects of its religious festivals because they were thought to have a defiling or polluting influence. On the other hand, the Israelite (Ex 12:44; Deut 12:12, 18) and early church communities included slaves in the worship setting. In the church their status was raised to equality "in Christ" (Gal 3:28; Col 3:22-25; 4:16).

3. *Release of Hebrew slaves after six years.* Biblical legislation (Lev 25:39-43; see also Jer 34:8-22) and the Code of Hammurabi are unique in prescribing the release of debt slaves after a certain number of years. This is a highly redemptive feature compared to most other ancient Near Eastern cultures.

4. *Provisions given to slaves upon release.* Material assistance for released slaves stands out as a generous act of biblical law (Deut 15:12-18); other law codes do not appear to include this act of compensation.

5. *Limitations on physical beatings; freedom for damaged slaves.* Biblical legislation limited the severity of physical beatings (Ex 21:20-21), and any slave who was damaged by her or his master automatically gained freedom (Ex 21:26-27). Other cultures did not limit the slave owner's power in this way. Indeed, torturous abuse (including crucifixion) of some slaves was often intended as an object lesson for others.

6. *Admonitions of genuine care.* Paul encouraged masters to turn away from harshness

---

[8]Domestic movement has to do with change in tradition or social norms within a single generation (e.g., the daughters of Zelophehad), where the start and finish of that movement are markers in the same covenant community. This type of measure is different from foreign-relations benchmarks and from epoch-crossing (and often covenant-crossing) canonical movement.

and to show genuine care for their slaves.[9] These words were powerful in a world that often left sick slaves to die without treatment.

7. *Condemnation of trading stolen slaves/people.* Scripture denounces foreign countries—Gaza and Tyre—for stealing people in order to trade them as slaves.[10]

8. *Refuge and safety for runaway slaves.* In the ancient world runaway slaves were sought for bounty. Captured slaves were at times executed along with their families and accomplices. The Code of Hammurabi prescribed the death penalty for aiding and abetting a runaway slave. Most nations had extradition treaties. In a radical departure from these prevalent views, Israel became a safety zone or refuge for foreign runaway slaves (Deut 23:15-16; cf. Is 16:3-4).

When these biblical modifications, which brought greater protection and dignity for the slave, are read in their ancient Near Eastern and Greco-Roman contexts, redemptive movement becomes increasingly clear. Admittedly, the biblical improvements did not liberate slaves into complete equality. Scripture moved the cultural "scrimmage markers" only so far. Yet the movement was sufficient to signal a clear direction for further improvements in later generations. This redemptive-movement meaning was—and is—absolutely crucial to contemporary application.

Women texts: Redemptive movement. As one compares the biblical texts about women to their surrounding context (and augments this foreign movement with domestic and canonical movement), a certain impression emerges. On the whole, the biblical material is headed toward an elevation of women in status and rights while reducing patriarchal power. An overall sense of redemptive spirit emerges from each of these examples.

1. *Improved rights for female slaves and concubines.* The ancient Near East permitted the sale of girls to any male, whether domestic or foreign, and often for sexual purposes. These young women had virtually no rights of their own. While the Old Testament permitted the sale of daughters as chattel slaves and concubines, it made a significant redemptive move against unchecked patriarchy by granting these female slaves rights normally afforded to the rest of Israel's daughters (Ex 21:7-11).

2. *No bodily punishment of a wife.* Babylonian codes stipulated drowning for women who, in opposition to their husbands, neglected their home. Assyrian law permitted husbands to scourge their wives, pluck out their hair, and bruise or pierce their

---

[9] Ephesians 6:9; Colossians 4:1; note especially Philemon 16, where Paul calls Philemon to treat Onesimus as "a beloved brother."

[10] Exodus 21:16; Deuteronomy 24:7; I Timothy 1:10 (NIV, "slave traders"); cf. Rev 18:13 ("human beings sold as slaves," TNIV).

ears. For more rebellious acts of insubordination, the husband had the right to mutilate or cut off certain parts of his wife's body and in a few cases was even permitted to kill her. Old Testament legislation took husband-wife relationships in a quite different direction. To this may be added an aspect of canonical development. In Ephesians 5:25 not only is it assumed that the husband will do no bodily harm, but he is instructed to sacrifice himself—his own body and life—for the sake of his wife.

3. *Women gain inheritance rights.* The daughters of Zelophehad initiated the inheritance question (Num 27:1-11). They were permitted to inherit land, but under limited circumstances (Num 36:1-13). Even though this change was incremental, it indicates movement toward greater freedoms for women. This domestic movement is augmented with one Old Testament incident of complete inheritance equality, Job 42:15.

4. *The right of women to initiate divorce.* The New Testament extends the right of initiating divorce to women (Mk 10:12; I Cor 7:10-16). This kind of canonical movement sets a clear direction for the emerging status of women in Jesus and the early church.

5. *Grounds for divorce favor Judeo-Christian women.* In comparison with other ancient Near Eastern cultures, Israelite males had at least some minimal red tape to work through in divorcing their wives (Deut 22:13-19; 24:1-4). While not adequate by modern standards, within its own day this legislation granted Israelite women a greater dimension of dignity. Jesus takes this movement one step further by narrowing the broad Mosaic grounds for divorce (Mt 5:32; 19:9), which had reflected extreme patriarchal power. He thereby increased the rights and status of women and significantly reduced male authority.

6. *Fairer treatment of women suspected of adultery.* Biblical law instructed a husband who suspected his wife of adultery to take her to the temple and have her pronounce a curse upon herself (Num 5:11-31). Compared to the ancient Near Eastern environment, where the wife was often subjected to an abhorrent "trial by water" and guilt was determined by her sinking or floating (with potential for an anger-driven drowning), the biblical rule is redemptive. The fact that Israel had a less easily abused approach yields a sense of quiet reduction in patriarchal power within its cultural context. Furthermore, canonical development demonstrates that the "one gender only" response to adultery falls away. The early (and later) church discontinued Israel's practice of scrutinizing suspected adulteresses and moved toward greater gender equality in dealing with adultery (Mt 5:27-30; cf. Jn 7:53–8:11).

7. *Elevation of female sexuality.* Women often functioned as prostitutes in the ancient world, at a terrible cost to their dignity as human beings. Comparatively, the Bible elevates female sexuality (Lev 19:29). Though the redemptive movement in the area of female sexuality was incremental,[11] the covenant community took major steps against the sexual exploitation of women. Indeed, the apostle Paul elevated the marriage bed to a place of full equality (I Cor 7:3-4: the wife has authority over her husband's body equal to her husband's over hers). Within their setting and time, these developments were significant.

8. *Improved rape laws.* Assyrian rape laws punished the female victim whether she was forced or seduced and at times held her guilty while the man went free. An unmarried male perpetrator merely paid a monetary fine. If the perpetrator was a married male, his own wife was taken out by others and sexually ravished for his crime. While justice may have been achieved in the eyes of men, such practices often created a double atrocity for women. Old Testament rape laws have their own inherent difficulties, but they are much improved over the harsher patriarchy that marks certain law codes of the ancient world. And from a canonical perspective Jesus not only moves toward greater gender equality but also radicalizes the whole issue by addressing the lust of men (Mt 5:27-30; cf. Jn 7:53–8:11).

9. *Softening the husband side of household codes.* For the first-century Greco-Roman audience, the striking component of the New Testament household codes was the material concerning the husband. As with slavery, Paul modifies the top end of the hierarchical structure more heavily than the bottom. Paul's word to husbands to "love [their wives], just as Christ loved the church and gave himself for her" (Eph 5:25) put their patriarchy on a different footing within the broader sociological setting.[12]

10. *Seed ideas and breakouts.* When read against the backdrop of the ancient culture, numerous biblical texts so dramatically advance the role and status of women that they might be labeled "seed ideas" and "breakouts": cases where God blesses women in roles that radically depart from the cultural norm of patriarchy (Judg 4:4-7; 5:1-31; cf. 2 Kings 22:14-20; 2 Chron 34:22-28), mutuality statements that at least soften patriarchy in their immediate setting (I Cor 11:11-12), mutuality statements that go further and embrace full equality for processing marital de-

---

[11]Cf. the earlier portrait of slaves (points 3 and 4) and women (points 4, 5 and 7).
[12]See chapter eleven in this volume for an elaboration of this point.

cisions (I Cor 7:3-5),[13] and profound new/equal status statements for slaves and women (Gal 3:28; cf. I Cor 12:13; Eph 2:15; Col 3:11).

Bringing together the three streams of biblical movement—foreign, domestic and canonical—one can clearly see where Scripture is moving on the issue of patriarchal power and women's rights and status. In broad terms, there was a liberalizing, freeing and less-dominating spirit in both the slavery and the women texts. Yet if, as the previous section illustrates, the biblical movement toward an improved social ethic was incremental (not absolute) in the case of slaves and women, then redemptive movement clearly needs to be taken further. It must become a crucial factor in shaping our contemporary application of the women texts. Just as the slavery texts contain a crucial element of redemptive movement, so the redemptive spirit within the women's texts must carry us to new and improved ways of thinking about the treatment of women.

To summarize hermeneutical insights from the texts illustrating redemptive movement in the biblical treatment of slaves and women:

- A redemptive-movement hermeneutic acknowledges movement meaning—foreign, domestic and canonical—as a legitimate component of meaning in biblical words.

- Movement or redemptive-spirit meaning is crucial: it should shape the course of our contemporary appropriation of the Bible, carrying us beyond bound-in-time applications.

- As with the slavery texts, the redemptive spirit within the women texts must prompt us to wrestle with new and improved ways of treating women.

The Realization of Redemptive-Movement Meaning

The New Testament as final revelation. Before offering suggestions for contemporary application of a redemptive-movement hermeneutic, we need to raise the very important question of its limits. Given that the New Testament is the final apex of revelation, should we conclude that it offers a completely finalized expression of redemptive-movement meaning in all concrete particulars? Or does the redemptive movement begun in the Old Testament and extended in the New Testament need

---

[13]Paul's mutual obligation (I Cor 7:3), mutual deference (I Cor 7:4) and mutual consent (I Cor 7:5) statements call for equality in the decision-making process along with a radicalized sense of caring for the other person's needs.

to be extended even further? Does our commitment to the New Testament as God's final word help decide these questions one way or the other?

For Christians, of course, the New Testament *is* the "final and definitive revelation"[14] by which we address all issues of faith and practice. Since the New Testament is God's final and definitive word spoken to his people in the last days (Heb 1:2), transmitted to the saints once and for all (Jude 3), we do not expect any further revelation until the coming of Jesus Christ.[15] This point is not at issue.

Rather, here is the crux of the matter: How does one relate the New Testament as final *revelation* with a further *realization* of its social ethic? Some authors unfortunately merge these two concepts into one affirmation, assuming that the New Testament revelation contains a fully realized ethic in all of its concrete "frozen-in-time" particulars. All agree that the New Testament moves beyond the Old Testament in its development or realization of ethic; that is, it takes the Old Testament redemptive spirit further. However, the New Testament is still *like* the Old Testament in expressing the unfolding of an ethic at certain points in an incremental (not absolute) fashion. In the end, therefore, the issue is not the New Testament's status as final revelation but *the degree to which the New Testament is similar or dissimilar to the Old Testament with respect to its realization of ethic.* Do contemporary Christians in some fashion need to move *with* the redemptive spirit of the New Testament toward a realization of that movement beyond certain concrete, frozen-in-time particulars?

The rest of this chapter will present a threefold rationale for seeing the New Testament as expressing an incremental (not ultimate) ethic in certain concrete particulars: (1) the Old Testament as precedent, (2) the New Testament slavery texts and (3) the New Testament women texts.

The Old Testament as precedent: Continuity and discontinuity. An appeal to redemptive-movement meaning in the Old Testament should inform appropriate expectations for the New Testament. Granted, the New Testament moves the Old Testament ethic further along in its concrete expressions, as the Old Testament itself moved

---

[14]These words are used often by Thomas R. Schreiner in a critique of my book. What he perhaps does not know is that I am in full agreement with him on this point. See Thomas R. Schreiner, "William J. Webb's *Slaves, Women and Homosexuals:* A Review Article," *Southern Baptist Journal of Theology* 6 (2002): 54-56, 63. For a more detailed discussion, see William J. Webb, "The Limits of a Redemptive-Movement Hermeneutic: A Focused Response to T. R. Schreiner," *EQ* 75, no. 4 (2003): 327-42.

[15]Ibid., p. 54.

incrementally beyond its foreign and domestic context. However, something very important has stayed the same between the Old and the New Testaments. The Old Testament was God's revelation to his covenant people within the constraints of a curse-laden and culturally shaped world, and the New Testament is *still* revelation from God within a curse-laden and culturally distinct world. Given that both of these factors—the fallen world context and an ancient world horizon—were still part of the equation at the time of the New Testament, one should be less quick to pronounce the movement within the New Testament "absolute" in all of its particulars rather than incremental like the Old Testament.

It is this "real world" continuity between Testaments that strongly suggests the likelihood of an incremental ethic within the New Testament and thus the need for a redemptive-movement hermeneutic.

The New Testament slavery texts: Further redemptive movement. Most agree that contemporary Christians need to have moved beyond the "frozen-in-time" words of the New Testament to a more ultimate ethic regarding slavery. Again, there is certainly movement within the New Testament slavery texts (beyond the Old Testament) toward a betterment of the institution. The status of slaves is basically elevated within the New Testament community, although household slaves with pagan masters are urged to follow Christ's example of suffering (1 Pet 2:18-25). The fact that slaves had salvific equality "in Christ" surely had subtle ways of increasing their social status within the covenant community. Indeed, Paul's letter to Philemon urges the transformation of relationship between a runaway slave and his owner: slave and master are first of all brothers in Christ.

But none of this, as redemptive as it is, amounts to an abolitionist position in the New Testament. There is no overt call for the abolition of slavery. Slaves are still instructed to submit and obey. Christian masters are simply called on to treat their slaves in a humane and Christian way, as those who themselves serve a heavenly Master. Try as we may, modern Christians simply "cannot get there from here" with a stationary approach to meaning in the text. That is, we can scarcely argue cogently for a proactive abolitionist position in today's world based on a words-on-the-page understanding of the New Testament texts on slaves.

However, if we understand biblical meaning to include the *redemptive spirit* of the text, the situation changes. Now one can construct a well-reasoned argument that abolitionism best reflects a reasonable outgrowth of the spirit of the New Testament (*and* that of the Old Testament!) and its movement meaning. Wherever slavery may occur in our modern world, Christians should have an ethical obligation based on the spirit of Scripture (a) to abolish slavery rather than simply (b) to treat slaves well but allow slavery. A static, words-on-the-page understanding of social ethics in the Bible leads to the second option (b); a redemptive spirit and movement understanding of social ethics in the Bible leads to the first option (a).

While the New Testament is our final and definitive revelation and its underlying redemptive spirit contains an absolute ethic, the *realization* of its redemptive movement is incremental (as in the Old Testament) and not a fully realized ethic. The abolition of slavery, a clearly better ethic than a call for a nicer form of slavery, can be achieved only through reading and applying Scripture with a redemptive-movement hermeneutic. Unless one embraces the redemptive spirit of Scripture, there is no biblically based rationale for championing an abolitionist perspective. An isolated-words or stationary approach to the New Testament simply will not take us there.

This is not a matter of simply "permitting" abolition as a social reform should it happen.[16] That would involve a confusion of categories. Rather, since there truly is a better treatment of human beings than slavery, Christians should have a passionate commitment, rooted in the Bible's redemptive spirit, to rid society of slavery.

The New Testament women texts: Further redemptive movement. In light of Old Testament precedent and a redemptive-movement hermeneutic applied to the New Testament as the only valid way to arrive at the abolition of slavery, we turn at last to the women texts themselves. As with the slavery texts, there is a need to embrace redemptive movement beyond certain concrete, frozen-in-time aspects of the New Testament texts on women. Here I offer a sample set of four New Testament women texts where there exists a good hermeneutical basis for taking the redemptive-movement spirit further in its realization. The first three examples are reasonably straightforward, and for the most part they have been conceded by virtue of church practice as nonprescriptive texts, at least on the level of their specific formulation of a woman's obligations in the home and church. The final example requires a more extensive development, since it is the passage around which almost all the present controversy swirls. While more samples from New Testament texts

---

[16]Hierarchicalists sometimes say that it is OK to accept abolitionism because abolitionism itself is not condemned by the Bible! But here they fail to see the terribly anemic nature of their ethics, for it disregards the redemptive movement in Scripture and fails to find *any* ultimate ethic within the pages of the New Testament, our final revelation. Alternatively, a redemptive-movement hermeneutic argues that the slavery texts express an ultimate ethic in their underlying redemptive spirit.

about women could be provided,[17] these four will suffice to make the point here.

Head coverings on women in worship. It is broadly conceded within the contemporary church that Paul's urging women to have some sort of head covering in worship (I Cor 11) reflects a cultural component of life in Corinth.[18] Most hierarchicalists willingly accept a movement away from the concrete, on-the-page specifics of the text here and accept some kind of attitudinal alternative. What they apparently do not realize is that such an applicational move extends the redemptive movement well beyond the New Testament setting. This application change, subtle though it may be, significantly reduces what is often perceived as an expression of patriarchy and encourages a less restrictive treatment of women. Such an applicational move is wonderfully consistent with the underlying spirit of the Bible.

Silenced women. The New Testament also instructs women to be silent and not to raise questions within congregational gatherings.[19] Should they have any questions, they are to ask their husbands at home. In short, women are to be silent, and the text assumes a gender perspective: the male/husband is the repository of biblical knowledge.

The church has largely abandoned the concrete form of these instructions, and for good reason. Over the years women as a sociological group have greatly increased their knowledge and educational status. In our contemporary world, the questions raised by women often show more insight and knowledge than questions raised by men. So any kind of gender-based restrictions on questions in church becomes an application problem. Furthermore, when a woman gets home, she need not ask her husband for his insight on some passage or issue. She can simply consult a commentary, perhaps one written by biblical studies expert Margaret E. Thrall, whose exegesis of texts is as detailed and careful as those of her male counterparts in the field.[20] While providing certain transcultural underlying principles, this "be silent and ask your husband at home" text is generally no longer applied

---

[17] A case could easily be made for a realization of redemptive-movement meaning beyond the concrete particulars of other New Testament women texts (e.g., I Cor 11:12; I Tim 2:14; 4:7). For I Corinthians 11:12, see William J. Webb, "Balancing Paul's Original-Creation and Pro-Creation Arguments: I Corinthians 11:11-12 in Light of Modern Embryology," *WTJ* 66, no. 2 (Fall 2004). For I Timothy 2:14, see Webb, *Slaves, Women and Homosexuals,* pp. 221-35, 263-68. For I Timothy 4:7, see Webb, "The Limits of a Redemptive-movement Hermeneutic," pp. 338-39.

[18] See the discussion in chapter eight in this volume.

[19] See the discussion in chapter nine in this volume.

[20] See, e.g., her acclaimed commentary on 2 Corinthians: Margaret E. Thrall, *The Second Epistle to the Corinthians,* 2 vols., ICC (Edinburgh: T & T Clark, 1994, 2001).

today in its concrete gender-restrictive particulars.

Calling one's husband "master/lord." One New Testament text (I Pet 3:5-6) instructs Christian wives with pagan husbands to follow Sarah's example of submission, concluding that she "obeyed Abraham and called him her master [or lord]." Whether the Christian wife is being urged to call her pagan husband "lord" or whether Sarah's doing so to Abraham is simply illustrating her submission is a matter of debate.[21] But at least the possibility of the former exists; and "lord" is the title slaves had to use with their masters.

In any case, contemporary hierarchicalists do not follow this New Testament "instruction" any more than egalitarians do. Knowingly or not, they have moved in their application to a far softer expression of patriarchy than what is found in the concrete configuration of the New Testament text. But this is a good thing, for it carries further the underlying spirit of both Testaments, bringing elevated status and treatment of women and a corresponding reduction in patriarchal power. Unwittingly the Christian community has applied movement meaning from the Old and New Testament women texts as a whole.

In some respects redemptive applications of the preceding three examples— head covering, silencing and calling one's husband "lord/master"—are a given in our world. Practice says as much about one's hermeneutic as does theory. However, the next example will push the theory discussion a little further. I will engage some hermeneutical tools of cultural/transcultural assessment. These tools augment a redemptive-movement hermeneutic, helping us spot certain features of the biblical text where redemptive movement can and should be taken further.

The submission of wives to husbands. In Paul's "household codes" he instructs women to "submit to" their husbands (Eph 5:22; Col 3:18). Some Christian interpreters water down the idea of submission in an attempt to make it more palatable today. It is sometimes difficult to tell if they are making a statement about the lexicography of ancient terms or about modern application. While recasting ancient lexical terms within a historical document is hardly honest, I would suggest that we do need to consciously change our contemporary application. We need to move with the Bible's redemptive spirit and go far beyond the first-century patriarchy evidenced by this "submit to" language.

Aside from the redemptive spirit within the biblical women texts, which is

---

[21]See the discussion by Peter Davids in chapter thirteen in this volume. It should be noted here that nowhere in the Old Testament itself does Sarah actually address Abraham as "lord." Very likely, as Davids points out, Peter is following a Jewish tradition that would have been known to his readers.

headed in a less restrictive direction, a decision to move beyond the patriarchy in this passage is informed by cultural/transcultural analysis. Two of the tools I will use might be called, respectively, "pragmatics between two cultures" and "the ladder of abstraction." Leviticus 19:9, "You shall not reap to the very edges of your field," offers a good neutral illustration of how pragmatic factors help us discover where the line is between cultural and transcultural components. It also shows how pragmatic factors generally affect the lower end of the ladder of abstraction. See figure 22.2.

Nonmoral pragmatic factors tend to shape the most concrete "on the page" expression or form of a biblical command. *Pragmatic factors* are often involved in the "down the ladder" components of a biblical command, whereas the *ultimate rationale* generally provides the basis for its "up the ladder" components. The pragmatic factors related to the original setting of the command of Leviticus 19:9 are at least twofold: the high percentage of the original Israelite population involved in farming and the close proximity between the population base and the farms.

These two pragmatic factors were part of the original setting, but they are *not* part of the agricultural and social configuration of our modern world. In our industrialized setting, the percentage of the population in cities is much greater, and farms are sometimes hundreds of miles removed from population centers. If modern farmers were to leave the corners of their fields unharvested, that grain would simply rot. Thus the pragmatic basis of the Leviticus text is lost in our setting. When we are moving between two cultures, a lack of sustained pragmatics serves as a clue to cultural components within the biblical text. When the bottom drops out of the pragmatic basis between two cultures, the Christian interpreter should be prepared to move up the ladder of abstraction to discover what is transcultural in a biblical command. Leviticus 19:9 provided a concrete way to express the biblical call "Love your neighbor as yourself."

Now we return to the New Testament instructions for wives to "submit to" their husbands. There are several reasons these commands made sense in the original culture: differences in spouses' ages (the female was often significantly younger), differences in amount of formal education, differences in opportunities to acquire and hold resources, lack of informational sources within the home, women's lack of social exposure.[22] These and other nonmoral pragmatic factors created an automatic and somewhat heavy hierarchy. Of course, these features of mar-

---

[22]For a fuller discussion, see Webb, *Slaves, Women and Homosexuals*, pp. 213-16.

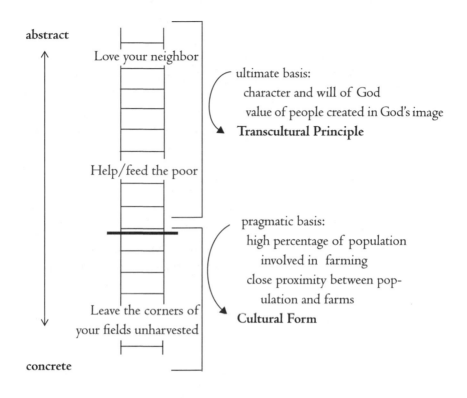

Figure 22.2. The ladder of abstraction

riage in the ancient world are not part of our contemporary world. Since the pragmatic situation no longer applies, we must be willing to move up the ladder of abstraction. When the "bottom falls out" of the pragmatics between two worlds, interpreters must be willing to rethink contemporary application.

So one must ask, what should a contemporary Christian marriage look like if we move to the top of the ladder of abstraction? An application of the transcultural principles of mutual submission, respect and self-giving love underlying Paul's exhortations in Ephesians 5 should lead to a marriage in which husband and wife submit to one another, with deference in decision making based on expertise in a particular area rather than on gender.[23]

---

[23]In *Slaves, Women and Homosexuals* I offer two models of marriage that meet this description, both of which utilize a redemptive-movement hermeneutic to avoid any gender-based hierarchy of authority. "Ultra-soft patriarchy" uses a redemptive-movement approach to apply a contemporary form of

Here is a summary of the hermeneutical insights derived from this crucial discussion of the realization of redemptive-movement meaning:

- We must make an important distinction between the New Testament as final *revelation* and the ethical *realization* of its redemptive spirit.

- There are three significant pieces of evidence that support an incremental (not absolute) ethic within the New Testament and thus commend a redemptive-movement hermeneutic within the New Testament. (1) Old Testament precedent within a cursed and culturally defined world should affect our social ethic expectations for the New Testament. (2) The New Testament slavery texts do not provide us with an ultimate social ethic in their concrete particulars, nor can one get to an abolitionist position based on a static "on the page" understanding of the words in these texts. (3) New Testament women texts show us—as seen in four brief examples—how we should permit the Bible's redemptive spirit to carry us beyond certain culture-based components of the New Testament's depiction and treatment of women.

- Christians need to ponder the Bible's underlying spirit and its redemptive-movement meaning to make good contemporary applications of New Testament texts.

"greater male honor" through much milder expressions of ritual/social honor (e.g., the wife and children taking the husband's last name) and not through gender-based leadership restrictions in the home or church. "Complementary egalitarianism" takes the redemptive movement in Scripture to complete male-female equality and so seeks out contemporary forms that express mutual deference and honor. There are no leadership role restrictions within the home or church in either model. In my view, whether one opts for ultra-soft patriarchy or an egalitarian position depends largely on one's understanding of gender components within the creation texts. See Richard Hess's examination of Genesis 1–3 in this volume (chapter four). For an alternative egalitarian approach to the creation narratives, see Webb, *Slaves, Women and Homosexuals*, pp. 110-51. While Hess's approach and mine differ somewhat, we share the conviction that the creation account is best understood not to support male authority as a God-ordained, transcultural ideal.

23

GENDER EQUALITY
AND HOMOSEXUALITY

William J. Webb

W hen Christians discuss the issue of gender equality, often someone will ask, "Doesn't acceptance of egalitarianism logically lead to acceptance of homosexuality?" Lying behind this question in part is a concern for consistency in how one interprets and applies the Bible. How is it, some argue, that egalitarians do not directly apply some very clear New Testament statements about women's submission yet still accept the Bible's prohibitions of same-sex relationships?[1] In response to these questions, this chapter will show that the hermeneutic by which egalitarians reject female subordination to male rule as transculturally normative is the same hermeneutic by which egalitarians affirm the Bible's prohibition of homosexual behavior as a universal norm.

The concern patriarchalists have about hermeneutical consistency gets voiced

---

[1]Another concern voiced by some patriarchalists is that an egalitarian position might lead to a blurring of gender distinctions altogether and thus lead to acceptance of a homosexual lifestyle. But the egalitarian claim that status differences between men and women are a cultural construct and not inherent in the sexual distinction hardly constitutes a move toward a wholesale rejection of male-female complementarity. Further, this concern seems to lack historical perspective, since several expressions of Christian faith in the late nineteenth and early twentieth centuries fully affirmed women in ministry without that leading to same-sex relationships (Quakers, Salvation Army, early Pentecostals, some early holiness groups). On this see chapter two of this volume. Biblical egalitarians affirm, appreciate and seek to maintain a distinction between the sexes that honors God's creation design. This includes not only the undisputed differences in sexual and reproductive function (which belie the claim that homosexual relations are somehow "natural") but also the general psychological differences that can be discerned in studies comparing groups of men and groups of women. One might well argue that the best way to celebrate these general differences is the inclusion of women in leadership, since women can bring a focus that complements that of men. In an integrative sense, egalitarians are stronger advocates of complementarity than are hierarchical complementarians! On gender differences, see chapter twenty-seven of this volume.

several ways. Doesn't departing from the (apparently) plain meaning of the text regarding the role of women in the church and home[2] open the door to doing something similar regarding homosexual behavior? If one understands gender hierarchy
as a culture-bound component of the biblical text, doesn't that encourage one to
view the homosexuality prohibitions within a culture-bound framework? If one
moves in a less restrictive direction in applying the Bible's women texts, doesn't that
naturally lead to becoming less restrictive in applying the Bible's homosexuality
texts?

Although these questions are like mixing oranges and bananas,[3] they often
come to us in the form of hermeneutical entanglements. Indeed, one of my purposes for writing *Slaves, Women and Homosexuals* was to unravel the interpretive relationship between these interrelated subjects.[4] This essay will show that an acceptance of an egalitarian view does not logically move one toward acceptance of
a homosexual lifestyle. Six biblical and theological reasons will serve to illustrate
the point: the core value of gender boundaries, the direction of redemptive movement, the vice/virtue and penal-code lists, the lack of canonical variance, biblical
purpose statements, and pragmatic clues. A seventh, nontheological reason will
highlight egalitarians who are producing major scholarly works against accepting
homosexuality.

The Core Value of Gender Boundaries

An examination of Scripture reveals that the core value in the commands prohibiting homosexuality is the need to maintain a clear demarcation between men and
women. There have been recent attempts to reduce the issue to a lack of lifelong
covenant relationships (thus making covenant homosexuality acceptable today),
but this is not the fundamental problem with homosexuality for the biblical authors. Rather, the *biblical* concern regarding same-sex sexuality is that Scripture
proclaims that in creating humankind in God's own image, God created them
"male and female" (Gen 1:27). In Genesis 2 this is reinforced in terms of God's

---

[2]I say "apparently plain" because patriarchalists assume that neither the texts themselves nor their own
readings of them are culturally conditioned.

[3]That is, being born a man or a woman is categorically not the same as adopting a homosexual lifestyle. One is a matter of birth pure and simple, while lifestyle issues (not sexual proclivities) are finally the result of moral choices, not accidents of birth.

[4]William J. Webb, *Slaves, Women and Homosexuals: Exploring the Hermeneutics of Cultural Analysis* (Downers
Grove, Ill.: InterVarsity Press, 2001).

having made men and women for *each other*. God did not make men for men, nor did he make women for women.

The biblical prohibitions against homosexuality (and against transvestite dressing, its ritual counterpart) repeatedly emphasize a concern for defining and maintaining male and female relationship boundaries as a way of honoring our Creator. We shall see this underlying concern for male-female boundaries in several key texts: Leviticus 18:22, Deuteronomy 22:5 and Romans 1:18-32.

Leviticus 18:22. The homosexuality prohibition in the holiness code of Leviticus 18 is found within a grouping of laws that relate either directly or indirectly to sexuality:

> incest (Lev 18:6-18)
>
> menstruation (Lev 18:19)
>
> adultery (Lev 18:20)
>
> sacrifice of children to Molech (Lev 18:21)
>
> ⇒ homosexuality (Lev 18:22) ⇐
>
> bestiality (Lev 18:23)

Those who argue that the holiness code refers to a specific type of homosexuality often appeal to the presence of the Molech prohibition (Lev 18:21), which immediately precedes the homosexual prohibition of Leviticus 18:22.[5] They suggest that after mentioning the cult practice of sacrificing children to Molech (Lev 18:21), the author reflects on another practice within pagan cults: homosexual prostitution (Lev 18:22). In this view, then, the prohibition of Leviticus 18:22 might be more narrowly applied today against cult or prostitution-type homosexuality.

While this cult option is tenable,[6] it is by no means the most probable explanation. Another understanding of the organization of Leviticus 18 is far more likely. The placement of the Molech verse within the sexual-intercourse list is probably related to the nature of the category groupings. Notice that the Molech verse

---

[5]Some limit the kind of homosexuality addressed in Leviticus 18–20 by suggesting that it is related to pagan cult prostitution and idolatry. For example, see Letha D. Scanzoni and Virginia R. Mollenkott, *Is the Homosexual My Neighbor?* rev. ed. (San Francisco: HarperSanFrancisco, 1994), pp. 63-66; S. F. Bigger, "The Family Laws of Leviticus 18 in Their Setting," *JBL* 98 (1979): 202-3; N. H. Snaith, *Leviticus and Numbers,* Century Bible (London: Thomas Nelson, 1967), p. 126.

[6]For biblical references to male cult prostitutes, see Deuteronomy 23:17; 1 Kings 14:24; 15:12; 22:46; 2 Kings 23:7; Job 36:14; and possibly Revelation 22:15.

comes immediately after the category of heterosexual intercourse and immediately
before nonheterosexual intercourse:

incest (Lev 18:6-18)	*heterosexual* intercourse
menstruation (Lev 18:19)	*heterosexual* intercourse
adultery (Lev 18:20)	*heterosexual* intercourse

----

sacrifice of children to Molech (Lev 18:21)

----

homosexuality (Lev 18:22)	*nonheterosexual* intercourse
bestiality (Lev 18:23)	*nonheterosexual* intercourse

It would be rather unusual for a list of seventeen sexual intercourse prohibitions
to be interrupted by a prohibition that has nothing to do with sexual intercourse.
Even so, the placement of the Molech prohibition at this point within the list
makes sense once one recognizes its connection to offspring from sexual intercourse. Heterosexual intercourse produces offspring; homosexual intercourse and
bestiality do not. Thus the prohibition against sacrificing one's child to Molech is
appropriately located after a discussion of heterosexual intercourse—the kind of
intercourse that could result in offspring and in the sacrifice of those children to
Molech. The author then finishes the list with two remaining intercourse taboos in
which offspring are not involved.

This explanation seems much more likely than the foreign cult view. The connection between Molech and the preceding laws that deal with heterosexual relationships is the children that come from those relationships. The Molech text
relates to homosexuality and bestiality as a transitional marker that naturally distinguishes between offspring-bearing intercourse and intercourse that produces
no offspring. The author may well have cult-prostitution homosexuality in view,
but only as one kind of homosexuality among others that fit within this wider
sense of the homosexual prohibition. The author's organizational categories relate to offspring and a distinction between heterosexual intercourse and nonheterosexual intercourse.

Furthermore, the composer of the holiness code appears to have a broader un-
derstanding of homosexuality, given the comparative terms used in the prohibition.
The prohibition compares homosexual intercourse with heterosexual intercourse:
"You shall not lie with a male *as [a man lies] with a woman*; it is an abomination" (Lev

18:22; see also 20:13). The author's concern in this verse reflects the point of the organizational structure for the entire passage: homosexuality, like bestiality, breaks with heterosexual patterns. The list as a whole thus reinforces the comparative point within the verse.[7]

In sum, the Leviticus 18 list is most likely organized around heterosexual versus nonheterosexual intercourse. If this structural analysis reveals the author's intent, then covenant homosexuality fits within the prohibition. The core issue is appropriate sexual boundaries. The incest laws, for example, focus primarily on a man's crossing the boundary with a woman who is a close relative, including a granddaughter (Lev 18:10).[8] The severity of punishment in the incest cases[9] relates to the degree to which one violates a "family member and close relative" boundary. After the incest laws in the list of Leviticus 18, one encounters two further areas for setting sexual boundaries—homosexuality and bestiality—similarly defined by nature-and-society structural issues. In other words, the author's concern in Leviticus 18 is rooted in *maintaining sexual boundaries* between humans and animals, between men and close female relatives, and between people of the same gender.

Deuteronomy 22:5. Deuteronomy 22:5 similarly focuses on the issue of sexual boundaries in its prohibition of cross-dressing: "A woman shall not wear a man's apparel, nor shall a man put on a woman's garment; for whoever does such things is abhorrent to the LORD your God." The verse appears to be a symbolic or external-ritual prohibition that correlates with the homosexuality prohibitions. Obviously the specific substance of gender distinctions expressed through clothing is cultural and subject to change. Yet most societies retain some kind of dress distinction between men and women. Many Old Testament scholars regard this text as a prohibition against not only transvestite activity (dressing and acting like the opposite sex) but

---

[7]One might also examine the parallel passage of Leviticus 20, which is organized in part around descending levels of punishment. Even though the sacrificing of children to Molech receives the same level of penalty as homosexuality (death), it is split off from homosexuality and placed ahead of the sexual taboo list in a separate discussion (Lev 20:1-5).

[8]This is as close as Leviticus 18:6-18 and 20:11-12, 17 get to an actual father-daughter relationship, but such an act is surely presupposed by the very nature of the laws as they are set out in chapter 18.

[9]Leviticus 20:11-12, 14, 17, 19-21. The incest prohibitions within Scripture establish sexual boundaries with several very positive purposes: (1) preserving lines of family honor and structure, (2) protecting against sexual exploitation of those with less power within the family and (3) protecting against sibling rivalry and broader family rivalry. We might add an additional purpose today: the genetic benefits of restricting sexual intercourse with (and potential offspring from) close relatives.

also the primary forum in which it would be expressed, homosexuality.[10]

This Deuteronomy text indicates, along with the holiness code material (Lev 18 and 20), that it makes little difference to the biblical prohibition whether or not homosexuality is expressed in a covenant/equal-status relationship. Just as incest laws are designed out of a concern not to cross close family relationship lines, so also the homosexual codes appear to be given in order to retain appropriate sexual boundaries.

Romans 1:18-32. This text voices similar concerns about celebrating creation-based differences between male and female within a Christian heterosexual ethic. Paul speaks against women who "exchanged natural sexual relations [heterosexuality] for unnatural ones [lesbian relations]" and against men who "also abandoned natural relations with women [heterosexuality] and were inflamed with lust for one another [gay relations]."

Some homosexuality advocates attempt to define *unnatural* as something against one's sexual orientation and to reduce Paul's concerns about homosexuality to strictly idolatry-related or lust-related problems. These attempts, however, have not been convincing[11] and seem to reflect a radical misunderstanding of the discourse of Romans 1:18-32. Paul is setting out to show how the Gentile (pagan) world, by rejecting what could have been known about God *from* creation (Rom 1:18-20), has chosen idolatry—the worship *of* creation itself (in the form of the creature) rather than the Creator (Rom 1:21-23). The ultimate expression of this rejection of the Creator is to be found in Gentiles' "believing a lie" about God and about themselves, and this has resulted in homosexual activity (Rom 1:24-27). Only after this scathing rebuke does Paul add a list of all kinds of other sins that come from the same rejection of God (Rom 1:28-32).

Romans 1 adds two significant contributions to a biblical discussion of homosexuality. First, the implied creation and procreation theology underlying Leviticus 18 is now made explicit in Romans 1. Paul appeals to God's intention for male-with-female sexuality as something that is clearly revealed in nature and thus, by

---

[10]Peter C. Craigie, *The Book of Deuteronomy* (Grand Rapids, Mich.: Eerdmans, 1976), pp. 287-88; Patrick D. Miller, *Deuteronomy* (Louisville, Ky.: John Knox, 1990), p. 162; P. J. Harland, "Menswear and Womenswear: A Study of Deuteronomy 22:5," *Expository Times* 110, no. 3 (1998): 73-76.

[11]See R. T. France, "From Romans to the Real World: Biblical Principles and Cultural Change in Relation to Homosexuality and the Ministry of Women," in *Romans and the People of God: Essays in Honor of Gordon D. Fee*, ed. S. K. Soderlund and N. T. Wright (Grand Rapids, Mich.: Eerdmans, 1999), pp. 234-53. Cf. Robert A. J. Gagnon, *The Bible and Homosexual Practice: Texts and Hermeneutics* (Nashville: Abingdon, 2001), pp. 229-303.

specific inference, within the complementary gender design of men and women. This observation about God's purposes being visible in creation around us again reflects the core biblical concern with gender boundaries, yet with greater clarity.

As a second contribution, Romans I provides the only explicit prohibition of lesbian sexuality within a biblical discussion of homosexuality. An inclusion of lesbian acts within the homosexuality prohibitions is extremely important for understanding biblical concerns; it shows that the range of the biblical prohibitions of homosexual activity is broader than what some would suggest. This text argues against a narrowing of biblical concerns to certain limited forms of homosexuality (such as pederasty—men with young boys). In the ancient setting Paul's comments about lesbian sexuality would certainly include homosexual acts among equal-status female participants. By inference, therefore, Paul's parallel comments about gay sexuality most likely includes, but is not limited to, equal-status participants in the case of two males. Thus the lesbian prohibition of Romans I further confirms the broad range of homosexual activity that falls within the biblical concerns.

The Romans I idea that God's revelation is clear in the created world around us verifies that the core biblical issue is sexuality that accords with God's creation of male and female. All three texts show that the biblical problem with homosexuality is not really about covenant or a lack of it; it is not really about equality or a lack of equality of sexual partners. The deepest issue for the biblical authors is a breaking of sexual boundaries that violates obvious components of male-and-female creation design.

The Direction of Redemptive Movement

Besides the transcultural core value of gender boundaries, there are a number of other reasons that acceptance of egalitarianism does not logically lead to accepting homosexuality. One of the clearest hermeneutical reasons for rejecting this logical-acceptance thesis is the dramatic difference in "movement" within biblical homosexuality texts compared to women texts. At this point we need to return to the idea that "movement provides meaning," developed in chapter twenty-two as part of an egalitarian hermeneutic. Some familiarity with this concept will assist in the discussion here.

The meaning of a biblical text should be understood not just through the isolated words on the page but also in light of the text's underlying spirit or movement. For instance, biblical texts placing limits on women and slaves within the broader social context of the ancient world generally show redemptive movement in a *less restrictive direction*, granting higher status to and improved treatment of women and slaves (and a corresponding reduction of patriarchal and slave-owner power). In many texts having to do with women's relationships to men (usually husbands), and in many slavery texts, the isolated words on the page do not reflect an ultimate social ethic; yet the redemptive movement within the text is certainly headed in a liberating direction.

On the other hand, when the texts prohibiting homosexual behavior are read against the backdrop of the ancient world, we discover a biblical spirit that creates movement in a *more restrictive* direction. The biblical text moves restrictively compared to the openness toward and acceptance of homosexuality in the social realm and in pagan worship of the day.[12] In other words, we encounter a freeing or less restrictive movement with respect to slavery and patriarchy but a more restrictive movement with respect to homosexuality.

A commitment to biblical authority means that our modern application honors the direction and meaning of the redemptive spirit within the Bible. Although this is not a popular answer to the homosexuality question in our society, only a sexual ethic that excludes homosexual behavior retains the spirit and redemptive movement found in Scripture, as its words are understood in light of the ancient world context.

The Vice/Virtue Lists and the Penal Codes

Brief, undeveloped references to homosexuality are found within the "vice lists" of I Corinthians 6:9-10 and I Timothy 1:9-10. While the cryptic nature of these lists makes it difficult to specify the kind of homosexuality in view (whether broad or specific), one term used in the lists, *arsenokoitēs*, is of particular importance. The word literally means "a male who goes to bed [has sexual intercourse] with males" and in all likelihood was derived intentionally by the apostle from the Septuagint translation of Leviticus 18:22 and 20:13. If so, then these vice lists may well reflect broad concerns about gender boundaries like those noted in my discussion of Leviticus 18.

---

[12]While in broad socioreligious terms the ancient Near East and Greco-Roman historical data might be described as mixed (some for and some against homosexuality), the biblical texts move clearly in one direction. The biblical authors move to a prohibition of any homosexual activity, and they likewise restrict their sexual metaphor depictions of Yahweh to the heterosexual realm (unlike ancient Near Eastern and Greco-Roman portraits, in which certain pagan gods are depicted in acts of bestiality and homosexuality).

Along with its occurrence within the vice lists, homosexuality makes the death-penalty list in Leviticus 20:13. As noted earlier, the author's concern in the companion text of Leviticus 18 is maintaining sexual boundaries between humans and animals (bestiality), between men and close female family members/relatives (incest) and between people of the same sex (homosexuality). Now in Leviticus 20 each of these actions—bestiality, homosexuality and (the worst cases of) incest—receives the death penalty. Due to the contextual connection between Leviticus 18 and 20, likely the same broad scope of homosexuality argued for in Leviticus 18 (above) is in view in the penalty text of Leviticus 20.

What is especially important for hermeneutics about the vice/virtue lists and the death-penalty lists is their contribution to cultural/transcultural discussions. Both the vice/virtue lists and the penal codes of Scripture reveal what might be called "near to the heart" or "to die for" values within the covenant community. For the most part the issues within these lists are highly transcultural in nature.

A major difference between the egalitarian issue and the homosexuality issue should now become apparent. Women serving in leadership roles is simply narrated (Judg 4–5; 2 Kings 22:11-20), and in one case it is forbidden (1 Tim 2:12), but it certainly never receives this sort of death-penalty or vice-list censure. In fact, there is considerable variance within the many texts dealing with women's roles. When compared to the biblical texts on women's submission, the homosexuality prohibitions are clearly in an entirely different category—a category of extreme weightiness. Biblical injunctions with light or no censure are far more apt to involve significant cultural components; texts with heavy censure (death-penalty and vice lists) are more likely to convey transcultural matters.[13]

The Lack of Canonical Variance

Within the biblical canon as a whole there is considerable variance among the texts that address women's roles in a patriarchal setting, while canonical variance is entirely lacking in the homosexuality texts.

Consider first the women texts. Sometimes the husband has the prerogative of making unilateral decisions that overturn his wife's decisions (patriarchy; Num 30:1-16), yet sometimes the husband is instructed to make decisions in the context of mutual deference and mutual consent (egalitarianism; 1 Cor 7:3-5). Sometimes

---

[13]See Webb, *Slaves, Women and Homosexuals*, pp. 172-79, 192-206. On the exceptions of menstrual and sabbath laws, which evidence a mixture of cultural and transcultural components, see pp. 168-70, 178 in that book.

women are not permitted to inherit property (patriarchy),[14] yet sometimes they are given property rights along with men (egalitarianism; Num 27:1-11; 36:1-13; Job 42:15). Sometimes women are not permitted leadership roles (patriarchy; 1 Tim 2:11-12), yet sometimes they have significant leadership opportunities within the covenant community (egalitarianism; Judg 4:4–5:31; 2 Kings 22:14-20; Acts 18:1-4, 18-19, 24-26; Rom 16:7). For egalitarians, this canonical variance conveys a sense of God's latitude in blessing women with various leadership gifts and opportunities.

While patriarchalists may not find this evidence as compelling as egalitarians do, one thing should be reasonably clear: there is a major difference in this regard between the women texts and the homosexuality texts of Scripture. Unlike the women texts, a canonical survey of the homosexuality texts fails to reveal one shred of variance.

Different Purpose Statements

The biblical texts affirming the subordination of slaves and the subordination of women—the "obey" and "submit to" texts—frequently include an explicit purpose statement about behaving thus in order to win a non-Christian husband or slave owner.[15] These subordination texts are purpose-driven by a passion *to make one's behavior attractive to society*. On the other hand, the purpose statements related to the homosexuality prohibitions reveal a concern *to make one's behavior distinct from the broader social setting* (Lev 18:3; 1 Cor 6:9-10; see also Lev 18:24-30; 20:22-24).

With the texts pertaining to slaves and women, one may retain the purpose meaning by rethinking the actual behavior in the modern context; with the homosexuality texts, one may retain the purpose meaning only by staying with the same behavior. The difference is significant—the two types of purpose statements in Scripture head in diametrically opposite directions. The countercultural component within the homosexuality prohibitions raises the likelihood that they express transcultural concerns.

Different Pragmatic Clues

Interpreters must often move up the ladder of abstraction, away from the particulars of a text, in order to cross the application bridge between the biblical world

---

[14]This is the standard pattern in Deuteronomy and elsewhere in the Old Testament.
[15]Slaves: 1 Timothy 6:1; Titus 2:9-10. Women: Titus 2:4-5; 1 Peter 3:1 (cf. 1 Pet 2:12).

and ours (see chapter twenty-two for a visual diagram). One of the reasons for moving to an abstracted principle is that at times the pragmatic rationale underlying a biblical text disappears within the modern setting. For instance, the biblical command "When you build a new house, you shall make a parapet [barrier/railing] for your roof" (Deut 22:8) makes little sense in much of the modern world, since the reason for the rule generally does not exist in our setting.[16] Most of our houses have peaked rather than flat roofs, and we generally do not entertain guests on these peaked roofs. It would be somewhat absurd for a Christian to look up and down their street for railings on rooftops in order to identify biblically based homes on the block. So one has to move up the ladder of abstraction and say that what is transcultural and binding from this text is the principle of constructing homes to ensure the safety of guests.

In the ancient world the New Testament commands for women to "submit to" their husbands (Eph 2:22; Col 3:18; 1 Pet 3:1; see also Tit 2:5) are built on a set of underlying cultural assumptions. The ancient world would have had a hierarchy between men and women whether the Bible said anything about it or not. Patriarchy was automatically established in the ancient world since women, compared to men, received far less formal education, had no access to the kinds of information sources now available in our homes,[17] had less economic independence, had less social exposure,[18] had less available time outside the home,[19] had less physical strength (significant in an agrarian setting), and wives had less maturity than their husbands (males were often ten to fifteen years older than their twelve-to-fourteen-year-old brides).

Since these circumstances generally no longer exist in our Western world, any application of the "submit to" commands must push up the ladder of abstraction, beyond patriarchal social customs and toward a mutual-deference relationship between women and men. Modern Christians should move away from the heavy

---

[16]The ultimate theological basis for the command—the character of God and the value of people—provides the basis for the more abstract transcultural principle underlying or embedded within the command.

[17]Information is now readily accessible in homes through electronic media (TV, radio, telephone, Internet, DVDs, CDs, etc.) and literature (books, newspapers, magazines).

[18]Their outside-the-home activities were often of practical necessity restricted to the well (for water) and the market (for food).

[19]The lack of available/discretionary time outside the home was due to a number of factors: economic poverty, large families, lack of modern technology within the home and shorter life spans (often one-third to one-half the lifespan of women today).

"submit to" instructions of these biblical texts. Changes in the pragmatic support for a biblical command must affect our applications today.

Now we come to the question of pragmatics and the biblical commands that prohibit homosexuality. Should we or should we not move up the ladder of abstraction to reconfigure our modern application of these commands? As we examine the homosexuality prohibition, we discover underlying reasons such as sexual-intercourse design, reproductive design and nurturing design.[20] These three patterns of human design have as much relevance in our setting as they did in the ancient setting.[21]

A fourth reason underlying the homosexual prohibitions is the benefit of raising children by a father and a mother, who can provide different yet complementary role models for their sons and daughters. Children raised by two parents of the same sex can certainly experience parental love; however, they lack a natural kinship setting in which each can derive modeling from and relationship with a parent of their own gender.[22] To this consideration one might add the benefits of having a relationship with an opposite-sex parent, as well as the benefits that different-gender spouses bring to a home through their providing gender-complementary (not monolithic) perspectives and ways of doing things. This latter benefit would extend also to a home consisting of a heterosexual couple without children.

These four pragmatic components underlying the Bible's homosexual prohibitions still apply as one moves from the ancient world to our modern world. An understanding of pragmatics between the two worlds pushes our contemporary application of women texts up the ladder, while the pragmatics of the homosexuality

---

[20]These underlying reasons may require explanation. (1) *Sexual-intercourse design:* the creative architecture of male and female sexuality with its part-and-counterpart configuration argues against same-sex relationships. Two males or two females can function sexually; they can produce sexual arousal and climax, but not in a way that utilizes the natural, complementary design of body parts. (2) *Reproductive design:* the mutually completing contribution of male-and-female chromosomes, the egg and sperm, and so on argues against gay and lesbian relationships. (3) *Nurturing design:* the physical design of female breasts, their function of nurturing and comforting infants, and the benefits of breast milk for a strengthened immune system argue for heterosexual relationships (and against homosexual relationships) in which the mother can breastfeed her children.

[21]One could well add the factor of the survival of the human race—which is dependent on heterosexuality—as an ongoing, transcultural pragmatic. However, this discussion is a complex one and requires extensive development if a persuasive case is to be built. See Webb, *Slaves, Women and Homosexuals,* pp. 216-20.

[22]At the very least one might consider all of the distinctly male and distinctly female changes across the life span of either gender. For example, see B. R. Wainrib, ed., *Gender Issues Across the Life Cycle* (New York: Springer, 1992). These life-span gender differences suggest a significant natural benefit of boys' being able to relate to a male father and girls' being able to relate to a female mother.

texts argues that the interpreter stay down the ladder with the concrete-specific commands prohibiting homosexuality. There are good reasons not to move up the ladder of abstraction here.

Scholarship Arguing a Heterosexuality-Only Thesis

Finally, the idea that egalitarianism logically leads to accepting homosexuality ought to be viewed as fallacious in light of major publications in recent decades. The best research and strongest argumentation for a heterosexuality-only position within a Christian sexual ethic are found in books written by egalitarians.[23] After reading these major egalitarian-authored works on homosexuality, one should be convinced that an egalitarian position truly does not lead to accepting homosexuality.

Conclusion

I conclude by coming back to the opening question: *Doesn't acceptance of egalitarianism logically lead to acceptance of homosexuality?* This essay has argued that the answer is "No, not at all." When the hermeneutics that lead to egalitarian conclusions are consistently applied to the homosexuality texts, the result is a strong argument *against* accepting homosexuality within a Christian sexual ethic.

Scripture's sexual-intercourse prohibitions are primarily concerned with maintaining sexual boundaries—boundaries between humans and animals (bestiality), between men and close female family members/relatives (incest), and between people of the same gender (homosexuality). Whether we speak of the ancient world or of our contemporary world, the concerns remain the same. Only in embracing and celebrating these sexual boundaries does the covenant community pay homage to God's design within creation. These creative-design considerations truly transcend time and culture.

---

[23]The most comprehensive and scholarly work to date in defense of an exclusively heterosexual Christian ethic has been written by an egalitarian: Robert Gagnon, *The Bible and Homosexual Practice*. A number of other noteworthy books against accepting homosexuality have also been written by egalitarians: Thomas E. Schmidt, *Straight and Narrow? Compassion and Clarity in the Homosexuality Debate* (Downers Grove, Ill.: InterVarsity Press, 1995); Marion L. Soards, *Scripture and Homosexuality: Biblical Authority and the Church Today* (Louisville, Ky.: Westminster John Knox, 1995); Donald J. Wold, *Out of Order: Homosexuality in the Bible and the Ancient Near East* (Grand Rapids, Mich.: Baker, 1998); Stanley J. Grenz, *Welcoming but Not Affirming: An Evangelical Response to Homosexuality* (Louisville, Ky.: Westminster John Knox, 1998); Webb, *Slaves, Women and Homosexuals*. One should add to this noteworthy grouping the hierarchicalist James B. DeYoung, *Homosexuality: Contemporary Claims Examined in the Light of the Bible and Classical Jewish, Greek and Roman Literature and Law* (Grand Rapids, Mich.: Kregel, 2000).

24

FEMINISM AND ABORTION

Sulia Mason and Karen Mason

Contrary to the prevailing feminist view, abortion rights are not necessarily linked to women's rights. In fact, abortion rights are antithetical to women's equality; thus prolife biblical egalitarians maintain a biblically[1] and logically consistent position on the relation between women's equality and abortion. Both historical and logical analyses of the abortion debate bear this out. Historically, the principles on which feminism was founded are just the opposite of those on which abortion rights are founded. Logically, the right to abortion as a means to equal rights for women is self-defeating.

The shift among feminists from a predominantly antiabortion to a predominantly proabortion stance is readily apparent when we compare the attitudes of early feminists to those of contemporary feminists. In 1869 Dr. Charlotte Lozier caused a man to go to jail for soliciting her to perform an abortion. Writing of the incident, the *Springfield Republican* anticipated that as more women entered the medical profession, physicians would follow Lozier's lead "if called upon to commit this crime. . . . We are sure most women physicians would lend their influence and their aid to shield their sex from the foulest wrong committed against it."[2] In a eulogy for Dr. Lozier, who died shortly after this event, suffragist and abolitionist Paulina Wright Davis called abortion infanticide and commended Lozier's sense of justice. Wright concluded, "The murder of the innocents goes on. Shame and crime after crime darkens the history of our whole land. Hence it was fitting that

---

[1] Although a small contingent of Christians contends that the Bible does not stand against abortion, this chapter will assume that the prevailing view among evangelical Christians—that abortion is biblically condemned—is true. For a defense of this view, see Francis J. Beckwith, *Politically Correct Death: Answering Arguments for Abortion Rights* (Grand Rapids, Mich.: Baker, 1993), pp. 137-50.

[2] Quoted in Mary Krane Derr, ed., *"Man's Inhumanity to Woman Makes Countless Infants Die": The Early Feminist Case Against Abortion* (Kansas City, Mo.: Feminists for Life Education Project, 1991), p. 2.

a true woman should protest with all the energy of her soul against this woeful crime."[3]

But by the 1980s the right to abortion had become such a pillar of the feminist agenda that prochoice feminist Zillah Eisenstein expressed indignation that some representatives of "revisionist feminism" were questioning abortion's place in feminism.

> Not only is feminism—in both its liberal and radical forms—under attack by different factions of the state, but this assault has begun to find its place *within* feminism itself. The basic (mainstream) liberal feminist demands for women's equality before the law (the Equal Rights Amendment), *the right to freedom of choice in regard to abortion,* and the right to affirmative action are being seriously questioned and attacked by . . . revisionist liberal feminists such as Betty Friedan, and revisionist left feminists such as Jean Elshtain.[4]

Today abortion rights are seen as part and parcel of mainstream feminism. What happened? Tracing feminist statements on abortion through the years will not reveal the source of the shift, because it occurred on a more philosophical level: both the moral principles on which prochoice feminists base their demand for rights and the very nature of the equality for which these feminists are fighting have departed dramatically from the moral principles and the type of equality for which early feminists fought. A framework for understanding these philosophical changes can be established by first exploring the differences between feminism's and abortion's founding principles.

Historical Analysis

As women have demanded recognition of their rights over the years, they have based these demands on certain moral principles concerning the nature of humanity and of equality. These principles are universally applicable to all those within the relevant category. The category at issue in women's rights is not womanhood but humanity. That is, women have demanded their rights on the basis that they are as much human beings as men are. Today, nearly all partisans of the abortion debate—prochoice and prolife alike—acknowledge the humanity of the unborn, that (at least biologically) the unborn is a human individual distinct from its

---

[3]Quoted in ibid., p. 4.
[4]Zillah R. Eisenstein, *Feminism and Sexual Equality: Crisis in Liberal America* (New York: Monthly Review Press, 1984), p. 12; emphasis added.

mother. Thus unborn humans fall into the same category as women with regard to these foundational moral principles; yet prochoice feminists deny the application of these principles to the unborn. To remove this apparent dichotomy of principles, prochoice feminists have devised some lines of reasoning that will be presented below, but their attempts have only dug them deeper into the quandary of the contradiction.

To give some historical evidence of the principles on which women's rights were based, which are contrary to the principles on which abortion rights are based, we will start with John Stuart Mill's classic defense of women's equality, *The Subjection of Women*. Published in 1869, Mill's thorough treatise is one of the first such defenses. It is still frequently cited today by feminists of all persuasions because of its substantive philosophical argument and its watershed status. Here are some of Mill's principles, each followed by an exposition of its contradiction of abortion advocates' principles.

1. *A woman's value is determined by her humanity, not by the value a man places on her.* By Mill's time, Western society had eliminated nearly all of the laws and mores under which individuals were kept in fixed social positions—with one glaring exception. The new principle guiding Mill's society was that "human beings are no longer born to their place in life, and chained by an inexorable bond to the place they are born to."[5] Mill argued that women likewise should not have their value or position in society determined by the holders of power in a patriarchal system: "But if the principle is true, we ought to act as if we believed it, and not to ordain that to be born a girl instead of a boy, any more than to be born black instead of white, or a commoner instead of a nobleman, shall decide the person's position through all life."[6]

Similarly, Augustine had long before pointed out that the utilitarian value placed on something does not affect its inherent value. Having rational souls places people over animals in inherent value, yet horses have sold for more than men: a slave may not be an effective mode of transportation, and thus his utilitarian value can be less than that of a horse.[7] Yet this utility does not degrade the man's inalienably higher value, which is part and parcel of his humanity. So, for example, if men are paid more in the workplace than women, this may affect fairness, but it does not destroy the truth of the equality of the sexes.

---

[5] John Stuart Mill, *The Subjection of Women* (Buffalo, N.Y.: Prometheus, 1986), p. 22.
[6] Ibid., p. 24.
[7] Augustine, *City of God*, trans. Gerald G. Walsh et al. (New York: Doubleday, 1958), pp. 223-24.

Prochoice feminists applaud the notion that neither a random selection of chromosomes nor utilitarian value should determine a woman's true value; yet they acknowledge no inherent value of the unborn, only the utilitarian value the mother chooses to assign. For example, in Judith Jarvis Thomson's well-known essay defending abortion rights, she claims that mothers and fathers do not have any responsibility for the unborn unless they have willingly assumed it. (Acknowledging one's responsibility for another entails a recognition that the other has value, that the other possesses some right because of his or her inherent value, and that therefore one has a responsibility to fulfill that right.) Thomson says:

> If a set of parents do not try to prevent pregnancy, do not obtain an abortion, and then at the time of birth of the child do not put it out for adoption, then they have assumed responsibility for it, they have given it rights, and they cannot now withdraw support from it at the cost of its life because they find it difficult to go on providing for it. But if they have taken all reasonable precautions against having a child, they do not simply by virtue of their biological relationship to the child who comes into existence have a special responsibility for it.[8]

Notice that on this view the child's rights are granted by the parents through the parents' actions; they are not inherent, nor are they tied to the child's humanity. Thus the child's value is an accident of its parentage. Prolife advocate Rosemary Botcher highlights the inconsistency of proabortion feminists who "resent that the value of a woman is determined by whether some man wants her, yet they declare that the value of an unborn child is determined by whether some woman wants him. They resent that women have been 'owned' by their husbands, yet insist that the unborn are 'owned' by their mothers."[9] How, then, can prochoice feminists maintain that moral principles and rights apply equally to women because of their humanity, but not to the unborn, whose humanity is generally no longer questioned?

---

[8]Judith Jarvis Thomson, "A Defense of Abortion," *Philosophy and Public Affairs* 1, no. 1 (1971). Reprinted in *Thirteen Questions in Ethics and Social Philosophy*, ed. G. Lee Bowie et al., 2nd ed. (Fort Worth, Tex.: Harcourt Brace College, 1998), p. 162. Notice that the parents have taken "reasonable precautions" not by abstaining from intercourse but by using some form of birth control, which is not 100 percent reliable. The notion of restricting oneself from sexual encounters is rarely even considered in prochoice arguments.

[9]Rosemary Botcher, "Pro-abortionists Poison Feminism," in *Pro-life Feminism: Different Voices*, ed. Gail Grenier Sweet (Toronto, Ont.: Life Cycle, 1985), p. 45.

2. *Differences between men and women are inconsequential to their humanity, which is the basis of their equal rights.* Mill contended against the view that since men are generally stronger than women, they ought to rule over women.[10] Men had obtained legal power because they had physical power. Mill pointed out that as human societies advanced in "the progress of civilization, and improvement of moral sentiments of mankind,"[11] this principle of "might making right" was abandoned—except in the case of women. Since the principle no longer applies to humanity in general, Mill argued, it should not apply in this instance, since the woman is also human. The irrelevance of physical differences between men and women with respect to human rights was extended by Mill not just to societal roles but to the home as well. Previously society had insisted that "a man's home was his castle" and society could not infringe on his territory. This argument granted men a right to privacy in the home, but the problem was that the man was not alone in his home. Privacy is insufficient grounds to subordinate women at home.

Prochoice feminists agree with Mill on this point, of course. Yet in order to deny the unborn's right to life, they use the argument Mill rejected. Women, they claim, have a right to retain power over their bodies, and what they choose to do with their bodies is their private affair. This argument was much easier to uphold when prochoice advocates could argue that the unborn was not a separate human being, but as noted earlier, this reasoning no longer holds. Thus the woman now must contend with the fact that two human beings—she and the unborn—are dependent on her body. The prochoice argument tries to handle this fact by clinging to possession—it's her body, after all. As Thomson argued, it would be *nice* for a woman to share her body with the unborn, but she is not *obliged* to do so—it's her body to do with as she chooses. But the same argument could be made about men's ownership of their homes, finances and the like. Feminists would not agree to such reasoning in that case.

If we extend Mill's principles to the unborn, we would hold that the unborn should not be left to the power of the woman merely because she has power over her body and the unborn does not. Neither should we grant a woman this power because of her right to privacy; she is no longer "alone" in her body. Furthermore, that society should intervene even in this allegedly private matter is easily demonstrated with a comparison to slavery. Imagine an abolitionist trying to free slaves

---

[10]Mill, *Subjection of Women*, p. 6.
[11]Ibid., pp. 6-7.

and reading one of our bumper stickers: "If you don't like slavery, don't own slaves." The politically weak in any society will always need the protection of the law.

With regard to other differences between men and women, Mill points out the same problem: women's equality cannot be denied on the basis of these differences. For example, it is clear that not all men are intellectually equal, but it has been supposed that all men are intellectually superior to all women.[12] Contrary to those who argued that women are not capable of the higher human processes—reasoning and morality—feminist pioneers argued that women were capable but were not given the opportunity to educate and express themselves. This was the point of Mary Wollstonecraft:

> It is vain to expect virtue from women till they are, in some degree, independent of men; nay it is vain to expect that strength of natural affection, which would make them good wives and mothers. Whilst they are absolutely dependent on their husbands they will be cunning, mean, and selfish, and the men who can be gratified by the fawning fondness of spaniel-like affection, have not much delicacy, for love is not to be bought, in any sense of the words, its silken wings are instantly shriveled up when any thing besides a return in kind is sought.[13]

Society was expecting women to be something it refused to enable women to be; then it measured women on their inability to be that.

When Hitler wanted to destroy Jews, he emphasized the (insignificant) physical differences between Jews and Germans, claiming Jews were less human due to those differences. In the same way, if it is deemed acceptable to deny a person's human rights because of the person's physical status at some stage in life, then each group ought to pray that it will always be strong enough to protect itself.

But prochoice feminists regularly point to the biological differences in the stages of human development as sufficient grounds to deny the unborn their rights. Ann Druyan and Carl Sagan, for example, use differences in brain activity and cite the presence of "recognizably human brain activity," beginning in the seventh month, as marking the point at which the unborn should be considered human.[14] This ap-

---

[12]Ibid., pp. 26-31.

[13]Mary Wollstonecraft, *A Vindication of the Rights of Woman*, 2nd ed. (London: J. Johnson, 1792); reprinted in *History of Ideas on Woman: A Source Book*, ed. Rosemary Agonito (New York: G. P. Putnam's Sons, 1977), p. 148.

[14]Ann Druyan and Carl Sagan, "The Question of Abortion," reprinted in *Thirteen Questions in Ethics and Social Philosophy*, ed. G. Lee Bowie et al., 2nd ed. (Fort Worth, Tex.: Harcourt Brace College, 1998), p. 150.

proach, however, undermines the woman's position even more than it does that of
the unborn: while the biological differences between unborn and born are tran-
sient, the biological differences between women and men are permanent. Thus if
one uses biological differences to distinguish human rights, one has developed an
argument that cannot possibly support equal rights for women.

To summarize: While prochoice advocates point to physical and other differences between born and unborn human beings, feminism itself was founded on the
principle that such differences between male and female individuals are inconsequential to their humanity, the basis of their rights. To be consistent, one must either (a) not object to granting men rights over women because of their physical differences as men or (b) grant the unborn rights because the difference between them
and the women who carry them is inconsequential to their human rights.

3. *A best-case scenario is insufficient to justify a hierarchical system.*[15] The best cases of
male hierarchy, Mill notes, have been used to defend male privilege. It has been
argued that since many a man exercises his authority in a loving manner and many
a woman submits lovingly, one should leave female subjection intact. Mill argues
against this position by pointing out that laws and institutions are required "to
be adapted, not to good men but to bad."[16] The fact that some people can use
privileges responsibly does not mean that no law should be made against such
privileges. Consequently, it is not wise to leave women unprotected by the law
simply because some men will refrain from taking advantage of their male privilege. Mill writes, "It is contrary to reason and experience to suppose that there
can be any real check to brutality, consistent with leaving the victim still in the
power of the executioner."[17]

Once again, prochoice feminists recognize that laws are needed to protect
women from the men who abuse institutionalized power, not from the men who
take no advantage of this power. These same advocates, however, hold fast to abortion on demand—which essentially allows for any and all abortions—pointing to
those women who use abortion only in the most dire of circumstances (the "best
case" scenario) as justification. Many prolife advocates agree that when the
mother's life is at stake, it is morally acceptable (although tragic) that the mother's
life be chosen over the unborn's. But this morally acceptable scenario does not justify lesser cases, such as when the unborn's life is weighed against the woman's fi-

---

[15]Mill, *Subjection of Women*, pp. 40-41.
[16]Ibid., p. 41.
[17]Ibid.

nancial disposition, or her desire for schooling, or even her emotional trauma over the pregnancy. Just as women must be protected from men who prioritize their own convenience over the woman's well-being, so the unborn must be protected from women who prioritize their personal convenience over the unborn's life. Contrary to the prochoice feminist position, this is the position that is morally and logically consistent with feminism's founding principles.

Logical Analysis

The weakness produced by the contradictions in the prochoice feminists' position is summarized by Rosemary Botcher, who says of their argument that "the pro-abortion feminists dilute the force of its persuasiveness by hypocritically refusing to grant the unborn the same rights they demand for themselves."[18] But prochoice feminists don't throw in the towel here. Instead they have devised two routes out of their quandary. By the first route, they assert a conflict between the woman's and the unborn's rights and prioritize the woman's rights over the unborn's. When two individuals' rights come into conflict, they aver, it is not immoral to choose one over the other. We see this kind of reasoning in Thomson's argument, mentioned earlier. The problem this reasoning creates, however, is that it is therefore the possessor of the right (woman over the unborn) rather than the kind of right (right to life over right to a certain lifestyle) that receives preference. Such prioritization establishes the same unacceptable value system as a male-female hierarchy where the man's rights are preferred because he is the man. By selectively applying moral principles and rights to women and not to the unborn, prochoice feminists taking this route have unwittingly validated their oppressors.

Some prochoice feminists therefore take another approach to maintain that the principles and rights apply to women because of their humanity but not to the unborn (whose humanity is generally no longer questioned). The second route attempts to remove the unborn from the category of humanity by differentiating a human *being* from a human *person* and asserting that only human persons possess human rights. But to make this distinction, the prochoice feminist must accept a moral system in which the basis for equality is no longer the one for which early feminists had fought.

In defining equality, feminism's pioneers saw that women, even though biologically different from men, possess the same measure of that which distinguishes hu-

---

[18]Botcher, "Pro-abortionists Poison Feminism," p. 45.

mans from the rest of the animal kingdom: rational souls. Men may be physically stronger, run faster and jump higher, but so do lions, cheetahs and antelopes. It is the soul that makes the difference. An antiabortion position naturally follows from this view: the unborn also possesses a rational soul. Its rationality may be unexpressed in the womb, but this rationality is nonetheless present in latent form.

This basis for equality held by the early feminists leads to two important corollaries. First, certain differences between the sexes can be acknowledged, because they are irrelevant to each human being's inherent value. Second, our inherent value as human beings entails a moral responsibility, which is shared equally among all (equally valuable) humans.

Prochoice feminists, on the other hand, have devised two new definitions of equality, which permit them to remove the unborn from the category of "possessor of rights" or "human person." These feminists acknowledge the inherent biological equivalence of the unborn and other human beings, but they believe that personhood is attached either to a specific developmental capacity (such as the first adult-type brainwave patterns in the unborn)[19] or to a legal status assigned by society.[20] Thus for prochoice feminists holding to modernist epistemology, inequality is established by a measurable difference between the unborn and born; conversely, the equality of the sexes is established by the lack of such differences between the sexes. For those espousing postmodernist epistemology, equality is determined by societal construct; since the value of the unborn (or anything else, for that matter) does not exist objectively, society may assign an unequal value to the unborn. The rights associated with equality are thus legally assigned, not inherent, for the postmodernist.

These revised definitions of equality negate the two corollaries of the early feminists' definition of equality, as mentioned above. If, on the one hand, equality is established through a lack of difference, then prochoice feminists must negate the differences between women and men. If, on the other hand, equality is established by societal fiat, then moral responsibility is also a societal construct, and women and men can be equally freed from such responsibility.

The self-defeating nature of proabortion feminism can now be elucidated. Three points will suffice to show how the new definitions of equality produce un-

---

[19]Druyan and Sagan, "Question of Abortion," pp. 145-51.

[20]Mary Anne Warren, "The Moral Significance of Birth," reprinted in *Thirteen Questions in Ethics and Social Philosophy*, ed. G. Lee Bowie et al., 2nd ed. (Fort Worth, Tex.: Harcourt Brace College, 1998), pp. 164-71.

tenable logical difficulties and entail an admission of sexual inequality.

I. *Inherent in the argument for abortion is an implicit admission of male superiority and an existential downgrading of motherhood entailing an inferior position of womanhood.* Because equality for some prochoice feminists is based on a lack of differences between women and men, this group downplays the relation of pregnancy and motherhood to a woman's other roles and the value of womanhood. Abortion on demand, in effect, achieves equality by making the woman a man: like a man, she can have sex without the problems of womanhood. Natural womanhood, which includes the capacity to bear children, is seen in this view as an imposed inferiority. As Francis Beckwith notes, this rationale "implies that women are naturally inferior to men, that they need abortion . . . in order to become equal with men."[21]

The question to be addressed here is whether prochoice feminism upholds women both as human beings and as women. Traditional society made the mistake of treating women as women without granting them their human rights. A pro-abortion society turns the tables, treating the woman as a human being without recognizing her womanhood. Prolife feminists finally get it right: "In opposing abortion we stand against society's devaluation of women as mothers and commit ourselves to giving women the support they need to bear children with dignity."[22]

2. *The goal of equality is undermined when it is defined in terms of similarity in weakness rather than similarity in strength.* Striving for their goal of moral freedom, prochoice advocates seek to grant women the same impunity from the consequences of sexual activity that men have enjoyed in the past. As philosopher Bertrand Russell believed, "It is only with the decay of the notion of sin in modern times that women have begun to regain their freedom."[23] But this move merely affirms an equality of weakness. Claiming to be as good a basketball player as Michael Jordan because one can miss shots would be ludicrous. Likewise, claiming to possess the virtue of King David because of one's extramarital affair is absurd. Yet in their quest for sexual equality, Rebecca Merrill Groothuis points out, "women have simply asserted their 'right' to sink to the same level of sin to which men have traditionally had the right to sink."[24]

---

[21]Beckwith, *Politically Correct Death*, p. 26.

[22]Gail Grenier Sweet and Nancy Randolph Pearcey, "HLA and ERA—Inedible Alphabet Soup?" in *Pro-life Feminism: Different Voices*, ed. Gail Grenier Sweet (Toronto, Ont.: Life Cycle, 1985), p. 39.

[23]Bertrand Russell, *Marriage and Morals* (New York: Horace Liveright, 1929); reprinted in *History of Ideas on Woman: A Source Book*, ed. Rosemary Agonito (New York: G. P. Putnam's Sons, 1977), p. 293.

[24]Rebecca Merrill Groothuis, *Women Caught in the Conflict: The Culture War Between Traditionalism and Feminism* (Grand Rapids, Mich.: Baker, 1994; reprint, Eugene, Ore.: Wipf & Stock, 1997), p. 76.

To claim equality by claiming a right to what is worst in a man, what he hates in himself and in his better moments condemns or relegates to his weakness, is not uplifting. Groothuis continues, "Now, women are still sex objects; they are simply more available than they used to be. . . . Now more than ever, a woman is a pawn in a man's world, a sex object whose use is dictated by the male rules of the sexual game."[25] And consequently, notes Gail Grenier Sweet, "pro-life feminists already see abortion as a roadblock to full rights for *women* as well as unborn children."[26]

Rather than uplifting women through the "moral freedom" that abortion allegedly provides, "abortion is the destruction of human life and energy that does nothing to eradicate the very real underlying problems of women," says Cecilia Voss Koch. "By encouraging society to consider a woman's child as a disposable piece of property, abortion reinforces the image of woman herself as disposable property and reusable sex object—a renewable sexual resource."[27]

3. *In removing earlier double standards for male and female sexual behavior, the ethic of "abortion rights" results in new, equally unacceptable double standards.* Recognizing society's double standards for women and men, feminist pioneers sought an equal sharing of moral responsibility between the sexes; but prochoice feminists today seek an equal freedom from moral responsibility. In the realm of sexual responsibility, abortion allegedly grants women the same freedom from sexual consequences as men. But in addition to the problem with equality of weaknesses noted above, proabortion feminists have traded one set of double standards for another.

Traditional societies protected women by teaching them to resist the advances of men. Their modesty was to be a kind of "barrier reef against which the waves of male sensuality crashed with predictable regularity."[28] Such societies recognized that women were more vulnerable because they bear the child; but the corrective for the double standard was to demand even more of women, not of men. Will Durant points out that in traditional societies "men have never thought of applying the same restrictions [of chastity] to themselves; no society in history has ever insisted on the premarital chastity of the male; no language has ever had

[25]Ibid., p. 77.

[26]Gail Grenier Sweet, "Introduction," *Pro-life Feminism: Different Voices,* ed. Gail Grenier Sweet (Toronto, Ont.: Life Cycle, 1985), p. 6.

[27]Cecilia Voss Koch, "Reflecting As FFL Celebrates Its Tenth Birthday," in *Pro-life Feminism: Different Voices,* ed. Gail Grenier Sweet (Toronto, Ont.: Life Cycle, 1985), p. 22.

[28]David Wells, *No Place for Truth: Or, Whatever Happened to Evangelical Theology?* (Grand Rapids, Mich.: Eerdmans, 1993), p. 28.

a word for a virgin man."[29] The double standard existed, in particular, in the realm of prostitution: men who fancied such places could still be considered honorable, but promiscuous women were not.

The moral system in such societies held responsible only the men who got "honorable" women pregnant. Extramarital sex per se was not viewed as wrong for men. For example, maidservants—who were often subject to sexual exploitation—were urged to remain chaste or at least to "demand, prior to intercourse, a written promise of marriage."[30] Such societies promoted "shotgun" marriages and the like, and they often produced in men a disparagement of marriage, such as in Greek society, where men preferred concubines to wives: "The one has on her side the law that compels you to retain her, no matter how displeasing she may be; the other knows that she must hold a man by behaving well, or else look for another."[31]

Christian morality, the morality of many of the pioneer feminists, sought to eliminate the traditional double standard by recognizing the equal moral responsibility of both men and women. This morality is based not solely on potential harm to society but on the character and authority of God.[32] Both men and women are thus held accountable for their sexual sins, whether or not a pregnancy results. The Christian position has always been to endeavor to raise men to a high standard of morality rather than to reduce women to the fallen level of men. As a result, the double standard is truly eliminated. However, this approach is by no means the popular one. As Groothuis notes, "Modern feminists, of course, have been more successful in their campaign than early feminists. It is always easier to allow sin than to enforce righteousness."[33]

Proabortion proponents of women's rights, like Russell, have sought to eliminate the double standard by giving women and men the same degree of sexual freedom, and abortion is part and parcel of this freedom. Russell acknowledges, "A

---

[29] Will Durant, *Our Oriental Heritage*, vol. 1 of *The Story of Civilization* (New York: MJF Books, 1935), p. 46.

[30] Marvin Olasky, *Abortion Rites: A Social History of Abortion in America* (Washington, D.C.: Regnery, 1992), p. 26.

[31] Will Durant, *Life of Greece*, vol. 2 of *The Story of Civilization* (New York: MJF Books, 1939), p. 467.

[32] Wherever Christianity went, it demanded the same moral responsibility from both men and women. Historian Durant writes, "When Christianity entered Japan, native writers complained that it disturbed the peace of families by insinuating that concubinage and adultery were sins" (*Our Oriental Heritage*, p. 860).

[33] Groothuis, *Women Caught in the Conflict*, p. 45.

very clear-cut issue is raised by this question of the new morality versus the old. If the chastity of girls and the faithfulness of wives is no longer to be demanded, it becomes necessary either to have new methods of safeguarding the family or else to acquiesce in the breakup of the family."[34] Russell's solution was twofold: (I) limiting procreation to marriage and making extramarital sex sterile (presumably through birth control and abortion), and (2) "the decay of fatherhood as an important social institution," coupled with surrogate fatherhood. In other words, if a man felt sure of paternity, he could go ahead and play the part of the father in the life of the child, but no law would force him to accept such responsibility.[35]

On the one hand, Russell has seemingly eliminated the original double standard: neither men nor women are required to become parents, since women can choose abortion and men can simply choose not to accept fatherhood. But in the process he has left intact a double standard in which the woman still must take responsibility for the unborn child: it is she who must decide whether to undergo an abortion, while the man can simply walk away, whatever her decision.[36] The male author of this chapter once asked his philosophy class how many times a man has had to go under a surgeon's scalpel because some woman with whom he had practiced free sex had gotten pregnant. They got the point.

As women have been given freedom to abort the unborn, an additional double standard has arisen. In asserting a right not to reproduce, abortion rights advocate Christine Overall restricts this right to women. Adopting Thomson's viewpoint, she argues that a woman is in control of her body. However, men are held responsible for where they put their sperm; if they impregnate a woman, they can no longer choose not to have children.[37] So while for women genetic parentage (conception) does not entail social parentage (motherhood or caring for a born child), this is not the case for men.[38] This approach, says Botcher,

---

[34]Russell, *Marriage and Morals*, p. 294.

[35]Ibid., p. 295.

[36]One might also question Russell's motives in advocating such a system. His life is a tale of open marriages, divorces, seduction, deception, broken hearts, broken lives and philandering, reports historian Paul Johnson. He was openly adulterous and manipulative toward his wife of many years, who "treated him throughout with great restraint, moderation and indeed affection, agreeing to go and live with her brother so he could carry on his affair with Lady Ottoline." He also slept with a family's young daughter while staying with them during a lecture trip. Paul Johnson, *Intellectuals* (New York: Harper & Row, 1988), pp. 212-18.

[37]Christine Overall, *Human Reproduction: Principles, Practices, Policies* (Toronto: Oxford University Press, 1993), pp. 20, 85-91, 122.

[38]Ibid., pp. 88-89.

expects and requires that a man provide for his children, even though doing so may cause him much inconvenience. He cannot demand that he be excused from his obligation because his career, schooling, health or emotional well-being might suffer. He knew what he was doing when he did it and should expect to be held accountable. Men are expected to be mature, and the mark of maturity is the willingness to accept the consequences of one's actions, even though doing so may cause sacrifice and even hardship. Women who want equality can demand no less.[39]

Interestingly, this double standard also implies the inferiority of women: while men are expected to parent under any circumstances, women cannot be good mothers except under ideal conditions. Only men are expected to behave as mature adults. Botcher concludes that this double standard "reinforces the traditional concept of women having 'diminished responsibility.' They cannot be held to the same standards as men because they are not as competent as men."[40]

Recommendations

Today "mainline" feminists reject the prolife stance as antifeminist. Interestingly, biblical traditionalists agree with them and therefore reject any feminist position as unbiblical. While mainline feminists have come to be viewed as the inheritors of orthodox feminism, they are only one branch of feminist thought—the radical branch.[41] This group associates abortion with women's rights because they seek an equality in which women can be as immoral as men. Even Bertrand Russell acknowledged that such was not part of the platform of the founders of feminism.[42]

In every battle we fight, our principles are either vindicated or invalidated.[43] Be-

---

[39]Botcher, "Pro-abortionists Poison Feminism," p. 47.

[40]Ibid.

[41]Groothuis discusses four types of feminist thought: liberal, psychoanalytic, Marxist and radical. The liberal type corresponds to the pioneers of feminism, "nineteenth-century classical liberalism," while radical feminists occupy the far end of the feminist spectrum. Groothuis writes that "liberal feminism attempts to implement laws that ensure socioeconomic parity between women and men, while radical feminism aims to create a legal theory that grants special rights and/or consideration to women as a class" (*Women Caught in the Conflict*, p. 93). Christina Hoff Sommers refers to the radical group as "gender feminists." See Sommers, *Who Stole Feminism? How Women Have Betrayed Women* (New York: Simon & Schuster, 1994).

[42]Russell, *Marriage and Morals*, p. 292.

[43]It is possible for me to violate my principle and simultaneously vindicate it. Such vindication comes through acknowledging that the principle is right and I am wrong. However, abortionists deny the rightness of the principle. Seneca is a good example of someone who upheld his principles despite violating them: "I persist in praising not the life that I lead but the one I ought to lead. I follow it at a great distance, crawling."

cause of their inconsistency, mainline feminists have invalidated their own principles. Biblical egalitarians can validate their principles by holding, consistently and
biblically, to certain nonnegotiables:

- The value of all human beings—women and men, born and unborn—is inherent and inalienable.

- Since one's humanity is the basis of one's rights, biological differences between men and women, born and unborn, are inconsequential to human
  rights.

- It is appropriate to seek laws protecting women and the unborn from those
  who would abuse them, even though some in the oppressive class may not
  choose to abuse them.

- Pregnancy and motherhood distinguish women from men biologically but
  not in terms of equality of human rights.

- Equality of the sexes can—and should—hold both sexes to the same *high*
  moral standard, not absolve both from moral responsibility.

- The equal moral responsibility of both sexes in a prolife philosophy entails
  the elimination of all double standards between the sexes.

While the abortion debate is fraught with emotionally bound thinking, occasional opportunities for reasoned discourse do occur. At these times prolife feminists can point out the historical grounding and logical consistency of their position, as well as the inconsistencies of the prochoice position. Let us pray for and
seek out such opportunities.

PART V

LIVING
IT OUT

Practical Applications

25

IN SEARCH OF HOLY JOY

Women and Self-Esteem

Joan Burgess Winfrey

Self-esteem is a human commodity that has substantial relevance to the ministry of Christian women. Although the concept of self-esteem is multifaceted and unwieldy, it is at the point of ministry that it should be taken up. Self-esteem, adequately defined, may well determine not only the ability of Christian women to follow God's call on their life but indeed the belief that God would call them at all. Some years ago Miriam Adeney wrote *A Time for Risking*,[1] in which she posed two crucial questions for women: "What have you come to the kingdom for?" and "What gives you holy joy in the doing of it?"

These questions, which should ignite thoughtful reflection in the mind of any Christian, have formed a kind of thematic core for the Psychology of Women class that I have designed and taught at Denver Seminary. The heart and intent of Adeney's challenge, taken together with the title of the book, can open windows of hope and redirection for the women (and I believe ultimately for the men as well) who sit in the class. It is my strong conviction that the work of ministry and the ministry of work are, for women, vital determinants of self-esteem; yet the internal and external constraints that drive their life choices will likely dilute their access to these sources of fullness and purpose. Later in this chapter I will summarize the subfactors and correlates of self-esteem as they have been distilled in bodies of research. It is worth noting here, however, that the two major substrates of self-esteem, sense of worth and sense of competence, touch on intrinsic human value as well as human agency, the work of our hands. Both aspects call forth significant biblical themes, and both hold fruitful possibility for discussing fullness of life for women.

---

[1]Miriam Adeney, *A Time for Risking: Priorities for Women* (Portland, Ore.: Multnomah Press, 1987).

In the Psychology of Women class, we explore a wide variety of ideas that relate to female development, concepts of femininity, and the formation of the self in girls and women. We ponder the tensions between the universal imperatives of biology and the arbitrariness of culture; the impact of the family, society and the church on female development; and the multiplicity of other factors that shape gender definitions and the gendered psyche. The task of untangling these elements is formidable. In the unraveling process we attempt always to bring what Mary Stewart Van Leeuwen called "biblical critique" to our discussions.[2] For women, as for men, an authentic view of the self evolves out of the knowledge that we are invited residents of a city whose builder and maker is God. There exists for each one, as the beloved, a God-breathed self-statement and job description. The pursuit and discovery of that divine intent hold the secrets of joy and the composition of self-esteem.

Pursuit and discovery, however, are tricky endeavors. For many Christian women the path is stony and imbued with chronic sorrow. I have found in my work with women, both in the classroom and in the counseling room, predictable and recurrent self-defeating thought patterns that arise out of negative self-evaluations. Women frequently hold the belief that they are less intelligent, less capable and less valuable than men.

If we would encourage women along the sacred road of positive self-regard and kingdom purpose, we must attempt to comprehend the psychological, cultural and theological phenomena that have placed women outside the gate for centuries, indeed millennia, rendering them anemic and sometimes powerless to flourish on their own behalf and on behalf of Christ and his kingdom. The diminished agency of one-half of the body of Christ, the hindering of the hands and feet and eyes of Jesus on earth, is, quite simply, grievous.

Not only is self-esteem an unwieldy topic, it often suffers from bad press among Christians. The concept reflects, presumably, the mindset of the therapeutic culture which has shaped American consciousness for decades. The comments of Paul C. Vitz characterize a prominent mode of evangelical thought that equates self-esteem with self-worship and narcissism. Speaking of "the curse of self-esteem," Vitz states that often the term is muddled in confusion and that no agreed-upon definition or measure of self-esteem exists. He maintains, further, that research shows

---

[2]Mary Stewart Van Leeuwen, *Gender and Grace: Love, Work and Parenting in a Changing World* (Downers Grove, Ill.: InterVarsity Press, 1990).

no relationship between self-esteem and human behavior.[3] But Vitz's conclusions are more than a little overdrawn. It is not helpful to uncritically lump together all research on the subject with the groupspeak of pop psychology. The remarks of Vitz do, however, serve to highlight several legitimate points. The term *self-esteem* is in need of a lucid, operational definition; additionally, it is in need of a proper conceptual home, one that draws together valuable, respectable research in psychology with teachings of Scripture as they relate to the many layers of the self. Ellen Charry states that "the autonomous, secular self, a product of enlightenment and popularized post-Freudian psychology, . . . stands in tension with the Christian view that we come from God, return to God, and are therefore to glorify God in thanksgiving."[4] The self in self-esteem is a psychospiritual reality, rich with biblical meaning.

Let us, then, keep the term *self-esteem*, acknowledging the murkiness of the waters in which we navigate.[5] For the word *esteem* Webster's Dictionary offers as one definition "to set a high value on." *Regard* is suggested as a synonym. To regard is "to show respect or consideration, or to recognize the worth of a person."[6] Surely the incarnation is the ultimate act of esteem or regard toward humans. Let us, with humility and thanksgiving, seek deeper understanding of that which Jesus esteemed—our selves, fearfully and wonderfully made and redeemed to be his trophies in the ages to come.

While there is much to mine from research in psychology, the "deep structure," to borrow a term from linguistics, of the meaning of self-esteem is uncovered when we bring theological discernment to bear on psychological theory. A thoughtful discussion that explores the warp and weave of this essentially psychospiritual concept takes us into a room with some unpacked boxes. The unpacking can be facilitated by a discussion of some of the complexities of the concept.

---

[3]Paul C. Vitz, "Leaving Psychology Behind," in *No God but God: Breaking with the Idols of Our Age*, ed. Os Guinness (Chicago: Moody Press, 1992), pp. 95-96.

[4]Ellen Charry, "Theology After Psychology," in *Care for the Soul*, ed. Mark R. McMinn and Timothy R. Phillips (Downers Grove, Ill.: InterVarsity Press, 2001), p. 199.

[5]A number of authors have noted that the term *self-esteem* is used interchangeably with other terms such as *self-concept*, *self-worth* and *self-respect*. See for example, Linda T. Sanford and Mary E. Donovan, *Self-Esteem: Understanding and Improving the Way We Think and Feel About Ourselves* (New York: Penguin, 1985), or Chris Mruk, *Self-Esteem: Research, Theory and Practice* (New York: Springer, 1995). Sanford and Donovan regard *self-concept* as the more encompassing term that may include many self-statements, while self-esteem is the measure of how much we approve of our self-concept. It is "the reputation we have with ourselves" (p. 7).

[6]*Webster's Seventh New Collegiate Dictionary* (Springfield, Mass.: G & C Merriam, 1971), p. 284.

Well-designed research in the behavioral sciences ideally begins with careful definition of the construct or theoretical idea to be studied. However, definition and measurement of psychological constructs are not at all the same as definition and measurement in the physical sciences. In psychology we are confronted with the slaying, as it were, of large hairy mammoths. Intelligence is such a creature, and self-esteem roams the same jungle. We cannot and should not attempt to stringently apply the rigors of the scientific method to the study of humans. When we separate a concept from variables to which it is relevant, we become reductionistic. This is unproductive and undesirable in psychology as well as theology. The development of the self is not one-dimensional; it is contextual. Methods of inquiry must rely on many kinds of data, including that which is phenomenological.

One of the few comprehensive pieces of research on women and self-esteem, that of Linda T. Sanford and Mary E. Donovan,[7] was built on clinical observations and testimonies from women. These researchers offer some compelling comments that should capture the attention of Christians. They conclude that our level of self-esteem affects everything we think, say and do. It affects the choices we make, our ability to receive and give love, and our ability to change things that need to be changed.

An analysis of studies that have summarized large bodies of research on self-esteem reveals two subsuming factors: sense of worth and sense of competence.[8] Chris Mruk offers a phenomenological definition of self-esteem: "the lived status of one's individual competence and personal worthiness at dealing with the challenges of life over time."[9] The definition is useful in providing a framework for considering self-esteem in relationship to psychological and behavioral correlates that can be studied in the lives of people, rather than as an internal, subjective experience of self-evaluation only. Correlates of self-esteem that have been studied include parental factors, birth order, success, agency, acceptance, shame, vulnerability, loneliness, self-awareness, depression and sense of inferiority. Concepts such as the false self, silencing the self, absence of voice and learned helplessness are prev-

---

[7]Sanford and Donovan, *Self-Esteem*, p. xix.

[8]Ibid.; see also Carol Gilligan, *In a Different Voice: Psychological Theory and Women's Development* (Cambridge, Mass.: Harvard University Press, 1982); Emily Hancock, *The Girl Within* (New York: Fawcett Columbine, 1989); Mary Pipher, *Reviving Ophelia: Saving the Selves of Adolescent Girls* (New York: Ballantine, 1994); Jean Baker Miller and Irene Pierce Stiver, *The Healing Connection: How Women Form Relationships in Therapy and in Life* (Boston: Beacon, 1997); Susan Harter, *The Construction of the Self: A Developmental Perspective* (New York: Guildford, 1999).

[9]Mruk, *Self-Esteem*, p. 21.

alent in studies of self-esteem in girls, adolescent females and women.[10]

Several organizing frameworks are helpful for understanding females and their life experiences. It is necessary to gain a historical perspective, exploring philosophical and theoretical trends that have helped shape notions about gender differences. It is crucial, furthermore, to comprehend the way these ideas have been absorbed into the grain of culture and communicated to females. Finally, it is essential to embrace a developmental perspective that places the formation of the gendered self in a social-cultural background. The complexity of humans and the contextual nature of beliefs and actions must be acknowledged. But lurking in the corner is the eight-hundred-pound gorilla, our legacy from the Fall.

The Fallen Self as a Central Motif

Several great themes of Scripture can serve as lanterns for efforts to summarize findings and construct meanings on the formation of the self and self-esteem in women. Without some discussion of the image of God in humanity and the implications of the fallen nature of humans, gender studies are a hopeless perplexity. I have been indebted for some years now to Mary Stewart Van Leeuwen for her cogent discussion of the richly textured meanings of image bearing and of the differential effects of the Fall on males and females.[11] Her valuable insights have brought order out of chaos many times as I have attempted to construct a sound conceptual base for viewing the psychology of women.

Van Leeuwen suggests that if we are to understand the pervasiveness of gender stereotypes and gender struggles, we must go beyond biological, familial and cultural explanations. Something deeper is at work. To be made in the image of God is to share some of the attributes of God. Two aspects of the image of God that are of particular importance to our discussion are sociability and accountable dominion. God is intrinsically social, and his clear intention is for male and female, both created in his image, to work in equality and interdependence. Both the male and the female are given accountable dominion and told to fill the earth and subdue it. Van Leeuwen states that well-trained evangelical scholars agree unanimously that God called both sexes equally to exercise this dominion and that both are joint heirs to creation as well as salvation.

Yet the Fall, though it affected both male and female, may have affected them

---

[10]Ibid.
[11]Van Leeuwen, *Gender and Grace*, pp. 38-50.

in different ways. As the consequences for each one are announced, Genesis 3:16 ("your desire shall be for your husband, and he shall rule over you") foretells an unreciprocated desire for intimacy on the part of the woman and a tendency to abuse power in the case of the man. The result for the male (well documented in history) is the propensity to let dominion run wild. The result for the female, whose inclination is toward relationship and affiliation (also well supported in decades of psychological literature), is surrendered responsibility. The particular female sin is to use the preservation of relationships as an excuse not to exercise accountable dominion. This may take several forms, including "peace at any price," the securing of unhealthy, even destructive relationships, and reducing all of womanhood to the nurturance of others at the expense of hearing the word of God and keeping it. Women "adopt silence as their gift for the harmony of the church."[12] But peace at the expense of justice is not peace at all.

Van Leeuwen refers us to Luke 11:27-28. A woman, in the midst of a large crowd that looked on as Jesus cast out a demon, called out to him, "Blessed is the womb that bore you and the breasts that nursed you!" Jesus' response to her is startling: "Blessed rather are those who hear the word of God and obey it!" (NRSV). Jesus is not disparaging motherhood. He, through whom all things were made, knew only too well the woman's plight, a predicament externally imposed by her culture and perpetuated by her own nature. She would all too easily "disallow the logos"[13] and entrench herself in domesticity. Was Jesus simply seizing the moment to invoke an abstract principle of truth? Or did Jesus, sent from the heart of God, care more deeply than we can comprehend about the wholeness of this woman, and the women of generations to follow? This Lover of our soul was ministering soul care. "Hearing and doing" are choices that heal us and that transcend gender stereotypes and roles.

The events of the Genesis account and Van Leeuwen's perceptive elucidation of their sad aftermath in our fallen race have been self-evident over the past century in American culture. It is easy to resent the assumptions of Sigmund Freud, especially as he presumed to speak for women; yet he made a statement that had far

---

[12]Faith Martin, *Call Me Blessed: The Emerging Christian Woman* (Grand Rapids, Mich.: Eerdmans, 1988), p. 4.

[13]This expression is used by James C. Neely in *Gender: The Myth of Equality* (New York: Simon & Schuster, 1981), pp. 213-29. *Logos* is not used exclusively to mean the Word of God as in John 1, though it may include that meaning. Neely refers also to knowledge of society and its institutions, intellectual knowledge, and a general awareness and knowing that comes from erudition and involvement in the world.

greater import than he could have imagined. He contended that the psychologically healthy person loves well and works well. Freud, who professed atheism throughout his writings, had more theology than he knew. Loving and working—living out the *imago Dei*—are the keys to a healthy self and self-esteem. Yet living in the full expression of both sides of the *imago*—relationship and dominion—is a balancing act of formidable proportions for women who historically have been restricted by the dictates of culture and their own propensity to relinquish the work of the kingdom. The words of our Lord to the woman in Luke 11 ring across the ages into our own century.

Sigmund Freud and the Church: Peculiar People

Although writings on gender have frequently reflected a secular worldview, the body of knowledge on the subject accumulated in the biological and social sciences is of much potential value to the church. The crisis of the American woman has touched every sector of our culture. It is imperative that Christians, whom God has called to be salt and light in the world, give painstaking consideration to the issues that affect not only body life in the church but the moral tapestry of society as well. The church has the duty of accumulating, interpreting and sifting scientific and cultural knowledge, and the privilege of speaking to the needs of society from God's truth. This is accomplished through the humility that ensues from the recognition of our finiteness and through persistent effort to discover truth, both from God's revealed Word and from his creation, which is also part of his revelation.

Because interest in gender and gender roles as they relate to women in the family, the church and the world of work is in some degree a consequence of the feminist movement, evangelicals often assume that these concerns represent a worldly, not a biblical, emphasis. But ironically, roles defined for women as biblically correct can be shown to derive from cultural values and cultural definitions of femininity that are not in concert with biblical teaching.

Prior to the 1960s, psychological research, in large measure, conceptualized masculinity and femininity as bipolar opposites. The view of male and female as opposites, having mutually exclusive qualities, has deep historical roots. Theory in psychology, particularly that of Freud, has taken male anatomy and masculinity as the human standard. Femininity has been viewed as "absence of" or "otherness." Traditionalists and hierarchical complementarians, with their emphasis on role theology, rely on an inherent-trait thesis reminiscent of the "anatomy as destiny" biological determinism of Freud.

In the year that Martin Luther King Jr. gave his immortal "I Have a Dream" speech, Betty Friedan wrote *The Feminine Mystique*,[14] considered by many to be the seminal piece of writing of the twentieth-century feminist revolution in the United States. Friedan does not hold a Christian worldview, but every Christian should read and reread *The Feminine Mystique*—and then weep. Chapter five, "The Sexual Solipsism of Sigmund Freud," brings an indictment of American culture that could have and should have been written to the church. The affluence, the materialism, the turning inward, the discrimination, the failure to assist people in their place of need—in short, the tragic missing of the mark, or what Paul Tournier referred to as "the disincarnation of the church"[15]—find portentous expression in the following words of Friedan:

> After the depression, after the war, Freudian psychology became much more than a science of human behavior, a therapy for the suffering. It became an all-embracing American ideology, a new religion. It filled the vacuum of thought and purpose that existed for many for whom God, or flag, or bank account were no longer sufficient— and yet who were tired of feeling responsible for lynchings and concentration camps and the starving children of India and Africa. It provided a convenient escape from the atom bomb, McCarthy, all the disconcerting problems that might spoil the taste of steaks, and cars, and color television and backyard swimming pools. It gave us permission to suppress the troubling questions of the larger world and pursue our own personal pleasures. And if the new psychological religion—which made a virtue of sex, removed all sin from private vice, and cast suspicion on high aspirations of the mind and spirit—had a more devastating personal effect on women than men, nobody planned it that way.[16]

We cannot diminish the great contributions of Freud to the field of psychology. These include the role of defenses in human behavior and his structural theory of personality, which identifies the existence of the unconscious. Freud's greatest contribution, his developmental schema of human growth (which ironically proved to be a two-edged sword for women), paved the way for decades of important work. Neo-Freudian theories such as object relations theory and self-psychology, which absorbed and expanded Freud's inchoate and reductionistic principles into a more

---

[14]Betty Friedan, *The Feminine Mystique* (New York: Dell, 1963).

[15]Paul Tournier, *The Whole Person in a Broken World: A Biblical Remedy for Today's World* (New York: Harper & Row, 1964), p. 160.

[16]Friedan, *Feminine Mystique*, p. 123.

psychosocial, relational context, have been significant gifts to the world.

Freud, however, was strangely incapable of extricating himself from the social milieu of Victorian Vienna. This is nowhere more strongly evidenced than in his misconstrued psychology of women, fashioned out of parochial observations that have no reference outside of his own perceptual world. The Victorian woman, whose degradation and inferiority were taken as the natural order of things, formed the basis for Freud's female psychology. American culture and, more shockingly deplorable, the church all too readily absorbed Freud's notions about females. Additionally, as Friedan aptly notes, Freud's pleasure principle provided a segue to the good life and the American dream.

The cult of the housewife, popularized by the likes of *Leave It to Beaver*, was given a biblical cloak by the church. The post-World War II years, with their growing affluence, were a fertile medium for this uniquely American phenomenon. Divided gender spheres, with the man "out there" performing the real work of the world and the woman thoroughly domesticated, were the unhappy, inevitable outcomes. Thus the man was fragmented from the mainstream of the family and the woman was largely excluded from public life.

In order to sustain the way of life that characterized the ideals of Americans in the middle of the twentieth century, a type of sociological functionalism was opted for, without consciousness and without critique, and within the church it wore the mask of Christian virtue. Functionalism draws its assumptions (as Freud did) from a biological model and defines humans and human institutions according to their structure and function. Utilitarian, yes. It smacks of the "optimalization" spoken of by Nicolas Davidson,[17] which seeks "first to utilize human capacities efficiently and harmoniously, and second to meet universal physical and emotional needs with a minimum of friction and waste of effort."[18] Human endeavors, according to Davidson, should be as efficient and functional as possible, like well-oiled machinery.

There is no kingdom purpose here. Friedan describes it in this way: "By giving absolute meaning and sanctimonious value to the term 'woman's role,' functionalism put American women into a kind of deep freeze."[19] Friedan draws on the illustration of Nora from Henrik Ibsen's *A Doll's House*, a play written in 1879. Nora's desire was to live and love as a full human being and to obtain an education. In

---

[17]Nicolas Davidson, *The Failure of Feminism* (Buffalo, N.Y.: Prometheus, 1988), p. 258.
[18]Ibid., p. 127.
[19]Friedan, *Feminine Mystique*, p. 128.

1963 Nora might have laughed at an old-fashioned grandpa who told her she could not become a scientist because woman's place was in the home. But Nora would not have laughed at the complex, mysterious language of functionalism or of Freudian psychology, which made much the same statement with "not much more basis than Grandpa."[20]

Proponents of role theology in the church have cranked up the deep-freeze dial for women. In a three-part study of role theology,[21] Del Birkey points out that "the Bible does not address femininity and masculinity as independent realities because they are constructed and reconstructed in learned relational behavior in the world's cultures. 'Role theology' rebaptizes secular sociocultural and radical biologically deterministic theories of gender power into a Christian theology. But 'role theology' is unequivocally not biblical doctrine."[22] Birkey emphasizes that spiritual gifts, agape love, servant leadership and mutual submission are the determinants of Christian ministry, not gender, gender roles, authority or hierarchy.

Faith Martin affirms this position. She laments the fact that while the church is comfortable with little girls, women who are gifted as speakers, as administrators or in any other role that would break the traditional role of silence are a problem. Women are relegated to a position in the church that is parallel to, if not worse than, their position in society—one that ignores their rights as children of God. "The doctrine of woman's spiritual equality is gradually bringing about a growing self-confidence among Christian women. We are ready to challenge the current theories restricting our service. Secure in the knowledge that our cornerstone was laid by God, we will take the Scriptures as our deed and reclaim our borders."[23]

Reclaiming our borders must occur in a context of reconciliation. The modern feminist response to traditional psychological theory on females did not have this goal. The gender literature of the 1960s and 1970s mirrored feminist ideology and represented a radical, antithetical departure from the anatomy-as-destiny psychology of Freud. In its extreme, it denied all differences between males and females except those that are explicitly biological. This body of writing tended to encompass an evolutionary, relativistic epistemology that was polemical, self-righteous

---

[20]Ibid., p. 128.
[21]Del Birkey, "Gender Authority," *Priscilla Papers* 15, no. 1 (2001); "The Intolerable Goal of Role Theology," *Priscilla Papers* 15, no. 2 (2001); "New Testament Limits of Authority and Hierarchical Power," *Priscilla Papers* 15, no. 3 (2001).
[22]Birkey, "Intolerable Goal," p. 5.
[23]Martin, *Call Me Blessed*, p. 27.

and antimale. The extreme cultural determinism of radical feminism served mostly to entrench traditionalists.

The biology-culture tightrope is always difficult to negotiate, but the 1980s brought new gleanings from science and women's studies that rendered inadequate the earlier feminist dichotomy between nature and nurture. Biology and culture do not exist apart from one another. Biological determinism creates a false division between the sexes, and cultural determinism denies the particular strengths and needs of women and men. Both extremes carry potentially perilous consequences for human beings.

Neuropsychology and psychoendocrinology, the branches of science that relate central nervous system function with psychological behaviors, are evolving fields. Behavior must be regarded as the end result of a complex interaction of many factors. While it seems unlikely that the observed differences between male and female brains and physiologies have nothing to do with behavioral differences, the relationships are not clearly understood.

Beyond Developmental Maps, Beyond Life Scripts

Historically, developmental theory in psychology has reflected patterns and norms equated with maleness. Prior to the 1980s, assumptions about female growth were based almost exclusively on models of male development. Sigmund Freud, Jean Piaget, Erik Erikson and Lawrence Kohlberg, whose ideas shaped developmental psychology in the United States, uniformly identified psychological attributes associated with masculinity as hallmarks of maturity and health. Erikson and Kohlberg did not include any female subjects in their studies. Healthy developmental task achievements typically were expressed through such terms as *separation, individuation* and *autonomy.* Terms such as *connection* and *affiliation,* which would characterize women's studies in the decades to come, were in short supply.

It must be noted that it is impossible, through studies conducted with either male or female subjects, to reach impeccable conclusions on what is intrinsic and what is culturally determined. Traits and behaviors that derive from one's status in society, whether privileged or subordinate, cannot indiscriminately be judged as innate or as representing a standard of measurement. Yet all of these theorists freehandedly drew conclusions about human development in general and female development in particular from their observations.

Brett Webb-Mitchell provides an interesting, well-formulated discussion of the impact of Enlightenment thinking on developmental psychology. Among the strains of Enlightenment thought is an overemphasis on individualism and logical categories. As an alternative perspective, Webb-Mitchell suggests the biblical metaphor of pilgrimage for development across the life span of the Christian. "Christian pilgrimage is different from developmental psychology because it takes place on a particular pathway among a particular community that is greater and older than an individual and is constituted and guided by a specific story, the Gospel of God."[24] He states further that the pilgrimage is a "mindbodyspirit"[25] act of the person, and it is through the grace of God that we come to maturity, to the measure of the full stature of Christ (Eph 4:13).

Webb-Mitchell's concerns about fragmentation and dualism in theories of human development are germane to this discussion of fullness of life for women, as are his insights on the significance of the role of community in human experience. Studies of the psychology of women that began to emerge in the late 1970s and early 1980s had a central theme of relationship. It is in relationship that core female identity is shaped, and concern for relationship underlies the life patterns and choices of females. Women's studies of the 1980s began to celebrate the distinctives of female development and the female voice as authentic, worthy subjects of inquiry.[26] But the relational context, which inevitably determines the developmental pathway of the female, is at once her strength and her vulnerability.

Many personal and social factors are woven through the fabric of women's self-esteem. The array of women's issues identified in research of the past several decades are invariably punctuated with a relationship constituent. For example, the negative experiences of women in corporations appear to result, in part, from avoidance of competitive actions that might jeopardize work relationships. The need to please others is played out also in eating disorders, which are almost exclusive to female populations. Additionally, the dynamics of depression in females reflect the vulnerability of females' relational core. And let us not overlook the relentless, shameless objectification of the female body in the media, from advertising, to

---

[24]Brett Webb-Mitchell, "Leaving Development Behind and Beginning Our Pilgrimage," in *Care for the Soul: Exploring the Intersection of Psychology and Theology,* ed. Mark R. McMinn and Timothy R. Phillips (Downers Grove, Ill.: InterVarsity Press, 2001), p. 91.

[25]Ibid., p. 95.

[26]For a brief summary of a number of these writings, see Joan Burgess Winfrey, "Pastoral Care for Abused Women," in *Women, Abuse and the Bible: How Scripture Can Be Used to Hurt or Heal,* ed. Catherine Clark Kroeger and James R. Beck (Grand Rapids, Mich.: Baker, 1996), pp. 154-56. See also the important works that have evolved from the Stone Center at Wellesley College by Jean Baker Miller, Irene Pierce Stiver, Judith Jordan, Janet L. Surrey and others.

loathsome television sitcoms, to NFL cheerleading with sports cameras zooming in like infrared missiles. The relational factor surfaces when we ask questions about females' tolerance and even complicity in these societal travesties. The internal codes that define the feminine self place girls and women at risk for humiliation, contempt, objectification, marginalization and sometimes life-threatening psychological symptoms.

I have a love-hate relationship with the findings of women's studies of recent decades. They are echoed consistently in my own clinical experiences with women. The relational context in which women live and move is warm and good, a thing to be cherished. It is God's gracious endowment to her, but it is easily exploited by significant others and by our predatory culture. In my initial interview sessions with women clients, almost without exception the word *codependent* is tossed out as part of the presenting problem. This has become a wastebasket term, and I always ask the client to tell me what the word means to her. Predictably, she acknowledges that she too is part of the problem. In some manner she gives herself away at the expense of her self-respect. This is frequently in close personal relationships, but almost as often it is in a work setting or in her faith community. Her self-esteem battle may exist alongside the anguish of a faith crisis. My work with her may include helping her reframe her internal representations of God, a crucial step in the healing of her soul.

I also have a foreboding apprehension about the potential application of gender literature that identifies the significance of relationship in the lives of girls and women. Perhaps it is part of our inheritance from the Garden that perpetuates our fondness for dichotomies and categories. Femininity and masculinity are more accurately depicted on a continuum. Categories can quickly take the shape of dualisms, and absolutes can take on the power of articles of faith. Dualism has several sharp edges for women. Mind-body dualism has tended to equate femaleness with the body, nature and the earth. Maleness has been equated with the spiritual, the intellectual and the cultural. The corporeal and the natural are regarded as inferior to the spiritual and the cultural. In our fallen state, human pride finds greater value in what is built, shaped and refined by human effort than in what is part of natural existence. Women continue to fashion their identity in relationship and, in large measure, interpret reality out of bodily experience, including the bearing and nurturing of children.[27]

---

[27]Winfrey, "Pastoral Care," pp. 153-54.

Instead of acclaiming the legitimate transformative power inherent in women's relational emphases in work, ministry and all of life, the church may once again opt for a Venus-Mars gender rubbish in the interest of cementing roles and putting up divider walls. Social-emotional realms, especially the home, and "godliness with contentment" are then the divine appointment for women. The comments of Webb-Mitchell are again helpful here. "In pilgrimage, the telos, the point of the journey, defines the method of the journey and the journey itself. . . . In sum, the telos is what matters in our understanding of what development is."[28] What have we come to the kingdom for?

Growing Up Gifted in the Name of Jesus

> May the favor of the Lord our God rest upon us;
>   establish the work of our hands for us—
> yes, establish the work of our hands. (Ps 90:17 NIV)

Psalm 90 is called "A Prayer of Moses the Man of God." To the name of Moses, a highly revered figure in the Old Testament history of redemption, is added a title of honor, an ancient name of the prophets which expresses an intimate fellowship with God.[29] As Israel stood on the threshold of the Promised Land, Moses recognized that human undertakings are the work of the Lord insofar as they are executed by him. It is the gracious rule of Yahweh that establishes our work. As his people, cast in his image, we need intimate fellowship with him and with other humans. Our sense of worth arises out of life together. And we need to work in his vineyards. Our sense of competence emerges as we work together, according to his purpose and grace.

The titles of books written in recent decades for women who are of the household of God suggest that family members need to sweep the corners to find some lost coins:

- *No Time for Silence*

- *Women in Travail and Transition: A New Pastoral Care*

- *A Costly Obedience*

- *Loving and Working: Reweaving Women's Public and Private Lives*

---

[28]Webb-Mitchell, "Leaving Development Behind," p. 96.
[29]Franz Delitzsch, *Psalms* in *Commentary on the Old Testament*, ed. C. F. Keil and Franz Delitzsch (reprint, Grand Rapids, Mich.: Eerdmans, 1986), pp. 48-59.

- *Ministry at the Margins*

- *A Time for Risking*[30]

These authors identify the need for women in ministry to confront injustice and bring compassion and agape love to the world. Staking claim to biblical principles and historical precedent, they urge women to say yes to what really matters and to pour out their energies for the sake of God's kingdom. They hold no illusions that these charges are easy. They boldly proclaim that God distributes gifts according to grace, not gender, and that his gifts and calling are irrevocable (Rom 11:29).

What Do Women Want?

Several years ago I was a guest speaker in a class on men's issues, having been asked to report some of the recent research in women's studies. One young man raised his hand and asked, "So just what is it that women want anyway?" I could barely contain my smile, which did not reflect any disrespect for the young man. It was the exact question that was asked repeatedly by Sigmund Freud in his lifetime.

We must first acknowledge what we need. We need a theological self-concept,[31] for only in the strength of God's truth can we begin to disentangle ourselves from the malignant messages of our culture and divest ourselves of the things that so easily beset us. Then, with integrity, we can request what we want.

Realizing that this is a lifelong endeavor, a pilgrimage, I will presume to speak for Christian women and state that the wish list could look like this:

- We want to enter the Promised Land and participate freely in the unfolding drama of redemption.

- We want to love and work as those who inhabit the City of God.

---

[30]Janette Hassey, *No Time for Silence: Evangelical Women in Public Ministry Around the Turn of the Century* (Minneapolis: Christians for Biblical Equality, 1986); Maxine Glaz and Jeanne Stevenson Morssner, eds., *Women in Travail and Transition* (Minneapolis: Fortress, 1991); Elizabeth Smith Bellinger, ed., *A Costly Obedience: Sermons by Women of Steadfast Spirit* (Valley Forge, Penn.: Judson, 1994); Rosemary Curran Barciauskas and Debra Beery Hull, *Loving and Working: Reweaving Women's Public and Private Lives* (Bloomington, Ind.: Meyer-Stone, 1989); Cheryl J. Sanders, *Ministry at the Margins: The Prophetic Mission of Women, Youth and the Poor* (Downers Grove, Ill.: InterVarsity Press, 1997); Adeney, *Time for Risking*.

[31]Jeffrey H. Boyd, "Self-Concept: In Defense of the Word *Soul*," in *Care for the Soul: Exploring the Intersection of Psychology and Theology*, ed. Mark R. McMinn and Timothy R. Phillips (Downers Grove, Ill.: InterVarsity Press, 2001), p. 106. Boyd submits an intriguing rationale for soul as the biblical parallel of the self. See also Jeffrey H. Boyd, "The 'Soul' of the Psalms Compared to the 'Self' of Kohut," *Journal of Psychology and Christianity* 19, no. 3 (Fall 2000), where he writes that it is the soul that longs for and calls out to God, and it is the empathy of God that restores the soul (pp. 291-31).

- We want to be honored as anointed vessels in God's plan of reconciliation for the world, free of internal and external reproach on our bodies and minds.

- We want honest dialogue with the men in our lives about the things we hold sacred.

- We want to listen and to be heard.

- We want to ripen into Christian adulthood and grow up gifted in the name of Jesus.

Kathleen Norris, in her poem "The Monastery Orchard in Early Spring" from the collection *Little Girls in Church*, says it well:

God's cows are in the fields,
safely grazing. I can see them
through bare branches,
through the steady rain,
fir trees seem ashamed
and tired, bending under winter coats.

I, too, want to be light enough
for this day: throw off impediments,
push like a tulip
through a muddy smear of snow.

I want to take the rain to heart
and feel it move
like possibility, the idea
of change, through things
seen and unseen,
forces, principalities, powers.

Newton named the force that pulls the apple
and the moon with it,
toward the center of the earth.
Augustine found a desire as strong: to steal,
to possess, then throw away.
Encounter with fruit is dangerous:
the pear's womanly shape forever mocked him.

A man and a woman are talking.
Rain moves down and

branches lift up
to learn again
how to hold their fill of green
and blossom, and bear each fruit to glory,
letting it fall.[32]

---

[32]Kathleen Norris, "The Monastery Orchard in Early Spring," in *Little Girls in Church* (Pittsburgh, Penn.: University of Pittsburgh, 1995), p. 45.

26

MARRIAGE AS A PARTNERSHIP
OF EQUALS

Judith K. Balswick and Jack O. Balswick

*Two are better than one, because they have a good reward for their toil. For if they fall, one will lift up the
other; but woe to one who is alone and falls and does not have another to help. Again, if two lie together,
they keep warm; but how can one keep warm alone? And though one might prevail against another, two
will withstand one. A threefold cord is not quickly broken.* ECCLES 4:9-12

A number of the chapters in this book give exegetical understandings of Scripture and theological support for marital equality. In this chapter we build on this
foundation and focus on the practical aspects of how marriage as a partnership of
equals can be a life-giving reality.

Languaging Marriage

The central issue and dividing line between marital equality and inequality is the
authority issue. And much of the controversy over marital authority is about the
language used to describe marriage in Christian circles. That marriage is a partnership is widely held, although partnership is defined and practiced in a variety of
ways. Three categories for describing and negotiating authority in the marital partnership are *male leadership, mutual submissiveness* and *equal regard.* It should come as no
surprise that each approach boasts the authority of Scripture when it comes to interpretation and application to the marital relationship.

Male leadership proponents regard authority as inherent in the position of the
husband. According to this view, decisions about marriage and family life are ultimately to be made by the husband. The corresponding implication is that the wife
must take a submissive role. Is it possible, one might ask, for marriage to be a partnership of equals according to this view? Answering this question requires some

understanding of how the concept of "male leadership" is used. At the risk of over-simplifying, we suggest that the male leadership model comes in two varieties—hard patriarchy and soft patriarchy.

Patriarchy refers to a social structural system that gives husbands an assumed position of authority over their wives. In hard patriarchy, husbands make critical and final decisions and wives willingly submit to the husband's authority over them. Soft patriarchy emphasizes a suffering servant model of the husband's leadership. Christian husbands are to emulate "servant leadership" in relationship to their wives, just as Christ laid down his life for the church.

The mutual submissiveness model calls for husbands and wives to be subject to one another (Eph 5:21). This model is applicable to relationships in the body of Christ, but specifically to the marital dyad.

Don Browning, director of the Religion, Culture and Family Project, describes Christian marriage as a relationship of equal regard.[1] The ethic of equal regard is a response to the feminist ideology and social science literature that stresses independence rather than mutuality and interdependence. The expressed concern is that language of submissiveness and self-sacrifice opens the door to personal abuse of power. It is further reasoned that since the biblical view of marital love is mutuality, each spouse should regard the other as she or he wants to be regarded. Browning is open to the concept of self-sacrifice in love if it is "derived from equal regard."[2]

While we agree with Browning in substance, we also affirm the concept of mutual submission and personal sacrifice. Circumstances like sickness, absence or incapacity require unequal sacrifice of one spouse. In this case one spouse is challenged to give much more than an equal share. Making the best interest of the other a priority is the essence of the extraordinary way of the cross and covenant love.

Perhaps it isn't so much the language we use but our actions that speak louder than words. While attitudes and beliefs certainly influence perceptions about marital roles, what truly makes a difference is how spouses experience their relationship in the day-to-day encounter. This is where the rubber meets the road! Should we conclude then that language is unimportant? Not at all, for behavior is a direct reflection of how spouses define themselves and their roles. However, we hasten to add that how one is treated determines marital satisfaction. Therefore the two

---

[1]Don S. Browning, Bonnie Miller-McLemore, Pamela Couture, K. Brynof Lyon and Robert Franklin *From Culture Wars to Common Ground: Religion and the American Family Debate,* 2nd ed. (Louisville, Ky.: Westminster John Knox, 2000).

[2]Ibid., pp. 238-84.

things, role definition and behavior, go hand in hand.

In fact, couples may use any one of these terms *(male leadership, mutual submissiveness* or *equal regard)* and practice inequality or equality in marriage. So authority must be understood in terms of how power is defined and used in each unique relationship.

Power in Marriage

Power is the ability to influence. Spousal power can be either achieved or ascribed. Achieved power is based on personal resources that are valued by both spouses. Each spouse has personal and relational qualities—such as emotional stability, wisdom, compassion, spirituality, knowledge, relational sensitivity—that have significant influence in the relationship and are valued by the other spouse. The greater one's resources, the greater the potential influence (power) in the relationship.

In contrast, ascribed power "comes with the position." In a patriarchal system the husband has power over the wife simply because he is male. This is a position of power that is culturally endowed, solely by virtue of gender. He has certain rights and privileges that go along with the position. He hasn't had to earn it or prove it, it is a given! In fact, he can do what he likes even if it's selfish. His wife may resent him because she is at his mercy, but she succumbs nonetheless. Ascribed power can also be thought of as contingency power, for it is dependent on both the husband's and wife's acceptance of the belief system that assigns power to the husband. A certain amount of power may also be ascribed to the woman in the role of mother or wife. She has power over her children or even over her husband in certain situations.

One common misunderstanding about power in marriage can be seen in the secular social-exchange model, in which each partner tries to maximize their personal interest. This model views the marital relationship as a zero-sum game in which there is a set number of units of power available in any relationship. Power in marriage can be represented as 100 units to be divided up between the husband and wife. If the husband has all the power (100 units), the wife has none (0 units). If the wife has slightly more power (60 units), then the husband is less powerful (40 units). According to this marital model, 50 units must be carefully allocated to each spouse. Scott Bartchy points out how this ludicrous scenario puts the husband effectively in command if he has 51 power units in contrast to the wife's 49 units.[3] Spouses keep score in a rat race of vying for one unit of

---

[3]S. Scott Bartchy, "Issues of Power and a Theology of the Family: Consultation on a Theology of the Family," seminar given at Fuller Theological Seminary, Pasadena, Calif., 1984; S. Scott Bartchy, "Issues of Power and a Theology of the Family," *Mission Journal* 21 (July-August 1987): 3-15.

power. Instead of spending all that energy over a one-point edge, it makes more sense for both spouses to be 100 percent powerful. In a marriage of mutual submission, both spouses reach full potential and together double their relationship satisfaction.

Dominant Husbands and Manipulative Wives

Marriages of mutual empowerment do not come naturally or automatically. The human tendency in marriage is to dominate in order to guarantee personal interests. The desire for power and self-preservation is obvious in the Genesis narrative. Adam and Eve act out of desire for power and disobey God's boundaries. When confronted by God, Eve points the finger at the serpent, while Adam says Eve made him do it and is even bold enough to blame God for bringing Eve into his life. They protect and defend themselves rather than admit their fault and face the consequences of their behavior.

Unbalanced marital power is based on self-interest and ascribed power. The dilemma it sets up is that the husband has most of the power and the wife has little power. The wife is automatically in the "one down" position and the husband in the "one up" position. Because the husband's power is ascribed, there is no way for a wife to have equal power. The tendency in any social system based on inequality is for the more powerful to coerce and the less powerful to manipulate. Whether inequality is based on race, age or gender, persons in subordinate positions are given one of two options: either submit or influence in indirect ways. In the case of marriage, the wife may find subtle ways to influence her husband. For example, she may form a coalition with her children or extended family members to gain strength and power in her position.

The not-too-subtle intent of many women's books is to teach wives how to manipulate their husbands in order to get what they want. This approach views the husband as the weak link because the subordinate wife can easily outsmart him. She is taught to use sex to get her way. The sexy wife can reduce her husband to compliance through sweet talk and finesse. In knowing and unknowing ways, she goes to extremely superficial and dishonest lengths to influence her husband. In truth, a husband whose masculine security is based on his wife's submission places himself in the position of actually being under her control. By merely disobeying him or refusing him sex, or showing little interest in the relationship, she brings his masculine ego into question. At this point his power is effectively reduced to zero, leaving him alone and desperate.

The Inherent Superiority of Equal Partnership Marriages

In his classic book *Love and Will* Rollo May identifies five types of power: (1) exploitative (influence by brute force), (2) manipulative (influence by devious social-psychological means), (3) competitive (influence based on the possession and use of personal resources), (4) nutritive (influence like that of a parent on a child—this power eventually outlives its usefulness) and (5) integrative (the use of personal power for another's sake).[4] What May calls integrative power is clearly what we refer to as empowerment. May points to Jesus as an example of one who used integrative power. In stating his central message Jesus said, "I came that they may have life, and have it to the full" (Jn 10:10).

The power of God is available in unlimited supply. Each spouse is given the fruit of the Spirit in full measure; each spouse is to be an imitator of Christ; every believer is to be filled with the Holy Spirit. God calls spouses to give of their life out of fullness, not out of deprivation. Spouses who are for each other want the best for each other. Both spouses have power, and neither has to lord it over, control or manipulate the other in order to express their wishes. Mutual empowerment means that two persons reach their fullest potential as God intended. They mesh their lives as individuals and partners in marriage, work, coparenting, life goals and service to the Lord.

In equal partnership marriages the locus of authority is placed in the relationship, not in one spouse or the other. Even though it may take longer to arrive at a joint decision, as the couple listens, honors and respects each other's opinion, they move toward a united stance. It adds the dimension of "we-ness" and mutual accountability as each one takes a responsible role in decisions that are made.

Carmen Martin-Knudson and Anne Mahoney have developed a measurement of marital equality based on four criteria: partners hold equal status; accommodation in the relationship is mutual; attention to the other in the relationship is mutual; and there is mutual well-being of the partners.[5] Several studies indicate the importance of equality in marriage as a success factor. In a study of 135 elderly married couples, Wallace Reynolds and Rory Rerner found different measurements of equality all to be associated with marital sat-

---

[4]Rollo May, *Love and Will* (New York: W. W. Norton, 1969).

[5]Carmen Martin-Knudson and Anne Mahoney, "Language and Processes in the Construction of Equality in New Marriages," *Family Relations: Interdisciplinary Journal of Applied Family Studies* 47, no. 1 (1998): 81-91.

isfaction.[6] In a crosscultural study of 186 cultures, Lewellyn Hendrix found role sharing to be strongly related to marital equality.[7] Drawing on extensive research and personal interviews in the United Kingdom, the United States and Israel, Claire Low Rabin found a correlation between marital inequality and marital distress.[8]

Living out mutual submission principles in the marital relationship requires ongoing refining. Dialoging about disagreements, honoring differences, communicating honestly, and facing the challenges of parenting and married life is a transforming process. The marital encounter becomes a crucible of sorts in which spouses are changed through their interaction. Each spouse must be brave enough to express personal needs as well as consider the needs of the spouse. The anxiety that occurs when things heat up and solutions are not easily found is often stressful. In fact, in their study of 150 Israeli married couples, Claire Low Rabin and Ofrit Shapira-Berman found that while equal role sharing and decision making were predictive of wives' marital satisfaction, these predicted marital *tension* for husbands.[9]

Working out an equal partnership takes time, effort and energy. Heartache and disappointment will be part of the refining process of living and loving in relationship. Spouses will be challenged to face themselves in new ways in the context of the other and the marriage. Admitting mistakes, becoming aware of one's faults and shortcomings, and making honest apologies can be grueling. It's not always easy to smooth out the rough edges that occur, but the very process of working it through creates character, personal strength and relationship growth. Transformation is the ultimate promise and hope for marriages that are sharpened on the grindstone of truthful interaction.

Behind the "two are better than one" Scripture is the idea that two independent persons have unique strengths to offer each other and the relationship. Without two separate identities, interdependence is not possible. Some hold to the false notion that dependency or fusion is the ideal: "I can't do it without you, and I must lean on you to be strong." Two overly dependent persons hanging on to each other for dear life have no solid ground on which to stand when things

---

[6]Wallace Reynolds and Rory Rerner, "Marital Satisfaction in Later Life: An Examination of Equity, Equality and Reward Theories," *International Journal of Aging and Human Development* 40, no. 2 (1995): 155-73.

[7]Lewellyn Hendrix, "Quality and Equality in Marriage: A Cross-Cultural View," *Journal of Comparative Social Science* 31, no. 3 (1997): 201-25.

[8]Claire Low Rabin, *Equal Partners, Good Friends: Empowering Couples Through Therapy* (London: Routledge, 1996).

[9]Claire Low Rabin and Ofrit Shapira-Berman, "Egalitarianism and Marital Happiness: Israeli Wives and Husbands on a Collision Course?" *American Journal of Family Therapy* 25, no. 4 (1997): 319-30.

get difficult or an unexpected stress hits.

Empowerment occurs when two equal partners influence each other. Interdependence is the intent. Spouses who are secure and self-confident can express themselves honestly and directly. In doing so, they have an opportunity to listen and to know the deeper feelings and thoughts of their spouse so they can come to a decision out of mutual respect and regard. Individual power is translated into relationship strength. When each spouse is able to stand solidly on his or her own feet, using the personal resources and relational strengths that have been developed, mutual empowerment happens.

Equal Partnership Parenting

In hierarchical marriages, the mother does most of the parenting. Yet few parents can do it well all by themselves. The Bible teaches the importance of both parents' involvement in the lives of their children. Nowhere does Scripture teach that mothering is more important than fathering. A healthy byproduct of marriage as an equal partnership is the emergence of a strong coparenting model. In fact, some researchers have identified the lack of fathers' involvement in the lives of their children as the source of major social problems today.[10] An accumulation of evidence demonstrates the benefits of coparenting to children and parents alike. When father and mother are jointly involved in parenting, a strong parental partnership enhances their leadership capacity. Together and separately, a mother and father can nurture as well as teach, equip, discipline and give wise counsel.

A study by Diane Ehrensaft reported a number of advantages for coparented children.[11] They had a more secure sense of basic trust, were better able to adapt to brief separations from the mother and had closer relationships with both mother and father. Coparented children developed better social discrimination skills and displayed greater creativity and moral development. Having less animosity toward the other gender, they were better able to develop strong friendship bonds with opposite-gender children and displayed fantasies of sustained connection with others.

Not surprisingly, sons seemed to benefit especially from coparenting. Boys who had a strong bond with both their father and mother were better able to display

---

[10]David Blankenhorn, *Fatherless America: Confronting Our Most Urgent Social Problem* (New York: BasicBooks, 1995).

[11]Diane Ehrensaft, *Parenting Together: Men and Women Sharing the Care of Their Children* (Chicago: University of Illinois Press, 1990).

empathy, affection and nurturing behavior; they thought highly of the way they were parented and were more likely to state that they wanted to "be a father" when they grew up. Strong fathering had a positive effect on how boys developed relational skills. Boys who grew up with fathers who connected emotionally were more nurturing and rational.

Girls who were coparented had a greater sense of self and personal boundaries. Also, when a father in particular took an active interest in his daughter's achievements, she was likely to succeed in her career goals. Mothers who modeled assertiveness and self-confidence, in addition to nurturing behaviors, gave their daughters permission to set firm boundaries as well as make emotional connections with others.

There is significant evidence to suggest that coparenting is beneficial to parents as well. The most obvious benefit is for working mothers whose husbands take the parenting role seriously. In these homes, working mothers are less likely to be enmeshed or overinvolved with their children. Fathers involved in the parenting process were more apt to develop their social-emotional and relational side. In contrast to the world of work outside the home, where decisions are largely based on rational rather than emotional skills, taking care of children inclined men toward personal and emotional issues. This inclination had a positive impact on the way they performed in work roles, since high empathy skills helped them relate better to coworkers.

Coparenting allows mothers and fathers to better understand and be involved with their children and to be more consistent and effective in discipline. In addition, it strengthens the marriage as they work in tandem as parents. Ideally, dual-earner parents will find ways to complement each other on a day-to-day basis throughout their parenting years. One parent may find helping with homework to be a special gift, while the other is best with activities. Dividing up parenting responsibility will ease the burden as long as both parents learn the needed skills, such as nurturing, setting rules and setting boundaries. Dual parenting is a rewarding investment that pays off in the end, as it benefits fathers, mothers, children and family life as a whole.

Equal Partnership Dual-Earner Marriage

It is estimated that two-thirds of two-parent families with dependent children are dual-earner families today. The Bureau of Labor Statistics in 1992 shows that 76 percent of women with children between the ages of six and seventeen, and 58 percent of all mothers with children under age six, were employed.[12] When both spouses are working outside the home, division of labor within the home becomes a very important issue. In hierarchical marriages, wives spend much more of their time working in the home than do husbands.

Marriage partners who both hold equally high commitments to work and home life need the agility of an acrobat to meet demands in both arenas. Wanting to do it all, they find that sooner or later something gives, whether it's work, the marriage, parenting or the emotional health of the acrobats.

To practice marital equality, dual-earner couples must be proactive in establishing and maintaining a rightful balance of work and family.[13] Rather than merely reacting to life circumstances and pressures, the couple must become intentional in forming an equal-participation marriage. Here are some important points:

- Establish a close relationship.

- Be flexible and adaptable to life circumstances.

- Agree on priorities.

- Focus on the essentials.

- Draw on all the resources you can muster to help meet the demands of parenting and family life.

Sometimes it is necessary to accommodate the individual strengths of each partner. One spouse pulls back from work commitments in order to give more time to family life at a particular family stage. Then, at another time, the other spouse makes adjustments by taking on more childcare and decreasing employment responsibilities. Whatever the arrangement, both spouses equally respect and honor each other's commitments to work and the home.

There are major benefits for both men and women in a dual-earner/dual role-sharing marriage. Based on responses to questionnaires from 815 dual-career couples, Janice Steil and B. A. Turetsky found that the greater the marital equality, the less wives reported negative psychological symptoms.[14] John M. Gottman reports

---

[12]Gayle H. Kimball, *Empowering Parents: How to Create Family-Friendly Workplaces, Schools and Governments* (Chicago: Equality, 1998).

[13]Jack O. Balswick and Judith K. Balswick, *The Dual-Earner Marriage: The Elaborate Balancing Act* (Grand Rapids, Mich.: Fleming H. Revell, 1995).

[14]Janice M. Steil and B. A. Turetsky, "Is Equal Better? The Relationship Between Marital Equality and Psychological Symptomatology," in *Applied Social Psychology Annual* 7, ed. Stuart Oskamp (Newbury

that doing housework may prove to be good for husbands' health. He found a correlation between the amount of housework a man did and his physical health four years later. Another important aspect for the man was that his involvement in the home led to validation and appreciation. This contributed to a mutually satisfying relationship with his wife and children.[15]

Relaxing perfectionist household and parenting standards is especially important for the woman. The couple must agree on the standards so they can cooperatively achieve their goals. When the wife is able to let go of certain areas as her domain, she will be able to appreciate her husband's efforts without setting up unrealistic expectations. Drawing on research of Claire Low Rabin and Pepper Schwartz, Gottman states that "when wives and husbands make what they both feel is a successful effort to divide chores fairly, both spouses benefit. Inequalities in household and childcare have profound consequences for marital satisfaction of women, which has to affect the quality of the marriage for the man as well."[16] The benefit of shared roles for the wife is that she can find fulfillment in work, marriage and mothering.

A hard lesson for all dual-earner couples to learn or admit is that they can't do everything! In prioritizing what needs to be done, they must learn to do a "good enough" job. By living in previously uncharted territories, dual-earner couples can represent marriage as a partnership of equals. They need support from family, friends and community as they work toward a satisfying and meaningful family life.

The Relational Embeddedness of Marital Equality

Marital equality can best be understood in a wider biblical context based on how our Creator God relates to us, the created ones. We offer four relationship principles—covenant, grace, empowerment and intimacy—as foundational to marriage as a partnership of equals.

The covenant principle. Marriage as a partnership of equals is based on covenant, a reciprocal, unconditional commitment. The vows exchanged in the wedding ceremony, "for better or worse, for richer or poorer, in sickness and health, till death do us part," have unconditional commitment as the focus. The couple makes a public covenant before God, family, friends and a community of faith,

---

Park, Calif.: Sage, 1987), pp. 73-97.

[15]John Mordechai Gottman and Nan Silver, *Why Marriages Succeed or Fail: What You Can Learn from Breakthrough Research to Make Your Marriage Last* (New York: Simon & Schuster, 1994), pp. 157-58.

[16]Ibid., p. 157.

fully intending to keep these promises.

God's love is seen in the Old Testament as a covenant established with Adam and Eve, Noah and his family, Abraham and Sarah, and the children of Israel: "I will make a covenant with you. I will be your God and you will be my people." God's unconditional commitment is given with an expressed desire that it be returned. God's faithful, steadfast, always-abounding love is sure and secure. God invites a response from those who are loved. God's love is perfect, but we are imperfect. After all, we are sinners saved by grace. Yet God desires a reciprocal love, waiting for a maturity of faith that makes giving back possible. In mature, marital love, we hope for a similar mutual, reciprocal love.

Human love, however, is typically conditional. Most of us commit ourselves to loving under certain requirements and conditions. A secular model of marriage is often based on a social exchange or quid pro quo model that promises love when one is loved back in equal measure. It's tit for tat: "I give something if I get something," "I will love you when you do this." Spouses who are invested in having and keeping power in a relationship find ingenious ways to increase their influence and lessen that of their spouse. Their way to gain power is to diminish the spouse's power. This battle puts the self at the center and the spouse at the periphery. A marriage that is based on conditional love soon turns into a deadly, legalistic war of keeping score.

In contrast, the Bible commands Christians to extend their view far beyond this self-focused perspective. Christians are directed to "do to others what you would have them do to you," "go the second mile" and "turn the other cheek." This extraordinary way of the cross is the deepest challenge of Christian marriage. The biblical concept of love requires an unconditional commitment given equally by both partners. Covenant love serves as the solid foundation of security. It is the backbone and relational strength of an equal-partnership marriage. Trust is the core reward that develops when spouses regard each other with a mutual respect that puts priority on the relationship, when each spouse treats the other as a cherished equal, one who is uniquely gifted as God's creation.

The grace principle. Equal-partnership marriage thrives on grace shown through mutual acceptance and forgiveness. Valuing each other's personality strengths as well as accepting differences brings a comforting, peaceful atmosphere to the marriage. Since human love is imperfect, partners will disappoint, offend and fail each other from time to time. However, grace allows spouses to approach marital differences and disappointments with confession and understanding that takes them beyond the failure toward responsible change. When spouses fail or make mistakes, forgiveness renews their spirit and gives them courage to make necessary amends. Grace keeps the couple open to ongoing reconciliation, restoration and renewal.

The opposite of a gracing response is a shaming one. This is the message that the spouse is not "good enough." Whereas guilt is the feeling that one has done a wrong, shame is the feeling that one *is* a wrong. Spouses who can't admit they are wrong will generally shame, blame or point the finger at the other. They have a hard time being accountable for their part or failure in any given situation.

Jack grew up in a shaming home and learned early on that being less than perfect meant there was something unacceptable about him. Obviously that made it hard for him to admit when he was at fault, so he conveniently blamed Judy when things went wrong. For example, whenever we got lost while driving, it became quite clear that it was Judy's fault. This tendency to blame dampened Judy's spirit and put distance between us.

When Judy spoke up about the pattern, however, Jack took another look at what was behind the blaming and took responsibility for his actions. He learned he could admit mistakes without jumping to the conclusion that he was a woebegone reprobate.[17] The dilemma of unequal partnership is that husbands carry the burden of having to know everything and always be right, while wives pretend not to know or suppress what they know is right.

Nonacceptance puts marriage on an unequal footing. It's a devastating way of keeping a spouse in a one-down position. Focusing on deficits draws out a critical spirit that breaks the connection. On the other hand, grace brings acceptance and appreciation for the spouse. Grace places value on how the spouse views things without judging their thoughts as inadequate or inferior. Therefore it eliminates the need to change the spouse into what is more acceptable according to one's self-centered assumptions.

In a gracing marriage each spouse feels appreciated for who they are. The relationship has a person-centered quality: spouses enjoy each other. A gracing spouse accepts the other spouse as being as important as oneself, recognizes there is more than one way (my way) to approach life and sees differences as complementary resources instead of deficits. Grace fosters equal partnership.

The empowering principle. Whereas the first two principles provide a solid founda-

---

[17]Early in our marriage it was difficult for Jack to realize his shaming tendencies, since he would justify his blaming as "spiritual correction."

tion, the third principle—mutual empowerment—is the core work of equal-partnership marriages. As we noted earlier, power is the ability of one spouse to influence the other. Power is based on resources, and resources are qualities valued by the other spouse. Power issues are inevitable in marriage, because each person is unique and spouses must learn to negotiate all kinds of life decisions from different perspectives. This naturally brings tension in the marriage.

The most problematic aspect of empowerment is how power is used in the marital relationship. An underlying assumption of social science research is that spouses will use power in controlling or manipulative ways to get what they want and maintain their position of influence. While power *is* often perceived this way, Jesus radically redefined power as giving oneself for the other. Mutual empowerment is described in 1 Corinthians 7 as a harmony that emerges when spouses listen to and consider each other when making decisions. We describe empowerment as a reciprocal process of building up, equipping, supporting, encouraging, affirming and challenging the other.

Empowerment can be seen as the ability to envision and encourage a spouse to be everything God created him or her to be. This includes personality, giftedness and reaching one's greatest potential. It is not simply yielding to the wishes of another person, nor is it giving up one's own power in the process of empowering the other. Rather, empowerment is an active, intentional process that affirms the spouse to be an effective and equal partner. Internal strength and relationship confidence come from knowing that your spouse believes in and desires your best, takes great delight in your development, encourages you to reach your full potential and supports your personal goals and growth.

The empowering principle seeks the full potential of each spouse through a synchronous rhythm of interaction and interdependence. Mutual support in coparenting, housekeeping and work roles enables both spouses to live out their purpose and calling. This partnership, unhampered by predetermined and restricted definitions of marital roles, is free to expand into something beyond what each can do alone—two are better than one.

A biblical model of empowerment can be seen in the person of Jesus Christ. What Jesus taught about power was central to his mission and meant to be imitated. Jesus modeled a new way of being personally powerful. He rejected the use of power to control others but used power to serve others, to lift up the fallen, to encourage responsibility and maturity. When James and John asked to sit on his right and left hand in glory, Jesus replied, "Whoever wants to become great among you must be your servant, and whoever wants to be first must be slave of all. For even the Son of Man did not come to be served, but to serve, and to give his life a ransom for many" (Mk 10:43-45).

Jesus' relationship to his disciples is a perfect example of empowerment. Preparing them for his leaving, Jesus encourages them to look to the Holy Spirit, who will give them strength to accomplish their ministry (Jn 16). He assures them, "But you will receive power when the Holy Spirit comes on you" (Acts 1:8). When Scripture asks ordinary spouses to respond in extraordinary ways, like forgiving seventy times seven, being a suffering servant, loving unconditionally, caring enough to confront and practicing mutual submission, we need the empowerment of the Holy Spirit to do so. The power of God's Spirit gives strength to live out the extraordinary way of the equal-partnership marriage.

The intimacy principle. The fourth principle of an equal-partnership marriage is to know and be known through emotional, physical, spiritual and intellectual intimacy. Marriages that are built on mutual unconditional love and lived out in an atmosphere of grace and empowerment have the greatest capacity for mutual intimacy.

The model of two becoming one flesh does not eradicate the individual. In fact, an individual spouse becomes even more defined through self-discovery within a relationship as intimate as marriage. Intimacy is best achieved when each person has regard for the other, for the self and for the relationship.

The deepest craving of every spouse is to be understood. There is great satisfaction in knowing that your spouse has truly listened and responded sensitively to what you have expressed. Intimate communication is not easily achieved. It takes an ongoing experience of making yourself available to your spouse. It means you stay emotionally connected even during anxious or fearful expressions. It means creating an atmosphere of safety so the heart can be laid bare. It requires the ability to stay with the agenda of the spouse without attempting to change, convince or fix him or her. It does not mean that you must betray your own views, but that you must set them aside for a time so your partner can fully express hers or his without fear or shame. In a profound way, intimate communication means giving up your life, dying to self, in order to be fully present to the spouse.

The bold action of receiving and giving to each other emotionally and sexually maximizes intimacy. The receiver is able to give up the familiar in order to understand the spouse's needs, wishes and desires. It takes heart and mind to give full attention, respect, sensitivity, compassion, awareness and understanding.

Only when spouses believe they will be understood will they dare to share their deepest pains, fears, dreams and hopes. Only when spouses are vulnerable with each other will they discover themselves. Self-disclosure deepens self-knowledge. Internal self-esteem grows out of clarifying personal values, beliefs and convictions. Intimate sharing helps spouses know themselves and the other in more profound and endearing ways. The intimate connection between spouses enhances a sense of belonging and secure attachment. To know and be known emotionally gives each a solid base to know and be known sexually.

We believe intimacy deepens marital bonding and sexual unity. "Men want sexual intimacy, women want emotional intimacy," goes the saying. A common belief is that men experience closeness mostly through sex while women experience closeness mostly through emotional sharing. It does seem to be generally true that sexual intimacy helps men feel emotionally connected while emotional connection opens women up to sexual intimacy. Every couple must find a good balance and create ways to achieve deeper intimacy in both areas.

Keeping both sexual and emotional intimacy alive in marriage increases the likelihood of mutual satisfaction, according to Jean Duncombe and Dennis Marsden.[18] They found that couples gain the best of both worlds by attending to both aspects of intimacy. When women realized that erotic energy moved their spouse toward deeper emotional connection and men made a stronger link between sexual and emotional intimacy, the couples' intimacy increased. As Paul Ricoeur notes, "When Eros is mated with tenderness and fidelity, authentic happiness and spiritual fulfillment follow."[19]

Spouses who are able to engage and respond to their spouse find mutual interdependence to be crucially important in all aspects of intimacy. Steil and Turetsky, in a longitudinal study of 130 husbands and wives, found that equality was positively related to sexual intimacy.[20] Cheryl Rampage found that marital intimacy is most achievable when there is equality between partners, empathy for each other's experience and willingness to collaborate in both meaning and action.[21]

---

[18]Jean Duncombe and Dennis Marsden, "Love and Intimacy: The Gender Division of Emotion and 'Emotion Work': A Neglected Aspect of Sociological Discussion of Heterosexual Relationships," *Sociology* 27, no. 2 (May 1993): 221-41; reprinted in *The Sociology of the Family: A Reader,* ed. G. A. Allan (Oxford: Blackwell, 1999).

[19]Paul Ricoeur, *Oneself as Another,* trans. Kathleen Blarney (Chicago: University of Chicago Press, 1994), p. 73.

[20]Steil and Turetsky, "Is Equal Better?"

[21]Cheryl Rampage, "Power, Gender and Marital Intimacy," *Journal of Family Therapy* 16, no. 1, special issue (February 1994): 125-37.

In the most tender moments, it is indeed a sacred experience to be seen, heard, known and responded to with love. In an equal partnership the spouse will be experienced as godly, as one who cares. The interdependency of mutual commitment, grace, empowerment and intimacy creates a holy place of communion between two who have become one flesh.

A delicate balance between separateness and togetherness emerges in an interdependent union. Marriage offers a profound place of personal, spiritual and relationship growth. As two unique persons support and commit themselves to each other throughout life's journey, they reap the deep rewards of equal partnership. Scripture promotes marriage as a union between two spouses who regard and relate to each other as equals. We believe that making the best interest of the spouse and the relationship a priority reflects God's design for marriage. Practicing equal partnership throughout marriage brings out the crucial essence of covenant commitment and bears the fruit of a grace-filled, mutually-empowered and intimate union.

Weaving two lives into a threefold cord that is not easily broken is possible when God is at the center. In Christ the potential for a vital and fulfilling equal-partnership marriage is at its height. Because intimacy, covenant, grace and empowerment are based on biblical principles, marriages like this are a powerful witness to the world of God's love.

27

NATURE, CULTURE AND
GENDER COMPLEMENTARITY

Cynthia Neal Kimball

Then God said, "Let us make humankind in our image, according to our likeness;
and let them have dominion . . . upon the earth."
So God created humankind in his image,
in the image of God he created them;
male and female he created them.
God blessed them, and God said to them, "Be fruitful and multiply, and fill the earth and subdue it;
and have dominion over . . . every living thing that moves upon the earth." . . .
And it was so. God saw everything that he had made, and indeed,
it was very good.
GENESIS 1:26-31

It was very good." The created order showed that both man and woman imaged God, both were called to rule, both were called to multiply and nurture children. And it was good.

There is a cost when this good is not realized. This cost is imaged in a poignant story I once heard from Sister Joan Chittister.

A trader in the Middle East went from bazaar to bazaar and bought rugs for export. One day he rode his horse past a stall where an elderly woman sat on a tiny prayer rug before a very, very large hand-woven rug. The trader drew up his horse suddenly and shouted, "Old lady, is that rug behind you for sale?"

Without looking up from her prayer rug, the woman simply said, "Yes, sir, it is."

He said, "How much do you want for that rug?"

She said, "One hundred rupees, sir. One hundred rupees."

He said, "One hundred rupees for that rug!"

She said, "Absolutely, sir, one hundred rupees. Not a single rupee less."

He looked at her. He looked at the rug. He said, "Old lady, in all the bazaars, in all the countries, in all the stalls in the Middle East, I have never seen a rug that beautiful."

She said, "I know that, sir. That's why I'm selling it for one hundred rupees, and not a single rupee less."

He said, "In the name of Allah, old lady, if you realize how beautiful your rug is, why would you ever sell it for only one hundred rupees?"

For the first time in the conversation the woman looked up at him, an expression of shock on her face. She thought for a moment and then said, "Because, sir, until this very moment I never knew that there were any numbers above 100."

"I never knew." All those years of weaving rugs and selling the fruits of her labor, and she never knew.

There *are* numbers above 100, and there is a terrible cost when people are kept ignorant of their possibilities. Hierarchies of domination over others have devastating effects on God's creation. Peter told us there were numbers above 100 when he proclaimed,

> In the last days, God says,
>   I will pour out my Spirit on all people.
> Your sons and daughters will prophesy,
>   your young men will see visions,
>   your old men will dream dreams.
> Even on my servants, both men and women,
>   I will pour out my Spirit in those days,
>   and they will prophesy. (Acts 2:17-18, quoting Joel 2)

Every age barrier, every gender barrier, every class barrier was broken that day. The new redemptive community that Christ wrought through the cross introduced us to the realization that all of God's people—regardless of age, class or gender—have gifts and contributions to make in proclaiming his gospel, and we can't ever go back to not knowing. There are numbers above 100. How should the family and the church respond to this call for a new redemptive community? How can we reclaim maleness and femaleness in a way that avoids the constructions of gender-based authority-subordination hierarchies?

The questions of male-female differences and their connection to the nature-nurture debate have been a part of developmental and social psychology for quite some time. What are the reasons (genetic versus cultural) for the broadly generalizable differences between males and females? Aside from clear anatomical differences, how does having a gender shape men and women's sexual identity? Perhaps a more fundamental question is, what difference does gender difference make at all? How we view sexual difference between men and women affects many personal and political decisions, including how we parent, how we educate, how we view marriage and our employee-employer relationships, even how we administer therapeutic interventions.

Historically, gender difference has cost women dearly in terms of opportunities for intellectual achievement. During the early nineteenth century, women's unique reproductive capacities and responsibilities were thought to take precedence over any cognitive pursuits. It was believed that there were vital forces individuals had to allocate between cognitive and biological functions—the "brain-womb" conflict. If a woman diverted some of that vital force toward cognitive functions rather than reproduction, then she could expect to experience deformity and certainly sterility. Clearly one can see the dangers of using sexual difference as a unit of analysis.

Nonetheless, when we look around at our own relationships, particularly male-female relationships, we often find differences. It is important that we recognize those differences and identify the experiences that encourage them. Is it truly something innate, or is it due to the manner in which we train our children? The challenge before us is to engage in dialogue with the important theoretical positions as we embark on the journey of discovering a redemptive vision for men and women in God's community.

A full understanding can be achieved only through exploring both developmental and cultural forces affecting gender socialization and behavior. It is no longer sufficient to ask "whether, and to what degree, the sexes (or, alternatively, feminine, masculine, and androgynous persons) differ in a specific trait, skill, or task performance. Rather, [we need] to ask *how, when,* and *why* it makes a difference to be male or female."[1] Understanding these many forces will affect how we think about role differentiation and, specifically, how these differences fit into a biblical model of gender complementarity.

This chapter will explore current theories held by those who work in the areas of nature/genetics and nurture/culture. I will present some of the current and relevant research concerning difference, and discuss how theory affects views on the source of that difference. I will begin with the research concerning gender differences found crossculturally, then present studies that examine the genetic forces in-

---

[1]Thomas Eckes and Hanns M. Trautner, *The Developmental Social Psychology of Gender* (Mahwah, N.J.: Lawrence Erlbaum Associates, 2000), p. 10.

fluencing gender difference, and move on to discuss the cultural forces shaping gender identity. I will also discuss some of the implications of gender role differentiation and suggest ways the church may serve as a buffer to these societal influences.

Crosscultural Gender Differences

Gender differences operate mainly in terms of their effects on social interactions. When observed alone, boys' and girls' behavior differs very little. But in larger same-sex social groups, the differences are dramatic. Exploring these implications is important for understanding key issues such as identity and interpersonal interactions.

When a behavior is found in many cultures, nature is most often thought to play the larger role. Most frequently social scientists note gender differences in the areas of early sex segregation (as early as three years of age), aggression, social dominance and mating behavior. On average, within a culture and across cultures, men are more aggressive and competitive than women and more concerned about their position in the dominance hierarchy. On average, women are less oriented toward promiscuous or polygamous sexual relationships and more concerned with finding older men who have attained financial resources and social status. On the other hand, men are more oriented toward promiscuity and finding a younger and attractive female partner.

Noted crosscultural researcher F. F. Strayer found that preschool-aged children—in many cultural settings, including villages in Mexico, Africa, the Philippines, India and the United States—practice sex segregation in their playmate choices.[2] In other words, same-sex friends are chosen above opposite-sex friends significantly more often. Although sex segregation does not occur among toddlers, it is a clear reality by three years of age. A leading developmental researcher in the area of gender difference, E. E. Maccoby, argues that sex segregation in the preschool and middle childhood years actually affords children different "cultures."[3] Boys tend to be more physical in their play than girls, engaging in a great deal of wrestling and mock fighting. This, too, has been found crossculturally. Maccoby suggests that this rough-and-tumble play may function to establish a group's social

---

[2]F. F. Strayer, "Peer Attachment and Affiliate Subgroups: Ethological Perspectives on Preschool Social Organization," *Memo de Recharche*, 1977, p. 5.

[3]E. E. Maccoby, *Two Sexes: Growing Up Apart, Coming Together* (Cambridge, Mass.: Harvard University Press, 1998).

dominance patterns. Social dominance is more salient for boys' groups than girls': "In preschool and kindergarten, then, we see the beginning of boys' concern not to appear weak in the eyes of their male peers."[4]

Girls have their share of conflict, but they tend toward a more relational aggression. Girls are more likely to use "social alienation" as a means of aggression.[5] This sharply increases with age and has also been a consistent crosscultural finding. Another consistent gender-difference finding has been in the conversations of preschool children. Girls are more likely than boys to sustain longer exchanges, take turns with their conversation partner, speak and maintain a theme, and use "extending statements" or "relevant turns." Boys are more likely to use imperatives ("don't do that," "get that," "stop it").[6]

This is but a small peek into the research, but it is quite evident that clear gender differences are present early in life. And these differences provide different "subcultures" for boys and girls that play a role in the development of their sexual identities, shaping how they view not only their own gender but also those of the other gender. Cultural norms also shape how boys and girls view adults. In cultures that confer a relatively high status on males, boys distance themselves from women and girls to a greater degree than in cultures where male status is not as high.[7]

Crosscultural data and the differences shaped by subcultures cannot be ignored. The question becomes: when is difference a healthy complementarity, and when does it become destructive and negatively influence both gender identity and relational interactions? In a later section I will address how the church may be affected by generalizable gender differences and how we might address these differences in such a way as to be a healthy body of Christ.

Nature / Genetic Forces

The difficulty in examining the genetic forces behind gender difference lies in our inability to disentangle nature from nurture. Obviously, both are operating in a developing child. Many studies of "environmental" influences have ignored the confounding variable of genetic influence because they used intact biologically related families. Factors that are influential in the environment may be linked with herita-

---

[4]Ibid., p. 38.
[5]R. B. Cairns et al., "Growth and Aggression: Part I, Childhood to Early Adolescence," *Developmental Psychology* 25 (1989): 320-33.
[6]Maccoby, *Two Sexes.*
[7]Ibid.

ble parental characteristics and passed on genetically to the child.[8]

In this section I will present one type of study examining genetic influence: children who are born with hormonal and biochemical disorders. Julianne Imperato-McGinley and her colleagues followed nineteen men who were raised as women because they had external female genitalia that resulted from a prenatal hormonal disorder, 5-alpha-reductase syndrome.[9] At puberty, when the men developed secondary sex characteristics, nearly all the men switched to a male identity and role. The authors suggest that these results demonstrate hormonal influence above environmental influences.

Studies examining prenatal androgen exposure in female fetuses indicate increased masculine behaviors such as "higher activity levels and lower levels of nurturance, greater 'tomboy' behavior, greater preference for male clothes, increased propensity toward aggressive behavior, and greater preference for male toys during play, though not for male playmates."[10]

When male fetuses have disorders that limit postnatal production of androgen, they show lower spatial abilities at puberty than boys without the disorder. Higher testosterone levels correlate with greater sensation-seeking behaviors, higher irritability and lower frustration tolerance in the male adolescent. Girls with lower estrogen and progesterone levels tend to evidence more mood swings and emotional behaviors.[11]

In sum, we cannot deny that there are hormonal and biochemical effects that have differential consequences in male and female behavior. Perhaps rather than asking what difference difference makes, we should be asking how difference can be recognized honestly and interpreted wisely.

Implications of Genetic and Crosscultural Differences

The physiological differences between the sexes are clear: body build, muscular development, hormonal patterns, childbearing capacity and longevity. Social differences include level of aggression, language styles and same-sex segregation. It is

---

[8]S. Scarr, "Developmental Theories for the 1990s: Development and Individual Differences," *Child Development* 63 (1992): 1-19.

[9]Julianne Imperato-McGinley, R. E. Peterson, T. Gautier and E. Sturla, "Androgens and the Evolution of Male-Gender Identity Among Male Pseudohermaphrodites with 5 alpha-Reductase Deficiency," *New England Journal of Medicine*, 300 (1979): 1233-37.

[10]T. D. Wachs, "Necessary but Not Sufficient: The Respective Roles of Single and Multiple Influences on Individual Development," *American Psychological Association*, 2000, p. 63.

[11]Ibid., p. 65.

clear from the crosscultural and genetic gender studies that God has fashioned men and women with certain differences. And yet both bear his image. Additionally, it is clear that God is beyond gender.

Too often gender differences are not understood or appreciated, and so they become barriers to a beneficial complementarity between women and men. We fear that which we don't understand. Although we are not governed by our genes, we are embodied, and our hormones and genes affect our behavior. The quest for the church is to better appreciate these differences and use them to build the church. If, as research seems to indicate, females use language earlier and use more affective language, how does that predispose them to greater self-regulatory behavior? How can such abilities in a woman be used to support and encourage her husband or the men with whom she works? How can the more direct conflict style of men be used to encourage women in more direct methods? In other words, how can we learn from the differences?

All crosscultural differences are not necessarily genetically determined. Mary Stewart Van Leeuwen writes that at creation both genders were made for community (sociability) and both were given dominion over the creation. In the Fall "the woman abused her dominion by eating of the 'tree of the knowledge of good and evil' (Gen 2:17). The man, in turn, abused his sociability by accepting some of the fruit from her even though he knew that their unity as man and woman was not to supersede their obedience to God."[12] The punishments that were pronounced on each one, then, became the opposite of the sin each committed. From that point forward, men have struggled with the temptation to dominate as opposed to exercising appropriate dominion. Women's sociability has tended to degenerate into social enmeshment. These tendencies are borne out in many of the crosscultural nature-and-nurture studies.

What this suggests is that to appreciate gender complementarity in the church, and in all relationships, is to recognize these differences in a way that will help men and women encourage each other toward the health of both and against the abuse of either. Not all men are aggressive rather than relational. Not all women are relational and not aggressive. Many differences reside within each gender as well. Perhaps true complementarity is marked by an acknowledgment of differences, accountability against abuse of differences and encouragement for those wanting to

---

[12]Mary Stewart Van Leeuwen, *Gender & Grace: Love, Work and Parenting in a Changing World* (Downers Grove, Ill.: InterVarsity Press, 1990), p. 43.

grow in both appropriate dominion and sociability.

Nurture / Cultural Forces

Gender schema theories cite developmental research demonstrating that from birth, sex-typed behavior is imposed on infants. From the first hours after birth, men and women view and describe female infants as different from male infants. Daughters are rated as smaller, with finer features, softer and less alert than sons. Sons are perceived as stronger and hardier than daughters, even when these infants do not actually differ in any physical attributes. The data indicate that parents, particularly fathers, attribute stereotypical characteristics to their infants solely as a function of infant gender.[13]

Some studies examining whether adults play differently with infants based on their gender found that adults offer dolls to a child they perceive to be a girl and male sex-typed toys (such as hammers) to a child they perceive to be a boy. The fact was that the same infant was used for both situations; the researchers simply dressed the child differently. These studies clearly show that adult response is independent of differences in the child's behavior and is governed solely by the assumed sex of the child. I must note, however, that a meta-analysis has not found consistent results in these types of studies.[14]

At approximately two to three years of age, children understand that they are either a boy or a girl. Sally knows that girls are different from boys and begins to organize information from the environment within this new "girl" schema. Around the age of four or five Sally realizes that she will always be a girl and that changes in clothes or hairstyle do not change the gender of a person. Gender is a permanent characteristic. Sally gains and organizes continual information from multiple sources in her social environment about what it means to be a girl. She translates this information into rules to which she must conform. Every child internalizes the gender lens embedded in the society, evaluates the different ways of behaving that the culture defines as appropriate, and rejects any behaviors that do not match her or his sex.

My own daughter discovered a rule in her social environment that didn't even match up with her real world experience. When she was four years old she told me

---

[13]J. Z. Rubin, F. J. Provenzano and Z. Lurio, "The Eye of the Beholder: Parents' View on Sex of Newborns," *American Journal of Orthopsychiatry* 44 (1974): 512-19.

[14]M. Stern and K. H. Karraker, "Sex Stereotyping of Infants: A Review of Gender Labeling Studies," *Sex Roles* 20 (1989): 501-22.

that women could not be doctors—this from a child who had always had a female pediatrician. What this shows is that once the gender lens is internalized, social reality as well as individual identity is constructed accordingly.

The hallmark of enculturation is the individual's inability to distinguish between reality and the cultural lens through which he or she perceives it. I believe that our boys and girls demonstrate how enculturated they have become within our gender-polarizing society. It is evident that during these early years, stereotypes are increasingly rigid. Children have much to learn, and they want to get it right! Children learn very early that what parents, teachers, peers and the church consider appropriate behavior varies as a function of sex, that toys, clothing, occupations, hobbies, domestic chores, even pronouns vary as a function of sex.

As children learn the contents of society's gender schema, they learn the selective attributes linked to their own sex. Children learn to apply these attributes selectively to the self, and this in turn organizes their self-concept. In effect, children learn to evaluate their adequacy as a person in terms of the gender schema. For example, it is not uncommon to hear that boys are good in sports, math and getting dirty. Johnny then examines whether he indeed is all the things boys are supposed to be. He will decide whether he is "good" based on how adequately he meets these expectations. Sally learns that to be female is to be thin, beautiful, never angry; in effect, to be female is to be under "the tyranny of nice and kind." She decides whether she is a "good" woman based on how well she fulfills these social expectations.

I was struck by an illustration of this recently. Another family was enjoying pizza with us one evening. After we had eaten, the seven-year-old daughter began running in place. I did not realize what the child was doing and joked about her seemingly high level of energy. The mother remarked that this was not just excess energy; the child always ran in place after eating high-calorie meals. This seven-year-old was worried about becoming fat!

No seven-year-old ought to be so concerned about her weight. However, these standards become internalized in children, so they seek to conform to the culture's definition of maleness or femaleness. As gender identity theory asserts, gender is so salient in our culture that it becomes the most central and important organizing component in one's self-concept.[15] Enculturated myths become self-fulfilling prophecy, molding personal behaviors and identities.

---

[15]Florence Geis, "Self-Fulfilling Prophecies: A Social Psychological View of Gender," in *The Psychology of Gender*, ed. A. E. Beall and R. J. Sternber (New York: Guilford, 1993).

Florence Geis demonstrates how self-fulfilling prophecies regarding gender ste-reotypes are perpetuated. We will never be certain which came first because beliefs and behavior can be circular—the "chicken and egg" problem. Nevertheless, "we are more likely to see what we expect to see, sometimes even if it is not actually there, and not see or reinterpret what we do not expect, sometimes even if it is there."[16] Geis provides case after case where males are viewed as more competent and better leaders than females though there is no empirical evidence to support these perceptions. Of course if perceptual biases occur beyond our awareness, we must ask what we can do to fight them.

What are these stereotypical norms? Studies of sex-role stereotyping have re-peatedly confirmed that men are viewed as the opposite of women. When people of both sexes are asked to characterize men and women, they agree that men are strong, independent, worldly, aggressive, ambitious and logical, as well as blunt, rough, loud, sloppy and unable to express tender feelings. In contrast, women are described as weak, dependent, not worldly, passive, unambitious and illogical, as well as tactful, gentle, understanding, neat in appearance and able to express tender feelings with ease. These findings, first reported by S. L. Bem,[17] were confirmed in a later study.[18] An analysis of the characteristics commonly attributed to men re-veals that the most highly valued masculine traits represent a "competency" cluster that includes objectivity, skill in business and self-confidence. The traits considered most valuable for women constitute a "warmth-expressiveness" cluster that in-cludes tenderness, understanding and concern for others.

As in the nature studies, there are many complementary and competing theories concerning the how and why of cultural influences on gender identity and differ-entiation.[19] I will turn now to the implications for strong gender differentiations. Here we begin to observe just what difference difference can make when culturally determined gender stereotypes govern our behavior.

Implications of Cultural Stereotypes

For women. Cultural norms that are based solely on perceived sexual difference place

---

[16]Ibid., p. 14.

[17]S. L. Bem, "The Measurement of Psychological Androgyny," *Journal of Consulting and Clinical Psychology* 42 (1974): 155-62.

[18]Geis, "Self-Fulfilling Prophecies."

[19]See Eckes and Trautner, *Developmental Social Psychology;* Maccoby, *Two Sexes;* Beall and Sternberg, eds., *Psychology of Gender.*

considerable constraints on people. Significant research has been done examining the effects of sex-role stereotyping on mental health. Bem cites a number of studies that show positive correlations between high femininity (on the Bem scale of masculinity-femininity) and high anxiety, low self-esteem and low social acceptance.[20] Women who score high on the femininity scale, and who have been socialized against developing such traits as ambition, independence and assertiveness, evidence significantly low self-esteem. Women clients consistently show general depression, passivity, anxiety, dependency and a need to please. Women who are victims of domestic violence reflect lower self-esteem and greater helplessness, passivity, dependency and acceptance of traditional male and female sex roles than nonvictims. High-achieving women with doctorates and professional accomplishments have evidenced an "impostor phenomenon," tending to attribute success to factors other than their own ability and fearing discovery as a phony, despite academic and professional accomplishments.

Recent research has described what is called the "lost voice" of women. Some girls who had felt a strong sense of themselves in early and middle childhood begin to experience a disavowal of their perceptions, beliefs, thoughts and feelings at adolescence.[21] Lyn Mikel Brown and Carol Gilligan found remarkable strength and courage in the voices of eight- to ten-year-old girls. These girls spoke passionately about their feelings of conflict and anger in relationships, believed in their own experience of knowledge, and could discuss differences as a normal part of relationships.[22] Between the ages of eleven and fifteen, however, many girls experience a deterioration of self-confidence. While the adolescent girl can often voice an opinion to herself, she chooses to shut off this part of herself in public for fear of offending others and losing valued relationships. These girls will speak of the conflict they feel between their emotions and the contrasting image of the "perfect girl"—that is to say, society's idealized vision of what makes a good woman.[23]

---

[20]See S. L. Bem, *Bem Sex-Role Inventory: Professional Manual* (Palo Alto, Calif.: Consulting Psychologists Press, 1981); S. L. Bem, *The Lenses of Gender: Transforming the Debate on Sexual Inequality* (New Haven, Conn.: Yale University Press, 1993); Bem, "Measurement of Psychological Androgyny."

[21]Carol Gilligan, Annie G. Rogers and Deborah L. Tolman, eds., *Women, Girls and Psychotherapy: Reframing Resistance* (Cambridge, Mass.: Harvard University Press, 1991).

[22]Lyn Mikel Brown and Carol Gilligan, *Meeting at the Crossroads: Women's Psychology and Girls' Development* (Cambridge, Mass.: Harvard University Press, 1992), p. 192 n. 26.

[23]Elizabeth Debold, Marie Wilson and Idelisse Malavé, *Mother Daughter Revolution: From Betrayal to Power* (New York: Addison-Wesley, 1993), p. 11.

At the threshold of adolescence, the eager young woman learns that to be a "good" woman she must get along with everyone and never have bad feelings such as anger, passion, sadness or even too much exuberance. Because it is not safe to talk about personal knowledge or belief that is less than "perfect," she sacrifices herself for the sake of her relationships. She tries to become the perfect girl because she feels that this is the kind of woman with whom everyone wants to be. The perception is that her perfect qualities make her worthy of inclusion. Brown and Gilligan call the trap of trying to live up to this idealized image the "tyranny of nice and kind."[24] These girls feel that they must choose between their strong self and their need for connection to others. Unfortunately, although they protect themselves from rejection, doing so makes it impossible for them to achieve honest, genuine relationships. This disavowing of the self can lead to the creation of an altered, inauthentic self, an attempt to avoid having to choose between self and relationship.

The disavowal of the self has also been linked to psychological symptoms, including eating disorders, anxiety, self-mutilation and depression.[25] James K. Zimmerman traced the suicide attempts of three girls to their desperate efforts to resist the image of traditional femininity that was being passed on to them by their mothers.[26] To be connected to their mothers would mean doing what was expected of them and losing connection with their own voices. It was necessary for them to reject this image of femininity in order to retain their voices, and yet they needed the support of their mothers to undertake this task.

For men. The male role also contains many constricting and limiting features from which men need to free themselves. Popular imagery about the male role is confusing and contradictory. For example, physical strength and accomplishment are dominant images of masculine achievement, but intellectual and interpersonal competencies are necessary for the kinds of achievement society most rewards in men. Males are expected to show greater emotional control than women and are often described as being more alienated from their feelings; but at the same time, men appear to become angry or violent more easily than women and are often rewarded for doing so.

---

[24]Brown and Gilligan, *Meeting at the Crossroads*, p. 53.

[25]Ibid., p. 105.

[26]James K. Zimmerman, "Crossing the Desert Alone: An Etiological Model of Female Adolescent Suicidality," in *Women, Girls and Psychotherapy: Reframing Resistance*, ed. Carol Gilligan, Annie G. Rogers and Deborah L. Tolman (Cambridge, Mass.: Harvard University Press, 1991), pp. 492-503.

William Pollack, a leading psychologist and researcher of boys' development, writes of the Boy Code: boys wear "this mask as an invisible shield, a persona to show the outside world a feigned self-confidence and bravado, and to hide the shame they feel at their feelings of vulnerability, powerlessness and isolation."[27] He asserts that there are four injunctions that provide the basis for the Boy Code: the sturdy oak, "give them hell," the big wheel and "no sissy stuff." A boy is not expected, or even allowed, to reach out to another when he needs comfort or reassurance. Doing so would violate the Boy Code. Because of strict adherence to this code, the boy (and eventually the man) becomes disconnected from his emotions. In fact, he will feel humiliated if he allows connection to his emotions or dares to express them. Even more important, boys and men police each other, thus maintaining the risk of isolation and shame. Pollack goes on to describe how boys and men are shamephobic, tuned in to any potential "loss of face." Boys intent on keeping the Code will do anything to avoid shame.

Messages sent to males include *perform, provide, protect.* If these roles in any way aren't played out successfully, men are seen as failures and inadequate. The stress from this can lead to domestic violence, alienation, alcohol and drug abuse, higher levels of coronary and pulmonary diseases, and suicide. Men can also suffer from the "impostor" phenomenon. Whether we are male or female, the temptation to evaluate ourselves based on how adequately we meet the expectations of our prescribed roles is strong and hard to resist.

The Role of the Church

The church is a socializing environment. Our children learn to conform to traditional role expectations or to transcend them based, in part, on their interaction with this environment. It is important to consider the church's response historically. Early church fathers were quite confident that women were different from men and that this difference was one of inferiority. Some of their words are quite painful:

> The woman herself alone is not the image of God: whereas the man alone is the image of God as fully and completely as when the woman is joined with him. (Augustine)[28]

---

[27]William Pollack, *Real Boys: Rescuing Our Sons from the Myths of Boyhood* (New York: Random House, 1999), p. 5.

[28]Augustine *On the Trinity* 7.7.10; quoted in Patricia Gundry, "Why We're Here," in *Women, Authority and the Bible*, ed. Alvera Mickelsen (Downers Grove, Ill.: InterVarsity Press, 1986), p. 21.

As regards the individual nature, woman is defective and misbegotten, for the active force in the male seed tends to the production of a perfect likeness in the masculine sex; while the production of women comes from a defect in the active force or from some material indisposition or even from some external influence. (Aquinas)[29]

God's sentence hangs still over all your sex and His punishment weighs down upon you. You are the devil's gateway; you are she who first violated the forbidden tree and broke the law of God. It was you who coaxed your way around him whom the devil had not the force to attack. With what ease you shattered that image of God: man! Because of the death you merited, the Son of God had to die. (Tertullian)[30]

Within the Christian church today, denominations and congregations hold a wide spectrum of beliefs about the "acceptable" roles of women. The view that a church holds will affect the way a girl or woman is expected to behave and may affect her development as well. A church's theology of gender will communicate what sort of difference gender differences make and whether or not those differences can be properly appreciated for their complementarity.

In traditional churches, women are taught that their submission to men is a mark of godliness. Leadership may not be encouraged or possible for women. A church that promotes more egalitarian beliefs, however, can provide girls and women with a forum in which to try out new roles and exercise their voices. Egalitarian churches that allow and encourage female leadership can provide nonstereotypical role models for young women. Regardless of their theological perspectives on gender, churches need to be challenged to provide women with resistance strategies to counter the cultural silencing of female voices.

Unfortunately, in our churches as well as in the culture at large, difference has often made the wrong sort of difference, with damaging results. A theology of complementarity without hierarchy, however, would help us celebrate gender differences in a way that supports and encourages each other's gifts and seeks to meet each other's needs.

We must ask ourselves some critical questions. How should our theology of both the human condition and redemption influence the manner with which we

---

[29]Thomas Aquinas *Summa Theologica* I.92.1; quoted in Nancy Tuana, *The Less Noble Sex* (Bloomington: Indiana University Press, 1993), p. 22.

[30]Tertullian *De Cultu Feminarum*; quoted in *Not in God's Image: Women in History from the Greeks to the Victorians*, ed. Julia O'Faolain and Lauro Martines (New York: Harper & Row, 1973), p. 132.

build our human relationships? With what transcendent values will we begin the work to change both the inner and outer realities that shape gender relationships? We need a vision that transcends roles and allows us to think in terms of what it means to be a redeemed human being. Van Leeuwen suggests that the fundamental issue for the church is not primarily "proper" gender roles for husbands and wives, particularly if "proper" roles are some historically determined way of organizing family economic, domestic and childrearing tasks. Rather, the fundamental question is priorities. Each Christian family contains particular talents, needs and limitations. How might these be taken into account as the family attempts to serve God's kingdom on earth? Responsible Christian freedom must be practiced during each season of a family's life.[31]

There is no one recipe that fits every family, and for that I am grateful. The last thing we need is a new standard by which to evaluate our competence. What is critical is that both women and men intentionally work out these kingdom priorities, modeling for and discipling their children in a way that celebrates redemption and responsible Christian freedom based on God's gracious gifts, not on rigid role expectations. What is important is that we are intentional in being authentic, full human beings, not mere replays of traditional role stereotypes of men and women.

The church, which is made up of Christian women and men, can and should respond as a community with the same kingdom priorities. The church needs to answer the question of priorities by facilitating a structure that utilizes all spiritual gifts and contributes to the advancement of God's kingdom on earth. The church should take the lead in formulating answers that bring emotional and spiritual health to the entire body.

The church is at a decision point about sex roles. We could slip back into restrictive rules that limit relationships and use of God's gifts—which would be tantamount to going back to not knowing there are numbers above 100. Or we could trip into a permissive, ruleless model that allows anything by anybody. Or we can look to kingdom priorities in formulating a new redemptive vision that is moral, healthy, just and empowering.

How should the family and the church respond to this call for a new redemptive community? Jesus tells us in Matthew 20:25-27:

You know that the rulers of the Gentiles lord it over them, and their high officials

---

[31]Van Leeuwen, *Gender & Grace*, p. 176.

exercise authority over them. Not so with you. Instead, whoever wants to become great among you must be your servant, and whoever wants to be first must be your slave—just as the Son of Man did not come to be served, but to serve, and to give his life as a ransom for many.

How can we reclaim maleness and femaleness in a way that avoids the constructions of domination-subordination hierarchies? What structures and supports are necessary to help us truly formulate this new redemptive vision? How can we be accountable to this vision in our relationships? What is needed at the church level to support and maintain this accountability? How might each of us be using power in a hurtful hierarchy? We all must answer these questions, first individually, then as a family, and finally as a church and a community.

In my times of meditation, I begin dreaming. I dream of a time when both men and women will truly communicate and learn from each other, when the notion of maleness and femaleness can be wrought from the fabric of creation, not from the trappings of our society. I dream of a time when both fathers and mothers are invested in their children's lives, when both are the holders of the schedule. I dream of a time when fathers are so involved that mothers no longer play the role of mediator or buffer between children and Dad, when Dad no longer goes to Mom to find out what is wrong with Sally or what Johnny needs. I dream of a time when moms no longer pass on "the tyranny of nice and kind" to their daughters, when women no longer give over the power of their voice, when they trust their perceptions and authorize their own voice. I dream of a time when women learn to speak with boldness. I dream of a time when little boys can enjoy girls for friends. I dream of a time when men can feel deeply and articulate those feelings. I dream of a time in which the church will take the lead in facilitating and promoting healing, redemptive relationships.

A poem by Nancy Smith reminds us that the liberation of women is also the liberation of men:

> For every woman tired of acting weak when she knows she is strong,
> there is a man weary of appearing strong when he feels vulnerable.
>
> For every woman sick of acting dumb,
> there is a man burdened with the constant expectation of "knowing everything."
>
> For every woman accused of being an emotional female,
> there is a man denied the right to weep.
>
> For every woman feeling tied down by children,

there is a man denied the full joy of sharing parenthood.

For every woman who takes a step toward her own liberation,
there is a man who finds the way to freedom made a little easier.[32]

---

[32]This poem, written by Nancy Smith, was found on a number of websites, but no date or place of
publication was given.

28

HELPING THE CHURCH
UNDERSTAND BIBLICAL EQUALITY

Mimi Haddad and Alvera Mickelsen

Teachings about the scriptural basis for the equality of men and women in the church and home have been circulating within Christendom for more than a hundred years. Yet many Christian churches are still practicing, either consciously or unconsciously, a "men preferred" or "male only" pattern of leadership and teaching. Why should this be true? Why hasn't biblical gender equality been more fully accepted?

While we acknowledge the reality of sinfulness that operates even in the church, we have come to see another element in the gender debate. Sociological research suggests that it is not enough to present the biblical facts. There are other significant factors that influence our thoughts and actions.

In *Diffusion of Innovations*, Everett Rogers notes that in the early days of long sea voyages, scurvy was a far more effective killer of sailors than war, pirates or accidents. In 1601 an English sea captain conducted an experiment that proved that citrus juice or fruits added to the diet would prevent scurvy. Though sailors were informed of these findings, it was not until two hundred years later—and thousands of needless deaths—that scurvy was finally conquered by the British Navy.[1]

This is a classic example of how simply telling the facts often does little to change behavior. What held back this simple and much-needed change in the behavior of sailors? Why didn't the sailors consume citrus products when they knew it might save their lives? Why did their behavior remain unchanged?

This dilemma brings us to the science of diffusion—the study of what causes a new idea or change in practice or belief to take hold in a social system. Rogers

---

[1]Everett M. Rogers, *Diffusion of Innovations*, 4th ed. (New York: Free Press, 1995), pp. 7-8.

outlines five basic elements needed for a new idea or change to be accepted. These principles are well worth the consideration of Christian leaders who want the church to embrace biblical teachings on gender equality. The diffusion of a new idea is facilitated when we

- speak the truths of the Bible in language like that of our Lord Jesus Christ—simple, direct and rich in personal stories

- show how life improves, in marriages and in the church, when gender barriers are broken

- connect the message to the core beliefs of Christians

- model the message in as many ways as possible

- find simple, safe ways for people to "sample" their freedom in Christ with no gender barriers

We will deal with each of these in some depth.

Eliminate Complexity: The Importance of Understandable Language

"Complexity is the degree to which an innovation is perceived as relatively difficult to understand and use. The higher the complexity, the lower the rate of adoption."[2]

The degree of perceived complexity will directly affect how quickly a new gadget, idea or behavior is embraced. For example, when home computers were first introduced into the market, they were fairly complex; therefore engineers and those with a technical background were the first to purchase them.[3] Technical hobbyists were not put off by the complexity of these early computers, but the "perceived complexity of the home computers was an important negative force in their rate of adoption"[4] among the general population. As "home computers became more user friendly,"[5] however, their adoption rate increased among those outside the technical community.

Many people find the biblical debate on gender to be as incomprehensible as early home computers. Although it is important for evangelical scholars, pastors and leaders to be acquainted with the arguments and issues, few laypersons have the educational background, time, patience or resources to learn the ancient lan-

---

[2]Ibid., p. 242.
[3]Ibid., p. 243.
[4]Ibid.
[5]Ibid.

guages or engage the complex principles of biblical interpretation and theology that are frequently taken up in the gender debate. Many people are unable or unwilling to sort through the maze of technical language and ideas used in discussions of these matters.

How can we help the average person in the pew? How do we communicate in a way that minimizes complexity while stating clearly and simply the truth of Scripture on gender that so many need to hear?

Some have discovered that complexity is best overcome by the use of simple language and many personal examples, as evidenced in the teaching style of Christ. Jesus knew that making matters personal helps everyone understand. Take the Lord's Prayer as recorded in Matthew 6:9-13. Here we see very profound ideas expressed in simple language. In English the entire prayer has fifty-eight words, and forty-six of them have only one syllable! Most of the teachings of our Lord are framed in similarly simple language. No wonder the masses of people followed him. They understood him!

When we discuss biblical equality, we often use words like *complementarianism, hermeneutics, traditionalism, exegesis, hierarchical* and *egalitarianism*. Many people have only vague concepts of what these words mean. To reach the average person in the pew, we must use language that is comprehensible. For example, instead of using the term *egalitarianism*, we can speak of "gift-based ministry."

Jesus said things like "Love your neighbor as yourself," "What God has joined together, let no one separate," "Many who are first will be last, and the last will be first." All of these teachings run counter to the way most of his hearers (and most of us) actually think and live, but the ideas are crystal-clear. There is no ambiguity and no jargon.

When we teach about equality, we probably should put more emphasis on the clear and simple teaching of Scripture, such as Christ's call to love one's neighbor as oneself. Or the teaching of Genesis 1 that men and women alike are made in the image of God and are to share responsibility for God's created world.

The call to love is very clear, just as is the call to care for God's created world. To fulfill our call as human beings created in God's image, we must care for the earth, the animals and one another—all of the things that make this world habitable. In our society, that includes caring for children, providing for a well-governed society, and what we commonly call work. And it surely includes making known the message of God and our responsibility to him.

This must be done in ways that are easily understandable to our fellow human beings. I recently listened to a fourth-grade girl recite memory verses, including Titus 2:11, "The grace of God has appeared, bringing salvation to all men" (KJV).

I asked her, "Does that include you?"

She answered, "No."

Fortunately she had a NRSV Bible with her, and I asked her to look it up in that translation. It read, "The grace of God has appeared, bringing salvation to all." Then I repeated my question, "Does that include you?"

She answered, "Yes."

It was a clear illustration of how important language is and why we need gender-accurate translations in which the language does not need further translation and explanation.

Or take I Corinthians 12, where we find clear teaching regarding God's gifts to all his people. God gives his gifts as he chooses, and all believers are to use their gifts for the good of the "body," his church. There is no suggestion that men get "leadership gifts" and women get "service gifts." Such passages are clear and do not need abstract theological language to explain them. They fit the Genesis account of men and women alike being created in the image of God and sharing responsibility for God's world.

If we who are involved in this biblical debate will express complex ideas simply, using easy-to-understand examples and personal stories, we will take an important step toward reaching all Christians with a vital and life-transforming message.

Show the Relative Advantage: How Biblical Equality Improves People's Lives

"The Relative Advantage is the degree to which an innovation is perceived as being better than the idea it supersedes."[6]

Although the thought patterns of the Western academic world are dominated by rationalism, this is probably not so true of most ordinary people. Most of us are more interested in entering into people's lives and sharing their feelings. There is good reason that *Guideposts* magazine has survived for so many years. Every article is a personal experience piece. Much of *Reader's Digest* is devoted to personal stories.

A large portion of the Bible recounts the experiences of individuals or of the nation Israel. We have four accounts of the life of Christ, and most of the rest of the New Testament consists of letters from individuals to churches or other individuals.

---

[6]Ibid., p. 212.

The Bible has often been called a case study of God's acts with human beings.

Seeing the success of churches and marriages that practice gender equality will probably persuade more people than will theological discussions. At the first Christians for Biblical Equality (CBE) marriage conference (2000), couples were greatly moved as they observed the joy and satisfaction of some whose marriages had been transformed by the practice of equality. Some remarked, "The Spirit of God was so present it was like a revival meeting."

One woman explained that she and her husband had been taught that wives were to submit to their husbands as "God's plan for marriage." They wanted to be in God's plan, so they revised their way of relating to each other so that the husband made most of the decisions and she became a "submissive wife." She said it almost destroyed their marriage, and she became very depressed. Not until they found CBE and saw with new eyes God's message of mutual submission were they able to salvage their relationship and experience deep joy. Their honest, moving testimony was a powerful agent in changing the attitudes of many. When people see the relative advantage of living out the biblical message of equality, theology moves into practice and lives are changed.

Conversely, we can show the relative *disadvantage* of hierarchical gender roles by asking: What kind of life do you want your talented, outgoing daughter to have? Or, what kind of life do you want your shy, talented son to have? Will the traditional view of male leadership and female submission provide for the fullest development of the gifts God has given them? Not all men enjoy leadership or have the gift. Not all women are quiet followers. In a truly biblical marriage, or in a church where everyone uses their God-given talents, each contributes what gifts they have in mutual submission to one another. Insisting that only men be leaders and that women only be followers denies the great differences between individuals in God's creation.

Most churches are looking for more gifted leaders to take charge of their programs. Churches that open leadership doors to women double their potential supply. Furthermore, many women are skilled at enlisting and working with volunteers because of their wide experience in organizing social and family activities. Most churches run largely on volunteer work. Women often have more experience than men in training and encouraging others. Many are skilled teachers with experience in motivating and directing. What a shame to have all of this lost to the church because of tradition. Churches that deny opportunity to women leaders are working with one hand tied behind their back. But where women and men demonstrate success and fulfillment in using their gifts in church, we observe firsthand the relative advantage of gift-based ministries.

A significant problem with ministry that is gender-based rather than gift-based is that it overlooks the successes women have had in foreign missions. In mission fields around the world women have preached, married, buried and baptized thousands, begun and administered hospitals, orphanages and schools, and planted hundreds of churches. The Women's Missionary Movement flourished between 1870 and 1920. It brought the good news of Christ to millions of people around the world—especially in countries such as India and Pakistan, where men could not teach or minister to women at all. Women have also been influential in building the church in countries such as China, South Korea and Africa.

By rehearsing the successes women have had on the mission field, we take another step toward bringing the message to life; we show the advantage of biblical equality in a vital way. Once we demonstrate this, we can ask: "What if women had not taken the initiative? Millions of people would never have heard the gospel. Were these women missionary leaders out of God's will?"

In pointing out the relative advantage of permitting women to serve in leadership, we should also note the biblical examples of powerful and successful women chosen by God to be leaders, prophets and evangelists. Deborah (Judg 4–5) was a judge (at that time the top leadership position in Israel), the commander-in-chief of the army, a poet, singer and prophet. God used her to deliver Israel from the tyranny of King Jabin of Canaan. The first evangelist in the New Testament was the Samaritan woman at the well. She was also the first person to whom Jesus revealed that he was the Messiah. Mary Magdalene was the first person to see the risen Christ. The list goes on and on.

Women were so active in the early church that Saul had them imprisoned along with men (Acts 9:1-2). Women participated in the Day of Pentecost, received the gift of tongues and proclaimed the risen Christ. Paul speaks of Euodia and Syntyche (Phil 4:2-3) as his coworkers who fought at his side in spreading the gospel.[7]

Freedom in Christ, including gender equality, furthers evangelism and missions. It brings joy and fruitfulness to those who practice and believe it. By showing the relative advantage of embracing biblical equality, we harness a powerful communication tool and help the church understand the biblical message that ministry should be based on gifts, not gender.

---

[7]For an in-depth discussion of women leaders in the Bible, see chapter six.

Increase Compatibility: Connecting to the Core Beliefs of Christians

"Compatibility is the degree to which an innovation is perceived as consistent with the existing values, past experiences, and needs of potential adopters."[8]

Health workers in Peru attempted to eliminate typhoid fever by teaching villagers to boil their drinking water. However, few adopted this practice. Had these health workers been familiar with Peruvian culture, they would have been aware of the common belief that "only the ill use hot water."[9] Villagers had been taught from an early age to dislike boiled water.[10]

Old ideas die hard because they function as the "main mental tools that individuals utilize to assess new ideas."[11] "One cannot deal with an innovation except on the basis of the familiar, what is known."[12] Previous practices serve as the standard by which a new idea is evaluated and interpreted.

For centuries many Christians have been taught that the submission of women to men in church, home and society is God's plan. Biblical egalitarians have come to understand that such a notion is rooted in sinful love of power; yet as we introduce people to a new, more biblically faithful model of men and women working together as equal partners, most people will interpret this "new" teaching through the old. How, then, ought we to proceed?

Researchers suggest we can effectively communicate a new belief that would otherwise be perceived as suspect if we connect to the core values of those who do not yet hold the belief. By beginning with what we already share as Christians, we help others accept what might otherwise be rejected as incompatible. Thus we need to begin by stating the values we hold in common.

Evangelicals who promote biblical equality can affirm the core values of fellow Christians who disagree with us on gender equality. What we have in common as Christians far outweighs our disagreements; we must therefore rehearse our shared values frequently and clearly. For example, some who oppose biblical equality say that egalitarians deny or diminish the authority of the Bible and other core beliefs of Christianity. This is not true. We do well to carefully and frequently communicate our belief in the authority of the Bible in all matters of faith and practice. Our differences lie in how we interpret certain passages of the

---

[8]Rogers, *Diffusion of Innovations*, p. 224.
[9]Ibid., p. 3.
[10]Ibid.
[11]Ibid., p. 225.
[12]Ibid., pp. 225-26.

Bible, not in our doctrine of the Bible.

Because some Christians fear that the message of biblical equality will undermine the sanctity of marriage and the well-being of the Christian family, egalitarians must regularly reiterate their support of family values and the responsibility of parents for their children. We believe that this responsibility is so great that it needs to be shared by fathers and mothers together, as well as the extended family.

The gospel message is so important that we can agree that all must work to share it with others whenever we can. Every Christian should be free to tell others of the love of Christ—regardless of factors such as gender, age or race. The same goes for public preaching and teaching. Many agree that there are some basic differences between how men and women generally see and experience life. For that very reason, it is helpful for both men and women to hear the gospel from the perspective of the other gender. It enlarges our understanding of God and of the gospel of Christ. The history of the church and the witness of Scripture show that God uses men and women alike to proclaim him and to serve as leaders in his kingdom work.

Because most Christians have a strong desire to see the gospel message adopted by people around the world, we can also speak of the rich tradition of women throughout the history of the church who brought many to faith by using their gifts of preaching and teaching. Pastor David Yonggi Cho in Korea, who leads the largest Protestant church in the world, says that his church began to grow when he released women to use their gifts.[13] Similarly, Loren Cunningham, president of Youth with a Mission, notes that foreign missions grew rapidly once women began using their gifts in preaching the gospel in foreign lands.[14] By affirming the commitment to evangelism of women such as Lottie Moon, Frances Willard, Anne Hasseltine Judson and the hundreds of female pastors of Cho's church, we help others embrace gift-based ministry as a successful model of spreading the gospel.

By pointing to our commitment to the authority of Scripture, the sacredness of the family and the centrality of evangelism and missions, we connect to the core values of those who are otherwise apprehensive of biblical equality. By carefully establishing the enormous ground we have in common, we build sturdy bridges to those who are unsure of our message. And on these bridges we lead our brothers and sisters into the Promised Land where all Christians are encouraged to use their

---

[13]Loren Cunningham, David Joel Hamilton and Janice Rogers, *Why Not Women?* (Seattle: YWAM Publishers, 2000), p. 68.

[14]Ibid.

God-given gifts to forward Christ's kingdom.

Improve Observability: Modeling the Message of Gender Equality

"Observability is the degree to which the results of an innovation are visible to others."[15]

For people to accept a new idea or product, they must see it in use.

How did cell phones become so popular? Cell phones were not introduced in the United States until 1983. At that time they cost about three thousand dollars, and their use was limited to executives and CEOs. As the price dropped and quality improved, their use grew dramatically, not only in the United States but also around the world. Soon people began seeing cell phones everywhere. As a result, people realized that they were a highly useful product. They ceased being a novelty and became widely used.

Similarly, gender equality has made rapid strides, is widely visible in the secular world and is a growing reality in the evangelical world. Those who are uncomfortable working for a woman are at a distinct disadvantage. Young women gain leadership experience in high school and college, where student body presidents and club leaders are often women. When they reach adulthood, they are unaccustomed to the restrictions that may be placed on them in the church. Where can we find living models of biblical equality in the church?

There are, of course, women pastors in some churches. Many Christian colleges and seminaries have women teaching Bible or theology or preaching in chapel services. These women serve as important role models to many. We cannot underestimate our need to observe women using their gifts in the church, as well as husbands and wives serving one another in mutual submission. Several practical ways to model the message of biblical equality are listed at the end of this section.

In churches that restrict women, modeling must begin gradually. Usually there is no difficulty with women teaching children in any church. Women leaders are often acceptable even for high school and college groups. The students rarely question this, since they have had women leaders and teachers in high school and college. Any objections usually arise from adults who have not been exposed to models of females working as equals with men.

The Scriptures provide many examples of women serving alongside men in the gospel. By pointing to these narratives, we allow the Bible to model the mes-

---

[15]Rogers, *Diffusion*, p. 244.

sage of equality. When Jesus visited the home of Mary and Martha in Bethany, Mary sat at Jesus' feet to listen to his teachings, just as male disciples did. When Martha complained, Jesus rebuked her and took the side of Mary (Lk 10:38-42).

Paul mentions Priscilla and Aquila more often than anyone else except Timothy. And in most instances he names Priscilla first, although that was contrary to the customs of the day. When people quote a few passages of Paul, often in isolation from the context, they must be helped to see the meaning of these passages in light of what Paul himself actually practiced.

Paul's practical counsel to married couples in 1 Corinthians 7 models an approach to marriage that is based on mutuality and equality. Here he gives identical instructions to husbands and wives regarding marital relations, explaining that each has authority over the other's body and each should yield to the other (1 Cor 7:2-5).

Through both the examples in the Bible and living models of biblical equality in our churches and our homes, ideas about equality come to life. This is an important part of communication. We all need models to understand an idea fully.

Practical ways of modeling the message include the following:

1. Use couples to serve as both greeters and ushers. After that is accepted, the church may be willing to use single women or women whose husbands do not come to church.

2. Have women read aloud the Scripture in church, during Bible study groups and other church functions.

3. Encourage or assign women to pray publicly when opportunities arise.

4. Ask couples and women to serve on church committees for which they are qualified.

5. Have couples share leadership of house groups, Bible studies and adult education. At times when the husband cannot be present (illness or business), the wife can lead or take over his duties. Or they can take turns. This prepares the way for greater equality.

6. Encourage women to participate in business meetings or on committees of which they are a part. Every committee needs women on it!

The appeal for change should be on the basis of using those most qualified and available rather than on the basis of choosing women specifically. However, there are some instances in which the appeal for women on a gender basis may be acceptable. On a church building committee, women are often better qualified than men to plan kitchens, nurseries, restrooms and childcare centers. Most men will agree to that! If a woman has an obvious gift the church is in need of, she should be encouraged to use that gift.

Offer Trialability: Safe, Simple Ways to Sample Biblical Equality

"Trialability is the degree to which an innovation may be experimented with on a limited basis. . . . The personal trying-out of an innovation is a way to give meaning to an innovation, to find out how it works under one's own conditions. This trial is a means to dispel uncertainty about the new idea."[16]

Looking again at the example of cellular phones, we can readily see how easy it was to try out a friend's cell phone. Because of this and other factors, cell phones quickly became part of everyone's life.

As new ideas are sampled on a trial or installment basis, they are often easier to embrace. By allowing an individual an opportunity to sample biblical equality, we give the message personal meaning, whereby one comes to understand how it works "under one's own conditions."[17] This is a critical step in the process of diffusion. The trying out of a new innovation is the last step toward making it our own.

By providing small, safe opportunities for others to take their first steps as egalitarians, we help Christians understand and embrace the joy of living as God intended. Some simple changes in behavior may offer a safe means of sampling equality in traditional situations.

How can equality be sampled in marriages where male leadership has been firmly taught and practiced? Husbands often consider certain tasks inherently male. One of these is the control of money. Yet practically speaking in America, if God intended men to be in control of money, he played a terrible trick on women! In our society, women on average outlive men by six or seven years, and husbands are usually a few years older than their wives. This means that a woman is likely to be a widow for eight to ten years.

Some men keep such control of money that their wives have little or no knowledge of their financial situation and no experience in making important financial decisions. Some don't know what the financial resources of the family are or where they are located. This can have tragic consequences. Men who love their wives should never let that happen.

Couples can learn to take turns or to share the tasks of keeping records, paying

---

[16]Ibid., p. 243.
[17]Ibid.

bills and handling financial affairs. No important financial decisions should be made by either one without consultation and agreement of the other. After all, both husband and wife must sign joint tax returns, and both are responsible for their accuracy.

Women can be equally controlling over areas perceived as theirs. They may not want to see their husband participate in childcare, school conferences, cooking, laundry and the like. If the wife needs to visit a sick relative or becomes ill herself, the husband is severely handicapped in his ability to help either her or himself.

Changes in these situations can be introduced without any appeal to "equality"—just to common sense.

Very often husbands and wives need safe, structured opportunities to make their first big decision as egalitarians. Christians for Biblical Equality offers marriage conferences and materials to help couples experience new ways of working together, in mutual submission, using their God-given gifts.

Egalitarians can help others embrace biblical equality by encouraging them to identify and use their gifts in their own churches. Where churches are closed to gift-based ministry, Christians eager to take their first step as egalitarians can proceed by learning to identify and sharpen their spiritual gifts in service to the community. There are many fine books, such as *Network*,[18] available through the Willow Creek Association, that help Christians identify their gifts. One's gifts often parallel the issues one feels strongly about.

Egalitarians can help their brothers and sisters in Christ try out or sample the message by empowering them to use their gifts. While the church may be closed to a woman's giftedness, the community at large is often open. Many organizations need mentors and volunteers. Women can serve others and fulfill God's intended purpose for them and their gifts by offering their services in schools, nonprofit ministries, short-term mission projects, shelters and neighborhood groups.

God will open a way. Pray, watch and get busy. You will know when the time comes. Perhaps God will even lead you to a church that is open to you and your gifts.

Conclusions

Changes in societal patterns are usually very slow and painful. This tends to be especially true in conservative churches. Change of any kind is often feared and con-

---

[18]Bruce Bugbee, Don Cousins and Bill Hybels, *Network* (Grand Rapids, Mich.: Zondervan, 1994).

sidered to be "the way of the world." Because Christians value the Bible, the Bible is often misused to prevent needed change and development. Most Christians have never really studied the biblical passages on gender for themselves; they believe what their pastor or Christian leader says these passages mean.

Meanwhile, like those sailors who died of scurvy although prevention was easily available, churches and individual Christians go on denying themselves the great joy and opportunity of serving the Lord in ways that are taught and modeled for us in Scripture, in history and in the lives of respected Christians around the world. So when we model the truths of biblical equality and encourage others to experience them in small ways, we help thousands of talented Christians find new ways to use their God-given gifts—gifts that are desperately needed by the church of Jesus Christ. And we help keep marriages from withering for lack of the true intimacy that is possible only in genuine equal-partnership relationships.

What can we do to encourage the acceptance and practice of biblical equality? Apply the principles of diffusion:

- Eliminate complexity; speak about biblical equality in simple, direct terms without using theological jargon.

- Show the relative advantage; demonstrate how life is improved in marriages and in the church with gender equality.

- Increase compatibility; connect with the core beliefs of those with whom you are working, and show how gender equality affirms those beliefs.

- Improve observability; model your beliefs in every situation, and open doors for others to do the same.

- Offer trialability; help those interested to find safe and easy ways to try out the concept of male-female equality in church and marriage.

29

TOWARD RECONCILIATION

Healing the Schism

Alice P. Mathews

Reconciliation is a term very much in vogue these days. In our litigious society, costly and destructive lawsuits have come to characterize the way even Christians handle differences. Yet the Bible shows us a better way.[1] Reconciliation is the Christian alternative for handling disputes between two parties who find themselves positioned against each other.[2]

Several decades of acrimonious labeling and infighting among conservative Christians over the place of women in the church and the home have led to what appears to be a hopeless chasm of difference between those who advocate gender equality and those who maintain hierarchical structures for male and female relationships. Can those who hold such opposing views be reconciled?

A Real and Significant Difference

If there is to be reconciliation, it must begin with the realization that the chasm between the two sides is real and significant. We must see and respect this conflict for what it is: a struggle for truth. No one in that struggle can dismiss opponents merely by labeling them—whether as power-hungry defenders of the status quo or as pawns of contemporary culture who are willing to compromise Scripture for the sake of a social agenda. Truth is on the line for God-fearing Christians on both

---

[1]This is the heart of 1 Corinthians, especially 6:1-11. It is also integral to our worship. In Matthew 5:23-24 Jesus regards reconciliation with any Christian who has something against us as essential before we can carry out our acts of worship to God.

[2]Resources for those who seek legal reconciliation include the Association of Christian Conciliation Services and the Christian Legal Society (PO Box 1492, Marrifield, VA 22116). See also Ken Sande, *The Peacemaker: A Biblical Guide to Resolving Personal Conflict* (Grand Rapids, Mich.: Baker, 1991).

sides of the chasm. When we fail to respect those who hold views that call our own beliefs into question, we miss the valid and ongoing struggle for truth. But in the effort to respect those with whom we disagree, we are faced with the painful necessity of doing so without abandoning this struggle.

This, of course, is not the first time in the history of the church that contrary understandings of biblical truth have faced the people of God. The great councils in the early centuries remind us that God-fearing Christians disagreed vigorously and often separated over core issues.[3] Later, in the sixteenth century, Martin Luther opposed certain teachings and practices of the Roman Catholic Church, launching the Reformation when he nailed his ninety-five theses to the Wittenberg door. Out of that act more than a hundred years of military warfare between Catholics and Protestants erupted in Europe.[4]

More recently, conservative Christians were divided over the issue of slavery, some using Scripture to defend the practice of owning other human beings and others using it to abolish that practice. Willard Swartley has helped us understand the ways the Bible has been used by groups opposing each other on this issue as well as on others, such as war and peace, sabbath keeping, and the subject of this book—the relationship between men and women in the home and the church.[5]

Even as we write in the twenty-first century, deep chasms exist between those who hold to an "open theism" and those who oppose it, and between those who believe all of the gifts of the Spirit should be operative in the church today and those who see some of those gifts as having been given to Christians in the first century only. All of this is to say that the church is no stranger to fracturing divisions in the name of truth.

Puzzled by the meaning or necessity of these fissures, we may ask why "the other

---

[3]Most twenty-first-century Christians assume that the church was clear about the nature of Christ from its earliest days. But it took the Council of Nicaea in 325 to formalize the church's understanding of Christ's divine nature (that God and Christ are of the same essence) and the Council of Chalcedon in 451 to formalize the understanding of the relation between the divine and human natures of Christ (one person in two natures). Long and bitter infighting over these doctrines led to permanent schisms in the church.

[4]After Luther's bold move and the quick formation of crowds of protesting followers around him, the Roman Catholic Church called the Council of Trent (1545, 1563) to deal with this new threat to its hegemony. Numerous wars based on this religious conflict broke out as Catholic governments tried to stop the spread of Protestantism in their countries: civil war in France (1562-1598), rebellion in the Netherlands (1565-1648), war between Spain and England (1585-1604) and the Thirty Years' War (1618-1648).

[5]Willard Swartley, *Slavery, Sabbath, War and Women* (Scottdale, Penn.: Herald, 1983).

side" cannot see what appear to us to be the *real* issues. Thomas Kuhn, examining the structure of scientific revolutions, concluded:

> The proponents of competing paradigms practice their trades in different worlds.
> . . . [They] see different things when they look from the same point in the same direction. Again, that is not to say that they can see anything they please. Both are looking at the world, and what they look at has not changed. But in some areas they see different things, and they see them in different relations one to the other. That is why a law that cannot even be demonstrated to one group of scientists may occasionally seem intuitively obvious to another.[6]

The extensive literature supporting male leadership and gender equality presents us with such competing paradigms.

Historian Anne Firor Scott, looking at the omission of women's accomplishments by earlier historians, reported:

> It is a truism, yet one easy to forget, that people see most easily things they are prepared to see and overlook those they do not expect to encounter. . . . Because our minds are clouded, we do not see things that are before our eyes. What clouds our minds is, of course, the culture that at any time teaches us what to see and what not to see.[7]

Our culture grinds the lens through which we look at all we see.

We may ask ourselves how people reading the same Scripture, and taking it as inspired and authoritative, can hold positions or paradigms as diverse as those represented by male-leadership and gender-equality views today. Or, to borrow Kuhn's words, we wonder why a position that cannot even be demonstrated to one group of sincere Christians seems intuitively obvious to another group of equally sincere Christians.

What is true for scientists and historians can also be true for theologians and biblical scholars. David Scholer puts his finger on a central problem for scholars in his discussion of starting points and the balance of texts. *The biblical text one chooses for one's starting point in the study of a doctrine or issue in Scripture becomes the lens through which one looks at all other texts.*[8] If, for example, an interpreter chooses 1 Timothy 2:12 as the

---

[6]Thomas Kuhn, *The Structure of Scientific Revolutions*, 2nd ed. (Chicago: University of Chicago Press, 1970), p. 150.

[7]Anne Firor Scott, "On Seeing and Not Seeing: A Case of Historical Invisibility," *Journal of American History* 71, no. 1 (June 1984): 7, 19.

[8]David Scholer, "1 Timothy 2:9-15 and the Place of Women in the Church's Ministry," in *Women, Authority and the Bible*, ed. Alvera Mickelsen (Downers Grove, Ill.: InterVarsity Press, 1986), pp. 193-219.

starting point, then other texts will be evaluated and interpreted (consciously or unconsciously) in the light of Paul's restrictive statement. On the other hand, if Galatians 3:28 is chosen as the starting point, texts such as 1 Timothy 2:12 will be read with Paul's declaration of "no distinctions" in mind.

If the starting text sets the boundaries or limits for what one is able to see in other texts, then the issue is more hermeneutical than exegetical. What, then, determines which texts are to function as starting texts? Scholer suggests that "our theological traditions tend to select our 'windows' for us."[9] Indeed, our particular culture and subculture have ground the lens through which we look at the Bible. As a result, a commentary written by a hierarchicalist will emphasize female subordination to male leadership, focusing almost exclusively on texts that appear to support subordination. On the other hand, those advocating gender equality focus on texts that their evangelical opponents often consider irrelevant.

When both groups use the same texts, it is often with a way of "seeing" that supports opposing views. For example, in discussions of Genesis 2, Stephen Clark sees the male as central to the narrative and therefore as the "head,"[10] whereas Perry Yoder argues that woman is the climax of the narrative, giving her an equal or even more important role.[11] We see what our lenses allow us to see.

One of the myths of modernity, accepted by physical and social scientists alike, was logical positivism—the idea that the investigator of any phenomenon could come to the investigative task with objectivity, uninfluenced by personal or cultural values. At the beginning of the twenty-first century, researchers in the natural and social sciences have come to understand that the way they personally view their world affects how they frame their questions. Those questions, in turn, determine the direction of their research. In effect, their assumptive world sets the limits for what they can or cannot see.

---

[9]David Scholer, "Feminist Hermeneutics and Evangelical Biblical Interpretation," *JETS* 30, no. 4 (December 1987): 417.

[10]Stephen B. Clark, *Man and Woman in Christ: An Examination of the Roles of Men and Women in the Light of Scriptures and the Social Sciences* (Ann Arbor, Mich.: Servant, 1980), p. 14. In this passage Clark cites three reasons that the partnership between man and woman should be understood as hierarchical: (1) "man is the center of the narrative," (2) "it is the man who is called 'Man' or 'human' and not the woman," and (3) man is created first, giving him as "firstborn" a natural precedence by birth. This synopsis of Clark is taken from Swartley, *Slavery, Sabbath, War and Women*, p. 154.

[11]Perry Yoder, "Woman's Place in the Creation Accounts," in *Study Guide on Women*, ed. Herta Funk (Newton, Kans.: Faith and Life, 1975), pp. 10-11. I am indebted to Swartley for the contrast in emphasis between Clark and Yoder (*Slavery, Sabbath, War and Women*, p. 154).

Theologians, too, bring their assumptive world to the questions they ask. Those who have spent their lives in service to Jesus Christ bring theological assumptions from their early training that continue to determine what they can and cannot see. Moreover, they are convinced that their assumptions are grounded in Scripture. Yet the history of the church should serve as a cautionary tale about assumptions that in fact were based at times more in political or social realities than in the core teachings of Scripture.

Therefore we must step back and ask ourselves hard questions about our assumptions.[12] As John Piper and Wayne Grudem acknowledge, "We have a thousand ways to justify with our brains the biases of the soul."[13] This is a good reminder to all who are concerned about women's roles in the home and church.

At the same time, we cannot ignore our differences. If we are committed to truth as the controlling principle, we must accept the reality that ideas divide people. When we know that we are to love one another, yet we have strong differences over crucial issues, the resulting cognitive dissonance may tempt us to try to paper over the chasm that divides us from our brothers and sisters in Christ. This can be dangerous to our commitment to truth.

"Truth" is not merely the content of a series of discourses or arguments; it also includes being true to oneself and to what is true in the opponent.[14] When we discard what we have come to accept as propositionally true merely to lower our cog-

---

[12]Lewis Wirth, in his introduction to Karl Mannheim's *Ideology and Utopia*, comments that "the most important thing that we can know about a man [sic] is what he takes for granted, and the most elemental and important facts about a society are those that are seldom debated and generally regarded as settled" ([San Diego, Calif.: Harcourt Brace Jovanovich, 1936], p. xxiii). More recently, Huston Smith expands on the importance of understanding our unexamined assumptions: "The dominant assumptions of an age color the thoughts, beliefs, expectations, and images of the men and women who live within it. Being always with us, these assumptions usually pass unnoticed—like the pair of glasses which, because they are so often on the wearer's nose, simply stop being observed. But this doesn't mean they have no effect. Ultimately, assumptions which underlie our outlooks on life refract the world in ways that condition our art and our institutions: the kinds of homes we live in, our sense of right and wrong, our criteria of success, what we conceive our duty to be, what we think it means to be a man or woman, how we worship our God or whether, indeed, we have a God to worship" (Huston Smith, *Beyond the Post-modern Mind*, 2nd ed. [Wheaton, Ill.: Theosophical Publishing House, 1989], pp. 3-4).

[13]John Piper and Wayne Grudem, "Charity, Clarity, and Hope," in *RBMW*, p. 419.

[14]Jesus referred to himself in John 14:6 as "the way and the truth and the life." Integral to living as "the truth" in first-century Palestine was being true not only to propositional truth but to his *being* God incarnate. It was his refusal to shade the truth of his being that put him on a collision course with the religious leaders.

nitive dissonance, we do violence to the integrity of our own mind and heart. And when we ignore or downplay serious differences in beliefs about propositional truth with someone who opposes us, we diminish or even nullify the worth of that person's mind and heart. As pompous old Polonius noted in Shakespeare's *Hamlet,* "To thine own self be true, and it follows as the day the night, thou canst not then be false to any man."

Truth can be a casualty when differences are trivialized in other ways as well. One means of trivializing real differences is to change nomenclature. For example, when the term *complementarian* was chosen to replace earlier designations of those who accept as biblical a hierarchical structure in male-female relationships, many people's perception of the debate changed. In defining their position, Piper and Grudem reject the terms *traditionalist* and *hierarchical,* arguing that *complementarian* is preferable because it "suggests both equality and beneficial differences between men and women."[15] This sounds like a significant change in the traditional position and, as such, a move toward reconciliation. But soon the reader discovers that the crux of the issue for "complementarians" is *difference* rather than equality and that "difference" refers primarily to an *in*equality in authority between women and men. The nomenclature misleads, and truth is trivialized.

As James Beck and Craig Blomberg note, "It is not clear that the idea of men and women playing complementary roles inherently suggests that certain roles are altogether prohibited for one gender. Some egalitarians have complained, rightly it seems, that their view can equally be described as complementarian," because they too reject unisex theories of gender development.[16]

The differences between opposing positions can also be trivialized by what Charles Long calls *significations.*[17] To signify is to name, and often by attaching pejorative names to movements or individuals, we can so color the perception of our opponents that it becomes impossible to carry on meaningful dialogue. For example, when an evangelical who supports gender equality is called a *feminist* without any further qualification (and sometimes in the tone and temper of an expletive), that naming confers a reality on the receiver that may not be true at all. It is a false

---

[15] Piper and Grudem, "Preface," *RBMW,* p. xiv.

[16] James R. Beck and Craig L. Blomberg, "Introduction," *Two Views on Women in Ministry,* ed. James R. Beck and Craig L. Blomberg (Grand Rapids, Mich.: Zondervan, 2001), p. 17.

[17] Charles Long, *Significations: Signs, Symbols and Images in the Interpretation of Religion* (Philadelphia: Fortress, 1988). Long's book is particularly germane for any reader pursuing a deeper understanding of the racial epithets or "namings" that demean and divide.

generalization that makes further discourse more difficult, if not impossible. It trivializes the issue by ignoring the actual content of the argument and removing the other person from inclusion in the conversation.

In a powerful essay on the abuse of language, German theologian Josef Pieper examines the purposes of human language and the words we use: "Word and language form the medium that sustains the common existence of the human spirit. . . . If the word becomes corrupted, human existence itself will not remain unaffected and untainted."[18] Because words convey reality, when we name or identify someone or something, we communicate a quality of reality to that person or thing.

But Pieper insists that a lie (outright or implied) can never be taken as true communication because "it withholds the other's share and portion of reality, to prevent his participation in reality."[19] It is a corruption of one's relationship to reality. A person who thus corrupts language can give fine speeches but is to a significant degree incapable of dialogue. This is a form of deceptive verbal artistry: superbly crafted, perfectly worded, brilliantly formulated, strikingly written, and at the same time false in its thrust and essence.[20] This is illustrated by a prominent Christian author who, in order to support her point, cites the first half of I Corinthians 7:4 ("The wife does not have authority over her own body but yields it to her husband") while omitting the second half of the same verse ("In the same way, the husband does not have authority over his own body but yields it to his wife"). This is patently dishonest no matter how elegantly stated.[21] Similarly, she offers two lists of "biblical commands" to husbands and to wives, in which she mingles loosely reworded biblical statements with other statements that are not found in Scripture.[22]

Our commitment to truth demands that we speak what is true and that we use language honestly. When we do this, we may discover that what we hold as true divides us from those who hold opposite views. If we are committed to truth as the controlling principle, then we must accept the reality that ideas can divide people.

Thus a genuine problem exists, and it is *our* problem. Jesus is clear in Matthew 5:23-24 that if we are in the family of God, we have an obligation before God to

---

[18]Josef Pieper, *Abuse of Language, Abuse of Power*, trans. Lothar Krauth (San Francisco: Ignatius, 1988), p. 15.

[19]Ibid., p. 16.

[20]Ibid., p. 19.

[21]Elisabeth Elliot, *The Mark of a Man* (Old Tappan, N.J.: Fleming H. Revell, 1981), p. 84.

[22]For example, she includes in the list of commands for wives the statement "Their role is to be receptive" (ibid.). By rephrasing quotations from Scripture in her own words, she implies that all of the statements have come from the Bible.

do all that we can to be reconciled to anyone in God's household who "has something against" us. Note that the text is not about our behavior when we have something against someone else. It is about our behavior when others have something against us. The problem belongs to all of us in the family of God, and it cannot be ignored.

Whether we are egalitarians or hierarchicalists, there are people who hold things against us. In the process of acting to defend their paradigm, people hurt other people within the body of Christ. In the pursuit of truth we demonstrate an un-Christian priority system when the idea becomes more important than the people holding that idea. We have only to scan the history of the church to discover how many paid dearly, often with their lives, as they found themselves caught in the crossfire of competing paradigms.

The chasm is real. Even more important, the way we often respond to it is a scandal to the church and a point of ridicule for the world. Jesus' prayer in John 17 shows us why this chasm is such a scandal. Crying out to the Father only hours before his trial and crucifixion, he prayed for the unity of all those who would follow him, then and in the ages to come, asking "that all of them may be one, . . . *so that the world may believe that you have sent me*" (Jn 17:21).

Do we understand that our oneness with each other and our mission of evangelism in the world are inseparable? Jesus' prayer was not a spiritual abstraction. Our unity is not simply for its own sake or because it would be pleasant or nice. In a profound way in this prayer our Lord links our unity with the success of our mission in the world. As J. Ramsey Michaels notes, "The unity of Jesus' followers challenges the world to believe."[23] This puts the matter of our unity in a different light. Yet the chasm is there, often using up time and energy and frequently diverting our attention from the fundamental mission of the church.

What Then Must Be Done?

We acknowledge that the chasm is real and that it comes from a struggle for truth. For these reasons we cannot trivialize it or water it down semantically. We attend to Jesus' prayer, and as his followers we acknowledge that the chasm often diverts us from the mission he gave us; moreover, it diverts unbelievers from taking our Lord seriously. What, then, must we do?

First, we all must continue to explore honestly the competing paradigms, using the tools of biblical

---

[23]J. Ramsey Michaels, *John*, NIBC (Peabody, Mass.: Hendrickson, 1984), p. 299.

theology, logic and courtesy. All Christians defending or forwarding one of the competing paradigms face the temptation of devoting their time to shoring up their own arguments while giving little attention or respect to the arguments of their opponents. We must adamantly resist this temptation.

A paradigm is like a closed box. Inside it are all of the pieces that make it a compelling explanation for the way things are or ought to be. To the extent that we enclose ourselves within the box, we fail to see the anomalies to our paradigm. Anomalies are like rocks piling up against the outer sides of our box. Kuhn has shown that we experience a *paradigm shift* only when the cumulative weight of anomalies pressing on the sides of the paradigm box forces it to collapse. All the major scientific discoveries of past centuries came about not because scientists were looking for a new theory but because significant anomalies overwhelmed their reigning paradigms.

What are the anomalies pressing against the sides of the respective paradigms? This book explores the anomalies pressing against the sides of the male-leadership paradigm, just as the contributors to Piper and Grudem's *Recovering Biblical Manhood and Womanhood* explored anomalies pressing against the sides of the gender-equality paradigm. Every paradigm has its anomalies.

Until we have explored the anomalies threatening both paradigms, we have not completed our task. This calls for the best efforts of our best scholars, as well as our best people working with women and men in the church and in the wider society. It means reviewing the biblical and theological studies to see what may still need to be explored. It involves listening to people in the pew and on the street. It includes hearing insights from the social sciences (historians, anthropologists, sociologists, psychologists and culture analysts). It means looking squarely at issues of abuse (sexual abuse, battering and the abuse of power in church and home). It means examining our own accommodations to the godless culture around us. When we thoroughly understand the anomalies as well as the paradigms, we can move to the next step.

Second, we are obligated to explain the competing paradigms at many levels. Just as educators develop textbooks adapted to the needs of various ages, audiences and educational levels, so must we develop tools that enable people at all levels to understand the issues at stake. What are the fundamental ideas in each of the paradigms? Where did these ideas come from? How long have they been with us? And most important, if we accept these ideas and adopt a particular paradigm as truth, what are the *implications* for the future?

Some would argue that such efforts have already been made. We can applaud the solid exegetical and hermeneutical work made available to wide audiences by biblical scholars and theologians. We are grateful for the Christian social scientists that have also helped us understand some of the implications of both paradigms for families and individuals in the home or church. But much remains to be done. As Kuhn observed, what is intuitively obvious to some is still opaque to others. How can we move beyond this impasse?

As the task of explaining the competing paradigms goes forward, the temptation is always to simplify issues to the point of being simplistic, to strip down the paradigms to such a point that the necessary nuancing of arguments disappears, resulting in a mere caricature of the paradigm. This happens, for example, when a young couple is frightened away from an egalitarian marriage by warnings of deadlock in decision making if one party (the husband) does not have the final word. Likewise it happens when a pastor warns that having a woman in a leadership role in the congregation starts that church down the slippery slope into a godless accommodation to the culture.

Proponents of either paradigm must understand both paradigms inside and out and know the anomalies pressing against the sides of each paradigm box. Then they must develop adequate, truthful, simple (but not simplistic) ways to communicate the paradigm to others to whom it is unfamiliar.

Third, while the first two steps are being carried out, we must acknowledge the chasm between the paradigms and embrace as fellow believers those on the other side of the chasm. We cannot ignore the existence of the chasm or minimize its significance with semantic games. If, in fact, our paradigm has emerged in a struggle to find the *truth* about men and women in the home and church, we are dishonest with ourselves (as well as with others) if we attempt to water down the points of disagreement. This places us in a state of cognitive dissonance.[24] We cannot pretend the differences do not exist. Yet our Lord calls us to unity. We are admonished to speak the truth in love (Eph 4:15).

Leon Festinger, in his work with cognitive dissonance, concluded that when we experience this tension we typically do two things. We try to reduce the dissonance, and we "actively avoid situations and information that would likely increase the dissonance."[25] The issue of truth concerns not only the truth we embrace but also

---

[24]This term was coined by Leon Festinger to describe the frustration or disequilibrium we experience when we are faced with inconsistencies between what we believe to be true and what we experience. See Leon Festinger, *A Theory of Cognitive Dissonance* (Evanston, Ill.: Row, Peterson, 1957), p. 3.
[25]Ibid.

our difficulty in living with the tension between truth and love. We actively avoid information and situations that increase the tension or dissonance between what we believe and what we experience in our lives.

Does this begin to explain how something that is intuitively obvious to one remains opaque to another? In view of this tendency, how can we maintain an awareness of the chasm between the two paradigms even as we embrace those whose ideas we reject?

The Gospel as the Basis of Our Relationship

Again, we recall Jesus' prayer that we may be one "so that the world may believe that you have sent me" (Jn 17:20-21). The unity for which he prayed in those last hours before dying on a Roman cross is not merely an agreement to sweep our differences under the carpet as if they did not matter. Nor is it a conformity that one group imposes on another in an effort to present an aura of unity. Jesus is clear about both the nature and the purpose of this unity. Just as the Father is in the Son and the Son is in the Father, so are we to be one in them. Our unity is in God, and the power to hold truth in love for one another lies first in our relationship to God. Reconciliation begins here.

Only the gospel has the power to convert our dissonance into consonance. But how does the gospel work to overturn our natural inability to hold the truth in love? The doctrine of reconciliation is clearly stated by Paul in 2 Corinthians 5:17-19:

> If anyone is in Christ, there is a new creation. The old has gone, the new has come! All this is from God, who reconciled us to himself through Christ and gave us the ministry of reconciliation: that God was reconciling the world to himself in Christ, not counting people's sins against them. And he has committed to us the message of reconciliation.

Thus reconciliation brings together in love and friendship those who have been enemies. God was in Christ reconciling us to himself, not counting our trespasses against us. Then he gave to us the evangelistic task of bringing other people into a relationship to himself through Jesus Christ. God knew the truth about us yet reached out to us in the atoning death of his Son to bring us into a relationship of love with him. God demonstrates how truth and love can coexist in our relationship to him. But can it coexist in our relationships to others with whom we disagree?

The pursuit of truth can never be a substitute for nurturing relationships within the body of Christ. We are called to care for the brother or sister with whom we disagree while at the same time holding to the truth as we understand it. The tension between the two is inherent, and the resulting discomfort may persuade us that it is not merely difficult to achieve but it is morally wrong to marry the two. We think we cannot hold to the truth we have embraced while nurturing relationships with those with whom we disagree. Yet our Lord calls us to truth *and* to oneness in him. He does not tell us it is easy, but he is clear that it is necessary.

On the eve of Jesus' crucifixion "a dispute . . . arose among [the disciples] as to which of them was considered to be greatest" (Lk 22:24). Jesus intervened, reminding them that his followers should not use power or authority in the manner of the "kings of the Gentiles." That dispute seemed minor, but Jesus knew that the spirit behind the dispute was the serpent's poison. It had the potential to destroy the work of God in the world. He could not ignore it and thus responded with a solemn rebuke. Why? Their oneness was essential to their work in the world for God's kingdom.

Paul faced factions tearing apart the believers in Corinth (petty infighting, sexual immorality, believers taking other believers to court, issues of relationships in and out of marriage, legalisms about eating and drinking, abuses of relationships at the Lord's Table, flaunting of spiritual gifts, etc.)—many seemingly intractable issues. While he ruled on or counseled certain attitudes and behaviors in each of the problem areas, he repeatedly pointed the Corinthians to Jesus Christ. When we talk about reconciliation, this is the only point of true unity. We are to be one in Christ even as the Father and the Son are one (Jn 17:20-23).

Working with mathematical set theory, anthropologist and missiologist Paul Hiebert offers a means of imaging how Jesus' prayer for oneness is realized in human life.[26] In set theory, a "set" is a kind of worldview, a way to understand what is or ought to be true in life. If you imagine a set as a circle, it has a circumference (boundary) and a center (target or goal).

Some people have what Hiebert calls "bounded sets." They focus on the *boundary* of their set, its circumference. A person with a "bounded set" believes what is most important is to maintain the boundaries of truth. Bounded sets are fundamental to our understanding of order, and in a bounded set the definition of righteousness and justice is to live within the law (the boundary) but not nec-

---

[26]Paul Hiebert, *Anthropological Reflections on Missiological Issues* (Grand Rapids, Mich.: Baker, 1994); see chapter six on bounded sets.

essarily to live in harmony with each other.

A different kind of set is the "centered" or "relational" set. Here the focus is
not on maintaining the boundaries but on the *relationship* of everyone and everything
to the center—the target or goal. Some are far from the center but are moving toward it. That makes them part of the set. Others may be near the center but are
moving away from it. Thus they are no longer seen as part of the set. The direction
of movement toward or away from the center determines who is "in" and who is
"out."

In "centered-set" thinking, more emphasis is placed on strengthening the relationship to the center than on maintaining the boundary. The boundary exists by
virtue of the members' relationship to the center. Hiebert sees Hebrew culture as
a centered set in which the people were in covenant relationship to God first, then
to one another as they moved toward the center. The theological worldview of Jesus
and Paul was also a centered set. How else could they envision and speak of all believers as forming one body?

We are one in Jesus Christ. Yes, we know the boundaries of our paradigms. But
as Christians wrestling with issues of gender limits or liberties in the church, we
know that the focus cannot be on boundaries. So we move from the image of a box
(our own paradigm) to the image of a circle (a centered or relational set). Why?
Because Jesus placed a priority on right relationships as absolutely integral to our
mission in the world.

It is never easy to care deeply for the brother or sister with whom we disagree
and at the same time to hold faithfully to the truth as we understand it. It can easily
throw us into such cognitive dissonance that we either let go of the truth we have
embraced or let go of any obligation for relationship with a disagreeing (and possibly disagreeable) brother or sister in Christ. It is a strange but hopeful reality,
however, that we most often grow and develop spiritually as we live within the tensions of the Christian life.[27]

If we are serious about healing the real schism between hierarchicalists and egalitarians, we will refuse to sacrifice the mission of the church (endangered by our
lack of unity) for the sake of the paradigm we embrace. But we will also refuse to
sacrifice the truth we have embraced, because we believe it is God's truth for the
welfare of his people. In the midst of the tension between the two, we will find a

---

[27]I am indebted to Old Testament professor John Worgul (Bethel Seminary of the East) who has
   helped me—and many of his students—come to grips with this paradoxical reality.

way to live within this tension as we stay focused on Christ, our Center. And we will discover that as we move toward him as Center, we move closer to others who are moving in the same direction. Even if we disagree about women's place in the home and church, we will at least be close enough to show love and care for those with a competing paradigm.

It is not a neat vision with a simple list of things to do that will guarantee unity. It has about it the raw and messy look of reality. But if the focus is on Christ, by his Spirit we can be one—and we will see things we had not seen before. We may even discover a completely different paradigm replacing both of the existing paradigms. But we can never make such discoveries as long as we insist on a bounded set with a focus on the boundaries. It becomes possible only when we are part of a centered set, with Christ and his kingdom as our priority, as we *all* move toward our Center.

There is an arrogance to which we are all liable. It is the arrogance of thinking that only we have the truth. God's truth may well be greater than all of our "truths." Until we come into that larger truth, we must be true to the truth we have embraced. But even as we embrace our paradigm, may God help us move toward an understanding of his true and perfect paradigm—which may well swallow up all earthly paradigms for the relationship of men and women in the church and home.

About the Contributors

Jack O. Balswick received his M.A. and Ph.D. from the University of Iowa. He is professor of sociology and family development at Fuller Theological Seminary. He coteaches with his wife Judith on gender and sexuality and coleads workshops across North America on relationship topics. Publications coauthored by the Balswicks include *The Family: A Christian Perspective on the Contemporary Home; Authentic Human Sexuality: An Integrated Christian Approach; Family Pain: Getting Through the Hurts of Family Life;* and *The Dual-Earner Marriage: The Elaborate Balancing Act.* Jack and Judy are members of Pasadena Covenant Church. They have two married children and four grandsons.

Judith K. Balswick received her M.A. from the University of Iowa and Ed.D. from the University of Georgia in counseling and human development. She is associate professor in and chair of the Marriage and Family Therapy Department, School of Psychology, Fuller Theological Seminary. Besides coteaching and coleading workshops with her husband Jack, she directs the Marriage and Family clinical training at Fuller. She has coauthored with her husband Jack the publications listed above.

Linda L. Belleville received her M.A. from Trinity Evangelical Divinity School and Ph.D. from the University of Toronto. She is professor of biblical literature at North Park Theological Seminary and an ordained minister with the Evangelical Covenant Church. Her publications include *2 Corinthians* (IVPNTC), *Women Leaders in the Church: Three Crucial Questions* and a contribution to *Two Views on Women in Ministry.*

Judy L. Brown received her M.A. from the Assemblies of God Theological Seminary and Ed.D. from Nova Southeastern University. She is ordained with the International Church of the Foursquare Gospel and is currently serving as ministries coordinator of the Great Lakes District as well as pastor of the Foursquare Church in Ferndale, Michigan. She has authored *Women Ministers According to Scripture, Structuring Sermons Step by Step* and the Old Testament study notes for the revised *Spirit-Filled Life Bible.*

Peter H. Davids received his M.Div. from Trinity Evangelical Divinity School and Ph.D. from the University of Manchester. An ordained minister, he is presently scholar-in-residence at the Vineyard Church in Stafford, Texas. He also serves as adjunct professor of New Testament at Tyndale Theological Seminary near Amsterdam. This follows his recent service in Innsbruck, Austria, with International Teams in Europe as an educational missionary and church adviser. His publications include *A Commentary on the Epistle of James* (NIGTC), *The First Epistle of Peter* (NICNT) and half of the New Testament part of *Hard Sayings of the Bible.*

Gordon D. Fee received his M.A. from Seattle Pacific University and Ph.D. from the University of Southern California. He is professor emeritus of New Testament studies at Regent College as well as an ordained minister with the Assemblies of God. His publications include *How to Read the Bible for All Its Worth; How to Read the Bible Book by Book; New Testament Exegesis: A Handbook; God's Empowering Presence: The Holy Spirit in the Letters of Paul; Listening to the Spirit in the Text;* and commentaries on I Corinthians and Philippians (NICNT) and the Pastoral Epistles (NIBC). He and his wife, Maudine, have four married children and twelve grandchildren.

Kevin Giles received his D.B. from Moore Theological College, Sydney, Australia, his M.A. from the University of Durham, England, and his Th.D. from the Australian College of Theology. He has served as an Anglican minister for more than thirty years and is currently the vicar of St Michaels, North Carlton, Diocese of Melbourne. His publications include *Women and Their Ministry; Created Woman; The Trinity and Subordinationism: The Doctrine of God and the Contemporary Gender Debate; What on Earth Is the Church?* along with contributions to *Dictionary of Jesus and the Gospels* and *Dictionary of the Later New Testament and Its Developments.* Kevin and his wife, Lynley, a marriage educator and counselor, have four children and four grandchildren.

Stanley J. Grenz received his M.Div. from Denver Seminary and D.Theol. from the University of Munich, Germany. He is Pioneer McDonald Professor of Theology at Carey Theological College, Vancouver, B.C. He is also an ordained minister with the Baptist Union of Western Canada. His publications include *The Social God and the Relational Self: A Trinitarian Theology of the Imago Dei; Renewing the Center: Evangelical Theology in a Post-theological Era; Theology for the Community of God; What Christians Really Believe . . . and Why; The Moral Quest: Foundations for Christian Ethics; A Primer on Postmodernism;* and, coauthored with Denise Muir Kjesbo, *Women and the Church: A Biblical Theology of Women in Ministry.* Stan and his wife, Edna, who is minister of worship at First Baptist Church, Vancouver, have two children.

Rebecca Merrill Groothuis is a freelance writer and editor. Her publications include the award-winning *Women Caught in the Conflict: The Culture War Between Traditionalism and Feminism* and *Good News for Women: A Biblical Picture of Gender Equality,* as well as articles and reviews in *Christian Scholar's Review, Christianity Today, ReGeneration Quarterly, Perspectives, Priscilla Papers, Christian Counseling Today, Christian Ethics Today, Eternity* and *The Denver Post.* She maintains a website with online articles <RebeccaMerrillGroothuis.com> and lives in the Denver area with her husband, Doug, who is a professor of philosophy at Denver Seminary.

Mimi Haddad received her M.A.T.S. from Gordon-Conwell Theological Seminary and is a Ph.D. candidate in historical theology at the University of Durham, England. She serves as president of Christians for Biblical Equality <www.cbeinternational.org> and is part of an intentional community in the inner city of Minneapolis. Mimi also serves on the steering committee and occasionally cochairs the Evangelicals and Gender Study Group at ETS.

Janette Hassey received her M.A. from Denver Seminary and Ph.D. from the University of Chicago. She is currently a missionary in the Philippines with Christus Victor Ministries. Her publications include *No Time for Silence: Evangelical Women in Public Ministry Around the Turn of the Century.*

Richard S. Hess received his M.Div. and Th.M. from Trinity Evangelical Divinity School and Ph.D. from Hebrew Union College. He is professor of Old Testament at Denver Seminary and editor of the *Denver Journal: An Online Review of Current Biblical and Theological Studies.* In addition to more than seventy articles published in various biblical and ancient Near Eastern journals and collections, he has edited ten books and written three, including *Studies in the Personal Names in Genesis 1-11* and *Joshua* (TOTC). He serves as an editor for a commentary series on the Septuagint and has in press commentaries on Leviticus and the Song of Songs. Rick and his wife, Jean, who is a pastor of a Presbyterian church, have three children.

Craig S. Keener received his M.A. and M.Div. from the Assemblies of God Theological Seminary and Ph.D. from Duke University. He is professor of New Testament at Eastern Seminary and ordained in the National Baptist Convention, USA. He has written twelve books, including *The IVP Bible Background Commentary: New Testament; Paul, Women and Wives; And Marries Another: Divorce and Remarriage in the Teaching of the New Testament; Black Man's Religion;* and commentaries on Matthew, John and Revelation. Craig and his wife, Médine, who teaches history, were married as this volume was being written.

Cynthia Neal Kimball received her Ph.D. from the University of New Mexico. She is associate professor in and chair of the Psychology Department at Wheaton College. Her publications include "Self-in-Relation: An Anabaptist, Feminist Theological and Psychological Model of Agency and Connection" in *Religion, Marriage and Family;* "Welfare Families" in *Welfare in America: Christian Perspectives on a Policy in Crisis;* and "Missing Voices: Professional Challenges for Academic Women," with T. Watson, S. S. Canning and J. L. Brady, in *Journal of Psychology and Christianity.* She and her husband, Douglas, have four children.

Walter L. Liefeld received his Ph.D. from Columbia University and Union Theological Seminary. He is distinguished professor emeritus of New Testament at Trinity Evangelical Divinity School in Deerfield, Illinois. He has held several pastorates and interim pastorates, most recently serving as senior pastor of Christ Church in Lake Forest, Illinois. Among his several books are *New Testament Exposition, Interpreting the Book of Acts* and (cowritten with Ruth Tucker) *Daughters of the Church.* He and his wife, Olive, have three grown children and seven grandchildren.

I. Howard Marshall received his B.A. from Cambridge, Ph.D. from Aberdeen and D.D. from Asbury. He is Honorary Research Professor of New Testament at the University of Aberdeen, where he has taught since 1964. His many publications include commentaries on the Gospel of Luke (NIGTC), Acts (TNTC), 1 and 2 Thessalonians (NBC), the Pastoral Epistles (ICC), and the Johannine Epistles (NICNT). Howard and his late wife,

Joyce, have four married children and seven grandchildren.

Karen Mason received her M.A. in philosophy of religion from Denver Seminary and was an instructor in writing at the University of Colorado at Boulder. She is a freelance writer and married to Sulia Mason.

Sulia Mason received his M.A. in philosophy of religion from Denver Seminary and has taught philosophy at Aurora Community College. He is currently a Ph.D. candidate in philosophy at the University of South Carolina and is married to Karen Mason.

Alice P. Mathews received her M.A. from Michigan State University and Ph.D. from the Iliff School of Theology and the University of Denver. She is the Lois W. Bennett Distinguished Associate Professor of Educational Ministries and Women's Ministries at Gordon-Conwell Theological Seminary. In addition, she is a regular participant in the daily radio program *Discover the Word* (RBC Ministries). She is the author of *A Woman God Can Use, A Woman Jesus Can Teach, Preaching That Speaks to Women* and *Marriage Made in Eden.* Alice and her husband, Randall, served in Europe for seventeen years as missionaries with the Conservative Baptist Foreign Mission Society. They have four children and six grandsons.

Alvera Mickelsen received her M.A. from Wheaton College and M.S. in journalism from Northwestern University. She taught writing for many years at Wheaton and Bethel Colleges. She and her late husband, Berkeley Mickelsen, wrote several articles and books together, including *The Family Bible Encyclopedia, Understanding Scripture* and *The Picture Bible Dictionary.* The two of them were among the founders of Christians for Biblical Equality. Alvera also served as editor for *Women, Authority and the Bible.*

Roger Nicole received his M.A. from the Sorbonne in Paris, B.D., S.T.M. and Th.D. from Gordon Divinity School in Boston, and Ph.D. from Harvard University. After forty-one years of teaching at Gordon-Conwell Theological Seminary, he is now professor of theology emeritus at Reformed Theological Seminary in Orlando. He is the author of numerous articles, including those published in book form in *Standing Forth* (twenty-three essays) and *Our Sovereign Saviour* (fourteen addresses). Roger is an ordained Baptist minister and lives with his wife, Annette, in Longwood, Florida.

Ronald W. Pierce received his M.Div. and Th.M. from Talbot School of Theology and Ph.D. from Fuller Theological Seminary. He is professor of biblical studies and theology in the Talbot School of Theology at Biola University, as well as an ordained minister with the Evangelical Free Church of America. His publications include *OT Interactive* (a computer learning program for Old Testament survey classes) as well as several articles in the *JETS, TrinJ* and *BBR.* He also serves on the steering committee and occasionally cochairs the Evangelicals and Gender Study Group at ETS. Ron and his wife, Pat, have directed Biola's travel-study program to the Holy Land for fifteen years. They currently reside in Fullerton, California, and have two children.

Aída Besançon Spencer received her M.Div. and Th.M. from Princeton Theological Seminary and Ph.D. from Southern Baptist Theological Seminary. She is professor of New Testament at Gordon-Conwell Theological Seminary and an ordained minister with the Presbyterian Church USA. She also serves as pastor of organization with Pilgrim Church, Beverly, Massachusetts. Her publications include *Beyond the Curse: Women Called to Ministry* and *Paul's Literary Style.* With her husband, William David Spencer, she has also written *The Global God, Joy Through the Night* and *The Prayer Life of Jesus.* Aída and William have one grown son.

Ruth A. Tucker received her M.A. from Baylor University and her Ph.D. from Northern Illinois University. She is associate professor of missiology at Calvin Theological Seminary. Before coming to CTS, she taught for seventeen years at Trinity Evangelical Divinity School. She was raised in northern Wisconsin in a Christian and Missionary Alliance Church and is now a member of LaGrave Avenue Christian Reformed Church. She is the author of fourteen books, including *Private Lives of Pastors' Wives; Walking Away from Faith: Unraveling the Mystery of Belief and Unbelief;* and the Gold Medallion award-winning *From Jerusalem to Irian Jaya.* She is the coauthor (with Walter L. Liefeld) of *Daughters of the Church.*

William J. Webb received his Ph.D. from Dallas Theological Seminary. He is an ordained minister with the Fellowship of Evangelical Baptists in Canada and currently serves as professor of New Testament at Heritage Seminary (Cambridge, Ontario). His writings include *Returning Home: New Covenant and Second Exodus as the Context for 2 Corinthians 6:14-7:1; Slaves, Women and Homosexuals;* and several articles in journals. Bill, his wife, Marilyn, and their three children live in Waterloo, Ontario.

Joan Burgess Winfrey received her Ph.D. from the University of Denver. She is a professor of counseling at Denver Seminary and a licensed clinical psychologist. She has contributed to a number of volumes on the subjects of domestic violence and abortion and is involved in a national research project on victim assistance and communities of faith in partnership with the Denver district attorney's office. She has served for a number of years as a deacon at Meadow Hills Church, a North American Baptist church in the Denver area. Joan is married and has two daughters.

Names Index

Subject Index